Microsoft® Office 97 Professional Edition

Illustrated A Second Course

Microsoft®

Office 97

Professional Edition

Illustrated A Second Course

Marie L. Swanson
Tara Lynn O'Keefe
Lisa Friedrichsen
David W. Beskeen
Elizabeth Eisner Reding

COURSE TECHNOLOGY

ONE MAIN STREET, CAMBRIDGE, MA 02142

an International Thomson Publishing company I(T)P®

Cambridge • Albany • Bonn • Boston • Cincinnati • London • Madrid • Melbourne • Mexico City
New York • Paris • San Francisco • Singapore • Tokyo • Toronto • Washington

Microsoft Office 97 Professional Edition—Illustrated A Second Course
is published by Course Technology

Managing Editor:	Nicole Jones Pinard
Product Manager:	Jeanne Herring
Production Editor:	Nancy Ray
Developmental Editors:	Cynthia Anderson, Rachel Bunin, Ann Marie Buconjic, Meta Chaya Hirschl, Katherine T. Pinard
Composition House:	GEX, Inc.
QA Manuscript Reviewers:	Gail Massey, Jean-Claire Shiely, Jeff Goding, John McCarthy, Brian McCooey, Chris Hall
Text Designer:	Joseph Lee
Cover Designer:	Joseph Lee

For more information contact:

Course Technology
One Main Street
Cambridge, MA 02142

International Thomson Publishing Europe
Berkshire House 168-173
High Holborn
London WC1V 7AA
England

Thomas Nelson Australia
102 Dodds Street
South Melbourne, 3205
Victoria, Australia

Nelson Canada
1120 Birchmount Road
Scarborough, Ontario
Canada M1K 5G4

International Thomson Editores
Campos Eliseos 385, Piso 7
Col. Polanco
11560 Mexico D.F. Mexico

International Thomson Publishing GmbH
Königswinterer Strasse 418
53277 Bonn
Germany

International Thomson Publishing Asia
211 Henderson Road
#05-10 Henderson Building
Singapore 0315

International Thomson Publishing Japan
Hirakawacho Kyowa Building, 3F
2-2-1 Hirakawacho
Chiyoda-ku, Tokyo 102
Japan

ISBN 0-7600-5135-6

Printed in the United States of America

10 9 8 7 6 5 4 3 2

From the Illustrated Series™ Team

At Course Technology we believe that technology will transform the way that people teach and learn. We are very excited about bringing you, instructors and students, the most practical and affordable technology-related products available.

The Development Process

Our development process is unparalleled in the educational publishing industry. Every product we create goes through an exacting process of design, development, review, and testing.

Reviewers give us direction and insight that shape our manuscripts and bring them up to the latest standards. Every manuscript is quality tested. Students whose backgrounds match the intended audience work through every keystroke, carefully checking for clarity and pointing out errors in logic and sequence. Together with our own technical reviewers, these testers help us ensure that everything that carries our name is as error-free and easy to use as possible.

The Products

We show both how and why technology is critical to solving problems in the classroom and in whatever field you choose to teach or pursue. Our time-tested, step-by-step instructions provide unparalleled clarity. Examples and applications are chosen and crafted to motivate students.

The Illustrated Series™ Team

The Illustrated Series™ Team is committed to providing you with the most visual introduction to microcomputer applications. No other series of books will get you up to speed faster in today's changing software environment. This book will suit your needs because it was delivered quickly, efficiently, and affordably. In every aspect of business, we rely on a commitment to quality and the use of technology. Each member of the Illustrated Series™ Team contributes to this process. The names of all our team members are listed below.

The Team

Cynthia Anderson
Chia-Ling Barker
Donald Barker
Ann Barron
David Beskeen
Ann Marie Buconjic
Rachel Bunin
Joan Carey
Patrick Carey
Sheralyn Carroll
Brad Conlin
Pam Conrad
Mary-Terese Cozzola
Carol Cram
Kim T. M. Crowley
Catherine DiMassa
Linda Eriksen
Jessica Evans
Lisa Friedrichsen
Jeff Goding
Michael Halvorson
Jamie Harper
Jeanne Herring
Meta Chaya Hirschl
Jane Hosie-Bounar
Steven Johnson
Bill Lisowski
Chet Lyskawa
Tara O'Keefe
Harry Phillips
Nicole Jones Pinard
Katherine T. Pinard
Kevin Proot
Elizabeth Eisner Reding
Art Rotberg
Neil Salkind
Gregory Schultz
Ann Shaffer
Dan Swanson
Marie Swanson
Jennifer Thompson
Sasha Vodnik
Jan Weingarten
Christie Williams
Janet Wilson

Preface

Welcome to *Microsoft Office 97 Professional Edition – Illustrated, A Second Course.* This highly visual book offers users a hands-on introduction to Microsoft Office and also serves as an excellent reference for future use. This book is a continuation of *Microsoft Office 97 Professional Edition-Illustrated, A First Course* and is for people who want more coverage of the Office programs and how they work together.

► Organization and Coverage

This text is divided into five sections as illustrated by the brightly colored tabs on the sides and tops of the pages. There are sections for Microsoft Word 97, Microsoft Excel 97, Microsoft Access 97, Microsoft PowerPoint 97, and Microsoft Office Integration.

► About this Approach

What makes the Illustrated approach so effective at teaching software skills? It's quite simple. Each skill is presented on two facing pages, with the step-by-step instructions on the left page, and large screen illustrations on the right. Students can focus on a single skill without having to turn the page. This unique design makes information extremely accessible and easy to absorb, and provides a great reference for after the course is over. This hands-on approach also makes it ideal for both self-paced or instructor-led classes. The modular structure of the book also allows for great flexibility; you can cover the units in any order you choose.

Each lesson, or "information display," contains the following elements:

This icon indicates a CourseHelp 97 slide show is available for this lesson. See the Instructor's Resource Kit page for more information.

Each 2-page spread focuses on a single skill.

Concise text that introduces the basic principles in the lesson and integrates the brief case study.

Excel 97

Changing Attributes and Alignment of Labels

Attributes are font styling features such as bold, italics, and underlining. You can apply bold, italics, and underlining from the Formatting toolbar or from the Font tab in the Format Cells dialog box. You can also change the alignment of text in cells. Left, right, or center alignment can be applied from the Formatting toolbar, or from the Alignment tab in the Format Cells dialog box. See Table C-2 for a description of the available attribute and alignment buttons on the Formatting toolbar. Excel also has predefined worksheet formats to make formatting easier. Now that he has applied the appropriate fonts and font sizes to his worksheet labels, Evan wants to further enhance his worksheet's appearance by adding bold and underline formatting and centering some of the labels.

Steps

CourseHelp

The camera icon indicates there is a CourseHelp available with this lesson. Click the Start button, point to programs, point to CourseHelp, then click Word 97 Illustrated. Choose the CourseHelp that corresponds to this lesson.

QuickTip

Highlighting information on a worksheet can be useful, but overuse of any attribute can be distracting and make a document less readable. Be consistent by adding emphasis the same way throughout a workbook.

Time To

✔ Save

1. Press [Ctrl][Home] to select cell A1, then click the Bold button on the Formatting toolbar
   The title "Advertising Expenses" appears in bold.
2. Select the range A3:J3, then click the Underline button on the Formatting toolbar
   Excel underlines the column headings in the selected range.
3. Click cell A3, click the Italics button on the Formatting toolbar, then click
   The word "Type" appears in boldface, italic type. Notice that the Bold, Italics, and Underline buttons on the Formatting toolbar are indented. You decide you don't like the italic formatting. You remove it by clicking again.
4. Click
   Excel removes italics from cell A3.
5. Add bold formatting to the rest of the labels in the range B3:J3
   You want to center the title over the data.
6. Select the range A1:F1, then click the Merge and Center button on the Formatting toolbar
   The title Advertising Expenses is centered across six columns. Now you center the column headings in their cells.
7. Select the range A3:J3 then click the Center button on the Formatting toolbar
   You are satisfied with the formatting in the worksheet.
   Compare your screen to Figure C-8.

TABLE C-2: Attribute and Alignment buttons on the Formatting toolbar

icon	description	icon	description
B	Adds boldface		Aligns left
I	Italicizes		Aligns center
U	Underlines		Aligns right
	Adds lines or borders		Centers across columns, and combines two or more selected adjacent cells into one cell.

► EX C-6 FORMATTING A WORKSHEET

Quickly accessible summaries of key terms, toolbar buttons, or keyboard alternatives connected with the lesson material. Students can refer easily to this information when working on their own projects at a later time.

Hints as well as trouble-shooting advice right where you need it – next to the step itself.

Clear step-by-step directions, with what students are to type in red, explain how to complete the specific task.

Other Features

The two-page lesson format featured in this book provides the new user with a powerful learning experience. Additionally, this book contains the following features:

- **Real-World Case**
  The case study used throughout the textbook, a fictitious company called Nomad Ltd, is designed to be "real-world" in nature and introduces the kinds of activities that students will encounter when working with Microsoft Office. With a real-world case, the process of solving problems will be more meaningful to students.

- **Integration Units**
  Three integration units provide hands-on instruction and meaningful examples for using Word, Excel, Access, and PowerPoint together. These integration units also reinforce the skills and concepts learned in the program sections.

- **End of Unit Material**
  Each unit concludes with a Concepts Review that tests students' understanding of what they learned in the unit. A Skills Review follows the Concepts Review and provides students with additional hands-on practice of the skills they learned in the unit. The Skills Review is followed by Independent Challenges, which pose case problems for students to solve. At least one Independent Challenge in each unit asks students to use the World Wide Web to solve the problem as indicated by a WebWork icon. The Visual Workshops that follow the Independent Challenges help students to develop critical thinking skills. Students are shown completed documents and are asked to recreate them from scratch.

Every lesson features large, full-color representations of what the screen should look like as students complete the numbered steps.

The innovative design draws the students' eyes to important areas of the screens.

Brightly colored tabs above the program name indicate which section of the book you are in. Useful for finding your place within the book and for referencing information from the index.

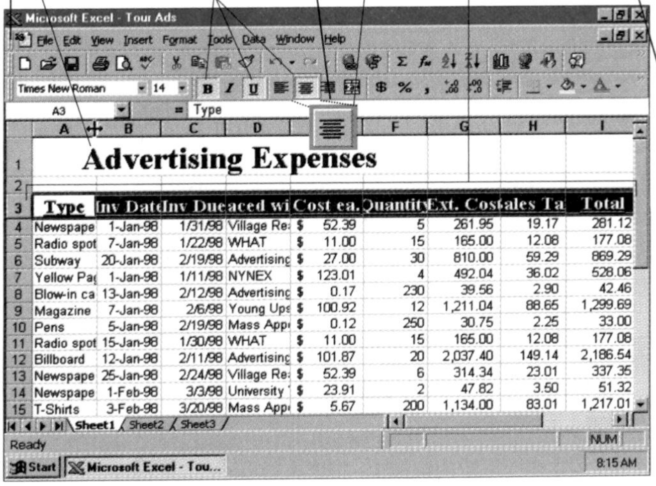

FIGURE C-8: Worksheet with formatting attributes applied

Title centered across columns

Buttons indented

Center button

Column headings centered, bold, and underlined

Excel 97

Clues to Use

Using AutoFormat

Excel provides 16 preset formats called AutoFormats, which allow instant formatting of large amounts of data. AutoFormats are designed for worksheets with labels in the left column and top rows and totals in the bottom row or right column. To use AutoFormatting, select the data to be formatted—or place your mouse pointer anywhere within the range to be selected—click Format on the menu bar, click AutoFormat, then select a format from the Table Format list box, as shown in Figure C-9.

FIGURE C-9: AutoFormat dialog box

List of AutoFormats

Sample of selected format

FORMATTING A WORKSHEET EX C-7

Clues to Use Boxes provide concise information that either expands on the major lesson skill or describes an independent task that in some way relates to the major lesson skill.

The page numbers are designed like a road map. EX indicates the Excel section, C indicates Excel Unit C, and 7 indicates the page within the unit. This map allows for the greatest flexibility in content – each unit stands completely on its own.

Instructor's Resource Kit

The Instructor's Resource Kit is Course Technology's way of putting the resources and information needed to teach and learn effectively into your hands. With an integrated array of teaching and learning tools that offer you and your students a broad range of instructional options, we believe this kit represents the highest quality and most cutting edge resources available to instructors today. Many of these resources are available online at www.course.com. The resources available with this book are:

CourseHelp 97 CourseHelp 97 is a student reinforcement tool offering online annotated tutorials that are accessible directly from the Start menu in Windows 95. These on-screen "slide shows" help students understand the most difficult concepts in a specific program. Students are encouraged to view a CourseHelp 97 slide show before completing that lesson. This text includes the following CourseHelp 97 slide shows:

- Understanding Mail Merge
- Using Macros

Adopters of this text are granted the right to post the CourseHelp 97 files on any standalone computer or network.

Course Test Manager Designed by Course Technology, this cutting edge Windows-based testing software helps instructors design and administer tests and pre-tests. This full-featured program also has an online testing component that allows students to take tests at the computer and have their exams automatically graded.

Course Faculty Online Companion This new World Wide Web site offers Course Technology customers a password-protected Faculty Lounge where you can find everything you need to prepare for class. These periodically updated items include lesson plans, graphic files for the figures in the text, additional problems, updates and revisions to the text, links to other Web sites, and access to Student Disk files. This new site is an ongoing project and will continue to evolve throughout the semester. Contact your Customer Service Representative for the site address and password.

Course Student Online Companion This book features its own Student Online Companion where students can go to access Web sites that will help them complete the WebWork Independent Challenges. This page also contains links to other Course Technology student pages where students can find task references for each of the Microsoft Office 97 programs, a graphical glossary of terms found in the text, an archive of meaningful templates, software, hot tips, and Web links to other sites that contain pertinent information. These new sites are also ongoing projects and will continue to evolve throughout the semester.

Student Files To use this book students must have the Student Files. See the inside front or inside back cover for more information on the Student Files. Adopters of this text are granted the right to post the Student Files on any stand-alone computer or network.

Instructor's Manual This is quality assurance tested and includes:

- Solutions to all lessons and end-of-unit material
- Unit notes with teaching tips from the author
- Extra Independent Challenges
- Transparency Masters of key concepts
- Student Files
- CourseHelp 97
- Task Reference

The Illustrated Family of Products

This book that you are holding fits in the Illustrated Series – one series of three in the Illustrated family of products. The other two series are the Illustrated Projects Series and the Illustrated Interactive Series. The Illustrated Projects Series is a supplemental series designed to reinforce the sills learned in any skills-based book through the creation of meaningful and engaging projects. The Illustrated Interactive Series is a line of computer-based training multimedia products that offer the novice user a quick and interactive learning experience. All three series are committed to providing you with the most visual and enriching instructional materials.

Brief Contents

Contents

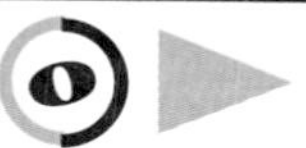

Office 97

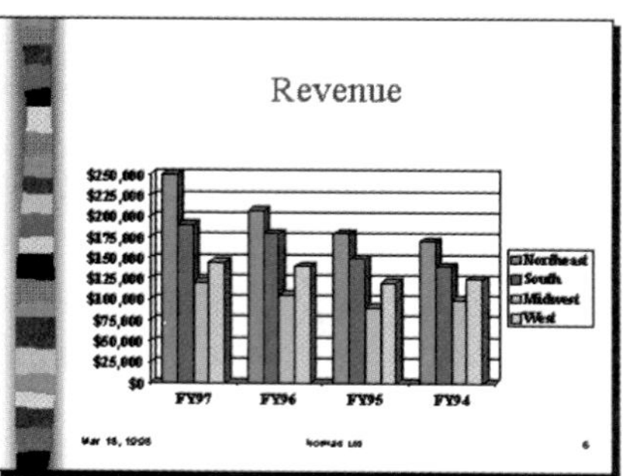

Word 97

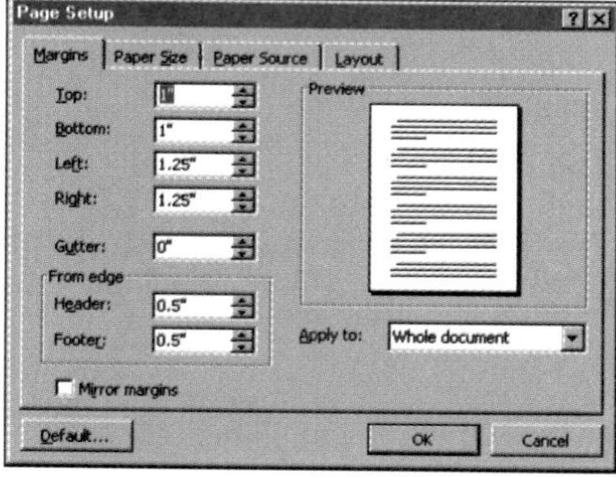

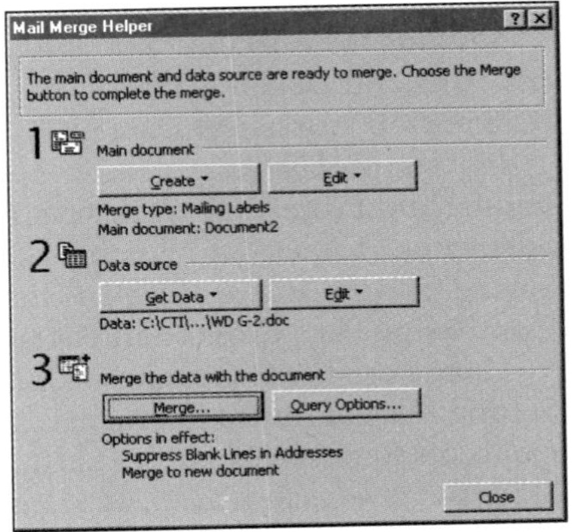

Mail Merge Helper
The main document and data source are ready to merge. Choose the Merge button to complete the merge.
1 Main document
Create
Edit
Merge type: Mailing Labels
Main document: Document2
2 Data source
Get Data
Edit
Data: C:\CTI\...\WD G-2.doc
3 Merge the data with the document
Merge...
Query Options...
Options in effect:
Suppress Blank Lines in Addresses
Merge to new document
Close

Picture

Excel 97

Contents

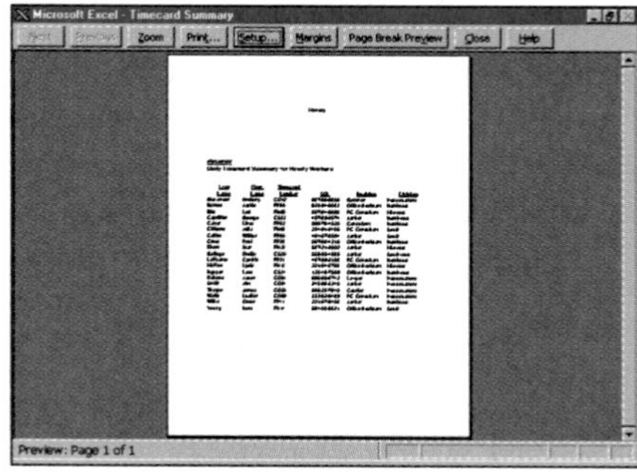

Microsoft Excel - Timecard Summary
Zoom
Print...
Setup...
Margins
Page Break Preview
Close
Help
Preview: Page 1 of 1

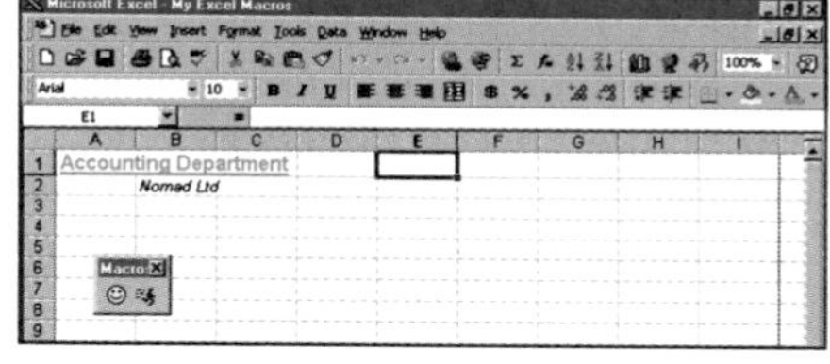

Microsoft Excel - My Excel Macros
Accounting Department
Nomad Ltd
Macro

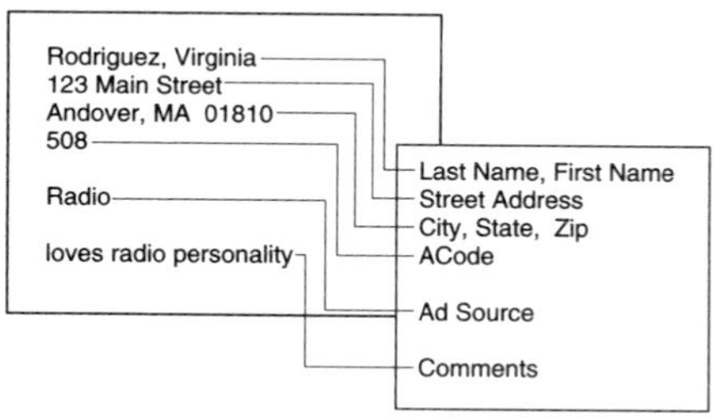

Rodriguez, Virginia
123 Main Street
Andover, MA 01810
508
Radio
loves radio personality
Last Name, First Name
Street Address
City, State, Zip
ACode
Ad Source
Comments

Integration

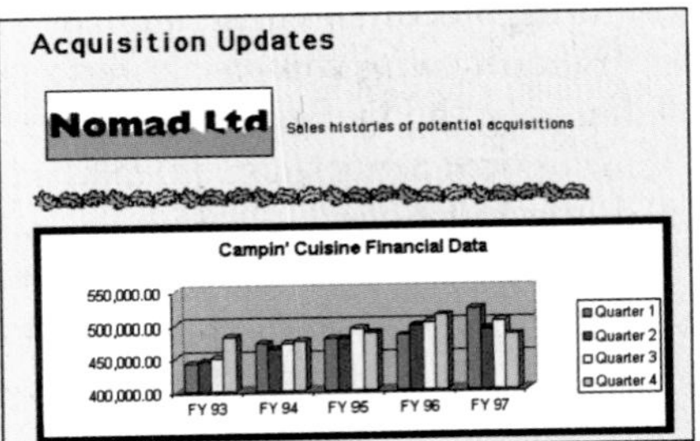

Access 97

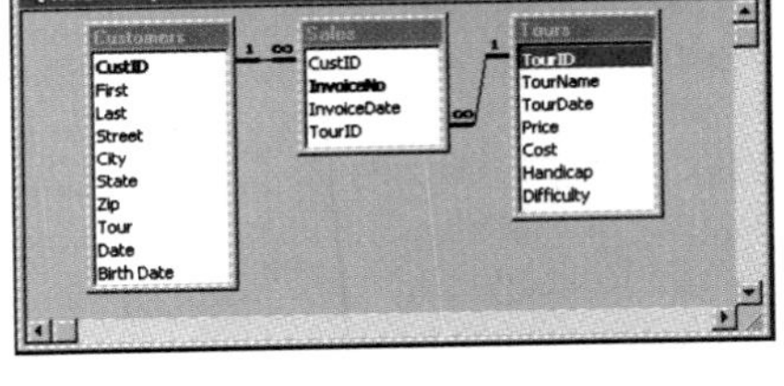

Contents

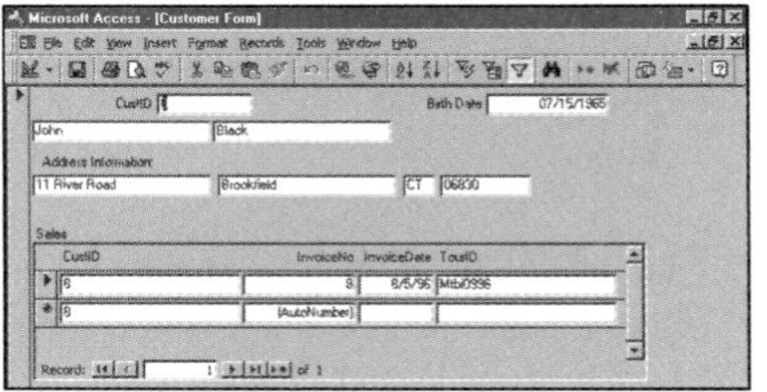

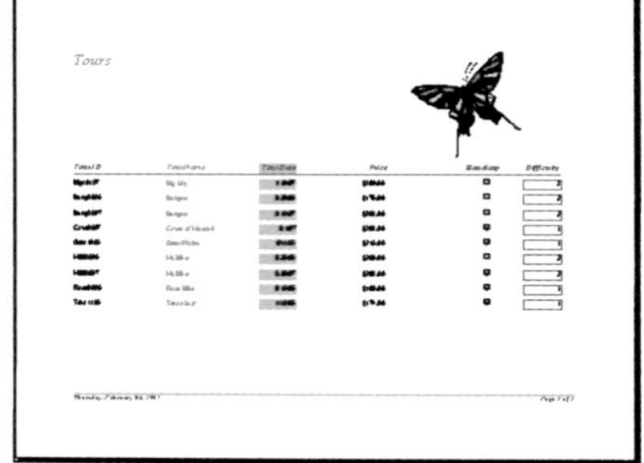

Integration

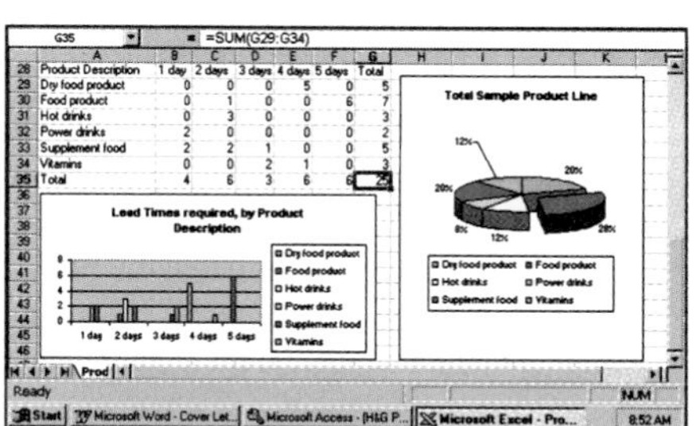

PowerPoint

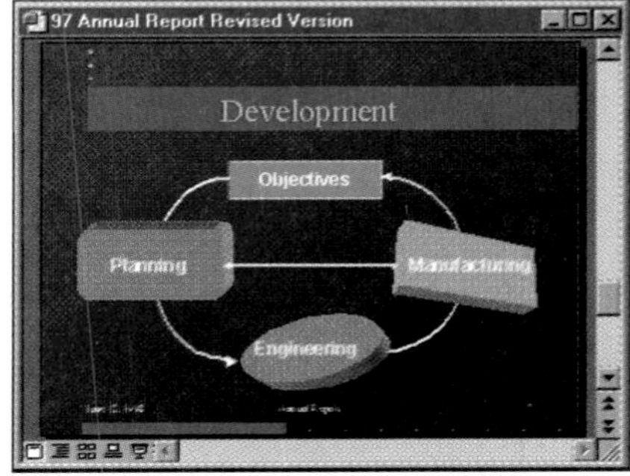

97 Annual Report Revised Version
Development
Objectives
Planning
Manufacturing
Engineering

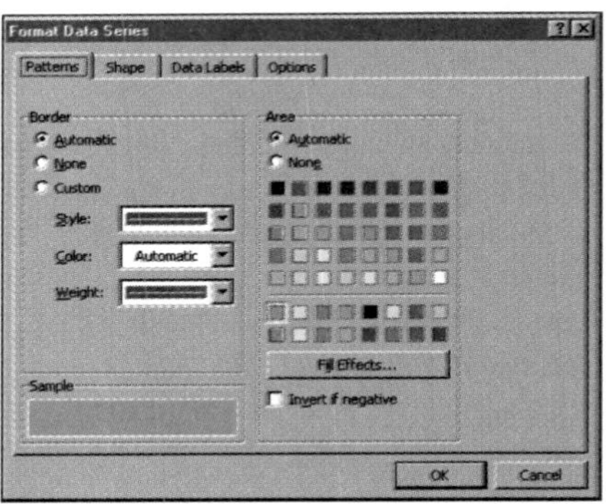

Format Data Series
Patterns
Shape
Data Labels
Options
Border
Automatic
None
Custom
Style:
Color:
Automatic
Weight:
Area
Automatic
None
Fill Effects...
Sample
Invert if negative
OK
Cancel

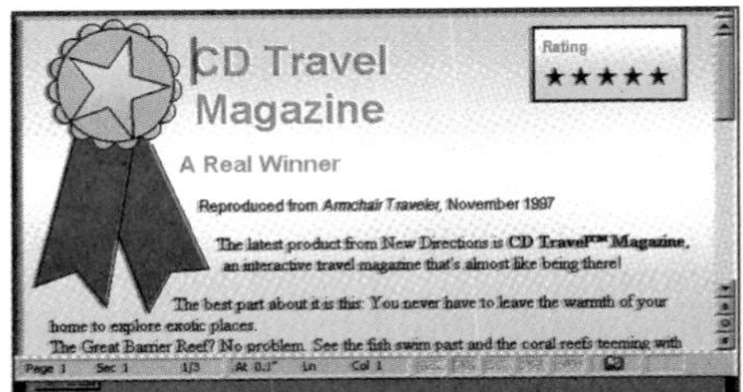

CD Travel Magazine
Rating
★★★★★
A Real Winner
Reproduced from Armchair Traveler, November 1997

Contents

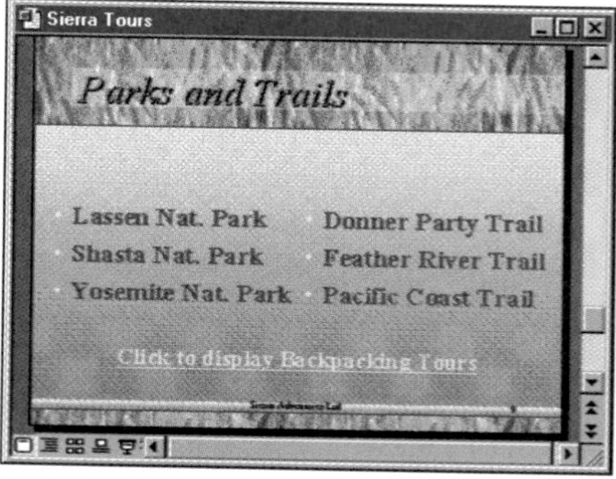

Integration

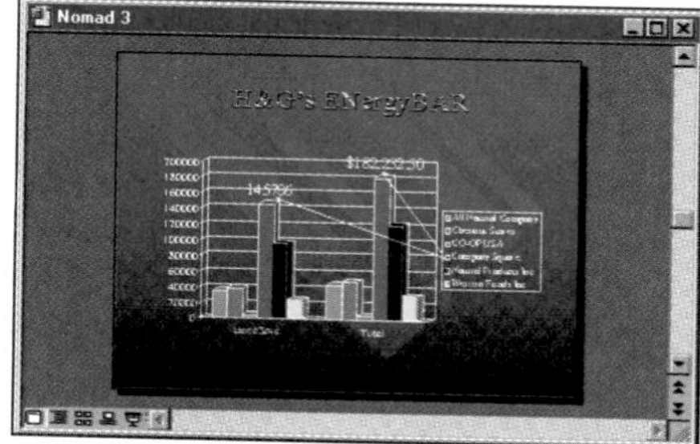

Reviewing

Microsoft Office 97 Professional

Objectives

- Plan the project and work efficiently
- Create a Word document
- Format a document
- Create an Excel worksheet
- Enhance an Excel worksheet
- Create an Access database
- Create an Access database query
- Create a PowerPoint presentation
- Modify a PowerPoint presentation
- Browse the Internet
- Create a Web page

You are already familiar with the basic skills necessary to use the Microsoft Office 97 Professional suite of programs. Using its **docucentric** approach, Office components help you complete tasks and work more efficiently, rather than show you how specific programs work. This unit reintroduces Nomad Ltd, an outdoor sporting gear and adventure travel company. In the past, Nomad Ltd's products have been available only in their own stores, but expanding growth has led it to seek outside vendors. Nomad employees will use Microsoft Office programs to create materials for an up-coming trade show, where the company hopes to attract new vendors.

Office 97

Planning the Project and Working Efficiently

The programs included in Microsoft Office 97 Professional provide all you need to complete common business tasks. Its **docucentric** approach concentrates on the efficient completion of tasks that result in professional-quality projects. To help you work better, Microsoft Office 97 Professional includes a variety of ways to create new documents and open existing ones, listed in Table B-1. Lynn Shaw, the executive assistant to the President of Nomad Ltd, is coordinating the trade-show project. Her team will use Microsoft Office components to prepare for the show.

Lynn's team has determined that the following materials are needed:

Formatted documents containing graphics and headers and footers

Existing Word documents can be modified to create new documents. Text can be formatted using AutoFormat, then text can be positioned around a graphic image using a frame. Headers and footers can be added to a multipage document so information is printed on each page.

Spreadsheets containing sales calculations, projections, and charts

Sales data can be entered and then totalled by division using Excel. The worksheet data can be formatted attractively using the AutoFormat feature. Increases in sales can be projected, and then the data can be charted.

Query an existing database for a list of potential vendors

A list of potential vendors can be obtained by querying Nomad's existing Access vendor database. By merging this query with a Word document, these vendors can be contacted before the trade show.

Create a presentation that runs unattended during the trade show

With PowerPoint, a dramatic slide show can be created that incorporates information about Nomad and its products, as well as dazzling special effects.

Combine data from Office components into a Web document

Elements from Office documents can be added to a Web page for instant, up-to-date access to all interested parties. Figure B-1 shows elements from a Word document included in a Web page.

FIGURE B-1: Word document included in a Web page

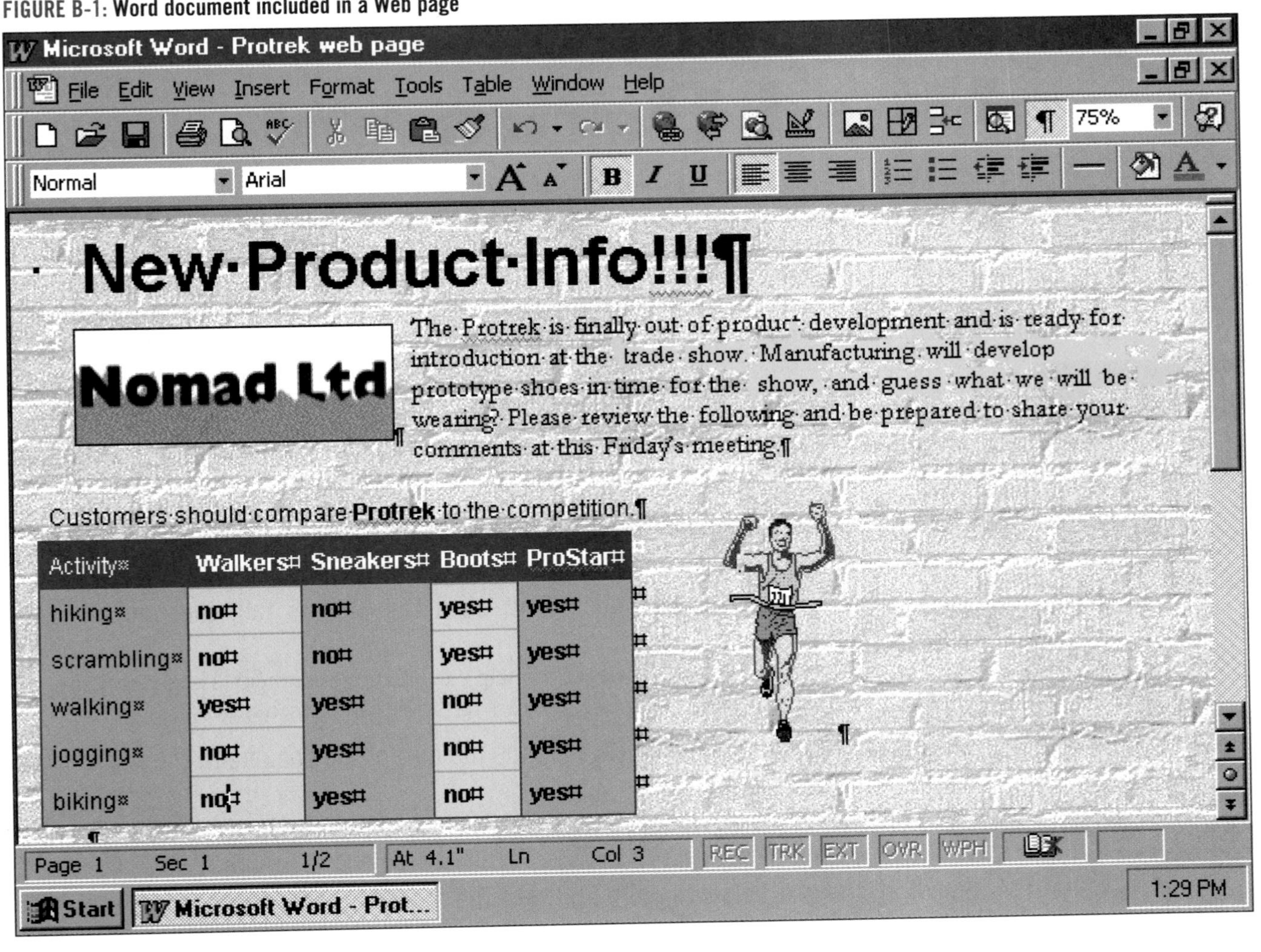

TABLE B-1: Methods to create and open documents

goal	using the desktop	using the shortcut bar	using the start menu
Create new document	Right-click Desktop, point to New, click the desired type of Microsoft document	Click [icon], click the icon for desired type of blank document, or click the tab for the desired type of document, then click OK	Click Start, point to Programs, then click desired Microsoft program icon or click New Office Document, then click the desired document type
Open an existing document		Click [icon], locate the folder and click the desired document, then click Open	Click Start, point to Documents, click filename or click Open Office Document, then click the desired document

Creating a Word Document

If you want to create a specific kind of document (such as a letter, memo, fax or résumé), you can use a template or wizard to help get you started. Although both templates and wizards provide the basic formatting you need to make attractive documents, wizards provide the added benefit of guiding you through the process of selecting preferences for specific features. As you type, the AutoCorrect feature corrects certain spelling mistakes as you make them and highlights other errors that you can correct later. In preparation for the trade show, Lynn needs to prepare a memo to other team members describing a new line of footwear at Nomad Ltd. She will use a template to help her prepare the memo.

1. Start Word
   When you first start Word, the program displays a document window in which you can begin typing your document. To get a head start creating a memo, start the new document using a template.
2. Click **File** on the menu bar, click **New**, click the **Memos tab**, then double-click **Elegant Memo**
   Each tab contains templates and wizards to help you create a document. The new document, based on the Elegant Memo template, appears in the document window.
3. Click each of the locations indicated in the top part of the document, then type in the text as shown in Figure B-2
   After typing in this basic information, you are ready to type the body of the memo. This text is already formatted in all caps, so you do not need to capitalize this text when you type it.
4. Select all the text below the line and type the following, being sure to press **[Enter]** when you are finished typing:
   The Protrek is finally out of product development and is ready for introduction at the trade show. Manufacturing will develop prototype shoes in time for the show, and guess what we will be wearing? Please review the following and be prepared to share your comments at this Friday's meeting.
   Pressing [Enter] creates a blank line. You can insert new text by simply placing the insertion point where you wish and typing additional text.
5. Place the insertion point after the word "following" (after the space), then type **information** and a **space**
   You can delete text you want to remove from the document.
6. Select the text **product**, then press **[Delete]**
   Replace existing text by selecting and then typing over the text you want to replace.
7. Select the text **Interoffice** at the top of the page, then type **Team**
   This text is already formatted in small caps, so you do not need to capitalize the word "team" when you type it.
8. Click the **Spelling button** on the Standard toolbar and correct any spelling errors you might have made; click **Ignore** to ignore the word "Protrek"
   It is good practice to save your document shortly after starting it. Compare your document to Figure B-3.
9. Click the **Save button** on the Standard toolbar, then save the document as **Protrek Memo**

QuickTip

Click the Show/Hide button so that you can better see spaces between words.

FIGURE B-2: Memo headings

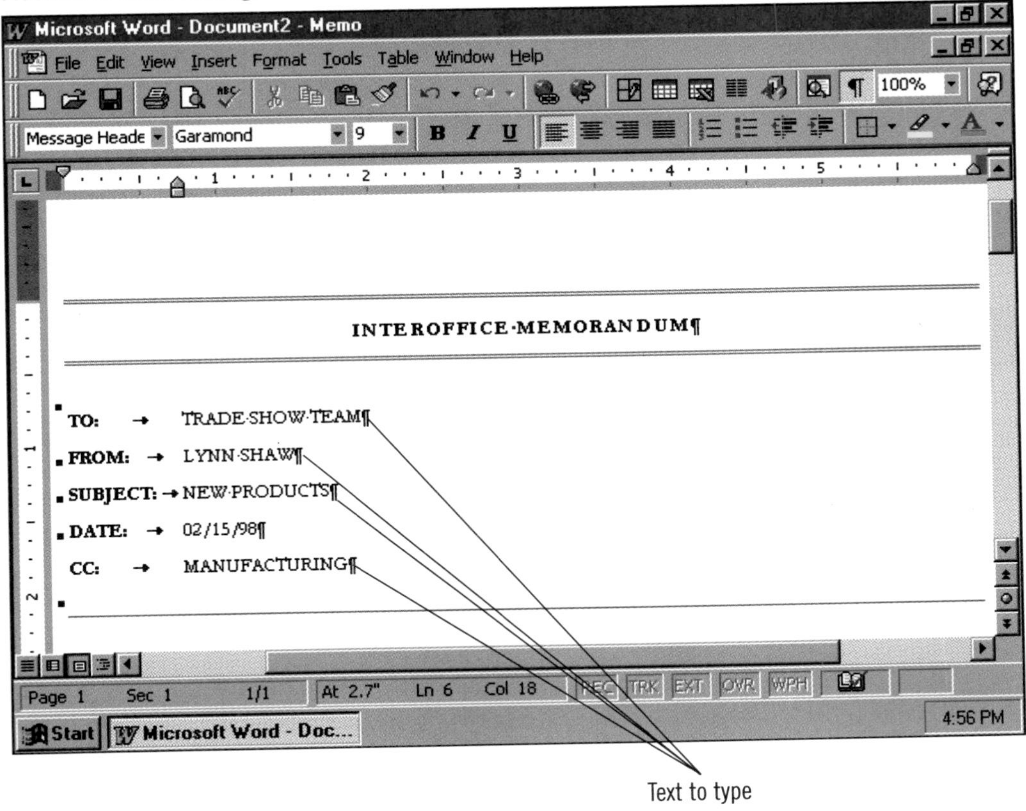

FIGURE B-3: Text in a memo

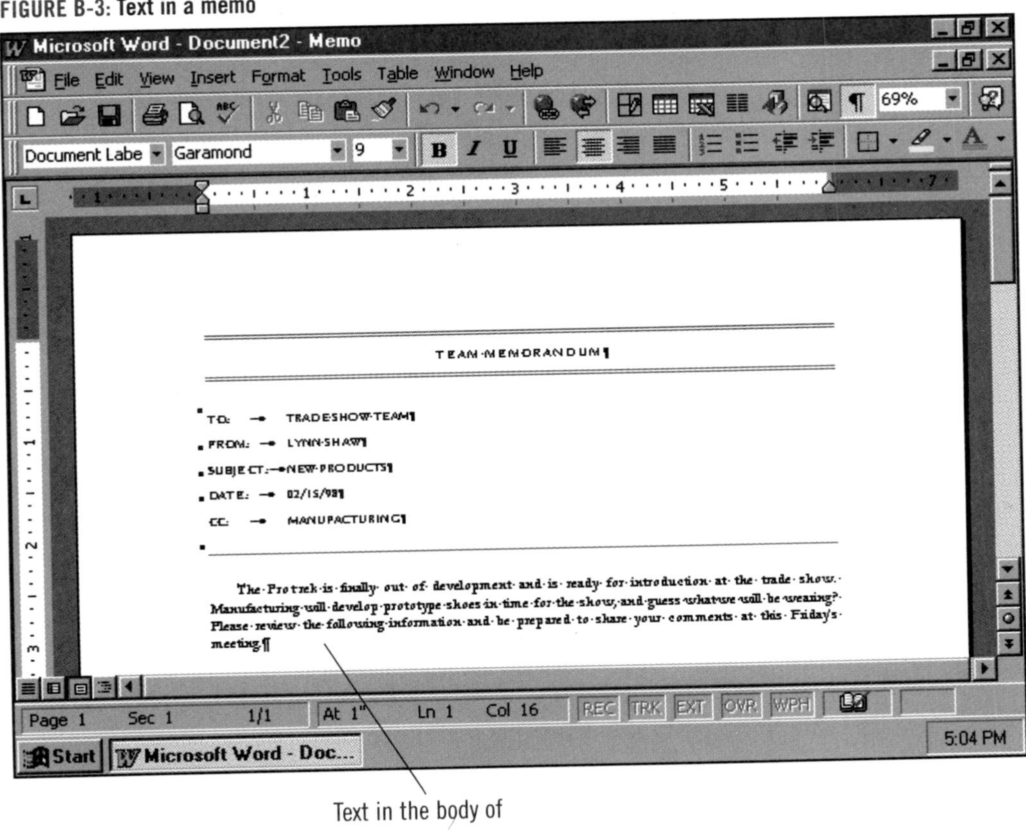

Office 97

Formatting a Document

Another way to add text to a document is to copy text from another document using the Clipboard. With the text of the document complete, you can format the document to improve its appearance. To make a table of numbers more attractive and easier to read, you can convert a tabbed list of numbers into a Word table. Lynn would like to use in her memo the text she read in another draft of the marketing document, so she opens the other document and copies the text into her memo.

1. Open the document OF B-1, triple-click in the **selection bar**, then click the **Copy button** on the Standard toolbar
   The text is copied to the Clipboard, and is ready for you to insert in the memo. This document contains the text you want to use in the memo. You will need to view the other document first.
2. Click **Window** on the menu bar, click **Document2 - Memo**, press **[Ctrl][End]** to place the insertion point at the end of the document, then click the **Paste button** on the Standard toolbar
   The copied text appears after the first paragraph. Now, you are ready to add formatting to your text. Begin by formatting the text in the headings.
3. Select the line that begins "Introducing Protrek: ...," click the **Font Size list arrow**, then choose **14 pts**; with the text still selected, click the **Bold button** on the Formatting toolbar, then apply bold formatting to the headings "The Sole of the Matter" and "Product Comparison," as shown in Figure B-4
4. Select the line that begins "Introducing Protrek: ...," then click the **Center button** on the Formatting toolbar. Click **Format** on the menu bar, click **Borders and Shading**, on the Shading tab, click **Gray 25%** (the second to last box in the bottom row), then click **OK**
   The line is centered between the margins and shaded, giving it the appearance of a heading. Now, improve the appearance of the bulleted list.
5. Scroll, if necessary; select the list of five items (each beginning with ">"); then click the **Bullets button** on the Formatting toolbar
   The >'s change to bullet symbols.
6. Select the **first bold heading** through the **last bold heading** (do not include the table in your selection) and click **Format** on the menu bar, click **Paragraph**, click the **Spacing after up arrow** to display 6pts, then click **OK**
7. Scroll to near the end of the document and select the tabbed list, then click the **Insert Table button** on the Standard toolbar
   The tabbed list is converted to a Word table arranged in a grid of rows and columns. Format the table with lines and borders to improve its appearance.
8. Click **Table** on the menu bar, then click **Table AutoFormat**; in the AutoFormat dialog box, click the **Columns 3** preset, then click **OK**
9. Click the **Print Preview button** on the Standard toolbar. (If the document does not fit on one page, click the **Shrink to Fit button** on the Preview toolbar.)
   Compare your document to Figure B-5.

QuickTip

Click the Zoom arrow, and increase the magnification to 100% to get a closer view of the text you are formatting.

Time To

- Save
- Close
- Exit

FIGURE B-4: Formatting headings

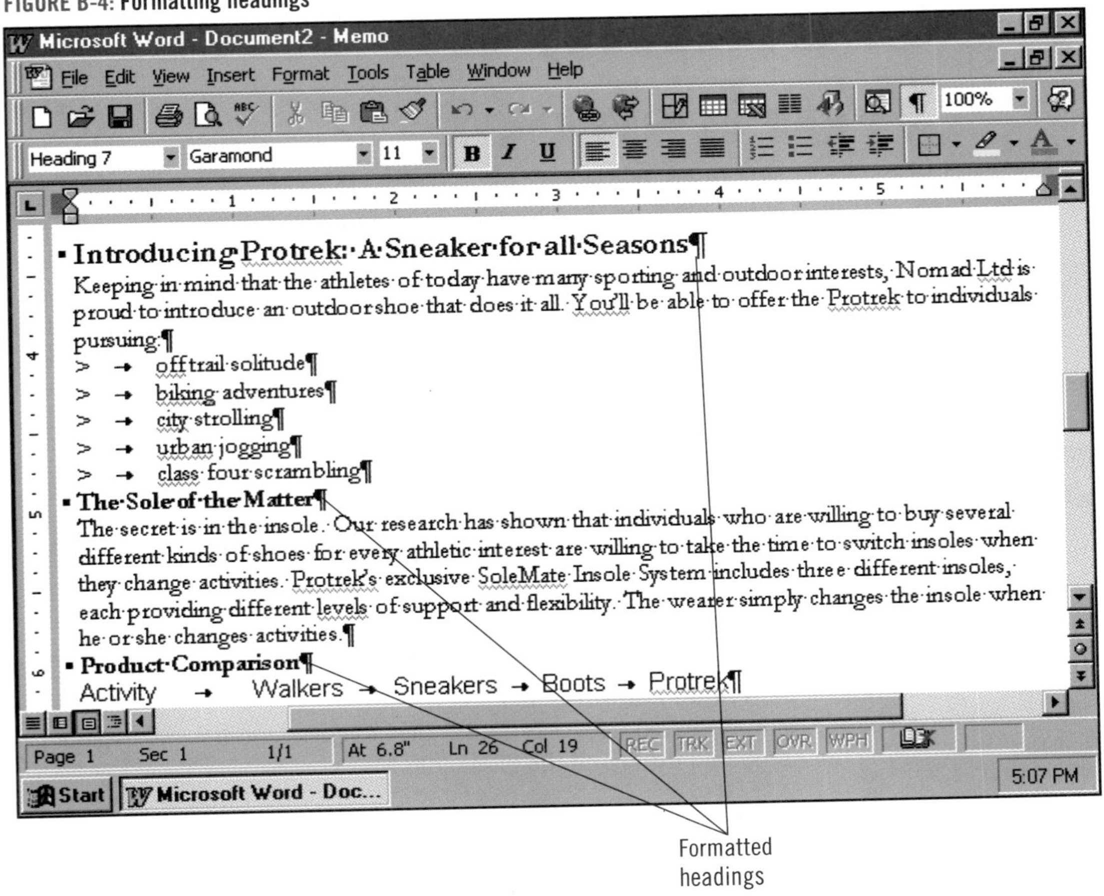

FIGURE B-5: Completed document

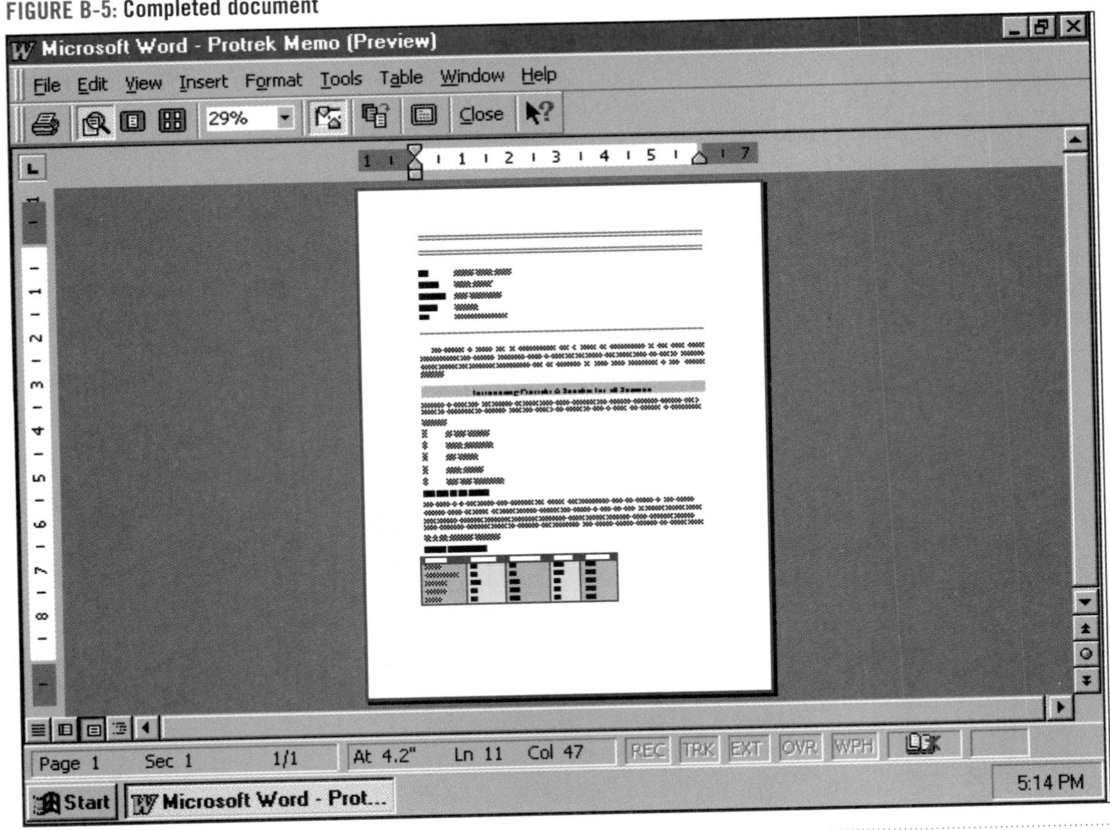

Office 97

Creating an Excel Worksheet

You can use an Excel worksheet to calculate numbers, make projections, and chart data. Formulas that automatically perform calculations can be added to a worksheet, and the AutoFormat feature makes raw data look more attractive. Charts—graphical representations of numeric data—can be used to help a reader focus on a particular aspect of the data. Enhancements, such as changing colors or patterns, shadowed text boxes, arrows, and text annotations, can be incorporated into a chart to make it more attractive and easier to read. To maximize efficiency when creating worksheets, you should follow a logical sequence of steps. Table B-2 gives an overview of the worksheet-development cycle. Clare Rothchild, a Nomad Ltd marketing intern, creates an attractive worksheet that shows potential vendors the company's net sales for the last four years.

Steps

1. **Start Excel, then, if necessary, open a new workbook**
   Enter the net sales data you received from the Accounting Department.

2. **Enter the data shown in Figure B-6 (be sure to include the commas), then save the workbook as Nomad Ltd Net Sales**
   Once the data is entered, create formulas that calculate annual and regional office totals using the AutoSum button and the fill handle.

Trouble?

Your initial entry of "Regional Offices" in cell A3 will not display completely once an entry is placed in cell B3. You will solve this screen discrepancy when you use AutoFormat.

3. **Click cell B9, create a formula to calculate the total for FY97 using the AutoSum button Σ, then use the fill handle to copy the formula to cells C9:E9**
   Use the same technique to create the regional office totals.

4. **Repeat Step 3, beginning in cell F4 and copying the formula to cells F5:F9**
   Cell F9 shows as ####### because the column is not wide enough to display the entire value, which will be rectified when you use AutoFormat. Now, make the data more attractive. Begin with the worksheet title, centering it across the columns of data, applying bold formatting and increasing its font size.

5. **Select the range A1:F1, click the Merge and Center button, click the Bold button B, click the Font Size list arrow, then click 12**
   Although you could assign individual colors and backgrounds to the remaining worksheet cells, you like using the AutoFormat feature because it's quick, easy, and visually effective.

QuickTip

Select the range or any cell within the range to be formatted before using AutoFormat.

6. **Select the range A3:F9, click Format, click AutoFormat, click Colorful 2, click OK, then press [Ctrl][Home]**
   The data is formatted using the Colorful 2 AutoFormat. Compare your worksheet to Figure B-7.

7. **Save your workbook, then preview and print the worksheet**
   Continue to the next lesson, where you create charts for the data.

FIGURE B-6: Net sales data for regional offices

	A	B	C	D	E	F
1	Nomad Ltd's Net Sales for Fiscal Years 1994 - 1997					
2						
3	Regional O	FY97	FY96	FY95	FY94	Total
4	Northeast	250,000	208,000	170,000	160,000	
5	Northwest	200,000	188,000	145,000	137,000	
6	Midwest	185,000	176,000	132,000	106,900	
7	South	145,000	132,000	130,000	123,000	
8	Southwest	170,000	156,000	151,000	146,000	
9	Total					

FIGURE B-7: Data enhanced using AutoFormat

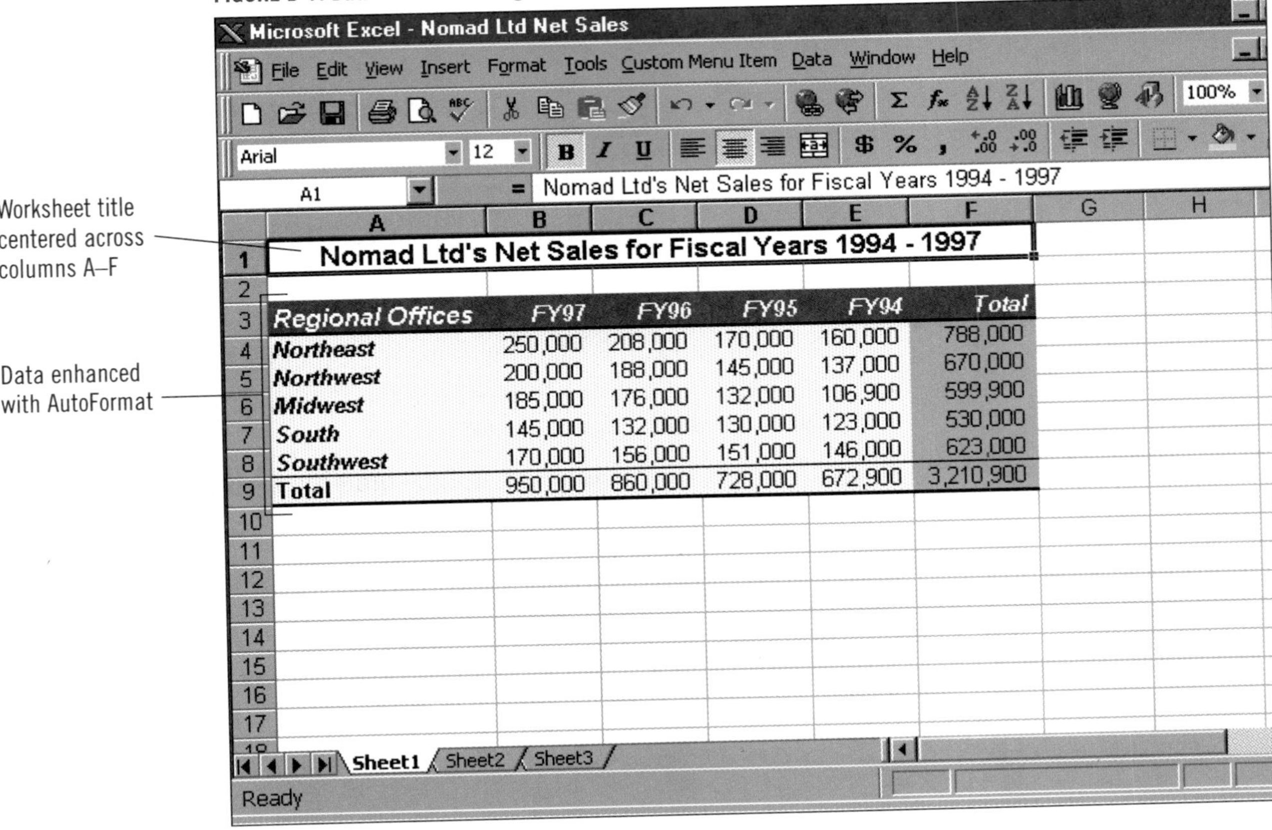

Regional Offices	FY97	FY96	FY95	FY94	Total
Northeast	250,000	208,000	170,000	160,000	788,000
Northwest	200,000	188,000	145,000	137,000	670,000
Midwest	185,000	176,000	132,000	106,900	599,900
South	145,000	132,000	130,000	123,000	530,000
Southwest	170,000	156,000	151,000	146,000	623,000
Total	950,000	860,000	728,000	672,900	3,210,900

TABLE B-2: Worksheet-Development Cycle

step	what to do
I. Plan and design the worksheet	Determine purpose of sheet; draw rough sketch.
II. Build the worksheet	Enter labels, values, and formulas into Excel.
III. Enhance the worksheet	Format data and add charts.
IV. Check for errors and print	Check spelling and data accuracy; choose page-setup options, then issue print command.
V. Perform final check	Read over printout for errors and reprint, if necessary.

Office 97

Enhancing an Excel Worksheet

Once you have entered and formatted the information, you can create charts to illustrate and dramatize the data. You can create multiple charts; remember that a variety of chart types can illustrate different trends within the data. As worksheet data is modified, a chart is updated automatically to reflect such changes. Clare uses the ChartWizard to create two charts for this data so that potential vendors can see the information graphically in several ways. She'll also add enhancements to make the charts look dramatic and call attention to chart data.

1. Select the range **A3:E8**, click the **ChartWizard button**, then create a 3-D Clustered Column chart titled **Net Sales by Regional Office** in the range **A10:H27**
   Add a drop shadow box around the chart title.
2. Right-click the **chart title**, click **Format Chart Title**, then use the **Patterns tab** to select Shadow
   The Midwest region's net sales figures rose dramatically in FY96. You want to call attention to that fact by using an arrowhead and text annotation.
3. Using the Drawing toolbar, add the text annotation **Dramatic improvement!** and an arrowhead pointing from the annotation to the Midwest's FY96 column, as shown in Figure B-8
   You also want to show the total net sales in a pie chart.
4. Select the ranges **A3:A8** and **F3:F8**, click the **ChartWizard button**, then create a 3-D Pie chart titled **Total Net Sales: FY94-FY97** in the range A29:G43
   You want to explode the Midwest pie slice to make it stand out.
5. Click the **Midwest pie slice twice** to select it, then drag the slice away from the pie center as shown in Figure B-9
   Add an annotation and an arrowhead to this chart.
6. Add the text annotation **Great profit potential** and an arrowhead pointing from the annotation to the Midwest's pie slice, as shown in Figure B-9
7. Save your workbook, then preview and print your worksheet
8. Exit Excel

QuickTip

To select nonadjacent ranges, select the first range, then press and hold [Ctrl] while you select the additional ranges.

FIGURE B-8: Net sales data in 3-D clustered column chart

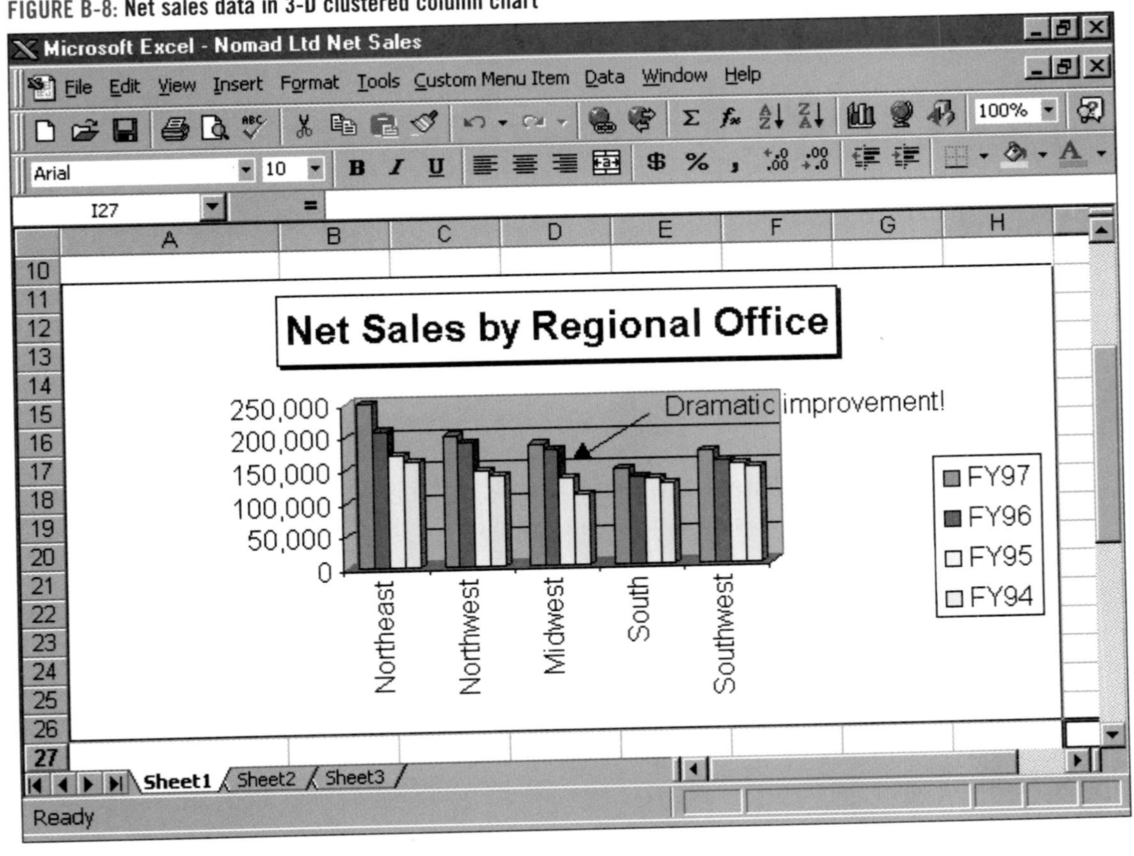

FIGURE B-9: Annotated and enhanced 3-D pie chart

Microsoft Excel - Nomad Ltd Net Sales

Total Net Sales: FY94-FY97

Northeast
Northwest
Midwest
South
Southwest

Exploded piece

Great profit potential

Office 97

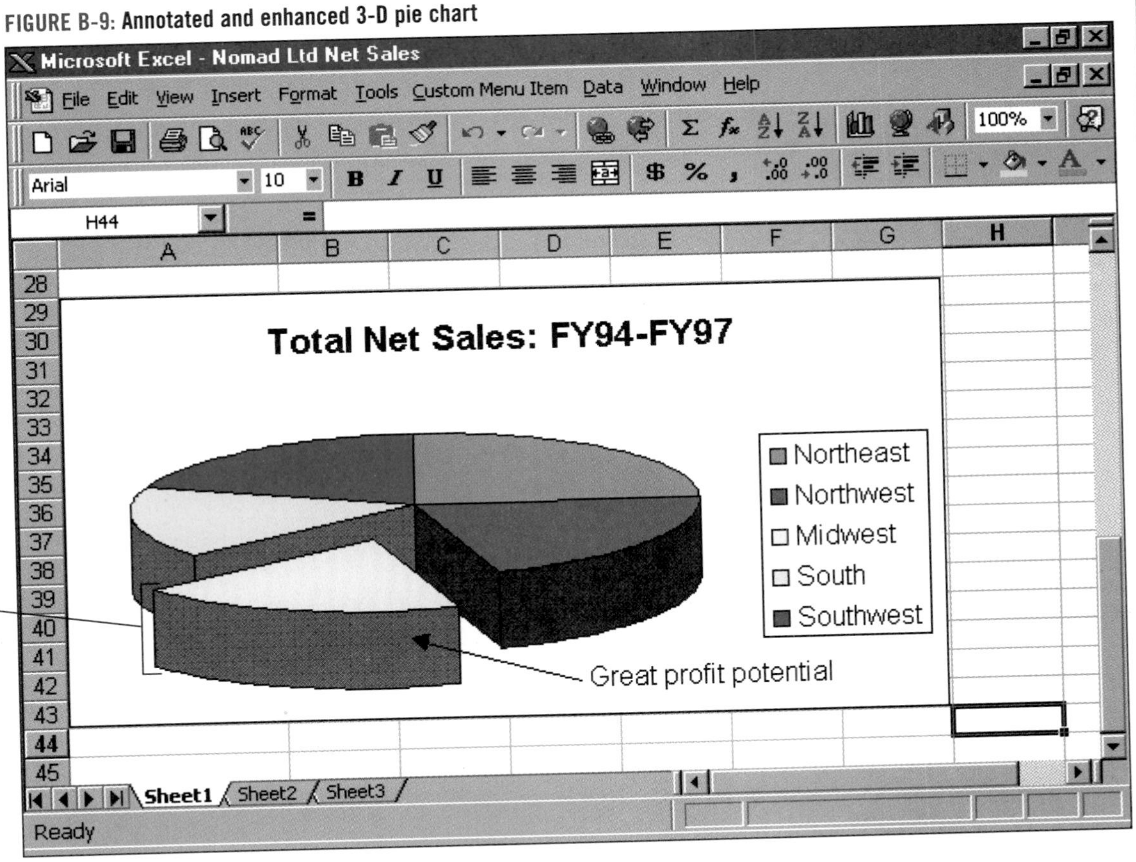

Office 97

Creating an Access Database

An Access database is used to store and manipulate lists of information organized as fields and records. To build an Access database, first you name the database, then you create tables to hold the information you wish to track. Aaron Douglas, a sales manager at Nomad Ltd, will develop a database to store vendor information on outside vendors that are considering selling Nomad products. The fields of information Aaron wishes to track are identified in Figure B-10.

Steps

1. Start Access, then create a new blank Access database and name it **Vendor**
   Now that the database is created, you proceed to define the fields in the table.
2. Create a new table in Design View
   Because you know exactly what fields of data you want to track, you will enter the fields directly into the table's Design view.
3. Enter the fields using the information in Figure B-10
   Be sure to identify the Potential field as a Currency data type. Every other field will be a Text data type. Because each vendor has a unique telephone number, you can use this field as the key field for the table.
4. Click **Phone**, then click the **Primary Key button** on the toolbar
   Now that you have identified the fields of your table, you will access the datasheet of the table and type the actual vendor information.
5. Click the **View button** on the toolbar, click **Yes** when prompted to save the changes, type **Vendor Master Table** as the table name, then click **OK**
   You will enter the records of information, using [Tab] to move from field to field across the record.
6. Enter the seven records as shown in Figure B-11
   With all seven records entered, you can close the Vendor Master Table.
7. Click **File**, then click **Close** to close the Vendor Master Table datasheet

QuickTip

Press [Ctrl] while pressing ' (the single apostrophe) to duplicate the field information from the previous record to the current record.

FIGURE B-10: Sketch of fields to be tracked in Vendor Master Table

Field Name	Data Type	Description
Name	Text	Company name of vendor
Street	Text	Street address
City	Text	
State	Text	
Zip	Text	
Phone	Text	
First	Text	First name of contact
Last	Text	Last name of contact
Potential	Currency	Potential annual revenue

Key Field

FIGURE B-11: Vendor Master Table datasheet

Fields

Vendor Master Table : Table

Name	Street	City	State	Zip	Phone	First	Last	Potential
Panthers	99 Ash	Casey	NY	11003	202-111-2222	Lois	Griffiths	$20,000.00
1st Team	77 Monroe	Linden	NY	11006	202-222-3333	Cindy	Ralston	$70,000.00
Sports Fever	222 Revere	Orient	NY	11007	202-222-5555	Riva	Noack	$80,000.00
Go For It	11 Main	Fontanelle	NY	11001	202-333-4444	Jeff	Larson	$20,000.00
Sports Team	44 Jefferson	Adair	NY	11003	202-555-1111	Brad	Michael	$150,000.00
Time Out	333 Taylor	Macksburg	NY	11003	202-666-7777	Doug	Allen	$10,000.00
All's Fair	88 Madison	Panora	NY	11003	202-777-8888	Mark	Arno	$75,000.00
								$0.00

Record: 7 of 7

Records

Seven total records

CLUES TO USE

Determining fields and data types

When designing a table in a database, break out each piece of information into its own field. For example, always create two fields to hold a contact's first name and last name. That way, you'll be able to sort on the last name field. When determining data types, use the text data type for any information that doesn't represent quantities or monetary values, even when the data contains only numeric characters such as Zip code, phone number, or Social Security number. By making these fields text fields, you'll have more control over how the fields are formatted later. In addition, you won't be able to inadvertently create a nonsensical, calculated total on a field that shouldn't be totaled, such as Zip code.

Office 97

Creating an Access Database Query

An **Access query** is a question you ask about the data in a database. Queries allow you to select the specific fields and records you wish to view and to sort the records in a certain order. You also can use a query to perform calculations on the data in the query such as totalling a numeric field of information. Aaron will create an Access query to pull a list of potential vendors that should be contacted before the upcoming trade show. He'll use the Zip field as his primary sort so that the list can be easily used by the Nomad sales representatives (whose territories are determined by Zip Codes). He'll use the Potential field (which represents potential sales volume) as his secondary sort so that the list of vendors within each state will be listed in a highest to lowest potential revenue order. Finally, because the trade show will be attended by only large vendors, Aaron will enter limiting criteria in the query to show only those vendors with potential annual revenue over $50,000.

Steps

1. Create a new query in Design View based on the Vendor Master Table
   You need only certain fields for the query: Name (vendor name), Zip, Phone, First (contact first name), Last (contact last name), and Potential (potential annual sales for the vendor). You will drag them to the query design grid for inclusion in the query's datasheet.

2. Click the **Name field** and drag it to the first column of the query design grid, then drag the **Zip**, **Phone**, **First**, **Last**, and **Potential fields** to the grid in order as shown in Figure B-12
   You will either scroll to the right in the query design grid to see all six fields or narrow the columns to view them all at one time. With the fields for the query in place, you will use the Zip field as the primary sort and the Potential field as the secondary sort. You will use a descending sort order in the Potential field so the vendors with the highest potential annual sales are listed first.

3. Click the **list arrow** of the Sort cell of the Zip field, click **Ascending**, click the **list arrow** of the Sort cell of the Potential field, then click **Descending**
   With the sorts in place, you will enter the limiting criteria to allow only those vendors who represent annual sales greater than $50,000 to display in the query.

4. Click the **Criteria cell** of the **Potential field**, then type **>50000**
   With the query defined as displayed in Figure B-13, you will view the resulting datasheet, print the datasheet, and save the query definition.

5. Click the **View button** to view the datasheet as shown in Figure B-14, then print the datasheet

6. Save the query as **Trade Show Query**, close the datasheet, then exit Access

QuickTip

You can double-click a name in the field list of the Query Design View to add the field to the next column of the query design grid.

CLUES TO USE

Sort order

Sort order is determined by the left-to-right order of the fields in the query design grid. The field on the far left is the primary (first) sort field, the next is the secondary sort field, and so on. You use the secondary sort field only when the data in the primary sort field is the same. For example, a telephone book displays its records by Last Name, the primary sort field. When two listings with the same last name are displayed, however, the secondary sort field of First Name determines which person's record is listed first.

FIGURE B-12: Query design view

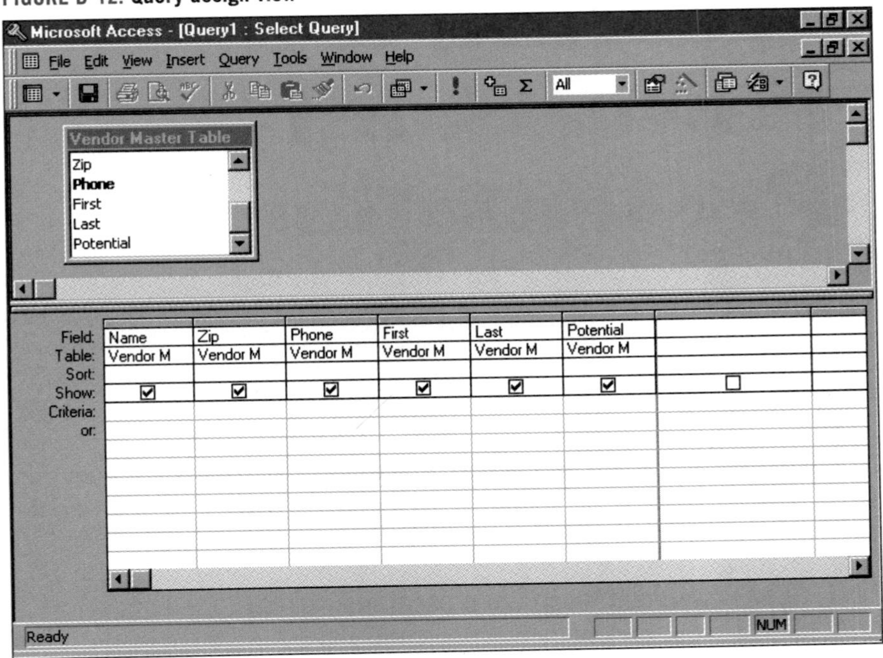

FIGURE B-13: Query design view with sorts and criteria

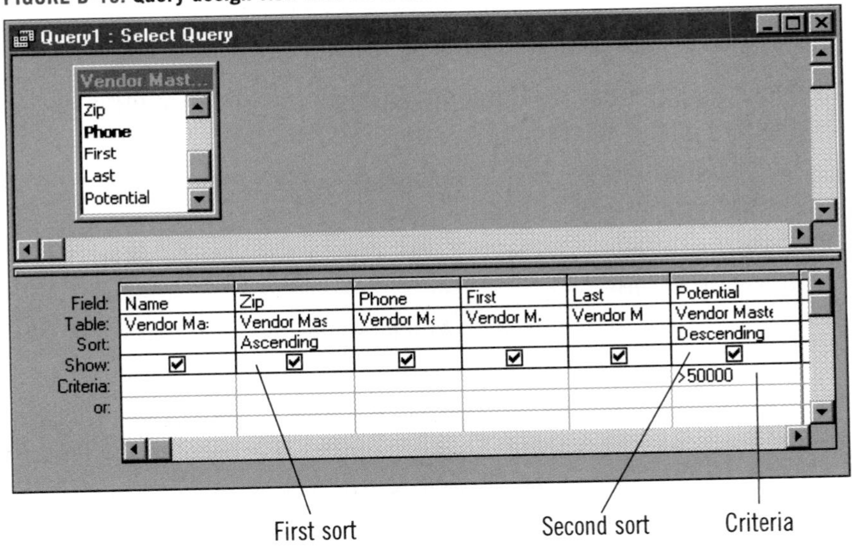

FIGURE B-14: Query datasheet

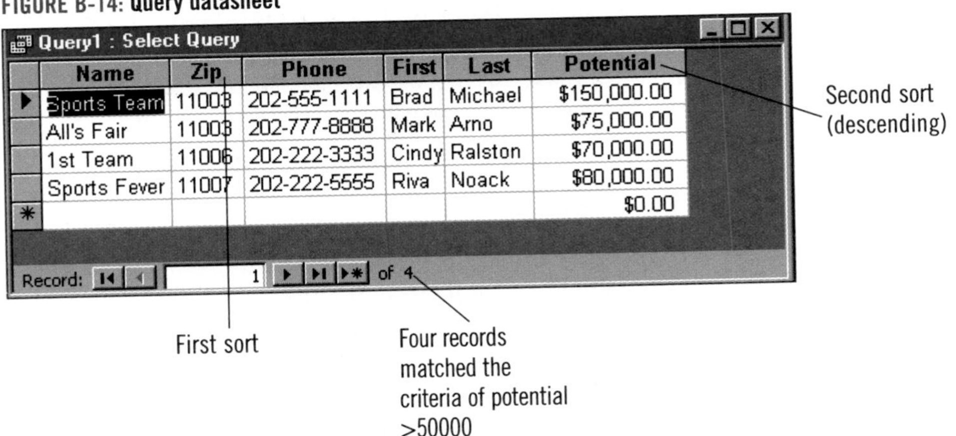

Office 97

Office 97

Creating a PowerPoint Presentation

A PowerPoint presentation is used to organize and display information. The two basic aspects of creating a presentation are (1)entering and editing information and (2)creating a slide design. You can create a presentation by entering your own information in Slide view or Outline view or by importing information from other sources, such as Microsoft Word or Microsoft Excel. To enhance the slides of your presentation, you can format text, add drawn objects, insert clip art, embed charts, or modify the color scheme. If you are planning to display your presentation using a computer, you can add special effects that allow you to manipulate your slides creatively in Slide Show view. Carrie Armstrong, the executive assistant to the president, finishes creating a brief presentation on Nomad Ltd that will run at the trade show.

1. **Start PowerPoint, open the presentation OF B-2, then save it as Trade Show 98**
   Slide 1 of the presentation appears. You add a PowerPoint template to the presentation.

2. **Click the Apply Design button on the Standard toolbar, then apply the Dads Tie template**
   Now, add a subtitle to the slide and format both text objects on the title slide.

QuickTip

The text size on your slide should be no smaller than 18 points to allow readability.

3. **Type "Quality Gear for Outdoors Enthusiasts" in the subtitle placeholder, then change the size and style of the title text**
   Compare your screen to Figure B-15. Add a new slide to your presentation with Nomad's company history.

4. **Click the Outline view button, create a new slide after Slide 2, then type the text shown in Figure B-16**
   Switch to Slide view and change the line spacing of the text you just entered to improve its appearance.

5. **Double-click the slide icon for Slide 3, press [Shift], click the text object, then click the Decrease Paragraph Spacing button once on the Formatting toolbar**
   The spacing between the lines of text decreases. Now, add an object to Slide 4 using a PowerPoint drawing tool.

QuickTip

You can customize the appearance of a drawn object by using the 3-D, Shadow, and Draw menu buttons on the Drawing toolbar.

6. **Click the Next Slide button, click the AutoShapes menu button AutoShapes on the Drawing toolbar, point to Stars and Banners, press [Shift], then draw a shape using the Vertical Scroll tool on the right side of the slide**
   Once you draw the scroll shape, you may need to adjust its position by dragging it or using the Arrow keys on your keyboard.

7. **Type Key Goals in the scroll shape, then format the object using the formatting tools on the Drawing toolbar**
   Use the scroll's sizing handles to make the scroll shape taller.

8. **Drag the scroll shape's top sizing handle until the object looks similar to Figure B-17**
   Your scroll shape may look different from Figure B-17, depending on the original size of the shape. Continue to the next lesson, where you'll work with Clipart, a chart, and slide show special effects.

FIGURE B-15: Slide showing applied template

Microsoft PowerPoint - [Trade Show 98]
File Edit View Insert Format Tools Slide Show Window Help
40%
Times New Roman
24
Nomad Ltd
"Quality Gear for Outdoors Enthusiasts"
Draw
AutoShapes
Slide 1 of 7
Dads Tie

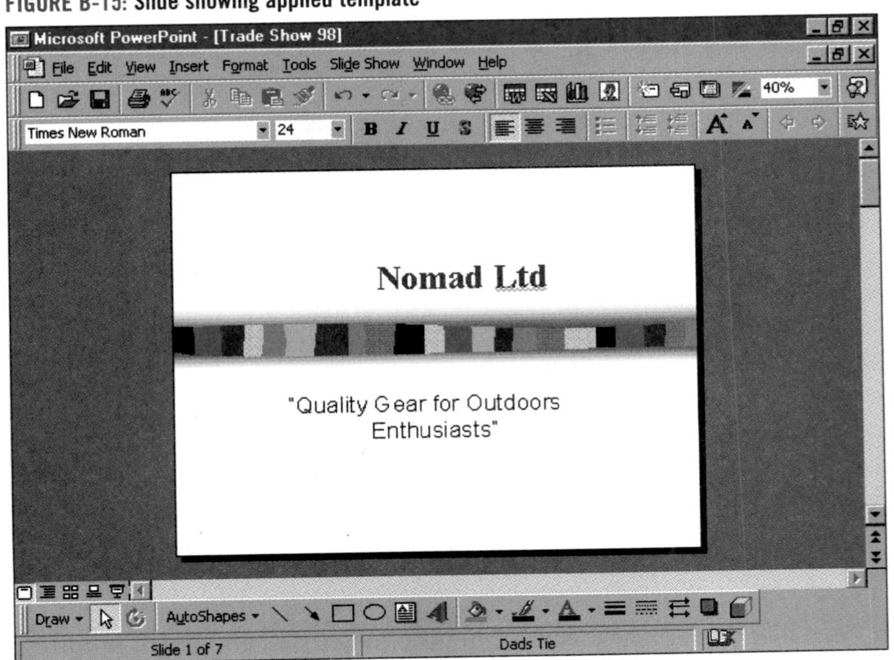

FIGURE B-16: New slide text

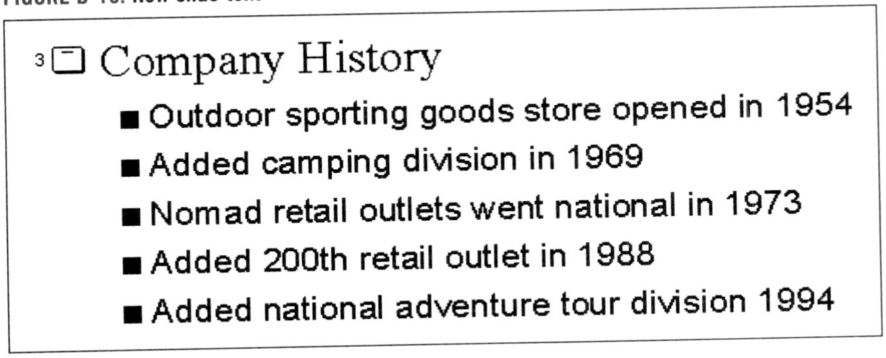

3 Company History
Outdoor sporting goods store opened in 1954
Added camping division in 1969
Nomad retail outlets went national in 1973
Added 200th retail outlet in 1988
Added national adventure tour division 1994

FIGURE B-17: Slide showing adjusted scroll object

Top Products for 97
New products
– Rollerblade Professional™
– SnowHiker ™ Boots
– OutBack Camping gear
New Travel tour
– Colorado River Kayak
Key Goals
Mar 18, 1998
Nomad Ltd
4

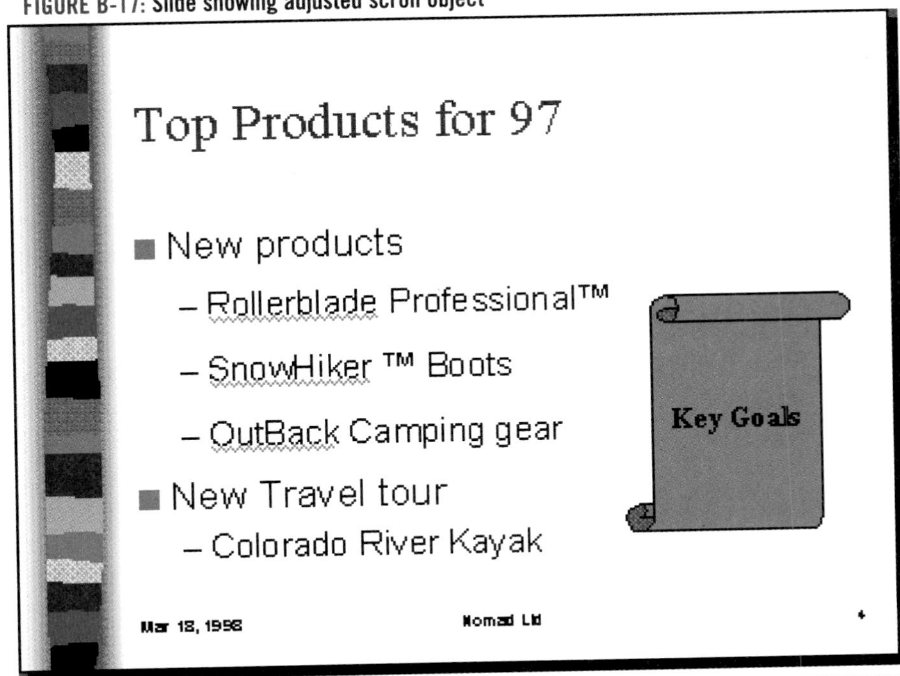

Office 97

Modifying a PowerPoint Presentation

Once you have the basic content and design of your presentation completed, you are ready to enhance your slides with supplemental objects such as Clipart, drawn shapes, and charts. Objects such as Clipart and charts can help clarify your message and make your slides more interesting. PowerPoint allows you to format and modify supplemental objects using its formatting and drawing tools. Carrie adds a piece of Clipart and a Microsoft Graph chart to finish her trade-show presentation, then sets slide show special effects so she can show the presentation on her computer.

QuickTip

If this picture is not available, choose another one.

QuickTip

After the Graph chart is selected, double-click any item in the Graph chart to open an editing dialog box for that item.

QuickTip

Click the Animation Effects button on the Formatting toolbar to open the Animation Effects toolbar.

1. Click the **Next Slide button**, then double-click the **Clipart placeholder**
   Place on the slide a piece of clip art that enhances the theme of the slide.
2. Click the **Transportation** category, then insert the **Yacht picture**
   Compare your screen to Figure B-18. Now, move to the next slide and embed a chart using Microsoft Graph.
3. Click , double-click the **graph placeholder**, clear the default datasheet contents, then enter the data shown in Figure B-19
   Format the numbers on the Value Axis.
4. Click the **datasheet Close button**, right-click the **numbers** on the Value Axis, then click **Format Axis**
   Change the scale and format of the axis.
5. Click the **Scale tab**, double-click the **number** in the Major unit text box, type **25000**, click the **Number tab**, in the Category list box, click **Currency**, then click **OK**
   Format the Value Axis numbers before you exit Microsoft Graph.
6. Click the **Decrease Decimal button** twice on the Formatting toolbar, then click in a blank part of the slide
   Compare your screen to Figure B-20. To finish your presentation, set animations, slide transitions, and slide timings.
7. Set text and object animations, slide transitions, and slide timings to the slides of your presentation, then preview the presentation in Slide Show view
   Use both Slide Sorter view and Slide view to accomplish these tasks. After setting slide show special effects, check your presentation for spelling mistakes.
8. Check the spelling, then print your presentation slides
   When PowerPoint finds a misspelled word or a word it doesn't recognize, the Spelling dialog box opens. Fix any misspelled words that the Spell Checker finds. Remember that PowerPoint does not catch misused words, only misspelled ones. This completes the trade show presentation.
9. Save and close the presentation, then exit PowerPoint

FIGURE B-18: Slide showing embedded clip art

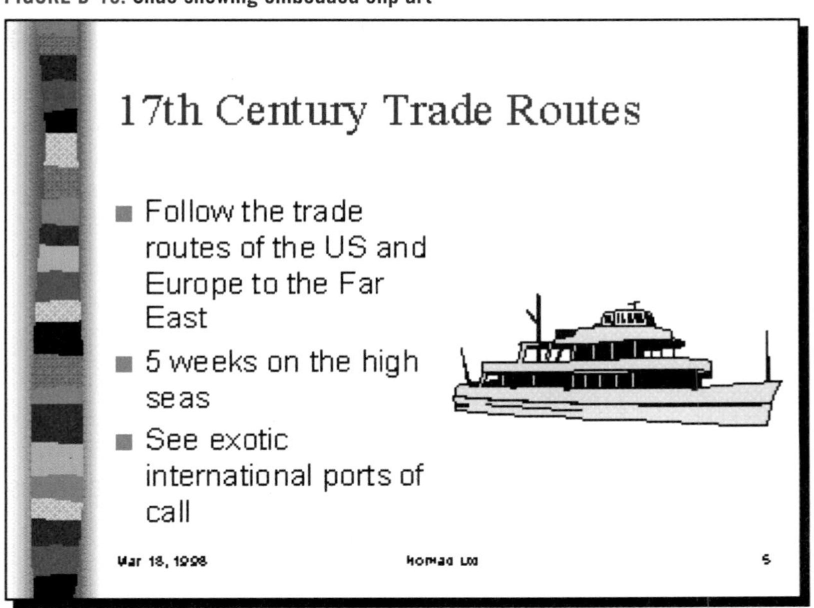

FIGURE B-19: Microsoft Graph data

Trade Show 98 - Datasheet

		A	B	C	D	E
	Regions	FY97	FY96	FY95	FY94	
1	Northeast	250000	207000	180000	170000	
2	South	190000	180000	150000	140000	
3	Midwest	120000	105000	90000	100000	
4	West	145000	140000	120000	125000	
5						

FIGURE B-20: Microsoft Graph chart on slide

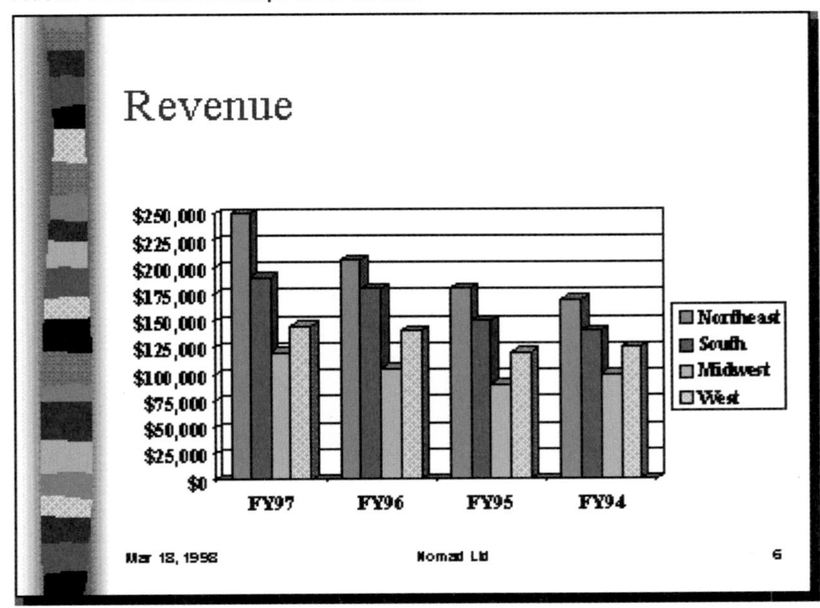

Office 97

Browsing the Internet

An Internet connection provides instant access to reference materials, current events, and almost unlimited topics of interest. Using a **Web browser** such as the Microsoft Internet Explorer, you can visit sites on the World Wide Web and obtain information for your business as well as personal uses. Lynn wants to get ideas from existing sites before setting up a Web page for her department.

Steps

QuickTip

You also can open Microsoft Internet Explorer by clicking Start, pointing to Programs, then clicking Internet Explorer.

Trouble?

Your list of matches may look different.

1. **Establish an Internet connection using established procedures from your instructor**
   Once your connection is open, open your Web browser.
2. **Double-click the Internet icon on your desktop**
   Use the Yahoo! search engine to locate relevant sites.
3. **Select the information in the Address text box, type http://www.yahoo.com, then press [Enter]**
   Once the Yahoo! Search engine is displayed, you look for sites about the Library of Congress to get design ideas for your Web page.
4. **Type Library of Congress in the Search text box, then click Search**
   The search reveals a variety of results. Compare your matches to Figure B-21. You decide to look at the direct Library of Congress site.
5. **Click Library of Congress, as shown in Figure B-22**
   You may have to scroll down the list to find the Library of Congress link. The address for this site is http://www.loc.gov. At the site, you notice the use of text, graphics, and links. Satisfied with how this page is laid out, you close the browser and end your Internet session.
6. **Click the Close button on the Microsoft Internet Explorer title bar, then disconnect your Internet connection using established procedures**

FIGURE B-21: Search results using Yahoo!

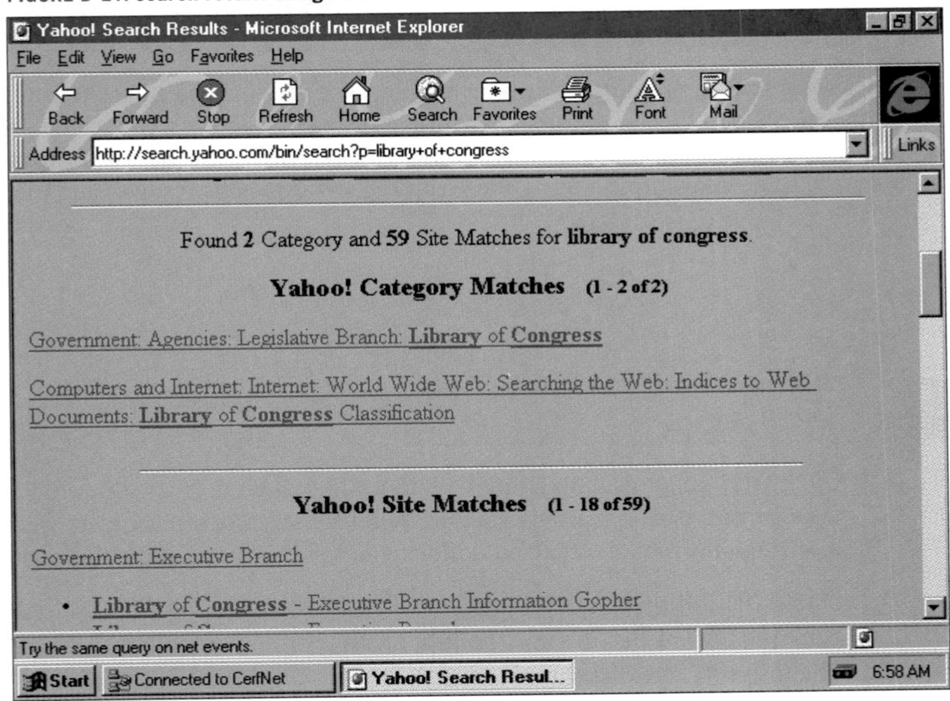

FIGURE B-22: Library of Congress home page

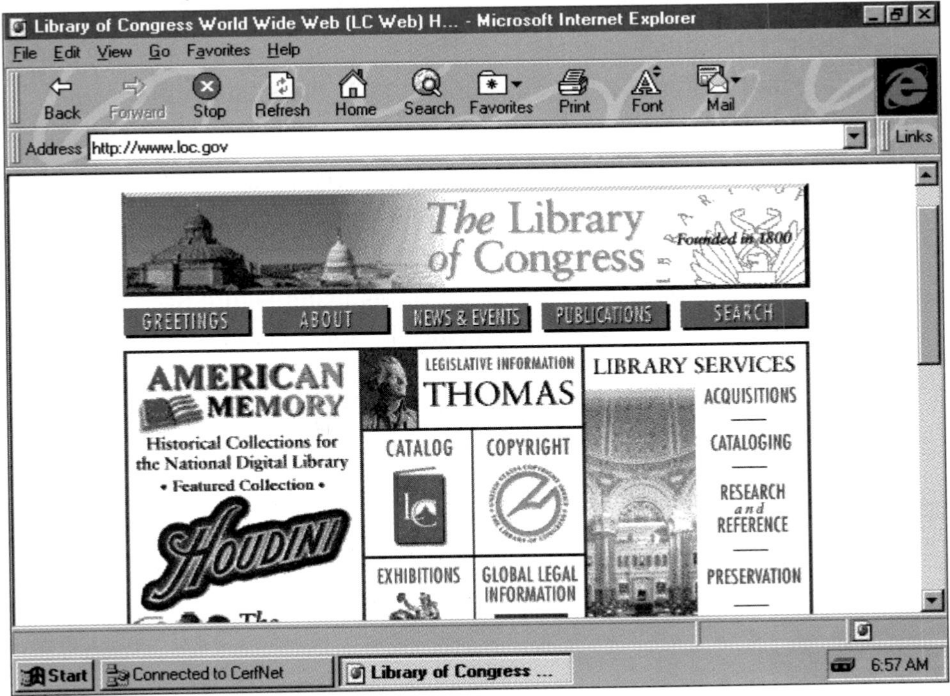

Using several search engines

A variety of search engines is available. Among the other tools are Bigfoot, Excite, HotBot, WebCrawler, or Yahoo!. Each engine searches in a slightly different way and may have different results. While you might find duplicate information using more than one search engine, it's a great way of finding the most information on any particular subject.

Office 97

Creating a Web Page

Microsoft Office 97 contains features that make it easy for you to create your own Web pages. You can create a Web page using the Word Web Page Wizard, which includes templates that add thematic formatting and graphics to your Web pages instantly. Lynn started a Web page for the trade-show project using the Web Page Wizard and is ready to add information to it.

Steps

1. Open Word, open the document OF B-3, then save it as **Trade Show Web page**
   When a Web page is created using the Web Page Wizard, placeholders are included to make inserting information easy. You decide to add the Nomad logo to the page.
2. Select the paragraph beginning with Replace, *excluding the concluding hard return*, click the **Insert Picture button** on the Standard toolbar
   The Insert Picture dialog box opens.
3. Click **Nomad** in the file list, then click **Insert**
   The Nomad logo file is displayed in the Web page, as shown in Figure B-23. Next, add text describing some highlights of the trade show.
4. Select the text **Type some text**, then type **The Protrek is finally out of product development and is ready for introduction at the trade show.**
   Add bulleted text to replace the existing placeholders.
5. Select the first Add a list item text, then type **Manufacturing will have the Protrek available two weeks after the trade show**
   Add bulleted text to replace the existing placeholders.
6. Replace the remaining **Add a list items** using Figure B-24 as a guide
   You decide to save the document, then print it and show it to colleagues. You'll complete it later.
7. Save and print your Web page, then exit Word

FIGURE B-23: Logo inserted into Web page

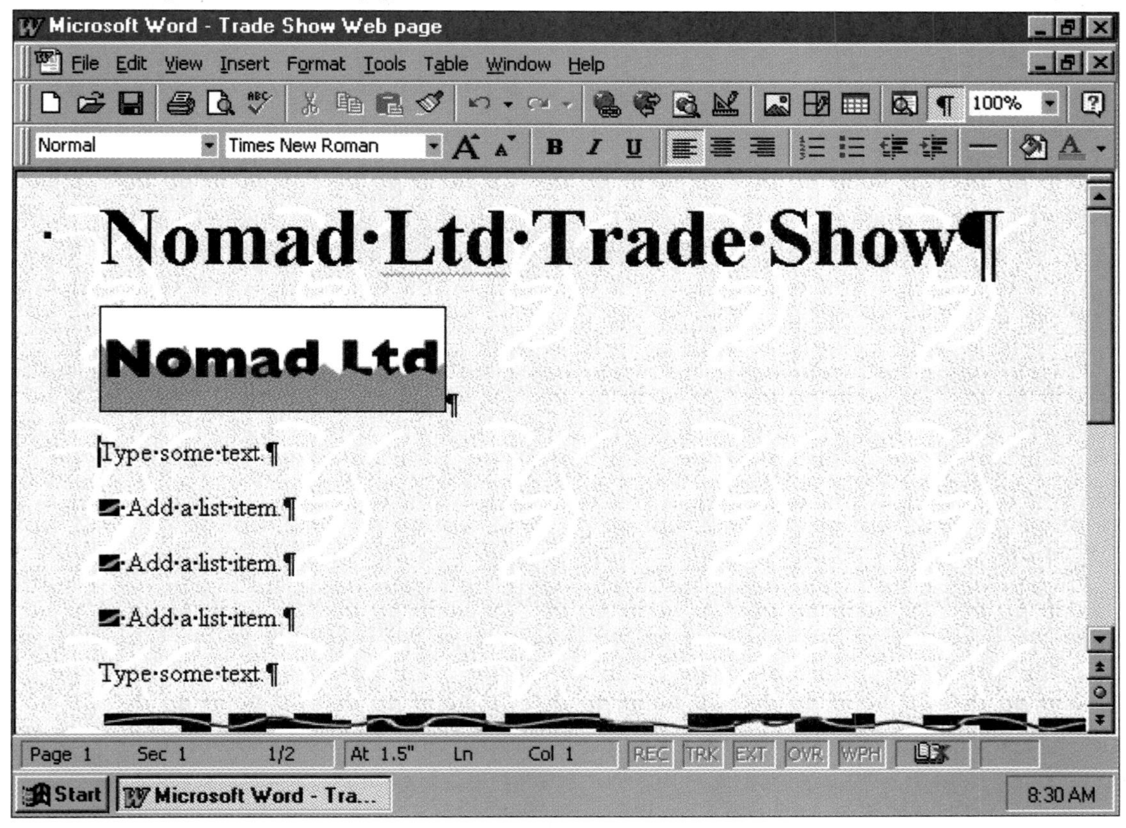

FIGURE B-24: Web page with text added

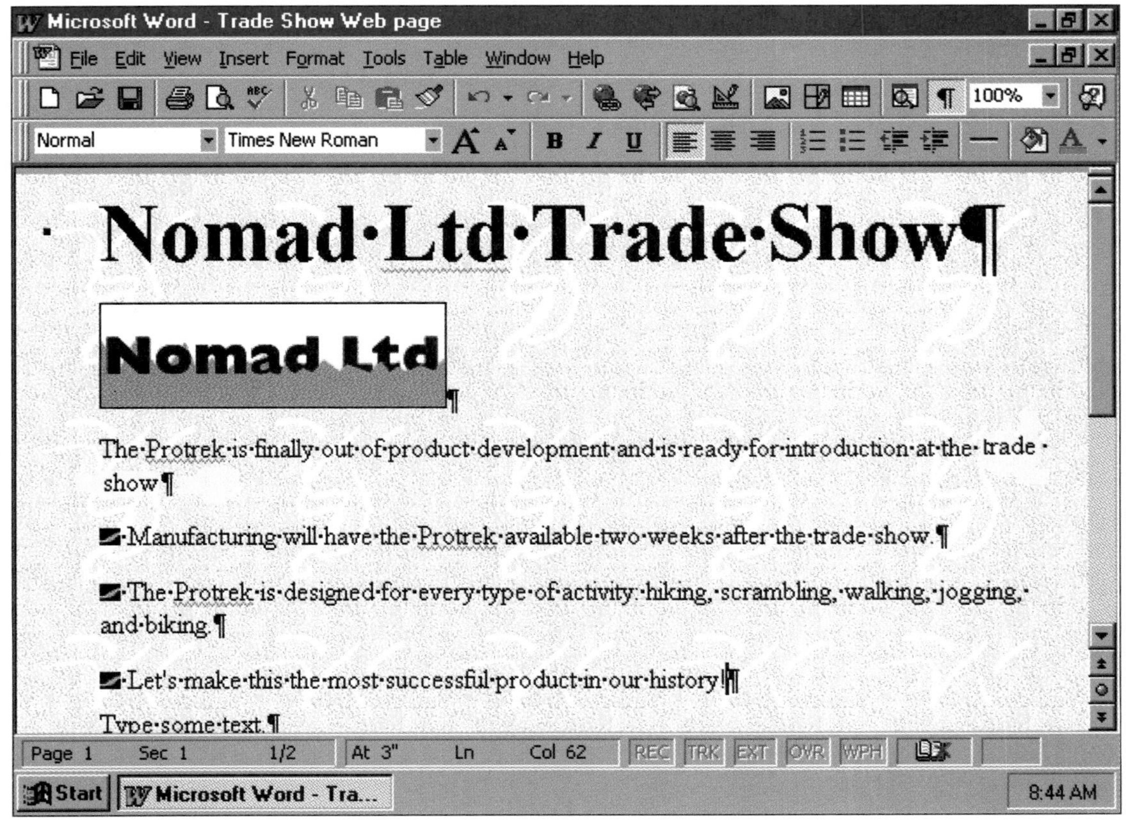

Independent Challenges

1. Recently, you have purchased an existing computer hardware and software retail store called Pentium Professionals. Before you can begin daily operations of the store, you must complete several tasks. Your primary goals include conducting a store inventory, an examination of last year's sales, and a presentation to the Chamber of Commerce to attract new customers. Apply your skills using Microsoft Office to complete these initial tasks.

To complete this independent challenge:

1. Create a Word document called "Pentium Pro Tasks" that lists the tasks outlined in this independent challenge, then save it.
2. Design a logo for this company using WordArt that can serve as a logo. Incorporate this logo into the Pentium Pro document, then print the document.
3. Create a new Access database called "Pentium Pros."
4. Add a table called "Existing Products" that contains at least 10 items. The table should include fields for Product Name, Quantity, Retail Price, and Manufacturer. (You can add more fields if you like.)
5. Create a query that displays the fields in Step 4 and sorts the table in ascending order by the Manufacturer, then in descending order by Product Name.
6. Name the query "Products by Manufacturer," then print the query.
7. Create a PowerPoint presentation consisting of at least five slides that describes the company and why local businesspeople should use your services. Name the presentation "Chamber Promotion," then save it. Add builds, transitions, sounds, and special effects where appropriate.
8. Print the slides as handouts (six slides to a sheet).
9. Create an Excel workbook called "Pentium Pro Sales," then save it. Rename Sheet 1 "Previous Year," then make up data for the months of the previous year. Include a 3-D pie chart to dramatize the data.
10. Print the worksheet and chart, then hand in your printed materials.

2. You've joined a local historical society. The members investigate events and share the information with other club members. Your interest in luxury liners and access to the Internet has made it possible to find out about an exciting chapter in history. Although the *Titantic* sank over 80 years ago, many facts surrounding the ships demise, as well as its passengers and crew remain intriguing. You decide to use your Microsoft Office skills and your access to the Internet to create a professional presentation.

To complete this independent challenge:

1. Log on to the Internet and use your Web browser to go to http://www.course.com, click the link for this textbook, then click the link for the Office Unit.
2. Use any of the following sites to compile your data: A Tribute to The R.M.S. Titanic and her crew, RMS Titanic: Her Passengers and Crew, or the MSNBC Titanic page. You also can point your Web browser to any other Titanic site using a search engine such as Yahoo!
3. Print any necessary Web pages.
4. Find out information about crew members and famous passengers. How many survivors were there? Were there any radio transmitters aboard the ship? If so, why wasn't the ship rescued?
5. Compile information you find in a Word document called "Titanic facts."
6. Create a PowerPoint presentation using the information you gathered from the Web.
7. Add timing, builds, transitions, sounds, and video clips to enhance your presentation.
8. Print the slides of your final presentation, then submit them.

Word 97

W

Formatting
Pages

Objectives

- ► Control text flow between pages
- ► Adjust document margins
- ► Insert headers
- ► Insert footers
- ► Modify text in a footer
- ► Change page orientation
- ► Change formatting in multiple sections
- ► Create headers for specific pages

In addition to formatting text and paragraphs, you can format the pages of your documents. **Page formatting** includes determining the margins between the text and the edge of the page. It also includes the size and orientation of a page. Additional formatting options allow you to specify the text flow on and between pages. Another feature allows you to add text that will appear at the top or bottom of each page in the document, in the form of headers and footers. To complete the formatting in her financial summary for Nomad Ltd, Angela Pacheco needs to adjust the document's margins, change the orientation for an additional page, and add headers and footers to her document.

Word 97

Controlling Text Flow between Pages

When the amount of text in a document fills a page, Word automatically creates a page break, which places any remaining text at the start of the next new page. Sometimes this break results in a line or two appearing alone at the bottom of the page with the rest of the paragraph continuing on the next page, giving the document an awkward appearance. Using text flow features, you can control how text flows on and between pages. Angela would like to have the Financial Results heading appear with the paragraph that follows it.

Steps

QuickTip

Turn off spelling and grammar checking. Display paragraph marks.

QuickTip

You can quickly insert your own page break anywhere in a document by pressing **[Ctrl][Enter]**. In normal view, this kind of break (sometimes called a hard page break) appears as a light gray line labeled "Page Break" in your document.

Trouble?

Do not be concerned if the amount of text you see in your own document does not match the amount of text shown in the figure. The exact amount of text you see can depend on the resolution of your monitor, or the type of printer connected to your computer.

1. **Start Word, open the document named WD E-1, then save it as Executive Summary**
   This document is the summary of the year's highlights at Nomad Ltd.
2. **Place the insertion point in the last heading, Financial Results**
   To control the flow of text affecting this heading and the next paragraph, you can use the Paragraph command.
3. **Click Format on the menu bar, then click Paragraph**
   The Line and Page Breaks tab contains the formatting option you want to use.
4. **Click the Line and Page Breaks tab**
   The Line and Page Breaks tab appears foremost in the dialog box. The Pagination area contains the options that affect the flow of text over the pages of the document. Table E-1 describes the text flow options. Choose the option to always keep this heading with the following paragraph.
5. **Click the Keep with next check box, then click OK**
   The heading (and the text that follows it) appears on the next page. To get a better picture of the flow of the document, preview it.
6. **Click the Print Preview button on the Standard toolbar**
   The document appears in the Preview window. Next, preview all the pages of the document.
7. **Click the Multiple Pages button on the Preview toolbar and click the second box in the first row of the grid to see the entire document**
   Compare your document to Figure E-1. The text in the legend that appears to run off the second page will be addressed later in this unit. If you see only one page of the document, click the Multiple Pages button again, and this time click to the first box in the second row. Click the Multiple Pages button one more time, and click to the second box in the first row.
8. **Click File on the menu bar, then click Save**
   The document is saved. Notice that several lines of text appear on the second page. Because you want all the headings in the summary document to appear on the first page, you will adjust the margins so that the text will appear on the first page.

FIGURE E-1: New text flow in document

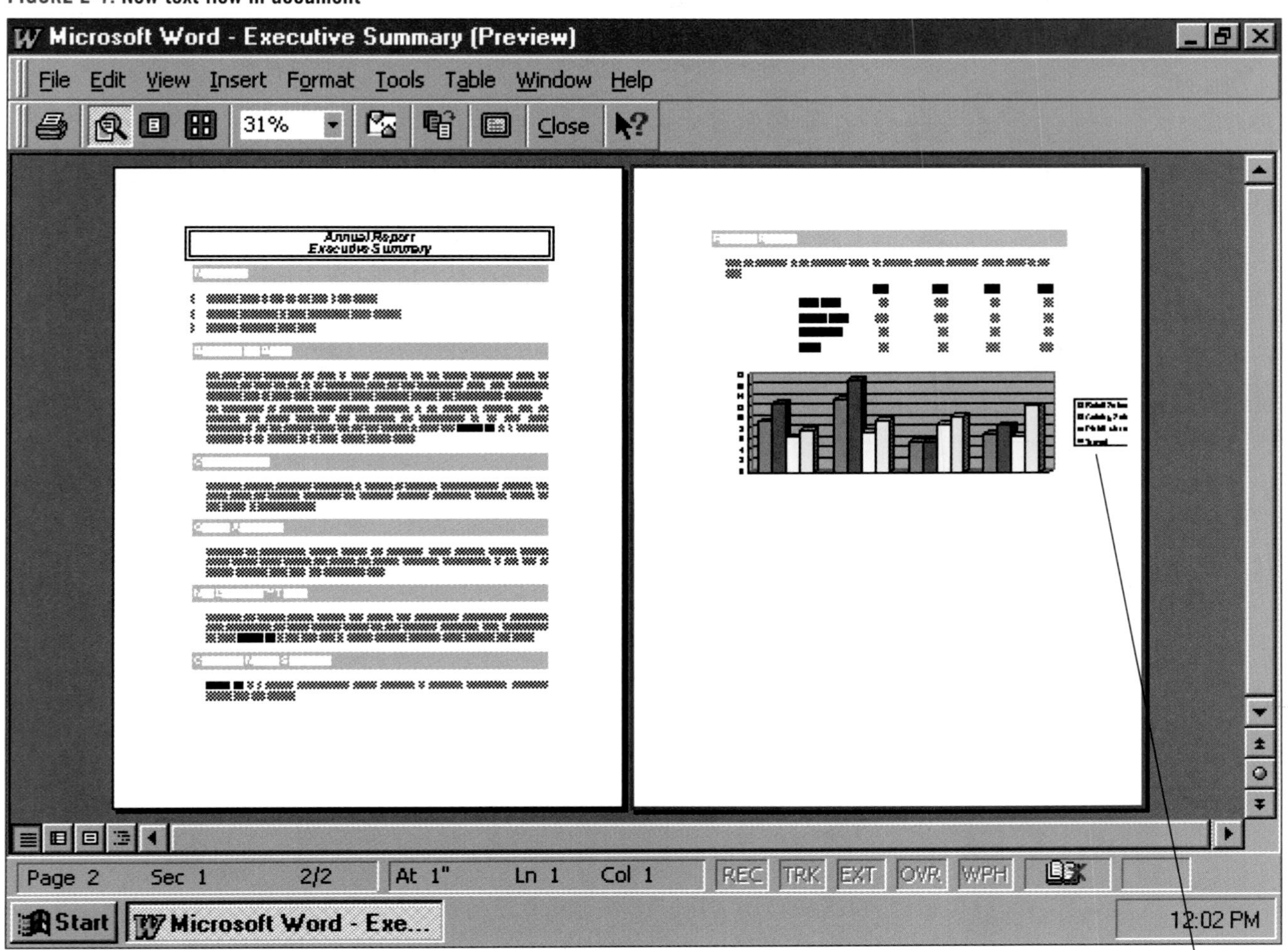

This problem will be corrected later in this lesson.

TABLE E-1: Pagination text flow options

choose this option	to
Widow/Orphan control	Prevent the last line of a paragraph from printing at the top of a page (widow), and the first line of a paragraph from printing at the bottom of a page (orphan)
Keep lines together	Prevent a page break within a paragraph
Keep with next	Prevent a page break between the selected paragraph and the paragraph after it
Page break before	Position the selected text at the top of the next page

Word 97

Adjusting Document Margins

The white space between the edge of the text and the edge of the page is called the **margin**. When you first create a document, the default size of the top and bottom margins is 1 inch, while the left and right margins are set to 1.25 inch, as shown in Figure E-2. However, you might decide to adjust margins to improve the appearance of the document or to manipulate the amount of text on a page. You can adjust the size of individual margins on the Margins tab of the Page Setup dialog box. Angela will adjust the margins in her document, so that all the main ideas of her summary document fit on the first page.

1. Click **File** on the menu bar, click **Page Setup**, then click the **Margins tab** (if it is not already foremost)
   The Page Setup dialog box appears, as shown in Figure E-3. On the Margins tab, you can determine the size of the margins for a document. First, decrease the size of the top margin.
2. Click the **Top down arrow** until **.8"** appears in the box, then click **OK**
   This reduces the size of the top margin, but it is not enough to move all the desired text from page 2 to the first page. Change the other margins to increase the amount of text that will fit on the first page.
3. Click **File** on the menu bar, then click **Page Setup**
   The Page Setup dialog box opens with the Margins tab displayed.
4. Click the **Bottom down arrow** until **.7"** appears, click the **Left down arrow** until **1"** appears, and then click the **Right down arrow** until **1"** appears
   Notice that the Preview area of the dialog box reflects your changes as you make them.
5. Click **OK**
   Adjusting the margins causes Word to move the text that previously appeared on the second page onto the bottom of the first page. The part of the chart that appears to run off the second page will be addressed later in this unit. To have the entire table appear on the next page with the chart, you can apply additional text flow formatting.
6. Click **Close** on the Preview toolbar
   The document appears in the normal view; you can now apply formatting to have all the lines of the entire table stay together on the same page.
7. Select all five lines of the table under the Financial Results heading, then click **Format** from the menu bar, then click **Paragraph**
8. On the Line and Page Breaks tab, click the **Keep with next check box**, then click **OK**
9. Click the **Print Preview button** on the Standard toolbar
   The document appears in the Preview window, as shown in Figure E-4.
10. Click **Close** on the Preview toolbar
    The document appears in the normal view.

Trouble?
Different screens at different resolutions might display the flow of text differently.

Time To
✓ Save

FIGURE E-2: **Margins in a document**

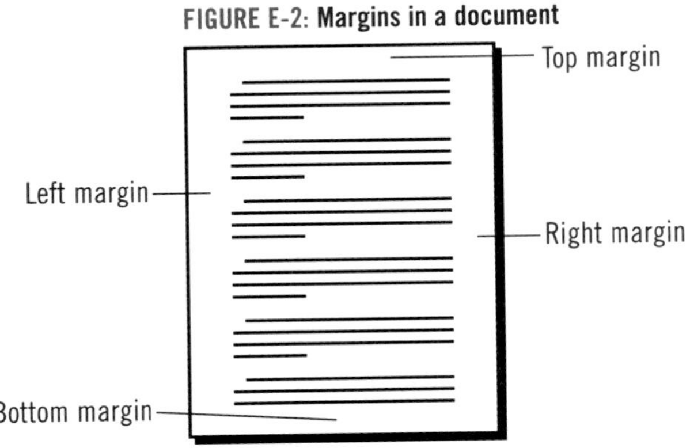

FIGURE E-3: **Margins tab in Page Setup dialog box**

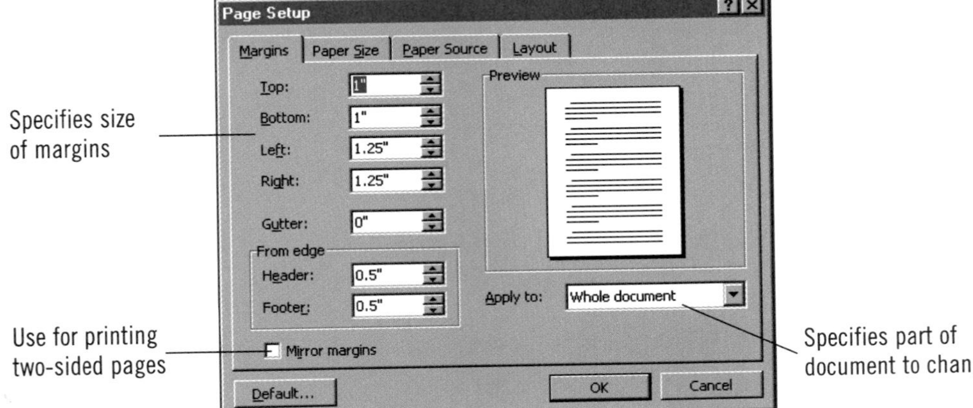

FIGURE E-4: **Preview of highlights document**

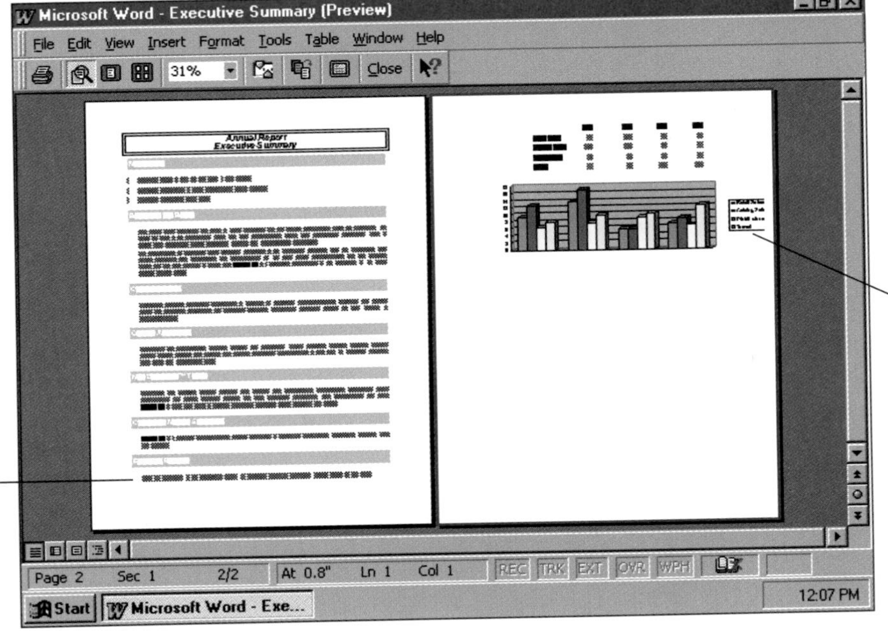

CLUES TO USE

Adjusting the Margins with the Ruler

You can adjust document margins in the page layout view or in the Preview window (if the ruler is displayed) by dragging the edges of the rulers. Position the pointer at an edge of a ruler until the pointer changes to ⟷, and then drag to the size you want. If you hold down [Alt] as you drag, you can see the exact margin size.

Word 97

Inserting Headers

In multiple page documents the top or bottom of every page typically contains information such as the page number, title, author's name, or date. Text that appears at the top of every page is called a **header**, while text appearing at the bottom of every page is called a **footer**, which you will learn about in the next lesson. You can use both headers and footers in your document. Angela would like the title of the Executive Summary to appear at the top of every page, so she begins by selecting and cutting the text she wants to use as a header.

Steps

1. **Select the first two lines in the document including the paragraph marks (enclosed in the double-box border) and click the Cut button on the Standard toolbar**
   Cutting this text removes the bordered title from the document and places it on the Clipboard. Because this is the text you want to appear at the top of every page, open the Header area of the document.
2. **Click View on the menu bar, then click Header and Footer**
   The document appears in Page Layout view but the text is dimmed. You cannot edit the body of the document while the Header or Footer area is displayed. This command also displays the Header and Footer toolbar, as shown in Figure E-5. In the Header area, you can type the text you want to appear at the top of every page, or you can paste the text you placed on the Clipboard.
3. **Click the Paste button on the Standard toolbar**
   Clicking the Paste button inserts the text from the Clipboard into the Header area. You can drag the Header and Footer toolbar to another area of the window if it obscures your view.
4. **Scroll down to the second page**
   The header also appears on the next page of the document. Compare your document to Figure E-6. You are now ready to create a footer, but save your work first before continuing.
5. **Click the Save button on the Standard toolbar**

FIGURE E-5: Inserting headers

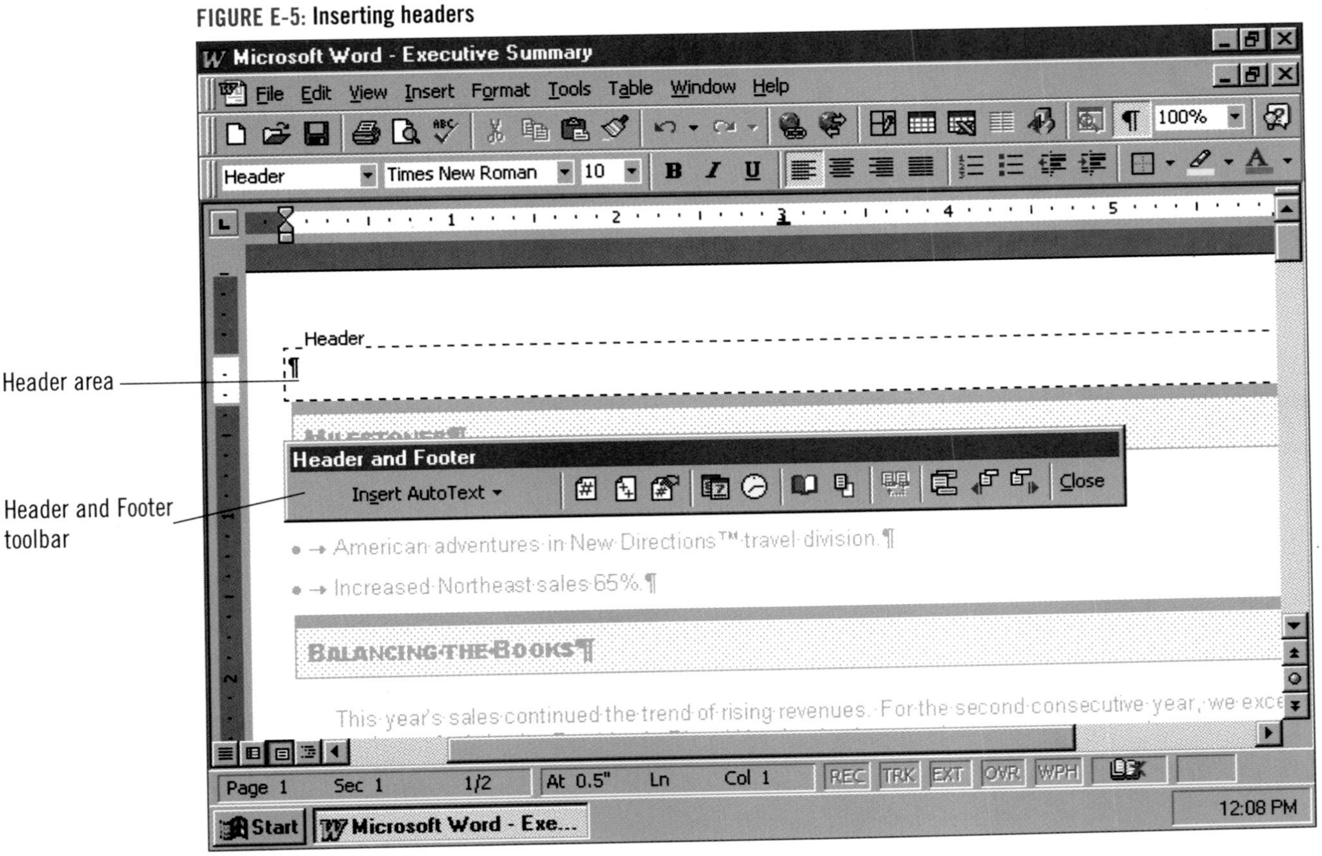

Header area

Header and Footer toolbar

FIGURE E-6: Text in a header area

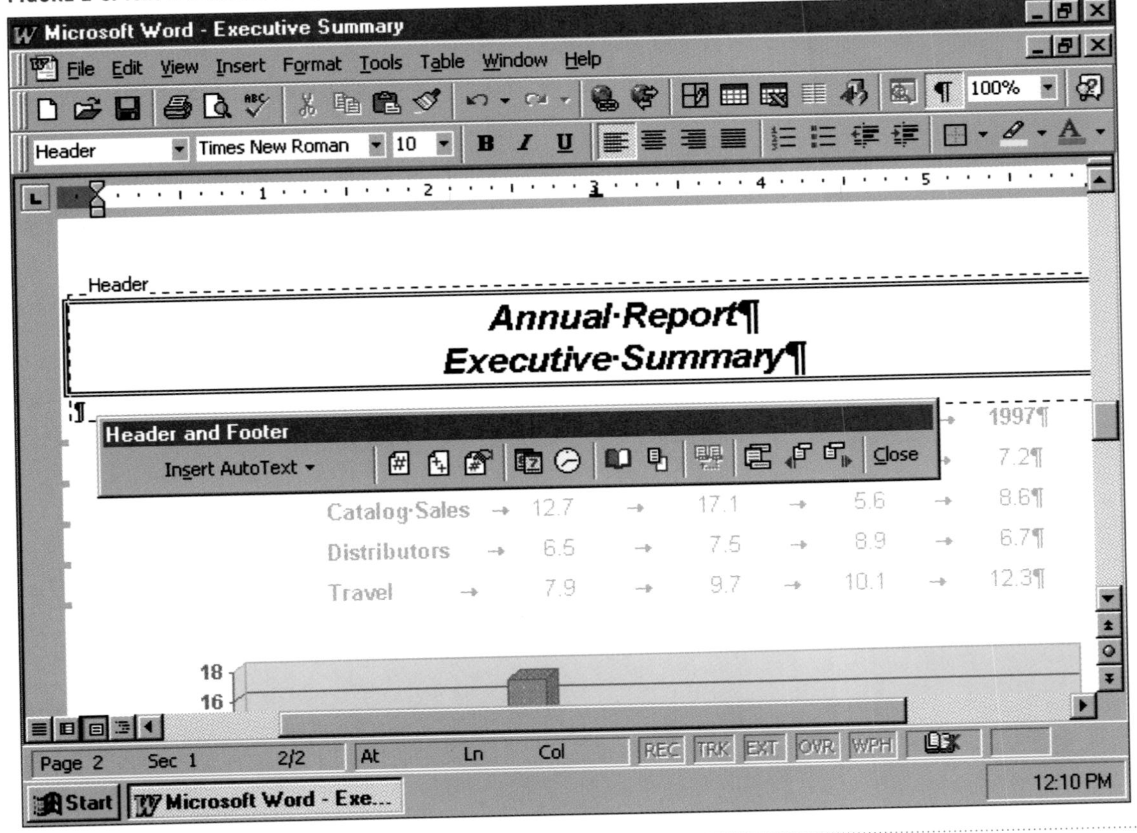

Word 97

Inserting Footers

In the same way headers display information at the top of every page, footers display information at the bottom of every page. You use the Header and Footer toolbar to switch between the header and footer areas. With the Header and Footer toolbar, the features you use most often when editing headers and footers are within easy reach. Table E-2 describes each of the buttons available on the Header and Footer toolbar. Angela would like the date and page number to appear at the bottom of every page. Because she is currently working in the header area, she begins by switching to the footer area.

Steps

1. **Click the Switch Between Header and Footer button on the Header and Footer toolbar**
   Clicking this button displays the Footer area, in which you can type or insert the information you want to appear at the bottom of every page.
2. **Click the Insert Date button on the Header and Footer toolbar**
   The current date appears in the footer. Use the preset tab stops already defined in the footer area to position text. You can also insert text that you want to precede the page number.
3. **Press [Tab] twice, type Page, then press [Spacebar]**
   With the text in the footer, you are ready to insert the page number.
4. **Click the Insert Page Number button on the Header and Footer toolbar**
   Clicking the Insert Page Number button inserts an instruction so that Word automatically supplies the correct page number on each page. Compare your footer to the one shown in Figure E-7. Now examine the footer on the following page.
5. **Scroll to the next page**
   The footer also appears on the next page of the document. You have finished working with headers and footers for now, so you can close the footer area.
6. **Click Close on the Header and Footer toolbar**
7. **Click Page Layout View button and scroll to the bottom of the page to see the footer in the document**
   Compare your document with Figure E-8. Notice that the text in the footer appears dimmed.
8. **Click the Save button on the Standard toolbar**

FIGURE E-7: Page numbers in a footer area

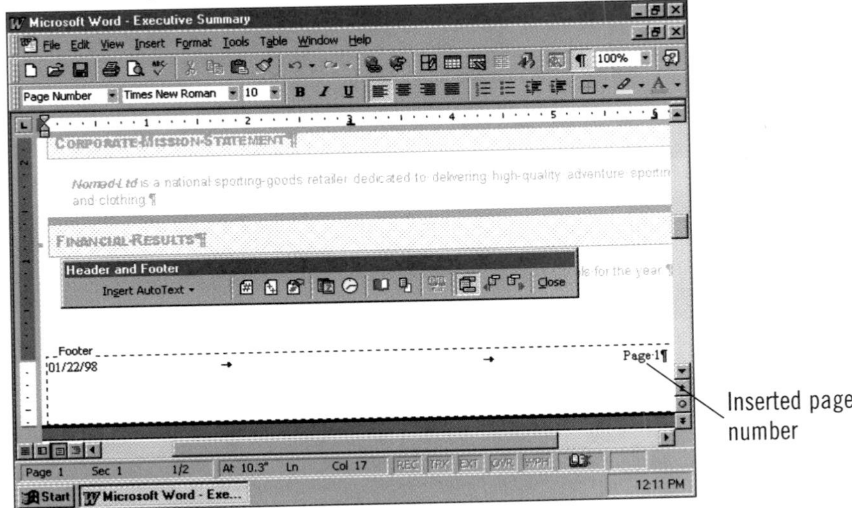

FIGURE E-8: Text in a footer

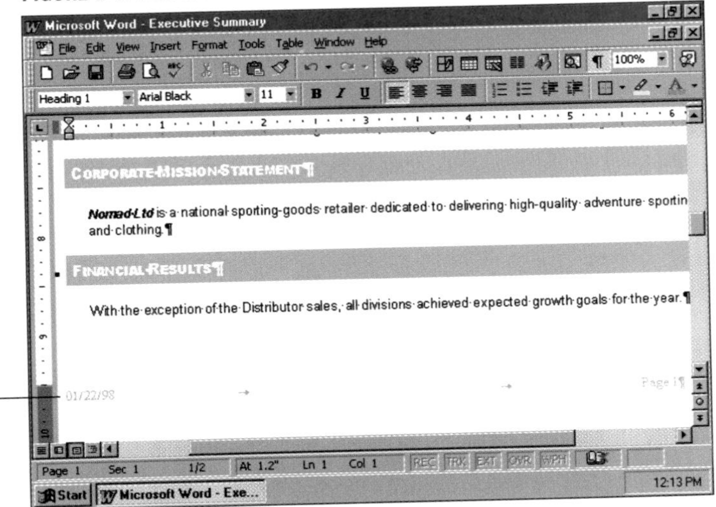

Word 97

TABLE E-2: Buttons on the Header and Footer toolbar

click	to
[button]	Move the insertion point between the header and footer areas
[button]	Move the insertion point to the previous header or footer area, when the document is divided into sections
[button]	Move the insertion point to the next header or footer area, when the document is divided into sections
[button]	Insert the header or footer from the previous section in the current section OR break the connection between sections, allowing different headers or footers to be created
[button]	Insert a field for sequential page numbers, starting with 1, that is updated when pages are added or deleted
[button]	Insert a field for the current date, based on the computer's clock, that is updated when the document is opened or printed
[button]	Insert a field for the current time, based on the computer's clock, that is updated when the document is opened or printed
[button]	Display the Page Setup dialog box, where you can modify the margins, paper source, paper size, and page orientation
[button]	Display or hide the document text while working in headers and footers

Word 97

Modifying Text in a Footer

When you need to edit the text in a header or footer, you simply display the header or footer area again. Although you can use the Header and Footer command on the View menu, when you are in page layout view, it is quicker to double-click in the area you want to edit. For example, to edit the footer in your document (which is displayed in page layout view), double-click the footer part of the document. Next, Angela decides to display the document name along with the page number. She uses a built-in AutoText entry to accomplish this.

Steps 1 2 3 4

1. **Scroll to display the footer in the document window, then double-click anywhere in the footer**
   The footer area opens. Now, you are ready to edit the footer.
2. **Place the insertion point in front of the word Page**
   Next, insert the document name using the AutoText feature.
3. **Click Insert AutoText on the Header and Footer toolbar, as shown in Figure E-9**
4. **Click Filename, type a comma, and press [Spacebar]**
   The filename of the document appears in the footer. If you change the name of the document, Word automatically updates this information in the footer. Because it is useful to know the total number of pages in a document, you can supply this information at the end of the footer.
5. **Place the insertion point after the page number, press [Spacebar], type of, then press [Spacebar] again**
6. **Click the Insert Number of Pages button on the Header and Footer toolbar**
   The total number of pages in the document appears in the footer, as shown in Figure E-10.
7. **Click Close on the Header and Footer toolbar**
   The Header and Footer toolbar closes. Compare your document to Figure E-11.
8. **Click the Save button on the Standard toolbar**

FIGURE E-9: Insert AutoText button

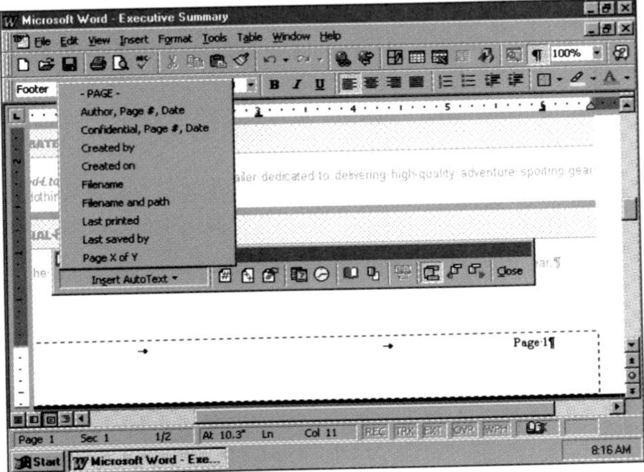

FIGURE E-10: Number of pages in footer

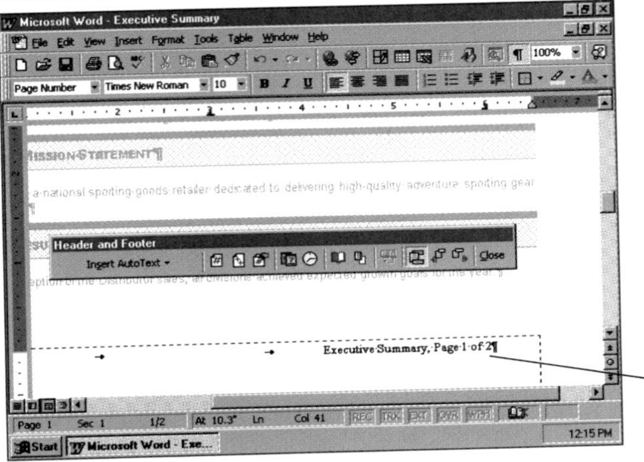

FIGURE E-11: Completed footer

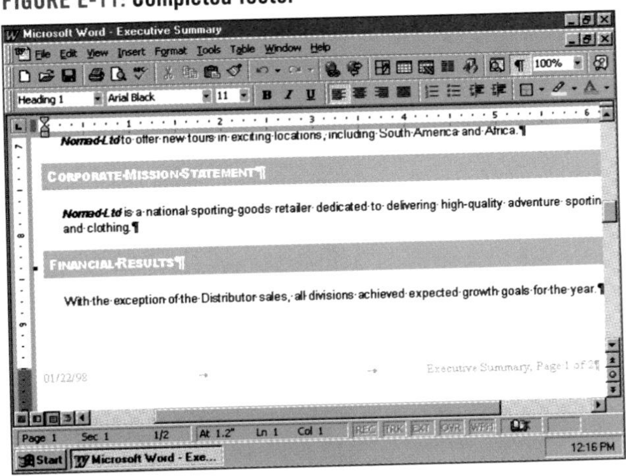

Using fields

You can use fields to insert and update information that Word retrieves from your document and your computer. A **field** is an instruction or code that tells Word what you want to insert. Word offers hundreds of fields, each inserting very specific information in the document. Some of the more common fields you might insert in a document include the document name, revision number, the date that the document was saved or printed, and information that appears in the Properties dialog box (available with the Properties command on the File menu).

Word 97

Changing Page Orientation

In most of the documents you create, the page itself is oriented such that it is taller than it is wide. This orientation is called **portrait**. When you arrange text on a page that is wider than it is tall, this orientation is called **landscape**. Figure E-12 illustrates the difference between portrait and landscape orientation. On the second page of the document, Angela noticed that the legend in the chart is too close to the edge of the page. She would like to change the orientation for the second page. She starts by displaying the document in normal view, so she can better locate the part of the document she wants to format.

Steps

1. Click the **Normal View button**
2. Scroll to and place the insertion point at the beginning of the text **Financial Results**
   Only the text from this point forward will be formatted with a new orientation.
3. Click **File** on the menu bar, then click **Page Setup**
   This command displays the Page Setup dialog box. The orientation settings are on the Paper Size tab.
4. Click the **Paper Size tab**
   Clicking this tab displays the Paper Size options in the Page Setup dialog box, as shown in Figure E-13. You can display the second page of the document in landscape orientation so that all of the chart appears when it is printed.
5. In the Orientation area, click the **Landscape option button**, click the **Apply to list arrow**, then click **This point forward**
   Clicking this button formats the contents of the second page in landscape orientation. Next, check the margins for this part of the document.
6. Click the **Margins tab**
   Notice that the previous settings for the top and bottom margins are now the settings for the left and right margins. You can change the margins so that they are consistent throughout the document.
7. In the Top box type **.8**, in the Bottom box type **.7**, in the Left box type **1**, and in the Right box type **1**
   Notice that the Preview area of the dialog box reflects your changes as you make them. Next, specify the part of the document you want formatted.
8. Click the **Apply To list arrow** and click **This point forward**
   This selection ensures that only this part (page two and after) of the document is affected by these changes.
9. Click **OK**, then click the **Save button** on the Standard toolbar
   Although you cannot see the changes in normal view, the second page is now formatted in landscape orientation with new margins. A double dotted line labeled "Section Break (Next Page)" was automatically inserted, as shown in Figure E-14. A section break allows you to format different parts of the same document with different page setup settings. Section breaks are inserted whenever you specify Page Setup options that affect only part of a document.

FIGURE E-12: Comparing page orientation

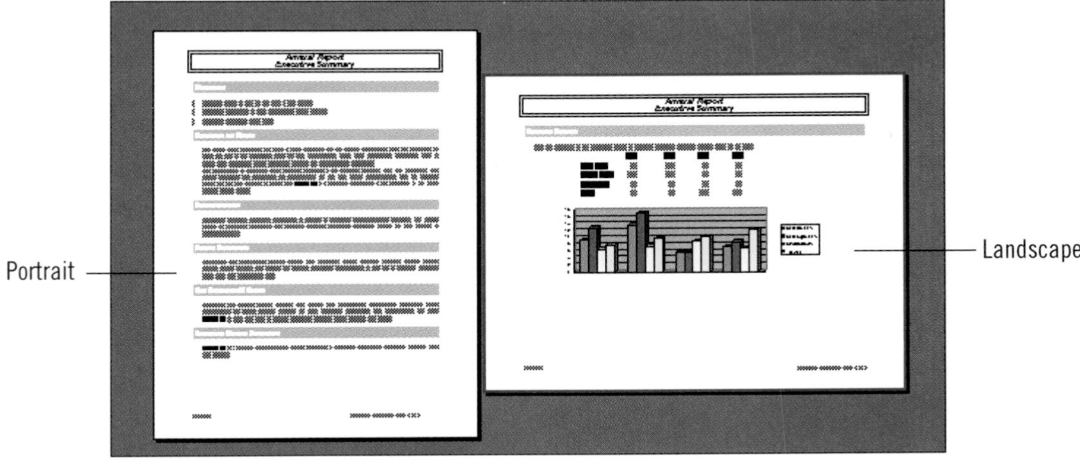

FIGURE E-13: Paper size options

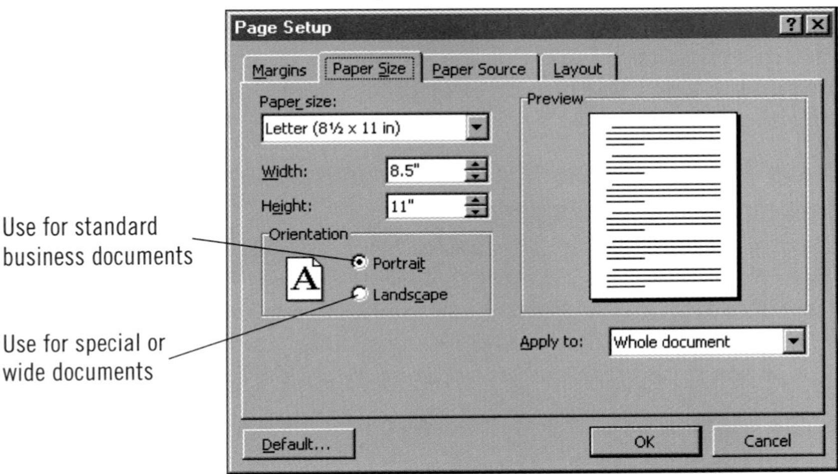

FIGURE E-14: Section break in a document

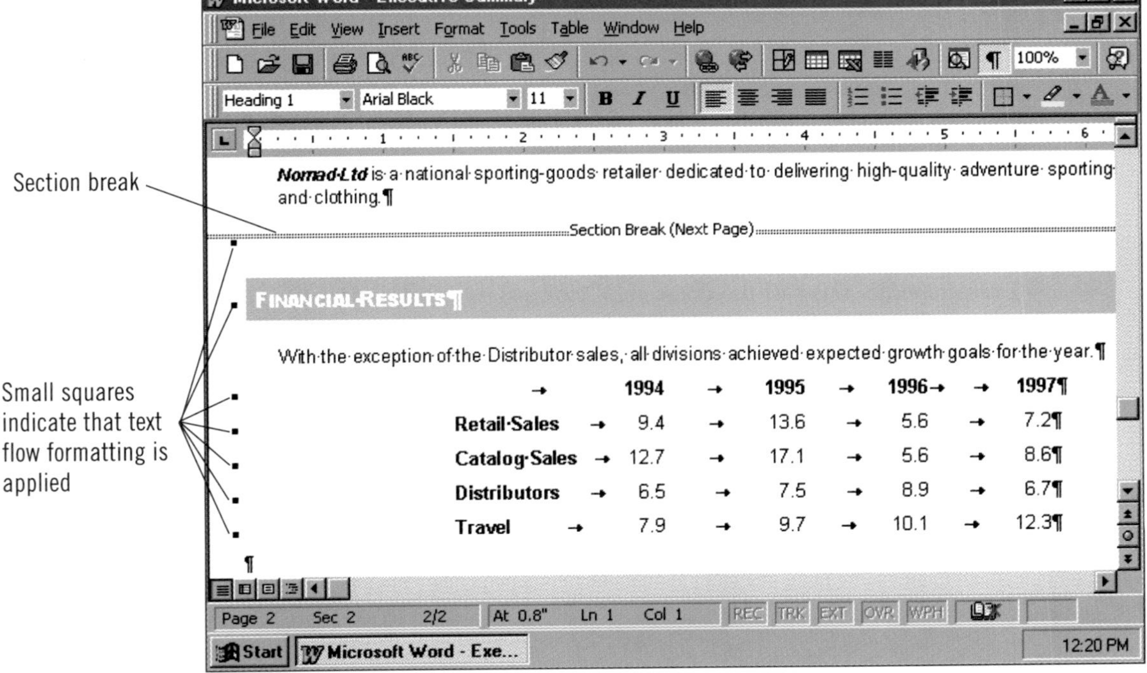

Word 97

Word 97

Changing Formatting in Multiple Sections

Whenever you format your document into sections and change the margins or orientation in different sections, you might also need to adjust the tab positions in the headers and footers. For example, suppose you inserted tabs to right-align text in a header or footer, and then you changed the width of the document by adjusting the document margins or orientation. You will want to adjust the tab position in the header or footer to match the new margins in the document, so that the text continues to be centered or right-aligned between the new margins. Angela wants to adjust the tab position in the footer for the second section to keep the page numbers aligned with the right margin.

Steps

1. **Place the insertion point in the second page of the document, click View on the menu bar, then click Header and Footer**
   The Header area for section two appears. Because the header is centered without a tab, it is unaffected by the changes to the page orientation and requires no adjustments. But the page number in the footer was placed with tabs and needs adjustment, so you can start by displaying the footer area.
2. **Click the Switch Between Header and Footer button on the Header and Footer toolbar, then scroll to the right margin**
   The Footer area for section two appears. Notice also that the Same as Previous button is indented on the Header and Footer toolbar, as shown in Figure E-15. By default, each section in a document uses the same footer information as the previous section. Because of the wider orientation in section two, you want to adjust the tab position for the footer in this section, so you must break this connection between the footers.
3. **Click the Same As Previous button on the Header and Footer toolbar, then scroll to the right margin again**
   The button is no longer indented and the connection is broken between the two sections. Now, you can adjust the position of the right-aligned tab stop.
4. **Drag the right-aligned tab in the horizontal ruler to the 9-inch mark**
   The page number information appears at the right margin in the footer. You have finished formatting the document for now, so you can close the Footer area.
5. **Click Close on the Header and Footer toolbar**
   The Footer area closes and you return to the document. Before closing and printing the document, preview the document to see how it will look.
6. **Click the Print Preview button on the Standard toolbar**
   Examine both pages of the document. Compare your document to Figure E-16.
7. **Click Close on the Preview toolbar**
   Return to the document window.
8. **Click the Save button on the Standard toolbar, then click the Print button on the Standard toolbar**
9. **Close the document**

FIGURE E-15: **Second section footer area**

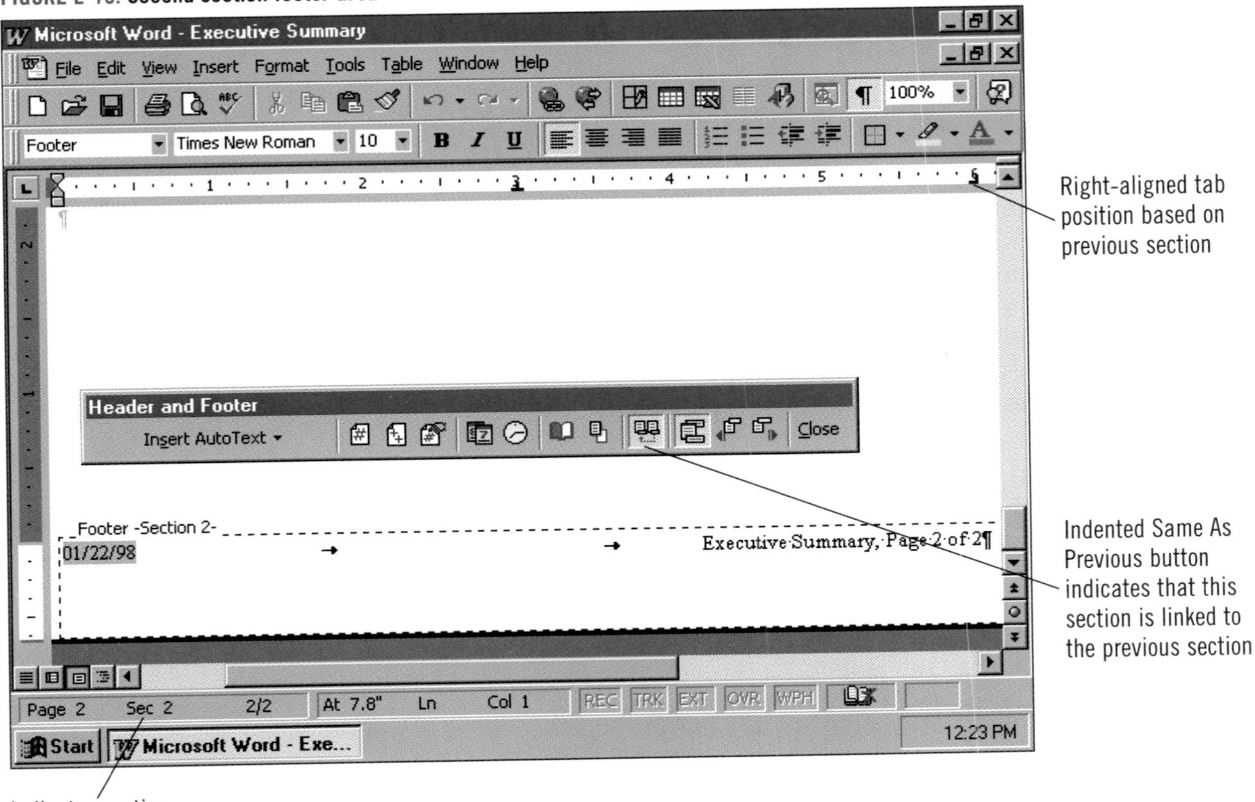

FIGURE E-16: **Different footers in the same document**

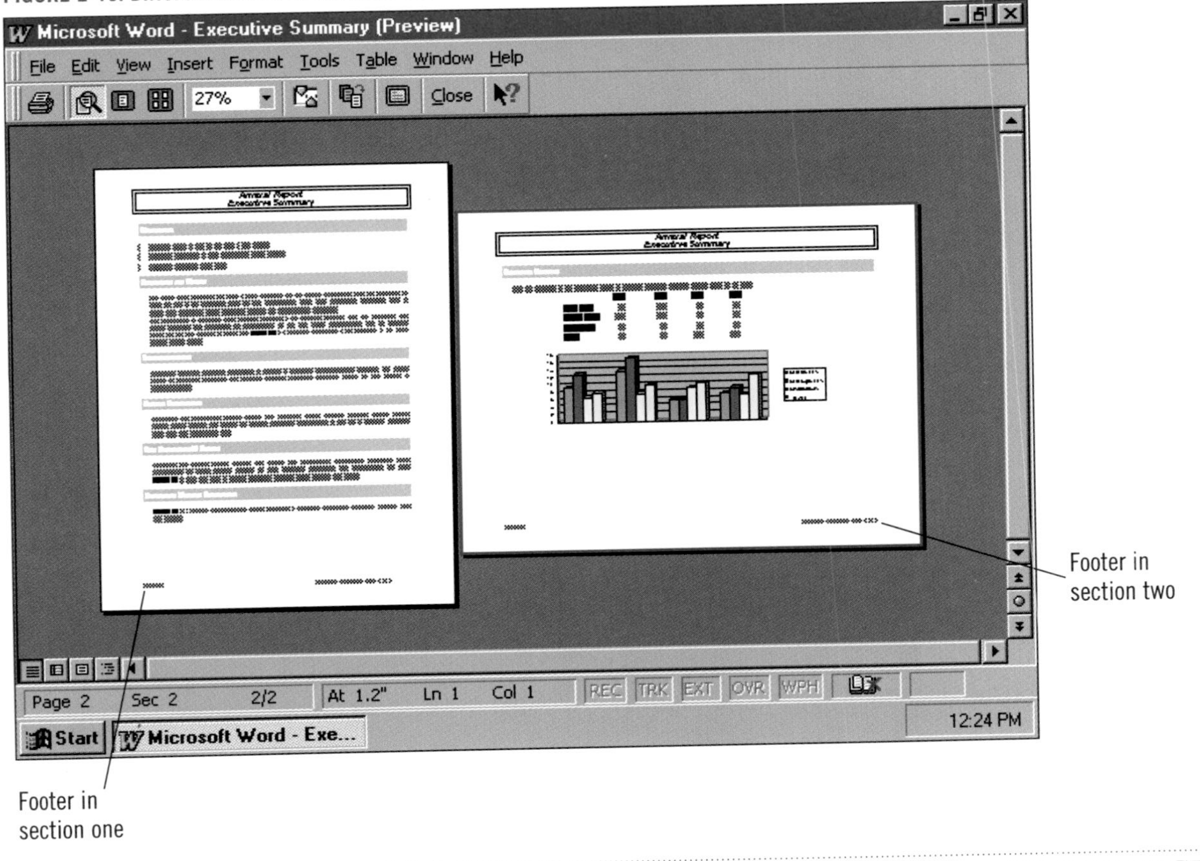

Word 97

Creating Headers for Specific Pages

Word also offers various header and footer formatting that is especially helpful in larger documents. Often when you create a large document, it will contain a title page on which you may not want to include the headers or footers. The Layout tab on the Page Setup command allows you to specify a different header or footer for the first page of the document. This tab also allows you to create different headers and footers for the even and odd pages of a document. Angela would like to add headers to the Nomad Annual Report. Since the report will be printed with the pages facing each other in a book format, Angela would like the page numbers to appear on the outside margin of the pages.

Steps

1. **Open the document named WD E-2, then save it as Nomad 1998**
   This document contains a more in-depth report of activities occurring at Nomad Ltd throughout the past year. You will add to the document headers containing the page numbers.
2. **Click File on the menu bar, then click Page Setup**
   The Page Setup dialog box opens. On the Layout tab, you can specify the header and footer options you want for the document.
3. **Click the Layout tab, then click the Different first page check box in the Headers and Footers box**
   Choosing this option will allow you to exclude the page number on the title page of your document. Since the page numbers always appear on the outside of facing pages, you will need to align the numbers on the even and odd pages differently.
4. **Click the Different odd and even check box, then click OK**
   The Page Setup dialog box closes. You are now ready to enter the page numbers in the headers.
5. **Place the insertion point in the second page, click View on the menu bar, then click Header and Footer**
   The Header and Footer areas and the Header and Footer toolbar are displayed in the document window. Notice the Header area is labeled Even Page Header. All the headers and footers are now labeled Even, Odd, or First Page. You will use Insert AutoText on the Header and Footer toolbar to insert page numbering information.
6. **With the insertion point left-aligned, click Insert AutoText on the Header and Footer toolbar, click Page X of Y, select the text, then press [F9]**
   Page X of Y AutoText entry automatically inserts the page number and the total number of pages in the document, as shown in Figure E-17. You need to press **[F9]** to update the header to reflect the number of pages in the document. Next insert this same information for the odd pages of your document.
7. **Scroll to the third page, with the insertion point in the Odd Page Header box, click the Align Right button on the Formatting toolbar, and then repeat step 6**
8. **Click Close on the Header and Footer toolbar**
9. **Click the Print Preview button on the Standard toolbar and display all four pages of the document, as shown Figure E-18. Then click Close on the Preview toolbar**

Time To

- Save
- Print the document
- Exit Word

FIGURE E-17: **Page X of Y AutoText entry**

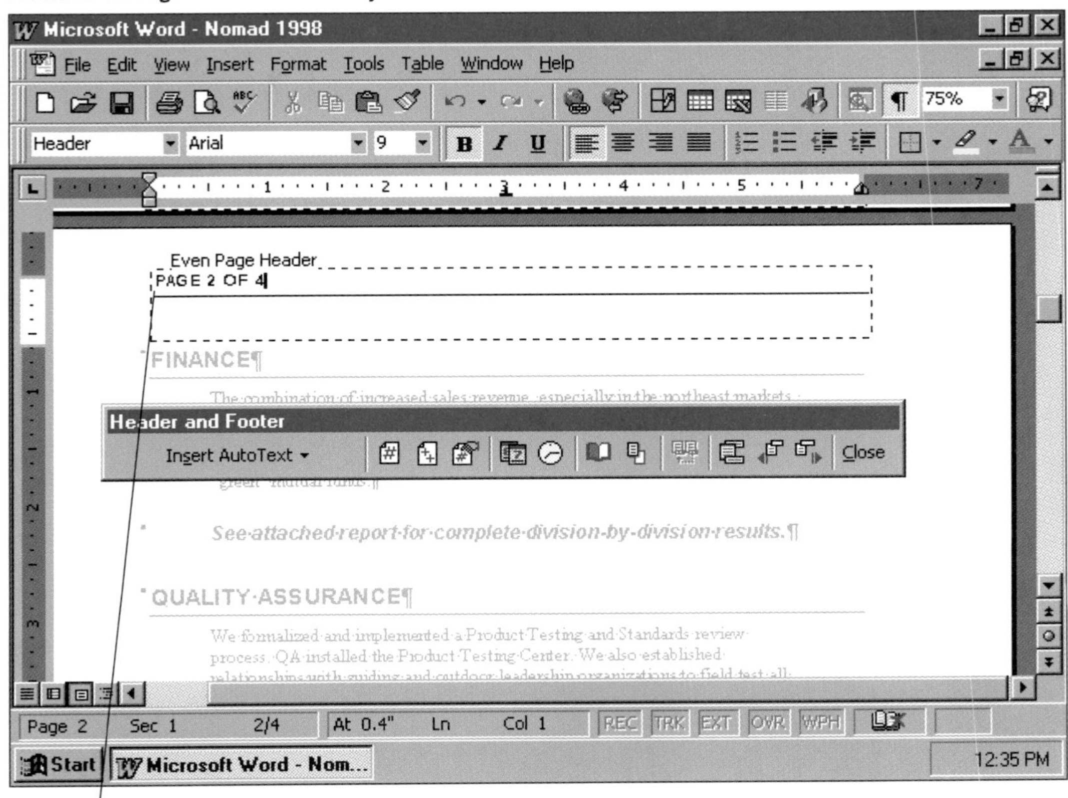

Page number and number of pages in document

No header on first page

FIGURE E-18: **Entire document in Print Preview**

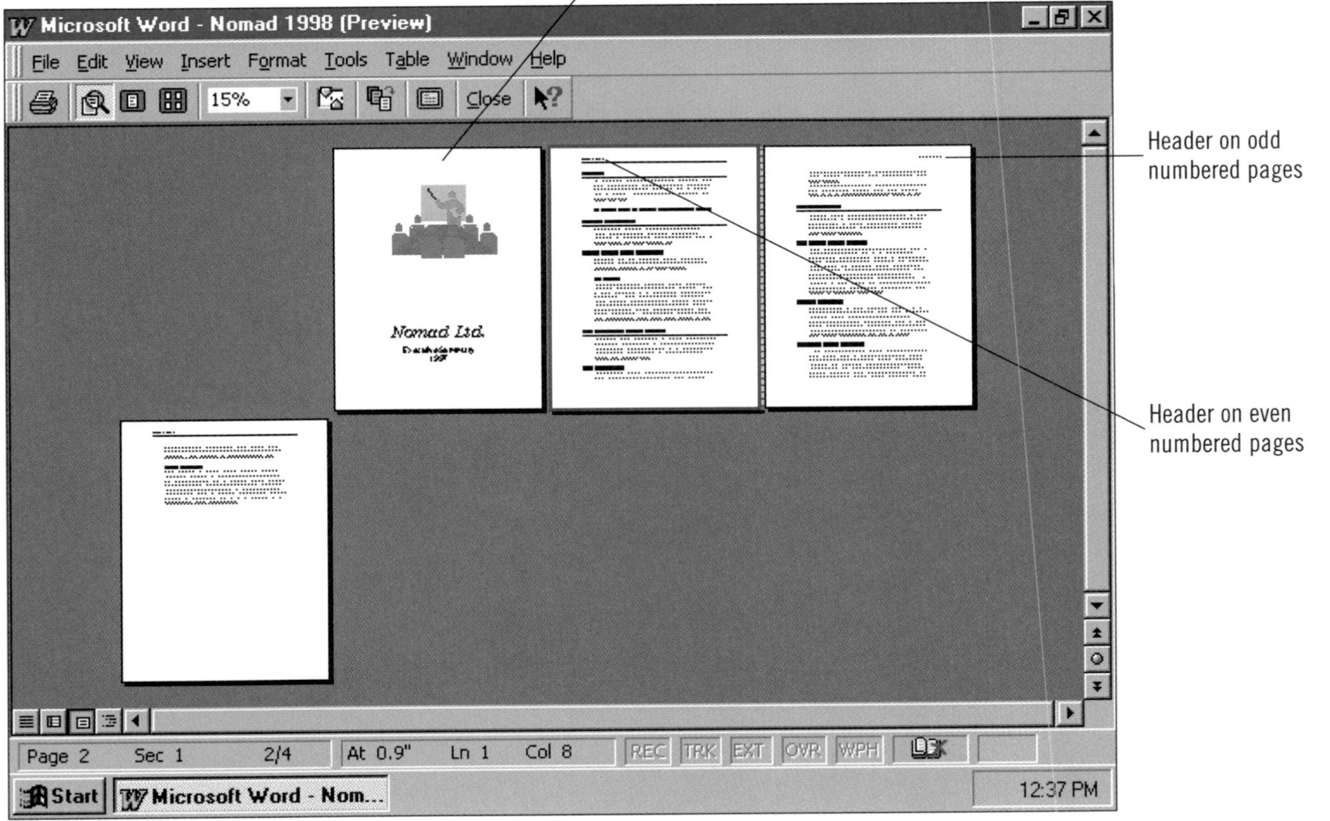

Header on odd numbered pages

Header on even numbered pages

Word 97

Practice

► Concepts Review

Label each of the elements in Figure E-19.

FIGURE E-19

Match each of the following terms with the statement that best describes its function.

6. **Footer**
7. **Header**
8. **Portrait orientation**
9. **Field**
10. **Margin**
11. **Landscape orientation**

a. Text that appears at the top of every page in a document
b. The white space between the edge of the text and the edge of the page
c. A page that is wider than it is tall
d. A special instruction or code for information that Word automatically updates
e. Text that appears at the bottom of every page in a document
f. A page that is taller than it is wide

Select the best answer from the list of choices.

12. Which of the following can you NOT accomplish in the Page Setup dialog box?
- a. Adjust the margins for the top, bottom, left, and right edges of a document.
- b. Adjust the tab settings for a header and footer.
- c. Apply unique page formatting options to multiple sections of a document.
- d. Select the page orientation.

13. When you decrease the size of all margins in a document:
- a. You increase the amount of text that will fit on the page.
- b. You decrease the amount of text that will fit on the page.
- c. The amount of text that will fit on the page does not change.
- d. You are not able to add headers and footers to the document.

14. Which of the following is NOT true about headers and footers?
  a. Clicking View, Header and Footer displays the Header and Footer toolbar.
  b. You can insert fields in a header or footer.
  c. You can paste existing information into a header or footer without having to retype it.
  d. You can edit document text while you are working in headers and footers.

15. Which of the following is NOT an example of a field you can enter in a header or footer?
  a. Document name
  b. Current date
  c. Total number of pages in the document
  d. Right-aligned tab stop

16. Which of the following is true when you create a new section with modified orientation and margin settings?
  a. Any existing tab settings in the header and footer areas are automatically adjusted to match the new margin settings.
  b. In normal view, there is no visible indication in the document that a new section has been created.
  c. You cannot create a new section with both modified orientation and margin settings.
  d. You may have to manually adjust headers and footers so that they align properly with the new margin settings.

17. To break the connection between a header or footer in multiple sections of a document, you:
  a. Click the Switch Between Header and Footer button on the Header and Footer toolbar.
  b. Double-click one of the headers with the right mouse button.
  c. Click the Same As Previous button on the Header and Footer toolbar.
  d. Click the New Section button on the Header and Footer toolbar.

18. Which of the following is a good reason to use landscape orientation in a document?
  a. You are formatting a long document.
  b. You are creating a document with unusually wide margins.
  c. A document requires that it is printed on a page that is wider than it is tall.
  d. Landscape orientation is useful only when creating graphics.

19. Which of the following is NOT a way to display the number of pages in a document?
  a. Numbering button on the formatting toolbar.
  b. Page Number button on the Header and Footer toolbar.
  c. NumPages field using Field command on the Insert menu.
  d. Insert Number of Pages button on the Header and Footer toolbar.

20. Which of the following is NOT true when you format part of a document in landscape orientation?
  a. You must change the position of the printer paper before printing the landscape page.
  b. After changing the orientation, you might need to adjust the width of the header and/or footer areas.
  c. You can see the different orientation in the print preview window.
  d. The landscape orientation option appears on the Paper Size tab in the Page Setup dialog box.

Skills Review

1. **Control text flow between pages.**
   a. Start Word and open the document named WD E-3. Save the document as "Software Letter".
   b. Place the insertion point in the heading "Reference Card…"
   c. Click Format on the menu bar, then click Paragraph.
   d. Click the Line and Page Breaks tab to bring it forward.
   e. Click the Page break before check box and click OK.

2. **Adjust document margins.**
   a. Click the Print Preview button on the Standard toolbar and examine all pages of the document.
   b. Click File on the menu bar, click Page Setup, then click the Margin tab.
   c. In the Top box, click the down arrow until .7 appears in the box. In the Bottom box, click the down arrow until .7 appears. In the Left box click the down arrow until 1 appears, and in the Right box click the down arrow until 1 appears. In the Header box, click the up arrow until .8 appears. Then click OK.
   d. Click Close on the Preview toolbar.

3. **Insert a header.**
   a. Select the first line in the document (the date), be sure to include the paragraph mark, and click the Cut button on the Standard toolbar.
   b. Click View on the menu bar, then click Header and Footer.
   c. Click the Paste button on the Standard toolbar.
   d. Scroll through the document to review your changes and save the document.

4. **Insert a footer.**
   a. Click the Switch Between Header and Footer button on the Header and Footer toolbar.
   b. Type "Page", press [Spacebar], then click the Insert Page Number button on the Header and Footer toolbar.
   c. Press[Spacebar], type "of", then press [Spacebar].
   d. Click the Insert Number of Pages button on the Header and Footer toolbar.
   e. Click Close on the Header and Footer toolbar, then save your work.

5. **Modify a footer.**
   a. Click the Page Layout View button, if not already in Page Layout view.
   b. Double-click the footer.
   c. Press [End], then press [Tab] twice and type "Continued on Next Page".
   d. Drag the right-aligned tab marker to the right, to the 6.5" mark.
   e. Scroll through the document to review your changes.
   f. Click Close on the Header and Footer toolbar, then save your work.

6. Change page orientation.

a. Scroll to and place the insertion point at the top of the second page.
b. Click File on the menu bar, then click Page Setup.
c. Click the Paper Size tab.
d. In the Orientation area, click the Landscape radio button.
e. Click the Apply To list arrow and click This point forward.
f. Click the Margins tab.
g. In the Top box, type ".7", in the Bottom box, type ".5", in the Left box type "1", and in the Right box type "1".
h. Click the Apply To List arrow and click This point forward.
i. Click the Layout tab.
j. Click the Section Start arrow and choose New Page, if it is not already selected.
k. Click OK and save your changes.

7. Use different footers in the same document.

a. Place the insertion point in the second page of the document, click View on the menu bar, then click Header and Footer.
b. With the insertion point in the Header area, click the Same as Previous button on the Header and Footer toolbar (to deselect it).
c. Select the date and press [Delete].
d. Click the Switch Between Header and Footer button on the Header and Footer toolbar.
e. Click the Same as Previous button.
f. Drag the right-aligned tab in the horizontal ruler to the 9" mark.
g. Delete the text "Continued on Next Page".
h. Type "Transport Express Inc., 1998".
i. Click the Close button on the Header and Footer toolbar.
j. Click the Print Preview button on the Standard toolbar and review your changes.
k. Click Close on the Preview toolbar.
l. Save your document and print it.
m. Close the document and exit Word.

Independent Challenges

1. The Mountain Top Tours travel company would like to create a more dramatic format to announce their upcoming tours in Switzerland. As their in-house publishing expert, you have been asked to create a new look for their brochure. Open the document WD E-4 and save it as "Mountain Landscape".

To complete this independent challenge:

1. Format the entire document in landscape orientation.
2. Adjust the top margin to be .4" and the footer margin to .3".
3. Insert a left-aligned header with the text "DRAFT 1.0"
4. Adjust the right-aligned tab in the footer so that it is even with the new right margin.
5. Preview, save, and print the document, then close it.

2. As co-chair for the Lake City High School Reunion entertainment committee, you want to help golfers attending the golf tournament find their way to the golf course. Add a map as a second page to a draft version of the golf announcement. Open the document WD E-5 and save it as "Golf Map". Make the following changes in the document.

To complete this independent challenge:

1. Format the second page in landscape orientation.
2. Adjust the top and bottom margins to be .7 inch each for the second page only.
3. Adjust the header margin to be .4 inch and the footer margin to be .3 inch for the second page only.
4. Create a footer in each section that includes a field for the name of the file at the left margin and the date at the right margin. Adjust the right-aligned tab in the footer in the second section.
5. Preview, save, and print the document, then close it.

3. As an intern in the Communications Department for a large manufacturer of microprocessors, you have been asked to improve the appearance of the analysis document of the company's financial statement. For quick access to this information, the company has placed an electronic version of the annual report on its Web site. After exploring the report highlights, you obtain a copy of the text (much of which is already complete) and add a few finishing touches to prepare the document for printing. Because this document will be printed on two sides of each page (to save paper), you will need to create different footers for odd and even numbered pages.

To complete this independent challenge:

1. Create a new blank document in Word and save it with the name "Financial Summary".
2. Log on to the Internet and use your browser to go to http://www.course.com. From there, click Student Online Companions, then click the link for this textbook, click the Word link for Unit E, then locate the 1995 Highlights page.
3. Click the Financial Statements link and finally click the link Managements Discussion and Analysis.
4. Select all the text in the document and copy it to the Clipboard. Paste it into the new blank document. Format the entire document in 12pts and 1.5 line spacing.
5. Add a title to the top of the document and add headings (use whatever text you wish) before every second paragraph. Format each of the headings so that they are never separated from the body of the following paragraph.
6. Adjust the top and bottom margins to be 1.25".
7. Specify different headers/footers for odd and even numbered pages.
8. Center the company name in the header for all pages. For odd numbered pages create a footer that contains the name of the document at the left margin, the date in the center, and page numbering information (use the Page X of Y format) at the right margin. Reverse this order for the footers in even numbered pages.
9. Preview, save, and print the document, then close it.

4. Your company has recently created a program to help the local food pantry collect food. Through this program employees are given longer lunch hours to volunteer at the food pantry, sorting donations and stocking shelves. You would like to give a certificate to all the employees who have volunteered over the past year. Using Figure E-20 as a guideline for formatting, create a new document and save it as "Volunteer Certificate".

To complete this independent challenge:

1. Use a border and indentation to create a signature line.
2. Experiment with different fonts, font sizes, and alignment.
3. Create a new first page by inserting a hard page break. On the new first page, create a cover memo to accompany the award.
4. Change the orientation of the last page of the memo (for the certificate) to print in landscape orientation.
5. Adjust the margins as necessary.

FIGURE E-20

MEMO

DATE:	06/23/97
TO:	ANDRA CARSON, VICE PRESIDENT
FROM:	YOUR NAME
RE:	ATTACHED CERTIFICATE

Here is my first attempt at creating an certificate that goes to all of the employees who have volunteered at the food shelf over the past year. Please share any comments or suggestions you have about the certificate. I would like to have the certificate printed and distributed by the end of the month

Enc. 1

IN APPRECIATION OF YOUR EFFORTS

Awarded to

Recipient

Food Shelf Volunteer

Presented by
Carson Associates

Wednesday, June 24, 1997

Your Name

Visual Workshop

As the conference coordinator for the upcoming Decorative Ideas Conference, you have been assigned the task of finalizing the conference menu. The caterer has supplied a menu for your approval. Open the document named WD E-6 and save it as "Final Menu". Using Figure E-21 as a guide, format the document so that the menu appears on a separate page and in landscape orientation. The letter should appear in portrait orientation. Also add a header containing the date, and a footer containing the document name and a page number. Adjust margins as necessary.

FIGURE E-21

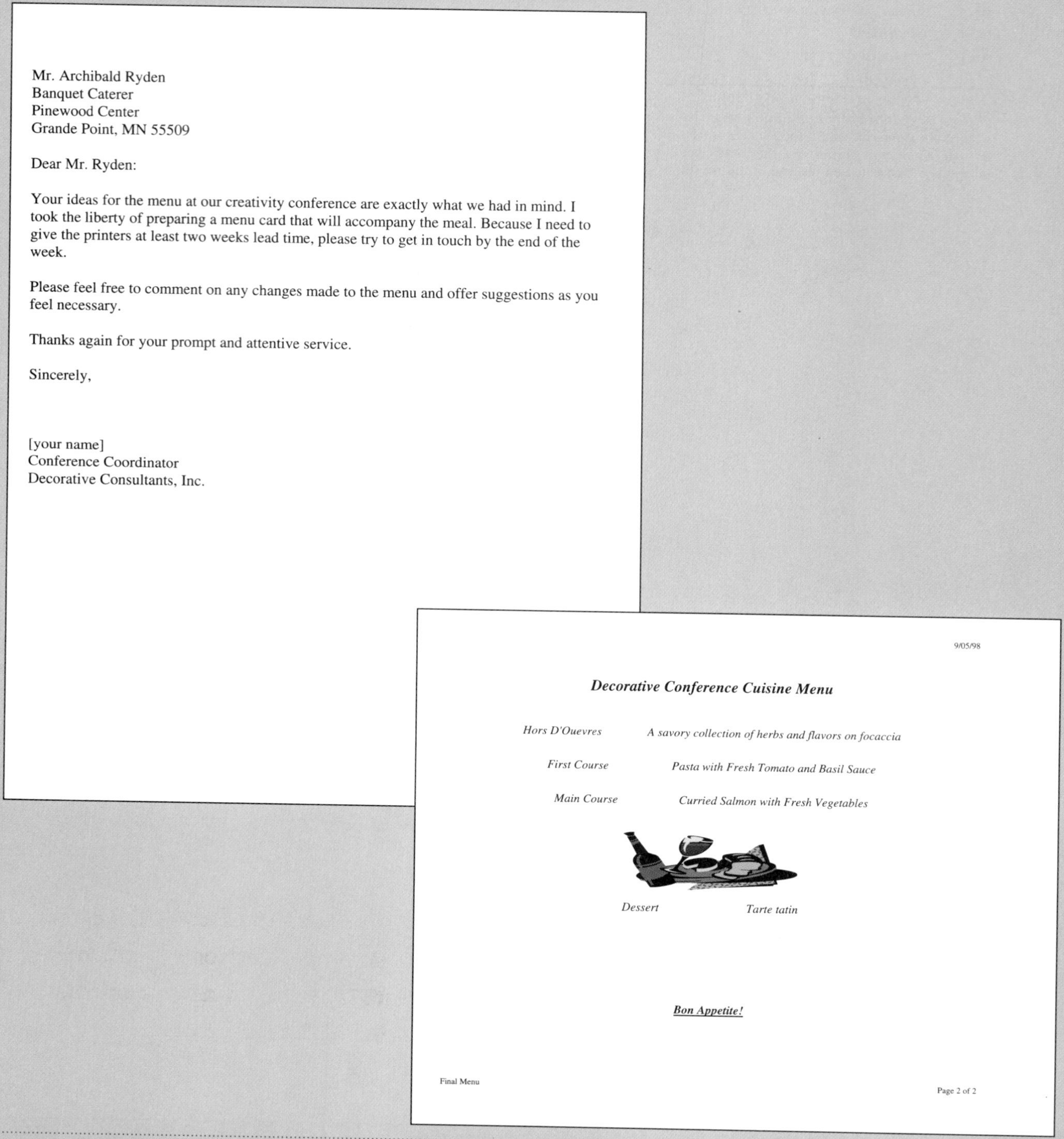

Mr. Archibald Ryden
Banquet Caterer
Pinewood Center
Grande Point, MN 55509

Dear Mr. Ryden:

Your ideas for the menu at our creativity conference are exactly what we had in mind. I took the liberty of preparing a menu card that will accompany the meal. Because I need to give the printers at least two weeks lead time, please try to get in touch by the end of the week.

Please feel free to comment on any changes made to the menu and offer suggestions as you feel necessary.

Thanks again for your prompt and attentive service.

Sincerely,

[your name]
Conference Coordinator
Decorative Consultants, Inc.

9/05/98

Decorative Conference Cuisine Menu

Hors D'Ouevres	*A savory collection of herbs and flavors on focaccia*
First Course	*Pasta with Fresh Tomato and Basil Sauce*
Main Course	*Curried Salmon with Fresh Vegetables*

Dessert	*Tarte tatin*

Bon Appetite!

Final Menu

Page 2 of 2

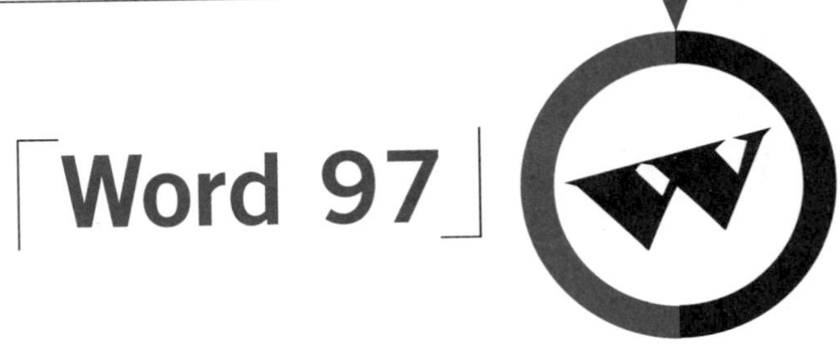

Formatting with AutoFormat and Styles

Objectives

- Create and apply character styles
- Use AutoFormat and the Style Gallery
- Modify styles
- Create and apply new paragraph styles
- Display style names in a document
- Move around with styles
- Replace styles
- Format as you type

There are many formatting features available in Word that provide a variety of ways to quickly format a document the way you want. By using **styles**, which are collections of format settings you store together, you can apply combinations of format settings quickly. And with the AutoFormat feature, Word automatically applies styles and improves formatting in an entire document for you. You can also use the Style Gallery to format a document, choosing from many built-in, professionally designed business documents provided with Word. You can even opt to format as you type. Angela will use a variety of techniques to improve the appearance of a cover letter to shareholders and an executive summary for the annual report.

Word 97

Creating and Applying Character Styles

Using styles can save a lot of time and reduce formatting errors. A **character style** is a stored set of font format settings. When you create a character style, you store the font format settings so that you can apply them quickly in one step, rather than applying each setting to each occurrence you want to format. Using character styles to format text ensures consistent formatting. For example, if you use bold, small caps, and italics formatting for product names in a brochure, you want all the product names to be formatted the same way. In the summary document, Angela would like to format *all* occurrences of the company name with identical format settings.

QuickTip

Turn off spelling and grammar checking. Display paragraph marks.

1. **Start Word 97, open the document named WD F-1 and save it as Nomad Report**
   Because the first occurrence of the company name, Nomad Ltd, is already formatted with the settings you want to use, you can create a style based on an example of existing character formatting.
2. **Select the first occurrence of the company name Nomad Ltd, click Format on the menu bar, then click Style**
   The Style dialog box opens in which you can view, modify, and create new character and paragraph styles. Here, you can create a new character style.
3. **Click New**
   The New Style dialog box opens, as shown in Figure F-1. In this dialog box, provide a name for the new style and specify the type of style you want to create.
4. **In the Name box, type CompanyName**
   This stores the format settings of the selected text in a style called "CompanyName." You can use uppercase or lowercase characters, punctuation, and spaces in a style name. Next, indicate that you are creating a character style rather than a paragraph style.
5. **Click the Style type list arrow, then click Character**
   Note that the Preview area shows how text will appear with the format settings, and the Description area lists the settings.
6. **Click OK to close the New Style dialog box, then click Apply in the Style dialog box**
   The dialog box closes. You won't see any change in the selected text, because it is already correctly formatted. The CompanyName character style is applied to the text. Now you can apply this style to other occurrences of the company name in the document.
7. **In the second-to-last body paragraph, select the company name, click the Style list arrow on the Formatting toolbar, then click CompanyName**
   The style list contains all the styles you can apply to text, including the new style you created, as shown in Figure F-2. In addition, character styles are followed by the a icon to distinguish them from paragraph styles, which are followed by a ¶.
8. **Repeat Step 7 for the next occurrence of Nomad Ltd**
   Compare your document to Figure F-3.
9. **Click the Save button on the Standard toolbar**

FIGURE F-1: New Style dialog box

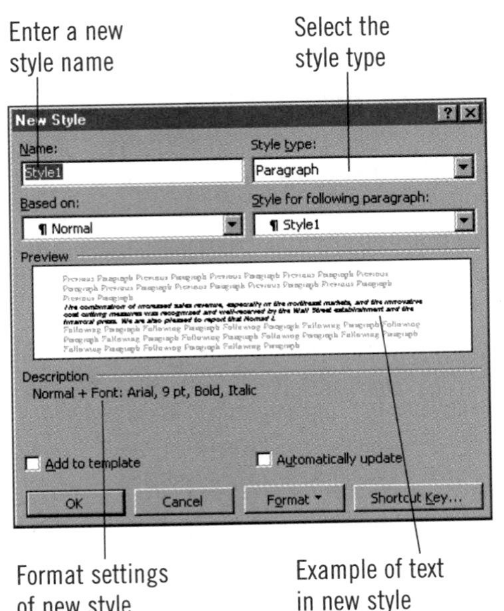

FIGURE F-2: Style list

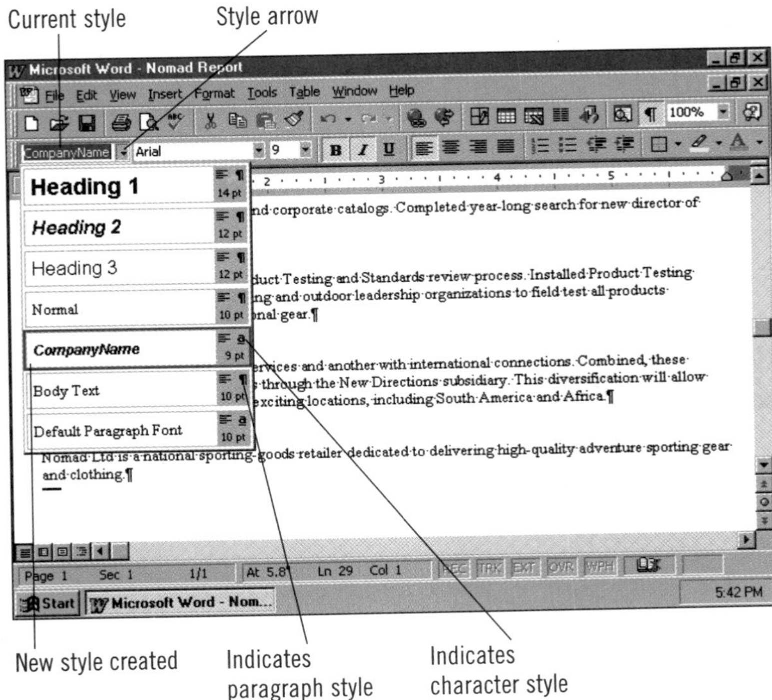

FIGURE F-3: Character styles applied

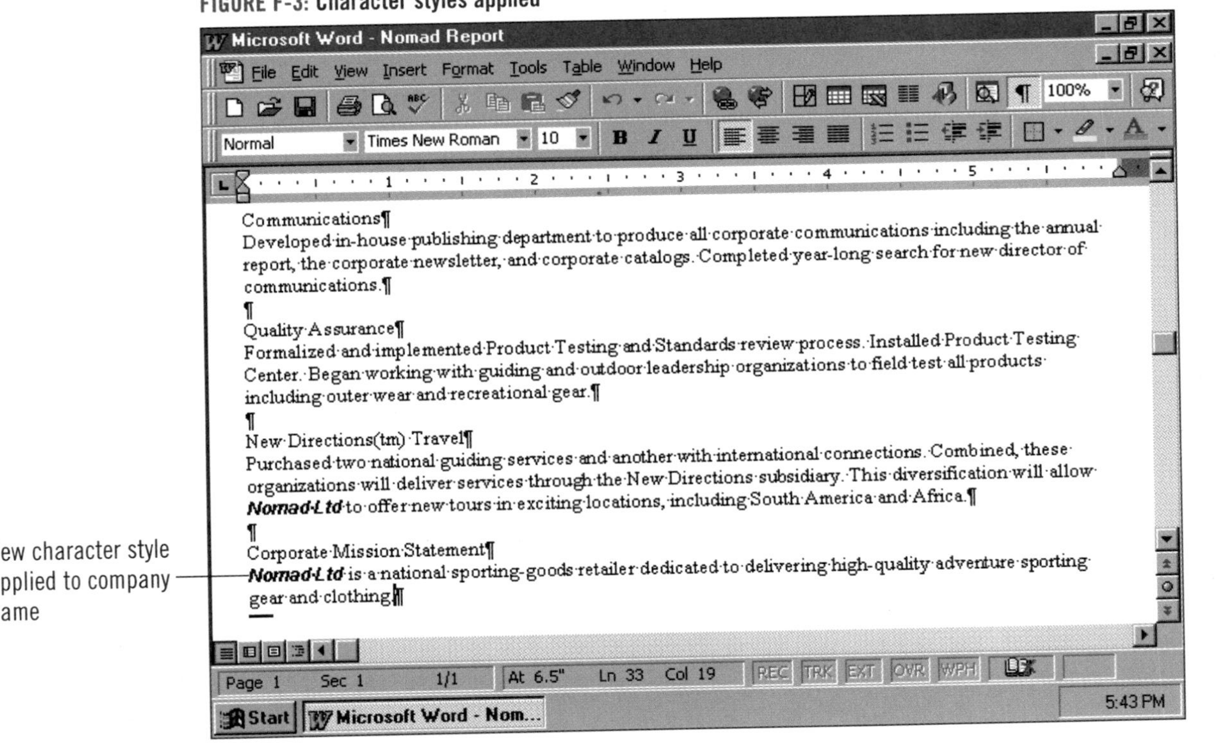

CLUES TO USE

Applying styles when creating them

When you create a style based on selected text, it is important to click Apply in the Style dialog box. By clicking Apply, you apply the style name to the text, so that this text is also updated if you later decide to change characteristics of the style.

Word 97

Using AutoFormat and the Style Gallery

With the AutoFormat feature, Word makes a number of changes, described in Table F-1, that improve the appearance of a document. In addition, certain paragraph styles found in the default template, Normal, are applied automatically. A **paragraph style** is similar to a character style, except that it contains format settings you can apply to paragraphs, rather than to selected words. Once styles are established in a document, you can use the Style Gallery to format your document in styles from the different templates provided. A **template** is a special document containing styles and other options you want to use in specific kinds of documents. Angela wants to add attractive formatting and paragraph styles to the summary document.

1. Press **[Ctrl][Home]**, click **Format** on the menu bar, then click **AutoFormat**
   The AutoFormat dialog box opens. This dialog box offers the option of accepting or rejecting changes after the document has been formatted (you won't use that option now) or of formatting the document without first reviewing each change. This default option is a fast way to format a document.
2. Select the **Auto Format now option button**, if necessary, then click **OK**
   AutoFormat enhances the appearance of the document, as shown in Figure F-4. Styles are applied throughout the document. To give the document a more professional look, choose a template from the Style Gallery.
3. Click **Format** on the menu bar, then click **Style Gallery**
   The Style Gallery dialog box opens. In this dialog box, you can choose from the list of templates and preview your document with styles from the selected template. Select a professional template and preview the document.
4. In the Template list box, scroll down, then click **Professional Memo**
   The Preview of box displays the document in styles from the Professional Memo template.
5. Click **OK**
   Word applies the styles defined in the template as shown in Figure F-5. To see which style was applied to the headings, place the insertion point in a heading.
6. Place the insertion point in the heading **Balancing the Books**
   Notice the style name that appears in the Style list box on the Formatting toolbar indicates that the Heading 1 style is applied to this paragraph. Because of its location under the large bold title, the text "Milestones" was not correctly analyzed as a heading during the AutoFormat process. You can format it with the same style as the other headings by applying the Heading 1 style.
7. Place the insertion point in the heading **Milestones**, then click the **Style list arrow** on the Formatting toolbar
   The Style list box now displays the styles available in the Professional Memo template. Notice that the style names are displayed with the style's formatting characteristics.
8. Scroll the Style list box, then click **Heading 1** (the first style displayed in the Style list)
   Compare your document to Figure F-6.
9. Click the **Save button** on the Standard toolbar

Trouble?

Do not be concerned if this step takes a few minutes.

FIGURE F-4: Document formatted with AutoFormat

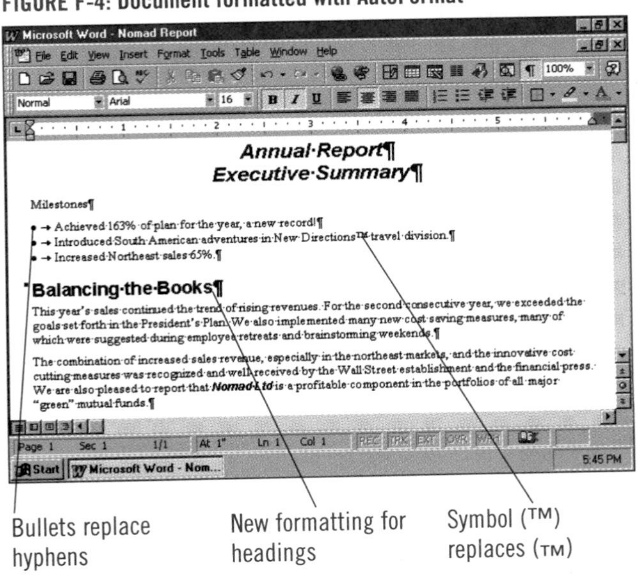

FIGURE F-5: Reformatted document with PROFESSIONAL MEMO styles

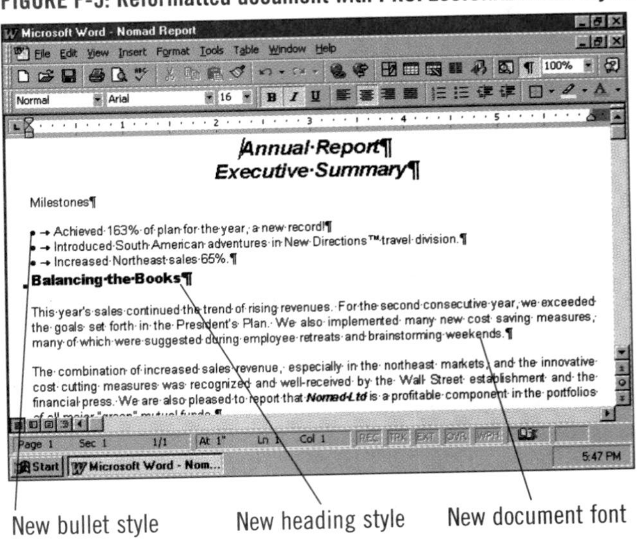

Word 97

FIGURE F-6: Updated style

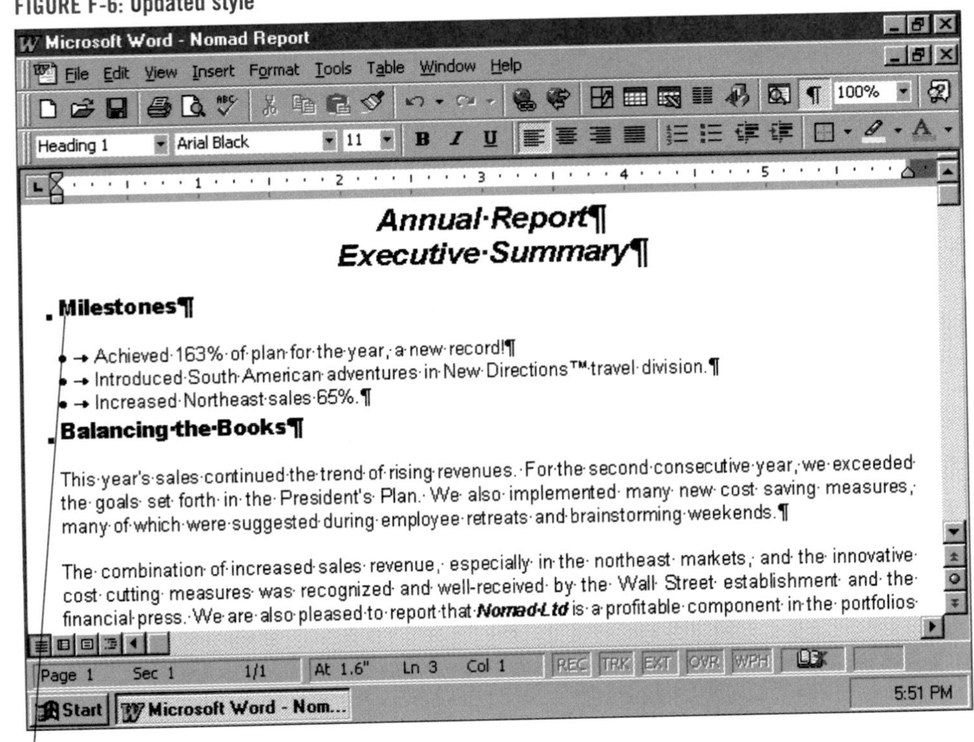

TABLE F-1: Changes made by AutoFormat

change	description
Applies styles	Applies paragraph styles to all paragraphs in a document, including headings, lists, body text, salutations, addresses, etc.
Adjusts spacing	Adds and removes extra paragraph marks as needed and replaces spaces and tabs with proper indentation
Replaces symbols and characters	Replaces hyphens and other symbols used to denote a list with bullets and replaces fractions entered as "1/2" with ½ symbol and inserts the trademark, registered trademark, and copyright symbols where indicated

Modifying Styles

When you use styles to format text, you can change format settings quickly and consistently for every occurrence of the style in the document. Modifying a style changes the appearance of all text formatted in that style. You save time and make fewer mistakes because you don't need to search for each occurrence of text that has formatting you want to change. The fastest way to modify a style is to change the formatting in a selected example and reapply the style. After reviewing the style of the Milestones heading, Angela decides to change the style of the font to small caps. After modifying the font style for the first heading, she'll update the Heading 1 style to change all the text formatted with this style.

Steps

1. Select the **Milestones** heading
2. Click **Format** on the menu bar, then click **Font**
   The Font dialog box opens. To make the heading text more distinctive, use the font effect called "small caps".
3. Click the **Small caps checkbox**
4. Click the **Shadow checkbox**, then click **OK**
   Now that you have adjusted the font formatting, you decide to increase the spacing before each heading.
5. Click **Format** on the menu bar, then click **Paragraph**
6. On the Indents and Spacing tab, click the **Spacing before up arrow** once to 6 pts, then click **OK**
   The space before this paragraph is increased. Now that this heading contains the formatting you want, modify the Heading 1 style, based on the modified "Milestones" heading, to format all the headings in the document in the same way. After changing the formatting, you can update a style by reapplying it to the same text.
7. Click the **Style list arrow** on the Formatting toolbar, then click **Heading 1**
   The Modify Style dialog box opens, as shown in Figure F-7. You can either update the style based on the selected text, or reformat the selected text with the original attributes of the style. In this case, modify the style based on the currently selected text.
8. Click **OK** to update the Heading 1 style based on the currently selected text
   All text formatted with the Heading 1 style now appears in small caps and is shadowed throughout the document. Deselect the text and compare your document to Figure F-8.
9. Click the **Save button** on the Standard toolbar

QuickTip

A fast way to apply a built-in heading style is to press [Alt][Ctrl] and the corresponding heading level. For example, to apply a Heading 1 style, press [Alt][Ctrl][1]. To apply a Heading 2 style, press [Alt][Ctrl][2], and so on.

FIGURE F-7: Modify Style dialog box

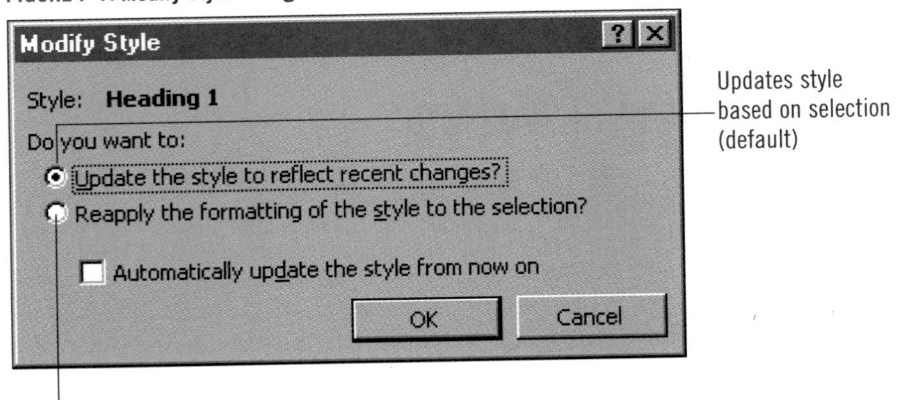

Updates style based on selection (default)

Reapplies previous style to selection

Word 97

FIGURE F-8: Updated style

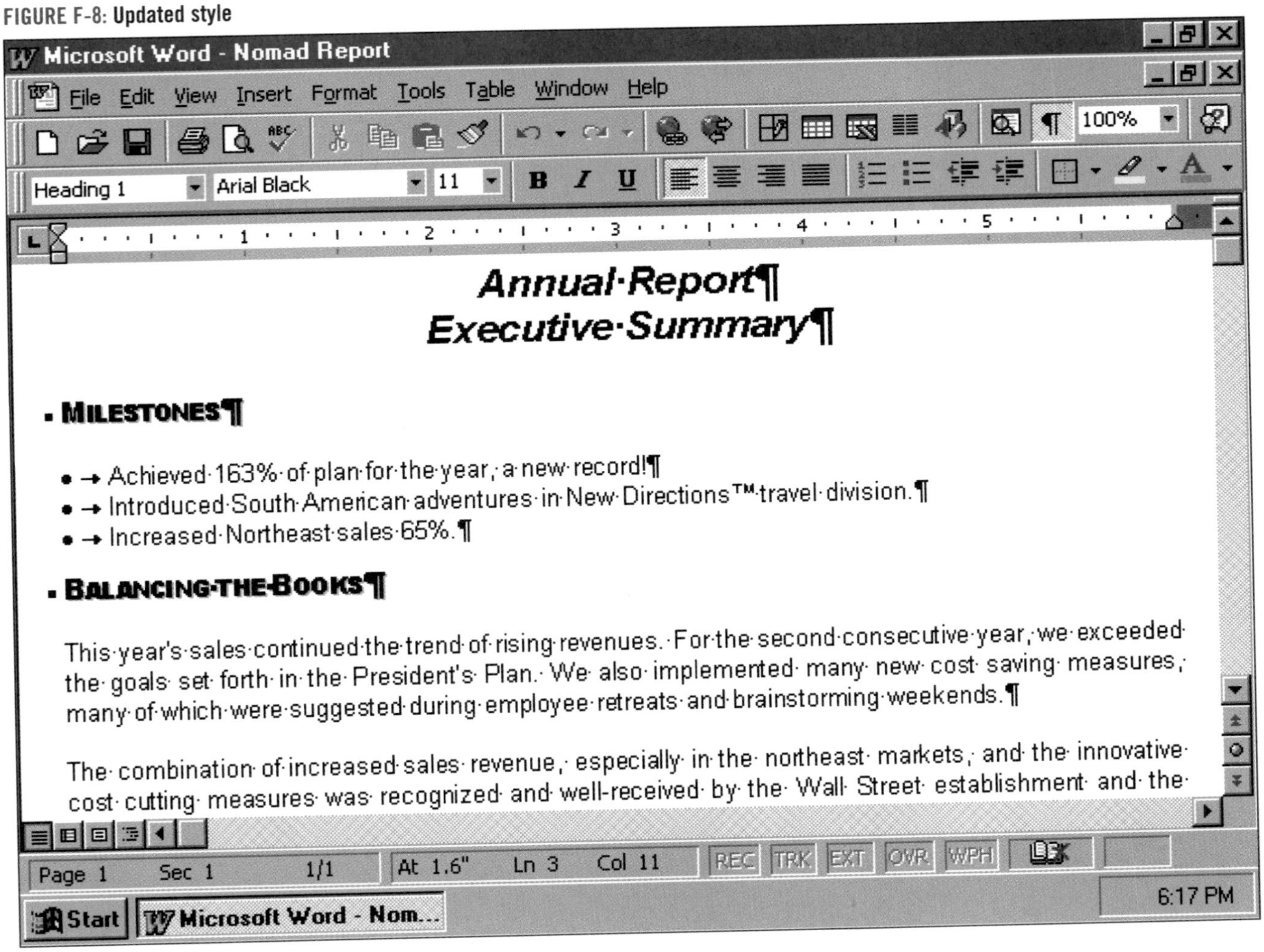

Microsoft Word - Nomad Report

File Edit View Insert Format Tools Table Window Help

Heading 1 | Arial Black | 11 | 100%

Annual·Report¶
Executive·Summary¶

▪ MILESTONES¶

- → Achieved·163%·of·plan·for·the·year,·a·new·record!¶
- → Introduced·South·American·adventures·in·New·Directions™·travel·division.¶
- → Increased·Northeast·sales·65%.¶

▪ BALANCING·THE·BOOKS¶

This·year's·sales·continued·the·trend·of·rising·revenues.·For·the·second·consecutive·year,·we·exceeded·the·goals·set·forth·in·the·President's·Plan.·We·also·implemented·many·new·cost·saving·measures,·many·of·which·were·suggested·during·employee·retreats·and·brainstorming·weekends.¶

The·combination·of·increased·sales·revenue,·especially·in·the·northeast·markets,·and·the·innovative·cost·cutting·measures·was·recognized·and·well-received·by·the·Wall·Street·establishment·and·the·

Page 1 Sec 1 1/1 At 1.6" Ln 3 Col 11 REC TRK EXT OVR WPH

Start | Microsoft Word - Nom... | 6:17 PM

Word 97

Creating and Applying New Paragraph Styles

You are not limited to using the paragraph styles provided by Word templates. In the same way you created a character style earlier in this unit, you can create your own customized paragraph styles. You can create a new style based on an example of selected text or you can specify the paragraph formatting you want in the Style dialog box. You can even assign a keyboard shortcut to a style. Angela would like to create a style to format the title of the Executive Summary so that it is distinctive.

Steps

1. **Select the first line of the document, click Format on the menu bar, then click Style**
   With the Style dialog box open, you are ready to create a new style.
2. **Click New, and in the Style Name box type NewTitle**
   The name "NewTitle" is the name of the new style. Next, identify that you want to create a paragraph style.
3. **Click the Style Type arrow and select Paragraph, if it is not already selected**
   To use a border as part of the NewTitle style, you need to specify additional format characteristics next.
4. **Click Format, then click Border on the list**
   The Borders and Shading dialog box appears. This is the same dialog box that appears when you select the Borders and Shading command on the Format menu. In this dialog box you can specify the settings that will be applied as part of the new style you are creating.
5. **From the Style list, click the double line, click the Width list arrow, click 3 pt, then click the Box border style in the Setting area on the left side of the dialog box, if it is not already selected**
   A preview of the border appears in the Preview area.
6. **Click OK until you return to the Style dialog box, then click Apply**
   The first line of the title appears with a border around it. Now, you can apply the NewTitle style to the next line of the title.
7. **Place the insertion point in the next line, click the Style arrow on the Formatting toolbar and click NewTitle**
   The next line of the title appears in the NewTitle style, as shown in Figure F-9.
8. **Click the Save button on the Standard toolbar**

QuickTip

You can quickly apply a style by pressing [Ctrl][Shift][S] to select the Style list on the Formatting toolbar. Type the name of the style in the Style list, then press [Enter].

FIGURE F-9: New style in document

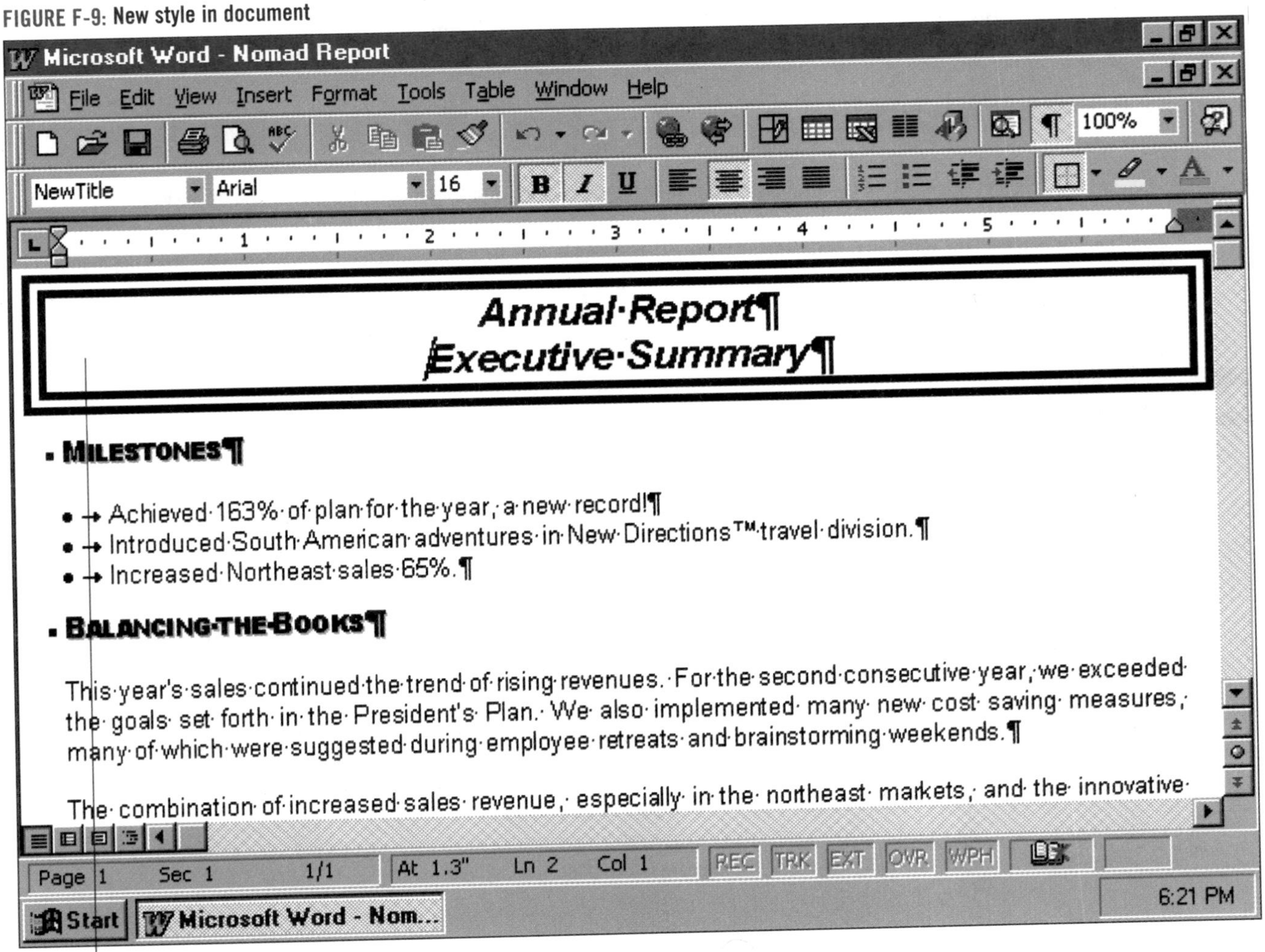

Microsoft Word - Nomad Report

Annual·Report¶
Executive·Summary¶

Milestones¶

- Achieved·163%·of·plan·for·the·year,·a·new·record!¶
- Introduced·South·American·adventures·in·New·Directions™·travel·division.¶
- Increased·Northeast·sales·65%.¶

Balancing·the·Books¶

This·year's·sales·continued·the·trend·of·rising·revenues.·For·the·second·consecutive·year,·we·exceeded·the·goals·set·forth·in·the·President's·Plan.·We·also·implemented·many·new·cost·saving·measures,·many·of·which·were·suggested·during·employee·retreats·and·brainstorming·weekends.¶

The·combination·of·increased·sales·revenue,·especially·in·the·northeast·markets,·and·the·innovative·

Title in new style

Word 97

Assigning keyboard shortcuts to styles

To apply styles even faster, you can assign a keyboard shortcut to a style. In the Style dialog box you choose the style to which you want to assign a keyboard shortcut. Then click the Modify button. Then click the Shortcut key button. Press the combination of keys you want to use as a shortcut and click Assign. Take care not to assign a keyboard shortcut that has already been assigned to another command. If you share a computer with others, click the Save Changes in arrow and select the document you are currently editing.

Word 97

Displaying Style Names in a Document

When formatting with styles it is often useful to see the name of the style applied to a paragraph. In the document's normal view, you can display the style names in the Style area at the left side of the window. You can also modify a style by double-clicking the style name in the Style area. These style names do not appear in the printed document, but you do have the option to print a separate document describing all the styles that are used. Angela would like to see the names of all the paragraph styles she is using in her document.

Steps

1. **Click Tools on the menu bar, click Options, then click the View tab**
   The View tab appears foremost in the dialog box, as shown in Figure F-10. On this tab, you can specify the width of the Style area in the document window.
2. **Click the Style area width up arrow until you see 1", then click OK**
   When you return to the document window, you see the names of the styles at the left edge of the window, as shown in Figure F-11. So that the Style area takes no more space than necessary, adjust the width of it.
3. **Position the pointer over the vertical line that separates the Style area from the rest of the document, and when the pointer changes to ⇹, drag the line so that the Style area is no wider than the longest style name**
   Depending on your computer system, you might need to increase or decrease the Style area. Next, make one last change to the Body Text style.
4. **Scroll (if necessary) to a paragraph formatted in the Body Text style and double-click the style name in the Style area**
   The paragraph that is formatted in Body Text style is selected. The Style dialog box opens, so you can now modify the style.
5. **Click Modify, click Format, then click Paragraph from the list**
   In the Paragraph dialog box, decrease the spacing after each body paragraph.
6. **In the Spacing After box, click the down arrow once, changing the spacing to 6 pt, then click OK until you return to the Style dialog box**
   Continue by applying these changes.
7. **Click Apply, then deselect the text**
   Clicking Apply closes the dialog box and updates the style throughout the document. Because you no longer need the Style area displayed, you can hide it.
8. **Position the pointer over the vertical line that separates the Style area from the rest of the document, and when the pointer changes to ⇹, drag to the left until the Style area disappears**
   Compare your document to Figure F-12. You have completed modifying your document for now, so you can save it.
9. **Click the Save button on the Standard toolbar**

FIGURE F-10: View tab in Options dialog box

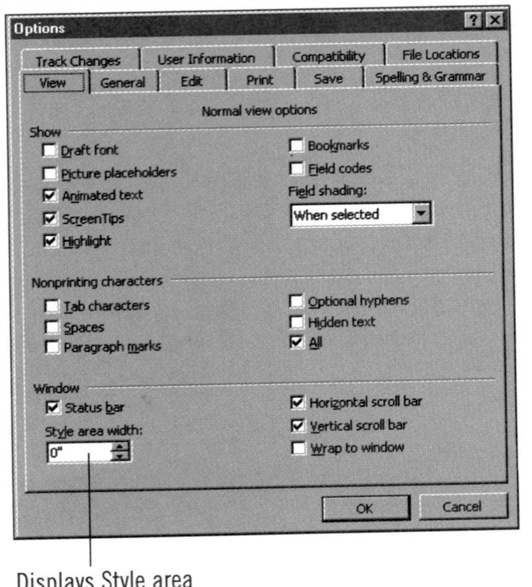

FIGURE F-11: Style area in document

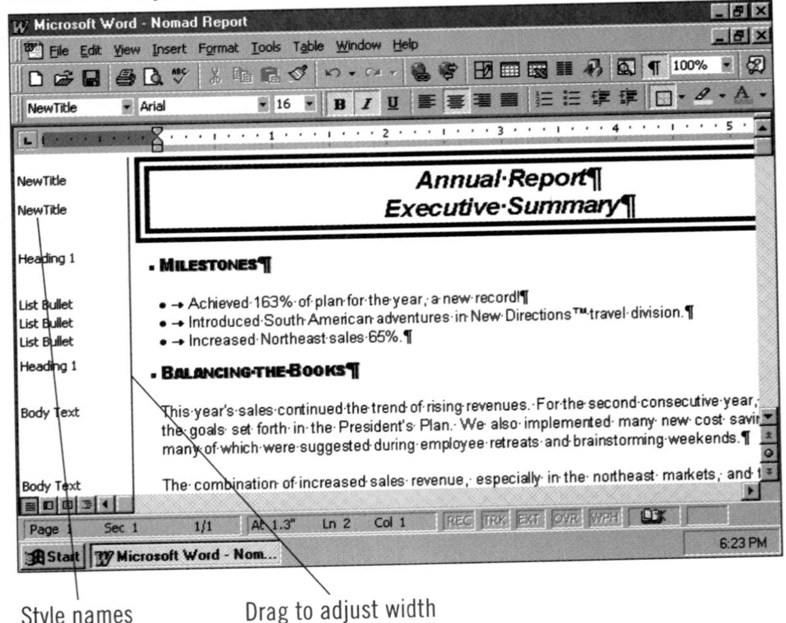

FIGURE F-12: Completed document

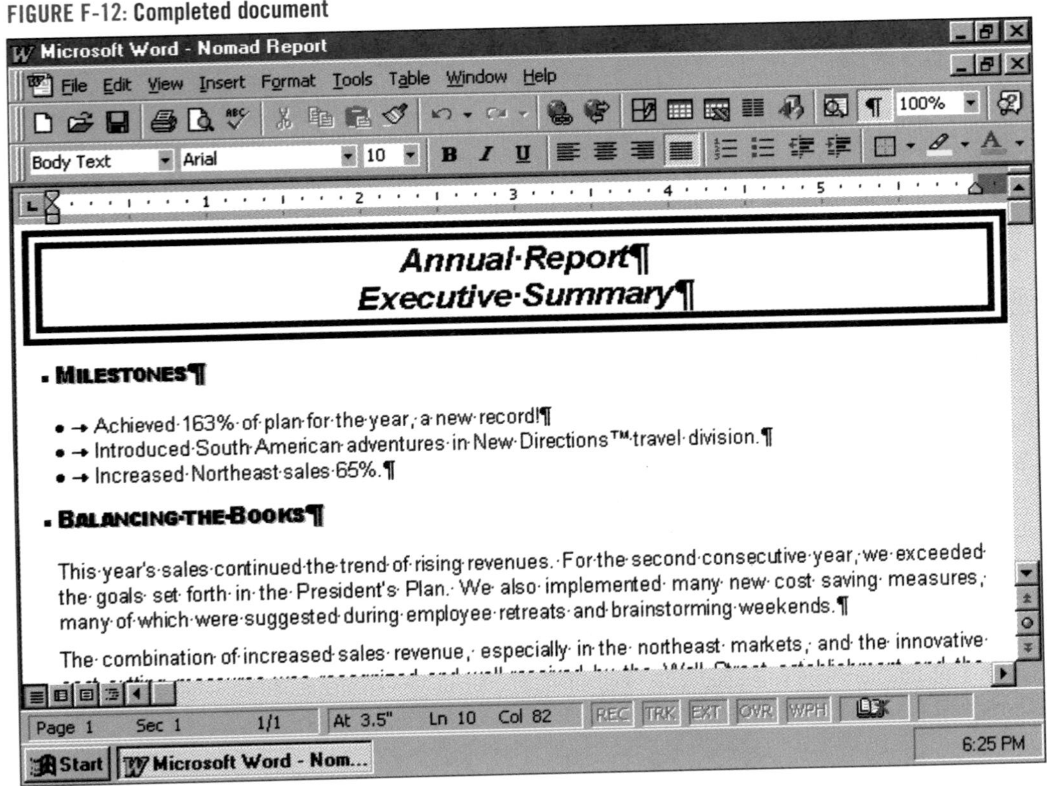

Word 97

Printing styles

You can get a hard copy document that contains a description of the formatting used in each of the styles in a document. When you print a document using the Print command, click the Print What arrow in the Print dialog box, then choose Styles from the list. This feature prints a list of styles and a description of each one. Use this feature when you want to keep track of the styles in your document.

Word 97

Moving Around with Styles

Styles can also play a valuable role as you move around in a longer document, because you can use styles to move to different parts of a document. For example, you can scroll through a document by "paging" through its headings. You can also use the Document Map to display headings on the left half of the window and the document text on the right half. By clicking a heading on the left, you can move the insertion point to the heading on the right. Angela wants to review each of the headings in the document, so will take advantage of the styles in the document to move to the locations she wants.

Steps 1 2 3 4

1. **Press [Ctrl] [Home] to place the insertion point at the beginning of the document**
2. **Click the Select Browse Object button at the bottom of the vertical scroll bar**
   This button displays a menu of items you can use to scroll through a document, as shown in Figure F-13. You want to scroll through the headings.
3. **Click the Browse by Heading button**
   The insertion point moves to the first heading in the document. Notice that the Previous and Next Page buttons in the scroll bar change color. The color indicates that clicking these buttons will move the insertion point from item to item, not from page to page as they normally do.
4. **Click the Next Heading button and Previous Heading button to move from heading to heading in the document, and back to the start of the document**
   To view all the headings at once and still see the text of the document, you can use the Document Map feature.
5. **Click the Document Map button on the Standard toolbar**
   The window splits into two parts. On the left side you see the headings in the document. On the right side is the document text, as shown in Figure F-14.
6. **On the left side of the window, click the last heading in the document, Corporate Mission Statement**
   The insertion point moves to that heading on the right side of the window. You can now edit the text in this heading.
7. **Select the text Mission Statement and type Vision**
   Notice that the heading on the left is also updated. Turn off the Document Map feature.
8. **Click the Document Map button on the Standard toolbar**
   Compare your document to Figure F-15.
9. **Click the Save button on the Standard toolbar**

FIGURE F-13: Search Items box

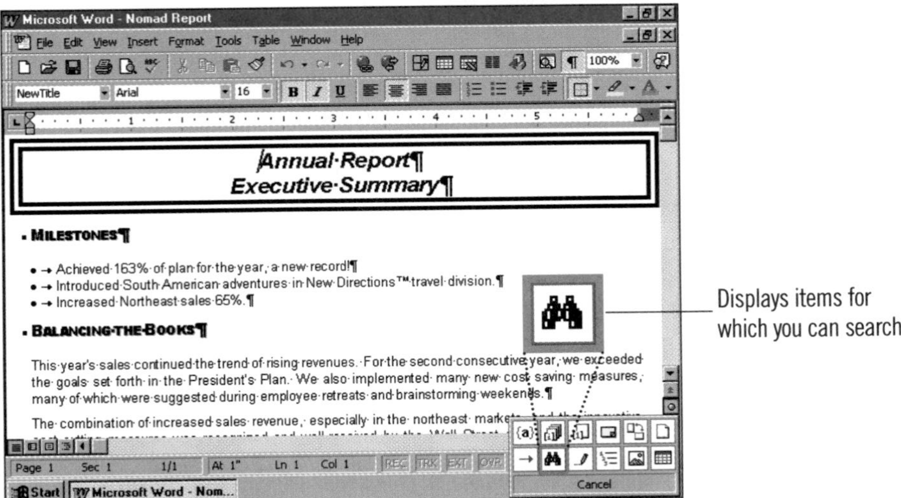

FIGURE F-14: Document Map

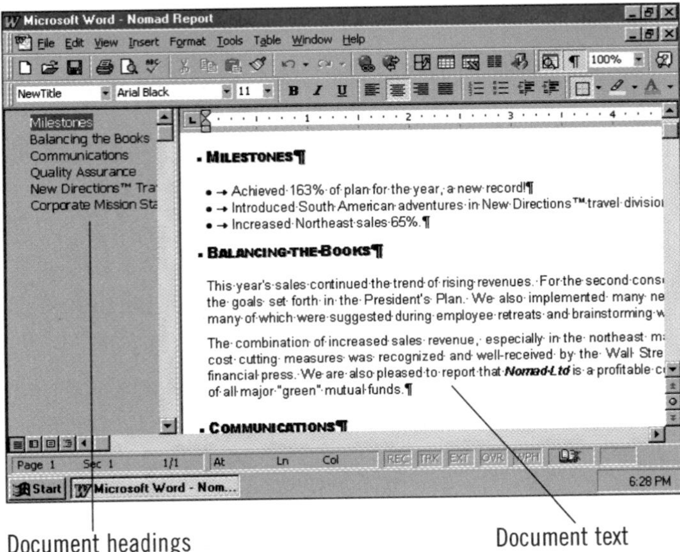

FIGURE F-15: Completed document

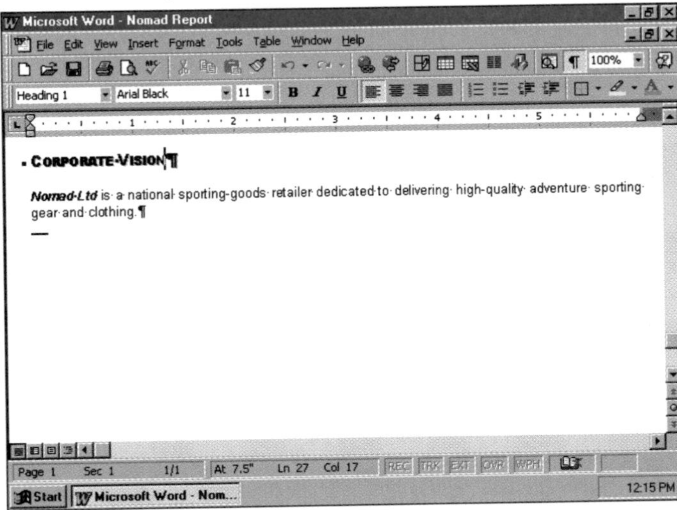

Word 97

Replacing Styles

The same way you search for and replace text and formatting in a document, you can use the Replace command to locate and replace each instance of a style. For example, suppose you decide to change all instances of the Heading 3 style with the Heading 2 style. With the Replace command you can instruct Word to search for text formatted in the Heading 3 style and format it in the Heading 2 style instead. Angela wants to align the body text in her document with the text (after the bullets) in the bulleted list at the start of the document. Because there is a Body Text Indent style available, she will use the Replace command to substitute this style for the current Body Text style throughout the document.

Steps

1. Press **[Ctrl][Home]** to place the insertion point at the start of the document
2. Click **Edit** on the menu bar, click **Replace**, then click **More** to extend the dialog box if all the options are not displayed
   The Find and Replace dialog box opens. You can specify the formatting you want to replace by clicking the Format button.
3. With the insertion point in the Find What box, click **Format** near the bottom of the dialog box, then click **Style** from the list
   The Find Style dialog box opens, as shown in Figure F-16. From this dialog box you can select the style for which you want to search. Select the current style applied to the body text in your document.
4. Click **Body Text**, then click **OK**
   The Format area below the Find What box indicates that you are searching for the Body Text style. Next, you can specify the style you want to use instead.
5. With the insertion point in the Replace With box, click **Format**, then click **Style** from the list
   You can select a new body text style.
6. Click **Body Text Indent**, then click **OK**
   The Format area below the Replace With box indicates that the text should be formatted in the Body Text Indent style, as shown in Figure F-17. You are now ready to replace the styles.
7. Click **Replace All**
   A message indicates the number of changes made.
8. Click **OK** to return to the dialog box, then click **Close**
   Compare your document to Figure F-18. Then save your changes and close the document.
9. Click the **Save button** on the Standard toolbar, then close the document

FIGURE F-16: Find Style dialog box

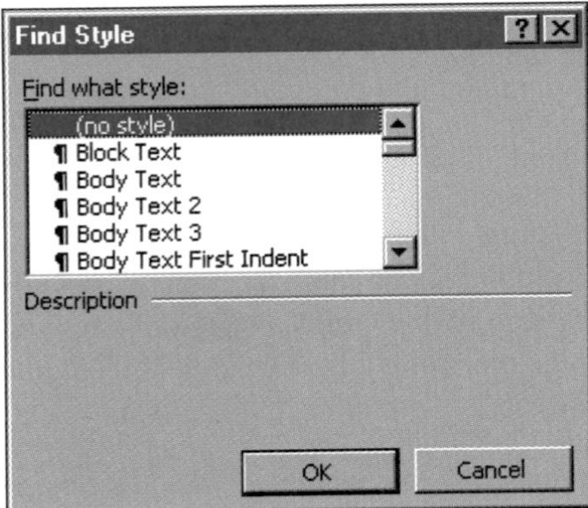

FIGURE F-17: Find and Replace dialog box

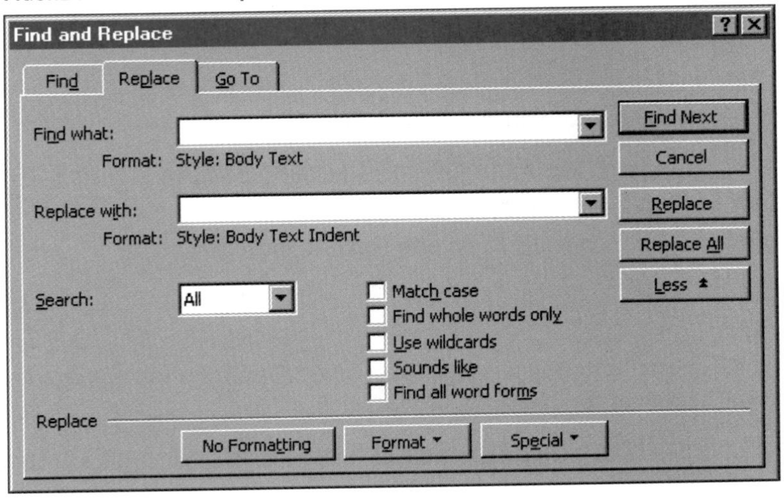

Find and Replace
Find | Replace | Go To
Find what:
Format: Style: Body Text
Replace with:
Format: Style: Body Text Indent
Search: All
Match case
Find whole words only
Use wildcards
Sounds like
Find all word forms
Find Next
Cancel
Replace
Replace All
Less
Replace
No Formatting | Format | Special

FIGURE F-18: Body Text Indent style in document

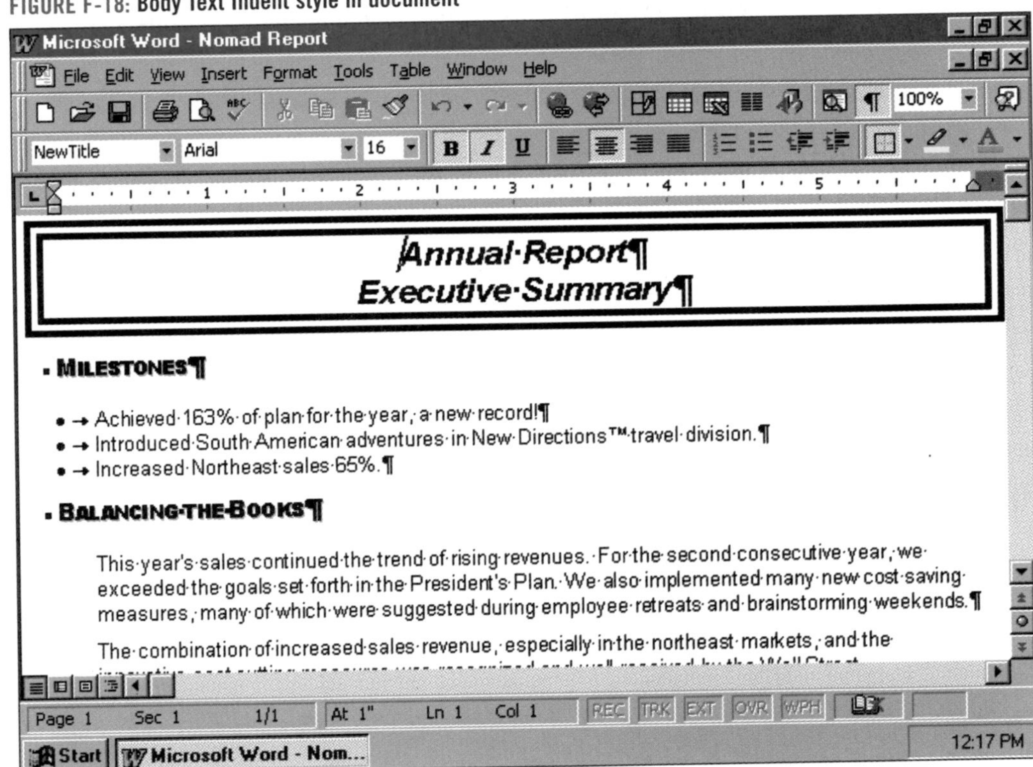

Formatting as You Type

Formatting a new document in Word can be as easy as typing. When you type certain combinations of text and formatting, Word formats the text as you type. For example, when you type a hyphen and then press the [Tab] key, Word formats the line with a bullet. The next document Angela would like to create is a draft document describing a new promotion. As she types the document, Word applies the appropriate formatting.

Steps

1. Click the **New button** on the Standard toolbar
2. Click **Tools** on the menu bar, click **AutoCorrect**
   In this case, verify the options for the AutoFormat As You Type feature.
3. Click the **AutoFormat As You Type tab** and compare the dialog box to Figure F-19, clicking any options not already enabled, then click **OK**
   The dialog box closes, and you are now ready to type the text of your document.
4. Type **Announcing new discount pricing for our "favorite" retailers** and press **[Enter]** twice
   When you press [Enter] twice after entering a line of text (that does not end in a punctuation mark), Word formats the line in the Heading 1 style.
5. Type **o** (a lowercase "o"), press **[Tab]**, then type **Sell at least 1/2 of your quota in the 1st week of each month** and press **[Enter]**
   Notice that as you type, the fraction "1/2" changes to a fraction symbol "½," the text "1st" changes to "1st" and bullets appear at the start of the line and at the beginning of the new line. Continue typing the document.
6. Type the following two lines, pressing **[Enter]** at the end of each line:
   Sell at least 3/4 of your quota in the 2nd week of each month
   Sell at least 100% of your quota in the 3rd week of each month
   Next, add a blank line.
7. Press **[Enter]** again at the end of the last line
   Pressing [Enter] twice stops the AutoFormatting in a bulleted list.
8. Type **Your store needs to meet only two of the above milestones to qualify**
   Compare your document to Figure F-20. You have completed typing and formatting your document for now, so print and save your work and close the document.

9. Print the document, click **File** on the menu bar, click **Close**, then click **Yes** and save the file with the name **Promotion**, then exit Word

FIGURE F-19: AutoFormat As You Type tab

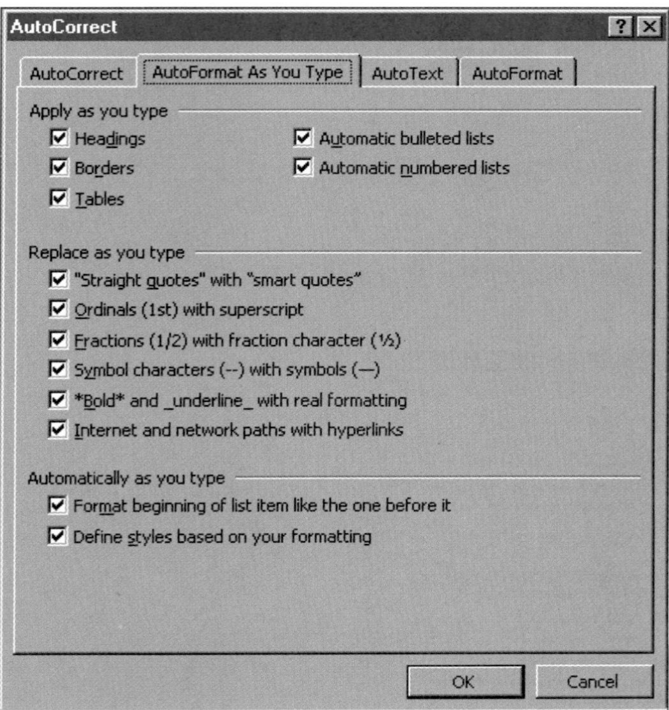

FIGURE F-20: Document formatted as you type

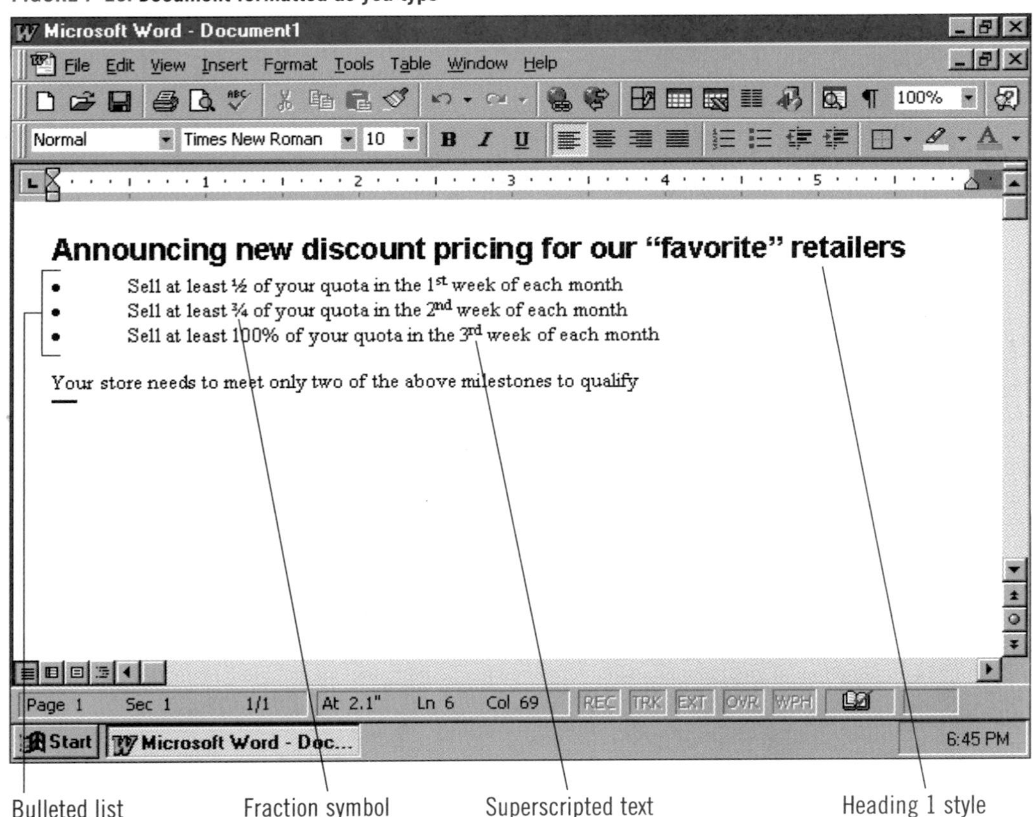

Word 97

Practice

► Concepts Review

Label and describe each of the parts of the document shown in Figure F-21.

FIGURE F-21

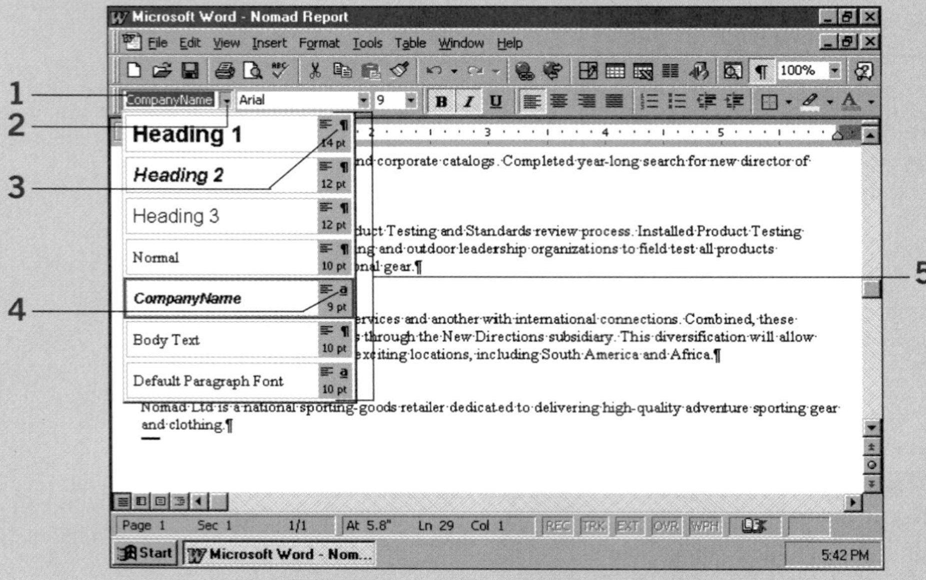

Match each of the following descriptions with the term that it describes best.

6. AutoFormat
7. Paragraph style
8. Templates
9. Style Gallery
10. Character style

a. A named set of paragraph format settings
b. Displays document in another set of styles
c. A named set of character format settings
d. Special documents containing styles and other options specific to different kinds of documents
e. Improves a document's appearance by applying styles and inserting symbols

Select the best answer from the list of choices.

11. Which of the following is true about replacing formatting in the Replace dialog box?
- a. You can click Replace All to review each occurrence of replaced formatting.
- b. To remove formatting from the search or replacement text, you click the Clear button.
- c. You can use buttons on the Formatting toolbar to select formatting options.
- d. You cannot use the Font or Paragraph dialog boxes to select formatting options.

12. To create a character style, you
- a. Type a name in the Style box on the Formatting toolbar and press [Enter].
- b. Click Format on the menu bar, then click Style.
- c. Click Format on the menu bar, then click Style Gallery.
- d. Select a style from the Style list on the Formatting toolbar.

13. **Which of the following is not a benefit of using styles?**
   a. Checks your document for proper grammar and word usage so it is appropriate for the kind of document you are creating
   b. Quickly applies format settings in one step
   c. Modifies style characteristics and reapply to all occurrences
   d. Previews a document in styles from other templates
14. **Which statement is not true about character styles?**
   a. You can create a character style using the Style dialog box.
   b. You can create a character style by using selected text as an example.
   c. Character styles affect the entire current paragraph.
   d. You can redefine a character style based on a selected example.
15. **Which statement best describes when to use styles in a document?**
   a. When text or paragraphs scattered throughout a document require similar and consistent formatting
   b. When text or paragraphs on the same page require the same format settings
   c. When text or paragraph formatting is not likely to change
   d. When text or paragraphs do not require many different format settings
16. **Which statement best describes the AutoFormat feature?**
   a. The AutoFormat command allows you to review changes before accepting them.
   b. AutoFormat corrects grammatical and spelling errors in a document.
   c. AutoFormat sorts items in a list for you.
   d. The AutoFormat command allows you to apply and reject formatting changes to improve the appearance of your document in one step.
17. **Which of the following changes is not made by AutoFormat?**
   a. Applies paragraph styles to all paragraphs in the document
   b. Adjusts spacing and inserts appropriate indentation
   c. Applies character styles to appropriate text
   d. Inserts appropriate symbols and characters
18. **Which of the following statements is NOT true about modifying styles?**
   a. You can modify a style based on the formatting in the current selection.
   b. You must open the Style dialog box and click the Modify button, and then open the dialog boxes for the type of formatting you want to use in the style.
   c. The Reapply Style dialog box gives you the option to redefine the style or apply original formatting.
   d. Redefining the style based on the current selection is the default option in the Reapply Style dialog box.

Skills Review

1. **Format text with AutoFormat.**
   a. Start Word and open the document named WD F-2. Save the document as "Healthy Home".
   b. Click Format on the menu bar, then click AutoFormat to apply standard styles and formatting to your document.
   c. Click OK.
   d. Scroll through the document and review the changes.
2. **Use the Style Gallery.**
   a. Click Format on the menu bar, then click Style Gallery.
   b. Select different templates and examine your document as it would appear with these templates.
   c. Click Elegant Memo in the list of templates.
   d. Click OK.
   e. Save your changes.

3. **Apply paragraph formatting and styles.**
   a. With the insertion point in the first paragraph in the body of the document, click Paragraph on the Format menu. In the Line spacing list, select 1.5 Lines, then click OK.
   b. Select the Body Text style from the Style list box on the Formatting toolbar.
   c. Make sure the first option for updating the style is selected in the Modify Style dialog box, then click OK.
   d. In the first list in the document (near the top of page 3, depending on your monitor), select the first line (yoga).
   e. Click Paragraph on the Format menu. Change the Spacing After to 3 pt. Click OK to close the dialog box.
   f. With the same line still selected, click Bullets and Numbering on the Format menu. On the Bulleted tab, change the bullet style to a diamond. Click OK to return to the document.
4. **Create and apply new styles.**
   a. Select the text "EnviroTech" near the beginning of the second page. Change the formatting of the text by choosing Arial from the Font box and 9 pt from the Font Size box then click the Bold button.
   b. Click Format on the menu bar, then click Style. Click New. In the Name box, type "EnviroTech" and from the Style Type list choose Character. Then click OK and in the Style dialog box, click Apply.
   c. Apply the EnviroTech character style to each occurrence of the company name "EnviroTech".
   d. Select the heading "Introduction" and apply the Document Label style.
   e. With the heading still selected, click Format on the menu bar, click Paragraph, then apply 18 pts of spacing after.
   f. Click the Lines and Page Breaks tab, then click the Keep with next checkbox. Click OK.
   g. Reapply the Document Label style and update the style to reflect these changes in formatting.
   h. Deselect the heading.
5. **Replace styles in a document.**
   a. Click Edit on the menu bar, then click Replace. Click Format and then click Style.
   b. Choose Heading 1 from the list of styles, click OK.
   c. Click in the Replace with box, then click the Format button and then click Style.
   d. Choose Document Label from the list of styles, click OK.
   e. Click Replace All. There were two replacements made.
   f. Close the dialog box and save the document.
6. **Display style names in the document.**
   a. Click Tools on the menu bar, click Options, then click the View tab.
   b. Click the up arrow in the Style area width box until you see 1", then click OK.
   c. Position the pointer over the vertical line that separates the Style area from the rest of the document and, when the pointer changes shape, drag the line so that the Style area is no wider than the longest style name.
   d. Scroll (if necessary) to a paragraph formatted in the List Bullet style and double-click the style name.
   e. Click Modify, click Format, then click Paragraph from the list.
   f. On the Indents and Spacing tab, type "6" in the Spacing After box, to change the spacing to 6 pt, then click OK until you return to the Style dialog box.
   g. Click Apply.
   h. Position the pointer over the vertical line that separates the Style area from the rest of the document and, when the pointer changes shape, drag to the left until the Style area disappears.
   i. Preview then print your document.
   j. Save your changes.
7. **Format text as you type.**
   a. Click the New button on the Standard toolbar.
   b. Click Format on the menu bar, click AutoFormat, then click the Options button.
   c. Click the AutoFormat As You Type tab, clicking any options not already enabled, then click OK twice.
   d. Type "Customer Satisfaction Survey Results" and press [Enter] twice.
   e. Type at least six hyphens in a row and press [Enter] (this creates a line border).

f. Type o (an "o"), press [Tab], then type "More than ½ of catalog customers received their orders within the 1st week of placing their order" and press [Enter].
g. Type the following two lines, pressing [Enter] at the end of each line:
   Just under ¾ of retail customers returned to make 2nd and 3rd purchases
   Over ½ of the customers surveyed expressed positive comments regarding their 1st purchase experience
h. Press [Enter] again at the end of the last line.
i. Type "These survey results mean that while generally positive, we must continue to pursue even higher customer satisfaction results. Let's all strive to ship orders within the 1st week for ½ of our customers, and increase positive purchase experiences to at least ¾ of the customers."
j. Save your document as "Sales Promotion" and print it.
k. Close both documents, saving any changes.
l. Exit Word.

Independent Challenges

1. As a member of the acquisitions team for an investment research company called Expansion Inc., you have been asked to improve the formatting of a summary analysis prepared by a colleague. Open the document named "WD F-3" and save it as "New Growth". Using Figure F-22 as a guide, apply the following formatting.

To complete this independent challenge:

1. Use the AutoFormat command to apply styles.
2. Use the Style Gallery to apply styles from the Professional Memo template.
3. Apply Heading 2 style to the headings "The Benefits of Growth", "Future Expansion", and "Initial Expansion."
4. Use the Replace command to format all occurrences of the name "World Travel Airlines" in bold italics.
5. Change the formatting for the Heading 1 style so that it appears with a bottom border and in 18 pts. Reapply and update the style.
6. Apply the Heading 2 style to the text "Cruise Lines Offer Opportunity for Growth" and the next two headings.
7. Preview, save, and print the document befroe closing it.

FIGURE F-22A

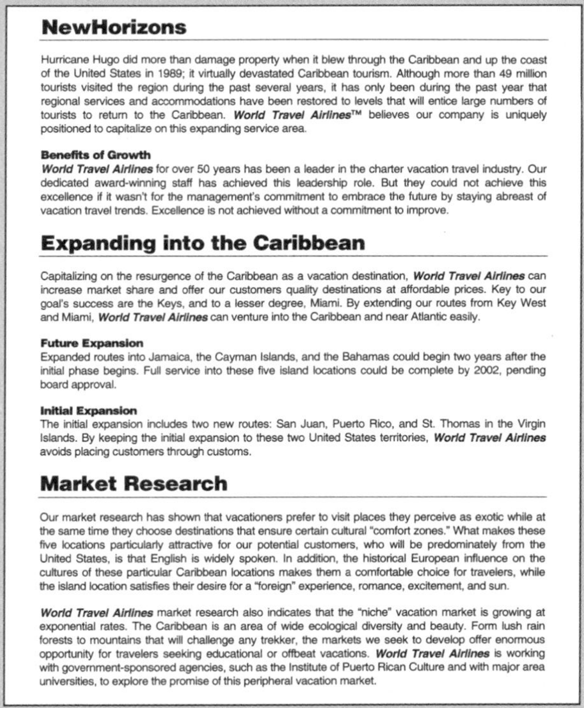

NewHorizons

Hurricane Hugo did more than damage property when it blew through the Caribbean and up the coast of the United States in 1989; it virtually devastated Caribbean tourism. Although more than 49 million tourists visited the region during the past several years, it has only been during the past year that regional services and accommodations have been restored to levels that will entice large numbers of tourists to return to the Caribbean. ***World Travel Airlines***™ believes our company is uniquely positioned to capitalize on this expanding service area.

Benefits of Growth

World Travel Airlines for over 50 years has been a leader in the charter vacation travel industry. Our dedicated award-winning staff has achieved this leadership role. But they could not achieve this excellence if it wasn't for the management's commitment to embrace the future by staying abreast of vacation travel trends. Excellence is not achieved without a commitment to improve.

Expanding into the Caribbean

Capitalizing on the resurgence of the Caribbean as a vacation destination, ***World Travel Airlines*** can increase market share and offer our customers quality destinations at affordable prices. Key to our goal's success are the Keys, and to a lesser degree, Miami. By extending our routes from Key West and Miami, ***World Travel Airlines*** can venture into the Caribbean and near Atlantic easily.

Future Expansion

Expanded routes into Jamaica, the Cayman Islands, and the Bahamas could begin two years after the initial phase begins. Full service into these five island locations could be complete by 2002, pending board approval.

Initial Expansion

The initial expansion includes two new routes: San Juan, Puerto Rico, and St. Thomas in the Virgin Islands. By keeping the initial expansion to these two United States territories, ***World Travel Airlines*** avoids placing customers through customs.

Market Research

Our market research has shown that vacationers prefer to visit places they perceive as exotic while at the same time they choose destinations that ensure certain cultural "comfort zones." What makes these five locations particularly attractive for our potential customers, who will be predominately from the United States, is that English is widely spoken. In addition, the historical European influence on the cultures of these particular Caribbean locations makes them a comfortable choice for travelers, while the island location satisfies their desire for a "foreign" experience, romance, excitement, and sun.

World Travel Airlines market research also indicates that the "niche" vacation market is growing at exponential rates. The Caribbean is an area of wide ecological diversity and beauty. Form lush rain forests to mountains that will challenge any trekker, the markets we seek to develop offer enormous opportunity for travelers seeking educational or offbeat vacations. ***World Travel Airlines*** is working with government-sponsored agencies, such as the Institute of Puerto Rican Culture and with major area universities, to explore the promise of this peripheral vacation market.

FIGURE F-22B

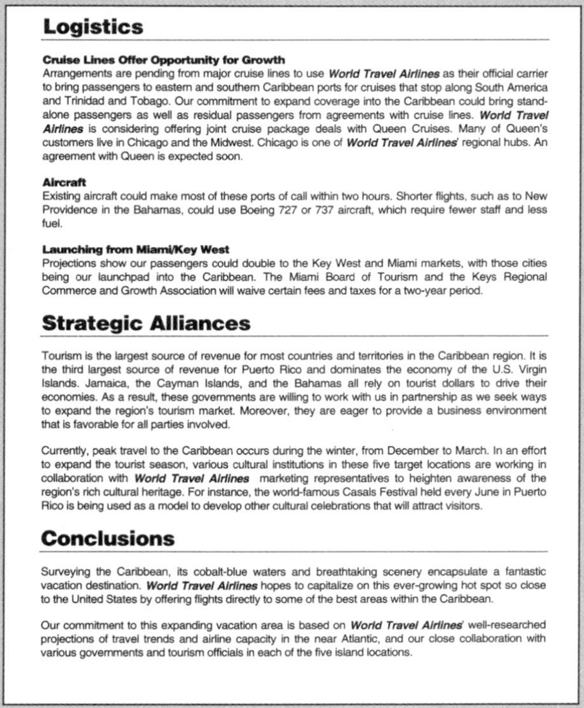

Logistics

Cruise Lines Offer Opportunity for Growth

Arrangements are pending from major cruise lines to use ***World Travel Airlines*** as their official carrier to bring passengers to eastern and southern Caribbean ports for cruises that stop along South America and Trinidad and Tobago. Our commitment to expand coverage into the Caribbean could bring stand-alone passengers as well as residual passengers from agreements with cruise lines. ***World Travel Airlines*** is considering offering joint cruise package deals with Queen Cruises. Many of Queen's customers live in Chicago and the Midwest. Chicago is one of ***World Travel Airlines***' regional hubs. An agreement with Queen is expected soon.

Aircraft

Existing aircraft could make most of these ports of call within two hours. Shorter flights, such as to New Providence in the Bahamas, could use Boeing 727 or 737 aircraft, which require fewer staff and less fuel.

Launching from Miami/Key West

Projections show our passengers could double to the Key West and Miami markets, with those cities being our launchpad into the Caribbean. The Miami Board of Tourism and the Keys Regional Commerce and Growth Association will waive certain fees and taxes for a two-year period.

Strategic Alliances

Tourism is the largest source of revenue for most countries and territories in the Caribbean region. It is the third largest source of revenue for Puerto Rico and dominates the economy of the U.S. Virgin Islands. Jamaica, the Cayman Islands, and the Bahamas all rely on tourist dollars to drive their economies. As a result, these governments are willing to work with us in partnership as we seek ways to expand the region's tourism market. Moreover, they are eager to provide a business environment that is favorable for all parties involved.

Currently, peak travel to the Caribbean occurs during the winter, from December to March. In an effort to expand the tourist season, various cultural institutions in these five target locations are working in collaboration with ***World Travel Airlines*** marketing representatives to heighten awareness of the region's rich cultural heritage. For instance, the world-famous Casals Festival held every June in Puerto Rico is being used as a model to develop other cultural celebrations that will attract visitors.

Conclusions

Surveying the Caribbean, its cobalt-blue waters and breathtaking scenery encapsulate a fantastic vacation destination. ***World Travel Airlines*** hopes to capitalize on this ever-growing hot spot so close to the United States by offering flights directly to some of the best areas within the Caribbean.

Our commitment to this expanding vacation area is based on ***World Travel Airlines***' well-researched projections of travel trends and airline capacity in the near Atlantic, and our close collaboration with various governments and tourism officials in each of the five island locations.

2. As an executive member of an organization dedicated to the improvement of media services called "Communication for the Future", you are in charge of planning the upcoming 1998 convention. While in town, many of your members will want the opportunity to explore the Boston area. You have contracted with a travel agency to prepare a visitor's guide. The travel agency has prepared a draft, and you have decided to make the document more attractive. Open document named WD F-4 and save it as "Tourist Info".

To complete this independent challenge:

1. Use the AutoFormat command to apply styles.
2. Change the formatting for the Heading 1 style so that the text is 18 pt and italics. Reapply and update the style.
3. Change the formatting for the Heading 2 style so that the text is 14 pt and 4 pts of spacing after. Reapply and update the style.
4. Change the List Bullet style so that it is formatted with the left indent of 0.50 inches, a hanging indent of 0.50 inches, and 2 pt spacing before and after. Reapply and update the style.
5. Create a character style called Highlight that is 9 pt, bold, Arial. When you create this style, assign a keyboard shortcut to the Highlight style, [Alt] + [Shift] + [H]. Apply this style (using the keyboard shortcut) to the first few words or phrase in each paragraph formatted in the List Bullet style. Be sure to save the shortcut in the document and not in the template.
6. Preview, save, and print the document before closing it.

3. As volunteer at your local health food co-op, you have signed up for producing a flyer that describes the co-op's features to new members. Using text already located on the co-op's Web site on the Internet, apply attractive formatting to improve the appearance of the document.

To complete this independent challenge:

1. Log on to the Internet and use your browser to find a Web page of a co-op in your area or of special interest to you. If you can't find one, go to http://www.course.com. From there, click Student Online Companions, click the link for this textbook, then click the Word link for Unit F. Click on one of the links provided, then copy all the text in the document that appears. Paste the contents of the clipboard into a new blank document. Save the document with the name Co-op Flyer.
2. First improve the appearance of the document using AutoFormat (in the AutoFormat dialog box, choose Letter as the document type), then apply the styles in the Contemporary Memo template in the Style Gallery.
3. Edit the list of items in the store's inventory so that each group of items appears on a separate line. Apply the List 2 style to the first list. Then change the Spacing after to 6 pts, click the Increase Indent button three times, apply bullets, then redefine the List 2 style. If your document does not have a list of products, format the second, third, and fourth paragraphs. Create a List Number that is similar to the List 2 style, but formatted with numbers.
4. Apply the List Number style to another list in the document. Or apply it to the first list if your document has only one.
5. Apply text flow formatting so that the lines of the store's address are never separated by a page break. Then create a new paragraph style called StoreAddress based on this formatting. Apply the StoreAddress style to the list of the hours at the end of the document.
6. Delete any extra paragraph marks that were used for spacing between paragraphs, and spell check the document.
7. Preview, save, and print the document before closing it.

4. As the marketing director for a small adventure travel agency, Majica Tours, you would like to announce a new tour offering. Using the AutoFormat As You Type in Word, create an attractive document that describes the tour features. Use Figure F-23 as a guide to complete this independent challenge:

1. Create a new blank document and save it as Majica Sea Tours. On the AutoFormat As You Type tab in the AutoCorrect dialog box, verify that all check boxes are checked.
2. Type "Announcing Seabreeze Sailing Adventures" and then press [Enter] twice to create a heading formatted in the Heading 1 style.
3. Change the Heading 1 style so that the font size is 18pts, and the paragraph formatting is 10 pts before and 18 points after, and centered.

4. Type ">" followed by a tab and then type the text shown in Figure F-23. Press [Enter] after each line.
5. Press [Enter] twice to stop bulleted formatting.
6. Under the heading, type 5 hyphens and then press [Enter] to create a solid line.
7. Change the formatting of the text in the bulleted list, so that it is formatted in Arial, 14 pts and 1.5 Line Spacing. Create a new paragraph style based on this formatting, name it Arrow List, and apply it to the bulleted list.
8. At the end of the document, type another set of hyphens and then press [Enter].
9. Type "Majica SeaTours Offices:" and apply the modified Heading 1 style to this text. Press [Enter] to create a new line.
10. Type the names of three cities (each on a separate line) and apply the Arrow List style to the list.
11. Preview, save, and print the document before closing it.

FIGURE F-23

Announcing Seabreeze Sailing Adventures

➢ Small groups, 8-10 guests
➢ Low cost, only $599 complete
➢ Gourmet meals, crew includes a gourmet chef
➢ Expert crew, 5 members with over 50 years of guiding and sailing experience

---

Majica SeaTours Offices:

➢ Lake of the Woods
➢ Big Mountain
➢ Lake Pacifica

Visual Workshop

As conference coordinator for Creative Consultants, Inc.'s 1998 Creativity Conference, you are in charge of developing an attractive document that describes the conference seminars to interested participants. A draft document contains the text you want to include. Open the document WD F-5 and save it as "Conference Overview". Figure F-24 serves as a guide for what your completed document should look like. Begin by using AutoFormat to apply consistent styles to the document. Then use the Style Gallery to apply the styles contained in the Contemporary Memo template. Create and apply a character style named "Planners" to the text "Artistic Planners." Continue formatting the document using the features you have learned in previous units, such as borders and shading, modifying bullets, and paragraph alignment. Remember to modify and reapply styles to quickly and consistently make changes throughout the document.

FIGURE F-24

Artistic Planners'

Creativity Conference

1998

Welcome to ***Artistic Planners'*** 1998 Creativity Conference™! This year's conference combines traditional creativity enhancing techniques with new methods tested in a variety of human endeavors. Learn how to become a more creative individual no matter what your field or interests. Today's sessions will help you:

- Learn to use guided imagery to focus your creative energies.
- Apply creativity enhancing techniques in everyday problem solving.
- Learn how to find your creative "zone" and stay in the zone through to the completion of a project.
- Discover how massage and relaxation techniques can enhance creativity.

Guided Imagination

Learn new techniques for finding the images that guide you towards your goals. Not all images work in every situation, so in this session you learn how to clarify your objectives to select the appropriate images. ***Artistic Planners'*** presenters will provide structures for interweaving images are also identified for gaining heightened integration.

Creativity Every Day

Creativity is not just for the traditional "artists" or traditional "artistic" endeavors. Employing creative thinking and creative problem-solving can help us achieve success in everyday activities at work, at home, and even at play. In this session, learn how to think "outside of the lines" no matter what you do.

The "Zone"

Sometimes our creativity comes unbidden, and if we are fortunate enough to take the time and energy to act on it, we are satisfied. But what to do when you "have" to be creative and your muse has abandoned you? In this session, we explore writer's block (and similar disabilities) in an effort to understand and triumph over them. Learn how to call up hidden stores of creativity, even when you feel dull and uninspired.

Enlightened Massage

View demonstrations of deep breathing, massage, and creative visualization exercises. Learn how various relaxation techniques can enhance your creative abilities. An informal dinner and discussion (with ***Artistic Planners'*** panel of experts) is scheduled after this final session.

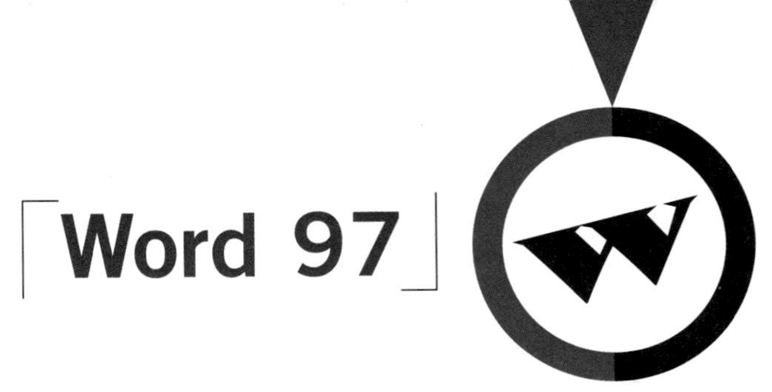

Merging
Word Documents

Objectives

- Create a main document
- Create a data source
- Enter records in a data source
- Insert merge fields
- Work with merged documents
- Create a label main document
- Merge selected records
- Format labels

Mail merge is widely used by companies who need to send similar documents to many individuals at once. The recipient's name and other personal information are often added to a document to create a more personal impression. The Word Mail Merge Helper guides you step-by-step through the **mail merge process**, which combines a standard document with customized information. Angela wants to respond to several customers' requests for information about upcoming alpine adventure tours. She'll use the Mail Merge Helper to create a form letter, enter names in a mailing list, and generate a mailing label for each envelope.

Word 97

Creating a Main Document

In the mail merge process, the **main document** contains **boilerplate text**, basic text that is common to all the versions of the merged document. The Mail Merge command on the Tools menu makes it easy to create and edit each of the merge elements. Table G-1 defines the basic elements of the mail merge process. Be sure to view the CourseHelp "Understanding Mail Merge" before completing this lesson. Instead of retyping each letter to each customer, Angela will use the Mail Merge Helper to modify a standard cover letter and merge it with a mailing list of customers, creating a personalized letter for each customer. First, she'll open the document that contains the boilerplate text for the letter.

CourseHelp

To view the CourseHelp for this lesson, click the Start button, point to Programs, point to CourseHelp, then click Microsoft Word 97 Illustrated. Choose the Understanding Mail Merge CourseHelp.

1. **Start Word, open the student file WD G-1, then save it as Response Letter Main**
   This document contains the boilerplate text for the main document. First you will insert today's date.
2. **With the insertion point at the beginning of the document, click Insert on the menu bar, then click Date and Time**
   The Date and Time dialog box opens.
3. **In the Available Formats box, verify that the Update Automatically check box is cleared, then click the fourth option in the list, and then click OK**
   The current date appears in the format you specified. Clearing the Update Automatically check box ensures that the date will not be updated each time you save or print the document. Now you are ready to start the Mail Merge Helper.
4. **Click Tools on the menu bar, then click Mail Merge**
   The Mail Merge Helper dialog box opens. Helpful instructions regarding the next step in the merge process appear at the top of the dialog box.
5. **In the Main Document section, click Create, then click Form Letters**
   You will create a form letter using Letter Main as the main document, which is already open and is the active window.
6. **Click Active Window**
   The merge type and main document name appear in the Main Document section of the Mail Merge Helper dialog box, as shown in Figure G-1.

TABLE G-1: Definition of mail merge elements

term	definition
Main document	The document containing the standard information that is the same for each merged document. It also contains the field names that represent the variable information to be inserted during the merge
Data source	The document containing the personalized information that varies for each merged document, such as name and address, payment due amount, appointment date and time, etc.
Data field	An attribute that describes an item or individual. A group of data fields that relate to a specific item is called a record
Merge field	The merge fields you insert in a mail merge main document instruct Word where to insert unique information from the selected data source. These fields appear with chevrons («») around the name
Record	The entire collection of fields related to an item or individual, contained in the data source
Header row	The field names, which appear in the first row of the data source
Boilerplate text	The text in the main document that is the same for each version of a merged document

FIGURE G-1: **Mail Merge Helper dialog box**

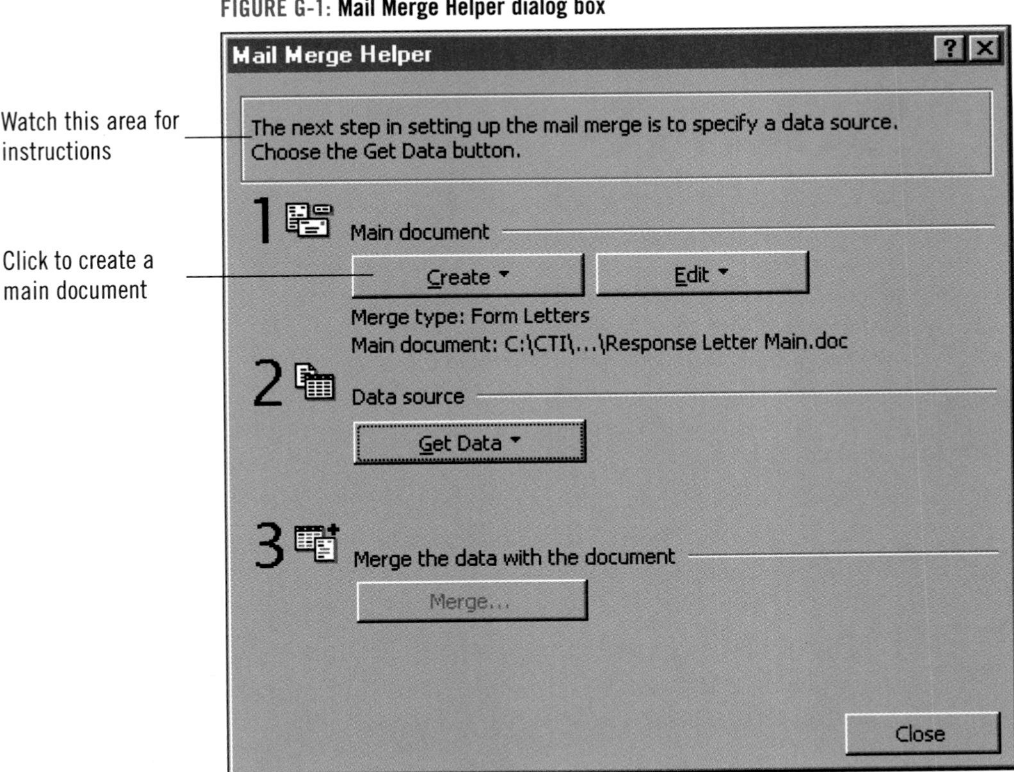

Viewing CourseHelp

The camera icon on the opposite page indicates there is a CourseHelp available for this lesson. CourseHelps are on-screen "movies" that bring difficult concepts to life, to help you understand the material in this book. Your instructor received a CourseHelp disk and should have installed it on the machine you are using. To start CourseHelp, click the Start button, point to Programs, point to CourseHelp, then click Microsoft Word 97 Illustrated. In the main CourseHelp window, click the topic that corresponds to this lesson. Because CourseHelp runs in a separate window, you can start and view a movie even if you're in the middle of completing a lesson. Once the movie is finished, you can click the Word program button on the taskbar and continue with the lesson, right where you left off.

Word 97

Creating a Data Source

Once you have specified a main document, you are ready to create the **data source**, which will contain the information that differs in each version of the merged document. The **data source** consists of fields related to an item or individual. A **field** is a specific item of data (such as a first name or a zip code) for a product or individual. A group of data fields that relate to a specific item is called a **record**. You can create a new data source, or specify an existing source that already contains the fields and information you would like in your form letter. Angela will create a new data source and specify the fields it will contain—in this case, the names and addresses of the Nomad customers to whom she wants to send the letter.

Steps 1 2 3 4

1. Click **Get Data**, then click **Create Data Source**
   The Create Data Source dialog box opens, as shown in Figure G-2. Several commonly used field names appear, and you can also create your own field names. First, you must remove any fields you don't need to use in the letter from the data source.
2. In the Field names in header row box, click **JobTitle**, then click **Remove Field Name**
   The JobTitle field is removed from the header row list and will not be included in the data source. Next, remove the other fields you don't need.
3. Repeat Step 2 to remove the following field names: **Company, Address2, Country, HomePhone**, and **WorkPhone**
   These fields are removed from the header row list. After removing or adding fields to the data source, you can close the Create Data Source dialog box.
4. Click **OK**
   The Save As dialog box opens. When you save your data source (which is a Word document) and give it a name, the data source becomes attached to the main document. Next, enter a name for the data source so that it is attached to the main document.
5. Type **Response Letter Data** in the File name box, then click **Save**
   Be sure to save the document in the same drive and folder as your other practice documents. After you click Save, the dialog box shown in Figure G-3 appears, indicating that there are currently no records in the data source. In the next lesson, you will add individual customer records to the data source.

Trouble?

If you accidentally remove a field name from the data source in the Create Data Source dialog box while the field name still appears in the Field name box, just click the Add Field Name button. If the Field name box shows a different name, type the name of the field you accidentally removed in the Field Name box, and then click the Add Field Name button.

FIGURE G-2: **Create Data Source dialog box**

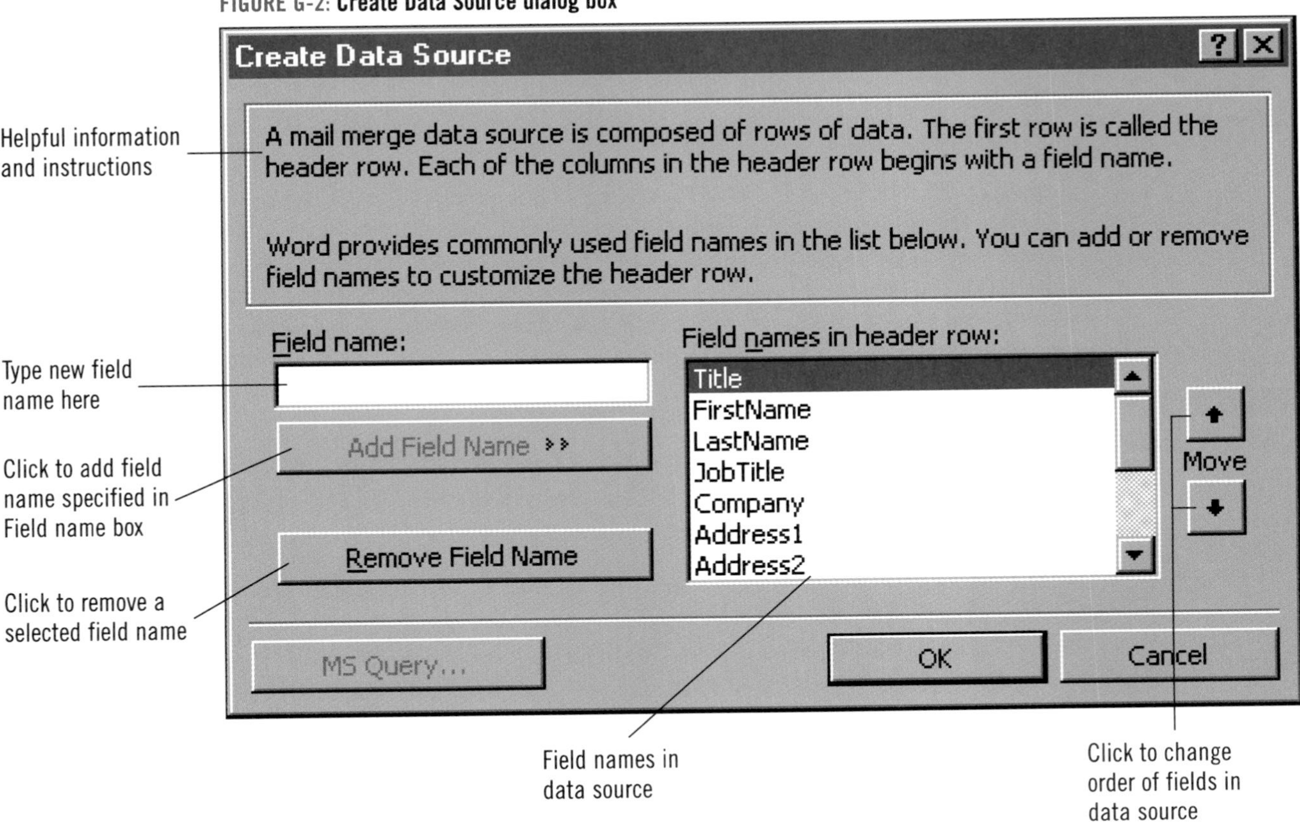

Word 97

FIGURE G-3: **Mail Merge dialog box**

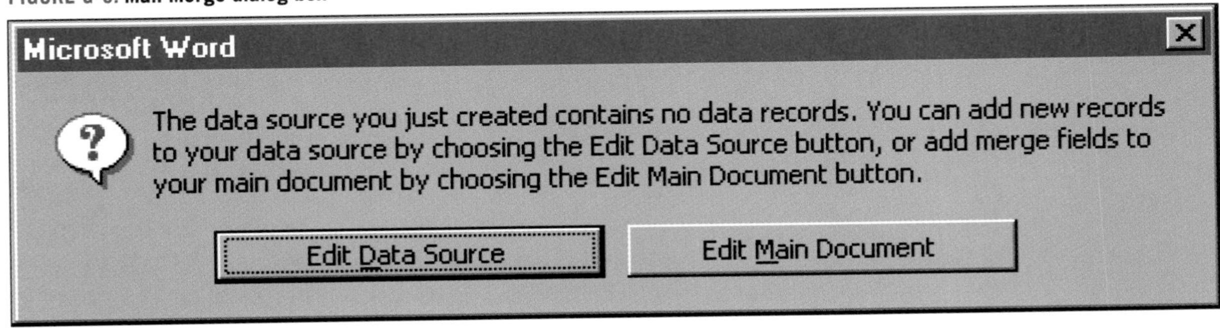

Word 97

Entering Records in a Data Source

Once you have created the fields for your data source, you are ready to add records. **Records** contain the information related to each individual to whom you want to send a letter. The Data Form dialog box makes it easy to quickly add records to a data source. This dialog box shows a form that includes text boxes corresponding to the field names in the data source. You can also edit a data source directly from the main document. Angela needs to enter records that contain the names and addresses of the Nomad customers who have requested alpine expedition information.

Steps 1 2 3 4

1. Click **Edit Data Source** to add the new records
   The Data Form dialog box opens, as shown in Figure G-4.
2. Place the insertion point in the Title field if it's not already there, type **Ms.**, then press **[Tab]** or **[Enter]**
   The text "Ms." appears in the Title field and the insertion point moves to the FirstName field. Pressing [Tab] or [Enter] moves the insertion point to the next field. Pressing [Shift][Tab] returns the insertion point to the previous field. You are now ready to enter more records.
3. Enter the following for the fields in the first record:

Title	FirstName	LastName	Address1	City	State	PostalCode
Ms.	**Lilly**	**Thomas**	**346 Lake St.**	**Cooper**	**MN**	**55321**

   Remember to press [Tab] or [Enter] to move to the next field.
4. Click **OK**
   Clicking OK closes the Data Form dialog box. You can always return to this dialog box.
5. Click **Tools** on the menu bar, click **Mail Merge**, then click **Edit** in the Data Source area
6. Choose **Response Letter Data**
   When you click Edit then Response Letter Data in the Data Source area, the Data Form dialog box opens.
7. Click **Add New** to show the blank data form, then enter the following data records:

Title	FirstName	LastName	Address1	City	State	PostalCode
Mr.	**Joe**	**Blondel**	**843 2nd St.**	**Midtown**	**TX**	**75150**
Ms.	**Leslie**	**Rauh**	**56311 S. Main Rd.**	**Canton**	**IL**	**60072**
Mr.	**Max**	**Bruni**	**358 Park Lane**	**Northport**	**WA**	**98023**

   Remember to click Add New after completing the data forms for the second and third records. Pressing [Enter] at the end of each record will also show a blank data form.
8. Click **OK** after completing the data form for the last record, then click Save on the Standard toolbar
   All records and changes to the data source are saved, and the dialog box closes. You return to the main document. Note that the Mail Merge toolbar appears in the document window, as shown in Figure G-5. This toolbar offers easy access to the commands you need when merging documents.

Trouble?

Take care not to press [Esc] or you will lose the record you are currently entering.

FIGURE G-4: Data Form dialog box

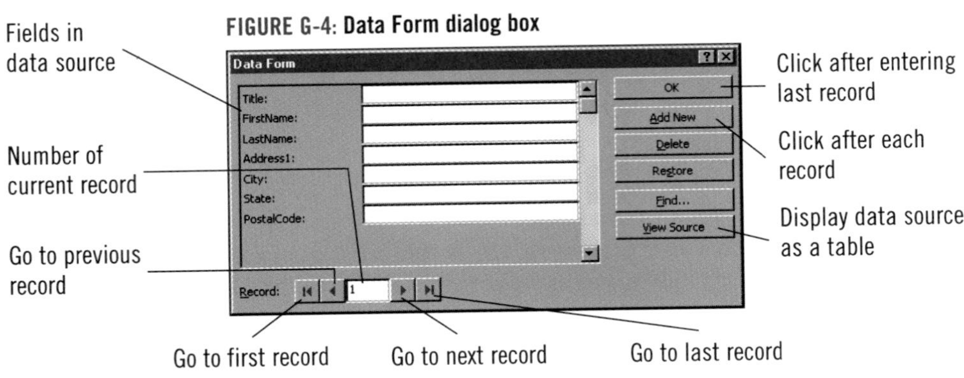

FIGURE G-5: Mail Merge Toolbar

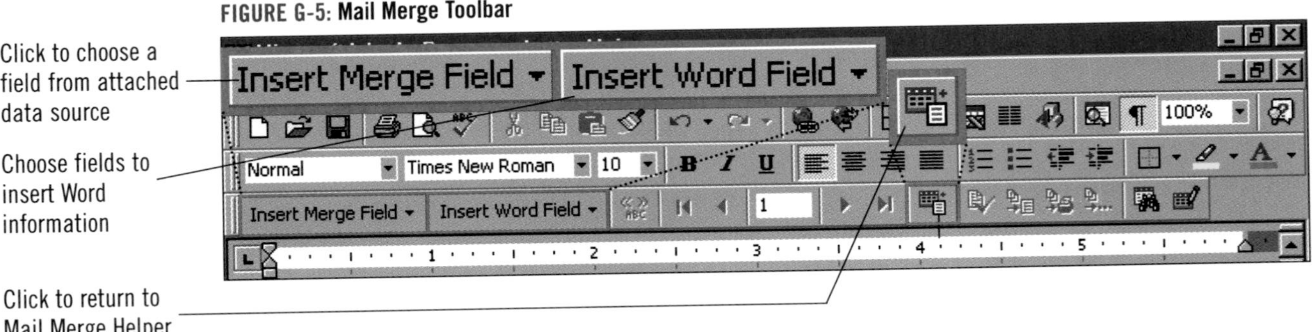

FIGURE G-6: Data records displayed in table format

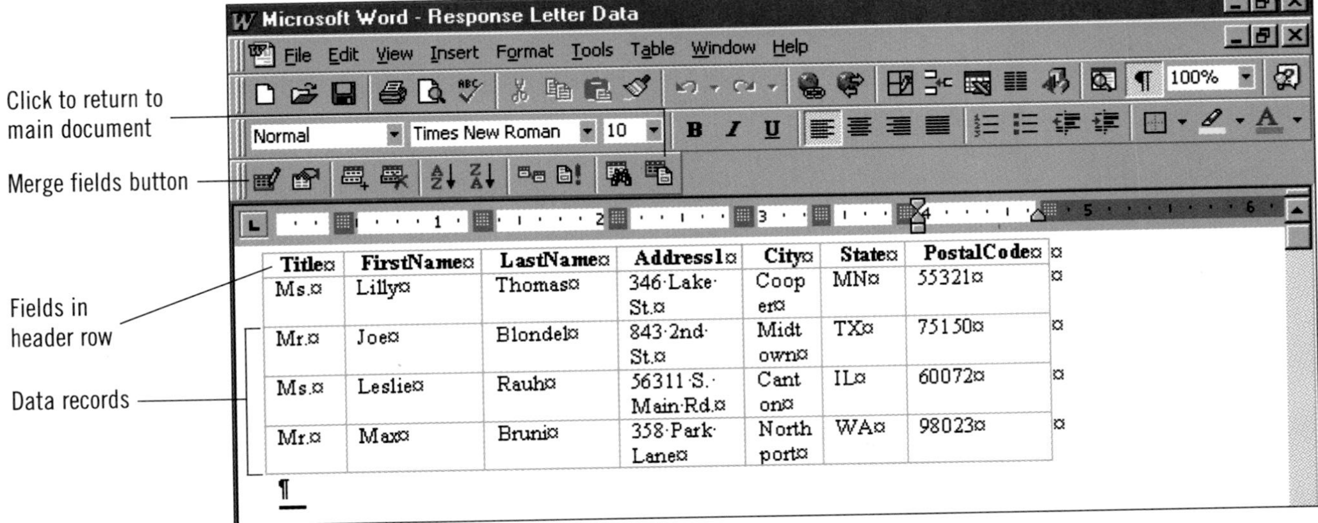

Title	FirstName	LastName	Address1	City	State	PostalCode
Ms.	Lilly	Thomas	346 Lake St.	Cooper	MN	55321
Mr.	Joe	Blondel	843 2nd St.	Midtown	TX	75150
Ms.	Leslie	Rauh	56311 S. Main Rd.	Canton	IL	60072
Mr.	Max	Bruni	358 Park Lane	Northport	WA	98023

Clues to Use

Editing the data source

It is easy to make changes to your data source. The Edit Data Source button on the Mail Merge toolbar, as shown in Figure G-5, shows the Data Form dialog box. Here you can click the View Source button to show the data records in table format, as shown in Figure G-6. Each field in the Data Form dialog box corresponds to a cell in the header row of the table. You can click the Manage Fields button in this view to add new fields or delete those you no longer need. Click the Mail Merge Main Document button when you are ready to return to the main document.

Word 97

Inserting Merge Fields

After specifying a data source, entering records, and returning to the main document, you see the Mail Merge toolbar. You can use this toolbar when you are ready to insert the field names from the data source into the main document. When you finish inserting fields, the main document will contain boilerplate text and the fields that indicate where variable information will be inserted during the merge. This is the last step before performing the actual merge. To merge her main document and the data source, Angela will insert the merge fields that make up the inside address and greeting of the letter to Nomad's customers.

Steps

1. **With the insertion point at the end of the date line, press [Enter] twice**
   Pressing [Enter] twice inserts a blank line between the date and the insertion point. In the next step, enter merge fields for the inside address.

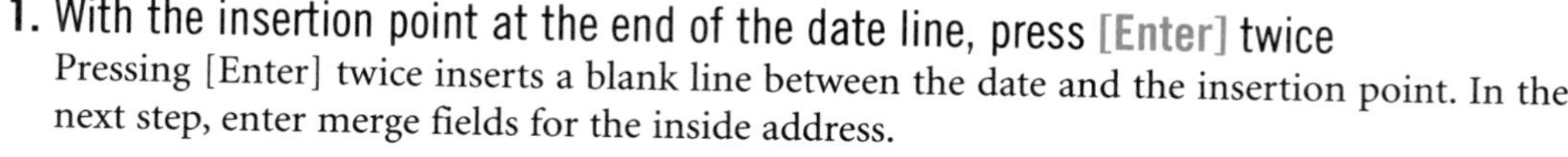

2. **Click Insert Merge Field on the Mail Merge toolbar, click Title in the list of fields, then press [Spacebar]**
   The Title field is inserted in the document, surrounded by chevrons (« »). The chevrons distinguish merge fields from the rest of the text in the main document. The space separates the Title field from the next field you enter.

3. **Click Insert Merge Field, click FirstName, then press [Spacebar]**
   The FirstName field is inserted in the document, followed by a space.
4. **Click Insert Merge Field, click LastName, then press [Enter]**
   The LastName field is inserted in the document. Pressing [Enter] places the insertion point in a new blank line.
5. **Insert the remaining merge fields for the inside address and greeting, as shown in Figure G-7**
   Be sure to insert proper punctuation, spacing, and blank paragraphs to format the inside address and greeting correctly.
6. **Click the Save button on the Standard toolbar**

QuickTip

Press **[Alt][Shift][F]** to show the Insert Merge Field dialog box. Use the arrow keys to select the desired field, then press **[Enter]** to insert the field in the main document.

FIGURE G-7: Main document with merge fields

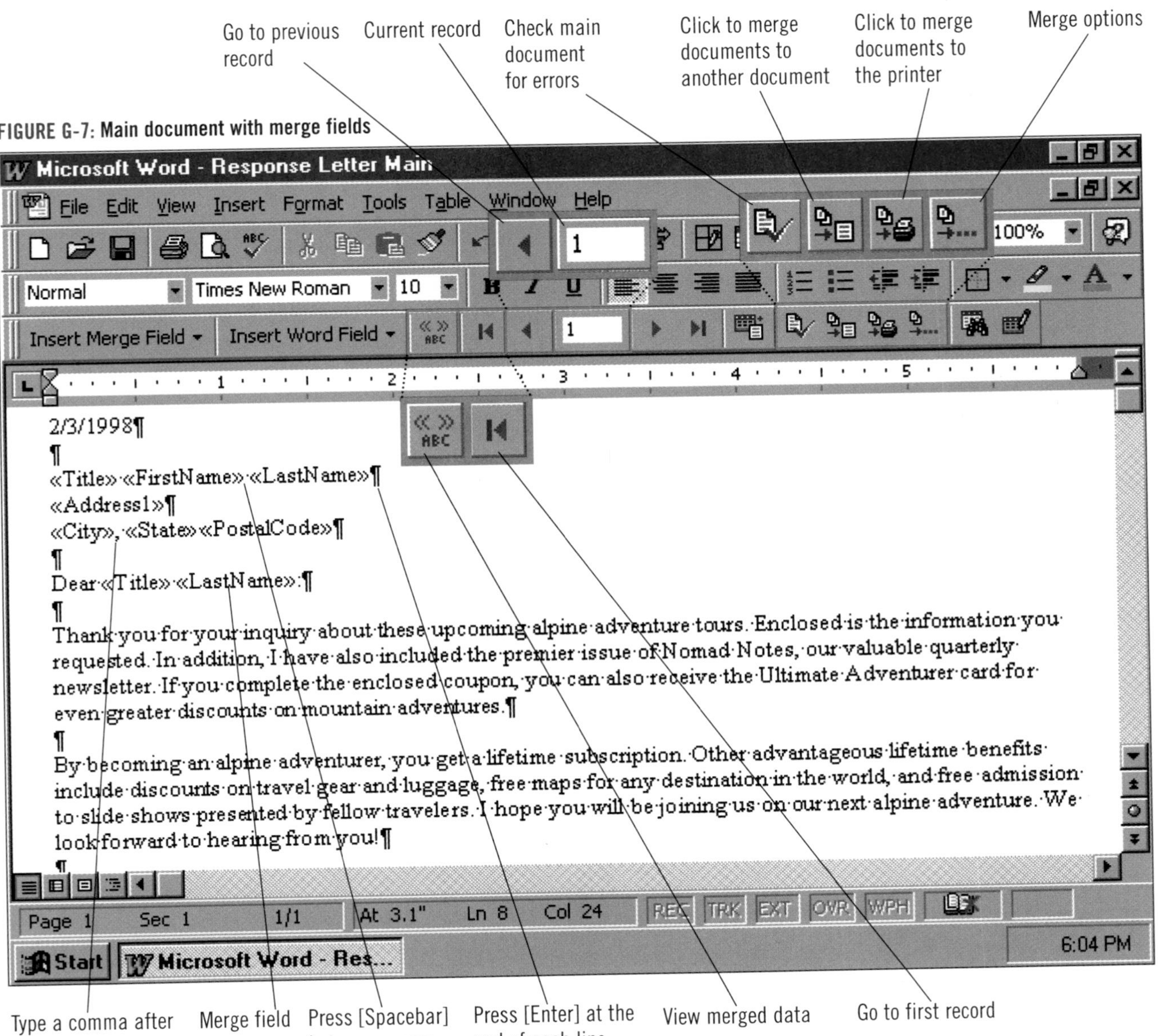

Word 97

Word 97

Working with Merged Documents

Performing the actual merge operation is as simple as clicking a button. You can merge all of your documents to a separate file or to a printer, or you can specify only certain records to merge. Even though merging to a separate file requires more disk space, you gain the ability to edit and review before printing. See Table G-2 for a summary of merge options. Angela will merge the Nomad letter to a separate file so she can view the merged documents in print preview, verify the page layout, and complete any necessary customization for individual merged documents.

QuickTip

You can save space on your hard disk by merging a large main document or many records directly to a printer rather than saving the merge in a new document. It is quick and easy to recreate the same merge at any time with the click of a button in the Mail Merge Helper dialog box.

1. **Click the Merge To New Document button on the Mail Merge toolbar**
   The main document and data source are merged to a new document called "Form Letters1". Each merged letter is separated with a section break, which you can see by scrolling through the document.
2. **Click the Print Preview button on the Standard toolbar**
   The document appears in print preview.
3. **Click the Multiple Pages button on the Print Preview toolbar, then drag to select four pages**
   You see all of the merged letters. In the Print Preview window, you can make last minute adjustments to customize a specific form letter.
4. **Double-click in the body text in the second page**
   The second merged letter appears close-up, as shown in Figure G-8. Because Mr. Blondel will be attending a travel exposition at which Nomad will have a booth, customize the last sentence of the letter to this customer.
5. **Click the Magnifier button on the Print Preview toolbar, then edit the last sentence to read: We look forward to seeing you at the Adventures Plus Convention in Dallas!**
6. **Click File on the menu bar, then click Save**
   The Save As dialog box opens.
7. **In the File name box, type Response Letter Merge, then click Save**
   The document containing all the merged letters (and the changes) is saved with the name Response Letter Merge. You can now print the letters.
8. **Click the Print button on the Print Preview toolbar, then click Close on the Print Preview toolbar after printing the documents**
   All the merged letters print on the printer connected to your computer. You can close all open documents.
9. **Hold down [Shift] while you click File on the menu bar, then click Close All**
   Click Yes in response to any messages asking you to save your changes.

FIGURE G-8: **Close-up of merged letter in print preview**

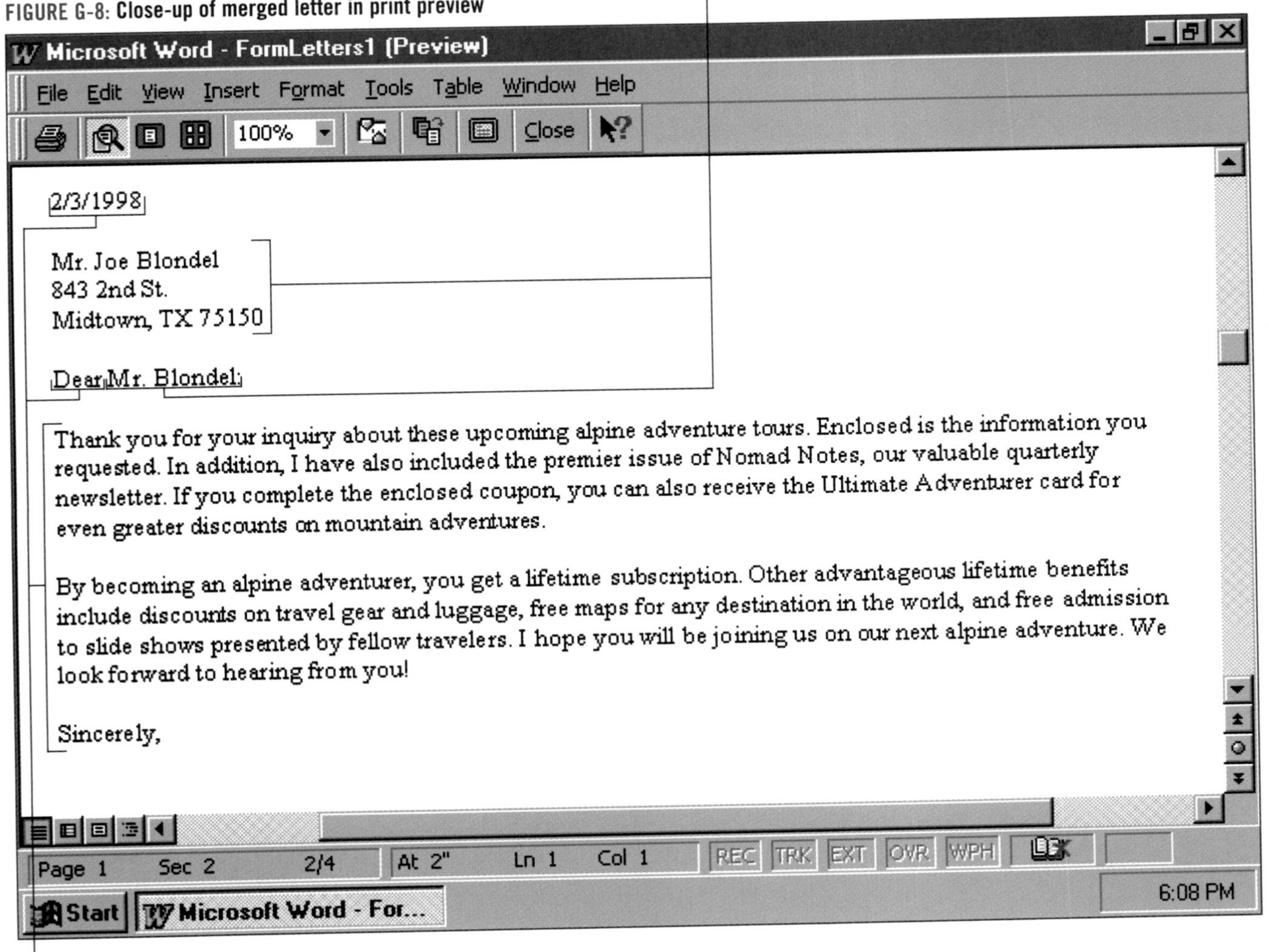

TABLE G-2: **Merge options**

click this button	or press	to
	[Alt][Shift][N]	Merge the main document and all records of the data source to a new file
	[Alt][Shift][M]	Send the merged main document and data source to the printer; does not create a new file
		Specify a range of records to include in the merge; also shows the Query options dialog box

Word 97

Creating a Label Main Document

Using the data source you created earlier in this unit, you can easily print envelopes or labels for mailing the letters. Simply specify a new main document, attach the existing data source, and select a setup format. You will learn about many standard formats that correspond to name brand business labels and envelopes, including index cards, postcards, name tags, and disk labels. You can also customize labels and envelope sizes. Angela will use a data source that her assistant has already created.

Steps

1. Click the **New button** on the Standard toolbar to create a new document
2. Click **Tools** on the menu bar, then click **Mail Merge**
   The Mail Merge Helper dialog box opens. Now create a new main document for the mailing labels.
3. Click **Create**, click **Mailing Labels**, then click **New Main Document**
   A temporary name for the main document appears in the Mail Merge Helper dialog box.
4. Click **Get Data**, then click **Open Data Source**
   The Open Data Source dialog box opens. You will use a data source that has already been created.
5. Click **WD G-2**, then click **Open**
   A message box appears, prompting you to finish setting up your main document.
6. Click **Set Up Main Document**
   The Label Options dialog box appears. In this dialog box, you need to select the appropriate type of label. The default brand name Avery standard appears in the Label Products box. You need to select the product number for the label.
7. In the Product number box, scroll to and click **5161 - Address**, then click **OK**
   The Create Labels dialog box opens. Here, you can enter the field names for the labels.
8. Click **Insert Merge Field**, click **Title**, press **[Spacebar]**, then continue entering the remaining merge fields and appropriate punctuation, as shown in Figure G-9
   Note that nonprinting characters (spaces and paragraph marks) are not visible in the Sample Label box.
9. Click **OK** to return to the Mail Merge Helper dialog box, as shown in Figure G-10
   In the next lesson, you will specify only selected records for the labels merge.

FIGURE G-9: Create Labels dialog box

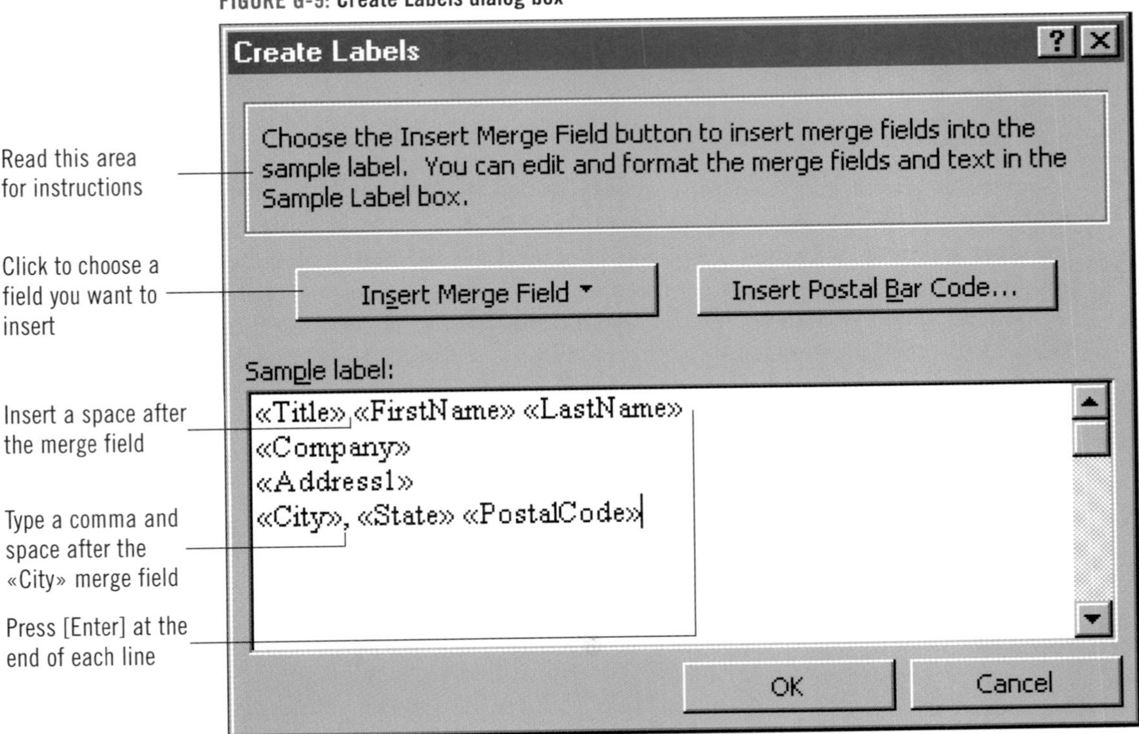

FIGURE G-10: Mail Merge Helper dialog box

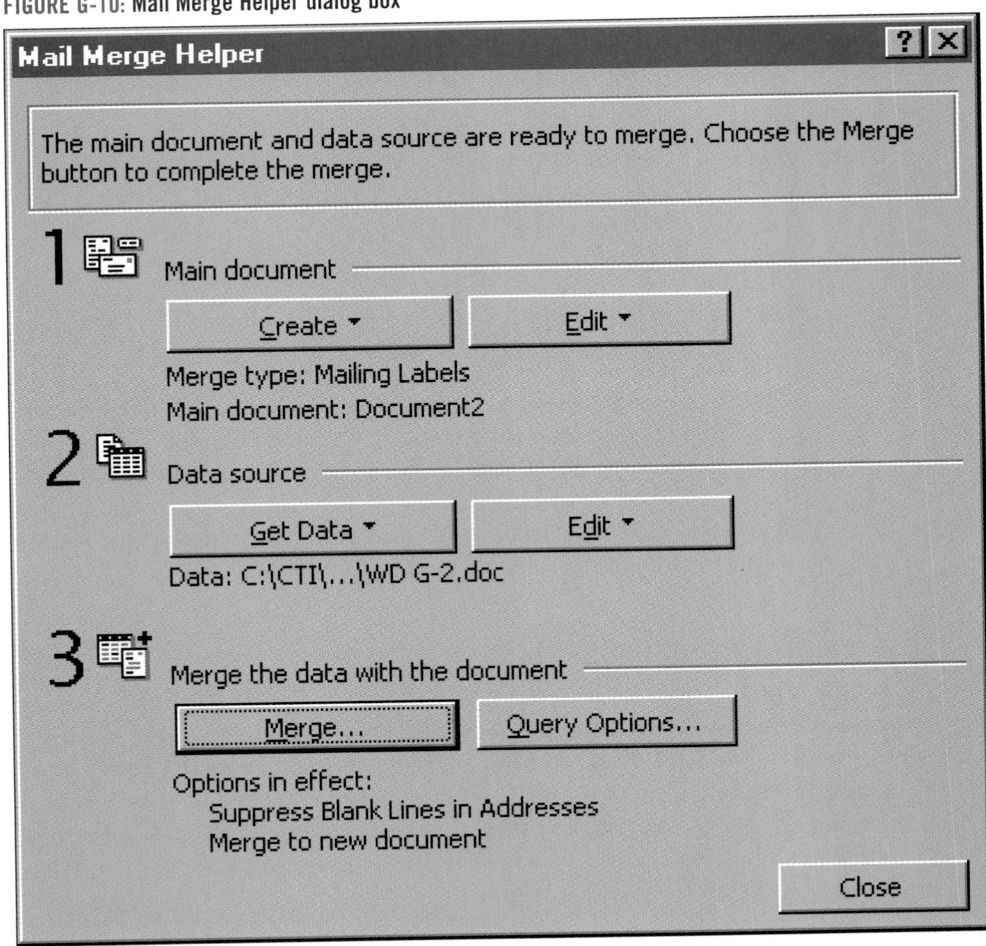

Word 97

Word 97

Merging Selected Records

Sometimes you do not want to send a document to all the individuals in a data source. For example, you might want one group of individuals to receive one kind of document, and another group of individuals to receive another. With the Mail Merge Query Options feature, you can specify the criteria for choosing which records in a data source should be merged with a main document. When you use Query Options, you can identify the fields and their contents that each record must match to be included in the merge. Angela is sending letters to Nomad customers in Massachusetts. She will only need labels for customers living in this state. In the Query Options dialog box, Angela puts MA in the state field to be included in this merge.

Steps 1 2 3 4

1. **In the Mail Merge Helper click Merge**
   The Merge dialog box opens. In this dialog box, indicate that you want to use Query Options to select records to merge.
2. **Click Query Options**
   The Query Options dialog box opens. In this dialog box, describe the criteria to use when selecting records to merge.
3. **In the Field column, click the fields list arrow and scroll down to select State**
   This is the field you want to include when selecting records. Next, verify how the field should be evaluated.
4. **In the Comparison column, be sure Equal to appears in the first box**
   This selection specifies that the contents of the State field in a record must exactly match the contents you will specify.
5. **In the Compare to column, type MA**
   Your selection criterion appears in the column. Compare your dialog box to Figure G-11. You can specify additional selection criteria in the subsequent rows of the dialog box. You have completed specifying your selection criteria, so continue with the merge process.
6. **Click OK**
   You return to the Merge dialog box, as shown in Figure G-12 so you can merge the records.
7. **Click Merge**
   The selected records are merged to a new document. The labels are arranged in a Word table. Each label appears in separate cells that are divided by grey (non-printing) gridlines. Notice that only those customers with an address in Massachusetts are merged on the labels. You have finished merging documents for now. Compare the merged label document to Figure G-13. With the labels in a Word table, you can quickly format the labels so they are easier to read.

Using multiple selection criteria

When you specify selection criteria for the data records to include in a merge, you are not limited to specifying a single field's contents. In fact, you can specify up to six criteria in the Query Options dialog box. After entering criteria in the first line of the dialog box, you click the operator arrow at the start of the next line. When you click the arrow, you can choose the And operator or the Or operator. Choose the And operator to identify additional required criteria that a record must match so that it is included in the merge. Choose the Or operator to identify additional optional criteria that a record can contain so that it is included in the merge.

FIGURE G-11: Query Options dialog box

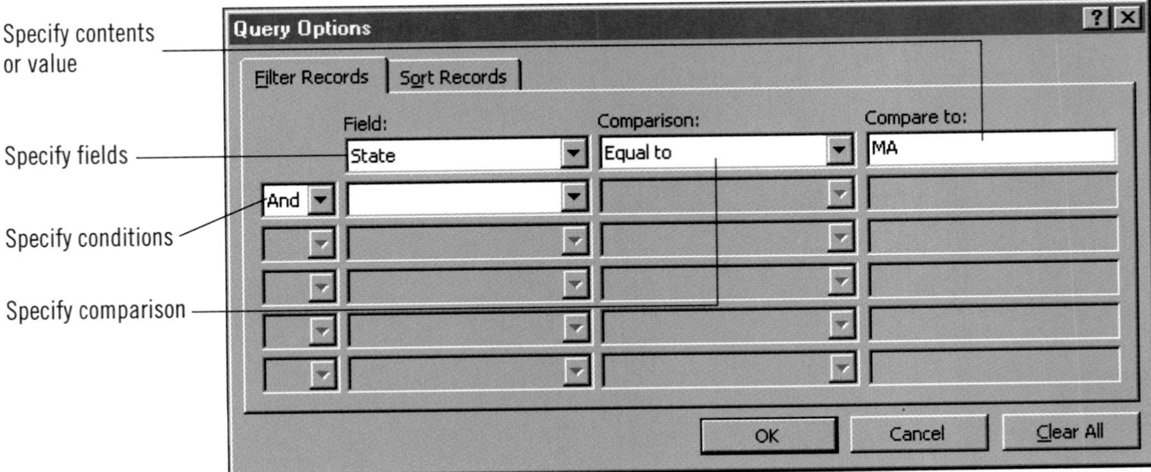

FIGURE G-12: Merge dialog box

FIGURE G-13: Merged label document

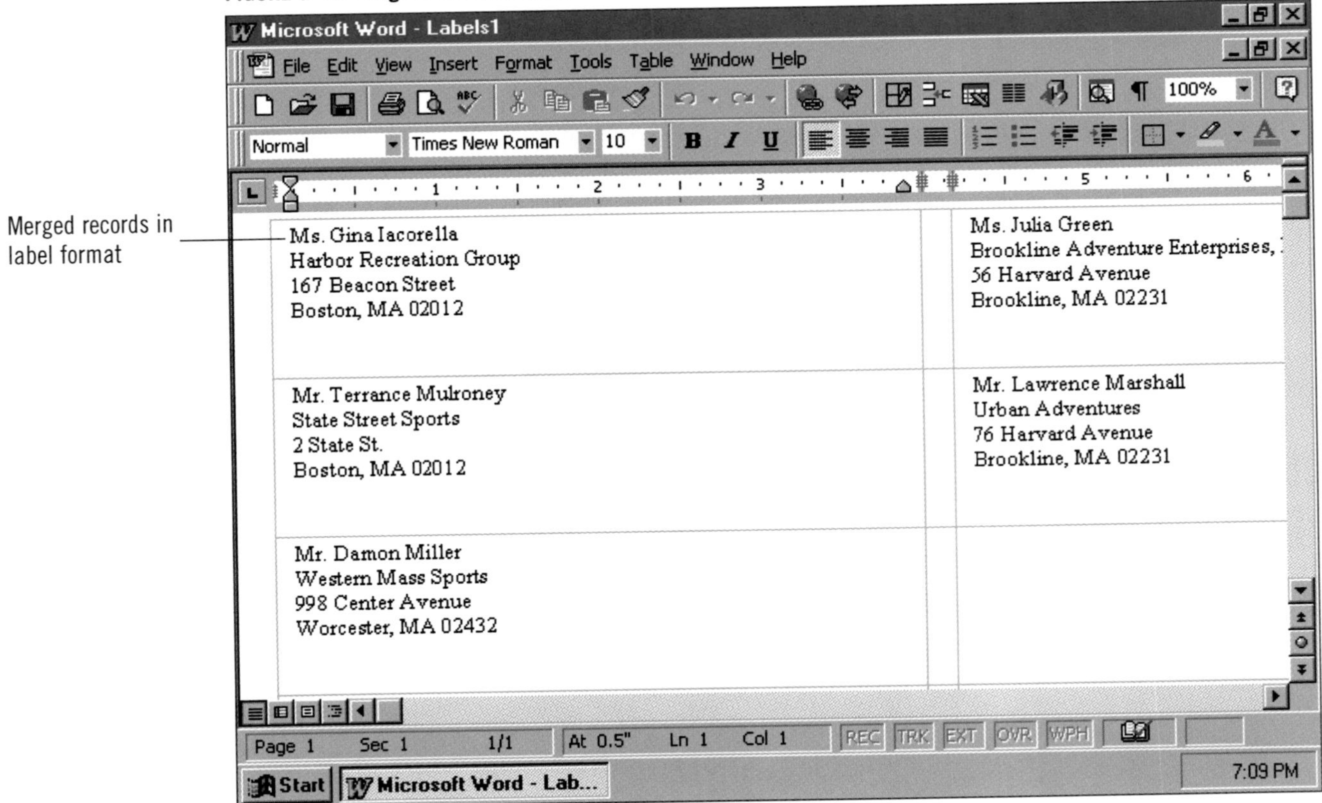

Word 97

Formatting Labels

If you have merged your main document and data source to a new file (rather than to a printer), you can format the merged documents to make them more attractive before printing them. To make her labels easier to read, Angela will format the label. After editing the merged label document, she will print the labels using ordinary paper in her printer.

Steps

1. Click **Edit** on the menu bar, then click **Select All**
   This command selects all the text in the merged label document.
2. Click the **Font Size arrow** on the Formatting toolbar, then click **14**, and click the **Bold button** on the Formatting toolbar
   Increasing the font size makes the labels clearer and easier to read. To get an overall view of the page, preview the document before printing it.
3. Deselect the text, then click the **Print Preview button** on the Standard toolbar
4. Click on the document
   Compare your document to Figure G-14.
5. Click the **Print button** on the Preview toolbar
   Remember you can print from print preview. Next, close all open documents. To choose this command, press and hold down [Shift] (otherwise, the Close command will appear on the File menu instead of Close All).
6. Hold down **[Shift]** while you click **File**, then click **Close All**
   When you choose the Close All command, you are prompted to save changes to any open documents and to name any unnamed documents before you close each file. Be sure to carefully watch for the message box that indicates which document is currently being closed and saved.
7. Click **Yes** in each message box that prompts you to save a document, save the files with the file names listed below, click **No** if you are asked to save any changes in the data source WD G-2, then Exit Word

Save this file	With this content	With this filename
Labels merged document	the final merge product, labels with customer information	**MA Only Labels Merge**
Labels main document	the document with the merge fields	**Labels Main**

The changes to each document are saved and all open documents are closed.

FIGURE G-14: Merged label document in print preview

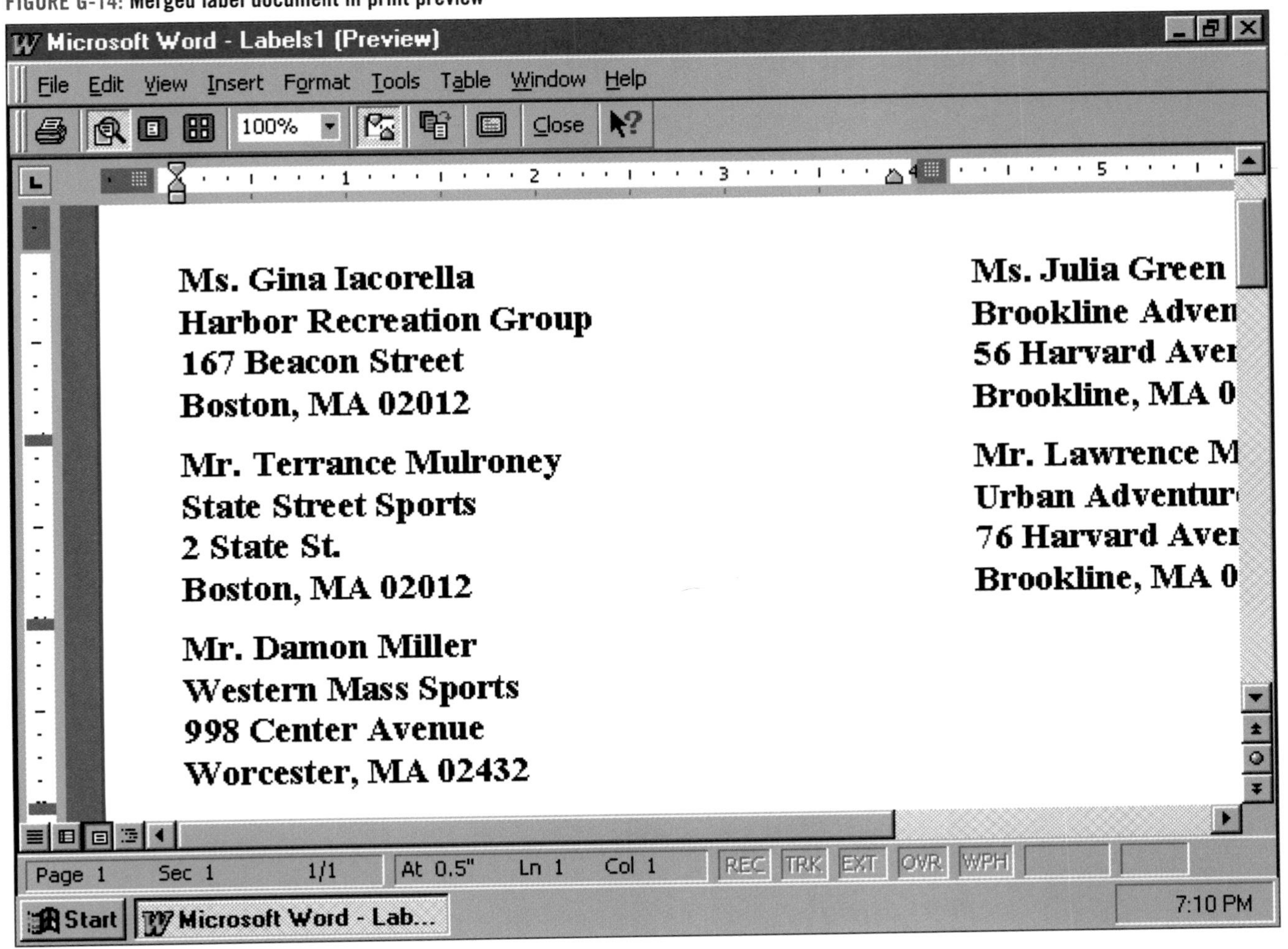

Word 97

Practice

► Concepts Review

Label each part of Figure G-15

FIGURE G-15

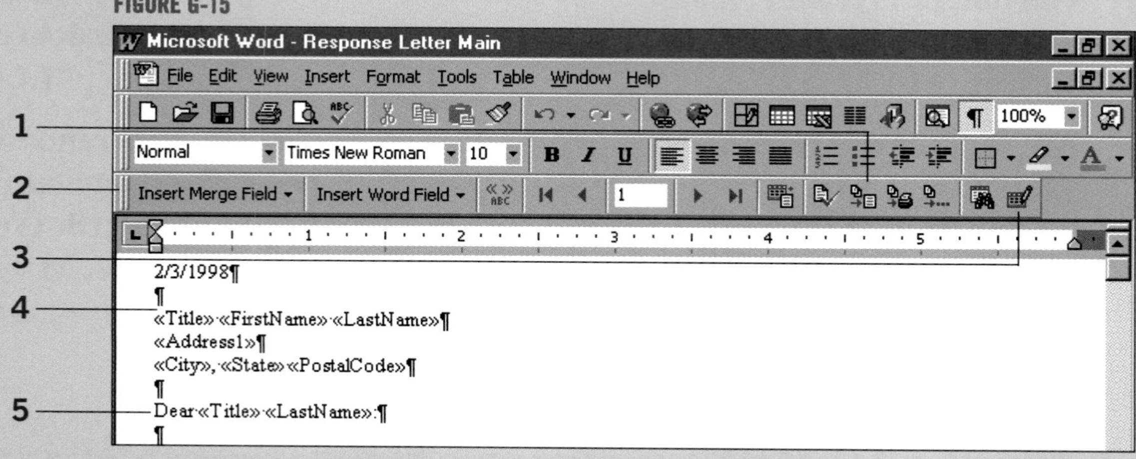

Match each of the following terms with the statement that best describes its function. Write the letter of the statement next to the appropriate term.

6. Data source
7. Data record
8. Boilerplate text
9. Main document
10. Field
11. View Source
12. Merge Field button
13. Mail Merge Helper
14. Data records

a. A piece of information specific to an item or individual
b. The entire collection of fields related to an item or individual
c. Contains the customized information that differs in each merged document
d. The text that is the same for each version of a merged document
e. Contains the common text for all versions of the merged document
f. Shows data records in table format
g. Are added to the data source in the Data Form dialog box
h. The Mail Merge command on the Tools menu shows this dialog box
i. Shows the list of fields to be entered in the main document

Select the best answer from the list of choices.

15. Which of the following is NOT a benefit of merging to a new file, rather than to a printer?

a. You can format the merged documents to enhance their appearance.
b. You can view the layout of merged documents in print preview.
c. You save space on your hard disk.
d. You can edit individual documents.

16. Which of the following statements best describes what you can accomplish when you show data records in table format?

a. Add merge fields to the main document
b. View one data record at a time
c. Edit the merged document
d. Add or delete fields from the data source

17. Which of the following tasks cannot be accomplished in the Query Options dialog box?

a. Sort records by fields in ascending or descending order
b. Save query specifications for future merge operations

c. Select fields to be included in the data source
d. Select records to be included in the merge operation

► Skills Review

1. Create a main document.

a. Start Word, open the document named WD G-3, then save it as "Ideas Main".
b. Select the text "[your name]" and replace it with your own name, then select the text "[Click here and type subject]" and replace it with "Ideas Wanted".
c. Open the Mail Merge Helper dialog box using Tools, then Mail Merge, and choose the Form Letters option to create a form letter main document based on the memo document in the active window.

2. Create a data source.

a. Click Get Data then click Create Data Source.
b. In the Field Names in Header Row box, remove all the fields except FirstName, LastName, and JobTitle.
c. In the Field Name box, type "Mailstation", click Add Field Name, then click OK.
d. Type "Ideas Data" in the File name box, then click Save.

3. Enter records in a data source.

a. Click Edit Data Source to add new records.
b. Enter the following information in the appropriate fields to complete the data form for each of the recipients of this memo.

	FirstName	LastName	JobTitle	Mailstation
Record 1	Jules	Martinez	Marketing Manager	34
Record 2	Carl	Ortez	Customer Service Manager	18
Record 3	Sandy	Woodward	Vice President of Sales	48
Record 4	Elizabeth	Lewis	Charter Sales Division	45

c. Click OK after completing the data form for the last record.
d. Click the Save button on the Standard toolbar.

4. Insert merge fields.

a. Place the insertion point after the tab character that follows the heading TO:.
b. Click Insert Merge Field on the Mail Merge toolbar and click FirstName, then press [Spacebar].
c. Click Insert Merge Field and click LastName. Then type a comma and press [Spacebar].
d. Click Insert Merge Field and click JobTitle.
e. Place the insertion point after the tab character that follows the Mailstation: heading.
f. Click Insert Merge Field and click Mailstation.
g. Click the Save button on the Standard toolbar.

5. Preview and edit merged documents.

a. Click the Merge To New Document button on the Mail Merge toolbar.
b. Click the Print Preview button on the Standard toolbar.
c. Click the Multiple Pages button on the Print Preview toolbar, and select four pages.
d. Click the magnifier pointer anywhere in the first page.

e. Click the Magnifier button on the Print Preview toolbar.
f. Select the last sentence of the letter and type "Please begin design for tour brochures". Close print preview, then print the first page.
g. Click File on the menu bar, click Close then click Yes.
h. In the File name box, type "Ideas Merge" and save the file.
i. Press and hold [Shift], click File on the menu bar, click Close All, then click Yes to save all versions.

6. Create a label main document.

a. Click the New button on the Standard toolbar, creating a new blank document.
b. Click Tools on the menu bar, then click Mail Merge.
c. Click Create, click Mailing Labels, then click Active Document Window.
d. Click Get Data, then click Open Data Source.
e. Click Ideas Data, then click Open.
f. Click Set Up Main Document.
g. In the Product Number box, click 5161-Address, then click OK.
h. Click Insert Merge Field, click FirstName, press [Spacebar], insert the LastName field, then press [Enter].
i. Click Insert Merge Field and click JobTitle. Press [Enter].
j. Click Insert Merge Field and click Mailstation.
k. Click OK to return to the Mail Merge Helper dialog box, then click Close.
l. Save the document as "Ideas Labels Main".

7. Merge and format labels.

a. Click the Merge to New Document button on the Mail Merge toolbar.
b. Click Edit on the menu bar, then click Select All.
c. Click the Font Size list arrow on the Formatting toolbar, then click 14.
d. Click the Bold button on the Formatting toolbar.
e. Preview the labels.
f. Close Print Preview.

8. Merge selected records.

a. Click Window on the menu bar, then click the Ideas Labels Main document.
b. On the Mail Merge toolbar, click the Mail Merge Helper button to show the Mail Merge Helper dialog box.
c. Click Query Options.
d. In the Field column, click the arrow and scroll down to choose Mailstation.
e. In the Comparison column, be sure "Equal to" appears in the first box, then in the Compare to column, type "45".
f. In the next line, click the operator arrow and choose Or.
g. In the Field column, click the fields list arrow and scroll down to choose Mailstation.
h. In the Comparison column, be sure "Equal to" appears in the first box, then in the Compare to column, type "34", then click OK.
i. Click Merge twice (be sure New Document is selected).
j. Click Edit on the menu bar, then click Select All.
k. Click the Font Size list arrow on the Formatting toolbar, then click 14. Click the Bold button on the Formatting toolbar.
l. Hold down [Shift] while you click File, then click Close All.
m. Click Yes and save your merged query label document with the name "Ideas Label Merge". You do not need to save the first merged document.
n. Click Yes to save Ideas Data.

o. Click Yes to save changes to Ideas Label Main.
p. Click File on the menu bar, then click Exit.

► Independent Challenges

1. As an account representative for Lease For Less, a company that rents office equipment such as fax machines and large copiers, you previously drafted a letter describing the corporate discount program to a current customer. Open the document named WD G-4 and save it as "Discount Main" and save WD G-5 as "Discount Data", then close "Discount Data". Complete the following steps to edit a main document, attach an existing data source, and create and edit a merged document.

To complete this independent challenge:

1. Open the Mail Merge Helper and specify Discount Main as the form letter main document.
2. Attach the existing data source Discount Data to the main document.
3. Insert today's date at the top of the main document, adding a blank line after the date. Edit the signature block to show your name.
4. In the main document, replace the placeholder text enclosed in brackets with the merge fields in the data source.
5. Merge the documents to a new file named "Discount Merge".
6. Preview the documents. Add the following sentence to the end of the last letter, "P.S. I hope the above information has answered your questions about Lease For Less services. If you have any further questions, please contact me at 666-2345".
7. Print the merged documents. Compare the later letter to Figure G-16. Save any changes to all open files before closing them.

FIGURE G-16

March 15, 1998

Ms. Brittany Brinig
Independent School Dist. 667
200 Gervais Pkwy.
Plains, NY 54012

Dear Ms. Brinig:

Thank you for your inquiry about a corporate discount for our copier rentals. Enclosed is the information you requested. In addition, I have also included the premier issue of WorkADay, our exclusive management newsletter.

To be eligible for a corporate discount, you must contact to rent 2 or more of our fax or copier machines for at least six months. Of course all of our machines come with unlimited service by our highly trained technicians. As a corporate customer, you will receive a 20% discount on general office rentals and a 30% discount for our industrial copiers including color copy machines. As your account representative, I would be pleased to discuss your office requirements with you. I will call you to arrange a time when we can meet.

Sincerely,

[your name]
Lease for Less
Account Representative

P.S. I hope the above information has answered your questions about Lease for Less services. If you have any further questions, please contact me at 666-2345.

2. As an executive assistant, you are responsible for the distribution of your company's newsletter to consultants at various other companies. Your company has just purchased a new printer that can print address labels. Using the printer for labels will save time when distributing the newsletter. Newsletter recipients in New York City will receive their documents via a hand-delivered courier (who has already provided the required labels), while the remaining companies will receive their documents via U.S. Mail and will require printed labels. Use the Mail Merge Helper to create a label main document named "Newsletter Main". You can also choose to create envelopes instead of labels if your printer has this option.

To complete this independent challenge:

1. Open the document WD G-6 and save it with the name "Newsletter Data" and close the document.
2. Use the Mail Merge Helper to attach the existing data source Newsletter Data to the label document.
3. If you are using labels, use the Avery label 5161-Address. If you are merging to envelopes, use the default envelope style. Insert the merge fields in the main document and save it as "Newsletter Main".
4. Enter your own address in the Return Address area (if you are creating envelopes, not labels).
5. Add an additional record to the data source using any name and address you wish.
6. Use the Query Options feature to specify a selection criterion. Use the "Not Equal To" comparison operator in your selection criterion to select records that do not contain "New York City" in the City field.
7. Merge the label (or envelope) and data source to another document named "Newsletter Merge".
8. Print your labels(or envelopes), then save any changes to all open files before closing them.

3. You are the fundraising coordinator for Companies for Kids, a non-profit organization that collects money and materials for children housed in local shelters. In response to requests for information from potential corporate sponsors, you previously drafted a short letter describing the benefits of being a sponsor. Open the letter named WD G-7 and save it as "Children Main". Complete the following steps to edit a main document, and create a data source and a merged document.

To complete this independent challenge:

1. Open the Mail Merge Helper and specify "Children Main" as the form letter main document.
2. Insert today's date at the top of the main document, adding a blank line after the date. Edit the signature block to show your name.
3. Create a new data source with the following merge fields: Title, FirstName, LastName, Company, Address1, City, State, PostalCode. Save the data source with the name "Children Data".
4. Add at least three records to the Data Form dialog box using any contact names, company names, and addresses you wish.
5. In the main document, replace the placeholder text (enclosed in brackets) with the merge fields created in Children Data.
6. Merge the documents to a new file named "Children Merge".
7. Preview and print the merged documents.
8. Create and print labels (or envelopes) to send with the letters, you do not need to save the labels. Use any label type you wish. Save any changes to all open files before closing them.

4. As a recent college graduate, you have just begun your search for a position requiring a background in business administration. Complete the following steps to edit a main document, create a new data source, and create a merged document.

To complete this independent challenge:

1. Create a new document that is a generic letter of inquiry. Leave blanks (or some other indicator) for where variable information (such as names, addresses, company names, and area of companies' specialization) belongs. Use Figure G-17 as a guide for inserting variable information that will be provided by your data source. Save the letter as "Inquiry Main".
2. Open the Mail Merge Helper and specify "Inquiry Main" as the form letter main document.

3. Use your Web browser to search for financial or investment companies and note their names and mailing addresses. Create a data source using the names and addresses of at least five companies for whom you would like to work. Be sure to include a field for an area of specialization to which you would refer in your letter.
4. For an example of a good web source for locating companies, log on to the Internet and use your browser to go to http://www.course.com. From there, click Student Online Companions, click the link for this textbook, then click Word for unit G. Follow the link to the Business BigBook.
5. Save the new data source as "Inquiry Data".
6. Attach the data source to the main document.
7. In the main document, replace the placeholder text with the merge fields in the data source.
8. Merge the documents to a new file named "Inquiry Merge".
9. Perform a second merge, this time generate letters for only those companies in your home state (or some other state in which you might wish to live). Use the Query feature to specify the criteria. Save this second merged document as "Home State Inquiry Merge".
10. Print the merged documents. Save any changes to all files before closing them.

FIGURE G-17

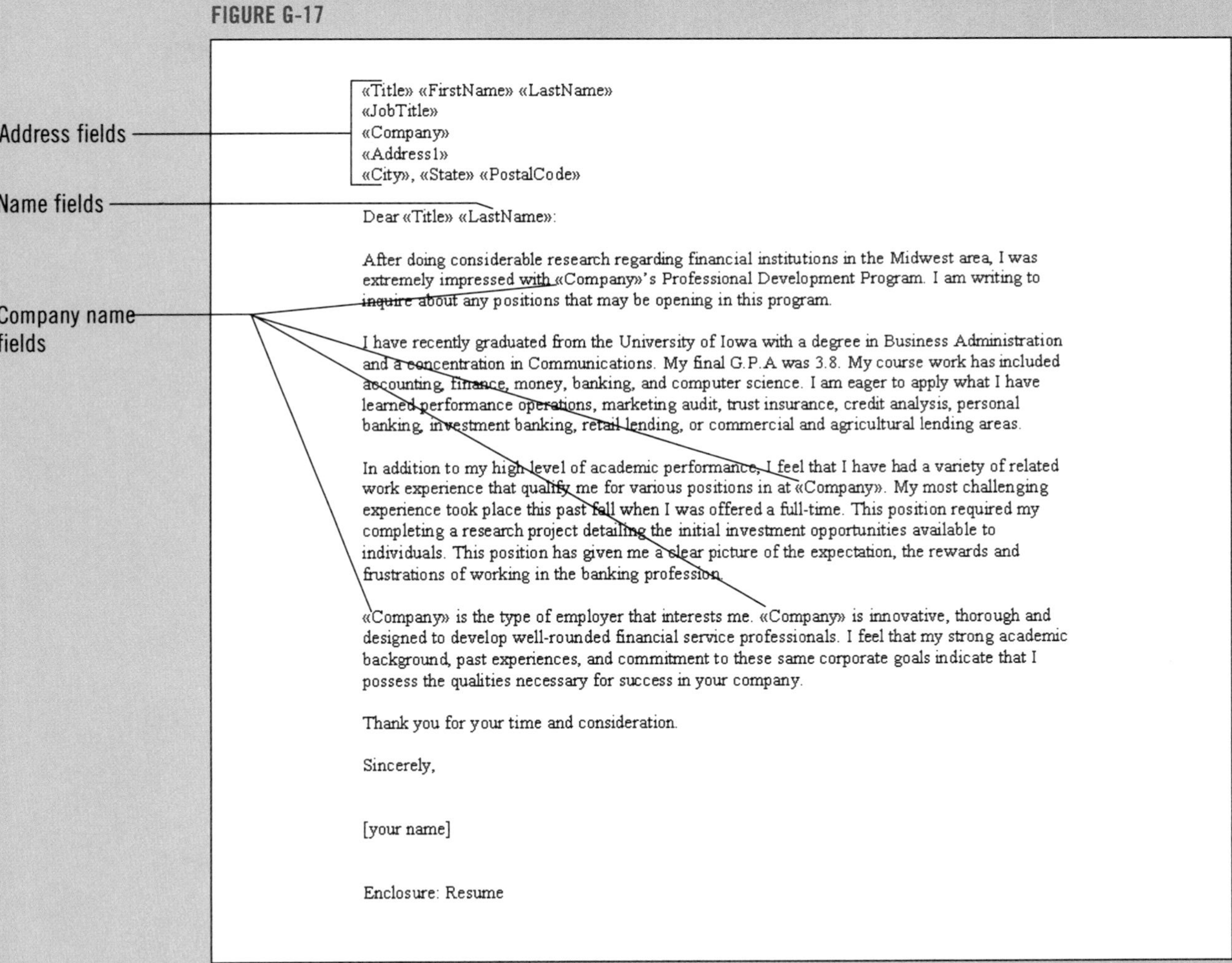

«Title» «FirstName» «LastName»
«JobTitle»
«Company»
«Address1»
«City», «State» «PostalCode»

Dear «Title» «LastName»:

After doing considerable research regarding financial institutions in the Midwest area, I was extremely impressed with «Company»'s Professional Development Program. I am writing to inquire about any positions that may be opening in this program.

I have recently graduated from the University of Iowa with a degree in Business Administration and a concentration in Communications. My final G.P.A was 3.8. My course work has included accounting, finance, money, banking, and computer science. I am eager to apply what I have learned performance operations, marketing audit, trust insurance, credit analysis, personal banking, investment banking, retail lending, or commercial and agricultural lending areas.

In addition to my high level of academic performance, I feel that I have had a variety of related work experience that qualify me for various positions in at «Company». My most challenging experience took place this past fall when I was offered a full-time. This position required my completing a research project detailing the initial investment opportunities available to individuals. This position has given me a clear picture of the expectation, the rewards and frustrations of working in the banking profession.

«Company» is the type of employer that interests me. «Company» is innovative, thorough and designed to develop well-rounded financial service professionals. I feel that my strong academic background, past experiences, and commitment to these same corporate goals indicate that I possess the qualities necessary for success in your company.

Thank you for your time and consideration.

Sincerely,

[your name]

Enclosure: Resume

Visual Workshop

As the conference coordinator for the annual Texas Educators Convention, you are in charge of creating nametags for conference attendees. Using the Mail Merge feature in Word, create a mailing labels main document named "Conference Main". Then create a data source with the following merge fields: FirstName, LastName, Grade/Subject. Save the data source with the name "Conference Data". Add at least four records in the Data Form dialog box. Using Figure G-18 as your guide, set up the main document by selecting the product 5095-Name Badge in the Label Options dialog box and inserting the merge fields in the Create Labels dialog box. Merge the labels to a new document named "Conference Labels". Use formatting to enhance the appearance of your nametags. Preview and print the labels on plain paper. Save any changes to all files, then exit Word.

FIGURE G-18

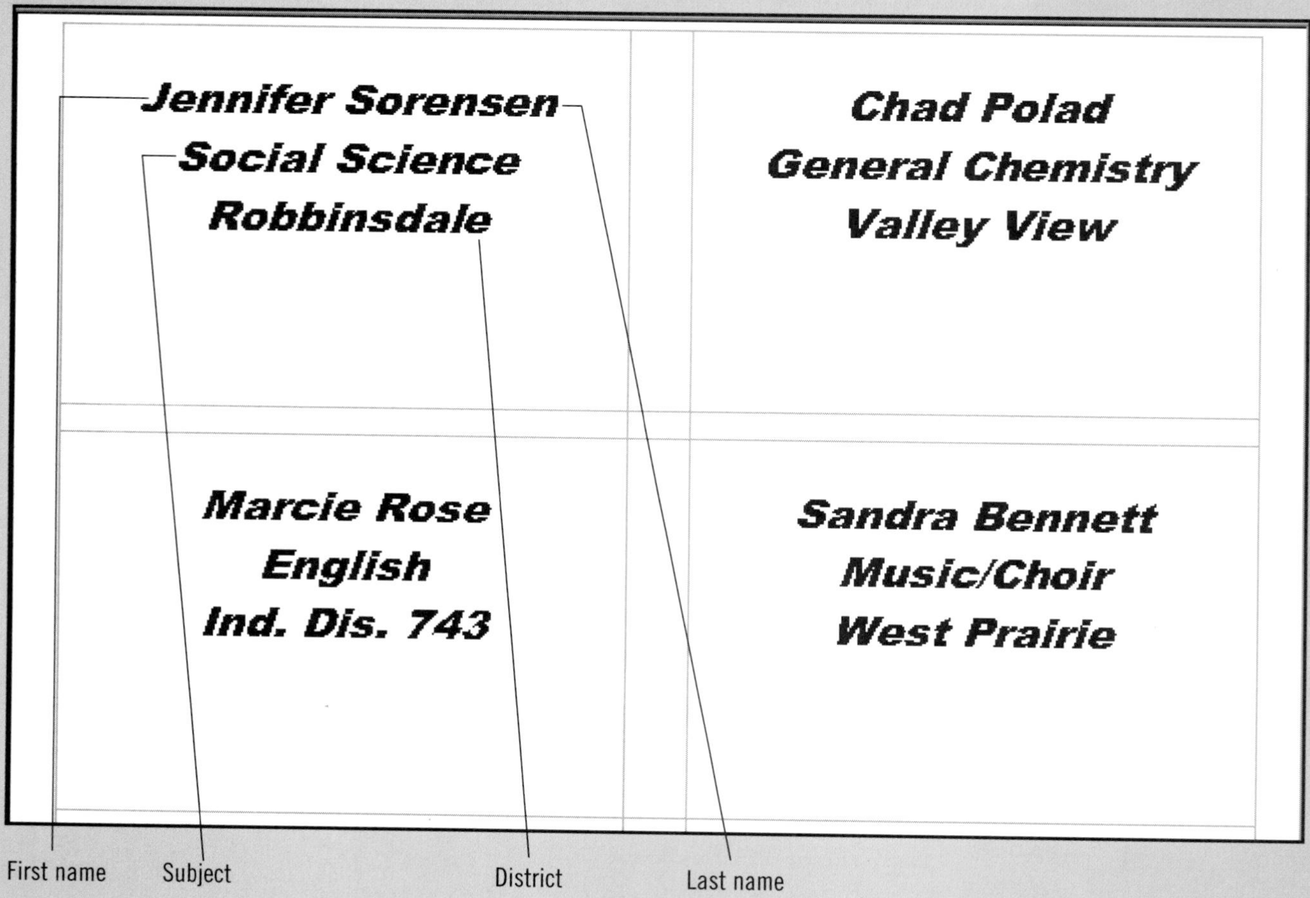

Jennifer Sorensen
Social Science
Robbinsdale

Chad Polad
General Chemistry
Valley View

Marcie Rose
English
Ind. Dis. 743

Sandra Bennett
Music/Choir
West Prairie

First name
Subject
District
Last name

Word 97 

Working with Graphics

Objectives

- Insert clip art graphics
- Modify clip art graphics
- Create custom graphics
- Modify custom graphics
- Apply special effects to graphics
- Position graphics and AutoShapes
- Insert a graphic from another program
- Create a callout

By adding and positioning graphics in a document, you can achieve dramatic effects. Graphics break up the monotony of large blocks of text and reinforce ideas presented in the text. Word provides many built-in graphics files (called **clip art**) covering a wide variety of topics, as well as decorative elements such as borders, bullets, and backgrounds. If the clip art collection provided with Word does not meet your needs, you can use the Drawing feature in Word to create your own graphics. Also, with the aid of the Drawing feature, you can create callouts, which draw your reader's attention to specific parts of a document. Angela has produced a simple report summarizing the year's highlights. Now she would like to spice up the text by inserting graphics and borders to create a flyer for Nomad Ltd senior management called *NomadNotes.*

Word 97

Inserting Clip Art Graphics

In Word you can insert pictures (in the form of graphics files, many of which are provided with the Word program) to better illustrate ideas and enhance your document. With Microsoft Clip Gallery 3.0, you can view available clip art graphics side-by-side. In addition, the Clip Gallery gives you easy access to recorded sound and video clips that you can insert in a document. After you insert a graphic, you can size and position it to fit where you want on the page. In the NomadNotes flyer, Angela wants to insert a graphic in the article about the new travel division. She would also like to insert a border under the name of the flyer.

1. Start Word
2. Open the document named **WD H-1** and save it as **Flyer Graphics**
   The document opens in page layout view.
3. Scroll to the top of the document and place the insertion point in front of the title **NomadNotes**, click **Insert** on the menu bar, click **Picture**, then click **Clip Art**
   The Microsoft Clip Gallery dialog box opens, as shown in Figure H-1. The pictures you see in this dialog box are the figures available in the currently selected category. If you see different pictures, it could be because another category is already selected on the left side of the dialog box. You can choose a category to view a collection of related pictures.
4. From the Categories list, click **Signs**, select a graphic that looks like a sign post with arrows pointing in several directions, and then click **Insert**
   The selected graphic appears in the document at the insertion point. After inserting a graphic, you often need to resize it to fit in the document. You can size a graphic object by dragging its sizing handles, which appear on all four sides and corners of a graphic.
5. Select the graphic (if necessary), position the pointer over the lower-right sizing handle, when the pointer changes shape ↘ then drag up and to the left until the graphic is about **1" wide** and **1.5" tall**
   The Picture toolbar appears when a picture is selected. Compare your document to Figure H-2. In addition to the pictures shown in Clip Gallery, you can also insert lines, backgrounds, and bullets. To better separate the title from the rest of the document, insert a decorative border.
6. Place the insertion point in front of the heading **Corporate Vision**, click **Insert** on the menu bar, click **Picture**, and then click **From File**
   The clip art folders include various folders with graphics and other decorative elements. Next locate the Lines folder.
7. Click the **Up One Level button** if necessary, then double-click the **Lines folder**
8. Select **Green and Black Stripe**, then click **Insert**
   Compare your document to Figure H-3. For now, don't be concerned about the position of your graphics in the document. You will learn how to position graphics later in this unit. For now save your changes to the document.
9. Click the **Save button** on the Standard toolbar

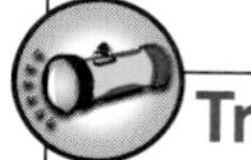

Trouble?

If you do not see the Clip Art command, click the From File command. Double-click the Popular folder.

Trouble?

If the Picture toolbar doesn't appear when the graphic is selected, click View on the menu bar, click Toolbars, then click Picture. If you accidentally moved the graphic, click Undo and be sure to drag the sizing handles, not the figure.

Trouble?

If you do not see the file in the Lines folder, it means that the correct graphics filters were not installed on your computer. You can continue working in this unit but your document will not contain the line shown in the figures.

FIGURE H-1: Clip Gallery dialog box

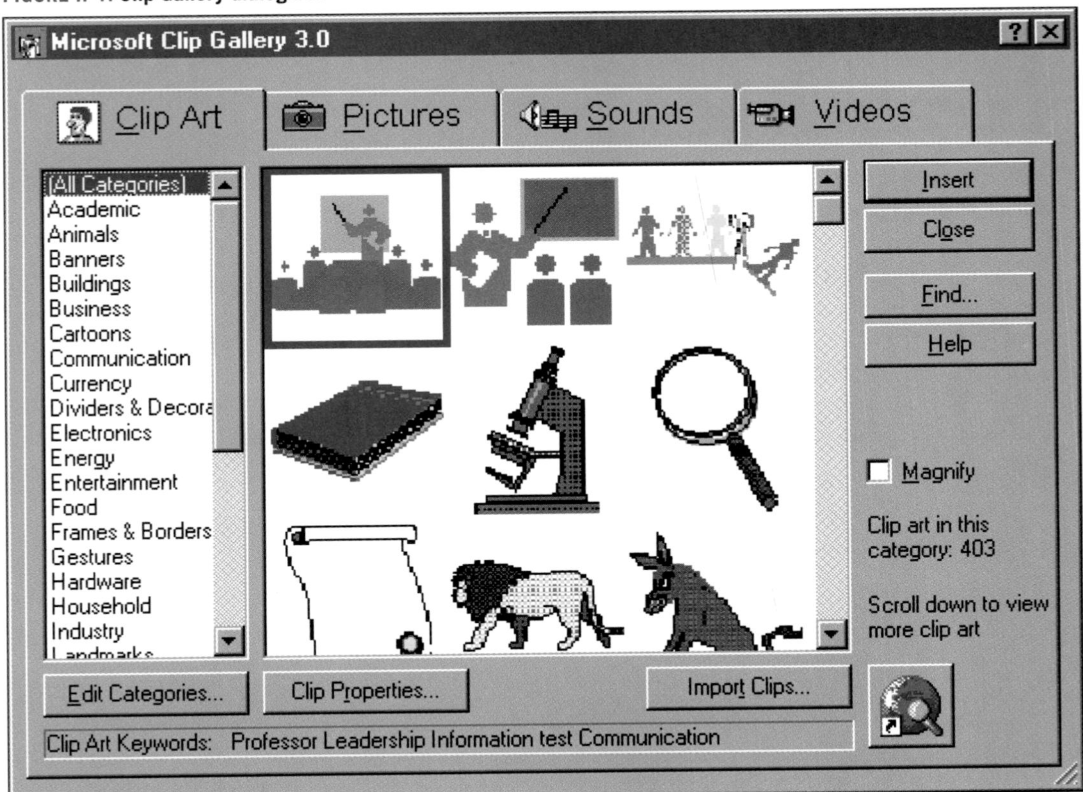

FIGURE H-2: Sized graphic

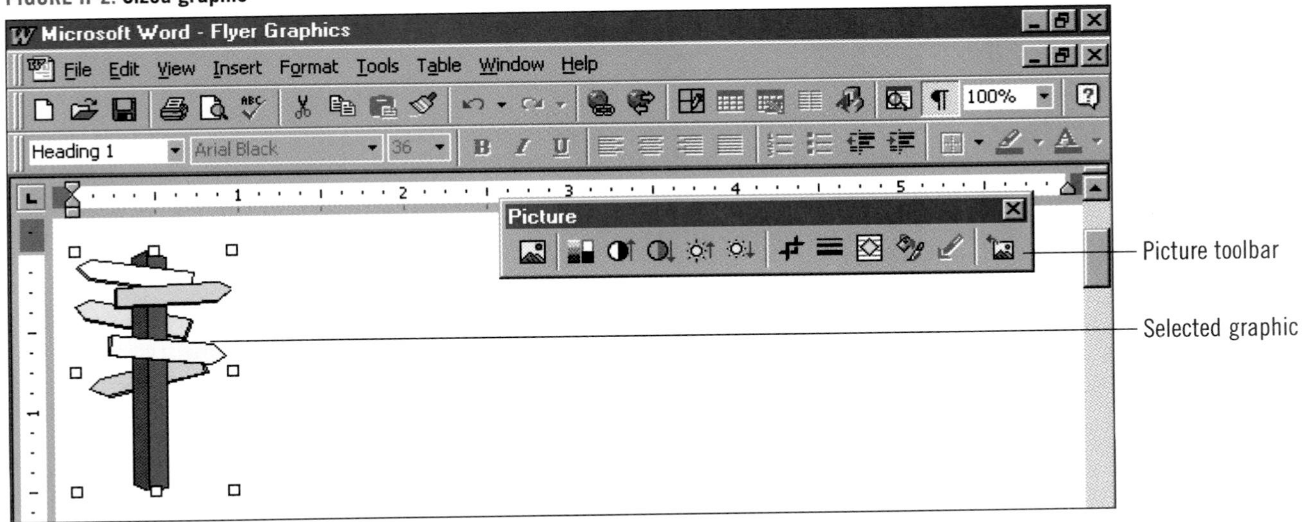

FIGURE H-3: Border graphic inserted

Word 97

Word 97

Modifying Clip Art Graphics

In Word you can modify clip art graphics to meet your needs. You might decide to change the color of the graphic or add a border around the picture. The Picture toolbar, as shown in Figure H-4, contains the buttons that provide easy access to the commands you need to modify clip art graphics. For example, with the Format Picture command on the Picture toolbar, you can specify color, line, position, and text wrapping options. Angela would like to modify the arrows sign graphic. Along with changing the color and adding a border, she would also like to modify the picture so that the text will wrap around the graphic instead of displacing the text.

Steps

1. Select the arrows sign graphic you inserted in the previous lesson
   The Picture toolbar appears in the document window. Because the document might not be printed on a color printer, change the image color.
2. Click the **Image Control button** on the Picture toolbar, then click **Grayscale**
   The color in the graphic changes to shades of gray. This option can be helpful if your printer does not print in color.
3. Click the **Text Wrapping button** on the Picture toolbar, then click **Square**
   The text wrapping feature allows you to specify how you would like the text to be arranged around the picture. Some text wrapping options include text being placed only above or below the picture, text going through or behind the picture, and text arranged tight against all sides of the graphic. With square text wrapping, the text will flow around all sides of the graphic evenly. You can add a border around a graphic to enhance its appearance.
4. Click the **Line Style button** on the Picture toolbar, then select the **3 pt double line**
   A double line border appears around the graphic. You can also change the color of a graphic.
5. Click the **Format Picture button** on the Picture toolbar
   The Format Picture dialog box opens. In this dialog box you can specify a variety of colors, patterns, and other characteristics for your picture. Next, you will change the background color of the graphic.
6. Click the **Colors and Lines tab**
   On the Colors and Lines tab, you can specify fill color, line style, and arrow styles as shown in Figure H-5.
7. In the Fill area, click the **Color list arrow**
   A color palette appears, allowing you to choose from a variety of colors. At the bottom of the palette, you see the More Colors and Fill Effects options. These options allow you to choose from a larger variety of colors or create your own hue and apply texture to your fill.
8. Choose the last color in the fourth row, then click **OK**
   The graphic now has a gray background. You have finished modifying this graphic for now. Compare your graphic to Figure H-6.
9. Click the **Save button** on the Standard toolbar

FIGURE H-4: Picture toolbar

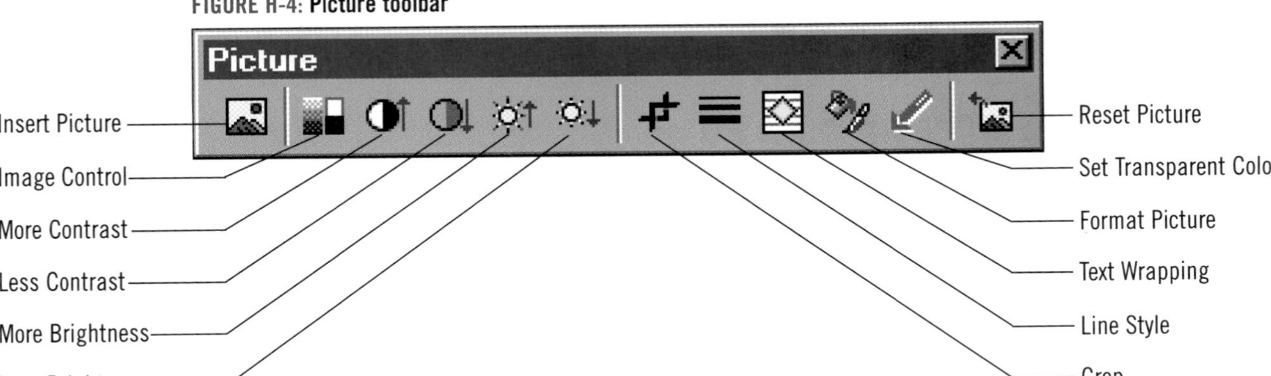

FIGURE H-5: Format Picture dialog box

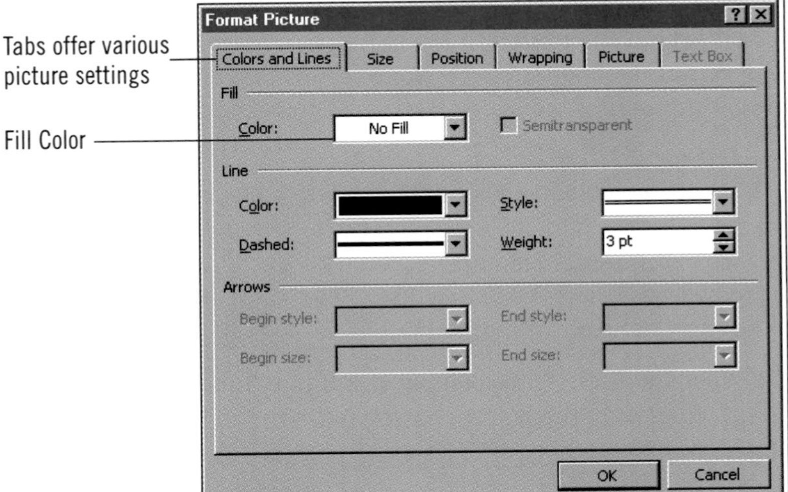

FIGURE H-6: Modified graphic

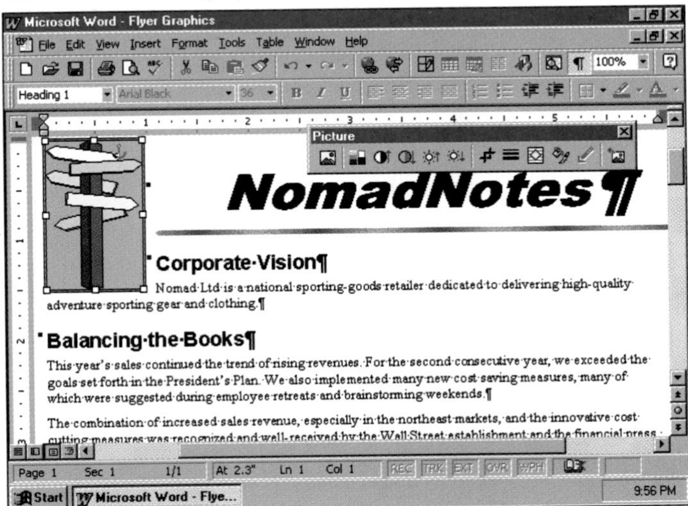

CLUES TO USE

Using the cropping tool to modify a graphic

Occasionally you will want to use only a small part of a graphic offered by Word. In this case you can use the cropping tool on the Picture toolbar to crop or cut away the undesired parts. To crop a picture, first select the graphic, then click the Crop button on the Picture toolbar. After clicking the Crop button the pointer will change to . Click this pointer on any of the sizing handles and drag over the areas you wish to crop.

Word 97

Creating Custom Graphics

When you want to insert graphics in your document, you are not limited to the clip art files provided by Word. In Word, you have the ability to create your own custom graphics using simple (but powerful) drawing tools on the Drawing toolbar. You can create lines and shapes, and apply colors to them. With the AutoShapes button on the Drawing toolbar you can create simple shapes quickly without having to draw them from scratch. AutoShapes include squares, triangles, lightning bolts, block arrows, and stars and banners. Angela would like to use a graphic to accompany the article about environmental relations in her newsletter. Because Word does not provide a graphic that she feels is relevant, she creates her own.

Steps

1. Click the **Drawing button** on the Standard toolbar
   The Drawing toolbar appears at the bottom of the Word document window, as shown in Figure H-7. You use the buttons on this toolbar to create your own graphics in your Word documents.
2. Click **AutoShapes** on the Drawing toolbar, click **Basic Shapes**, then click the **Isosceles Triangle** in the second row
   When you click an AutoShape feature, the pointer changes shape to +. With this pointer, you can drag and draw the selected shape to a desired size. The AutoShape option on the Drawing toolbar offers a variety of presets you can draw.
3. Scroll to the end of the document, click the pointer in a blank area (below the text) at the bottom of the page, then drag the pointer down and to the right until you have a triangle with a **1" base** and **1" tall** (you do not need to be very exact).
   Compare your shape to Figure H-8. Just as you can copy and paste text, you can also copy and paste selected graphics and AutoShapes.
4. Select the triangle shape, if it is not already selected, click the **Copy button** on the Standard toolbar, then click the **Paste button** on the Standard toolbar
   Another triangle shape appears near the original shape.
5. With the second shape selected, drag the bottom right sizing handle up and to the left so the new shape is just slightly smaller than the first shape
   With the shape selected you can drag it to a new position.
6. With the second shape still selected, position the pointer near the shape until the pointer changes to ✥, then drag the second shape so that it overlaps the first shape, as shown in Figure H-9
   The overlapping triangles will represent the mountains in the graphic.
7. Click the **Oval button** on the Drawing toolbar
   You can use this tool to draw circles, as well as ovals.
8. Press and hold down **[Shift]** and, near the top of the triangle shapes, drag a circle that is about one-half inch across
   Holding down the [Shift] key as you drag with the Ellipse tool creates a perfect circle. Compare your document to Figure H-10.
9. Click the **Save button** on the Standard toolbar

Trouble?

If you don't see the second shape, it is because Word pasted it exactly on top of the first shape. Click the shape and then drag it to the right, so you can work with the new one.

FIGURE H-7: Drawing toolbar

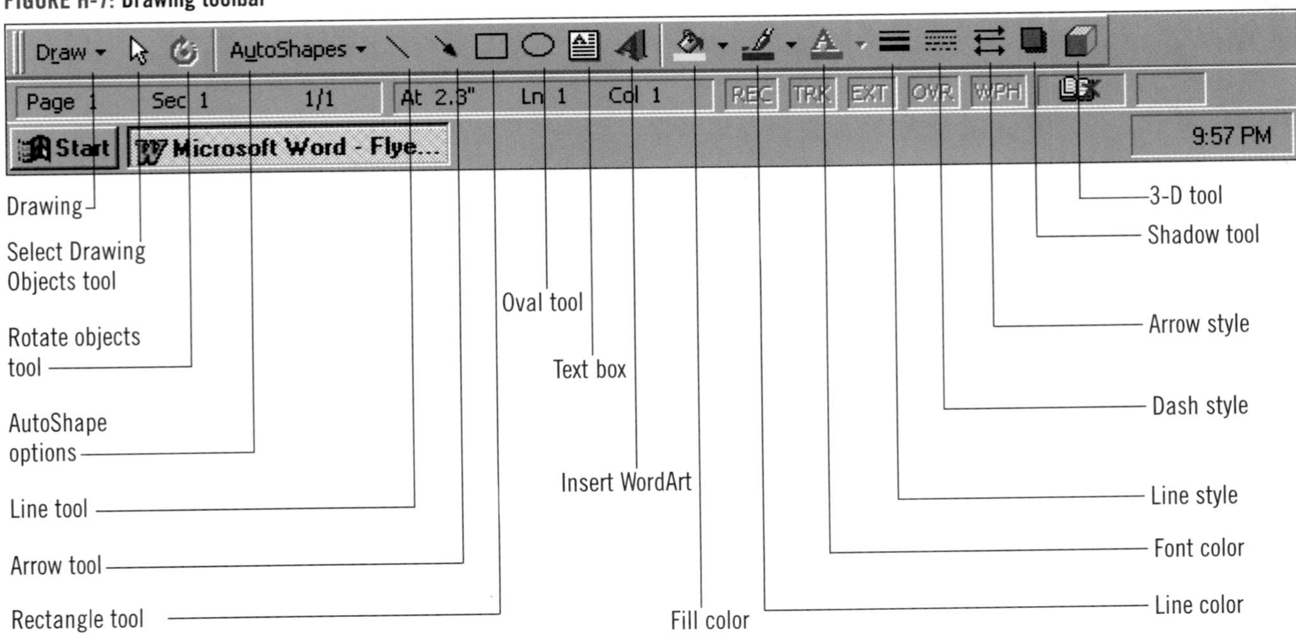

FIGURE H-8: AutoShape

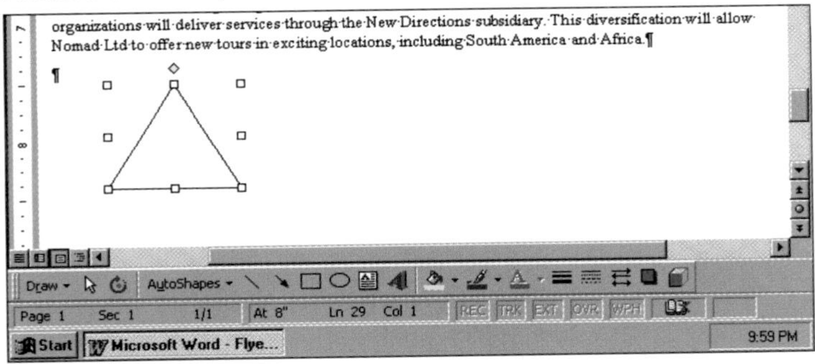

FIGURE H-9: Overlapping shapes

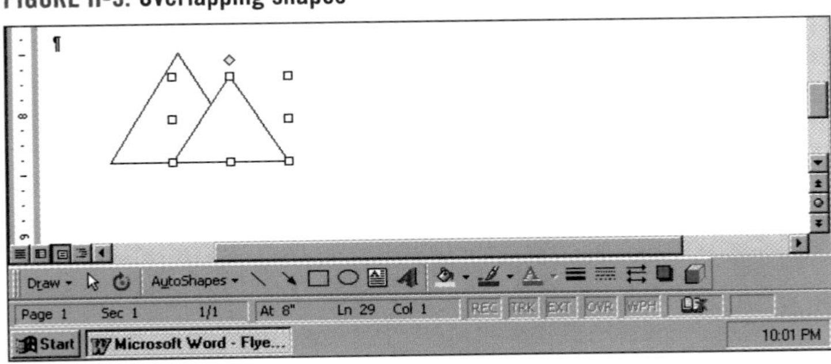

FIGURE H-10: Completed custom graphic

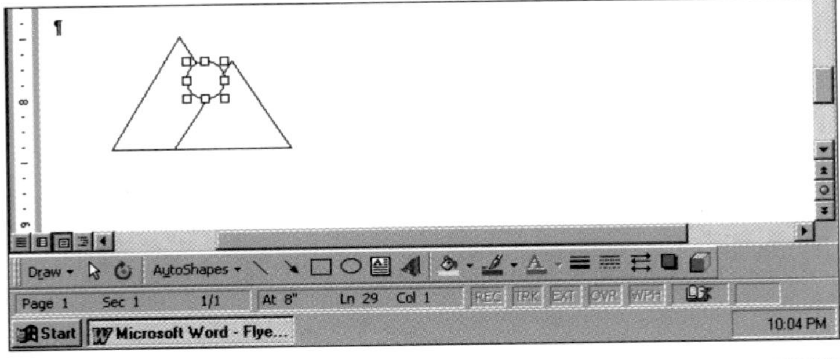

Word 97

Word 97

Modifying Custom Graphics

You are not limited to only drawing lines and shapes in your custom graphics. You can also fill your shapes with colors and rearrange shapes (as well as make many other modifications) to make your creations look the way you want. Angela's drawing needs color to make it look more realistic. Angela adds color to her shapes and makes other changes to her graphic to achieve the effect she wants. First, she adds color to the circle shape.

Steps 1 2 3 4

1. **Select the circle in the drawing, then click the Fill Color list arrow on the Drawing toolbar**
   Clicking the Fill Color button shows a palette of colors from which you can choose to fill the selected shape, as shown in Figure H-11.
2. **Click the Yellow color on the Palette**
   The circle is filled with the yellow color, as shown in Figure H-12. Only the circle will be filled with yellow because this is the selected shape.
3. **Select the larger triangle and click the Fill Color list arrow on the Drawing toolbar, then click a Dark Blue color on the Palette**
   The triangle is filled with dark blue. Now, fill the other triangle with another color.
4. **Repeat step 3 for the other triangle, this time choosing the Dark Green color**
   The second triangle is filled with dark green. Objects you draw appear in layers, one on top of another. The sequence in which you draw a shape determines the order in which the shapes are layered. For example, because the circle is the last object you drew, the circle appears on top of the other shapes. The Drawing button on the Drawing toolbar offers options for placing shapes in relation to each other and to text.
5. **Click the circle shape, click Draw on the Drawing toolbar, click Order, then click Send to Back**
   The circle appears behind the triangle, giving the appearance of a sun setting between two mountains.
6. **Adjust the position of each of the shapes (as necessary) by clicking and dragging them so that your picture approximates the illustration in Figure H-13**
   Do not be concerned if the colors for your two mountains are reversed. What is important is that your mountains are different colors from the sun shape and from each other. After you have finished modifying the various shapes in a custom graphic, you can group the shapes together, so that you can work a group of objects as a single shape.
7. **Click the Select Objects button on the Drawing toolbar, then drag a rectangle to surround all the objects**
   With all the shapes selected, you see the sizing handles for each of the objects. So that you can work with the objects as a single item, you group the objects together.
8. **Click Draw on the Drawing toolbar, then click Group**
   With the objects grouped, you see only one set of sizing handles as shown in Figure H-14. Grouping the shapes makes a single drawing object, so you can now select the entire arrangement by clicking only one shape. Having the shapes grouped together will make it easier to move the graphic in the document.
9. **Click the Save button on the Standard toolbar**

FIGURE H-11: Fill Color palette

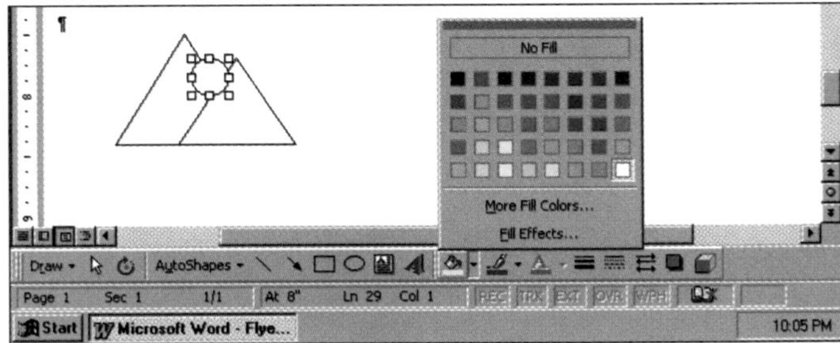

FIGURE H-12: Filled circle

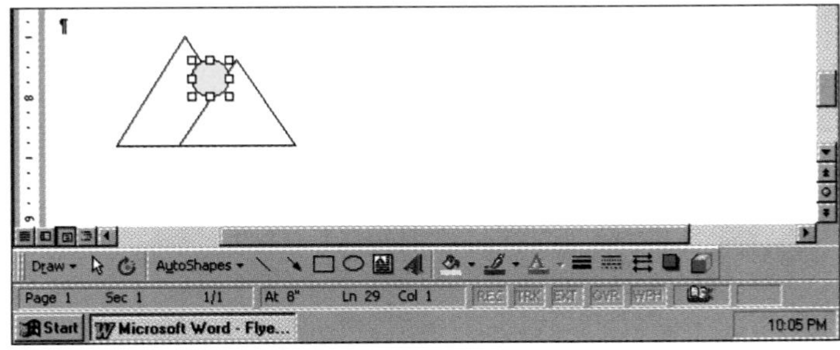

FIGURE H-13: Circle object sent to back

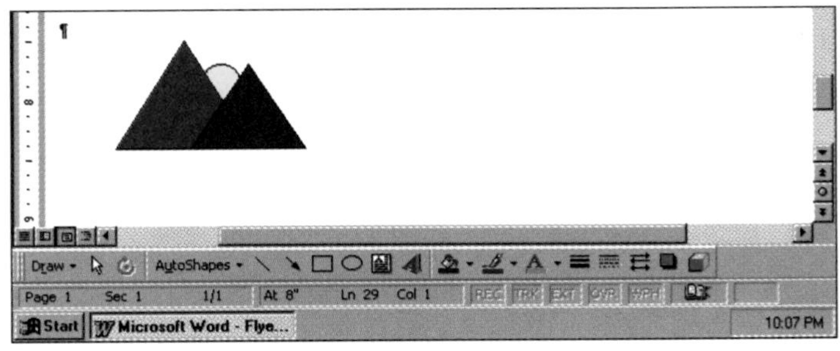

FIGURE H-14: Grouped drawing objects

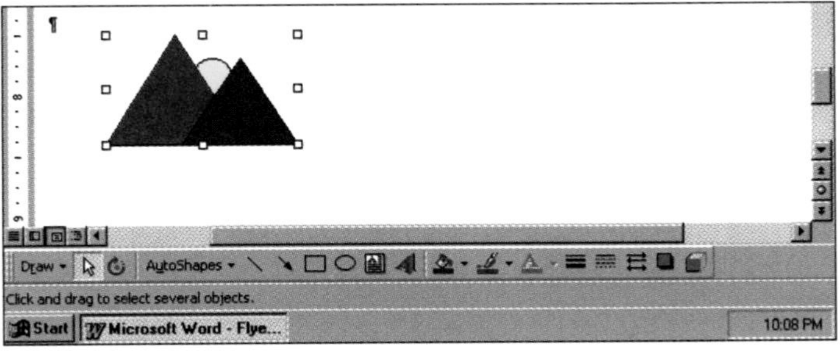

CLUES TO USE

Sizing shapes with precision

As you size shapes, you might have noticed that the lines in the shapes appear to "jump" as your pointer moves. This is because the shapes are automatically aligned to an invisible grid. The **Snap to Grid**, which is turned on by default, aligns shapes along a very tightly spaced grid. This feature makes it easier to align shapes with one another. If you want more flexibility to create and drag shapes exactly where you wish, you can turn off the **Snap to Grid** feature. Click the Draw button on the Drawing toolbar and then click Grid. Clear the **Snap to Grid** check box and click OK.

Word 97

Applying Special Effects to Graphics

The Drawing toolbar contains many features you can use to enhance the shapes you insert in a document. For example, you can give a shape a unique appearance by adding special fill patterns, such as gradient. You can display a shape in three-dimensions. You can even rotate the shape to an exact angle you choose. Angela would like to add a block arrow to emphasize the section on Balancing the Books. She would also like to experiment with some of the more dramatic fill effects found in the Fill Effects Dialog box.

Steps

1. Click **AutoShapes** on the Drawing toolbar, click **Block Arrows**, then select the **Down Arrow**
   After selecting an AutoShape, the pointer will change to +. With this pointer, you can click and drag the selected shape to any size and anywhere in the document.
2. In the white space at the end of the document, click and drag down **1"** and to the right **.5"**
   Just as you modify custom graphics, you can modify AutoShapes using the Drawing toolbar.
3. Click the **Fill Color list arrow** on the Drawing toolbar, then click **Fill Effects**
   The Fill Effects dialog box opens as shown in Figure H-15.
4. Select the **Gradient tab** if it is not already selected, then click the **Preset option button** in the Color area
   Notice the Variants and Shading styles at the bottom of the dialog box. You can also preview the fill effects in the sample box in the lower right corner. You can choose from a list of preset color options.
5. Click the **Preset colors list arrow**, select **Desert**, then click **OK**
   The arrow is filled with the Desert fill effect.
6. Click the **Line Color list arrow** on the Drawing toolbar, choose **Red**
   You can use the Line Style arrow to choose new colors and patterns for the lines outlining your AutoShapes. The 3-D feature can add an even greater dramatic effect to AutoShapes.
7. Click the **3-D button** on the Drawing toolbar, then select **3-D Style 1**
   The arrow appears with a 3-D effect. With the Free Rotate feature, you can rotate your figure to point in any direction that you choose.
8. Click the **Free Rotate button** on the Drawing toolbar, click any **rotate handle**, drag the arrow around until it points up, then click the **Free Rotate button** again to turn it off
   You can also change the size of the pointed part of the arrow. For example, you can squeeze down the top part of the arrow. (You need to turn off the Free Rotate feature to see the yellow sizing diamond you use in the next step.)
9. Position the pointer over the **yellow diamond** under the pointed part of the arrow and drag up a short distance
   Compare your document to Figure H-16.

QuickTip

Drag when the green dot appears in the center of the pointer.

Time To

✔ Save

FIGURE H-15: Fill Effects dialog box

Fill Effects
Gradient
Texture
Pattern
Picture
OK
Cancel
Colors
One color
Two colors
Preset
Shading styles
Horizontal
Vertical
Diagonal up
Diagonal down
From corner
From center
Variants
Sample:
Color styles
Preset styles
Shading styles
Preview

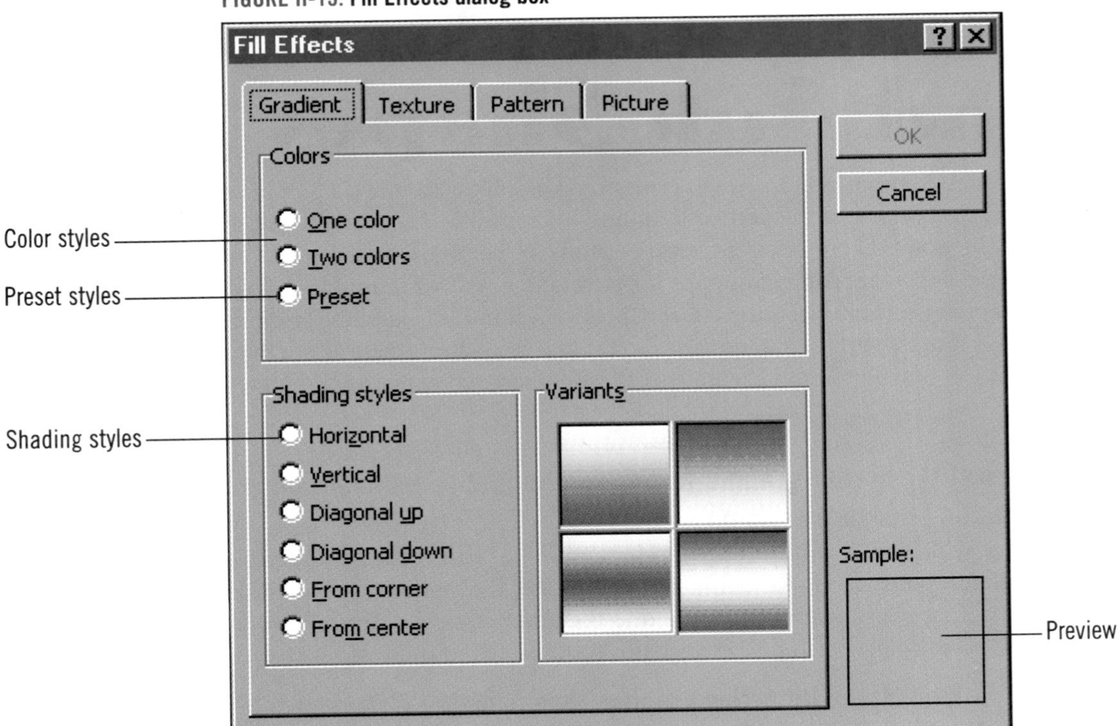

FIGURE H-16: Modified AutoShape

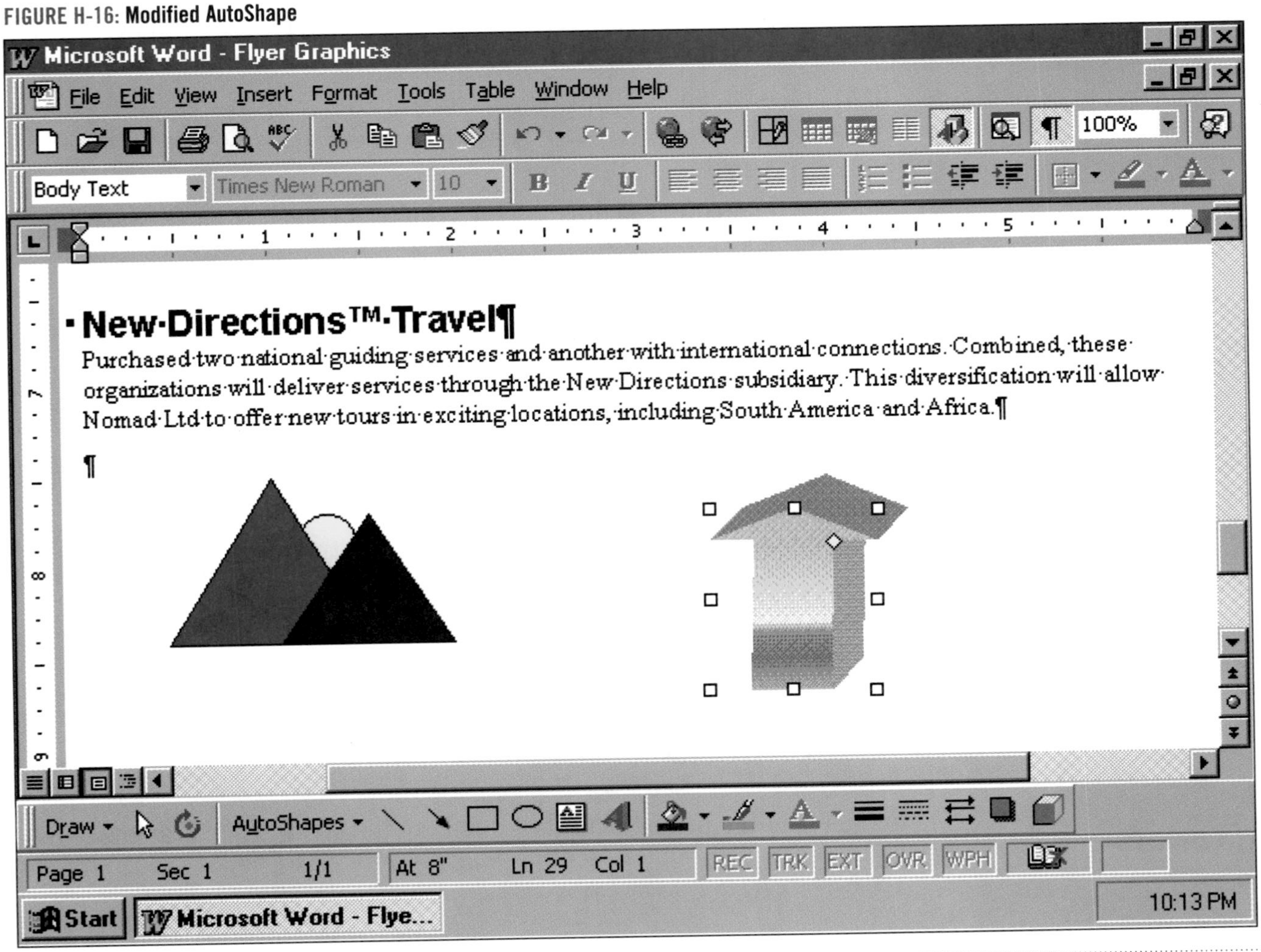

Microsoft Word - Flyer Graphics
File Edit View Insert Format Tools Table Window Help
Body Text
Times New Roman
10
100%
New·Directions™·Travel¶
Purchased·two·national·guiding·services·and·another·with·international·connections.·Combined,·these·organizations·will·deliver·services·through·the·New·Directions·subsidiary.·This·diversification·will·allow·Nomad·Ltd·to·offer·new·tours·in·exciting·locations,·including·South·America·and·Africa.¶
¶
Draw
AutoShapes
Page 1 Sec 1 1/1 At 8" Ln 29 Col 1
REC TRK EXT OVR WPH
Start
Microsoft Word - Flye...
10:13 PM

Word 97

Positioning Graphics and AutoShapes

Word offers various options when positioning graphics. To move a graphic, you simply select the graphic and drag it to the desired location. When positioning a graphic near text, you can specify how you would like the text to wrap around the graphic. The Format AutoShapes and Format Object dialog boxes contain options for positioning, text wrapping, and other types of formatting for graphics. You can open these dialog boxes by double-clicking the graphic. Angela has finished modifying her graphics and would like to position them throughout the document. She will specify how she would like the text to wrap before moving the graphics.

Steps

1. Select the **border graphic** and drag it so it appears under the paragraph below the heading **Corporate Vision**
   You will need to position the border about .25" below the paragraph. Placing graphics can often require several attempts before you get the results you want. Keep positioning it by releasing the mouse and re-selecting the graphic until it appears in the proper location. If text is misplaced, simply reselect and position the graphic again.
2. Double-click the **Up Arrow** graphic, then click the **Wrapping tab** (if it is not already in front)
   Double-clicking an AutoShape opens the Format AutoShape dialog box, as shown in Figure H-17. The Format AutoShape dialog box offers various formatting options such as positioning, text wrapping, and size.
3. Select **Tight** in the Wrapping Style area and **Right** in the Wrap to area, then click **OK**
   After you have specified the text wrapping style, you can move the graphic to the desired position.
4. Click inside the **Up Arrow graphic**, drag the graphic and place it under the heading **Balancing the Books**
   Make sure the heading is above the graphic with the paragraph text to the side of the graphic, as shown in Figure H-18. Notice the text wraps to the shape of the AutoShape.
5. Double-click the **custom mountain graphic**
   Double-clicking a custom graphic opens the Format Object dialog box. The Format Object dialog box offers the same options as the Format AutoShape dialog box.
6. Select **Tight** in the Text Wrapping area, select **Left** in the Wrap To area, then click **OK**
   With the wrapping options specified, you can position the custom graphic.
7. Drag the graphic to the right of the paragraph below the **Environmental Relations** heading
   The text flows to the left of the mountain graphic. To enhance the effect, format the paragraph so that both left and right edges of the paragraph are even.
8. Click anywhere in the paragraph below the **Environmental Relations** heading, then click the **Justify button** on the Formatting toolbar
   Compare your document to the illustration shown in Figure H-19.
9. Scroll to the top of the page, then select and drag the **arrow signs graphic** so that it is to the left of the heading **New Directions Travel**
   Compare your document to Figure H-20.

QuickTip

You do not need to be concerned if your text does not wrap exactly the same as shown in the figure. You can adjust the size of the arrow, if you wish.

Time To

✓ Save

FIGURE H-17: Format AutoShape dialog box

Text wrapping options

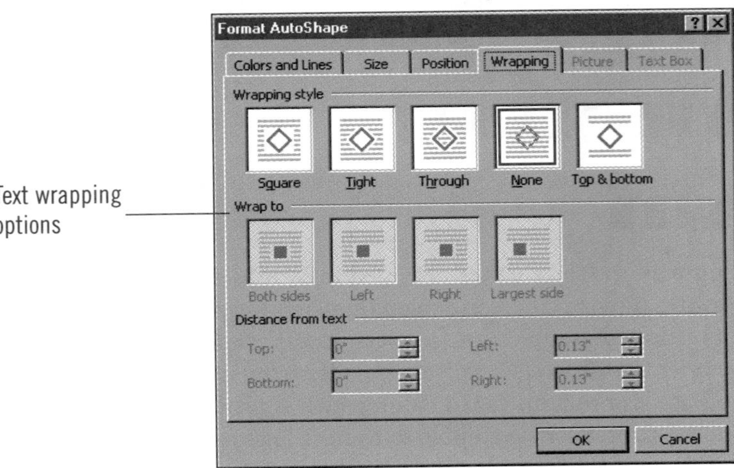

FIGURE H-18: Positioned graphic

Text wraps tight and to the right

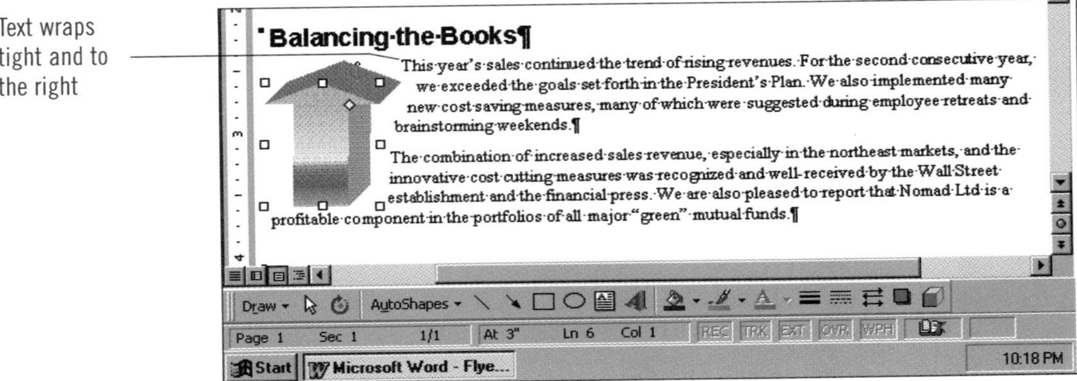

FIGURE H-19: Custom graphic positioned

Justified paragraph

Text wraps tight and to the left

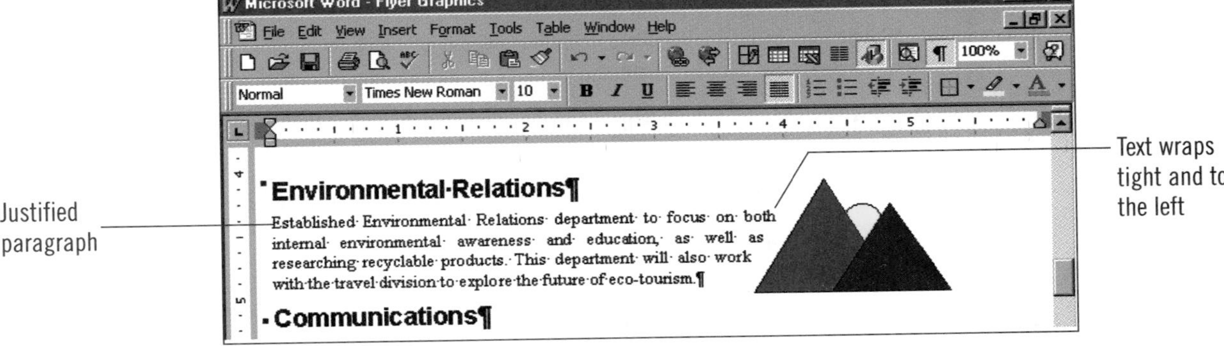

FIGURE H-20: Clip art positioned in document

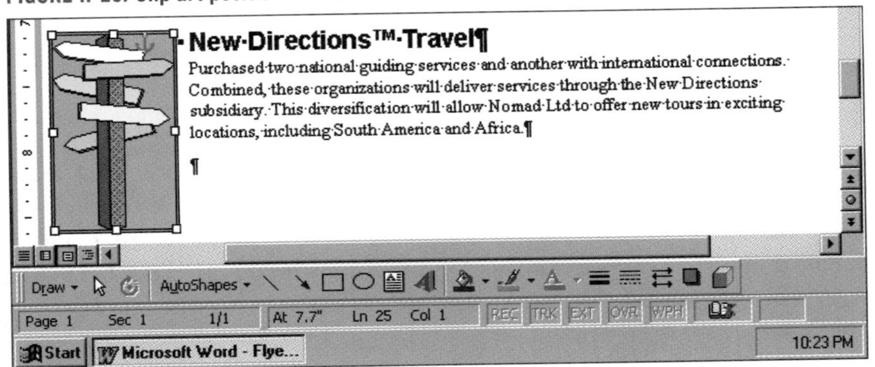

Word 97

Inserting a Graphic from Another Program

You are not limited to working with graphics either provided in Word's clip art collection or those you create with the Drawing toolbar. There are many drawing programs on the market with which you can create sophisticated graphics, and you can insert graphics created in these programs into your Word documents. The advertising department at Nomad has been busy creating a new logo in a graphics program called Paint, which is provided with Microsoft Windows 95. Michael Belmont has created a new graphic to use as a logo for Nomad Ltd, which Angela would like to insert in the newsletter.

Steps 1 2 3 4

1. Place the insertion point at the end of the title **NomadNotes**
2. Click **Insert** on the menu bar, then click **Object**
   The Object dialog box opens. You can click the Create from File tab to help locate a file. The Nomad logo file is located on your Student Disk.
3. Click the **Create from File tab**
   The Create from File tab is now foremost in the dialog box, as shown in Figure H-21. On this tab you can locate the Paint file.
4. Click **Browse**, then locate and double-click the drive that contains your student files
   With the appropriate drive selected, you can select the file you want to insert.
5. Click the **Preview button** (if it's not already selected), scroll to and select the file **WD Logo**, click **OK** in the Browse dialog box
   The logo filename appears in the File Name dialog box.
6. Click **OK** in the Object dialog box
   The picture appears in the document.
7. Select the Paint object, click the **Text Wrapping button** on the Picture toolbar, then click **Square**
   The Picture toolbar appears when you select an object, as it does when you select a picture.
8. Drag the object to the right of the title **NomadNotes**
   Compare your document to Figure H-22.
9. Click the **Save button** on the Standard toolbar

Modifying a Paint object

When you insert an object that was created in another program, you can edit the object in the original program (provided that the program is installed on your computer). For example, if you insert a Paint file as an object, you can modify the graphic using Paint without actually leaving Word. To edit an object, you simply double-click the object to display the object's original program environment. You will still be able to see the Word document in the original program window. To move back to the Word program simply click outside the object.

FIGURE H-21: Create from File tab in Object dialog box

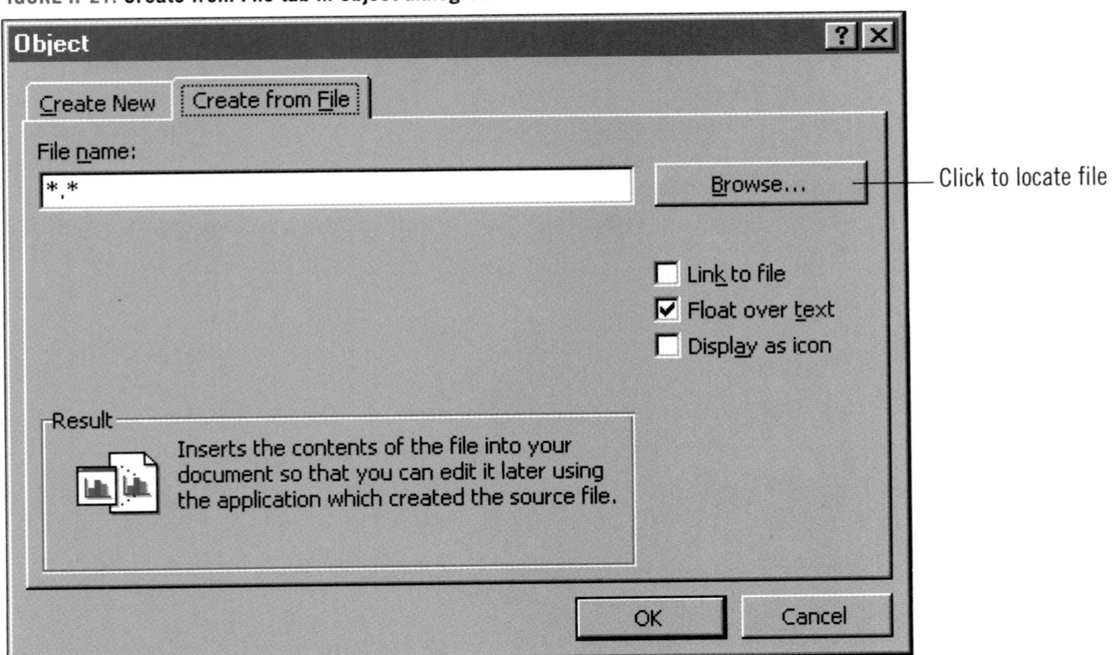

FIGURE H-22: New picture in document

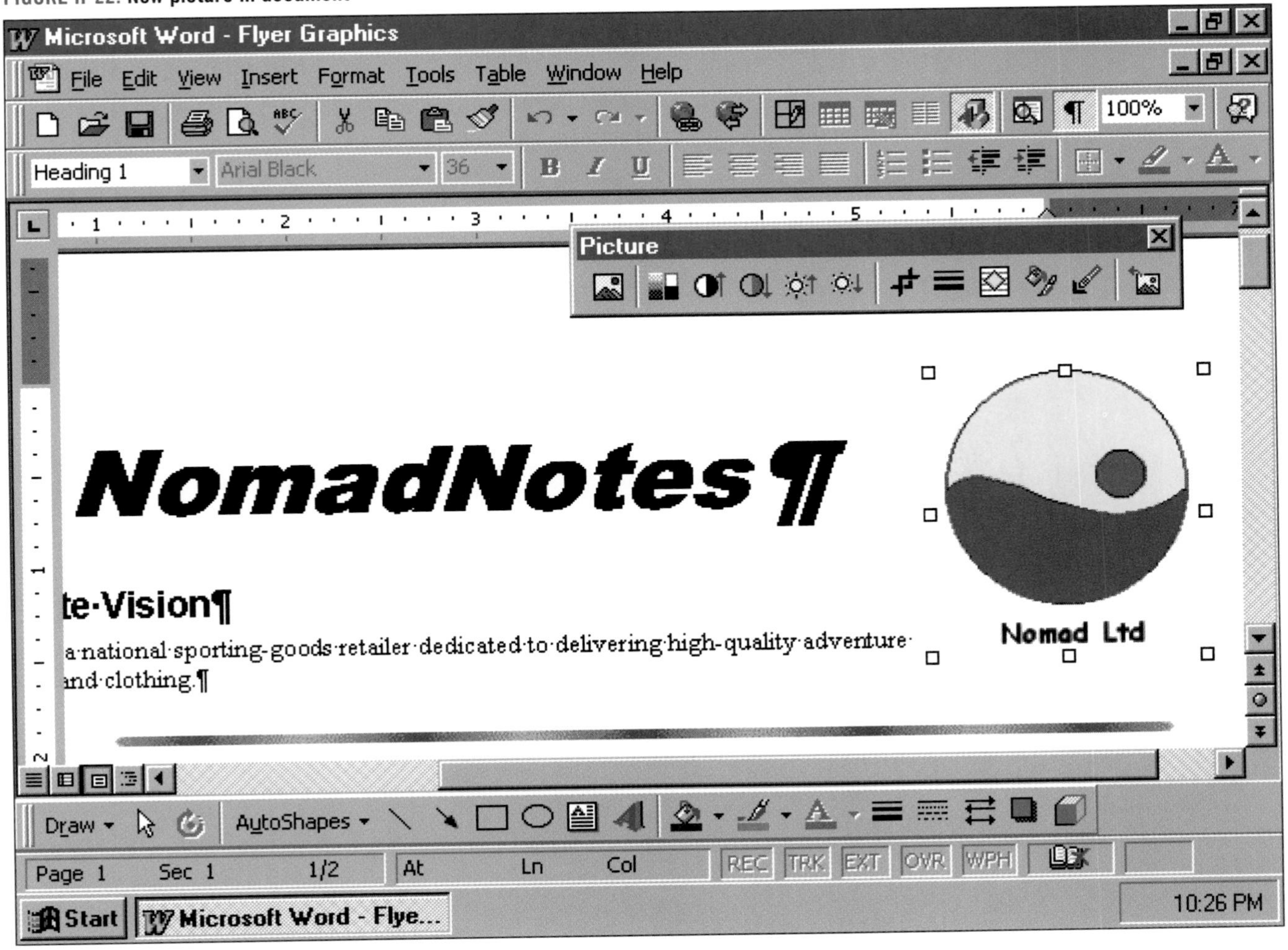

Word 97

Creating a Callout

When you want to draw your reader's attention to a specific item in a document, you can create a callout to that item. A **callout** is a graphic object containing text and a line pointing to a location in a document. You can enter any text you want in a callout. In addition, you can position it exactly where you wish. Angela would like to make sure her readers notice the new tour destinations available in the upcoming year, so she creates a callout to this part of the document.

Steps 1 2 3 4

1. Click **AutoShapes** on the Drawing toolbar, click **Callouts**, then select **Line Callout 2**
   With the Callout tool selected, you can drag your callout anywhere in the document.
2. Click the pointer near the end of the **New Directions** paragraph, and drag down and to the right about one-half inch
   A callout appears next to the text, as shown in Figure H-23. Immediately after you insert a callout, you can enter text.
3. Type **New for 1998!**
   You can use the yellow sizing handles to adjust the callout position.
4. Click the **callout frame** to select it and display its sizing handles, then drag the yellow sizing handle connected to the text box and pull down and to the left
   Notice that the first yellow sizing handle stays anchored.
5. Click the callout and drag the bottom sizing handle up so that the callout box is not larger than the text, then drag the right sizing handle until the text appears on one line
   With the callout still selected you can use the buttons on the Drawing toolbar to modify the text box itself.
6. Click the **Dash Style button** on the Drawing toolbar, and select the **Round Dot line**
   The callout appears with dashed lines.
7. Select the text in the callout, then click the **Bold button** **B** on the Formatting toolbar, then click the **Font list arrow** on the Formatting toolbar and click **Arial**
   To display the callout more clearly without the paragraph marks, you can hide the nonprinting characters.
8. Click the **Show/Hide button** ¶ on the Standard toolbar, then deselect the callout
   Compare your document to Figure H-24. You have finished working with graphics in your document, so you can hide the Drawing toolbar and save your changes.
9. Click the **Drawing button** on the Standard toolbar and save your changes
   The Drawing toolbar is hidden.

Time To

- Save
- Print the document
- Close
- Exit Word

FIGURE H-23: Creating a callout

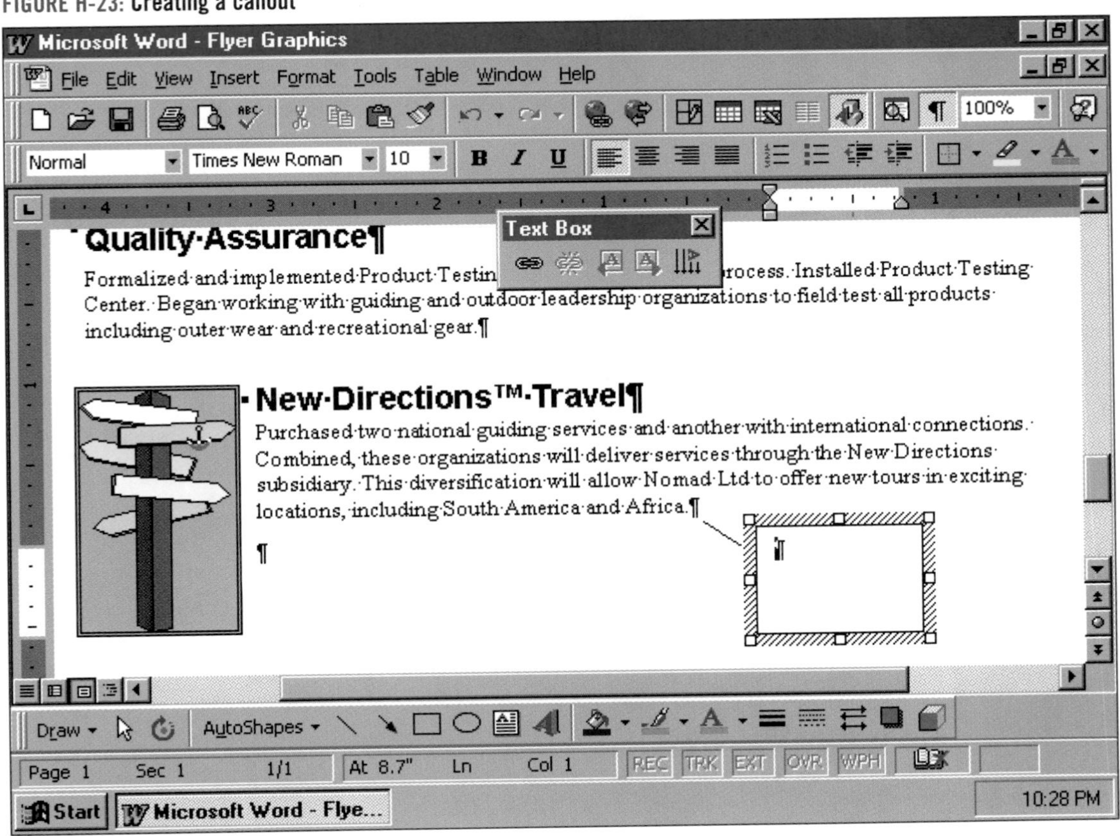

FIGURE H-24: Completed callout

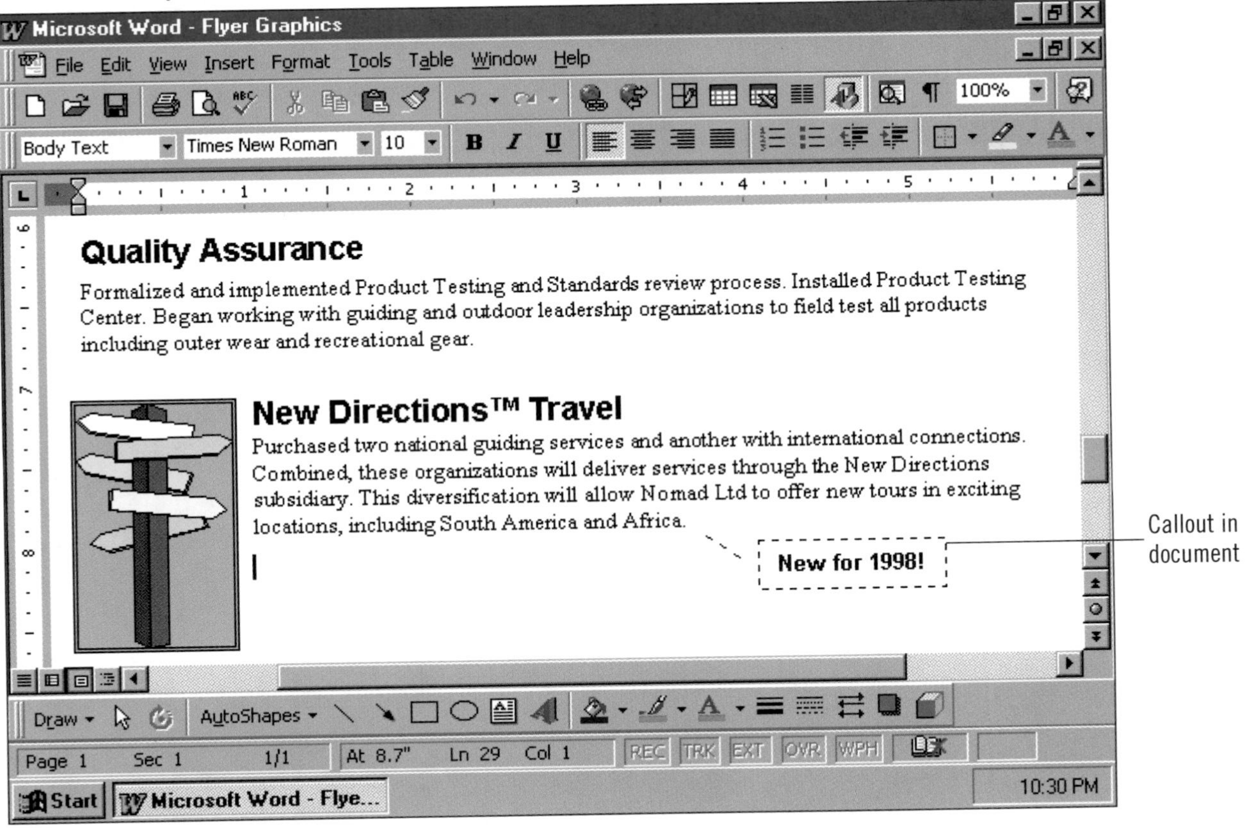

Practice

► Concepts Review

Label each of the elements in Figure H-25.

FIGURE H-25

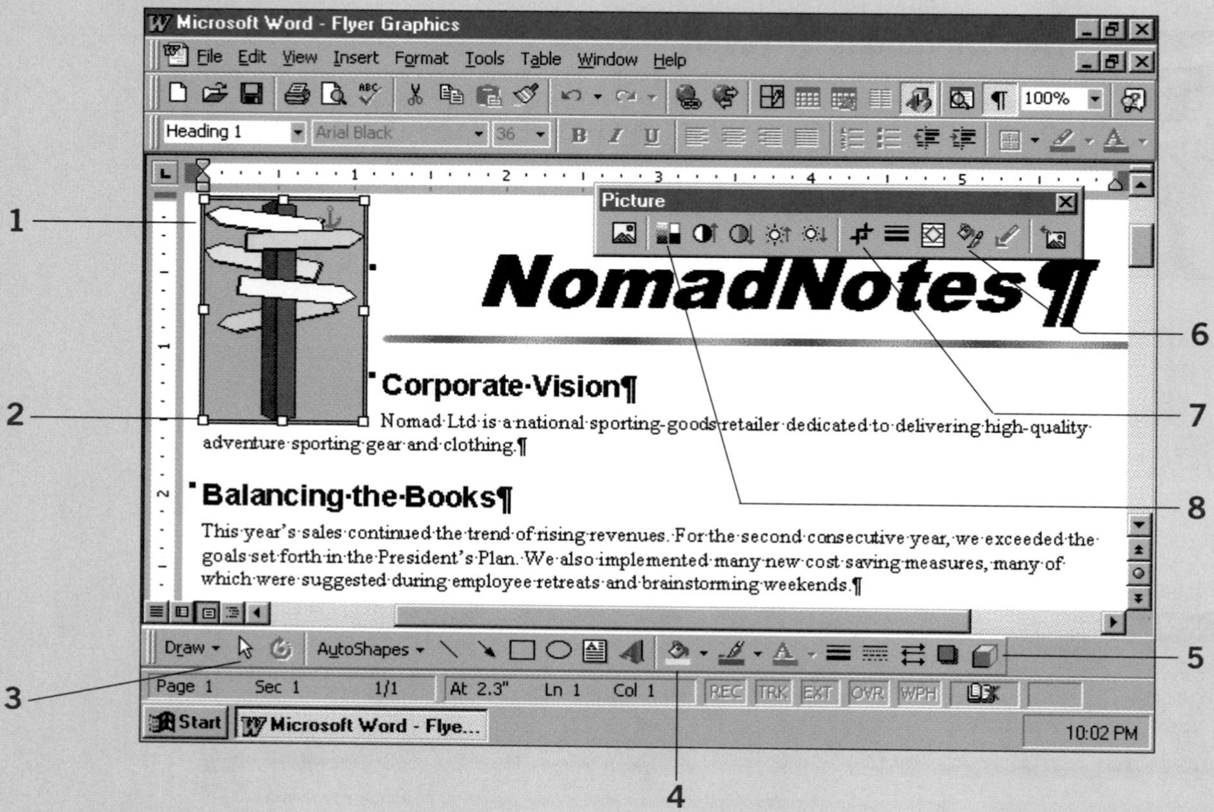

Match each of the following features with the correct descriptions.

9. Callout
10. Oval button
11. Select Objects button
12. Sizing handle
13. Drawing toolbar

a. Allows you to draw a circle or oval shape
b. Allows you to group custom shapes or AutoShapes into one graphic
c. Contains buttons you can use to create custom graphics
d. Framed text pointing to an area in a document
e. Allows you to size an object

Select the best answer from the list of choices.

14. To insert a graphic provided by Word, you
- **a.** Click Insert, then click Picture.
- **b.** Click the Drawing button on the Standard toolbar.
- **c.** Click the Picture button on the Drawing toolbar.
- **d.** Click View, then click Picture.

15. To draw your own custom graphic, you must first
- **a.** Click Insert, then click Picture and select the picture you want.
- **b.** Click the Drawing button on the Standard toolbar.
- **c.** Click the Picture button on the Drawing toolbar.
- **d.** Click View, then click Picture.

16. Which of the following is NOT true about using graphics in Word?
- **a.** You can create your own graphics in another program and insert them in Word.
- **b.** You can select graphics from Word's collection of clip art.
- **c.** You cannot modify graphics you insert in Word.
- **d.** You can edit graphics created in another program.

17. To modify a graphic, you need to
- **a.** Click Edit, then click Graphic.
- **b.** Exit Word and start the program that was used to create the graphic.
- **c.** Select the graphic and use the Picture toolbar.
- **d.** Triple-click the graphic.

18. To change the color of a shape, you
- **a.** Select the Fill Color button on the Drawing toolbar.
- **b.** Select the shape then click the Fill Color button.
- **c.** Delete the shape, click the Fill Color button and redraw the shape.
- **d.** Select the shape, click the Fill Color button, then select a new color.

19. To draw a perfect circle, you
- **a.** Click the Circle button and drag a circle.
- **b.** Click the Oval button and press [Ctrl] as you drag a circle.
- **c.** Click the Freeform button and carefully draw a circle.
- **d.** Click the Oval button and press [Shift] as you drag a circle.

20. To insert an AutoShape, you
- **a.** Click Insert, then click AutoShapes.
- **b.** Click AutoShapes on the Drawing toolbar.
- **c.** Click Tools, then click AutoShapes.
- **d.** Choose AutoShapes in the Picture dialog box.

Skills Review

1. Insert a graphic.
   a. Start Word.
   b. Open the document named WD H-2 and save it as "Theatre Graphics".
   c. Place the insertion point at the beginning of the document.
   d. Click Insert, click Picture, then click Clip Art.
   e. In the Screen Bean category, select the graphic that looks like someone scratching his head, then click OK.

2. Modify a graphic.
   a. Select the graphic and drag individual sizing handles until it is .75" wide and 1.25" tall.
   b. Click the Line Style button on the Picture toolbar, then select a 1 ½ pt line.
   c. Click the Format Picture button on the Picture toolbar.
   d. Click the Wrapping tab, click the Tight option, then Wrap to the Right option.
   e. In the Distance form text area, click the down arrow until 0" is shown in the Right box.
   f. Click the Color and Lines tab, click the Fill Color list arrow, select Lavender.
   g. Click OK.
   h. Position the graphic to the left of the bulleted list under the heading Still Can't Decide?

3. Create a custom graphic using AutoShapes.
   a. Click the Drawing button to display the drawing toolbar, if necessary, click Rectangle tool, and on the blank area of the document (if needed, create a blank page), draw a square by holding down [Shift] as you draw. The square should be about two inches on each side.
   b. Click the Fill Color list arrow and select a dark blue color.
   c. Click the Oval tool, and below the square, draw a circle by holding down [Shift] as you draw. The circle should be about two inches in diameter.
   d. Click the Fill Color list arrow and select a bright pink color.
   e. With the circle selected, drag it to place it over the square.
   f. Click AutoShapes on the Drawing toolbar, click Basic Shapes, then select the Diamond.
   g. Holding down [Shift] drag a diamond 2" by 2".
   h. Click the Fill Color list arrow and select a dark green color.
   i. Position the diamond over the circle.
   j. Click the Select Objects button and drag a rectangle around all three objects (if you cannot drag a rectangle around all of the objects, hold down [Shift] as you click each shape).
   k. Click Draw on the Drawing toolbar, then click Group.
   l. Hold down [Shift] and drag a corner sizing handle so that the graphic is about 1.5" on all sides.
   m. Double-click the graphic, click the Wrapping tab, click Tight, then click OK.
   n. Position the graphic to the left of the title.

4. Insert a Paint object.
   a. Place the insertion point near the middle of the page and click Insert on the menu bar, then click Object.
   b. Click the Create from File tab.
   c. Click the Browse button.
   d. Locate the student file called WD LOGO2, then click OK until you return to the document.
   e. Position the graphic to the left of the paragraph that is under the heading Othello, then size it attractively.
   f. Click the Text Wrapping button on the Picture toolbar, then click Tight.

5. **Create a callout.**
   a. Click the AutoShapes button on the Drawing toolbar, then click Callouts.
   b. Select Line Callout 3 (No Border), the third callout in the fourth row.
   c. Drag the callout down and to the right just under the shaded paragraph at the end of the document.
   d. Enter the text "Experience the classics in a modern setting!"
   e. Drag the sizing handles on the callout to fit just the text.
   f. Preview, save, and print the document, then close it.

Independent Challenges

1. As the communications coordinator for the annual Students for Peace Conference, you are responsible for designing attractive note paper for the staff. Begin by creating a new document and save it as "Peace Paper". Use Figure H-26 as a guide for how the completed note paper should look.

To complete this independent challenge:

1. Draw a rounded-rectangle 1.5" high and about 7" wide. (Hint: Use the Rounded Rectangle AutoShape found under Basic Shapes.) Position the rectangle just below the top of the page. Fill the rectangle with the sky blue color.
2. Insert the Dove graphic in the Animals category.
3. Size the graphic and position it so that it fits in the left side of the rectangle.
4. Using the Lines Autoshape, draw a long line down the left edge of the page. Format the line so it is 6 pts thick. Apply the sky blue color to the line.
5. Draw two horizontal lines near the bottom of the vertical line. Apply the color yellow to both these lines. Format them so that they are 6 pts thick. Send the upper yellow line behind the other lines.
6. Select all three lines and group them. Copy the grouped shapes and paste the graphic near the right edge of the page.
7. Select the second group of lines, click the Rotate or Flip command on the Draw button, then click Flip Horizontal. Position the lines so that the vertical line is aligned with right edge of the rectangle.
8. Preview, save, and print the document, then close it.

FIGURE H-26

2. As marketing communications specialist for The Magic Shop, a chain of stores selling magic supplies and costumes, you have decided to create your business card. Begin by creating a new document and saving it as "Magic Card". Use Figure H-27 as a guide for how the completed card should look.

To complete this independent challenge:

1. Type the company name, your name, an address, and a phone number, each on a separate line.
2. Format the text in the font you wish. Size the name of the shop at 14 pt. Right-align all the text.
3. Insert the graphic that looks like a magic hat in the Entertainment category.
4. Size the graphic to be about 1" by 1".
5. Apply tight and wrap to the right text wrapping. (Hint: Use the Format Picture dialog box, not the toolbar.)
6. Position the graphic to the right of the text so that the magic wand extends over the store name slightly.
7. Create a border around the graphic and text using the Rectangle tool. Modify the Rectangle so that it has no fill and 3 pt double-lines.
8. Preview, save, and print the document, then close it.

FIGURE H-27

3. As the marketing communications specialist at Sunset Travel, an international travel agency, you have been asked to design a new company logo that will adorn all company documents. You can begin your design using the Drawing toolbar. Create a new document and save it as "Sunset Logo". Use Figure H-28 as a guide for how the completed logo should look.

To complete this independent challenge:

1. Draw a rectangle 2" wide and 1" high.
2. Copy the rectangle and position it directly under the first shape.
3. Fill the bottom rectangle with the dark blue color.
4. Size the bottom rectangle so that it is only ¾" high. The top edge of the bottom rectangle should still be touching the bottom edge of the top rectangle.
5. Fill the top rectangle with the preset Late Sunset fill Effect. (Hint: Use the Gradient tab in the Fill Effects dialog box.)
6. Draw an oval about .5" across and fill it with the gold color.
7. Position the oval over the two rectangles.
8. Select the bottom rectangle and choose the Bring to Front option.
9. Group the three objects together.
10. Preview, save, and print the document, then close it.

FIGURE H-28

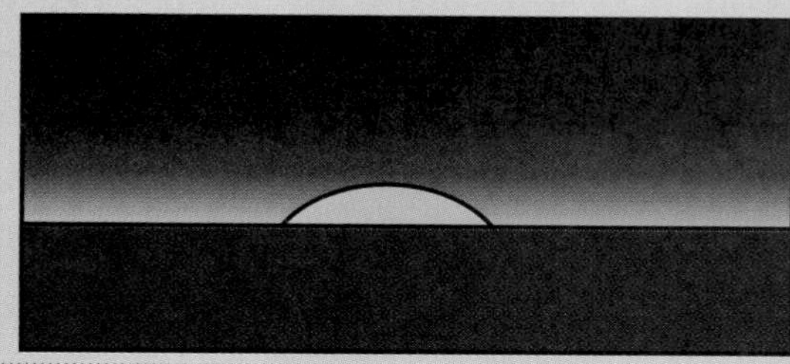

4. As communications director of the City of Boston's tourism department, you have recently written the text for a flyer for city visitors. Now you would like to add graphics to make the document look more attractive. Open the document called WD H-3 and save it as "Boston Graphics".

To complete this independent challenge:

1. Insert the graphic line Neighborhood. Size the graphic so that it is the width of the text on the page, not including margins, and position it above the title.
2. Insert the champagne bottle graphic, size it so that it is about 1" by 1".
3. Adjust the text wrapping around this graphic to be tight and to the right.
4. Position the graphic next to the heading Night Life.
5. Log on to the Internet and use your browser to search for information about Boston. Search for museums in the Boston area and add at least one name to the bulleted list in your document. If you can't locate a Boston museum, use your browser to go to http://www.course.com. From there, click Student Online Companions, click the link for this textbook, then click the Word link for Unit H. Insert another graphic of your choice (preferably a graphic that reflects the name of a museum you've identified). Size the graphic so that it is about one inch on each side and position it near the bulleted list.
6. Preview, save, and print the document, then close it.

Visual Workshop

Your work at the local state tourism office has taught you a great deal about what your state has to offer in the area of tourism and outdoor recreation. Every quarter you print a newsletter to promote exploration of your state. It's time to publish the Spring/Summer Issue. Use the draft document WD H-4 and save it as "Tourism Graphics". Figure H-29 serves as a guide for how your completed document should look. Use AutoShapes to create the triangle and sun graphics. You'll also insert the sailboat graphic from the transportation category.

FIGURE H-29

Spring/Summer Issue

EXPLORER

State Office of Tourism

Don't let summer pass you by without experiencing some of the special times only this season can bring. Set some time aside out of your busy schedule and give yourself a week or two to do some of these things you like to do best, or to explore someplace new. Plan a real vacation. Squeeze in a few long weekends of fun as well. It's never too early to make a few plans.

This issue or the Outdoor Explorer is full of ideas to help you on your way to a great vacation. For additional information to plan your trip or getaway. See the article on page 6 for details on the kinds of travel information services available in the north woods.

So put on those sandals, grab that oil, and kick back. Let the warmth of the summer sun melt away that tension and stress. Let this be one summer you'll never forget!

The first half of the newsletter features stories on what's new in the state, plus ideas on where to stay when you're traveling. On page 10 is a comprehensive, statewide Calendar of Events for April through August.

What's Inside

800-999-9999

In the local Metro Area

800-999-9000

From USA and Canada

For the most up to date info

Working
with Formulas and Functions

Objectives

- ► Create a formula with several operators
- ► Use names in a formula
- ► Generate multiple totals with AutoSum
- ► Use dates in calculations
- ► Build a conditional formula with the IF function
- ► Use statistical functions
- ► Calculate payments with the PMT function
- ► Display and print formula contents

Without formulas, Excel would simply be an electronic grid with text and numbers. Used with formulas, Excel becomes a powerful data analysis software tool. As you learn how to analyze data using different types of formulas, including those that call for functions, you will discover more ways to use Excel. In this unit, you will gain a further understanding of Excel formulas and learn how to build several Excel functions. Top management at Nomad Ltd has asked Evan Brillstein to analyze various company data. To do this, Evan will create several worksheets that require the use of formulas and functions. Because management is considering raising salaries for level-two managers, Evan's first task is to create a report that compares the payroll deductions and net pay for level-two managers before and after a proposed raise.

Excel 97

Creating a Formula with Several Operators

You can create formulas that contain a combination of cell references (for example, Z100 and B2), operators (for example, * [multiplication] and - [subtraction]), and values (for example, 99 or 1.56). You also can create a single formula that performs several calculations. If you enter a formula with more than one operator, Excel performs the calculations in a particular sequence based on algebraic rules called **precedence**; that is, Excel performs the operation(s) within the parentheses first, then performs the other calculations. See Table E-1. Evan has been given the gross pay and payroll deductions for the first payroll period and needs to complete his analysis. He also has preformatted, with the Comma style, any cells that are to contain values. Evan begins by entering a formula for net pay that subtracts the payroll deductions from gross pay.

QuickTip

If you make a mistake while building a formula, press [Esc] and begin again.

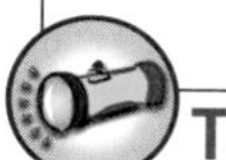

Trouble?

If you receive a message box indicating "Parentheses do not match," make sure you have included both a left and a right parenthesis.

1. **Start Excel if necessary, open the workbook titled XL E-1, then save it as Pay Info for L2 Mgrs. Next build the first part of the net pay formula in cell B11**
2. **Click cell B11, then type =B6-**
   Remember that you can type cell references in either uppercase or lowercase letters. (Excel automatically converts lowercase cell reference letters to uppercase.) You type the equal sign (=) to tell Excel that a formula follows, B6 to reference the cell containing the gross pay, and the minus sign (-) to indicate that the next entry will be subtracted from cell B6. Now, complete the formula.
3. **Type (B7+B8+B9+B10) then click the Enter button on the formula bar**
   The net pay for Payroll Period 1 appears in cell B11, as shown in Figure E-1. Because Excel performs the operations within parentheses first, you can control the order of calculations on the worksheet. (In this case, Excel sums the values in cells B7 through B10 first.) After the operations within the parentheses are completed, Excel performs the operations outside the parentheses. (In this case, Excel subtracts the total of range B7:B10 from cell B6.) Next, copy the formula across row 11.
4. **Copy the formula in cell B11 into cells C11:F11, then return to cell A1**
   The formula in cell B11 is copied to the range C11:F11 to complete row 11. See Figure E-2.
5. **Save the workbook**
   Evan is pleased with the formulas that calculate net pay totals. Next, he adds employee names to his worksheet.

TABLE E-1: Example formulas using parentheses and several operators

formula	order of precedence	calculated result
=36+(1+3)	Add 1 to 3; then add the result to 36	40
=(10-20)/10-5	Subtract 20 from 10; divide that by 10; then subtract 5	-6
=(10*2)*(10+2)	Multiply 10 by 2; add 10 to 2; then multiply the results	240

FIGURE E-1: Worksheet showing formula and result

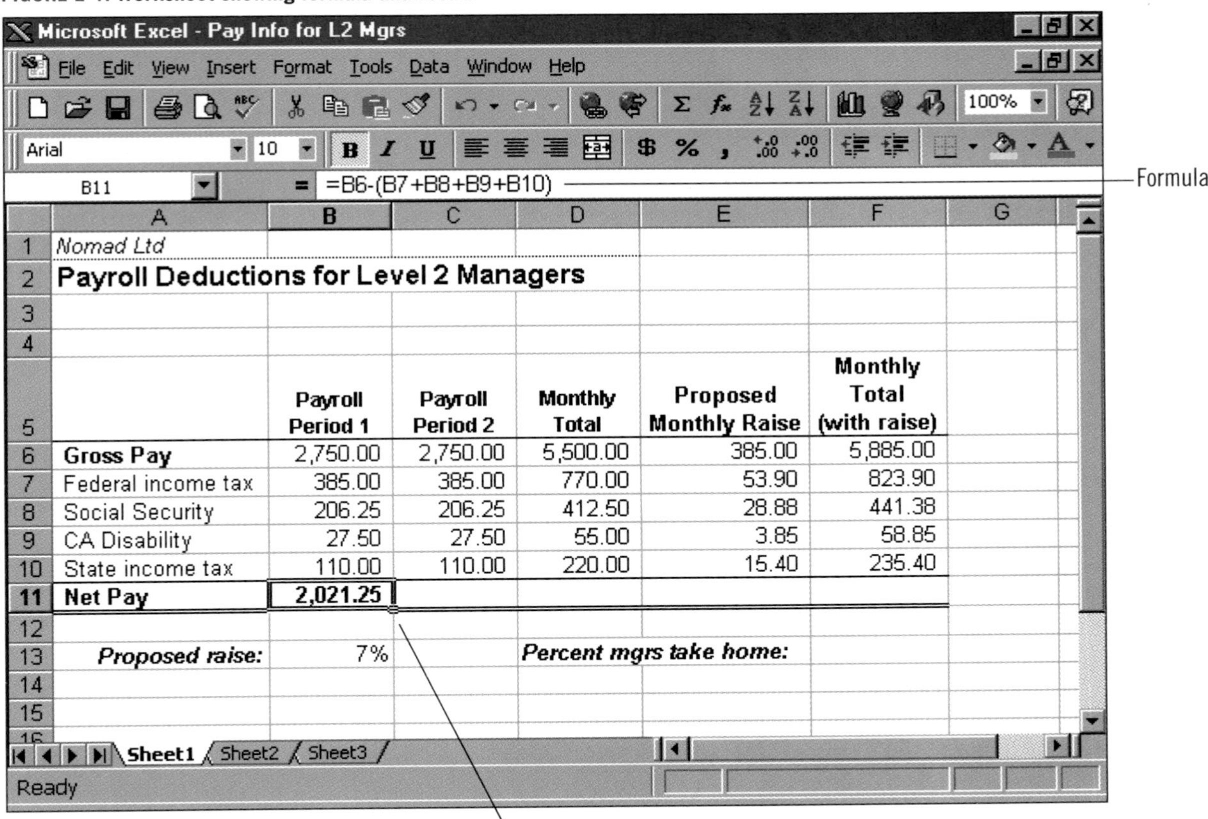

FIGURE E-2: Worksheet with copied formulas

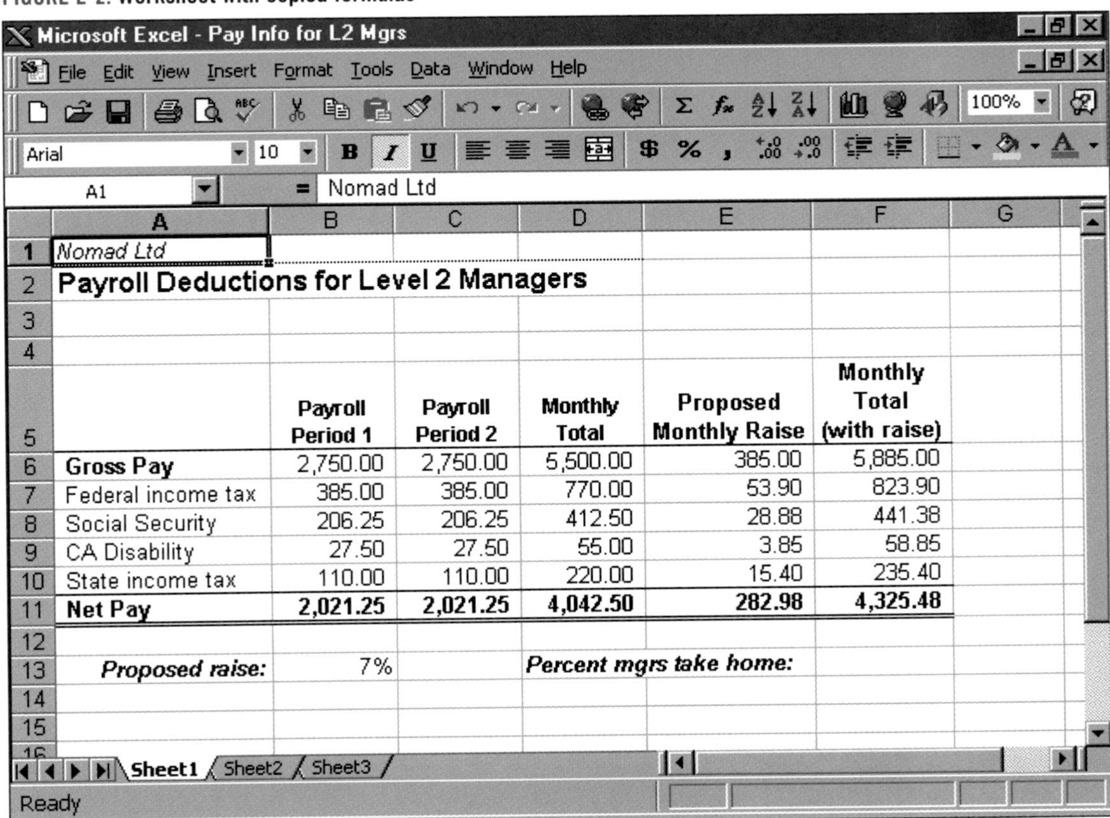

Excel 97

Using Names in a Formula

You can assign names to cells and ranges. Doing so reduces errors and makes a worksheet easier to follow. You also can use names in formulas. Using names in formulas facilitates formula building and provides a frame of reference for formula logic—the names make formulas easy to recognize and maintain. The formula Revenue - Cost, for example, is much easier to comprehend than the formula A2 - D3. You can produce a list of workbook names and their references at any time. Evan wants to include a formula that calculates the percentage of monthly gross pay the managers would actually take home (net pay) if a 7% raise is granted.

Steps

1. **Click cell F6, click the name box on the formula bar to select the active cell reference, type Gross_with_Raise, then press [Enter]**
   The name assigned to cell F6, Gross_with_Raise, appears in the name box. Note that you must type underscores instead of spaces between words. Cell F6 is now named Gross_with_Raise to refer to the monthly gross pay amount that includes the 7% raise. The name box displays as much of the name as fits (Gross_with_...). Next, name the net pay cell.
2. **Click cell F11, click the name box, type Net_with_Raise, then press [Enter]**
   Now that the two cells are named, you are ready to enter the formula.
3. **Click cell F13, type =Net_with_Raise/Gross_with_Raise, then click the Enter button ✓ on the formula bar (make sure you begin the formula with an equal sign)**
   The formula bar now shows the new formula, and the result 0.735 appears in the cell. See Figure E-3. If you add names to a worksheet after all the formulas have been entered, you must click Insert on the menu bar, click Name, click Apply, click the name or names, then click OK. Now format cell F13 as a percent.
4. **Format cell F13 using the Percent Style button % on the Formatting toolbar**
   Notice that the result shown in cell F13 (74%) is rounded to the nearest whole percent as shown in Figure E-3. Save and print the completed worksheet.
5. **Return to cell A1, then save and print the worksheet**
6. **Close the workbook**

QuickTip

To delete a name, click Insert on the menu bar, point to Name, then click Define. Select the name, click Delete, then click OK.

QuickTip

You can use the Label Ranges dialog box (Insert menu, Name submenu, Label command) to specify and name cells using column and row labels in your worksheet.

FIGURE E-3: Worksheet formula that includes cell names

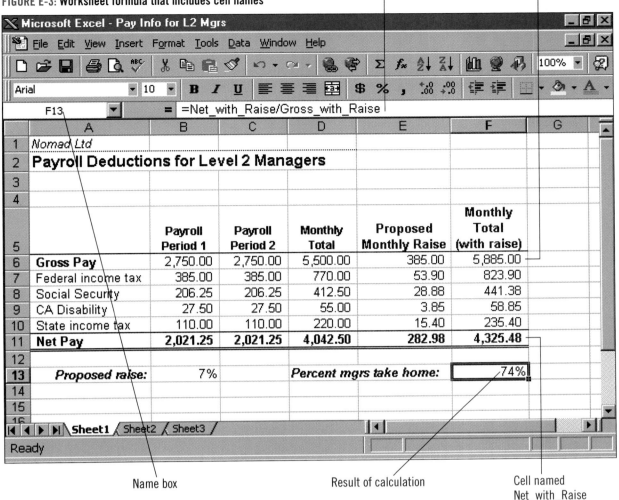

Formula with cell names

Cell named Gross_with_Raise

Microsoft Excel - Pay Info for L2 Mgrs

F13 =Net_with_Raise/Gross_with_Raise

	A	B	C	D	E	F	G
1	*Nomad Ltd*						
2	**Payroll Deductions for Level 2 Managers**						
3							
4							
5		**Payroll Period 1**	**Payroll Period 2**	**Monthly Total**	**Proposed Monthly Raise**	**Monthly Total (with raise)**	
6	**Gross Pay**	2,750.00	2,750.00	5,500.00	385.00	5,885.00	
7	Federal income tax	385.00	385.00	770.00	53.90	823.90	
8	Social Security	206.25	206.25	412.50	28.88	441.38	
9	CA Disability	27.50	27.50	55.00	3.85	58.85	
10	State income tax	110.00	110.00	220.00	15.40	235.40	
11	**Net Pay**	**2,021.25**	**2,021.25**	**4,042.50**	**282.98**	**4,325.48**	
12							
13	***Proposed raise:***	7%		***Percent mgrs take home:***		74%	
14							
15							

Sheet1 / Sheet2 / Sheet3

Ready

Name box

Result of calculation

Cell named Net_with_Raise

Excel 97

Producing a list of names

You might want to verify the names you have in a workbook and the cells they reference. To paste a list of names in a workbook, select a blank cell that has several blank cells beside and beneath it. Click Insert on the menu bar, point to Name, then click Paste. In the Paste Name dialog box, click Paste List. Excel produces a list that includes the sheet name and the cell or range the name identifies. See Figure E-4.

FIGURE E-4: Worksheet with pasted list of names

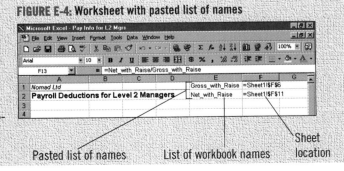

Microsoft Excel - Pay Info for L2 Mgrs

F13 =Net_with_Raise/Gross_with_Raise

	A	B	C	D	E	F	G
1	*Nomad Ltd*				Gross_with_Raise	=Sheet1!$F$6	
2	**Payroll Deductions for Level 2 Managers**				Net_with_Raise	=Sheet1!$F$11	
3							
4							

Pasted list of names

List of workbook names

Sheet location

Excel 97

Generating Multiple Totals with AutoSum

In most cases, the result of a function is a value derived from a calculation. Functions also can return results such as text, references, or other information about the worksheet. You enter a function, such as AVERAGE, directly into a cell; you can use the Edit Formula button; or, you can insert it with the Paste Function. You can use cell references, ranges, names, and formulas as arguments between the parentheses. As with other cell entries, you can cut, copy, and paste functions from one area of the worksheet to another and from one workbook to another. The most widely used Excel function, SUM, calculates worksheet totals and can be entered easily using the AutoSum button on the Standard toolbar. Evan's manager has asked him for a report summarizing annual bicycle sales. She wants the report to compare sales of competitor's brands to sales of Nomad Ltd's bikes. Evan has entered the data for units of bicycles sold. Now he needs to complete the worksheet totals.

1. **Open the workbook titled XL E-2, then save it as Bicycle Sales**
   You need to generate multiple totals with AutoSum. You can use the [Ctrl] key to select multiple, nonadjacent ranges.
2. **Select range B5:E10, press and hold [Ctrl], then select range B12:E14**
   To select nonadjacent cells, you must press and hold [Ctrl] while selecting the additional cells. Compare your selections with Figure E-5. Now, you are is ready to total the columns in the two selected ranges.
3. **Click the AutoSum button Σ on the Standard toolbar**
   When the selected range you want to sum (B5:E10 and B12:E14, in this example) includes a blank cell with data values above it, AutoSum enters the total in the blank cell. Next, generate annual totals in column F and grand totals in row 16.
4. **Select range B5:F16, then click Σ**
   Whenever the selected range you want to sum includes a blank cell in the bottom row or right column, AutoSum enters the total in the blank cell. In this case, Excel ignores the data values and totals only the SUM functions. Although Excel generates totals when you click the AutoSum button, it is a good idea to check the results.
5. **Click cell B16**
   The formula bar reads =SUM(B14,B10). See Figure E-6. When generating grand totals, Excel automatically references the cells containing SUM functions with a comma separator between cell references. Excel uses commas to separate multiple arguments in all functions, not just in SUM. You are ready to save and print your work.
6. **Save and print the worksheet, then close the workbook**

Trouble?

If you select the wrong combination of cells, simply click on a single cell and begin again.

FIGURE E-5: Selecting nonadjacent ranges using [Ctrl]

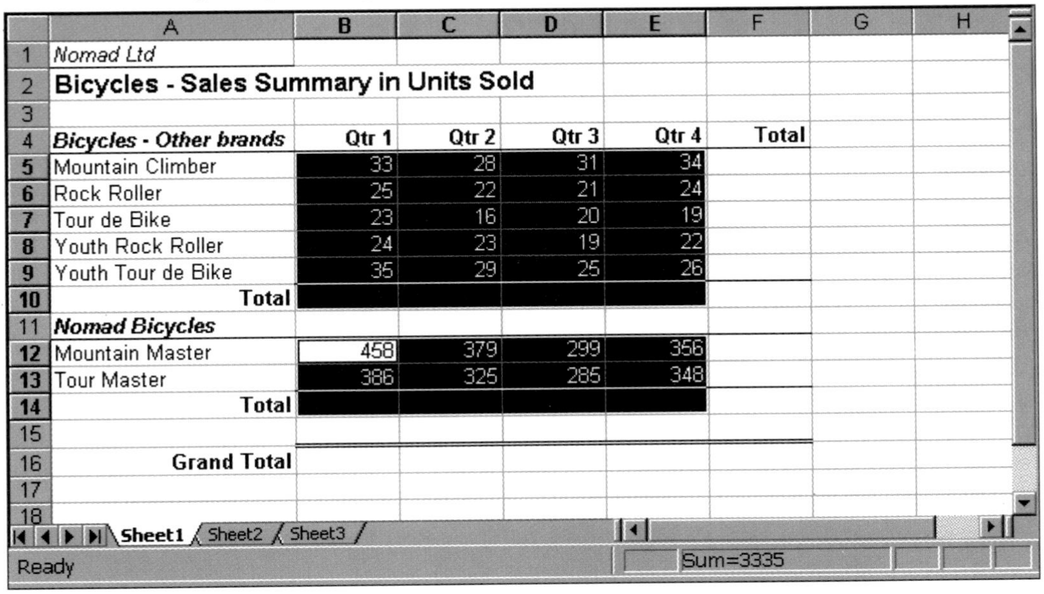

	A	B	C	D	E	F	G	H
1	*Nomad Ltd*							
2	**Bicycles - Sales Summary in Units Sold**							
3								
4	***Bicycles - Other brands***	**Qtr 1**	**Qtr 2**	**Qtr 3**	**Qtr 4**	**Total**		
5	Mountain Climber	33	28	31	34			
6	Rock Roller	25	22	21	24			
7	Tour de Bike	23	16	20	19			
8	Youth Rock Roller	24	23	19	22			
9	Youth Tour de Bike	35	29	25	26			
10	**Total**							
11	***Nomad Bicycles***							
12	Mountain Master	458	379	299	356			
13	Tour Master	386	325	285	348			
14	**Total**							
15								
16	**Grand Total**							
17								
18								

Sheet1 / Sheet2 / Sheet3

Ready Sum=3335

FIGURE E-6: Completed worksheet

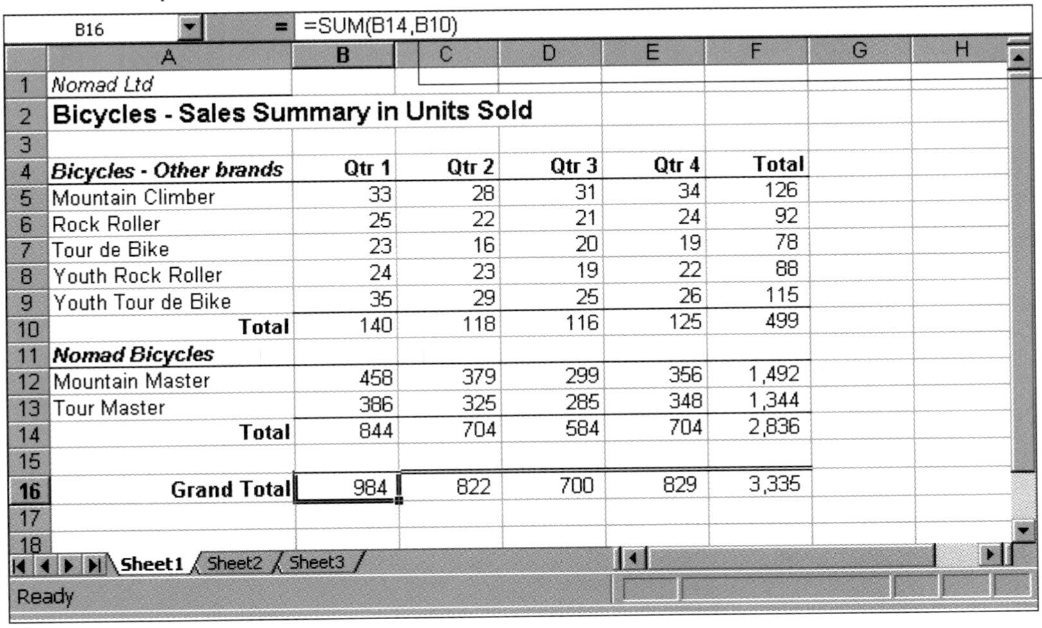

B16 = =SUM(B14,B10)

	A	B	C	D	E	F	G	H
1	*Nomad Ltd*							
2	**Bicycles - Sales Summary in Units Sold**							
3								
4	***Bicycles - Other brands***	**Qtr 1**	**Qtr 2**	**Qtr 3**	**Qtr 4**	**Total**		
5	Mountain Climber	33	28	31	34	126		
6	Rock Roller	25	22	21	24	92		
7	Tour de Bike	23	16	20	19	78		
8	Youth Rock Roller	24	23	19	22	88		
9	Youth Tour de Bike	35	29	25	26	115		
10	**Total**	140	118	116	125	499		
11	***Nomad Bicycles***							
12	Mountain Master	458	379	299	356	1,492		
13	Tour Master	386	325	285	348	1,344		
14	**Total**	844	704	584	704	2,836		
15								
16	**Grand Total**	984	822	700	829	3,335		
17								
18								

Sheet1 / Sheet2 / Sheet3

Ready

Comma used to separate multiple arguments

CLUES TO USE

Quick calculations with AutoCalculate

To check a total quickly without entering a formula, just select the range you want to sum, and the answer appears in the status bar next to SUM=. You also can perform other quick calculations, such as averaging or finding the minimum value in a selection. To do this, right-click the AutoCalculate area in the status bar and select from the list of options. The option you select remains in effect and in the status bar until you make another selection. See Figure E-7.

FIGURE E-7: Using AutoCalculate

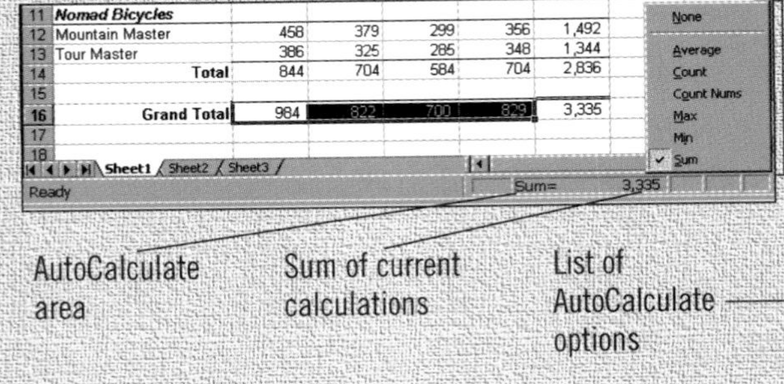

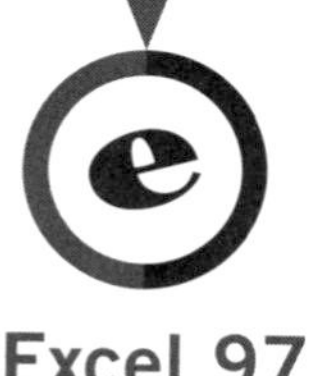

Excel 97

Using Dates in Calculations

If you enter dates in a worksheet so that Excel recognizes them as dates, you can sort (arrange) the dates and perform date calculations. For example, you can calculate the number of days between your birth date and today, which is the number of days you have been alive. Commonly used date formats that Excel recognizes are listed in Table E-2. When you enter a date in any of these formats, Excel considers the entry a date function, converts the date to a serial date number, and stores that number in the cell. A date's converted serial date is the number of days to that date. The serial date of January 1, 1900; for example, is 1; the serial date of January 1, 1998 is 35431. Evan's next task is to complete the Open Accounts Receivable worksheet for Adventure Tours in the Southwest. He remembers to enter the worksheet dates in a format that Excel recognizes, so that he can take advantage of date calculation.

Steps

1. Open the workbook titled **XL E-3**, then save it as **Southwest Tour Receivables** to the appropriate folder on your Student Disk
   Begin by entering the current date, the date that is critical to worksheet calculations.
2. Click cell **C4**, type **9/1/98**, then press **[Enter]**
   The date appears in cell C4 just as you typed it. You want to enter a formula that calculates the invoice due date, which is 30 days from the invoice date. The formula adds 30 days to the invoice date.
3. Click cell **F7**, type **=**, click cell **B7**, type **+30**, then click the **Enter button** on the formula bar
   Excel calculates the result by converting the 8/1/98 invoice date to a serial date number, adding 30 to it, then automatically formatting the result as a date. See Figure E-8. Because this same formula will calculate the due date for each invoice, you can copy the formula down the column using the fill handle.
4. Copy the formula in cell F7 into cells **F8:F13**
   Cell referencing causes the copied formula to contain the appropriate cell references. You are pleased at how easily Excel calculated the invoice due dates. Now you are ready to enter the formula that calculates the age of each invoice. You do this by subtracting the invoice date from the current date. Because each invoice age formula must refer to the current date, you must make cell C4, the current date cell, an absolute reference in the formula.
5. Click cell **G7**, type **=**, click cell **C4**, press **[F4]** to add the absolute reference symbols ($), type **-**, click **B7**, then click
   The formula bar displays the formula $C$4-B7. The numerical result, 31, appears in cell G7 because there are 31 days between 8/1/98 and 9/1/98. Again, copy the formula down the column.
6. Click cell **G7**, drag the fill handle to select range **G7:G13**, then press **[Ctrl][Home]** to deselect the range
   The age of each invoice appears in column G, as shown in Figure E-9.
7. Click the **Save button** on the Standard toolbar

QuickTip

You also can perform time calculations in Excel. For example, you can enter an employee's starting time and ending time, then calculate how many hours and minutes he or she worked. You must enter time in a format that Excel recognizes; for example, 1:35 PM (h:mm AM/PM).

QuickTip

If you perform date calculations and the intended numeric result displays as a date, format the cell(s) using a number format.

FIGURE E-8: Worksheet with formula for invoice due date

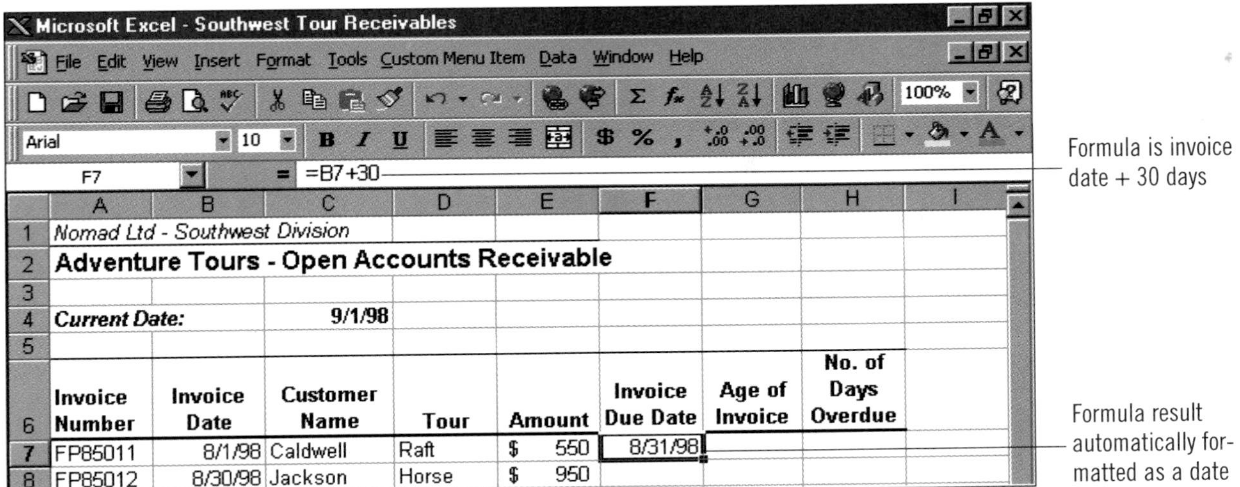

FIGURE E-9: Worksheet with copied formulas

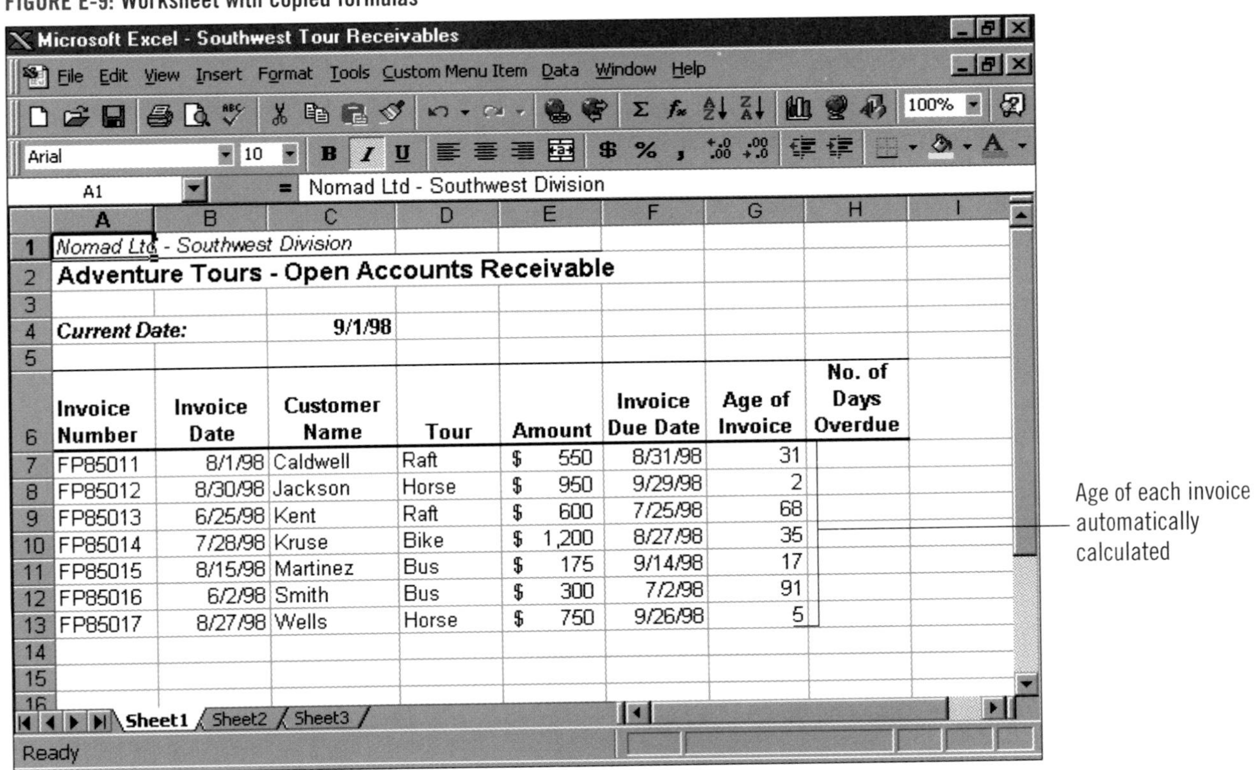

TABLE E-2: Commonly used date formats

format	example
M/d/yy	1/1/98
d-mmm-yy	1-Jan-98
d-mmm	1-Jan
Mmm-yy	Jan-98

Excel 97

Building a Conditional Formula with the IF Function

You can build a conditional formula using an IF function. A **conditional formula** is one that makes calculations based on stated conditions. For example, you can build a formula to calculate bonuses based on a person's performance rating. If a person is rated a 5 (the stated condition) on a scale of 1 to 5, with 5 being the highest rating, he or she receives 10% of his or her salary as a bonus; otherwise, there is no bonus. When the condition is a question that can be answered with a true or false response, Excel calls this stated condition a **logical test**. The IF function has three parts, separated by commas: a condition or logical test, an action to take if the logical test or condition is true, then an action to take if the logical test or condition is false. Another way of expressing this is: IF(test_cond,do_this,else_this). Translated into an Excel IF function, the formula to calculate bonuses would look something like: IF(Rating=5,Salary*0.10,0). The translation would be: If the rating equals 5, multiply the salary by 0.10 (the decimal equivalent of 10%), then place the result in the selected cell. If the rating does not equal 5, place a 0 in the cell. When entering the logical test portion of an IF statement, typically you use some combination of the comparison operators listed in Table E-3. Evan is almost finished with the worksheet. To complete it, he needs to use an IF function that calculates the number of days each invoice is overdue.

Steps 1 2 3 4

1. **Click cell H7**
   The cell pointer is now positioned where the result of the function will appear. You want the formula to calculate the number of days overdue as follows: If the age of the invoice is greater than 30, calculate the days overdue (Age of Invoice - 30), and place the result in cell H7; otherwise, place a 0 (zero) in the cell. The formula will include the IF function and cell references.
2. **Type =IF(G7>30, (make sure to type the comma)**
   You have entered the first part of the function, the logical test. Notice that you used the symbol for greater than (>). So far, the formula reads: If Age of Invoice is greater than 30 (in other words, if the invoice is overdue). Next, tell Excel the action to take if the invoice is over 30 days old.
3. **Type G7-30, (make sure to type the comma)**
   This part of the formula, between the first and second commas, is what you want Excel to do if the logical test is true; that is, if the age of the invoice is over 30. Continuing the translation of the formula, this part means: Take the Age of Invoice value and subtract 30. Finally, tell Excel the action to take if the logical test is false (that is, if the age of the invoice is 30 days or less).
4. **Type 0, then click the Enter button on the formula bar (you do not have to type The) to complete the formula**
   The formula is complete and the result, 1 (the number of days overdue), appears in cell H7. See Figure E-10. Next, Copy the formula.
5. **Copy the formula in cell H7 into cells H8:H13**
   Compare your results with Figure E-11, then save and print your work.
6. **Save, then print the workbook**

FIGURE E-10: **Worksheet with IF function**

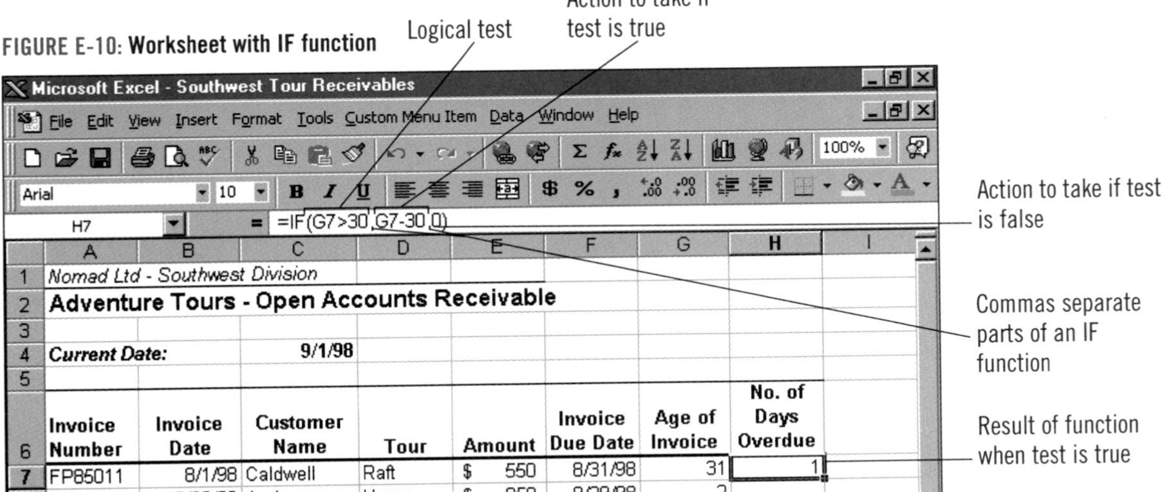

FIGURE E-11: **Completed worksheet**

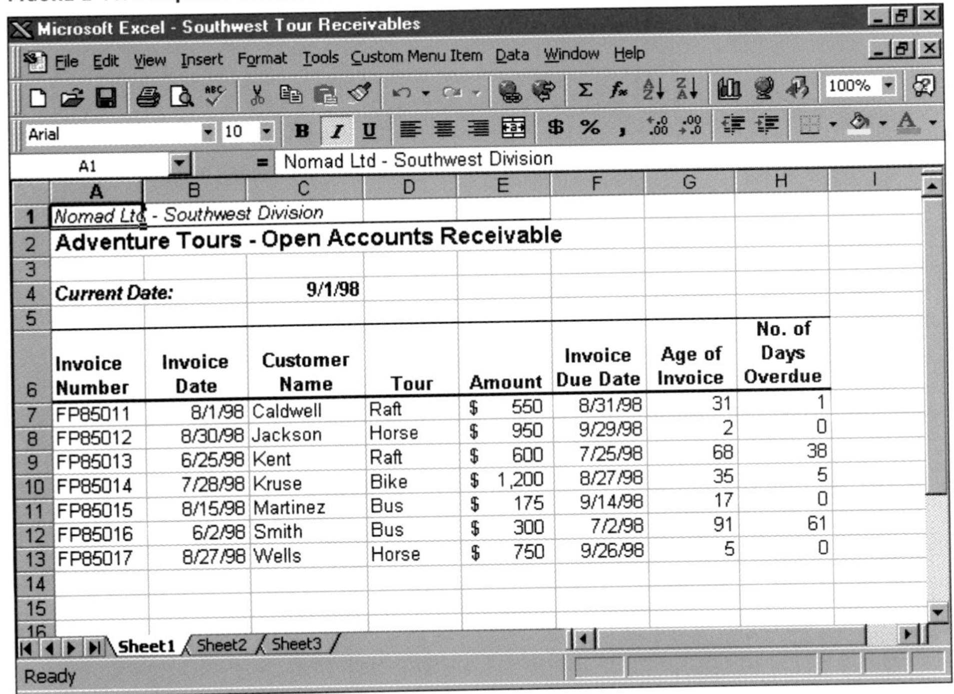

TABLE E-3: **Comparison operators**

operator	function
<	Less than
>	Greater than
=	Equal to
<=	Less than or equal to
>=	Greater than or equal to
<>	Not equal to

Excel 97

Excel 97

Using Statistical Functions

Excel offers several hundred worksheet functions. A small group of these functions calculates statistics such as averages, minimum values, and maximum values. See Table E-4 for a brief description of these commonly used functions. 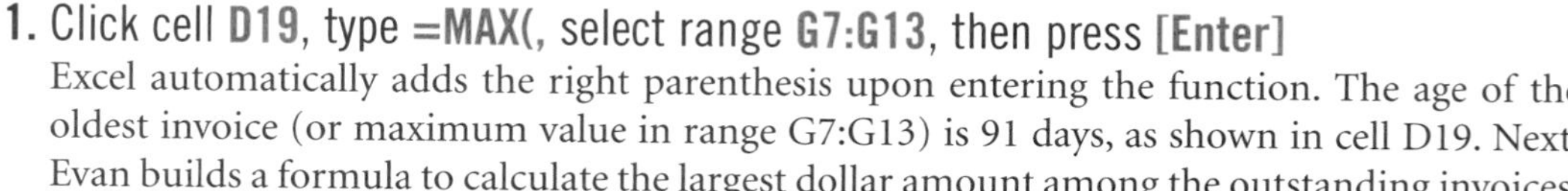 Evan's manager has asked him to present detailed information about open accounts receivable. To do this, Evan adds some statistical functions to the worksheet. He begins by using the MAX function to calculate the maximum value in a range.

Steps

Trouble?

If you have difficulty clicking cells or ranges when you build formulas, try scrolling to reposition the worksheet area until all participating cells are visible.

1. Click cell **D19**, type **=MAX(**, select range **G7:G13**, then press **[Enter]**
   Excel automatically adds the right parenthesis upon entering the function. The age of the oldest invoice (or maximum value in range G7:G13) is 91 days, as shown in cell D19. Next, Evan builds a formula to calculate the largest dollar amount among the outstanding invoices.
2. In cell D20, type **=MAX(**, select range **E7:E13**, then press **[Enter]**
   Note that the largest amount owed is $1,200, as shown in cell D20. Now you can use the MIN function to find the smallest dollar amount and the age of the newest invoice.
3. In cell D21, type **=MIN(**, select range **E7:E13**, then press **[Enter]**; in cell D22, type **=MIN(**, select range **G7:G13**, then press **[Enter]**
   The smallest dollar amount owed is $175, as shown in cell D21, and the newest invoice is two days old. In the next step, you use a function to count the number of invoices by counting the number of entries in column A.

QuickTip

If you don't see the desired function in the Function name list, scroll to display more function names.

4. In cell D23, type =, then click the **Paste Function button** on the Standard toolbar to open the Paste Function dialog box
5. Under Function category, click **Statistical**, then under Function name click **COUNT**
   After selecting the function name, notice that the description of the COUNT function reads, "Counts the number of cells that contain numbers . . ." Because the invoice numbers (for example, FP85011) are considered text entries, not numerical entries, the COUNT function will not work. There is another function, COUNTA, that counts the number of cells that are not empty and therefore can be used to count the number of invoice number entries.
6. Under Function name, click **COUNTA**, then click **OK**
   Excel automatically opens the Formula Palette and automatically references the range that is directly above the active cell as the first argument (in this case, range D19:D22, which is not the range you want to count). See Figure E-12. You need to select the correct range of invoice numbers. Because the desired invoice numbers are not visible, you need to collapse the dialog box so that you can select the correct range.
7. With the Value1 argument selected in the Formula Palette, click the Value1 **Collapse Dialog Box button**, select range **A7:A13** in the worksheet, click the **Redisplay Dialog Box button**, then click **OK**
   Compare your worksheet with Figure E-13.
8. Save, print, then close the workbook

FIGURE E-12: Formula Palette showing COUNTA function

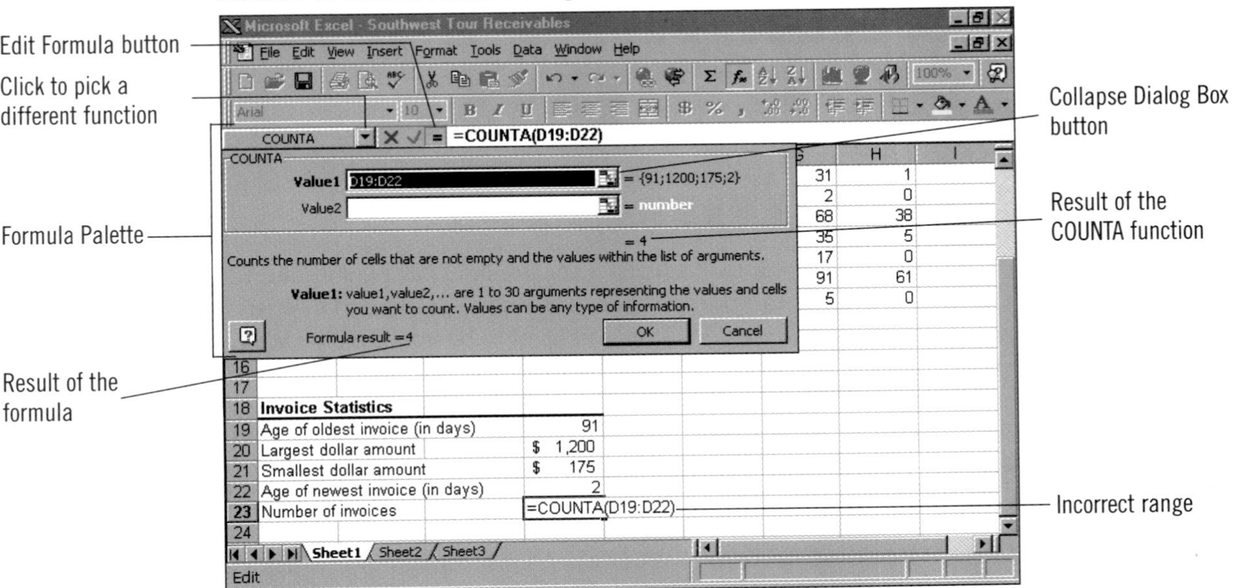

FIGURE E-13: Worksheet with invoice statistics

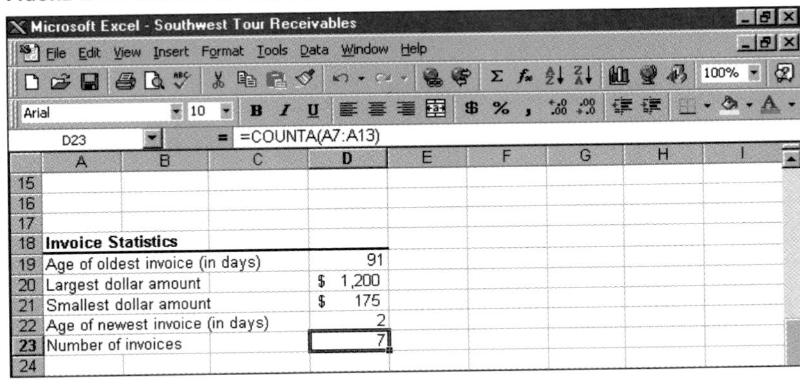

TABLE E-4: Commonly used statistical functions

function	worksheet action
AVERAGE	Calculates an average value
COUNT	Counts the number of values
COUNTA	Counts the number of nonblank entries
MAX	Finds the largest value
MIN	Finds the smallest value
SUM	Calculates a total

Using the Formula Palette to enter and edit formulas

When you use the Paste Function to build a formula, the Formula Palette displays the name and description for the function and each of its arguments, the current result of the function, and the current result of the entire formula. You also can use the Formula Palette to edit functions in formulas. To open the Formula Palette from either a blank cell or one containing a formula, click the Edit Formula button on the formula bar.

Excel 97

Calculating Payments with the PMT Function

PMT is a financial function that calculates the periodic payment amount for money borrowed. For example, if you want to borrow money to buy a car, the PMT function can calculate your monthly payment on the loan. Let's say you want to borrow $15,000 at 9% interest and pay the loan off in five years. Excel's PMT function can tell you that your monthly payment will be $311.38. The parts of the PMT function are: PMT(rate, nper, pv, fv, type). See Figure E-14 for an illustration of a PMT function that calculates the monthly payment in the car loan example.

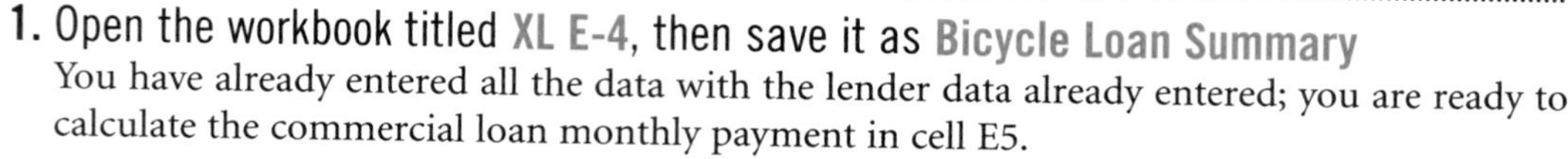

For several months, the management at Nomad Ltd has been planning the development of a new mountain bike. Evan's manager has asked him to obtain quotes from three different lenders on borrowing $25,000 to begin developing the new product. He obtained loan quotes from a commercial bank, a venture capitalist, and an investment banker. Now Evan can summarize the information using Excel's PMT function.

1. Open the workbook titled **XL E-4**, then save it as **Bicycle Loan Summary**
   You have already entered all the data with the lender data already entered; you are ready to calculate the commercial loan monthly payment in cell E5.
2. Click cell **E5**, type **=PMT(C5/12,D5,B5)** (make sure you type the commas); then click the **Enter button** on the formula bar
   Note that the payment of ($543.56) in cell E5 is a negative amount. (It appears in red on a color monitor.) Excel displays the result of a PMT function as a negative value to reflect the negative cash flow the loan represents to the borrower. You must divide the annual interest by 12 because you are calculating monthly, not annual, payments. Because you want to show the monthly payment value as a positive number, you can convert the loan amount to a negative number by placing a minus sign in front of the cell reference.
3. Edit cell E5 so it reads **=PMT(C5/12,D5,-B5)**, then click
   A positive value of $543.56 now appears in cell E5. See Figure E-15. Now, copy the formula to generate the monthly payments for the other loans.
4. Click cell **E5**, then drag the fill handle to select range **E5:E7**
   A monthly payment of $818.47 for the venture capitalist loan appears in cell E6. A monthly payment of $1,176.84 for the investment banker loan appears in cell E7. You are surprised that the monthly payments vary so much. You will not know the entire financial picture until you take one more step and calculate the total payments and total interest for each lender.
5. Click cell **F5**, type **=E5*D5**, then press **[Tab]**; in cell G5, type **=F5-B5**, then click
6. Copy the formulas in cells F5:G5 into cells **F6:G7**
   You can experiment with different interest rates, loan amounts, or terms for any one of the lenders; the PMT function generates a new set of values automatically. Compare your results to Figure E-16.
7. Save the workbook, then print the worksheet

QuickTip

It is important to be consistent about the units you use for *rate* and *nper*. If, for example, you express *nper* as the number of *monthly* payments, then you must express the interest rate as a *monthly* rate, not an annual rate.

FIGURE E-14: **Example of PMT function for car loan**

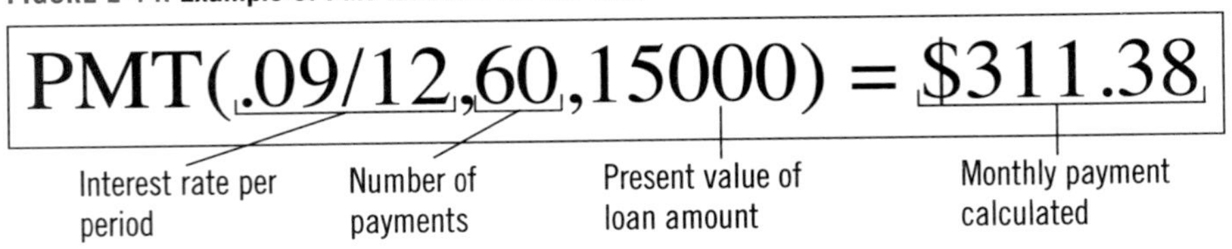

FIGURE E-15: **PMT function calculating monthly loan payment**

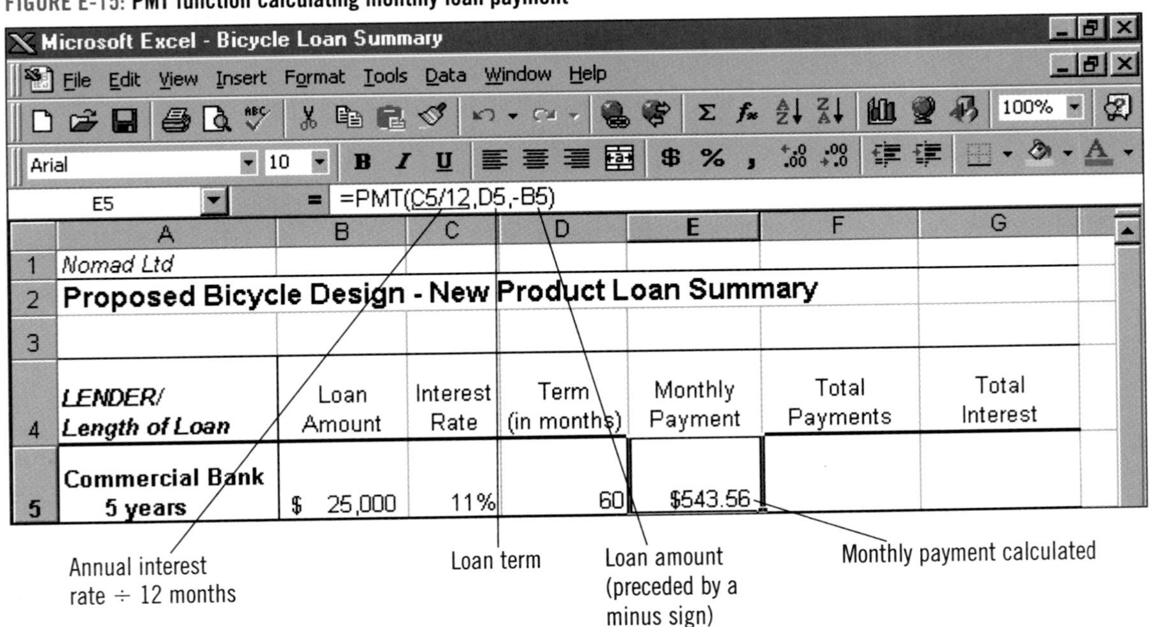

FIGURE E-16: **Completed worksheet**

Microsoft Excel - Bicycle Loan Summary

A1 = Nomad Ltd

Nomad Ltd

Proposed Bicycle Design - New Product Loan Summary

LENDER/ Length of Loan	Loan Amount	Interest Rate	Term (in months)	Monthly Payment	Total Payments	Total Interest
Commercial Bank 5 years	$ 25,000	11%	60	$543.56	$ 32,613.63	$ 7,613.63
Venture Capitalist 3 years	$ 25,000	11%	36	$818.47	$ 29,464.85	$ 4,464.85
Investment Banker 2 years	$ 25,000	12%	24	$1,176.84	$ 28,244.08	$ 3,244.08

Sheet1 / Sheet2 / Sheet3

Ready

Excel 97

Excel 97

Displaying and Printing Formula Contents

Excel usually displays the result of formula calculations in the worksheet area and displays formula contents for the active cell in the formula bar. However, you can instruct Excel to display the formulas directly in the worksheet locations in which they were entered. You can document worksheet formulas in this way: by first displaying the formulas then printing them. These formula printouts are valuable paper-based worksheet documentation. Because formulas are often longer than their corresponding values, landscape orientation is the best choice for printing formulas. Evan is ready to produce a formula printout to submit with the worksheet.

1. Click **Tools** on the menu bar, click **Options**, then click the **View tab**
   The View tab of the Options dialog box appears, as shown in Figure E-17.
2. Under Window options, click the **Formulas** check box to select it, then click **OK**
   The columns have widened and retain their original formats. You need to scroll horizontally to see that the column widths adjust automatically to accommodate the formulas.
3. Scroll horizontally to bring columns D through G into view
   Instead of formula results appearing in the cells, Excel shows the actual formulas. See Figure E-18. In order to see how this worksheet will print, you can preview it.
4. Click the **Print Preview button** on the Standard toolbar
   The status bar reads Preview: Page 1 of 3, indicating that the worksheet will print on three pages. You want to print it on one page and include the row number and column letter headings. You can do this by selecting several Page Setup options.
5. Click the **Setup button** in the Print Preview window, then click the **Page tab**
   Select the Landscape orientation and the Fit to scaling options.
6. Under Orientation, click the **Landscape option button**; then under Scaling, click the **Fit to option button**
   Selecting Landscape instructs Excel to print the worksheet sideways on the page. The Fit to option ensures that the document is printed on a single page. Finally, select the Sheet tab to turn on the printing of row number and column letters.
7. Click the **Sheet tab**, under Print click the **Row and Column Headings check box**, click **OK**, then position the Zoom pointer over column A and click
   The worksheet formulas now appear on a single page, in landscape orientation, with row (number) and column (letter) headings. See Figure E-19. Notice that the contents of cell A2 are slightly hidden.
8. Click the **Print button** in the Print Preview window, then click **OK**
   After you retrieve the printout, you want to return the worksheet to display formula results. You can do this by pressing [Ctrl][`] (grave accent mark) to toggle between displaying formula results and displaying formula contents.
9. Press **[Ctrl][`]** to re-display formula results, save and close the workbook, then exit Excel

QuickTip

All Page Setup options—such as landscape orientation, fit to scaling, and printing row and column headings—apply to the active worksheet and are saved with the workbook.

FIGURE E-17: View tab of the Options dialog box

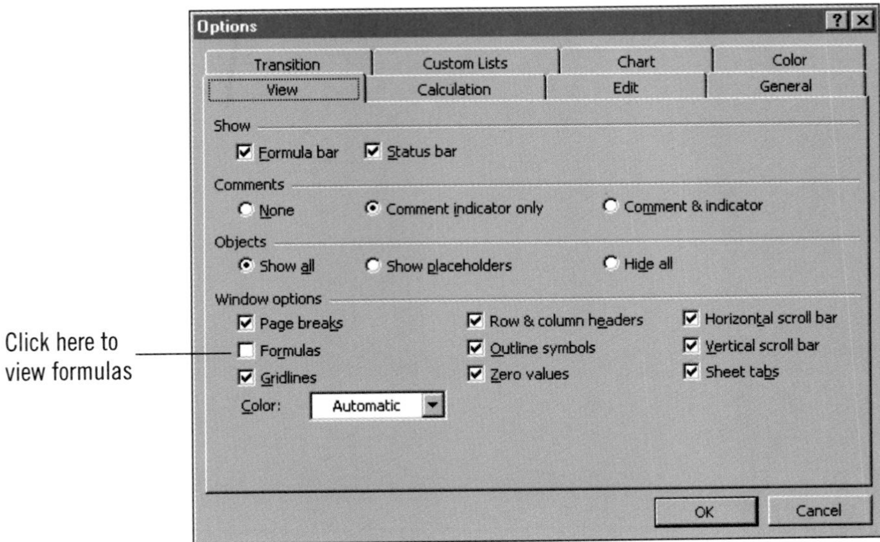

FIGURE E-18: Worksheet with formulas visible

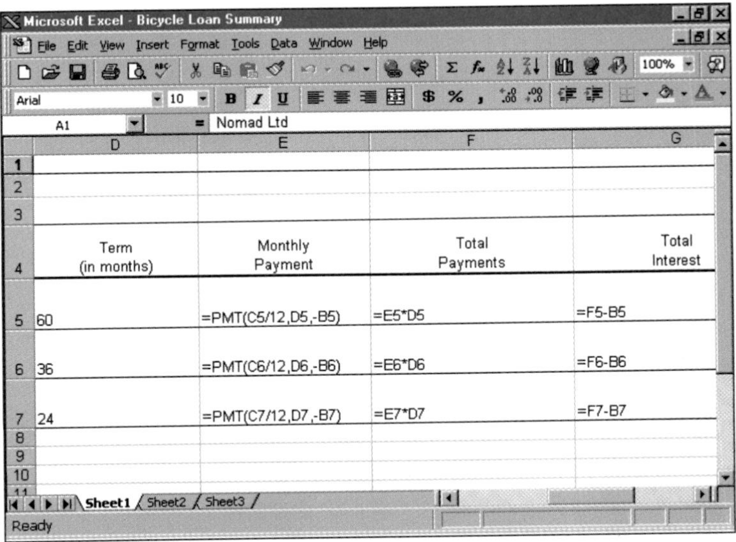

FIGURE E-19: Print Preview window

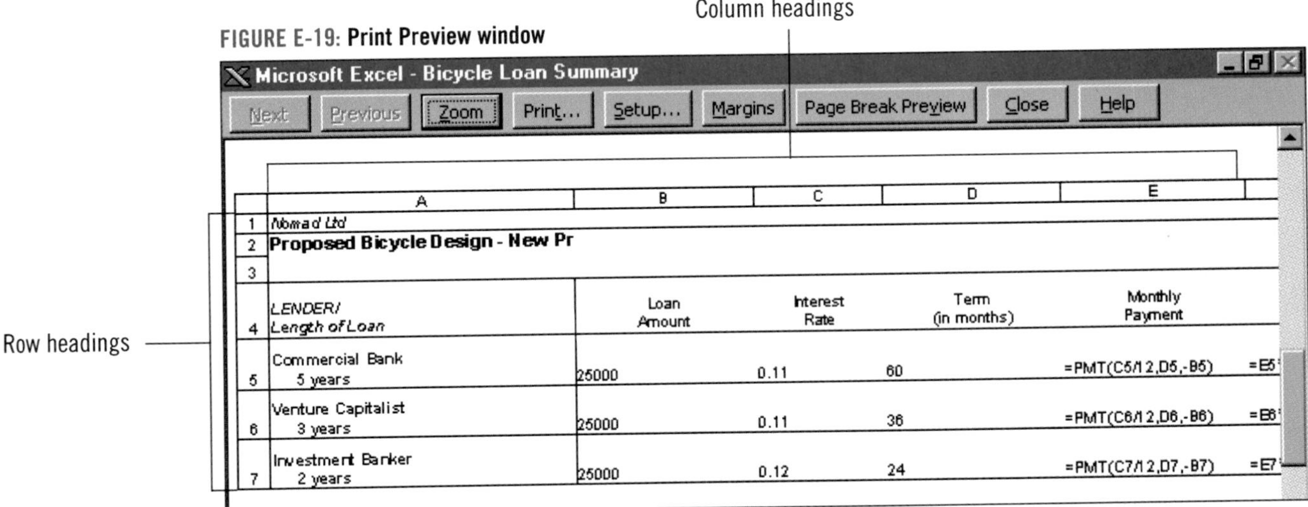

Practice

► Concepts Review

Label each of the elements of the Excel screen shown in Figure E-20.

FIGURE E-20

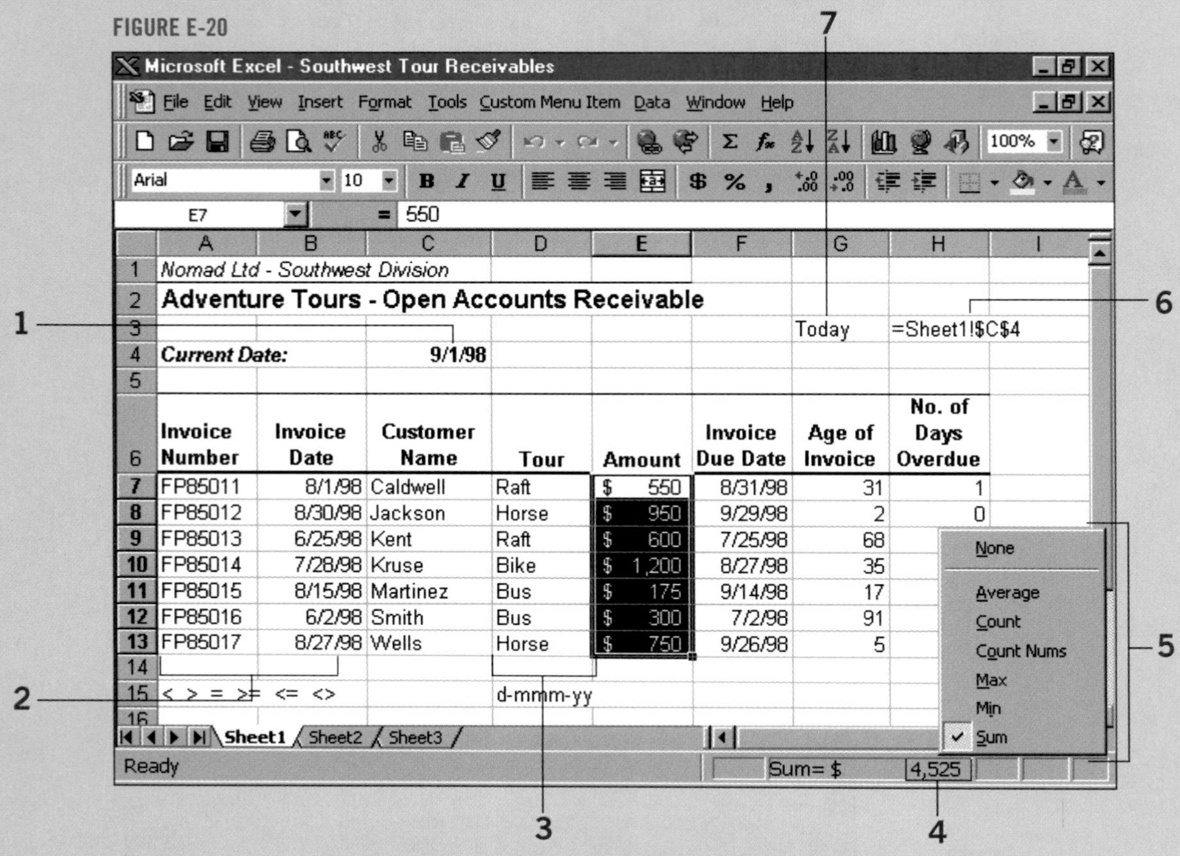

Match each of the terms with the statement that best describes its function.

8. Parentheses
9. COUNTA
10. test_cond
11. COUNT
12. pv

a. Part of the IF function in which the conditions are stated
b. Function used to count the number of numerical entries
c. Part of the PMT function that represents the loan amount
d. Function used to count the number of nonblank entries
e. Symbols used in formulas to control formula calculation order

Select the best answer from the list of choices.

13. **To generate a positive payment value when using the PMT function, you must**
    a. Enter the function arguments as positive values.
    b. Enter the function arguments as negative values.
    c. Enter the amount being borrowed as a negative value.
    d. Enter the interest rate divisor as a negative value.

14. **When you enter the rate and nper arguments in a PMT function**
    a. Multiply both units by 12.
    b. Be consistent in the units used.
    c. Divide both values by 12.
    d. Use monthly units instead of annual units.

15. **To express conditions such as less than or equal to, you can use a(n)**
    a. IF function.
    b. Comparison operator.
    c. AutoCalculate formula.
    d. PMT function.

► Skills Review

1. **Create a formula with several operators.**
    a. Open workbook XL E-5, and save it as "Annual Bonuses".
    b. In cell C15, enter the formula C13+(C14*7).

2. **Use names in a formula.**
    a. Name cell C13 "Dept_Bonus".
    b. Name cell C14 "Project_Bonus".
    c. In cell E4, enter the formula Dept_Bonus*D4+Project_Bonus.
    d. Copy formula in cell E4 into the range E5:E10.
    e. Format range E4:E10 with the Comma Style button.
    f. In cell F4, enter a formula that sums C4 and E4.
    g. Copy the formula in cell F4 into the range F5:F10.
    h. Return to cell A1, then save your work.

3. **Generate multiple totals with AutoSum.**
    a. Select range E11:F11.
    b. Enter the totals using AutoSum.
    c. Format range E11:F11 using the Currency Style button.
    d. Save your work, preview, then print the worksheet.

4. **Use dates in calculations.**
    a. Make the Merit Pay sheet active.
    b. In cell D6, enter the formula B6+183.
    c. Copy the formula in cell D6 into the range D7:D14.
    d. Save your work.

5. **Build a conditional formula with the IF function.**
   a. In cell F6, enter the formula IF(C6=5,E6*0.05,0).
   b. Copy the formula in cell F6 into the range F7:F14.
   c. Save your work.

6. **Use statistical functions.**
   a. In cell C19, enter a function to calculate the average of range E6:E14.
   b. In cell C20, enter a function to calculate the largest value in range F6:F14.
   c. In cell C21, enter a function to calculate the smallest value in range C6:C14.
   d. In cell C22, enter a function to calculate the number of entries in range A6:A14.
   e. Save, preview, then print this worksheet.

7. **Calculate payments with the PMT function.**
   a. Make the Loan sheet active.
   b. In cell B9, enter the formula PMT(B5/12,B6,-B4).
   c. In cell B10, enter the formula B9*B6.
   d. AutoFit column B, if necessary.
   e. In cell B11, enter the formula B10-B4.
   f. Save, then print the worksheet.

8. **Display and print formula contents.**
   a. Click Tools on the menu bar, click Options, then click the View tab, if necessary.
   b. Turn formulas on, then click OK.
   c. Adjust the column widths as necessary.
   d. Save, preview, and print this worksheet in landscape orientation with the row and column headings.
   e. Close the workbook.

Independent Challenges

1. As the store manager of Heavenly Cones Ice Cream Parlor, you have been asked to create a worksheet that totals the monthly sales of all the stores products. Your monthly report should include the following:

- Sales totals for the current month for each product
- Sales totals for the last month for each product
- The percent change in sales from last month to this month

To document the report further, you decide to include a printout of the worksheet formulas.

To complete this independent challenge:

1. Open the workbook titled XL E-6, then save it as "Heavenly Sales" to the appropriate folder on your Student Disk.
2. Complete the headings for weeks 2 through 4. Enter the weekly totals and the current month's totals, then copy them where appropriate. Calculate the percent change in sales from last month to this month. (*Hint:* The formula in words would be (Current Month-Last Month)/Last Month.) After you enter the percent change formula for regular ice cream, copy the formula down the column.
3. Save, preview, then print the worksheet on a single page. If necessary, print in landscape orientation. If you make any page setup changes, save the worksheet again.
4. Display and print the worksheet formulas with row and column headings. Again, print the formulas on one page.
5. Close the workbook without saving the changes for displaying formulas.
6. Submit your printouts.

2. You are an auditor with a certified public accounting firm. High Rollers, a manufacturer of skating products including roller skates and skateboards, has contacted you to audit its financial records. They have asked you to assist them in preparing their year-end sales summary. Specifically, they want to add expenses and show the percent each expense category represents of annual expenses. They also want to show what percent each expense category represents of annual sales. You should include a formula calculating the difference between sales and expenses and another formula calculating expenses divided by sales. The expense categories and their respective dollar amounts are as follows: Building Lease $36,000; Equipment $235,000; Office $24,000; Salary $350,000; Taxes $315,000. Use these expense amounts to prepare the year-end sales and expenses summary for High Rollers.

To complete this independent challenge:

1. Open the workbook titled XL E-7, then save it as "High Rollers Sales".
2. Name the cell containing the formula for annual expenses "Annual_Expenses". Use the name Annual_Expenses in the first formula calculating percent of annual expenses. Copy this formula as appropriate. Make sure to include a formula that sums all the values for percent of annual expenses, which should equal 1 or 100%.

3. Enter a formula calculating what percent of annual sales each expense category represents. Use the name Annual_Sales in the formula. Enter formulas calculating annual sales minus annual expenses and expenses divided by sales using only the names Annual_Sales and Annual_Expenses. Add formulas for totals as appropriate.
4. Format the cells using the Currency, Percent, or Comma style. Widen the columns as necessary to increase readability.
5. Save, preview, then print the worksheet on a single page. If necessary, use landscape orientation. Save any page setup changes you make.
6. Display and print worksheet formulas on a single page with row and column headings.
7. Close the workbook without saving the changes for displaying formulas.
8. Submit your printouts.

3. As the owner of Build-To-Fit, a general contracting firm specializing in home-storage projects, you are facing yet another business challenge at your firm. Because jobs are taking longer than expected, you decide to take out a loan to purchase some new power tools. According to your estimates, you need a $5,000 loan to purchase the tools. You check three loan sources: the Small Business Administration (SBA), your local bank, and your parents. Each source offers you a loan on its own terms. The local bank offers you the loan at 9.5% interest over four years. The SBA will loan you the money at 9% interest, but you have to pay it off in three years. Your parents offer you an 8% loan, but they require you to pay it back in two years, when they expect to retire. To analyze all three loan options, you decide to build a tool loan summary worksheet. Using the loan terms provided, build a worksheet summarizing your options.

To complete this independent challenge:

1. Open a new workbook, then save it as "Loan Options".
2. Enter labels and worksheet data. You need headings for the loan source, loan amount, interest rate, term or number of payments, monthly payment, total payments, and total interest. Fill in the data provided for the three loan sources.

3. Enter formulas as appropriate: a PMT formula for the monthly payment; a formula calculating the total payments based on the monthly payment and term values; and a formula for total interest based on the total payments and the loan amount.
4. Format the worksheet as desired.
5. Save, preview, then print the worksheet on a single page using landscape orientation. Along with the worksheet, submit a printout of worksheet formulas showing row and column headings. Do not save the worksheet with these settings.
6. Submit your printouts.

4. You can get up-to-date information on nearly any major company on the World Wide Web (WWW). When you get ready to make a major purchase, such as a vehicle, you can search the Web to gather the latest information available on the desired product. You have decided to purchase a new vehicle, and you are excited about logging on to the Web to research your planned purchase. Your self-imposed spending limit is $30,000, including purchase price and total interest on the loan. Create a spreadsheet using vehicle information found on the WWW to support your purchase decision.

To complete this independent challenge:

1. Open a new workbook, then save it as "My New Car" to the appropriate folder on your Student Disk.
2. Decide which features you want your ideal vehicle to have, and list these somewhere in your spreadsheet.
3. Log on to the Internet and use your web browser to go to http://www.course.com. From there, click the link Student Online Companions, click the link for this textbook, then click the Excel link for unit E.
4. Use any of the following sites to compile your data: Cadillac, Ford, GM, Honda, Toyota, or any other site with related information.
5. Compare at least three vehicles showing the automaker, the vehicle make and model year, the number of doors, color, and list sales price. Also compare the three vehicles based on the financing available. Specifically, calculate a loan amount (include list sales price, tax, and license fees), a monthly payment based on a five-year loan at 10.25% interest, the total of the payments, and the total interest paid. Make sure the total payments do not exceed your limit of $30,000.
6. Indicate on the worksheet your final purchase decision and the rationale behind that decision.
7. Save, print, then submit your printout.

► Visual Workshop

Create the worksheet shown in Figure E-21. (Hint: Enter the items in range C9:C11 as labels by typing an apostrophe before each formula.) Save the workbook as "Mortgage Payment Calculator" to the appropriate folder on your Student Disk. Preview, print, then submit the worksheet.

FIGURE E-21

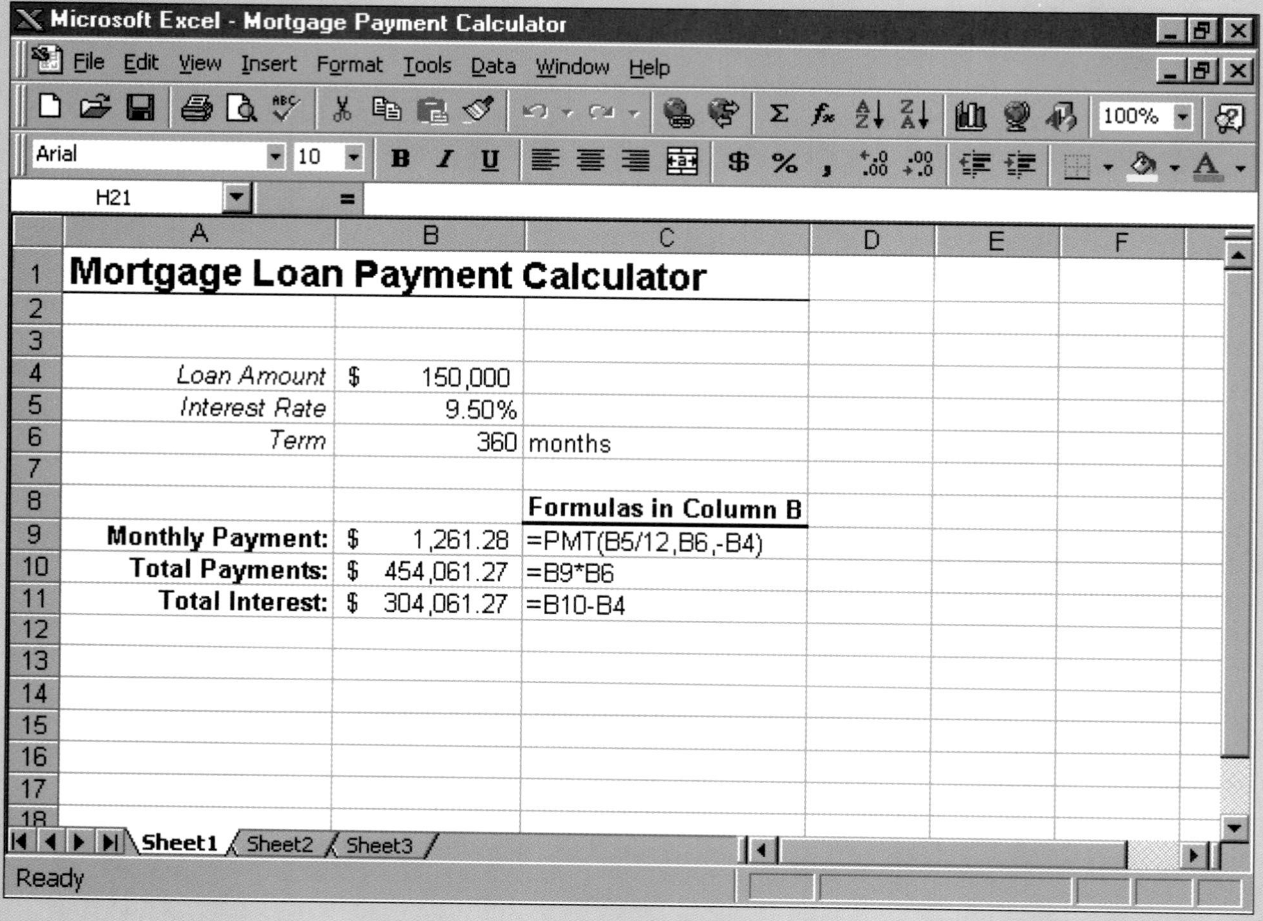

Microsoft Excel - Mortgage Payment Calculator

File Edit View Insert Format Tools Data Window Help

Arial 10 100%

H21 =

	A	B	C	D	E	F
1	**Mortgage Loan Payment Calculator**					
2						
3						
4	*Loan Amount*	$ 150,000				
5	*Interest Rate*	9.50%				
6	*Term*	360	months			
7						
8			**Formulas in Column B**			
9	**Monthly Payment:**	$ 1,261.28	=PMT(B5/12,B6,-B4)			
10	**Total Payments:**	$ 454,061.27	=B9*B6			
11	**Total Interest:**	$ 304,061.27	=B10-B4			
12						
13						
14						
15						
16						
17						
18						

Sheet1 / Sheet2 / Sheet3

Ready

Excel 97

e

Managing

Workbooks

Objectives

- Freeze columns and rows
- Insert and delete sheets
- Reference worksheet data
- Hide and protect worksheet areas
- Specify headers and footers
- Save custom views of a worksheet
- Control page breaks and page numbering
- Set margins and alignment

In this unit, you will learn several Excel features to help you manage and print workbook data. Nomad Ltd has increased the number of its hourly workers by 50% over the past year. Evan Brillstein's manager has designed a timecard summary worksheet to track salary costs for hourly workers. She turned the management of this worksheet over to Evan. In doing so, she has alerted him that she will need several reports generated from the worksheet data.

Excel 97

Freezing Columns and Rows

As rows and columns fill up with data, you might need to scroll through the worksheet to add, delete, modify, and view information. Looking at information without row or column labels can be confusing. In Excel, you can temporarily freeze columns and rows, which enables you to view separate areas of your worksheets at the same time. **Panes** are the columns and rows that **freeze**, or remain in place, while you scroll through your worksheet. The freeze feature is especially useful when you're dealing with large worksheets. Sometimes, though, even freezing is not sufficient. In those cases, you can create as many as four areas, or panes, on the screen at one time and move freely within each of them. Evan has been asked to verify the hourly pay rate, total hours worked, and total pay for two janitors at Nomad Ltd, Wilbur Collins and Orson Wilks. Because the worksheet is becoming more difficult to read as its size increases, Evan decides to freeze the column and row labels. To gather the requested information, Evan needs to view simultaneously a person's last name, total number of hours, hourly pay rate, and total pay. To do this, he will freeze columns A, B, and C and rows 1 through 5.

Steps

1. **Open the workbook titled XL F-1, save it as Timecard Summary, then scroll through the Monday worksheet to view the data**

2. **Return to cell A1, then click cell D6**
   Position the pointer in cell A1 to reorient the worksheet, then move to cell D6 because you want to freeze columns A, B, and C. By doing so, you can still view the last name when you scroll to the right. Because you want to be able to scroll down the worksheet and read the column headings, you also freeze the labels in rows 1 through 5. When instructed to do so, Excel freezes the columns to the left and the rows above the cell pointer.

3. **Click Window on the menu bar, then click Freeze Panes**
   Everything to the left and above the active cell is frozen. A thin line appears along the column border to the left of the active cell, and another line appears along the row above the active cell indicating that columns A through C and rows 1 through 5 are frozen.

4. **Scroll to the right until columns A through C and L through P are visible**
   Because columns A, B, and C are frozen, they remain on the screen; columns D through K are temporarily hidden from view. Notice that the information you are looking for in row 12 (last name, total hours, hourly pay rate, and total pay for Wilbur Collins) is readily available. You jot down Wilbur's data but still need to verify Orson Wilks's information.

5. **Scroll down until row 23 is visible**
   Notice that in addition to columns A through C, rows 1 through 5 remain on the screen as well. See Figure F-1. Evan jots down the information for Orson Wilks. Even though a pane is frozen, you can click in the frozen area of the worksheet and edit the contents of the cells there, if necessary.

6. **Press [Ctrl][Home]**
   Because the panes are frozen, the cell pointer moves to cell D6, not A1. Now that you have gathered the requested information, you are ready to unfreeze the panes.

7. **Click Window on the menu bar, then click Unfreeze Panes**
   The panes are unfrozen. You are satisfied with your ability to navigate and view the worksheet and are ready to save the workbook.

8. **Return to cell A1, then save the workbook**

Trouble?

If you do not see a thin vertical line in the worksheet area between columns C and D and a thin horizontal black line between rows 5 and 6, click Window on the menu bar, click Unfreeze Panes, then repeat Steps 2 and 3.

QuickTip

When you open an existing workbook, the cell pointer is in the cell it was in when you last saved the workbook. Press [Ctrl][Home] to return to cell A1 prior to saving and closing a workbook.

FIGURE F-1: Scrolled worksheet with frozen rows and columns

Microsoft Excel - Timecard Summary

File Edit View Insert Format Tools Data Window Help

Arial 10 100%

D6 = 887569856

	A	B	C	L	M	N	O	P
1	*Nomad Ltd*							
2	**Daily Timecard Summary for Hou**							
3								
4								
5	**Last Name**	**First Name**	**Timecard Number**	**Time Out**	**Total Hours**	**Hourly Pay Rate**	**Total Pay**	
23	Wilks	Orson	FP41	5:30 PM	8:00	$ 12.50	$ 100.00	
24	Young	Kara	FN14		3:00	$ 8.75	$ 26.25	
25								
26						**Total**	$ 2,051.25	
27								
28								
29								
30								
31								
32								
33								
34								

Monday / Tuesday / Wednesday / Friday / Saturday

Ready

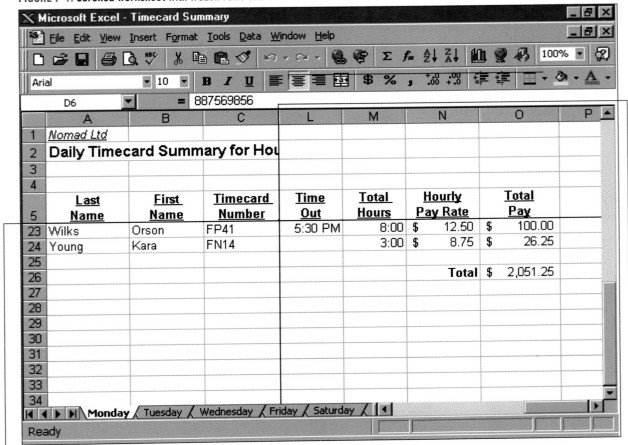

Break in row numbers due to frozen rows 1–5

Break in column letters due to frozen columns A–C

Excel 97

CLUES TO USE

Splitting the worksheet into multiple panes

Excel provides a way to split the worksheet area into vertical and/or horizontal panes so that you can click inside any one pane and scroll to locate desired information in that pane without any of the other panes moving. See Figure F-2. To split a worksheet area into multiple panes, drag the split box (the small box at the top of the vertical scroll bar or at the right end of the horizontal scroll bar) in the direction you want the split to appear. To remove the split, move the mouse over the split until the pointer changes to ÷, then double-click.

FIGURE F-2: Worksheet split into two horizontal panes

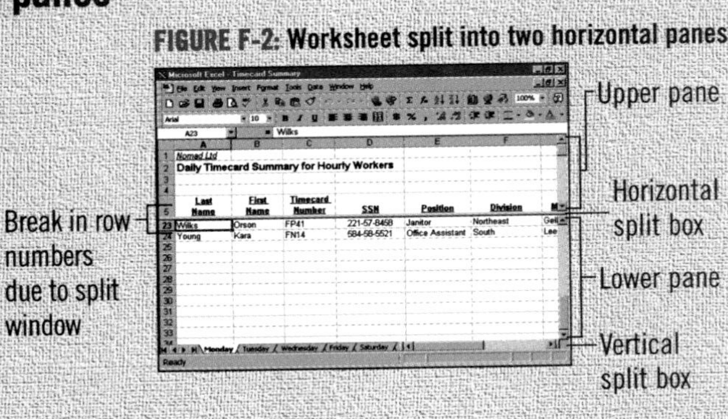

Excel 97

Inserting and Deleting Sheets

You can insert and delete worksheets in a workbook as needed. For example, because new workbooks open with only three sheets available (Sheet1, Sheet2, and Sheet3), you need to insert at least one more sheet if you want to have four quarterly worksheets in an annual financial budget workbook. As for other Excel features, you can do this by using commands on the menu bar or pop-up menu. Evan was in a hurry when he added the sheet tabs to the Timecard Summary workbook. He needs to insert a sheet for Thursday and delete the sheet for Sunday because hourly workers do not work on Sunday.

Steps

QuickTip

You also can copy the active worksheet by clicking Edit on the menu bar, then clicking Move or Copy Sheet. You choose the sheet the copy will precede, then select the Create a copy check box.

1. **Click the Friday sheet tab, click Insert on the menu bar, then click Worksheet**
   Excel automatically inserts a new sheet tab labeled Sheet1 to the left of the selected sheet. See Figure F-3. Next, rename the inserted sheet to something more meaningful.
2. **Rename the Sheet1 tab Thursday**
   Now the tabs read Monday, Tuesday, Wednesday, Thursday, Friday, and Saturday. The tabs for Sunday and Weekly Summary are not visible, but you still need to delete the Sunday worksheet.
3. **Scroll until the Sunday sheet tab is visible, move the pointer over the Sunday tab, then click the right mouse button**
   A pop-up menu appears. See Figure F-4. The pop-up menu allows you to insert, delete, rename, move, or copy sheets, select all the sheets, or view the code in a workbook.
4. **Click Delete on the pop-up menu**
   A message box warns that the selected sheet will be deleted permanently. You must acknowledge the message before proceeding.
5. **Click OK**
   The Sunday sheet is deleted. Next, to check your work, you view a menu of sheets in the workbook.

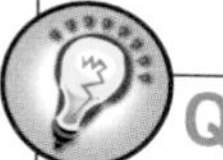

QuickTip

You can scroll several tabs at once by pressing [Shift] while clicking one of the middle tab scrolling buttons.

6. **Move the mouse pointer over any tab scrolling button, then right-click**
   When you right-click a tab scrolling button, Excel automatically opens a menu of the sheets in the active workbook. Compare your list with Figure F-5.
7. **Click Monday, return to cell A1, then save the workbook**

FIGURE F-3: Workbook with inserted sheet

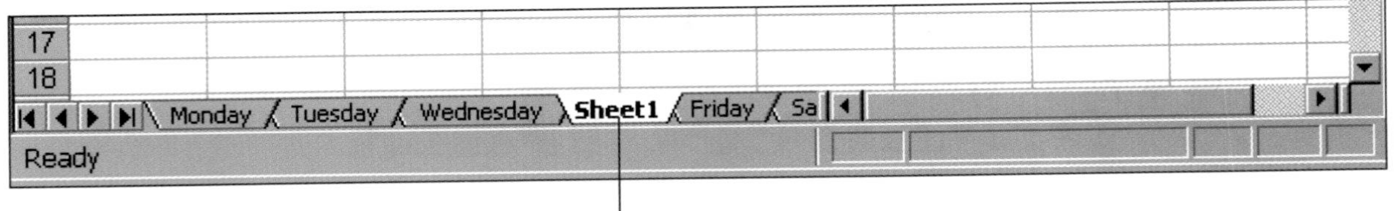

Inserted sheet

FIGURE F-4: Sheet pop-up menu

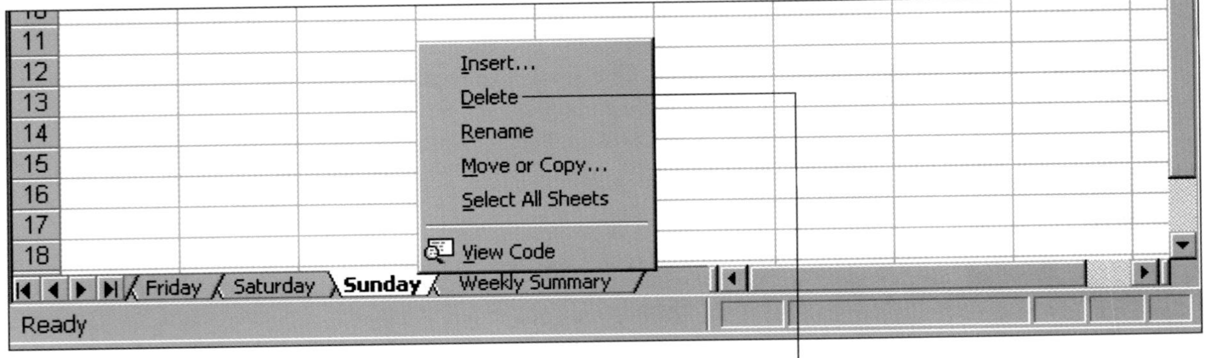

Click to delete selected sheet

FIGURE F-5: Workbook with menu of sheets

Microsoft Excel - Timecard Summary

File Edit View Insert Format Tools Data Window Help

Arial 10 100%

A1 = Nomad Ltd

	A	B	C	D	E	F	
1	*Nomad Ltd*						
2	**Daily Timecard Summary for Hourly Workers**						
3							
4							
5	**Last Name**	**First Name**	**Timecard Number**	**SSN**	**Position**	**Division**	**M**
6	Alexander	Anthony	CO12	887-56-9856	Gardner	Headquarters	Sto
7	Barnes	Jackie	FP55	023-94-5683	Office Assistant	Northeast	Gell
8	Bird	Lori	FN05	557-84-5698	PC Consultant	Midwest	Lee
9	Caprillian	George	CS33	457-89-2574	Janitor	Northwest	San
10	C		FP02	598-78-4525	Consultant	Northeast	Lee
11	C		FN03	234-91-3456	PC Consultant	South	Lee
12	C		FP06	484-57-8594	Janitor	South	Gell
13	C		FP28	557-58-4215	Office Assistant	Northeast	Gell
14	E		FN20	587-21-3692	Janitor	Midwest	Lee
15	G		CS30	558-65-4985	Janitor	Southwest	San
16	L		FP21	487-59-2158	PC Consultant	Northeast	Gell
17	M		FN13	221-54-8798	Office Assistant	Midwest	Lee

Menu: ✓ Monday, Tuesday, Wednesday, Thursday, Friday, Saturday, Weekly Summary

Tabs: Monday, Tuesday, Wednesday, Thursday, Friday

Ready

Active sheet

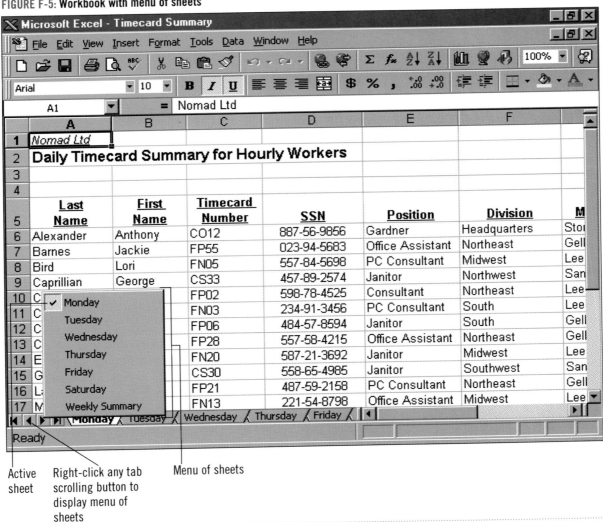

Right-click any tab scrolling button to display menu of sheets

Menu of sheets

Excel 97

Excel 97

Referencing Worksheet Data

You can reference data within a worksheet, between sheets, and between workbooks. For example, you can reference data within a worksheet if you want to reference a calculated total elsewhere in the sheet. Retyping the calculated result in another cell is not recommended because the data values on which the calculated total depend might change. Referencing data between sheets might be necessary if you have quarterly worksheets and an annual summary worksheet in the same workbook. Although Evan does not have timecard data for the remaining days of the week, he wants to try out the Weekly Summary sheet. He does this by creating a reference from the total pay data in the Monday sheet to the Weekly Summary sheet. First, he freezes panes to improve the view of the worksheets prior to initiating the reference between them.

Steps

1. **Click cell D6, click Window on the menu bar, click Freeze Panes, then scroll horizontally to bring columns L through O into view**
   Next, you right-click a tab scrolling button to access the pop-up menu for moving between sheets.

2. **Right-click a tab scrolling button, then click Weekly Summary**
   Because the Weekly Summary sheet will contain the reference, the cell pointer must reside there when the reference is initiated. A simple **reference** within the same sheet or between sheets is made by positioning the cell pointer in the cell to contain the reference, typing = (equal sign), positioning the cell pointer in the cell containing the contents to be referenced, and then completing the entry. You complete the entry either by pressing [Enter] or clicking the Enter button on the formula bar.

Trouble?

If you have difficulty referencing cells between sheets, press [Esc] and begin again.

3. **While in the Weekly Summary sheet, click cell C6, type =, activate the Monday sheet, click cell O6, then click the Enter button on the formula bar**
   The formula bar reads =Monday!O6. See Figure F-6. *Monday* references the Monday sheet. The ! (exclamation point) is an **external reference indicator** meaning that the cell referenced is outside the active sheet; O6 is the actual cell reference in the external sheet. The result $41.00 appears in cell C6 of the Weekly Summary sheet showing the reference to the value displayed in cell O6 of the Monday sheet. You are ready to copy the formula reference down the column.

4. **While in the Weekly Summary sheet, copy cell C6 into cells C7:C24**
   Excel copies the contents of cell C6 with its relative reference down the column. Test the reference for Anthony Alexander in cell C6 by correcting the time he clocked out for the day.

5. **Make the Monday sheet active, edit cell L6 to read 3:30 PM, then activate the Weekly Summary sheet**
   Cell C6 now shows $20.50. By changing Anthony's time-out to two hours earlier, his pay dropped from $41.00 to $20.50. This makes sense because Anthony's hours went from four to two and his hourly salary is $10.25. Additionally, the reference to Monday's total pay was automatically updated in the Weekly Summary sheet. See Figure F-7.

6. **Preview, then print the Weekly Summary sheet**

7. **Activate the Monday sheet, then unfreeze the panes**
   You are ready to save the workbook.

8. **Save the workbook**

FIGURE F-6: Worksheet showing referenced cell

	A	B	C	D	E	F	G	H	I
1	*Nomad Ltd*								
2	**Weekly Timecard Summary for Hourly Workers**								
3									
4			**Total Pay for the days of the week**						
5	**Last Name**	**Timecard Number**	**Mon**	**Tues**	**Wed**	**Thur**	**Fri**	**Sat**	**Weekly Total**
6	Alexander	CO12	$ 41.00						
7	Barnes	FP55							
8	Bird	FN05							
9	Caprillian	CS33							
10	Carter	FP02							
11	Childers	FN03							
12	Collins	FP06							
13	Cross	FP28							
14	Ebert	FN20							
15	Gallego	CS30							
16	LaFuente	FP21							
17	McFee	FN13							

FIGURE F-7: Weekly Summary worksheet with updated reference

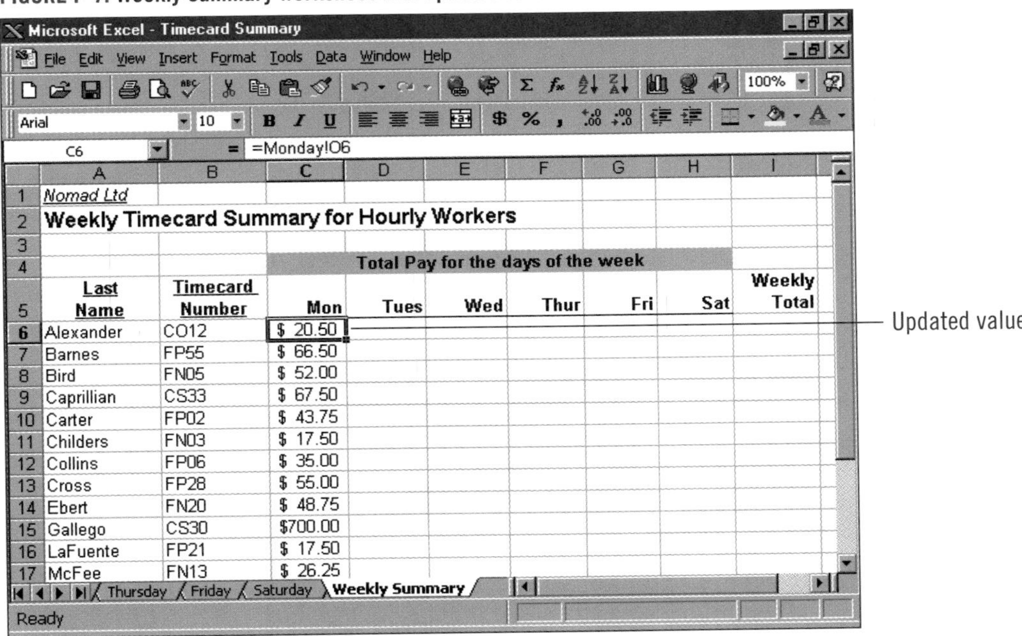

	A	B	C	D	E	F	G	H	I
1	*Nomad Ltd*								
2	**Weekly Timecard Summary for Hourly Workers**								
3									
4			**Total Pay for the days of the week**						
5	**Last Name**	**Timecard Number**	**Mon**	**Tues**	**Wed**	**Thur**	**Fri**	**Sat**	**Weekly Total**
6	Alexander	CO12	$ 20.50						
7	Barnes	FP55	$ 66.50						
8	Bird	FN05	$ 52.00						
9	Caprillian	CS33	$ 67.50						
10	Carter	FP02	$ 43.75						
11	Childers	FN03	$ 17.50						
12	Collins	FP06	$ 35.00						
13	Cross	FP28	$ 55.00						
14	Ebert	FN20	$ 48.75						
15	Gallego	CS30	$700.00						
16	LaFuente	FP21	$ 17.50						
17	McFee	FN13	$ 26.25						

Excel 97

Linking workbooks

Just as you can reference data between cells in a worksheet and between sheets, you can reference data between workbooks dynamically so that any changes made in one workbook are reflected immediately in the other workbook. This dynamic referencing is called **linking.** To link a single cell between workbooks, simply open both workbooks, select the cell to receive the linked data, press = (equal sign), select the cell containing the data to be linked, then press [Enter]. If you are linking more than one cell, you can copy the linked data to the Clipboard, select the upper-left cell to receive the link, click Edit on the menu bar, click Paste Special, then click Paste Link.

Excel 97

Hiding and Protecting Worksheet Areas

Worksheets can contain sensitive information that is not intended to be altered or even viewed by all users. In Excel, you can hide individual formulas, rows, columns, or entire sheets. In addition, you can **protect** selected cells so they cannot be changed while allowing other cells in the worksheet to be altered. See Table F-1 for a list of options you can use to hide and protect a worksheet. Cells that are protected so that their contents cannot be altered are called **locked cells**. You lock and unlock cells by clicking the Locked check box in the Format Cells dialog box. A common worksheet protection strategy is to unlock cells that will be changed, sometimes referred to as the **data entry area**, and to leave the remaining cells locked. Because Evan will assign someone to enter the sensitive timecard information into the worksheet, he plans to hide and protect selected areas of the worksheet.

Steps 1 2 3 4

1. **Make sure the Monday sheet is active, select range I6:L25; click Format on the menu bar, click Cells, then click the Protection tab**
   You include row 25, even though it does not contain data, in the event that new data is added to the row later. Notice that the Locked box in the Protection tab is checked, as shown in Figure F-8. By default, the Locked check box is selected, which indicates that all the cells in a new workbook start out locked.
2. **Click the Locked check box to deselect it, then click OK**
   Excel stores time as a fraction of a 24-hour day. In the formula for total pay, hours must be multiplied by 24. This concept might be confusing to the data entry person, so you hide the formulas before you protect the worksheet.
3. **Select range O6:O25; click Format on the menu bar, click Cells, click the Protection tab, click the Hidden check box to select it, then click OK**
   The screen data remains the same (unhidden and unlocked) until you set the protection in the next step.
4. **Click Tools on the menu bar, point to Protection, then click Protect Sheet**
   The Protect Sheet dialog box opens. You choose not to use a password.
5. **Click OK**
   You are ready to put the new worksheet protection status to the test.
6. **Click cell O6**
   Notice that the formula bar is empty because of the hidden formula setting. Now you attempt to change the cell contents of O6, which is a locked cell.
7. **In cell O6, type T to confirm that locked cells cannot be changed, then click OK**
   When you attempt to change a locked cell, a message box reminds you of the protected cell's read-only status. See Figure F-9. Next, you attempt to make an entry in the Time In column to make sure it is unlocked.
8. **Click cell I6, type 9, and notice that Excel allows you to begin the entry; press [Esc] to cancel the entry, then save the workbook**
   Evan is satisfied that the Time In and Time Out data can be changed as needed.

QuickTip

To turn off worksheet protection, click Tools on the menu bar, point to Protection, then click Unprotect Sheet. If prompted for a password, type the password, then click OK. Keep in mind that passwords are case sensitive.

FIGURE F-8: Protection tab in Format Cells dialog box

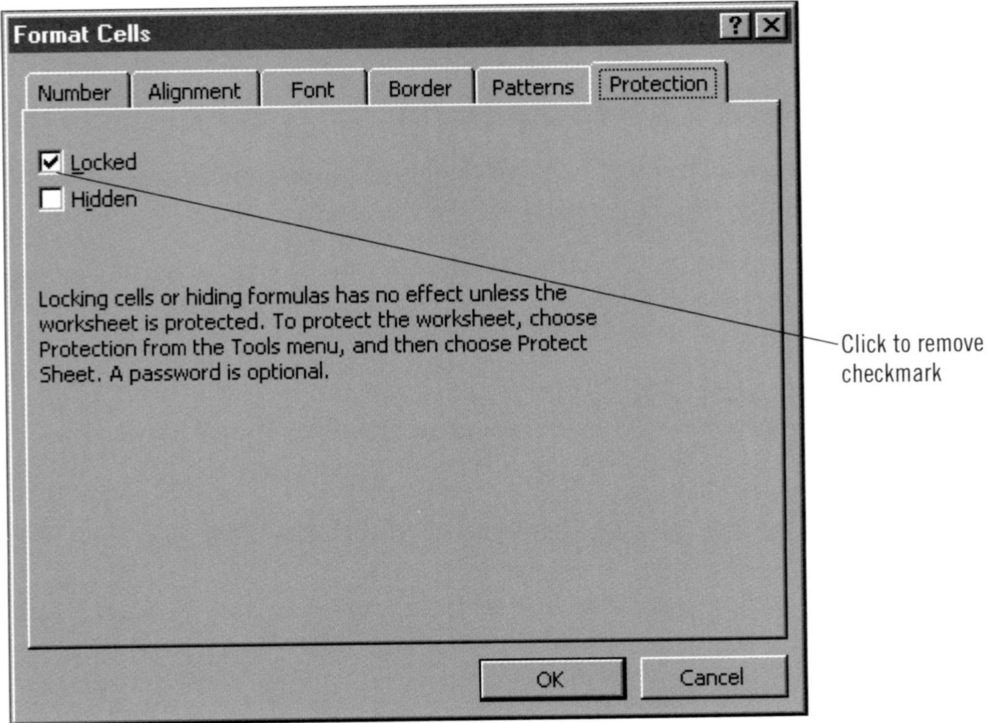

FIGURE F-9: Message box reminder of protected cell's read-only status

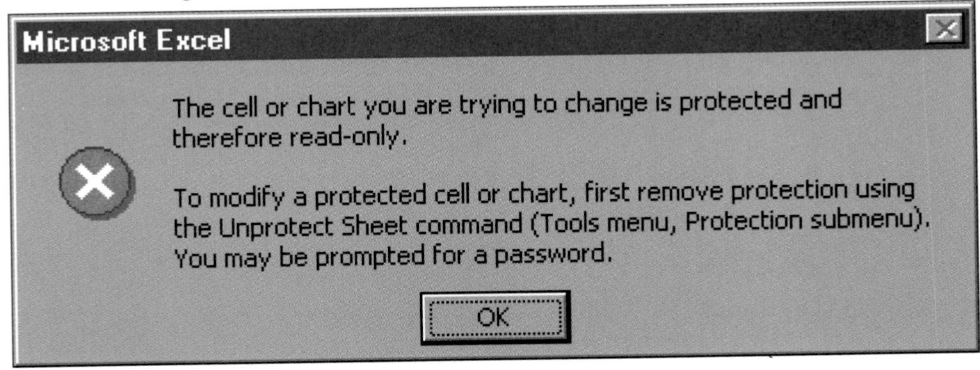

Excel 97

TABLE F-1: Options for hiding and protecting worksheet elements

task	menu commands
Hide/Unhide a column	Format, Column, Hide, or Unhide
Hide/Unhide a formula	Format, Cells, Protection tab, select/deselect Hidden check box
Hide/Unhide a row	Format, Row, Hide, or Unhide
Hide/Unhide a sheet	Format, Sheet, Hide, or Unhide
Protect workbook	Tools, Protection, Protect Workbook, assign optional password
Protect worksheet	Tools, Protection, Protect Sheet, assign optional password
Unlock/Relock cells	Format, Cells, Protection tab, deselect/select Locked check box

Note: *Some of the hide and protect options do not take effect until protection is enabled.*

Excel 97

Specifying Headers and Footers

A **header** is information that appears at the top of each printed page, and a **footer** is information that appears at the bottom of each printed page. You do not see headers and footers on the screen, except in the Print Preview window. By default, in Microsoft Excel 97 the header and footer are set to "none" in new worksheets. You can override the default of no headers and footers by creating your own. Excel provides a group of buttons that you can use to print specific information in your headers and footers. See Table F-2 for a description of these buttons. Evan remembers that his manager will use the Timecard Summary sheet as part of a report to upper management. He wants to include the date and filename in the footer, and he thinks it will improve the report to make the header text larger and more descriptive.

Steps

1. With the Monday sheet active, click **File** on the menu bar, click **Page Setup**, then click the **Header/Footer tab**
   The Header/Footer tab of the Page Setup dialog box opens. Notice that Excel automatically sets the header and footer to none. First, you customize the header.
2. Click **Custom Header**
   The Header dialog box opens, as shown in Figure F-10. By entering your header information in the Center section box, Excel automatically centers this information on the printout.
3. Click the **Center section box**, then type **Monday – 8/4**
   In the case of a long header, header text might wrap to the next line in the box but will appear on one line in the printout. Next, you change the font size and style.
4. Drag to select the header text **Monday – 8/4**, then click the **Font button** in the Header dialog box; in the Size box click **12**, in the Font style box click **Bold**, click **OK**, then click **OK** to return to the Header/Footer tab
   The new header appears in the Header box. You are ready to customize the footer.
5. In the Header/Footer tab, click **Custom Footer**
   The Footer dialog box opens. The information you enter in the Left section box is left-aligned on the printout. The text you enter in the Right section box is right-aligned on the printout.
6. Click the **Right section box**, type **Workbook:** and press **[Spacebar]**, then click the **File Name button** in the Footer dialog box to insert the filename code **&[File]**, then click **OK**
   You return to the Page Setup dialog box, and the revised footer appears in the Footer box. See Figure F-11.
7. Preview, print, then save the worksheet
   Evan is ready to submit the report to his manager.

QuickTip

You can easily turn off the header and/or footer in a worksheet by clicking the header or footer list arrow on the Header/Footer tab, scrolling to the top of the list, then choosing (none).

FIGURE F-10: Header dialog box

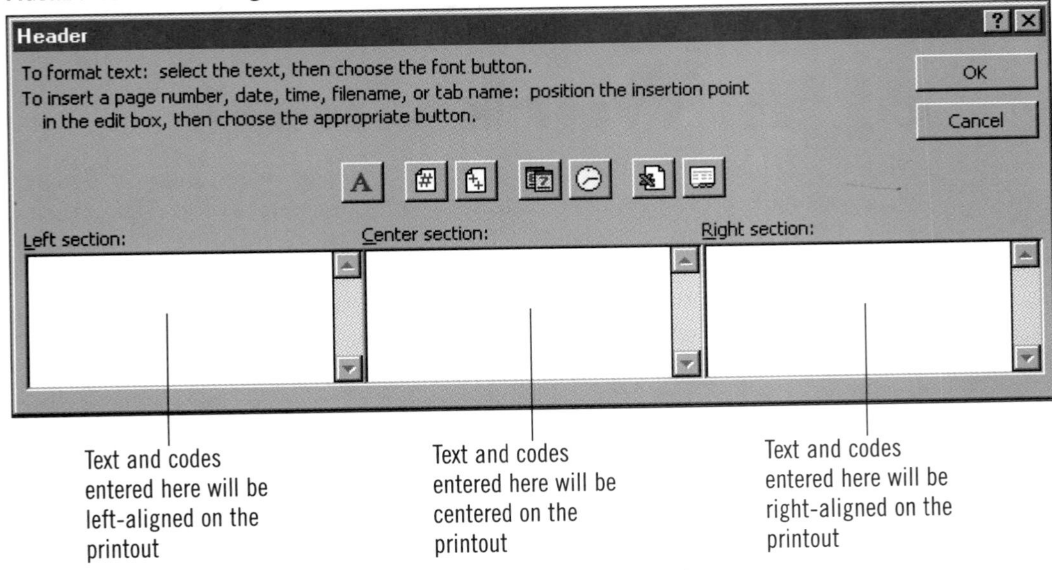

FIGURE F-11: Header/Footer tab with revised header and footer information

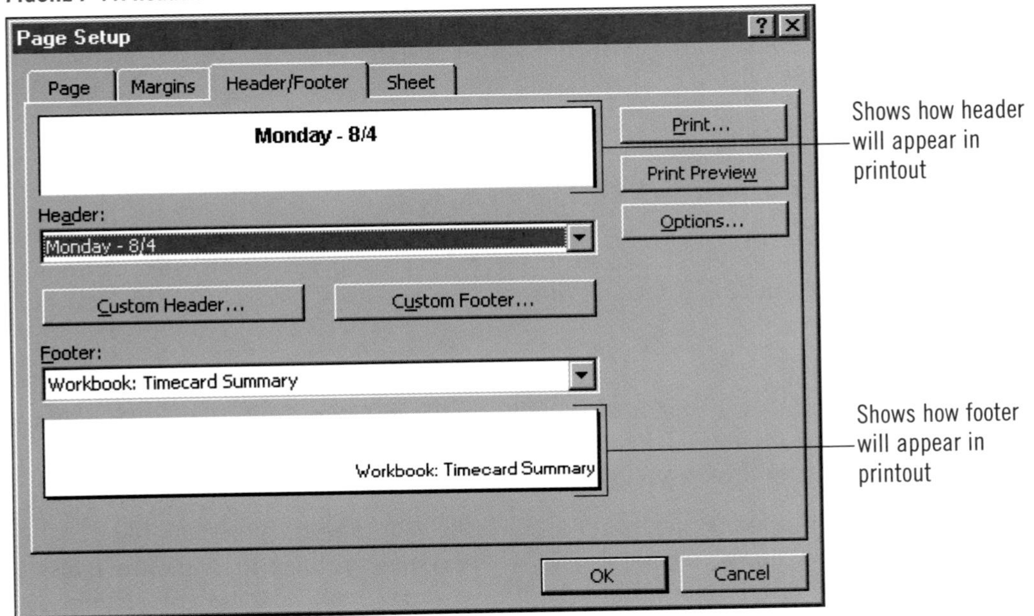

Excel 97

TABLE F-2: Buttons for customizing headers and footers

button	button name	code	result
A	Font	None	Displays the Font dialog box in which you choose attributes for the header or footer
	Page Number	&[Page]	Inserts current page number
	Total Pages	&[Pages]	Inserts total number of printed pages
	Date	&[Date]	Inserts the current date as it is stored in your computer
	Time	&[Time]	Inserts the current time as it is stored in your computer
	File Name	&[File]	Inserts the name of the workbook file
	Sheet Name	&[Tab]	Inserts the name of the worksheet

Excel 97

Saving Custom Views of a Worksheet

A **view** is a set of display and/or print settings that you can name and save, then access at a later time. By using Excel's Custom Views feature, you can create several different views of a worksheet without having to save separate sheets under separate filenames. For example, if you often switch between portrait and landscape orientations when printing different parts of a worksheet, you can create two views with the appropriate print settings for each view. You define the display and/or print settings first, then name the view.  Because Evan will be generating several reports from this data, he will save the current print and display settings as a custom view. In order to better view the data to be printed, Evan decides to use the Zoom box to display the entire worksheet on one screen. The Zoom box has a default setting of 100% magnification and appears on the Standard toolbar.

Steps

QuickTip

With **Report Manager add-in**, you can group worksheets and their views to be printed in sequence as one large report.

1. With the Monday sheet active select range **A1:O26**, click the **Zoom box list arrow** on the Standard toolbar, click **Selection**, then press **[Ctrl][Home]** to return to cell A1 and deselect the worksheet

   Excel automatically adjusts the display magnification so that the data selected fit on one screen. See Figure F-12. After selecting the **Zoom box**, you also can pick a magnification percentage from the list or type the desired percentage. Now that you have set up the desired view of the data, you are ready to save the current print and display settings as a custom view.

2. Click **View**, then click **Custom Views**

   The Custom Views dialog box opens. Any previously defined views for the active worksheet appear in the Views box. In this case, Evan's manager had created a custom view named Generic containing default print and display settings. See Figure F-13. Next, you choose Add to create a new view.

QuickTip

To delete views from the active worksheet, select the view in the Views list box, then click Delete.

3. Click **Add**

   The Add View dialog box opens, as shown in Figure F-14. Here, you enter a name for the view and decide whether to include print settings and hidden rows, columns and filter settings. Leave these two options checked.

4. In the Name box, type **Complete Daily Worksheet**, then click **OK**

   After creating a custom view of the worksheet, you return to the worksheet area. You are ready to test the two custom views. First, you turn off worksheet protection in case the views require a change to the worksheet.

5. Click **Tools** on the menu bar, point to **Protection**, then click **Unprotect Sheet**

   With the worksheet protection turned off, you are ready to show your custom views.

6. Click **View** on the menu bar, then click **Custom Views**

   The Custom Views dialog box opens, listing both the Complete Daily Worksheet and Generic views.

Trouble?

If you receive the message, "Some view settings could not be applied," repeat Step 5 to ensure worksheet protection is turned off.

7. Click **Generic** in the Views list box, click **Show**, then preview the worksheet

   The Generic custom view returns the worksheet to Excel's default print and display settings. Now, you are ready to test the new custom view.

8. Click **View** on the menu bar, click **Custom Views**, click **Complete Daily Worksheet** in the Views list box, click **Show**, then save the workbook

   Evan is satisfied with the custom view of the worksheet he created.

FIGURE F-12: Worksheet at 48% magnification

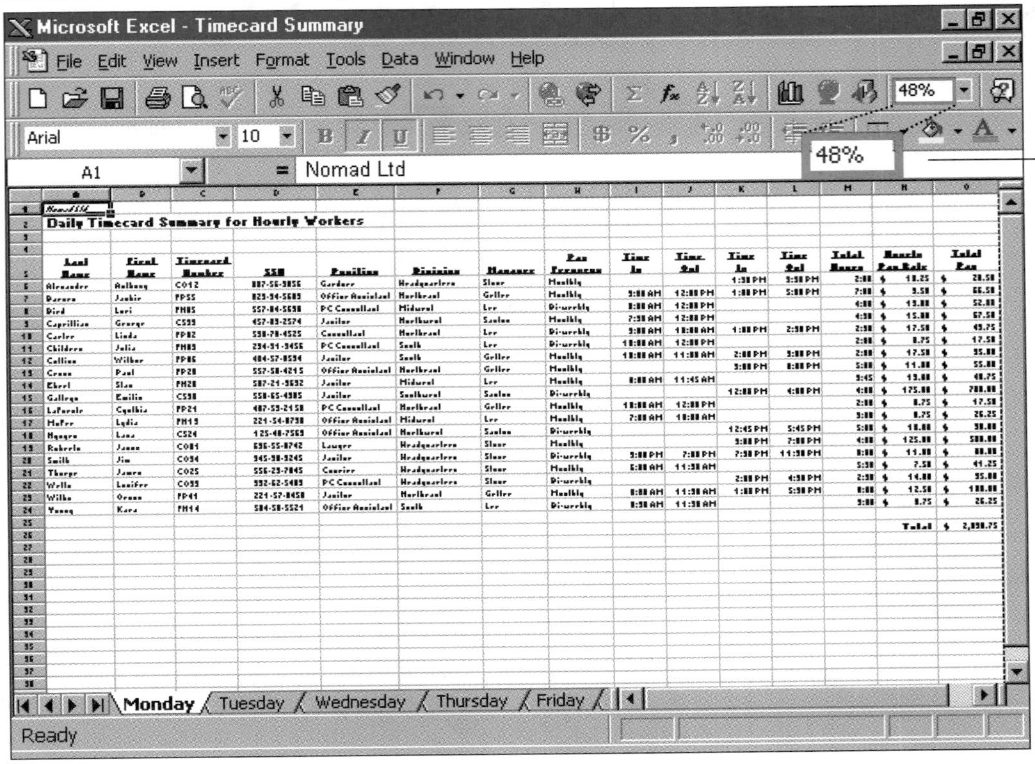

Zoom box showing current magnification

FIGURE F-13: Custom Views dialog box

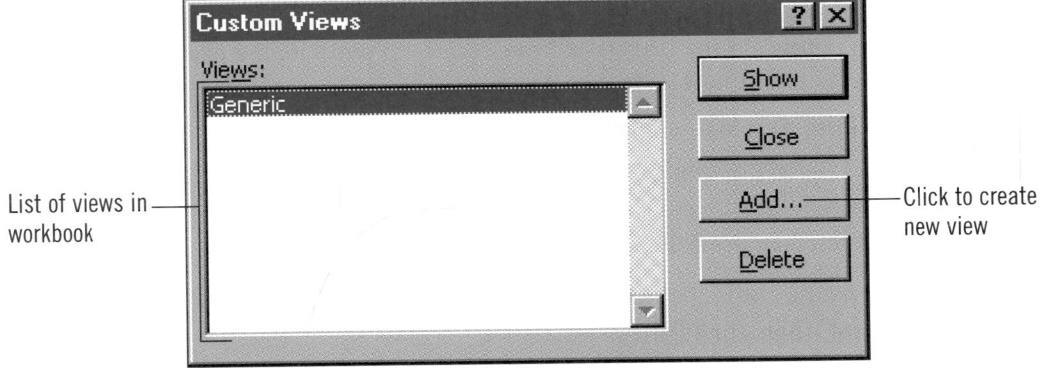

FIGURE F-14: Add View dialog box

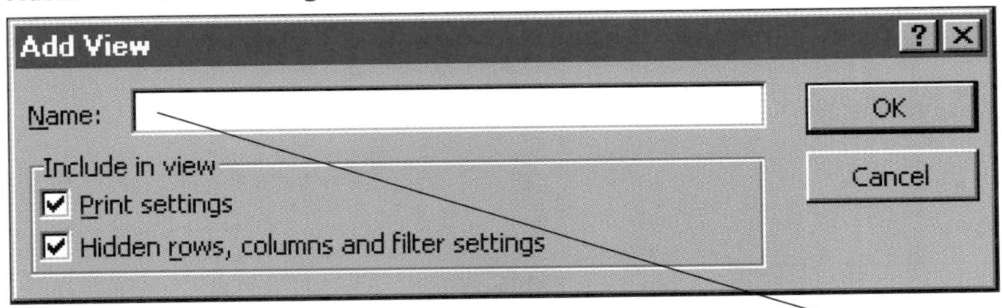

Excel 97

Controlling Page Breaks and Page Numbering

The vertical and horizontal dashed lines in your worksheets indicate page breaks. Excel automatically inserts a page break when your worksheet data doesn't fit on one page. These page breaks are **dynamic**, which means they adjust automatically when you insert or delete rows and columns and when you change column widths or row heights. Everything to the left of the first vertical dashed line and above the first horizontal dashed line is printed on the first page. You can override the automatic breaks by choosing the Page Break command on the Insert menu. Table F-3 describes the different types of page breaks you can use. Evan's manager wants another report displaying no more than half the hourly workers on each page. To accomplish this, Evan must insert a manual page break. He begins by returning the screen display to 100% magnification.

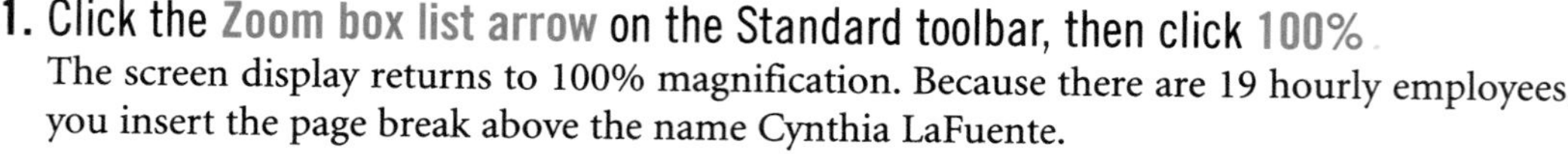

Trouble?

If you don't see the page breaks inserted by Excel, click Tools on the menu bar, click Options, then click the View tab. Make sure the Page breaks check box is selected.

QuickTip

To remove a manual page break, select any cell directly below or to the right of the page break, click Insert on the menu bar, then click Remove Page Break.

1. **Click the Zoom box list arrow on the Standard toolbar, then click 100%**
   The screen display returns to 100% magnification. Because there are 19 hourly employees, you insert the page break above the name Cynthia LaFuente.
2. **Click cell A16, click Insert on the menu bar, then click Page Break**
   A dashed line appears between rows 15 and 16 indicating a horizontal page break. See Figure F-15. Next, you preview the worksheet.
3. **Preview the worksheet, then click Zoom**
   Notice that the status bar reads "Page 1 of 2" and that the data for the employees up through Emilio Gallego appear on the first page. Evan decides to reinstate the page number in the footer because the report now spans two pages.
4. **While in the Print Preview window, click Setup, click the Header/Footer tab, click Custom Footer, click the Center section box, click the Page Number button, then click OK**
   Check your footer, then print the worksheet.
5. **In the Header/Footer tab, click OK, check to make sure both pages show page numbers, click Print, then click OK**
   Next, you save a custom view with the current display and print settings.
6. **Click View on the menu bar, click Custom Views, click Add, type Half N Half, then click OK**
7. **Save the workbook**

TABLE F-3: Page break options

type of page break	where to position cell pointer
Both horizontal and vertical page breaks	Select the cell below and to the right of the gridline where you want the breaks to occur
Only a horizontal page break	Select the cell in column A that is directly below the gridline where you want the page to break
Only a vertical page break	Select a cell in row 1 that is to the right of the gridline where you want the page to break

FIGURE F-15: Worksheet with horizontal page break

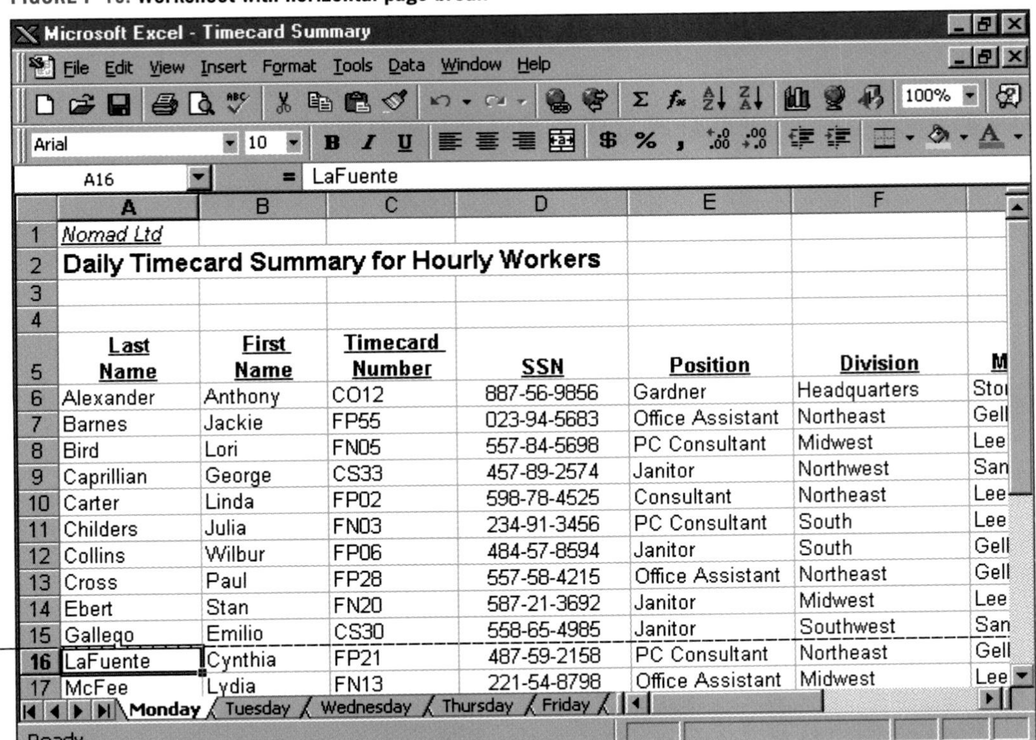

	A	B	C	D	E	F	
5	Last Name	First Name	Timecard Number	SSN	Position	Division	M
6	Alexander	Anthony	CO12	887-56-9856	Gardner	Headquarters	Stoı
7	Barnes	Jackie	FP55	023-94-5683	Office Assistant	Northeast	Gell
8	Bird	Lori	FN05	557-84-5698	PC Consultant	Midwest	Lee
9	Caprillian	George	CS33	457-89-2574	Janitor	Northwest	San
10	Carter	Linda	FP02	598-78-4525	Consultant	Northeast	Lee
11	Childers	Julia	FN03	234-91-3456	PC Consultant	South	Lee
12	Collins	Wilbur	FP06	484-57-8594	Janitor	South	Gell
13	Cross	Paul	FP28	557-58-4215	Office Assistant	Northeast	Gell
14	Ebert	Stan	FN20	587-21-3692	Janitor	Midwest	Lee
15	Gallego	Emilio	CS30	558-65-4985	Janitor	Southwest	San
16	LaFuente	Cynthia	FP21	487-59-2158	PC Consultant	Northeast	Gell
17	McFee	Lydia	FN13	221-54-8798	Office Assistant	Midwest	Lee

Dashed line indicates horizontal break after row 15

Excel 97

Using Page Break Preview

CLUES TO USE

By clicking View on the menu bar, then clicking Page Break Preview, or clicking Page Break Preview in the Print Preview window, you can view and change page breaks manually. Simply drag the dashed page break lines to the desired location. See Figure F-16.

FIGURE F-16: Page Break Preview window

Cell pointer in cell A16

Dashed page break line

Excel 97

Setting Margins and Alignment

You can set top, bottom, left, and right margins for a worksheet printout and determine the distance you want headers and footers to print from the edge of a page. Also, you can align data on a page by centering it horizontally and/or vertically between the margins. Evan has been asked to print selected information from the Timecard Summary. His manager wants an additional report showing last name, first name, timecard number, social security number, position, and division. First, Evan returns to the Generic custom view of the worksheet.

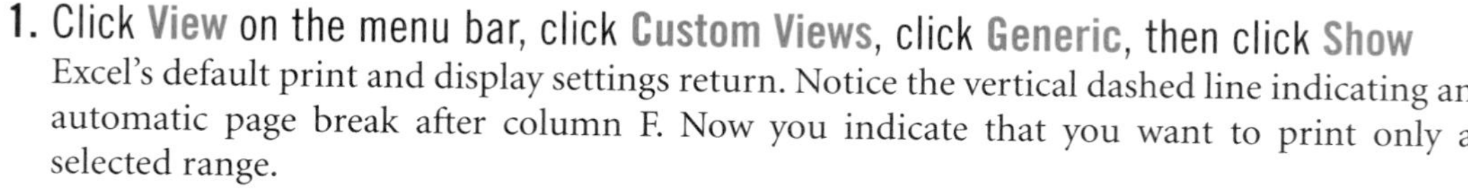

Steps

1. **Click View on the menu bar, click Custom Views, click Generic, then click Show**
   Excel's default print and display settings return. Notice the vertical dashed line indicating an automatic page break after column F. Now you indicate that you want to print only a selected range.

2. **Select range A1:F24, click File on the menu bar, click Print, under Print what click Selection, then click Preview**
   The Print Preview window displays only the selected cells. Next, center the data horizontally and start printing farther down the page.

3. **From the Print Preview window, click Setup, click the Margins tab, double-click the Top text box to select the 1, then type 3**
   Notice that the top margin line darkens in the Preview section of the dialog box. The Preview section reflects your activity in the Margins tab. Next, change the header so it prints 1.5" from the top edge of the page.

4. **Double-click the Header text box, then type 1.5**
   Finally, center the report horizontally on the page.

5. **In the Center on page section, click the Horizontally check box to select it**
   You have completed the changes in the Margins tab. See Figure F-17. Because all the data fits nicely on one page, you decide to set the footer to "none".

6. **Click the Header/Footer tab, click the Footer list arrow, scroll to the top of the list, then click (none)**
   Check the report to ensure that it begins farther down from the top of the page, is centered horizontally, and does not include a page number. Because the report is complete, preview and print the worksheet.

7. **Click OK to preview the worksheet, then print the worksheet**
   Compare your screen with Figure F-18. Because Evan will be switching between reports, he first prints this latest report, and then creates a custom view called Employee Info.

8. **Click View on the menu bar, click Custom Views, click Add, type Employee Info, then click OK**

9. **Save the workbook**

QuickTip

You can group multiple worksheets to print by selecting nonadjacent worksheets using [Ctrl] or by selecting adjacent worksheets using [Shift] before issuing the print command.

QuickTip

You can adjust page margins, header and footer margins, and column widths manually. When you click the Margins button in the Print Preview window, horizontal and vertical guides appear on the worksheet. Drag these margin guides to adjust the format of the sheet.

FIGURE F-17: **Margins tab with changed settings**

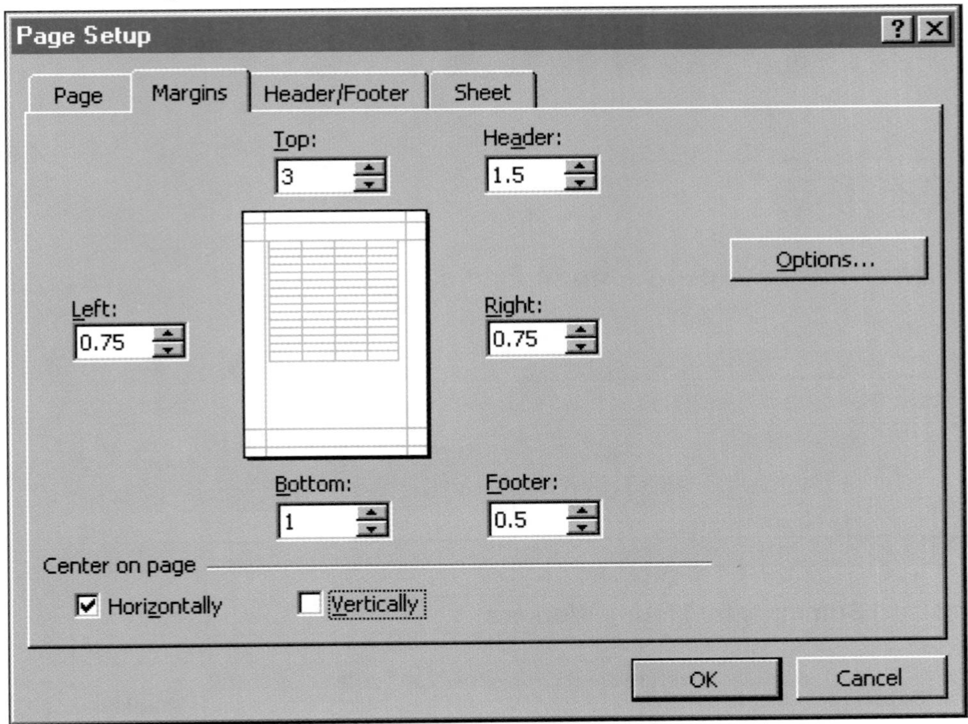

FIGURE F-18: **Print Preview window showing employee information**

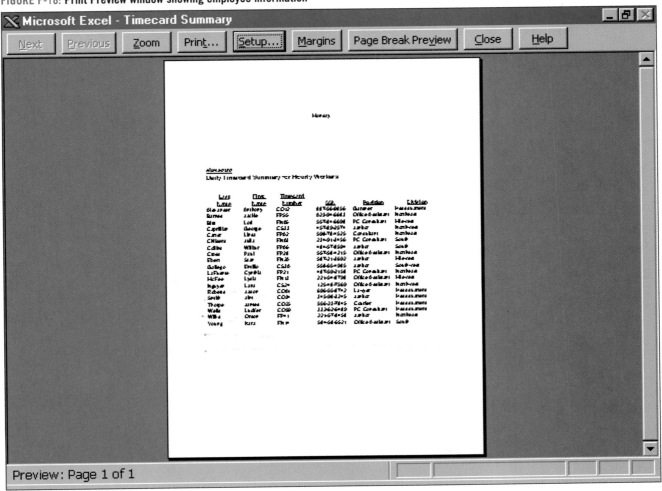

Practice

Concepts Review

Label each of the elements of the Excel screen shown in Figure F-19.

FIGURE F-19

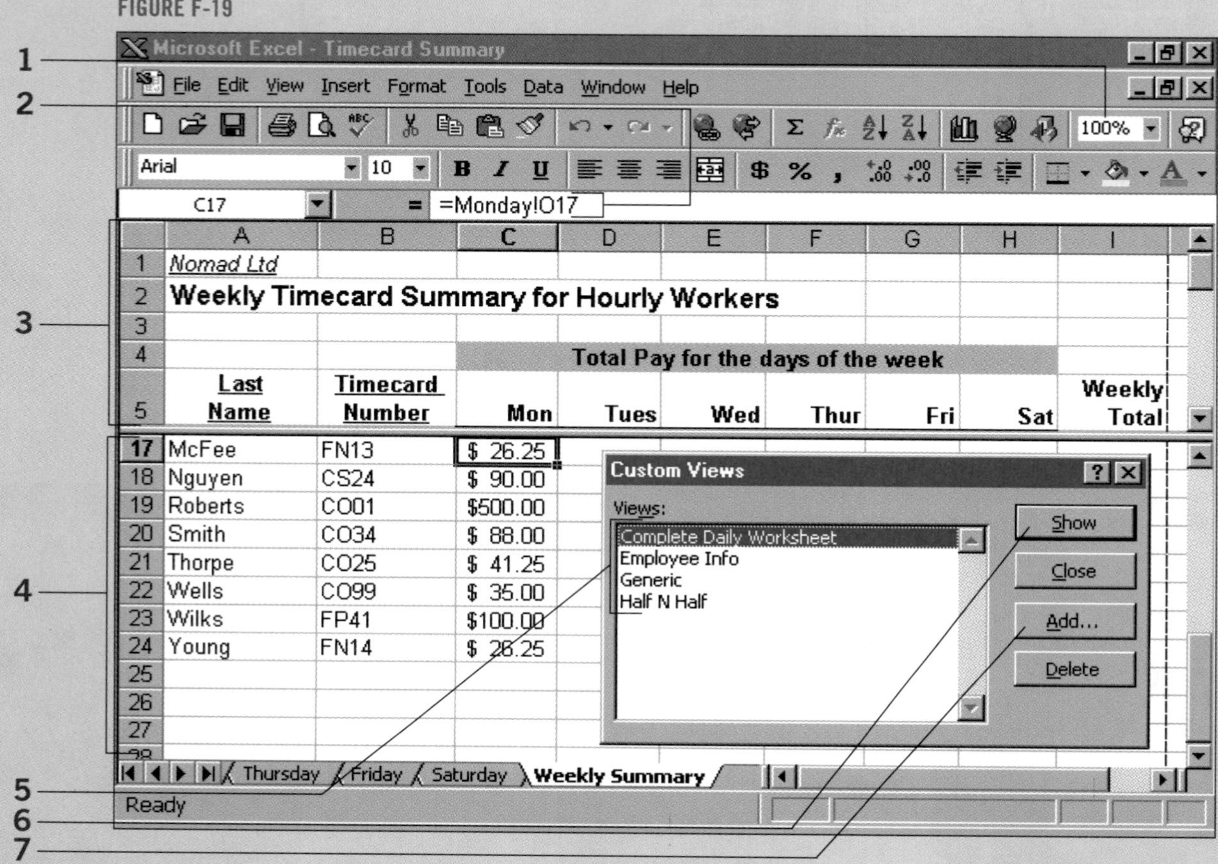

Match each of the terms with the statement that describes its function.

8. Inserts a code to print the total number of pages
9. Indicates how far down the page to start printing worksheet data
10. Indicates a page break
11. Inserts a code to print the sheet tab name in a header or footer
12. Indicates a selection to be printed

a. Dashed line
b. [icon]
c. Top margin
d. [icon]
e. Print what

Select the best answer from the list of choices.

13. You can save frequently used display and print settings by using the ________ feature.
a. Report Manager b. View menu c. Custom Views d. Save command

14. You freeze areas of the worksheet to________.
a. Freeze data and unlock formulas.
b. Lock open windows in place.
c. Freeze all data in place so that you can see it.
d. Lock column and row headings in place while you scroll through the worksheet.

15. To protect a worksheet, you must first unlock those cells that ________, and then issue the Protect Sheet command.
a. never change
b. the user will be allowed to change
c. have hidden formulas
d. are locked

Skills Review

1. Freeze columns and rows.
a. Open the workbook titled XL F-2, then save it as "Quarterly Household Budget".
b. Freeze columns A through B and rows 1 through 4 for improved viewing. (*Hint:* Click cell C4 prior to issuing the Freeze Panes command.)
c. Scroll until columns A through B and F through H are visible.
d. Press [Ctrl][Home] to return to cell C4.
e. Unfreeze the panes.

2. Insert and delete sheets.
a. With the 1997 sheet active, use the sheet pop-up menu to insert a new Sheet1.
b. Activate Sheet1.
c. Delete Sheet1.

3. Reference worksheet data.
a. In the 1997 sheet, click cell C22.
b. Type =, click cell G7, then press [Enter].
c. In cell C23, type =, click cell G18, then press [Enter].
d. To link data between the two worksheets, first activate the 1998 worksheet.
e. Click cell C4.
f. Type =.
g. Activate the 1997 worksheet.
h. Click cell F4, then press [Enter].
i. In the 1998 worksheet, copy the contents of cell C4 into cells C5:C6.
j. Preview, then print the 1998 worksheet.
k. Save the workbook.

4. Hide and protect worksheet areas.

a. In the 1997 worksheet, select row 16.
b. Issue the Hide Row command.
c. To unlock the expense data so you can make changes, first select range C10:F17.
d. Using the Protection tab of the Format Cells dialog box, turn off the locked status.
e. Using the Tools, Protection menu options, protect the sheet.
f. To make sure the other cells are locked, click cell D4.
g. Type 3.
h. Confirm the message box warning.
i. To change the first-quarter mortgage expense to $3,400, click cell C10, then type 3400.
j. Save the workbook.

5. Specify headers and footers.

a. Activate the 1997 worksheet. Using the File, Page Setup menu options, customize the Center Section of the Header to read "Lowe Family".
b. Further customize the header by changing it to appear in 12 pt bold type.
c. Set the footer to (none).
d. Preview, then print the 1997 worksheet.
e. Save the workbook.

6. Save custom views of a worksheet.

a. In the 1997 worksheet, select the range A1:H23.
b. Using the Zoom box, set the magnification so that the entire selection appears on the screen.
c. Using the View, Custom Views menu options, add a new view called "Entire Budget".
d. Save the workbook.

7. Control page breaks and page numbering.

a. Click cell A9.
b. Using the Insert, Page Break menu options, insert a page break.
c. Customize the footer to include a page number.
d. Preview and print the worksheet.
e. Save the workbook.

8. Set margins and alignment.

a. Activate the Generic custom view.
b. Select range A1:C20.
c. Using the Print menu option, under Print what, click Selection.
d. Preview the worksheet.
e. From the Print Preview window, click Setup; using the Margins tab, change the left margin to 2", and center the worksheet vertically on the page.
f. Preview, then print the worksheet.
g. Save the workbook.

Independent Challenges

1. You own PC Assist, a software training company. You have added several new entries to the August check register and are ready to enter September's check activity. Because the sheet for August will include much of the same information you need for September, you decide to copy it. Then you will edit the new sheet to fit your needs for September check activity. You will use sheet referencing to enter the beginning balance and beginning check number. Using your own data, you will complete five checks for the September register.

To complete this independent challenge:

1. Open the workbook entitled XL F-3, then save it as "Update to Check Register".
2. Delete Sheet2 and Sheet3, then create a worksheet for September by copying the August sheet.
3. With the September sheet active, delete the data in range A6:E24.
4. To update the balance at the beginning of the month, use sheet referencing from the last balance entry in the August sheet.
5. Generate the first check number. (*Hint:* Use a formula that references the last check number in August and adds one.)
6. Enter data for five checks.
7. Add a footer that includes your name left-aligned on the printout and the system date right-aligned on the printout. Add a header that displays the sheet name centered on the printout.
8. Save the workbook. Preview the September worksheet, then print it in landscape orientation on a single page.
9. Submit your printout.

2. You are a new employee for a computer software manufacturer. Your responsibility is to track the sales of different product lines and determine which computer operating system generates the most software sales each month. Although sales figures vary from month to month, the format in which data is entered does not. Use Table F-4 as a guide to create a worksheet tracking sales across personal computer (PC) platforms. Use your own data for the number of software packages sold in the DOS, Windows, and Macintosh columns. Create a summary report with all the sales summary information, then create three detailed reports for each software category: Games Software, Business Software, and Utilities Products.

To complete this independent challenge:

1. Create a new workbook, then save it as "Software Sales Summary".
2. Enter row and column labels, your own data, and formulas for the totals.

TABLE F-4

	DOS	Windows	Macintosh	Total
Games Software				
Space Wars 99				
Safari				
Flight School				
Total				
Business Software				
Word Processing				
Spreadsheet				
Presentation				
Graphics				
Page Layout				
Total				
Utilities Products				
Antivirus				
File recovery				
Total				

3. Create a summary report that includes the entire worksheet. Customize the header to include your name and the date. Set the footer to (none). Center the page both horizontally and vertically. Save the workbook. Preview and print the report.
4. Create three detailed report pages. Insert page breaks so that each software category is printed on a separate page. Number the report pages consecutively as follows: Games Software, page 1; Business Software, page 2; Utilities Products, page 3. Include your name and the date in the header of each page and the page number in the footer of each page. Save the workbook. Preview and print the report.
5. Submit your printouts.

3. You are a college student with two roommates. Each month you receive your long-distance telephone bill. Because no one wants to figure out who owes what, you split the bill three ways. You are sure that one of your roommates makes two-thirds of the long-distance calls. In order to make the situation more equitable, you decide to create a spreadsheet to track the long-distance phone calls each month. By doing so, you hope to determine who is responsible for each call. Create a spreadsheet with a separate area for each roommate. Track the following information for each month's long-distance calls: date of call, time of call, (AM or PM), call minutes, location called, state called, area code, phone number, and call charge. Total the charges for each roommate. Print a summary report of all three roommates' charges, and print a report for each roommate totaling his or her charges for the month.

To complete this independent challenge:

1. Create a new workbook, then save it as "Monthly Long Distance" to the appropriate folder on your Student Disk.
2. Enter column headings and row labels to track each call.
3. Use your own data, entering at least three long-distance calls for each roommate.
4. Create a report that prints all the call information for the month. Use the filename as the header. Format the header to make it stand out from the rest of the text. Enter your name and the date in the footer.
5. Create a report page for each roommate. Insert appropriate page breaks to print out a report for each roommate. Use the roommate's name as the header, formatted in 14-point italic type. Enter your name and the date in the footer. Center the reports on the page both horizontally and vertically. Save the workbook.
6. Preview, print, then submit the reports.

4. The World Wide Web can be used as a research tool to locate information on just about every topic imaginable, including careers. You have decided to conduct a job search using the Web. Currently, you are taking classes on computer programming, specializing in the C++ language and the Internet tool called Java. You plan to perform a search for jobs requiring these skills tracking the following information: position title, company name, city and state where company is located, whether experience is required, and salary. Your goal is to locate and list in a worksheet at least five jobs requiring C++ knowledge, and, in a separate worksheet, at least five jobs requiring Java knowledge.

To complete this independent challenge:

1. Open the workbook titled XL F-4, then save it as "Job Research – PC Programming".
2. Log on to the Internet and use your Web browser to go to http://www.course.com. From there, click Student Online Companions, click the link for this textbook, then click the Excel link for Unit F.
3. Use any combination of the following sites to search for and compile your data: Online Career Center, America's Job Bank, or The Monster Board.
4. Fill in information on at least five positions in each of the two above-mentioned worksheets.
5. Name the two sheets based on their content and copy sheets where appropriate.
6. Using your own judgment, customize the header, footer, margins, and alignment of each sheet.
7. Save the workbook, print both worksheets, then submit your printouts.

► Visual Workshop

Create the worksheet shown in Figure F-20. Save the workbook as "Generations of PCs". Preview, print, then submit the worksheet.

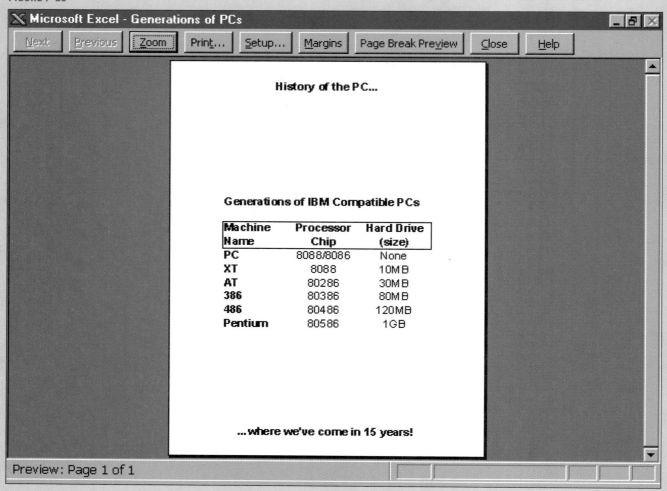

FIGURE F-20

Microsoft Excel - Generations of PCs

Next | Previous | Zoom | Print... | Setup... | Margins | Page Break Preview | Close | Help

History of the PC...

Generations of IBM Compatible PCs

Machine Name	Processor Chip	Hard Drive (size)
PC	8088/8086	None
XT	8088	10MB
AT	80286	30MB
386	80386	80MB
486	80486	120MB
Pentium	80586	1GB

...where we've come in 15 years!

Preview: Page 1 of 1

Automating
Worksheet Tasks

Objectives

- ► Plan a macro
- ► Record a macro
- ► Run a macro
- ► Edit a macro
- ► Use shortcut keys with macros
- ► Use the Personal Macro Workbook
- ► Add a macro as a menu item
- ► Create a toolbar for macros

A **macro** is a set of instructions that performs tasks in the order you specify. You create macros to automate frequently performed Excel tasks that require a series of steps. For example, if you usually type your name and date in a worksheet footer, Excel can record the keystrokes in a macro that types the text and insert the current date automatically. In this unit, you will plan and design a simple macro, then record and run the macro. Then you will edit the macro. You will also create a macro to run using shortcut keys, store a macro in the Personal Macro Workbook, add a macro option to the Tools menu, and create a new toolbar for macros. First, Evan Brillstein wants to create a macro that adds a stamp to his worksheets to identify them as originating in the accounting department.

Excel 97

Planning a Macro

As mentioned earlier, you create macros for tasks that you perform on a regular basis. For example, you can create a macro to enter and format text or to save and print a worksheet. To create a macro, you record the series of actions or write the instructions in a special format. Because the sequence of actions is important, you need to plan the macro carefully before you record it. Commands used to record, run, and modify macros are located on the Tools menu. Make sure to view the CourseHelp, "Using Macros," for more information before completing this lesson.

Evan wants to put a stamp on all his worksheets that identifies them as originating in the accounting department. He records a macro to automate this process. Evan plans the macro using the following guidelines:

CourseHelp

To view the CourseHelp for this lesson, click the Start button, point to Programs, point to CourseHelp, then click Microsoft Excel 97 Illustrated. Choose the Using Macros CourseHelp.

1. **Assign the macro a descriptive name, and write out the steps the macro will perform**
   This preplanning helps eliminate careless errors. Evan decides to name the macro DeptStamp. He writes a description of the macro, as shown in Figure G-1. See Table G-1 for a list of macros Evan might create.
2. **Decide how you will perform the actions you want to record**
   You can use the mouse, the keyboard, or a combination of the two methods. Evan decides to use a combination of the mouse and the keyboard.
3. **Practice the steps you want Excel to record and write them down**
   Evan wrote down the sequence of actions as he performed them and he is now ready to record and test the macro.
4. **Decide where to locate the description of the macro and the macro itself**
   Macros can be stored in an unused area of the active workbook, in a new workbook, or in the Personal Macro Workbook. Evan stores the macro in a new workbook.

TABLE G-1: Possible macros and their descriptive names

description of macro	descriptive name
Enter a frequently used proper name, such as Evan Brillstein	EvanBrillstein
Enter a frequently used company name, such as Nomad Ltd	CompanyName
Print the active worksheet on a single page, in landscape orientation	FitToLand
Turn off the header and footer in the active worksheet	HeadFootOff
Show a frequently used custom view, such as a generic view of the worksheet, setting the print and display settings back to Excel's defaults	GenericView

FIGURE G-1: Paper description of planned macro

Macro to create stamp with the department name

Name:	DeptStamp
Description:	Adds a stamp to the top-left of worksheet identifying it as an accounting department worksheet
Steps:	1. Position the cell pointer in cell A1
	2. Type Accounting Department, then click the Enter button
	3. Click Format on the menu bar, click Cells
	4. Click Font tab, under Font style click Bold, under Underline click Single, and under Color click Red, then click OK

Excel 97

Viewing CourseHelp

The camera icon on the opposite page indicates there is a CourseHelp available for this lesson. CourseHelps are on-screen "movies" that bring difficult concepts to life, to help you understand the material in this book. Your instructor received a CourseHelp disk and should have installed it on the machine you are using. To start CourseHelp, click the Start button, point to Programs, point to CourseHelp, then click Microsoft Excel 97 Illustrated. In the main CourseHelp window, click the topic that corresponds to this lesson. Because CourseHelp runs in a separate window, you can start and view a movie even if you're in the middle of completing a lesson. Once the movie is finished, you can click the Word program button on the taskbar and continue with the lesson, right where you left off.

Excel 97

Recording a Macro

The easiest way to create a macro is to record it using Excel's Macro Recorder. You simply turn the Macro Recorder on, enter the keystrokes, select the commands you want the macro to perform, then stop the recorder. As you record the macro, each action is translated into programming code that you can later view and modify. Evan wants to create a macro that enters a department stamp in cell A1 of the active worksheet. He creates this macro by recording his actions.

Steps

1. If necessary, click the **New button** on the Standard toolbar, then save the blank workbook as **My Excel Macros**
   Now you are ready to start the macro recording process.

QuickTip

If information in a text box is selected, you can simply type new information to replace it. This saves you from having to delete the existing entry before typing the new entry.

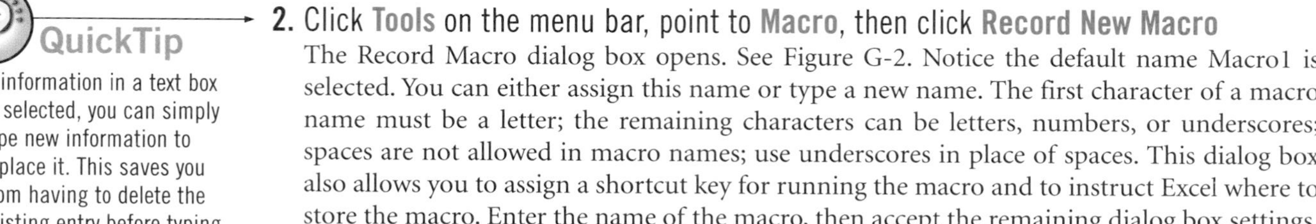

2. Click **Tools** on the menu bar, point to **Macro**, then click **Record New Macro**
   The Record Macro dialog box opens. See Figure G-2. Notice the default name Macro1 is selected. You can either assign this name or type a new name. The first character of a macro name must be a letter; the remaining characters can be letters, numbers, or underscores; spaces are not allowed in macro names; use underscores in place of spaces. This dialog box also allows you to assign a shortcut key for running the macro and to instruct Excel where to store the macro. Enter the name of the macro, then accept the remaining dialog box settings.
3. In the Macro name box, type **DeptStamp**, then click **OK**
   The dialog box closes. Excel displays the small Stop Recording toolbar containing the Stop Recording button, and the word "Recording" appears on the status bar. Take your time performing the steps because Excel records every keystroke, menu option, and mouse action that you make. Next, execute the steps that create the department stamp.
4. Press **[Ctrl][Home]**
   The cell pointer moves to cell A1. When you begin an Excel session, macros record absolute cell references. By beginning the recording in cell A1, you ensure that the macro includes the instruction to select cell A1 as the first step.
5. In cell A1, type **Accounting Department**, then click the **Enter button** on the formula bar
6. Click **Format** on the menu bar, then click **Cells**
   Now, you change the font style and attributes of the text.
7. Click the **Font tab**, in the Font style list box click **Bold**, click the **Underline list arrow** and click **Single**, then click the **Color list arrow** and click **red** (third row, first color on left)
   See Figure G-3. Confirm the changes in the dialog box, then stop the macro recording.
8. Click **OK**, click the **Stop Recording button** on the Stop Recording toolbar, click cell **D1** to deselect cell A1, then save the workbook
   Compare your results with Figure G-4.

Trouble?

If your results differ from Figure G-4, clear the contents of cell A1, then repeat Steps 2 through 8. When prompted to replace the existing macro, click Yes.

FIGURE G-2: **Record Macro dialog box**

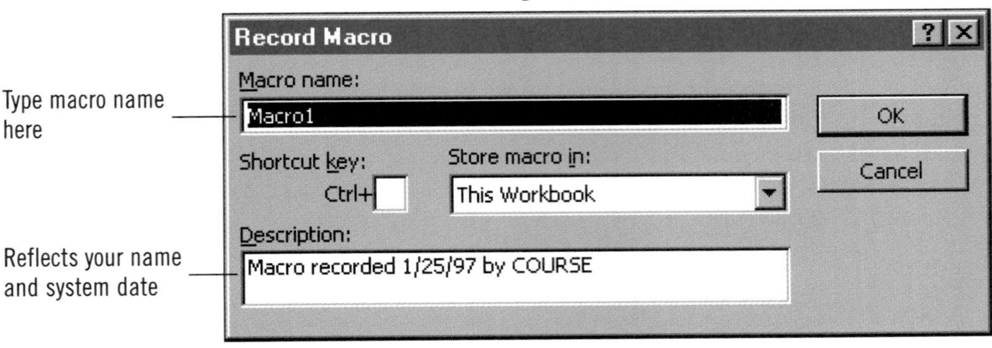

FIGURE G-3: **Font tab of the Format Cells dialog box**

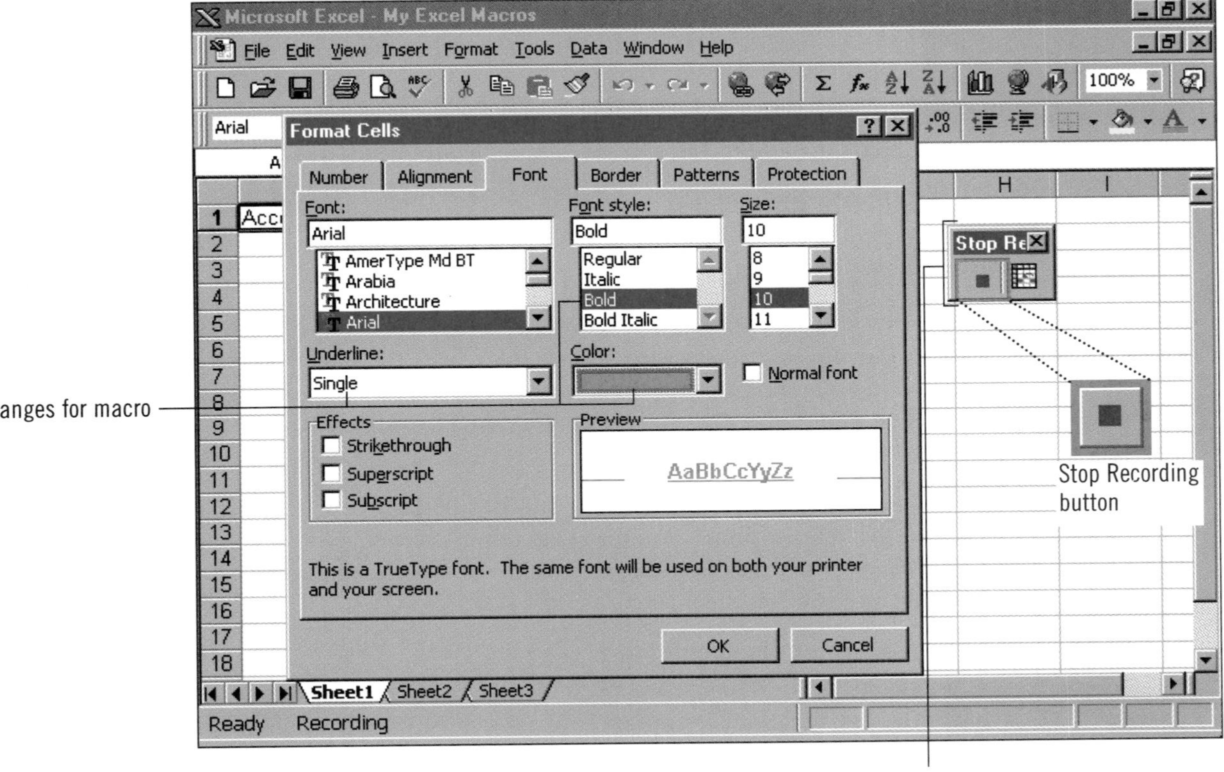

FIGURE G-4: **Personalized department stamp**

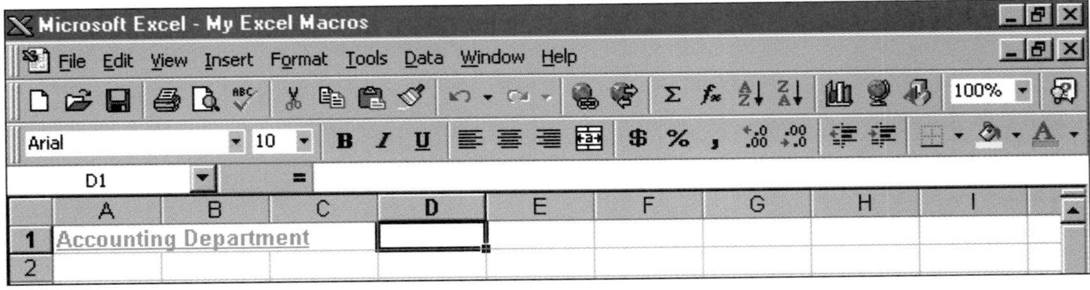

Excel 97

Excel 97

Running a Macro

Once you record a macro, you should test it to make sure that the actions performed are correct. To test a macro, you **run** or execute it. One method of running a macro is to select the macro in the Macros dialog box, then click Run. Evan clears the contents of cell A1 and then tests the DeptStamp macro. After he runs the macro from the My Excel Macros workbook, he decides to test the macro once more from a newly opened workbook.

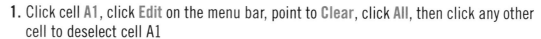

1. **Click cell A1, click Edit on the menu bar, point to Clear, click All, then click any other cell to deselect cell A1**
   When you delete the contents of a cell, any formatting still remains in the cell. By using the Clear All option on the Edit menu, you can be sure that the cell is free of contents and formatting.
2. **Click Tools on the menu bar, point to Macro, then click Macros**
   The Macro dialog box, shown in Figure G-5, lists all the macros contained in the open workbooks.
3. **Make sure DeptStamp is selected, click Run, then deselect cell A1**
   Watch your screen as the macro quickly plays back the steps you recorded in the previous lesson. When the macro is finished, your screen should look like Figure G-6. As long as the workbook containing the macro remains open, you can run the macro from any open workbook. Now you test this.
4. **Click the New button on the Standard toolbar**
   Because the new workbook automatically fills the screen, it is difficult to be sure that the My Excel Macros workbook is still open. Use the Window menu to display a list of open workbooks before you run the macro.
5. **Click Window on the menu bar**
   A list of open workbooks displays underneath the menu options. The active workbook name (in this case, Book2) appears with a checkmark to its left. See Figure G-7. Confirming that My Excel Macros is still open, you run the macro from this new workbook.
6. **Deselect cell A1 if necessary, click Tools on the menu bar, point to Macro, click Macros, make sure 'My Excel Macros.xls'!DeptStamp is selected, click Run, then deselect cell A1**
   Cell A1 should look like Figure G-6. Notice that when multiple workbooks are open, the macro name includes the workbook name between single quotation marks, followed by an exclamation point indicating that the macro is outside the active workbook. Because you do not need to save the new workbook in which you tested the macro, you close the file without saving it.
7. **Close Book2 without saving changes, then return to the My Excel Macros workbook**

QuickTip

To delete a macro, select the macro name in the Macro dialog box, click Delete, then click OK to confirm.

To stop a macro while it is running, press **[Esc]**.

FIGURE G-5: Macro dialog box

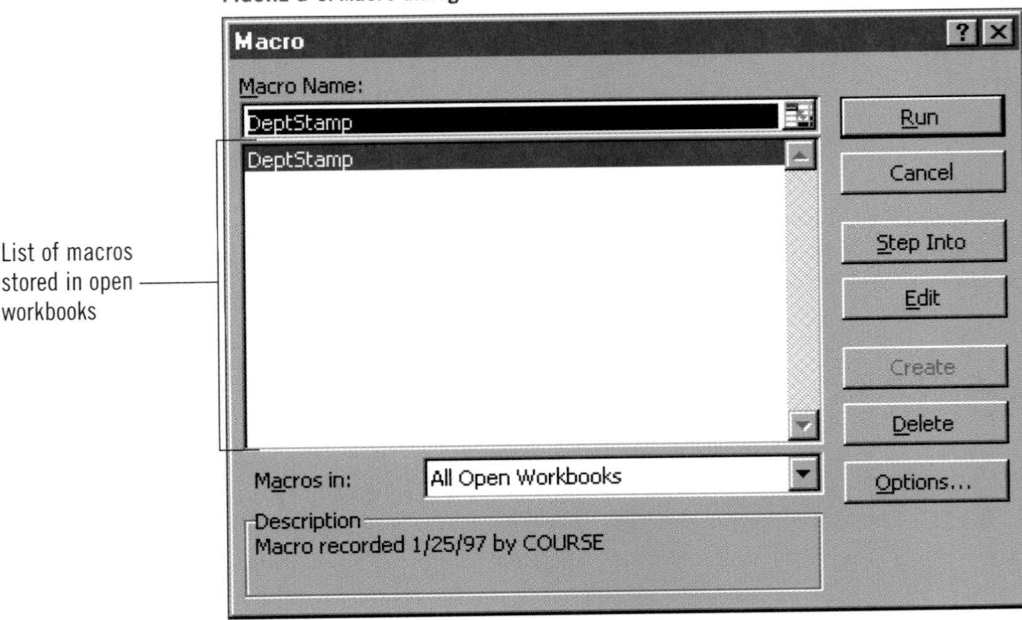

List of macros stored in open workbooks

FIGURE G-6: Result of running the edited DeptStamp macro

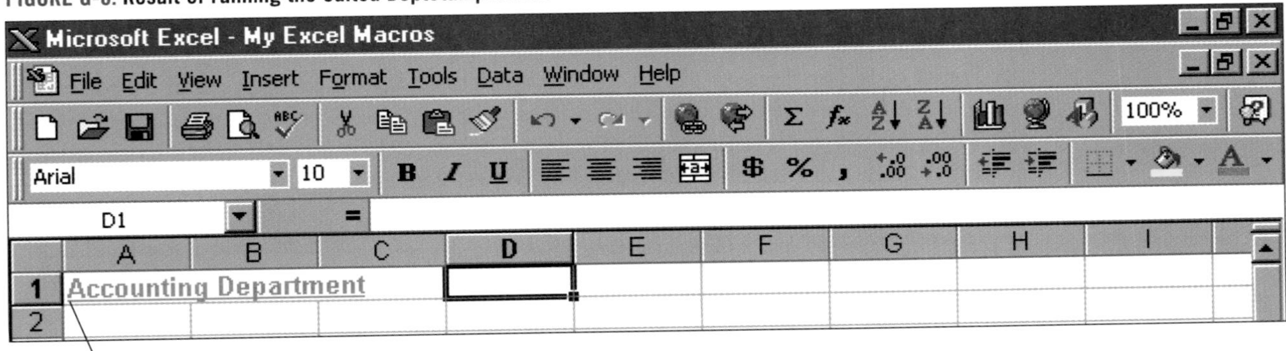

First macro instruction positions pointer in cell A1

FIGURE G-7: Window menu showing list of open workbooks

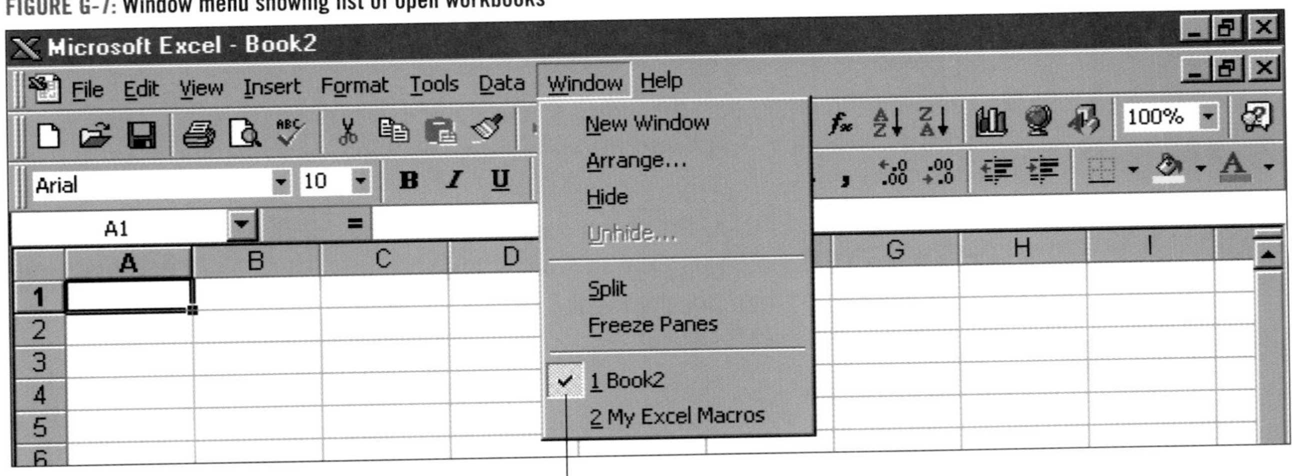

Check mark indicates active workbook

Excel 97

Excel 97

Editing a Macro

When you use the Macro Recorder to create a macro, the instructions are recorded automatically in Visual Basic for Applications programming language. Each macro is stored as a **module**, or program code container, attached to the workbook. Once you record a macro, you might need to change it. If you have a lot of changes to make, it might be best to re-record the macro. If you need to make only minor adjustments, you can edit the macro code, or program instructions, directly using the Visual Basic Editor. Evan wants to modify his macro to change the point size of the department stamp to 12.

QuickTip

You can also start the Visual Basic Editor by clicking Tools on the menu bar, pointing to Macro, then clicking Visual Basic Editor or by pressing [Alt][F11].

1. **Make sure the My Excel Macros workbook is open, click Tools on the menu bar, point to Macro, click Macros, make sure DeptStamp is selected, then click Edit**
   The Visual Basic Editor starts showing the DeptStamp macro steps in a numbered module window (in this case, Module1). You can maximize the module window to get a better look at the macro code.
2. **Maximize the window titled My Excel Macros.xls – [Module1 (Code)], then examine the steps in the macro**
   See Figure G-8. The name of the macro and the date it was recorded appear at the top of the module window. Notice that Excel translates your keystrokes and commands into words, known as macro **code**. For example, the line .FontStyle = "Bold" was generated when you clicked Bold in the Format Cells dialog box. When you make changes in a dialog box during macro recording, Excel automatically stores all the dialog box settings in the macro code. You also see lines of code that you didn't generate directly while recording the DeptStamp macro; for example, .Name = "Arial".
3. **In the line .Size = 10, double-click 10 to select it, then type 12**
   Because Module1 is attached to the workbook and not stored as a separate file, any changes to the module are saved automatically when the workbook is saved. Next, print the change to Module1.
4. **In the Visual Basic Editor, click File on the menu bar, click Print, then click OK to print the module**
   Review the printout of Module1, then return to Excel.
5. **Click File on the menu bar, then click Close and Return to Microsoft Excel**
   You want to rerun the DeptStamp macro to view the point size edit you made using the Visual Basic Editor.
6. **Click cell A1, click Edit on the menu bar, point to Clear, click All, deselect cell A1, click Tools on the menu bar, point to Macro, click Macros, make sure DeptStamp is selected, click Run, then deselect cell A1**
   Compare your results with Figure G-9.
7. **Save the workbook**

FIGURE G-8: Visual Basic Editor showing Module1

Name of the macro

Code window

Microsoft Visual Basic - My Excel Macros.xls - [Module1 (Code)]

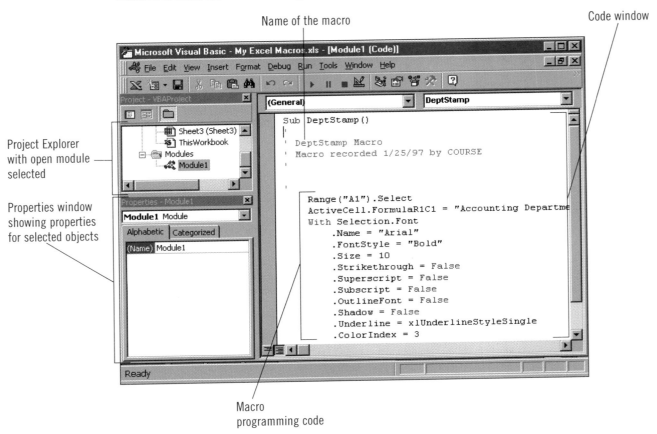

Project Explorer with open module selected

Properties window showing properties for selected objects

```
Sub DeptStamp()
'
' DeptStamp Macro
' Macro recorded 1/25/97 by COURSE
'

'
    Range("A1").Select
    ActiveCell.FormulaR1C1 = "Accounting Departme
    With Selection.Font
        .Name = "Arial"
        .FontStyle = "Bold"
        .Size = 10
        .Strikethrough = False
        .Superscript = False
        .Subscript = False
        .OutlineFont = False
        .Shadow = False
        .Underline = xlUnderlineStyleSingle
        .ColorIndex = 3
```

Macro programming code

Excel 97

FIGURE G-9: Result of running the edited DeptStamp macro

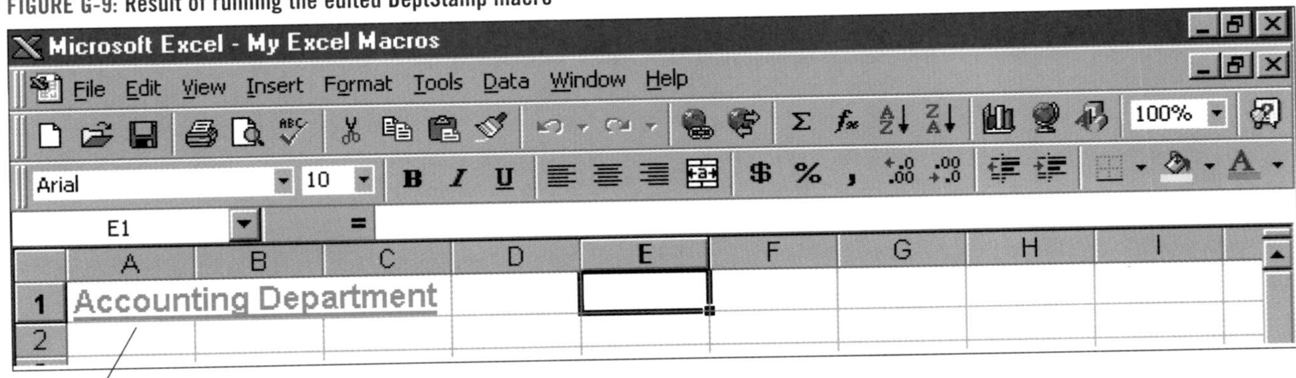

Font size enlarged to 12pt

CLUES TO USE

Adding comments to code

With practice, you will be able to interpret the lines of code within your macro. Others who use your macro, however, might want to know the function of a particular line. You can explain the code by adding comments to the macro. Comments are explanatory text added to the lines of code. When you enter a comment, you must type an apostrophe (') before the comment text. Otherwise, Excel thinks you have entered a command. On a color monitor, comments appear in green after you press [Enter]. See Figure G-8. You also can insert blank lines in the macro code to make the code more readable. To do this, type an apostrophe, then press [Enter].

Excel 97

Using Shortcut Keys with Macros

In addition to running a macro from the Macro dialog box, you can run a macro by assigning a shortcut key combination. Using shortcut keys to run macros reduces the number of keystrokes required to begin macro play back. You assign shortcut key combinations in the Record Macro dialog box. Evan also wants to create a macro called CompanyName to enter the company name into a worksheet. He assigns a shortcut key combination to run the macro.

Steps

1. **Click cell B2**
   You will record the macro in cell B2. You want to be able to enter the company name anywhere in a worksheet. Therefore, you will not begin the macro with an instruction to position the cell pointer as you did in the DeptStamp macro.

2. **Click Tools on the menu bar, point to Macro, then click Record New Macro**
   The Record Macro dialog box opens. You notice the option Shortcut key: Ctrl+ followed by a blank box. You can type a letter (A–Z) in the Shortcut key box to assign the key combination of [Ctrl] plus a letter to run the macro. Use the key combination [Ctrl][Shift] plus a letter. Doing this avoids overriding any of Excel's previously assigned [Ctrl]+[letter] shortcut keys, such as [Ctrl]+[C] for Copy.

3. **With the default macro name selected, type CompanyName, click the Shortcut key box, press and hold [Shift], then type C**
   Compare your screen with Figure G-10. You are ready to record the CompanyName macro.

4. **Click OK to close the dialog box, then start recording the macro**
   By default, Excel records absolute cell references in macros. Beginning the macro in cell B2 causes the macro code to begin with a statement to select cell B2. Because you want to be able to run this macro in any active cell, you need to instruct Excel to record relative cell references while recording the macro. You can do this before recording the macro keystrokes by selecting the Relative Reference button on the Stop Recording toolbar.

QuickTip

When you begin an Excel session, the Relative Reference button is toggled off, indicating that Excel is recording absolute cell references in macros. Once selected, and until it is toggled back off, the Relative Reference setting remains in effect during the current Excel session.

5. **Click the Relative Reference button on the Stop Recording toolbar**
   The Relative Reference button appears indented to indicate that it is selected. See Figure G-11. This button is a toggle and retains the relative reference setting until it is clicked off.

6. **In cell B2, type Nomad Ltd, click the Enter button on the formula bar, press [Ctrl][i] to italicize the text, click the Stop Recording button on the Stop Recording toolbar, then deselect cell B2**
   Nomad Ltd appears in italics in cell B2. You are ready to run the macro in cell A5 using the shortcut key combination.

7. **Click cell A5, press and hold [Ctrl][Shift], type C, deselect the cell**
   The result appears in cell A5. See Figure G-12. Because the macro played back in selected cell (A5) instead of the cell where it was recorded (B2), Evan is convinced that the macro recorded relative cell references.

8. **Save the workbook**

FIGURE G-10: **Record Macro dialog box with shortcut key assigned**

Record Macro

Macro name:

CompanyName

Shortcut key: Ctrl+Shift+ C

Store macro in: This Workbook

Description:

Macro recorded 1/25/97 by COURSE

OK

Cancel

Shortcut to run macro

FIGURE G-11: **Stop Recording toolbar with Relative Reference button selected**

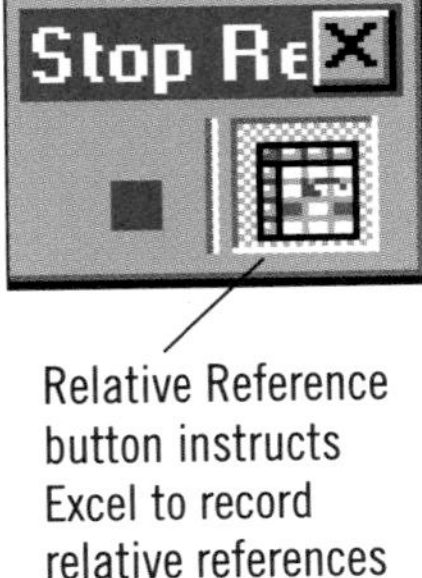

Relative Reference button instructs Excel to record relative references

FIGURE G-12: **Result of running CompanyName macro**

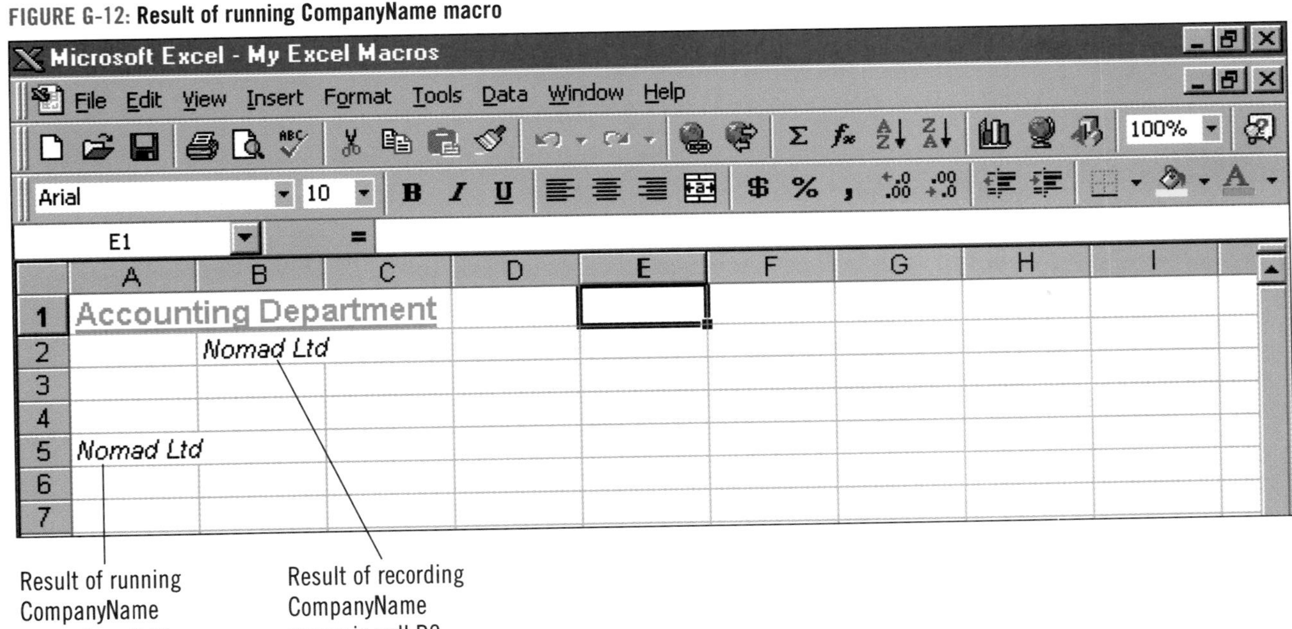

Result of running CompanyName macro in cell A5

Result of recording CompanyName macro in cell B2

Excel 97

Using the Personal Macro Workbook

You can store commonly used macros in a **Personal Macro Workbook**. The Personal Macro Workbook is always available, unless you specify otherwise, and gives you access to all the macros it contains, regardless of which workbooks are open. The Personal Macro Workbook file is created automatically the first time you choose to store a macro in it. Additional macros are added to the Personal Macro Workbook when you store them there. Evan often finds himself adding a footer to his worksheets identifying his department, the workbook name, the sheet name, the page number, and current date. He saves time by creating a macro that automatically inserts this footer. Because he wants this macro to be available whenever he uses Excel, Evan decides to store this macro in the Personal Macro Workbook.

Steps

1. From any cell in the active worksheet, click **Tools** on the menu bar, point to **Macro**, then click **Record New Macro**
   The Record Macro dialog box opens. Name the macro FooterStamp. You also want to assign a shortcut key.
2. In the Macro name box, type **FooterStamp**, click the **Shortcut key box**, press and hold **[Shift]**, type **F**, then click the **Store macro in list arrow**
   Notice that This Workbook is selected by default, indicating that Excel automatically stores macros in the active workbook. See Figure G-13. You also can choose to store the macro in a new workbook or in the Personal Macro Workbook.
3. Click **Personal Macro Workbook**, then click **OK**
   The recorder is on, and you are ready to record the macro keystrokes.
4. Click **File** on the menu bar, click **Page Setup**, click the **Header/Footer tab** (make sure to do this even if it is already active), click **Custom Footer**, in the Left section box, type **Accounting**, click the **Center section box**, click the **File Name button**, press **[Spacebar]**, type **/**, press **[Spacebar]**, click the **Sheet Name button**, click the **Right section box**, click the **Date button**, click **OK** to return to the Header/Footer tab
   The footer stamp is set up, as shown in Figure G-14.
5. Click **OK** to return to the worksheet, then click the **Stop Recording button** on the Stop Recording toolbar
   You want to ensure that the macro will set the footer stamp in any active worksheet. To test this, you activate Sheet2, type some sample text, run the FooterStamp macro, then preview the worksheet.
6. Activate Sheet2, in cell A1 type **Testing the FooterStamp macro**, press **[Enter]**, press and hold **[Ctrl][Shift]**, then type **F**
   The FooterStamp macro plays back the sequence of commands. Preview the worksheet to ensure the macro worked.
7. Preview, then save the worksheet
   Evan is satisfied that the FooterStamp macro works on any active worksheet. Next, Evan adds the macro as a menu item on the Tools menu.

Trouble?

If you are prompted to replace an existing macro named FooterStamp, click Yes.

QuickTip

Once created, the Personal Macro Workbook file is usually stored in the XLSTART folder under the name "Personal".

QuickTip

You can copy or move macros stored in other workbooks to the Personal Macro Workbook using the Visual Basic Editor.

FIGURE G-13: Record Macro dialog box showing Store macro in options

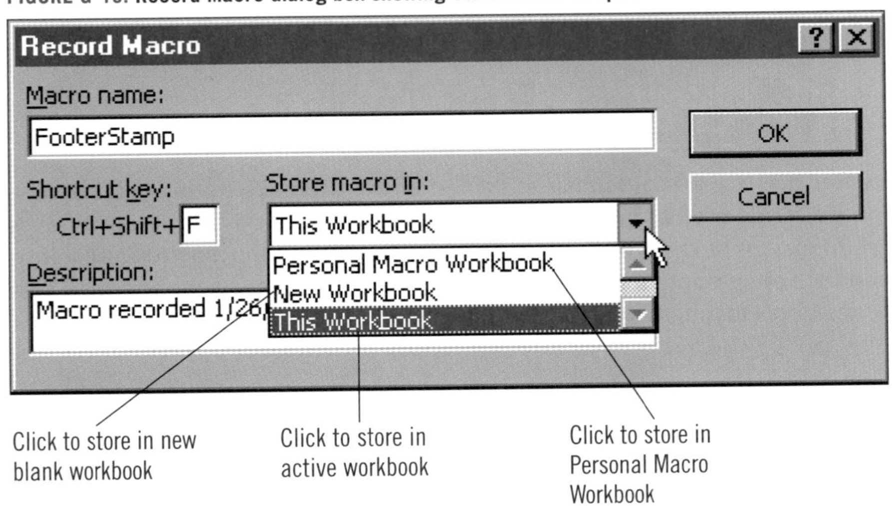

FIGURE G-14: Header/Footer tab showing custom footer settings

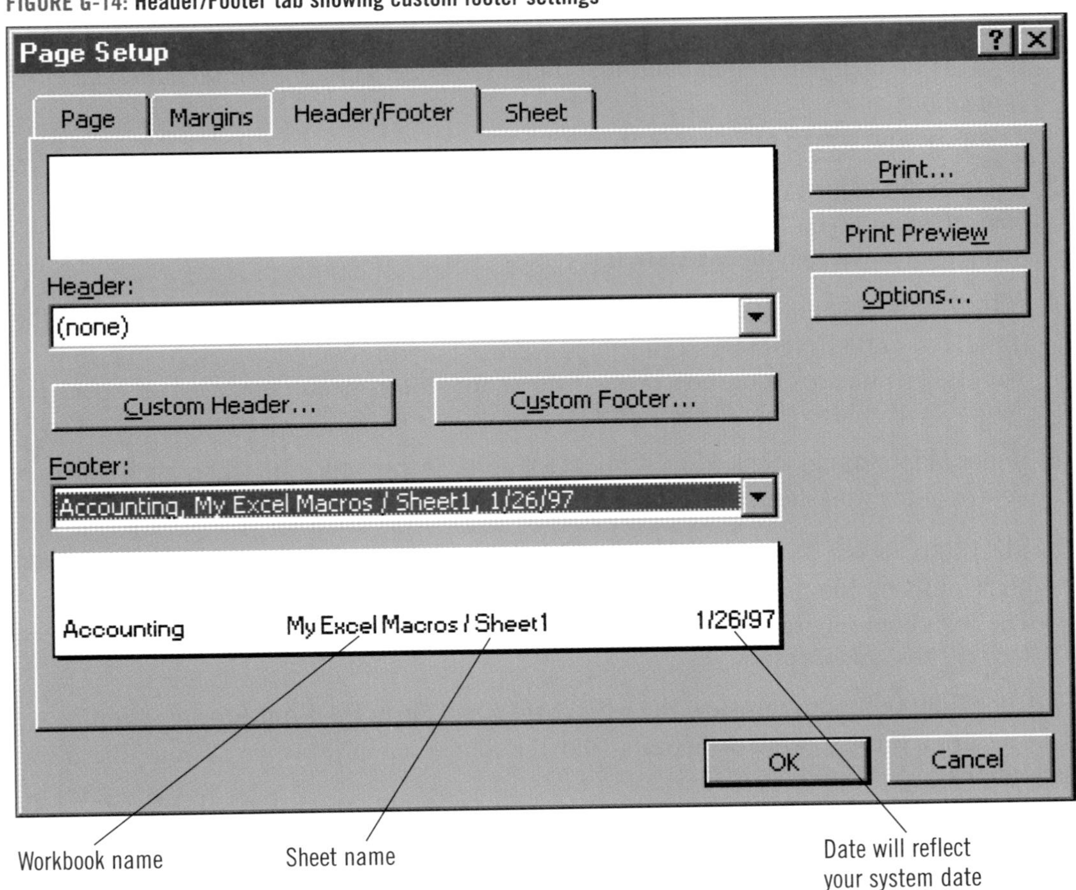

Excel 97

CLUES TO USE

Working with the Personal Macro Workbook

Once created, the Personal Macro Workbook automatically opens each time you start Excel. By default, the Personal Macro Workbook is hidden as a precautionary measure. You can add macros to the Personal Macro Workbook when it is hidden, but you cannot delete macros from it.

Excel 97

Adding a Macro as a Menu Item

The **Worksheet menu bar** is a special toolbar at the top of the Excel screen that you can customize. In addition to storing macros in the Personal Macro Workbook so that they are always available, you can add macros as items on a menu. To increase the macro's availability, Evan decides to add the FooterStamp macro as an item on the Tools menu. First, he adds a custom menu item to the Tools menu, then he assigns the macro to that menu item.

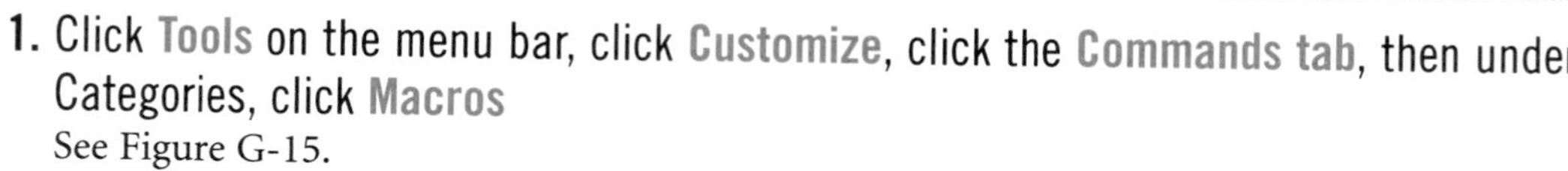

Steps

QuickTip

If you want to add a command to a menu bar, the first step is to display the toolbar containing the menu to which you want to add the command.

Trouble?

If you don't see 'PERSONAL.XLS'!FooterStamp under Macro name, try repositioning the Assign Macro dialog box.

1. **Click Tools on the menu bar, click Customize, click the Commands tab, then under Categories, click Macros**
   See Figure G-15.
2. **Under Commands, click Custom Menu Item, drag the selection to Tools on the menu bar (the menu opens), then point just under the Wizard option, *but do not release the mouse button***
   Compare your screen to Figure G-16.
3. **Release the mouse button**
   Now, Custom Menu Item is the last item on the Tools menu. Next, edit the name of the menu item and assign the macro to it.
4. **With the Tools menu still open, right-click Custom Menu Item, select the text in the Name box (&Custom Menu Item), type Footer Stamp, then click Assign Macro**
   The Assign Macro dialog box opens behind the Tools menu. You need to select the FooterStamp macro from the list.
5. **Under Macro name, click PERSONAL.XLS!FooterStamp, click OK, then click Close**
   Return to the worksheet, and test the new menu item in Sheet3.
6. **Click the Sheet3 tab, in cell A1 type Testing macro menu item, press [Enter], then click Tools on the menu bar**
   The Tools menu appears with the new menu option at the bottom. See Figure G-17. You can now test this menu option.
7. **Click Footer Stamp, preview the worksheet, then close the Print Preview window**
   The Print Preview window appears with the footer stamp. Now, you'll reset the menu options.
8. **Click Tools on the menu bar, click Customize, click the Toolbars tab, click Worksheet Menu Bar to select it, click Reset, click OK to confirm, click Close, then click Tools on the menu bar to ensure the custom item has been deleted**
   Because you did not make any changes to your workbook, you don't need to save it. Next, you create a toolbar for macros and add macros to it.

FIGURE G-15: Commands tab of the Customize dialog box showing macro options

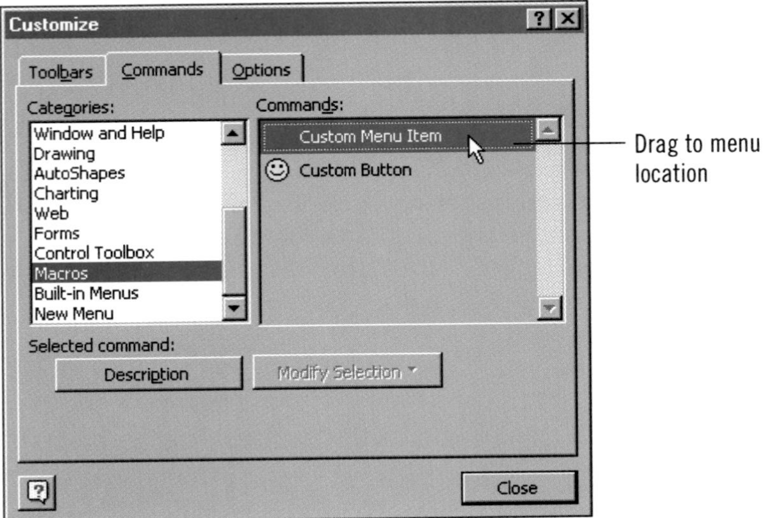

FIGURE G-16: Tools menu showing placement of Custom Menu Item

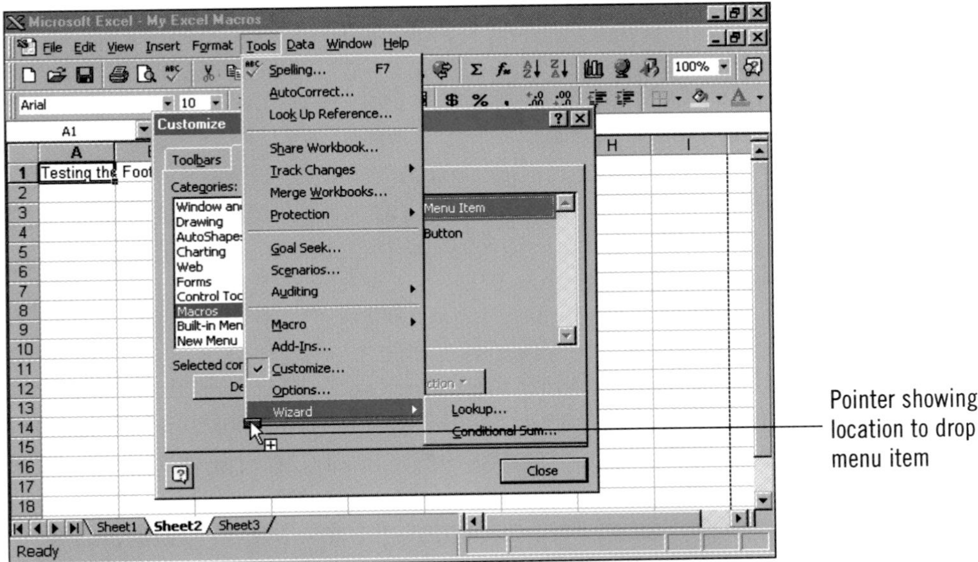

FIGURE G-17: Tools menu with new Footer Stamp item

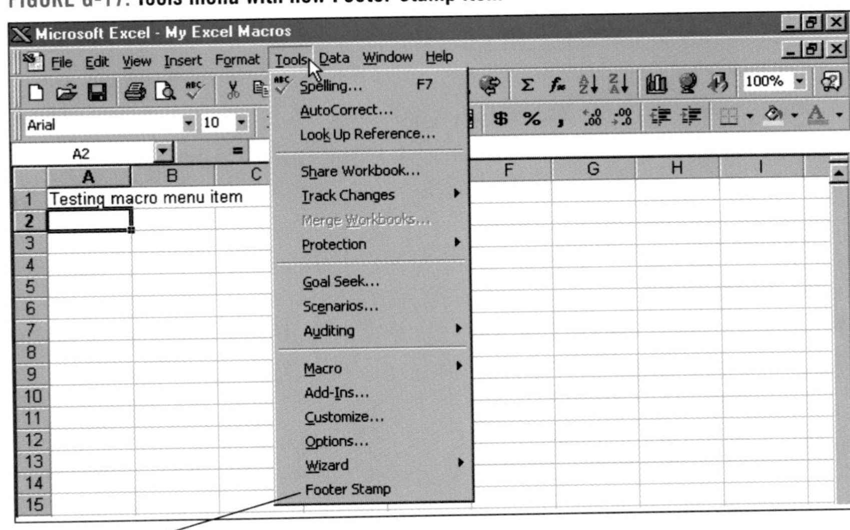

Excel 97

Creating a Toolbar for Macros

Toolbars contain buttons that allow you to access commonly used commands. You can create your own custom toolbars to organize commands so that you can find and use them quickly. Once you create a toolbar, you then add buttons to access Excel commands such as macros. Evan has decided to create a custom toolbar called Macros that will contain buttons to run two of his macros.

Steps

QuickTip

Toolbars you create or customize are available to all workbooks on your own PC. You also can ensure that a custom toolbar is available with a specific workbook by attaching the toolbar to the workbook using the Toolbar tab in the Customize dialog box.

1. With Sheet3 active, click **Tools** on the menu bar, click **Customize**, click the **Toolbars tab** if necessary, then click **New**
   The New Toolbar dialog box opens, as shown in Figure G-18. Under Toolbar name, a default name of Custom1 is selected. You name the toolbar Macros.
2. Type **Macros**, then click **OK**
   Excel adds the new toolbar named Macros to the bottom of the list and a small, empty toolbar named Macros opens. See Figure G-19. Notice that you cannot see the entire toolbar name. A toolbar starts small and automatically expands to fit the buttons assigned to it. Now you are ready to add buttons to the toolbar.
3. If necessary, drag the **Macros toolbar** off the Customize dialog box and into the worksheet area; in the Customize dialog box, click the **Commands tab**, under Categories click **Macros**, then drag the Custom Button over the new Macros toolbar
   The Macros toolbar now contains one button. Because you want the toolbar to contain two macros, you add an additional Custom Button to the toolbar.
4. Drag the **Custom Button** over the Macros toolbar again
   With the two buttons in place, you customize the buttons and assign macros to them.
5. Right-click the leftmost on the Macros toolbar, in the Name box select **&Custom Button**, type **Department Stamp**, click **Assign Macro**, click **DeptStamp**, then click **OK**
   With the first toolbar button customized, you are ready to customize the second button.
6. With the Customize dialog box open, right-click the rightmost on the Macros toolbar, edit the name to read **Company Name**, click **Change Button Image**, click (bottom row, third from the left) in the Macros dialog box, right-click , click **Assign Macro**, click **Company Name** to select it, click **OK**, then close the Customize dialog box
   The Macros toolbar appears with the two customized macro buttons. Next, you test the buttons.
7. Move the mouse pointer over on the Macros toolbar to display the macro name (Department Stamp), then click to run the macro; click cell **B2**, move the mouse pointer over on the Macros toolbar to display the macro name (Company Name), click , then deselect the cell
   Compare your screen with Figure G-20. Notice that the DeptStamp macro automatically replaces the contents of cell A1. Now remove the toolbar.
8. Click **Tools** on the menu bar, click **Customize**, click the **Toolbars tab** if necessary, under Toolbars click **Macros** to select it, click **Delete**, click **OK** to confirm the deletion, then click **Close**
9. Save, then close the workbook

Trouble?

If you are prompted to save the changes to the Personal Macro Workbook, click Yes.

FIGURE G-18: New Toolbar dialog box

FIGURE G-19: Customize dialog box with new Macros toolbar

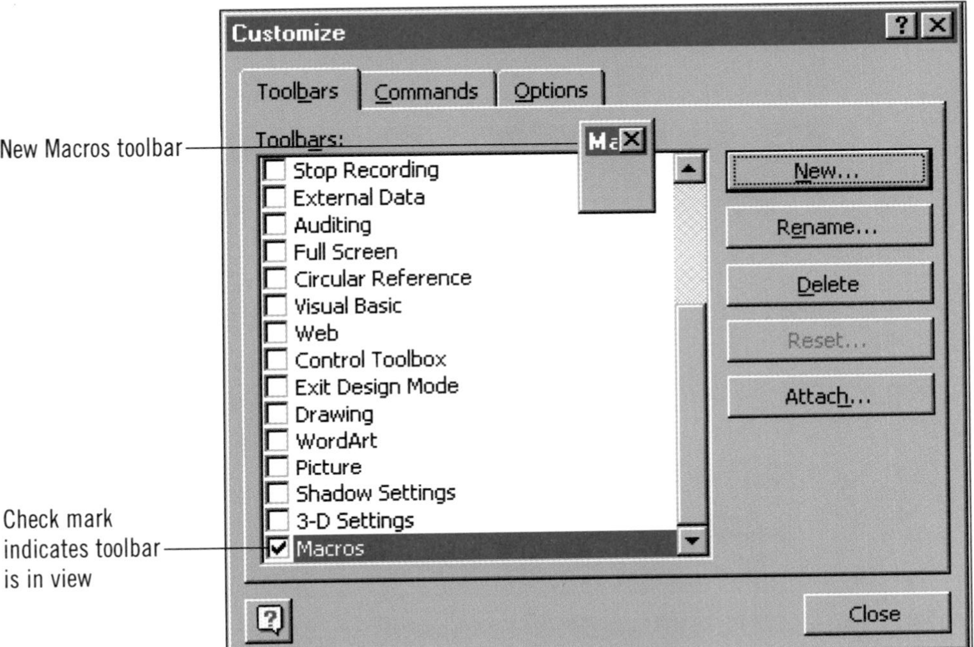

FIGURE G-20: Worksheet showing Macros toolbar with two customized buttons

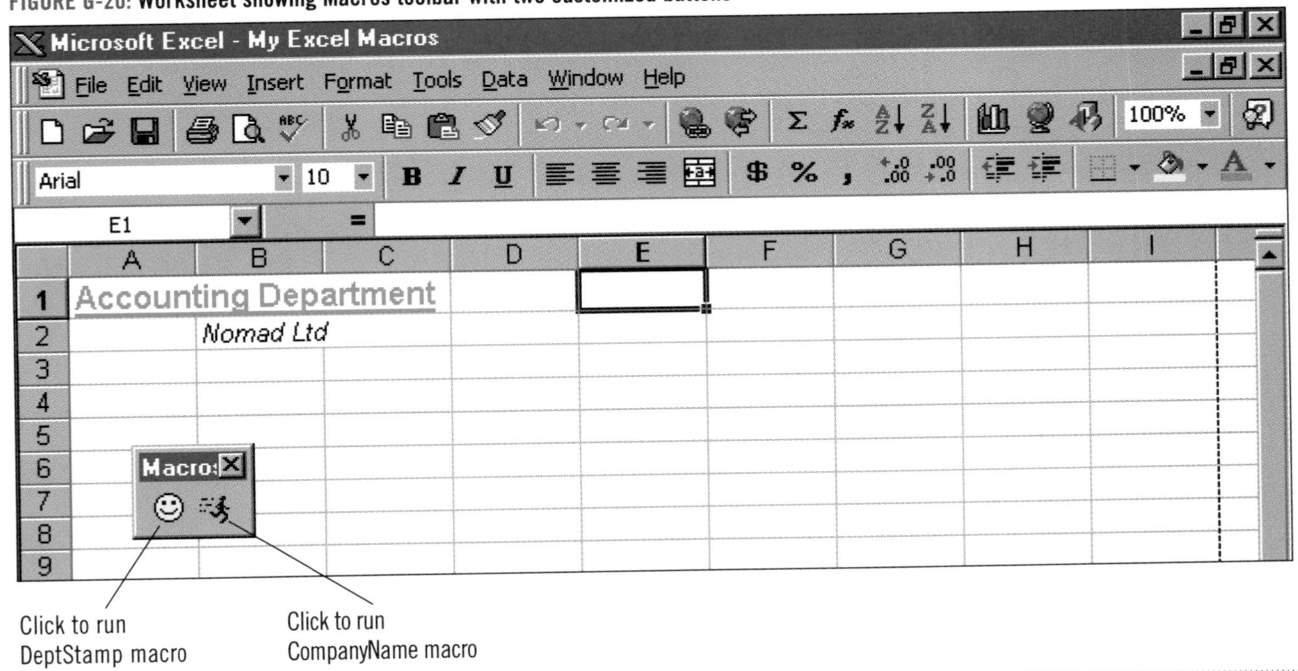

Practice

► Concepts Review

Label each of the elements of the Excel screen shown in Figure G-21.

FIGURE G-21

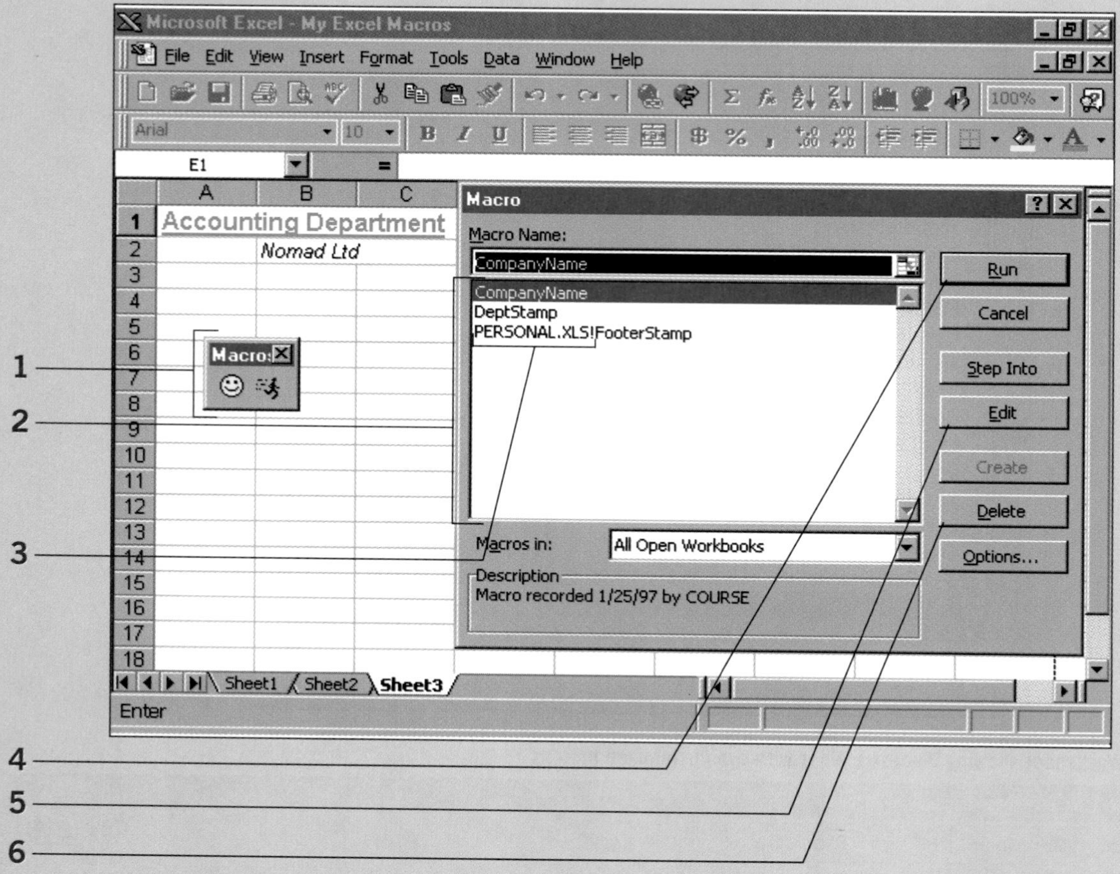

Select the best answer from the list of choices.

7. Which of the following is the best candidate for a macro?

a. One-button or one-keystroke commands
b. Often-used sequences of commands or actions
c. Seldom-used commands or tasks
d. Nonsequential tasks

8. When you are recording a macro, you can execute commands by using

a. Only the keyboard.
b. Only the mouse.
c. Any combination of the keyboard and the mouse.
d. Only menu commands.

9. A macro is stored in
- **a.** The body of a worksheet used for data.
- **b.** An unused area to the far right or well below the worksheet contents.
- **c.** A module attached to a workbook.
- **d.** A Custom Menu Item.

10. Which of the following is *not* true about editing a macro?
- **a.** You edit macros using the Visual Basic Editor.
- **b.** A macro cannot be edited and must be recorded again.
- **c.** You can type changes directly in the existing macro code.
- **d.** You can make more than one editing change in a macro.

11. Why is it important to preplan a macro?
- **a.** Macros won't be stored if they contain errors.
- **b.** Planning helps prevent careless errors from being introduced into the macro.
- **c.** It is very difficult to correct errors you make in a macro.
- **d.** Planning ensures that your macro will not contain errors.

12. Macros are recorded with relative references
- **a.** Only if the Relative Reference button is selected.
- **b.** In all cases.
- **c.** Only if relative references are chosen while recording the macro.
- **d.** Only if the Absolute Reference button is not selected.

13. You can run macros
- **a.** From the Macro dialog box.
- **b.** From shortcut key combinations.
- **c.** As items on menus.
- **d.** Using all of the above.

Skills Review

1. Record a macro.
- **a.** Create a new workbook, then save it as "Macros".
- **b.** You will record a macro to enter and format your name, address, and telephone number in a worksheet. Click Tools on the menu bar, point to Macro, then click Record New Macro.
- **c.** In the Macro name box, type "MyAddress", click the Store macro in list arrow and click This Workbook, then click OK to begin recording.
- **d.** Ensure that the Relative Reference button on the Stop Recording toolbar is toggled off.
- **e.** Enter your personal information as follows: Type your name in cell A1; type your street address in cell A2; type your city, state, and ZIP code in cell A3; then type your telephone number in cell A4.
- **f.** Select range A1:D4, then format it to be 14-point Arial bold.
- **g.** Add a border and color of your choice to the selected range.
- **h.** Click the Stop Recording button on the Stop Recording toolbar.
- **i.** Save the workbook.

2. **Run a macro.**
   a. Make sure range A1:D4 is selected. Using the menu commands Edit, Clear, All, clear the cell entries.
   b. Click Tools on the menu bar, point to Macro, click Macros, in the list box click MyAddress, then click Run.
   c. Clear the cell entries generated by running the MyAddress macro.
   d. Save the workbook.

3. **Edit a macro.**
   a. Click Tools on the menu bar, point to Macro, click Macros, click MyAddress, then click Edit.
   b. Locate the line of code that defines the font size, then change the size to 18 points.
   c. Edit the selected range to A1:E4 (increasing it by one column to accommodate the changed label size).
   d. Add a comment line that describes this macro.
   e. Print the module, then return to Excel.
   f. Test the macro in Sheet1.
   g. Save the workbook.

4. **Use shortcut keys with macros.**
   a. While in Sheet1, using the Tools menu, open the Record Macro dialog box.
   b. In the Macro name box, type MyName.
   c. In the Shortcut key box, press and hold [Shift], then type N.
   d. Click OK to begin recording.
   e. Enter your full name in cell G1. Format as desired.
   f. Click the Stop Recording button on the Stop Recording toolbar.
   g. Clear cell G1.
   h. Use the shortcut key to run the MyName macro.
   i. Save the workbook.

5. **Use the Personal Macro Workbook.**
   a. Open the Record Macro dialog box.
   b. Name the macro FitToLand.
   c. Choose to store the macro in the Personal Macro Workbook, then click OK. If you are prompted to replace the existing FitToLand macro, click Yes.
   d. Record a macro that sets print orientation to landscape, scaled to fit on a page.
   e. Stop the macro recording.
   f. Activate Sheet2, and enter some test data in cell A1.
   g. Run the FitToLand macro.
   h. Preview Sheet2.

6. **Add a macro as a menu item.**
   a. Click Tools on the menu bar, click Customize, click the Commands tab, under Categories click Macros, then under Commands click Custom Menu Item.
   b. Drag the Custom Menu Item to the Tools menu, point to Macro, then release the mouse button.
   c. Right-click Custom Menu Item on the Tools menu, then rename the item "Fit to Landscape".
   d. Click Assign Macro, click PERSONAL.XLS!FitToLand, then click OK.
   e. Close the Customize dialog box.
   f. Activate Sheet3, then enter some test data in cell A1.
   g. Run the Fit to Landscape macro from the Tools menu.
   h. Preview the worksheet.
   i. Using the Tools, Customize menu options, reset the toolbar titled Worksheet menu bar.
   j. Save the workbook.

7. Create a toolbar for macros.

a. Make sure the Macros workbook is activated, click Tools on the menu bar, click Customize, click the Toolbars tab, then click New.
b. Name the toolbar "My Info", then click OK.
c. Click the Commands tab, click Macros, then drag the new toolbar onto the worksheet.
d. Drag the Custom Button to the My Info toolbar.
e. Again, drag the Custom Button to the My Info toolbar.
f. Right-click the first button, rename it My Address, click Assign Macro, click MyAddress, then click OK.
g. Right-click the second button, edit the name to read My Name, click Change Button Image, click the button image of your choice; right-click the new button, click Assign Macro, change the store option to This Workbook, click MyName, then click OK.
h. Close the dialog box.
i. Clear the cell data, then test both macro buttons on the My Info toolbar.
j. Use the Toolbars tab of the Customize dialog box to delete the toolbar named My Info.
k. Save, then close the workbook.

Independent Challenges

1. As a computer-support employee of an accounting firm, you are required to develop ways to help your fellow employees work more efficiently. Employees have asked for Excel macros that will do the following:

- Delete the current row and insert a blank row
- Delete the current column and insert a blank column
- Format a selected group of cells with a red pattern, in 12-point Times bold italic

To complete this independent challenge:

1. Plan and write the steps necessary for each macro.
2. Create a new workbook, then save it as "Excel Utility Macros".
3. Create a new toolbar called Helpers.
4. Create a macro for each employee request described above.
5. Add descriptive comment lines to each module.
6. Add each macro to the Tools menu.
7. On the Helpers toolbar, install buttons to run the macros.
8. Test each macro by using the Run command, the menu command, and the new buttons.
9. Save, then print the module for each macro.
10. Delete the new toolbar, reset the Worksheet menu bar, then submit your printouts.

2. You are an analyst in the finance department of a large bank. Every quarter, you produce a number of single-page quarterly budget worksheets. Your manager has informed you that certain worksheets need to contain a footer stamp indicating that the worksheet was produced in the finance department. The footer also should show the date, the current page number of the total pages, and the worksheet filename. You decide that the stamp should not include a header. It's tedious to add the footer stamp and to clear the existing header and footer for the numerous worksheets you produce. You will record a macro to do this.

To complete this independent challenge:

1. Plan and write the steps to create the macro.
2. Create a new workbook, then save it as "Header and Footer Stamp".
3. Create the macro described above. Make sure it adds the footer with the department name, and so forth and also clears the header.
4. Add descriptive comment lines to the macro code.
5. Add the macro to the Tools menu.
6. Create a toolbar titled Stamp, then install a button on the toolbar to run the macro.
7. Test the macro to make sure it works from the Run command, menu command, and new button.
8. Save and print the module for the macro.
9. Delete the new toolbar, reset the Worksheet menu bar, then submit your printout.

3. You are an administrative assistant to the marketing vice-president at Sweaters, Inc. A major part of your job is to create spreadsheets that project sales results in different markets. It seems that you are constantly changing the print settings so that workbooks print in landscape orientation and are scaled to fit on one page. You have decided that it is time to create a macro to streamline this process.

To complete this independent challenge:

1. Plan and write the steps necessary for the macro.
2. Create a new workbook, then save it as "Sweaters Inc Macro".
3. Create a macro that changes the page orientation to landscape and scales the worksheet to fit on a page.
4. Test the macro.
5. Save and print the module sheet.
6. Delete any toolbars you created, reset the Worksheet menu bar, then submit your printout.

4. Research conducted using the World Wide Web (WWW) usually yields vast amounts of information and can generate up-to-the-minute data in every field imaginable. Because macros are often shared among PC users, they are prone to develop viruses. Think of a virus as software that is intended to harm computers or files. Using the WWW, you can gather up-to-date information about computer viruses, particularly those known to appear as macros in Excel workbooks. You have decided to collect information on Excel macro viruses. Using a selection of Web search engines, you will gather detailed data on at least five viruses associated with Excel macros.

To complete this independent challenge:

1. Open a new workbook, then save it as "Excel Macro Viruses".
2. Log on to the Internet and use your browser to go to http://www.course.com. From there, click Student Online Companions, click the link for this textbook, then click the Excel link for Unit G.
3. Use any combination of the following sites to search for and compile your data: Yahoo!, WebCrawler, or Alta Vista.
4. Fill in information on at least five viruses known to exist in Excel macros. Possible column headings are Name of Virus, Date Discovered, Name of Macro, Who Discovered, Where Discovered, How it Gets Transmitted, Damage it Causes, and Recovery Tips.
5. Format the worksheet as desired to increase readability. (*Hint*: To word wrap text in cells, you can use the wrap text feature located in the Alignment tab of the Format Cells dialog box.)
6. Save the workbook, print the worksheet, then submit your printout.

► Visual Workshop

Create the macro shown in Figure G-22. (*Hint:* Save a blank workbook as "File Utility Macros", then create a macro called SaveClose that saves a previously named workbook. Finally, include the line ActiveWorkbook.Close in the module, as shown in the figure.) Print the module. Test the macro. Submit your module printout. (The line "Macro recorded...by ..." will reflect your system date and name.)

FIGURE G-22

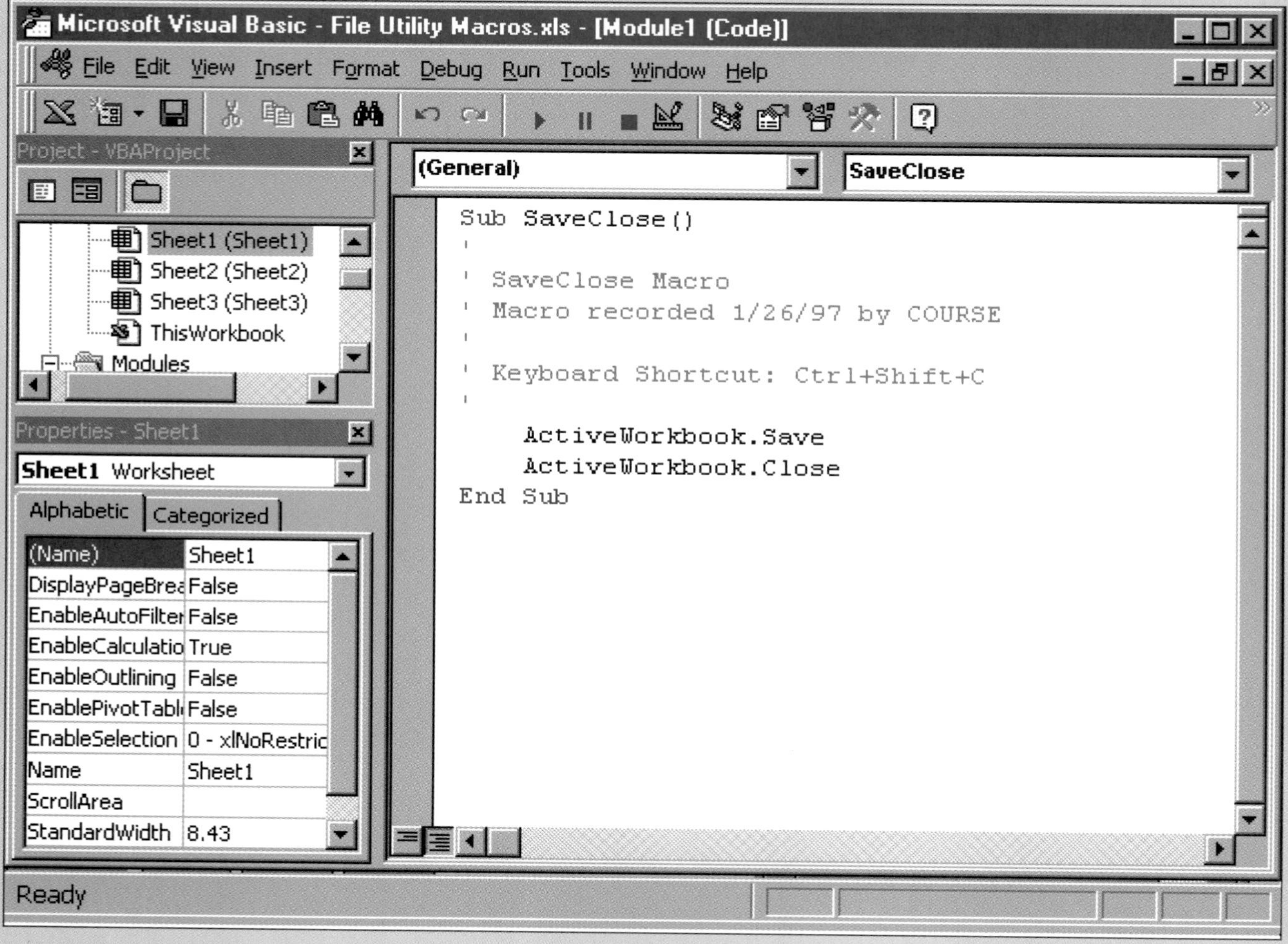

Microsoft Visual Basic - File Utility Macros.xls - [Module1 (Code)]

File Edit View Insert Format Debug Run Tools Window Help

Project - VBAProject: Sheet1 (Sheet1), Sheet2 (Sheet2), Sheet3 (Sheet3), ThisWorkbook, Modules

Properties - Sheet1: Sheet1 Worksheet

Alphabetic	Categorized
(Name)	Sheet1
DisplayPageBrea	False
EnableAutoFilter	False
EnableCalculatio	True
EnableOutlining	False
EnablePivotTabl	False
EnableSelection	0 - xlNoRestric
Name	Sheet1
ScrollArea	
StandardWidth	8.43

(General) — SaveClose

```
Sub SaveClose()
'
' SaveClose Macro
' Macro recorded 1/26/97 by COURSE
'
' Keyboard Shortcut: Ctrl+Shift+C
'
    ActiveWorkbook.Save
    ActiveWorkbook.Close
End Sub
```

Ready

Using
Lists

Objectives

- Plan a list
- Create a list
- Add records with the data form
- Find records
- Delete records
- Sort a list by one field
- Sort a list by multiple fields
- Print a list

A **database** is an organized collection of related information. Examples of databases include a telephone book, a card catalog, and a roster of company employees. Excel refers to a database as a **list**. Using an Excel list, you can organize and manage worksheet information so that you can quickly find needed data for projects, reports, and charts. In this unit, you'll learn how to plan and create a list; add, change, find, and delete information in a list; and then sort and print a list. Nomad Ltd uses lists for analyzing new customer information. Evan's manager has asked him to build and manage a list of new customers as part of the ongoing strategy to focus the company's advertising dollars.

Excel 97

Planning a List

When planning a list, consider the information the list will contain and how you will work with the data now and in the future. Lists are organized into records. A **record** contains data about an object or person. Records, in turn, are divided into fields. **Fields** are columns in the list; each field describes a characteristic about the record, such as a customer's last name or street address. Each field has a **field name**, a column label that describes the field. See Table H-1 for additional planning guidelines. Also, make sure to view CourseHelp "Using Databases" before completing this lesson. At his manager's request, Evan will compile a list of new customers. Before entering the data into an Excel worksheet, he uses the following guidelines to plan the list:

CourseHelp

The camera icon indicates there is a CourseHelp available with this lesson. Click the Start button, point to Programs, point to CourseHelp, then click Excel 97 Illustrated. Choose the CourseHelp entitled Using Databases.

1. **Identify the purpose of the list.**
   Determine the kind of information the list should contain. Evan will use the list to identify areas of the country in which new customers live.

2. **Plan the structure of the list.**
   Determine the fields that make up a record. Evan has customer cards that contain information about each new customer. A typical card is shown in Figure H-1. Each customer in the list will have a record. The fields in the record correspond to the information on the cards.

3. **Write down the names of the fields.**
   Field names can be up to 255 characters in length (the maximum column width), although shorter names are easier to see in the cells. Field names appear in the first row of a list. Evan writes down field names that describe each piece of information shown in Figure H-1.

4. **Determine any special number formatting required in the list.**
   Most lists contain both text and numbers. When planning a list, consider whether any fields require specific number formatting or prefixes. Evan notes that some Zip codes begin with zero. Because Excel automatically drops a leading zero, Evan must type an apostrophe (') when he enters a Zip code that begins with 0 (zero). The apostrophe tells Excel that the cell contains a label rather than a value. If a column contains both numbers and numbers that contain a text character, such as an apostrophe ('), you should format all the numbers as text. Otherwise, the numbers are sorted first, and the numbers that contain text characters are sorted after that; for example, 11542, 60614, 87105, '01810, '02115. To instruct Excel to sort the Zip codes properly, Evan enters all Zip codes with a leading apostrophe.

Lists versus databases

If your list contains more records than can fit on one worksheet (that is, more than 65,536), you should consider using database software rather than spreadsheet software.

FIGURE H-1: Customer record and corresponding field names

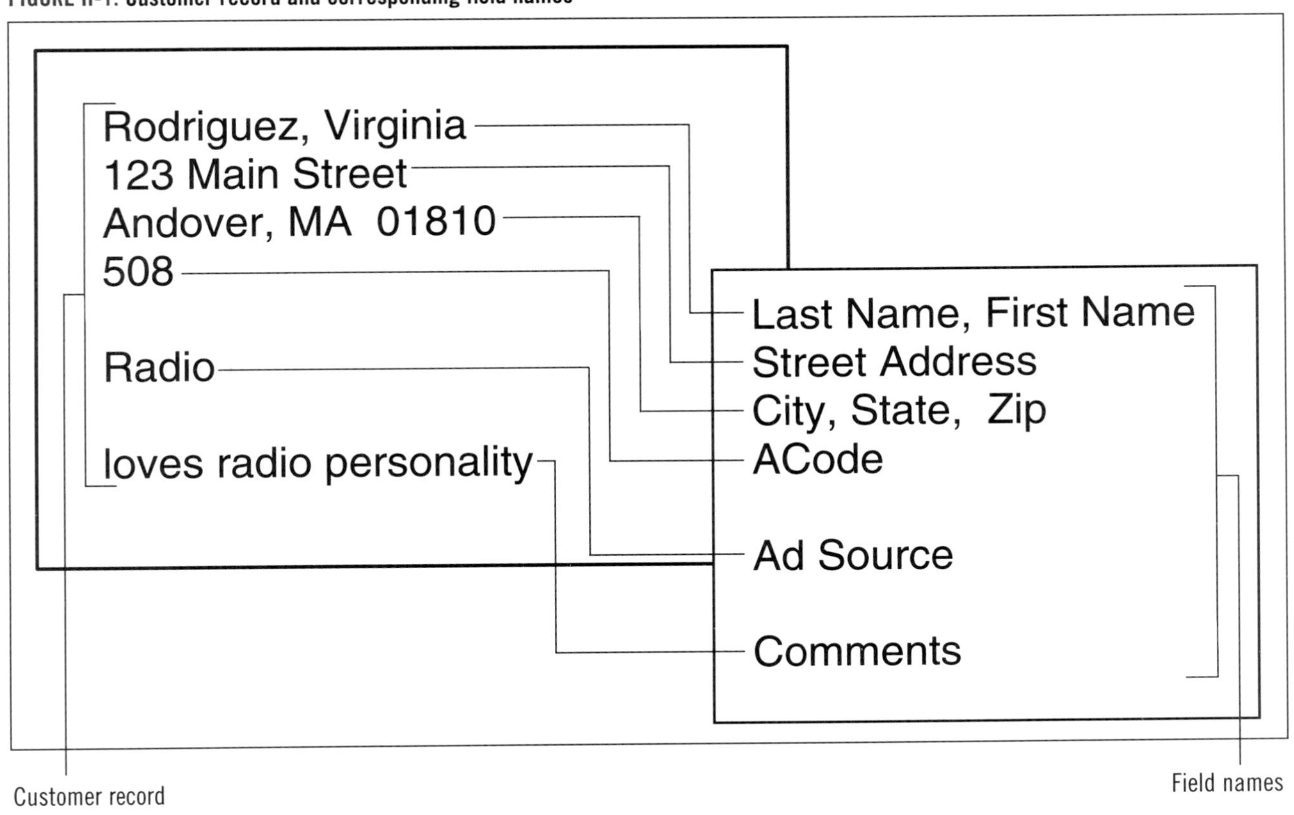

TABLE H-1: Guidelines for planning a list

size and location guidelines	row and column content guidelines
Devote an entire worksheet to your list and list summary informationbecause some list management features can be used on only one listat a time.	Plan and design your list so that all rows have similar items in the same column.
Leave at least one blank column and one blank row between your list and list summary data. Doing this helps Excel select your list when it performs list management tasks such as sorting.	Do not insert extra spaces at the beginning of a cell because that can affect sorting and searching.
Avoid placing critical data to the left or right of the list.	Use the same format for all cells in a column.

Excel 97

Creating a List

Once you have planned the list structure, the sequence of fields, and any appropriate formatting, you need to create field names. Table H-2 provides guidelines for naming fields. Evan is ready to create the list using the field names he wrote down earlier.

Steps

1. **Open the workbook titled XL H-1, save it as New Customer List, then rename Sheet1 as Practice List**
   It is a good idea to devote an entire worksheet to your list.
2. **Beginning in cell A1 and moving horizontally, type each field name in a separate cell, as shown in Figure H-2**
   Always put field names in the first row of the list. Don't worry if your field names are wider than the cells; you will fix this later. Next, format the field names.
3. **Select the field headings in range A1:I1, then click the Bold button B on the Formatting toolbar; with range A1:I1 still selected, click the Borders list arrow, then click the thick bottom border (second item from left in the second row)**
   Next, enter three of the records in the customer list.
4. **Enter the information from Figure H-3 in the rows immediately below the field names, using a leading apostrophe (') for all Zip codes; do not leave any blank rows**
   If you don't type an apostrophe, Excel deletes the leading zero (0) in the Zip code. The data appears in columns organized by field name. Next, adjust the column widths so that each column is as wide as its longest entry.
5. **Select range A1:I4, click Format on the menu bar, point to Column, click AutoFit Selection, click anywhere in the worksheet to deselect the range, then save the workbook**
   Automatically resizing the column widths this way is faster than double-clicking the column divider lines between each pair of columns. Compare your screen with Figure H-4.

QuickTip

If the field name you plan to use is wider than the data in the column, you can turn on Wrap Text to stack the heading in the cell. Doing this allows you to use descriptive field names and still keep the columns from being unnecessarily wide. If you prefer a keyboard shortcut, you can press **[Alt][Enter]** to force a line break while entering field names.

TABLE H-2: Guidelines for naming fields

guideline	explanation
Use labels to name fields.	Numbers can be interpreted as parts of formulas.
Do not use duplicate field names.	Duplicate field names can cause information to be incorrectly entered and sorted.
Format the field names to stand out from the list data.	Use a font, alignment, format, pattern, border, or capitalization style for the column labels that is different from the format of your list data.
Use descriptive names.	Avoid names that might be confused with cell addresses, such as Q4.

FIGURE H-2: Field names entered and formatted in row 1

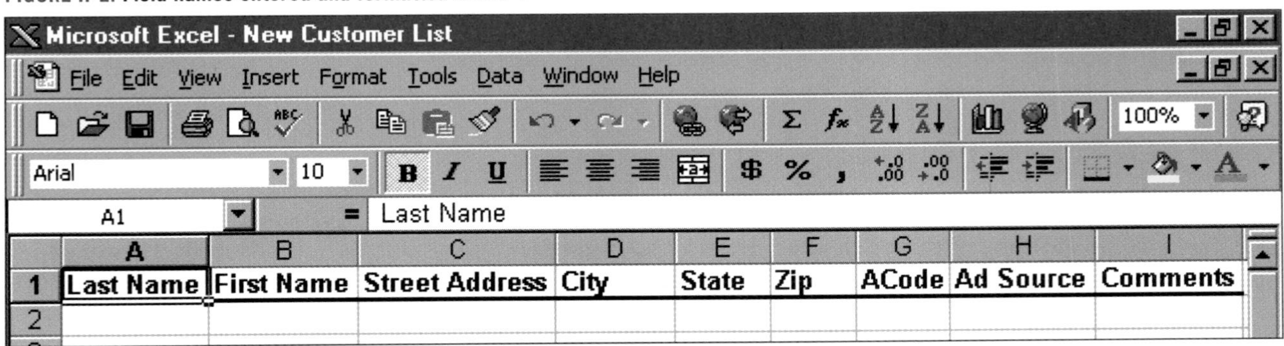

FIGURE H-3: Cards with customer information

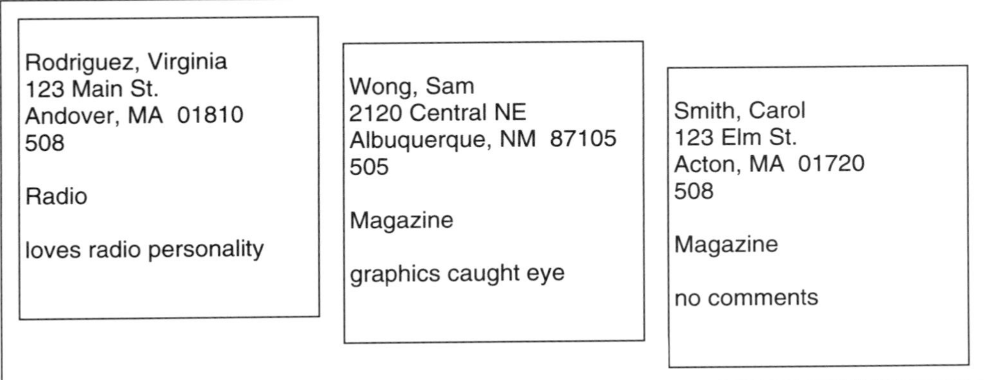

FIGURE H-4: List with three records

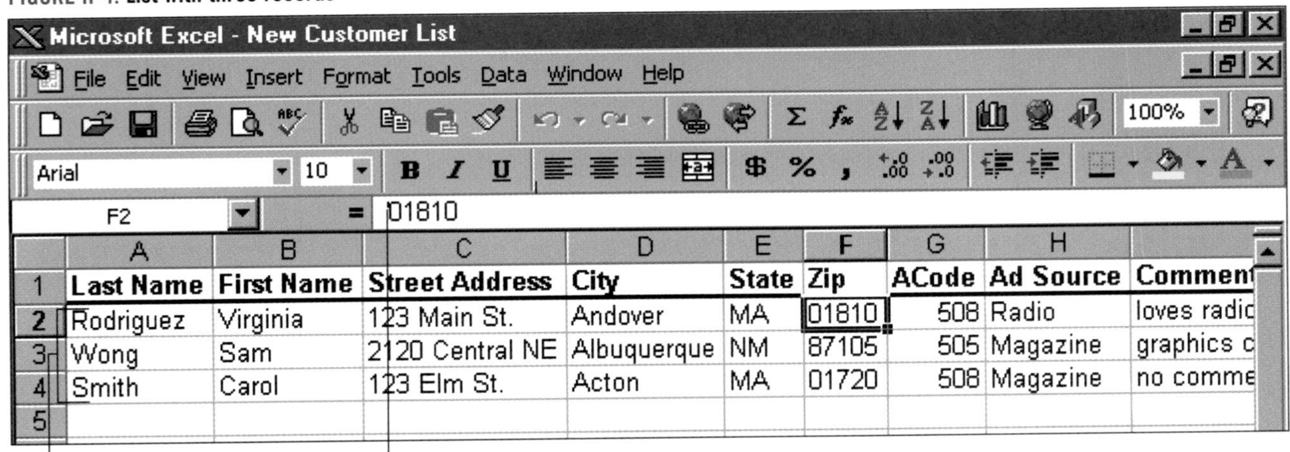

Maintaining the quality of information in a list

To protect the list information, make sure the data is entered in the correct field. Stress care and consistency to all those who enter the list data. Haphazardly entered data can yield invalid results later when it is manipulated.

Excel 97

Adding Records with the Data Form

You can add records to a list by typing data directly into the cells within the list range. Once the field names are created, you also can use the data form as a quick, easy method of data entry. By naming a list range in the name box, you can select the list at any time, and all new records added to the list will be included in the list range. Evan has entered all the customer records he had on his cards, but he received the names of two more customers. He decides to use Excel's data form to add the new customer information.

Steps

QuickTip

You can select the database quickly using the **[End]** key. Start in cell A1, press and hold **[Shift]**, press **[End]** [→], then press **[End]** [↓].

1. Make sure the New Customer List is open, then rename Sheet2 as **Working List**
   Working List contains the nearly complete customer list. Before using the data form to enter the new data, define the list range.
2. Select range **A1:I45**, click the **name box** to select **A1**, type **Database**, then press **[Enter]**
   The Database list range name appears in the name box. When you assign the name Database to the list, the commands on Excel's Data menu default to the list named "Database". Next, enter a new record using the data form.
3. While the list is still selected, click **Data** on the menu bar, then click **Form**
   A data form containing the first record appears, as shown in Figure H-5.
4. Click **New**
   A blank data form appears with the insertion point in the first field.

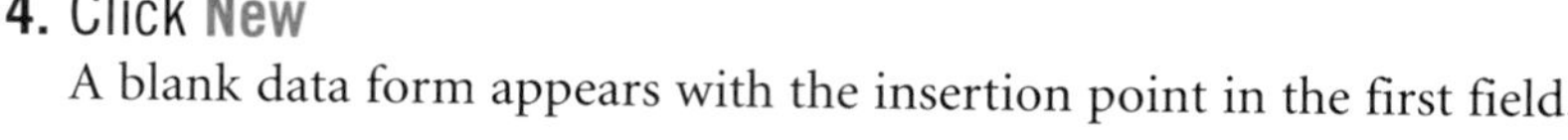

Trouble?

If you accidentally press [↑] or [↓] while in a data form and find yourself positioned in the wrong record, press [↑] or [↓] until you return to the desired record.

5. Type **Chavez** in the Last Name box, then press **[Tab]** to move the insertion point to the next field
6. Enter the rest of the information for Jeffrey Chavez, as shown in Figure H-6
   Press [Tab] to move the insertion point to the next field, or click in the next field's box to move the insertion point there.
7. Click **New** to add Jeffrey Chavez's record and open another blank data form, enter the record for Cathy Relman as shown in Figure H-6, then click **Close**
   The list records that you add with the data form are placed at the end of the list and are formatted like the previous records. Verify that the new records were added.
8. Scroll down the worksheet to bring rows 46 and 47 into view, confirm both records, return to cell A1, then save the workbook

FIGURE H-5: Data form showing first record in list

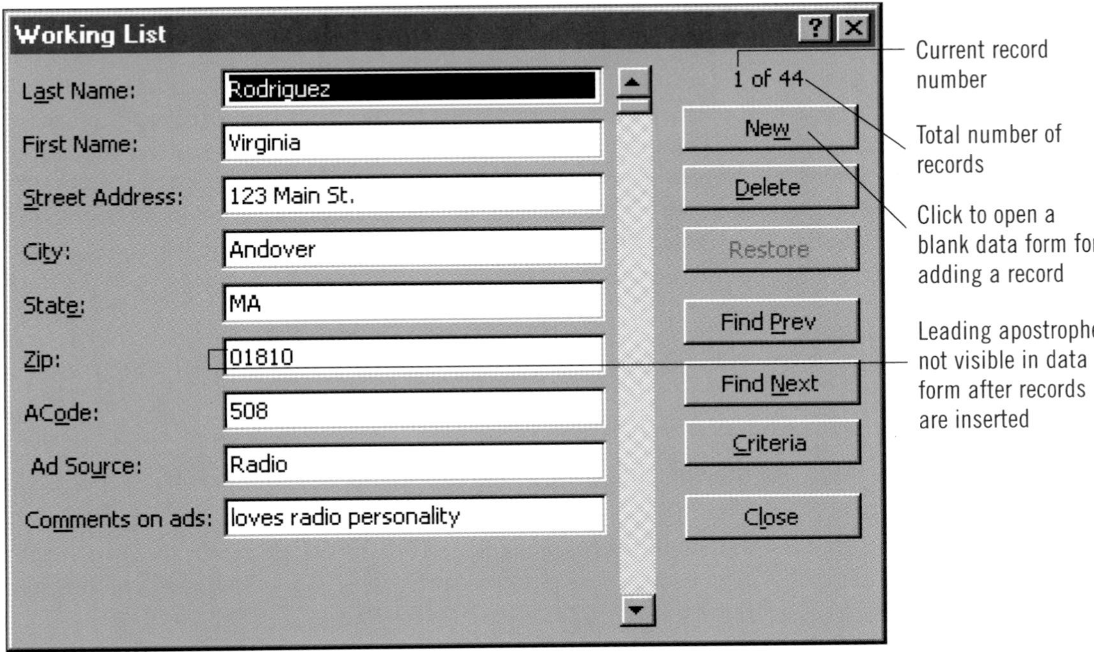

FIGURE H-6: Two data forms with information for two new records

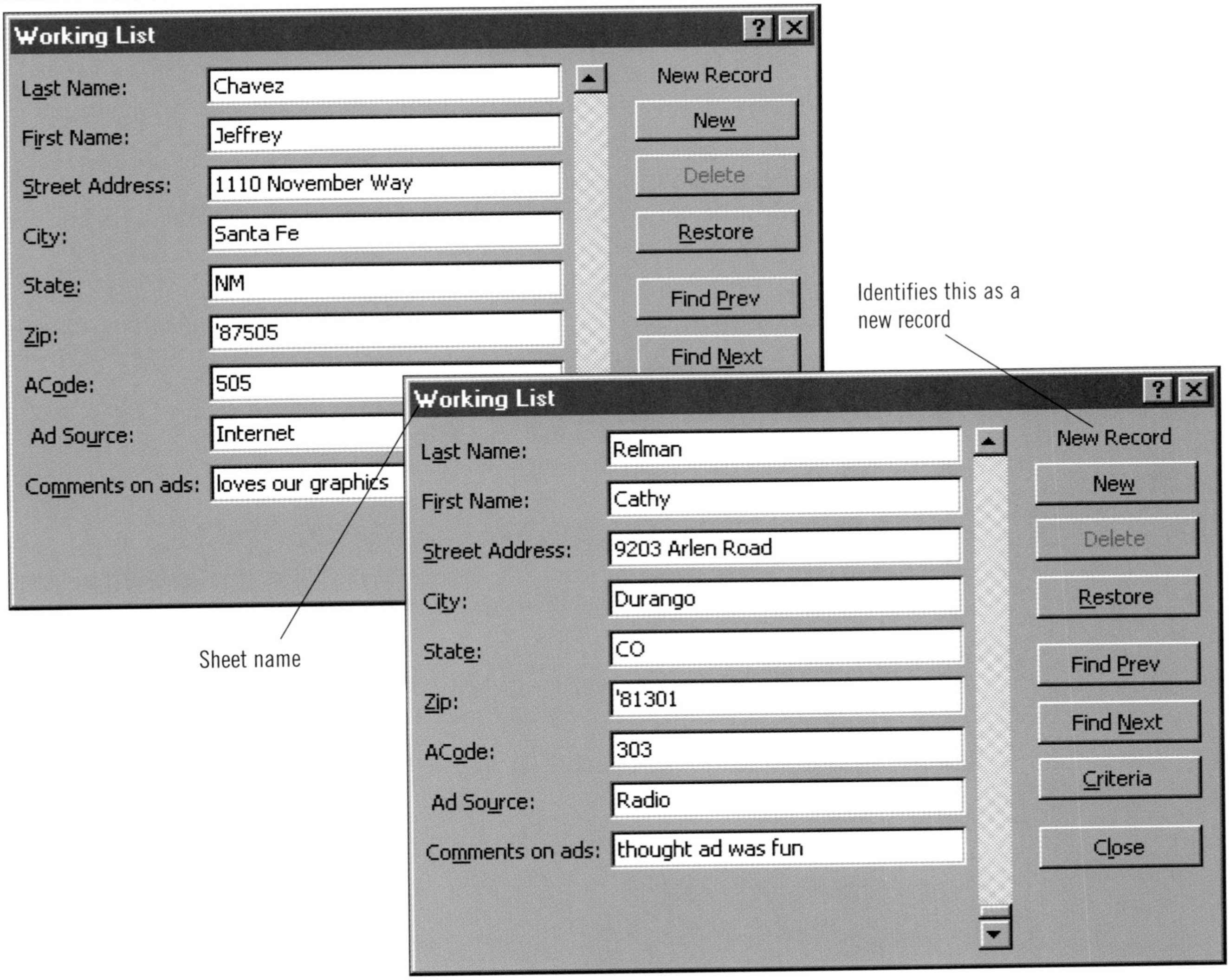

Excel 97

Finding Records

From time to time, you need to locate specific records in your list. You can use Excel's Find command on the Edit menu or the data form to perform searches in your list. Also, you can use the Replace command on the Edit menu to locate and replace existing entries or portions of entries with specified information. Evan's manager has asked him to list the specific Ad Source for each new customer rather than list the general ad category. She also wants to know how many of the new customers originated from the company's Internet site. Evan begins by searching for those records with the Ad Source "Internet".

Steps

Trouble?

If you receive the message, "No list found", simply select any cell within the list, then repeat Step 1.

QuickTip

You also can use comparison operators when performing a search using the data form. For example, you could specify >50,000 in a Salary field box to return those records whose value in the Salary field is greater than 50,000.

1. From any cell within the list, click **Data** on the menu bar, click **Form**, then click **Criteria**
   The data form changes so that all fields are blank and "Criteria" appears in the upper-right corner. See Figure H-7. You want to search for records whose Ad Source field contains the label "Internet".
2. Press **[Alt][U]** to move to the Ad Source box, type **Internet**, then click **Find Next**
   Excel displays the first record for a customer who learned about the company through the Internet site. See Figure H-8.
3. Click **Find Next** until there are no more matching records, then click **Close**
   There are six customers whose Ad Source is the Internet. Next, change the Ad Source entries that currently read "Radio" to "KWIN Radio".
4. Return to cell A1, click **Edit** on the menu bar, then click **Replace**
   The Replace dialog box opens with the insertion point located in the Find what box. See Figure H-9.
5. In the Find what box, type **Radio**, then click the **Replace with box**
   Next, instruct Excel to search for entries containing "Radio" and replace them with "KWIN Radio".
6. In the Replace with box, type **KWIN Radio**
   You are about to perform the search and replace option specified. Because you notice that there are other list entries containing the word "radio" with a lowercase "r", you choose the option "Match case" in the dialog box.
7. Click the **Match case box** to select it, then click **Find Next**
   Excel moves the cell pointer to the first occurrence of "Radio". Next, instruct Excel to replace all existing entries with the information specified.
8. Click **Replace All**
   The dialog box closes, and you complete the replacement and check to make sure all references to radio in the Ad Source column now read "KWIN Radio".
9. Make sure there are no entries in the Ad Source column that read "Radio", then save the workbook

FIGURE H-7: Criteria data form

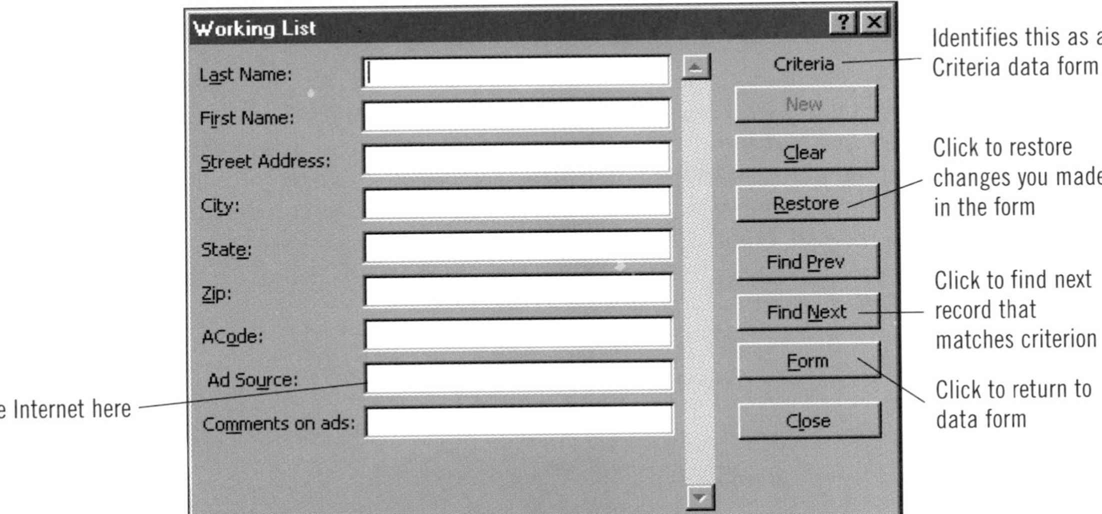

FIGURE H-8: Finding a record using the data form

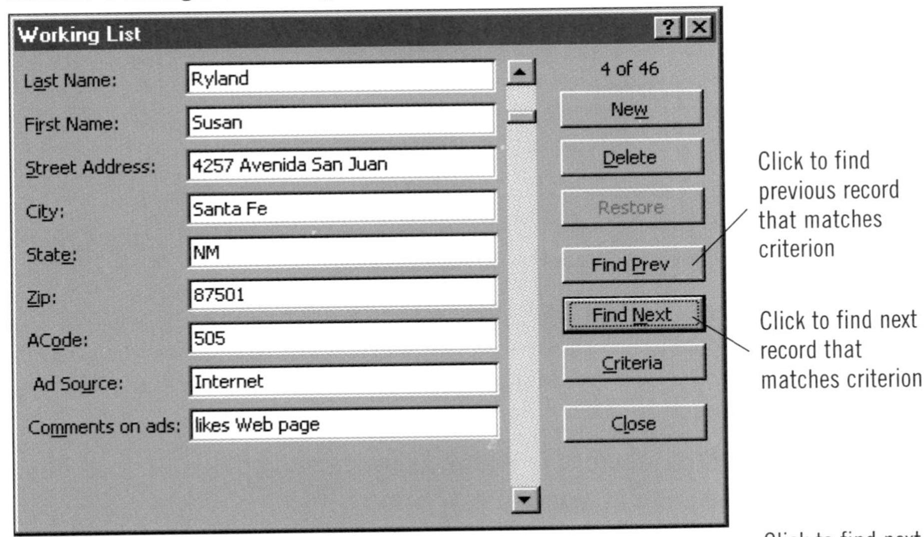

FIGURE H-9: Replace dialog box

Replace

Find what:

Replace with:

Search: By Rows

Match case

Find entire cells only

Find Next

Close

Replace

Replace All

Type Radio here

Type KWIN Radio here

Click to find exact case matches

Click to find next occurrence of item in Find what box

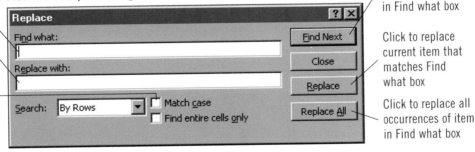

Click to replace current item that matches Find what box

Click to replace all occurrences of item in Find what box

Using wildcards to fine-tune your search

You can use special symbols called **wildcards** when defining search criteria in the data form or Find dialog box. The question mark (?) wildcard stands for any single character. For example, if you do not know whether a customer's last name is Paulsen or Paulson, you can specify Pauls?n as the search criteria to locate both options. The asterisk (*) wildcard stands for any group of characters. For example, if you specify Jan* as the search criteria in the First Name field, Excel locates all records with first names beginning with Jan (for instance, Jan, Janet, Janice, and so forth).

Excel 97

Deleting Records

You need to keep your list up to date by removing obsolete records. One way to remove records is to use the Delete button on the data form. You also can delete all records that meet certain criteria—that is, records that have something in common. For example, you can specify a criterion for Excel to find the next record containing Zip code 01879, then remove the record using the Delete button. If specifying one criterion does not meet your needs, you can set multiple criteria. After she noticed two entries for Carolyn Smith, Evan's manager asked him to check the database for additional duplicate entries. Evan uses the data form to delete the duplicate record.

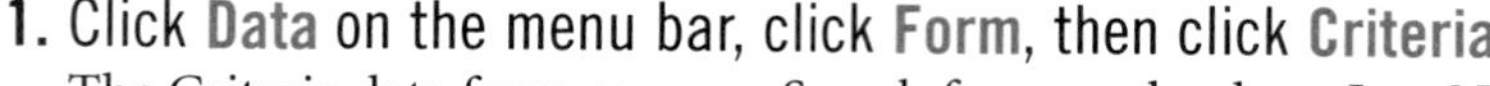

QuickTip

Besides using the data form to add, search for, and delete records, you also can use the data form to edit records. Just find the desired record and edit the data directly in the appropriate box.

1. **Click Data on the menu bar, click Form, then click Criteria**
   The Criteria data form appears. Search for records whose Last Name field contains the label "Smith" and whose First Name field contains the label "Carolyn".
2. **In the Last Name box, type Smith, click the First Name box, type Carolyn, then click Find Next**
   Excel displays the first record for a customer whose name is Carolyn Smith. You decide to leave the initial entry for Carolyn Smith (record 5 of 46) and delete the second one once you confirm it is a duplicate.
3. **Click Find Next**
   The duplicate record for Carolyn Smith, record number 40, appears as shown in Figure H-10. You are ready to delete the duplicate entry.

QuickTip

Clicking Restore on the data form will not restore deleted record(s).

4. **Click Delete, then click OK to confirm the deletion**
   The duplicate record for Carolyn Smith is deleted, and all the other records move up one row. The new record, Manuel Julio, is shown in the data form. Next, view the worksheet to confirm deletion of the duplicate entry.
5. **Click Close to return to the worksheet, scroll down until rows 40–46 are visible, then read the entry in row 40**
   Notice that the duplicate entry for Carolyn Smith is gone and that Manuel Julio moved up a row and is now in row 41. You also notice a record for K. C. Splint in row 43, which is a duplicate entry.
6. **Return to cell A1, and read the record information for K. C. Splint in row 8**
   After confirming another duplicate entry, you decide to delete the row.
7. **Click cell A8, click Edit on the menu bar, then click Delete**
   The Delete dialog box opens as shown in Figure H-11. Choose the option to delete the entire row.
8. **Click the Entire row option button, then click OK**
   You are pleased that the duplicate record for K. C. Splint is deleted and that the other records move up to fill in the gap.
9. **Save the workbook**

FIGURE H-10: Data form showing duplicate record for Carolyn Smith

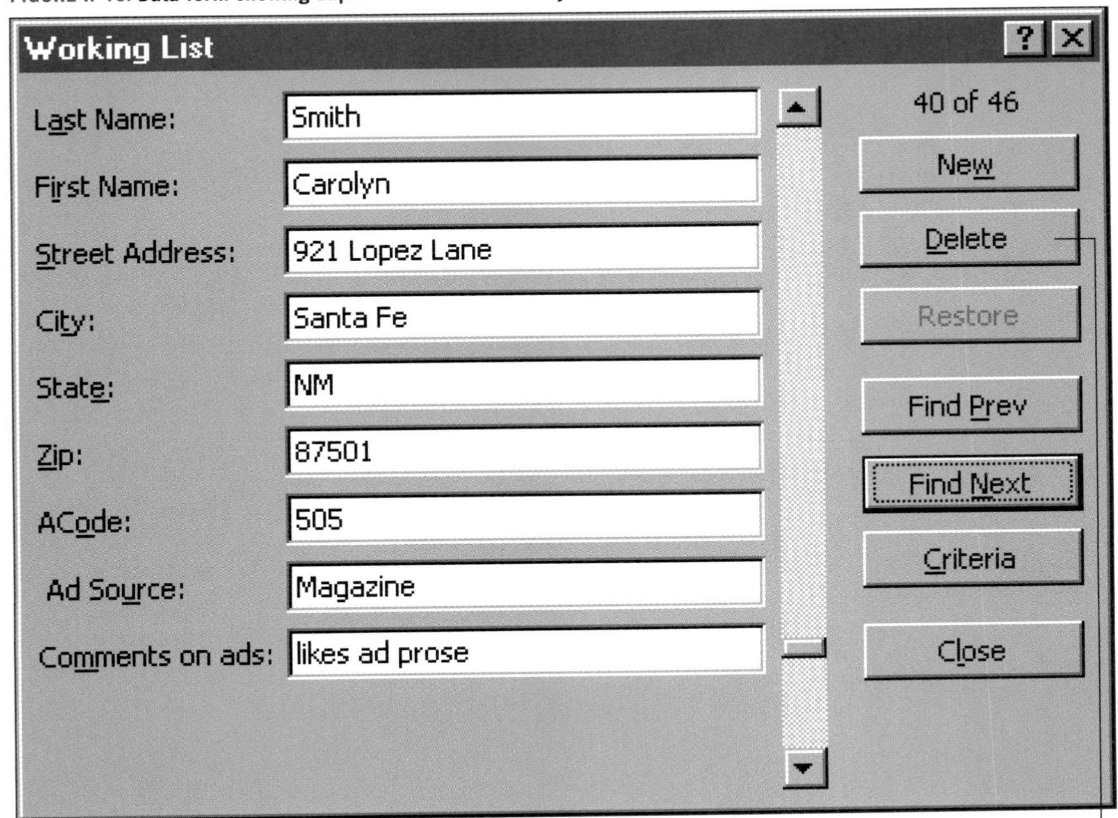

Click to delete current record from list

FIGURE H-11: Delete dialog box

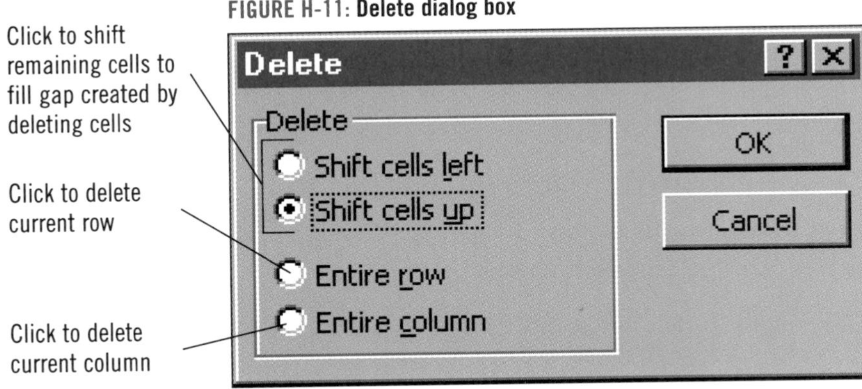

Click to shift remaining cells to fill gap created by deleting cells

Click to delete current row

Click to delete current column

Excel 97

Deleting records using the data form versus deleting rows from the worksheet area

When you delete a record using the data form, you cannot undo your deletion. When you delete a record by deleting the row in which it resides inside the worksheet area, however, you can immediately restore the record by using the Undo command on the Edit menu, the Undo button, or by pressing [Ctrl][Z].

Excel 97

Sorting a List by One Field

Usually, you enter records in the order in which they are received, rather than in alphabetical or numerical order. When you add records to a list using the data form, the records are added to the end of the list. Using Excel's sorting feature, you can rearrange the order in which the records appear. You can use the sort buttons on the Standard toolbar to sort records by one field, or you can use the Sort command on the Data menu to perform more complicated sorts. Alternatively, you can sort an entire list or any portion of a list, or you can arrange sorted information in ascending or descending order. In ascending order, the lowest value (the beginning of the alphabet, or the earliest date) appears at the top of the list. In a field containing labels and numbers, numbers come first. In descending order, the highest value (the end of the alphabet, or the latest date) appears at the top of the list. In a field containing labels and numbers, labels come first. Table H-3 provides examples of ascending and descending sorts. Because Evan wants to be able to return the records to their original order following any sorts, he begins by creating a new field called Entry Order. Then he will perform several single field sorts on the list.

QuickTip

Before you sort records, it is a good idea to make a backup copy of your list or create a field that numbers the records so you can return them to their original order, if necessary.

QuickTip

If your sort does not perform as intended, press **[Ctrl][Z]** immediately to undo the sort and repeat the step.

1. In cell J1, enter the text and format for cell J1 as shown in Figure H-12, then AutoFit column J
   Next, fill in the entry order numbers for all records.
2. In cell J2 type **1**, press **[Enter]**, in cell J3 type **2**, press **[Enter]**, select cells **J2:J3**, drag the fill handle to cell **J45**, then return to cell A1
   With the Entry Order column complete as shown in Figure H-12, you are ready to sort the list in ascending order by last name. You must position the cell pointer within the column you want to sort prior to issuing the sort command.
3. While in cell A1, click the **Sort Ascending button** on the Standard toolbar
   Excel instantly rearranges the records in ascending order by last name, as shown in Figure H-13. Next, sort the list in descending order by area code.
4. Click cell **G1**, then click the **Sort Descending button** on the Standard toolbar
   Excel sorts the list, placing those records with higher-digit area codes at the top. Next, update the list range to include original entry order.
5. Select range **A1:J45**, click the **name box**, type **Database**, then press **[Enter]**
   You are now ready to return the list to original entry order.
6. Click cell **J1**, click the **Sort Ascending button** on the Standard toolbar, then save the workbook
   The list is back to its original order, and the workbook is saved.

TABLE H-3: Sort order options and examples

option	alphabetic	numeric	date	alphanumeric
Ascending	A, B, C	7, 8, 9	1/1, 2/1, 3/1	12A, 99B, DX8, QT7
Descending	C, B, A	9, 8, 7	3/1, 2/1, 1/1	QT7, DX8, 99B, 12A

FIGURE H-12: List with Entry Order field added

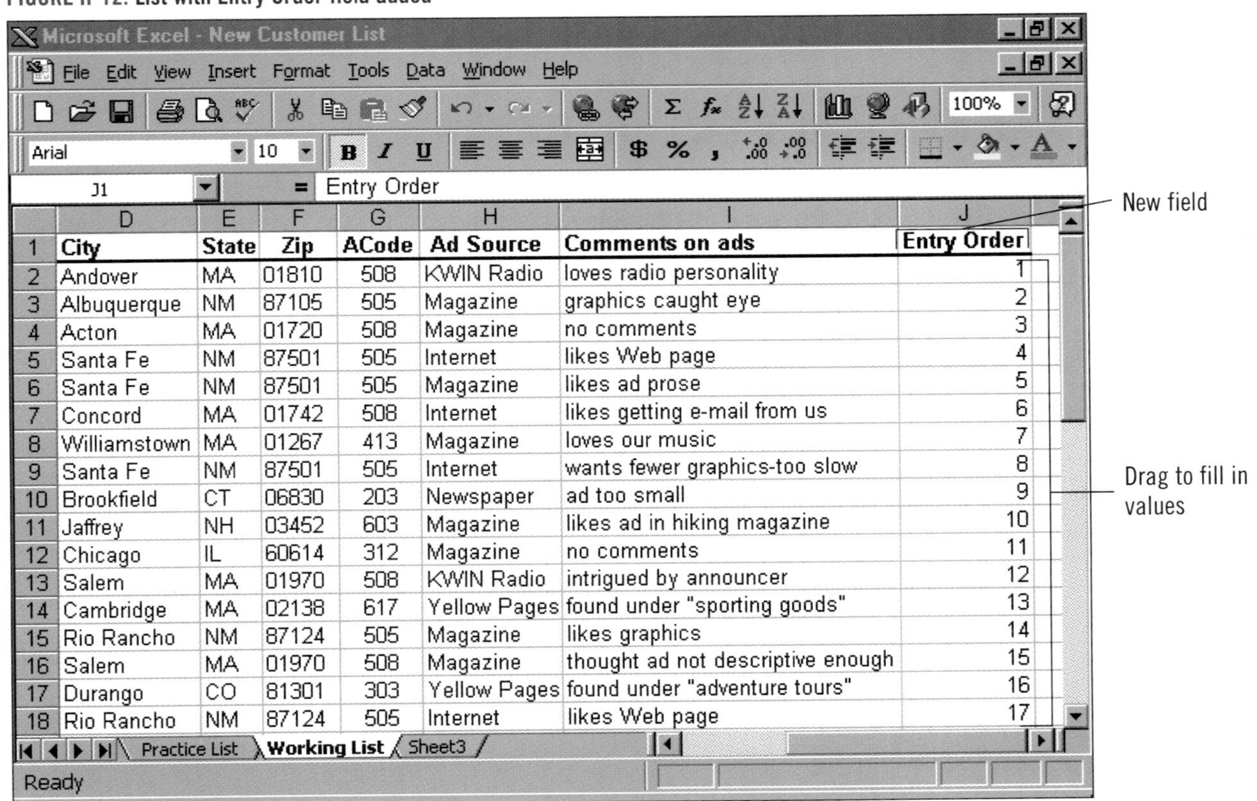

	D	E	F	G	H	I	J
1	**City**	**State**	**Zip**	**ACode**	**Ad Source**	**Comments on ads**	**Entry Order**
2	Andover	MA	01810	508	KWIN Radio	loves radio personality	1
3	Albuquerque	NM	87105	505	Magazine	graphics caught eye	2
4	Acton	MA	01720	508	Magazine	no comments	3
5	Santa Fe	NM	87501	505	Internet	likes Web page	4
6	Santa Fe	NM	87501	505	Magazine	likes ad prose	5
7	Concord	MA	01742	508	Internet	likes getting e-mail from us	6
8	Williamstown	MA	01267	413	Magazine	loves our music	7
9	Santa Fe	NM	87501	505	Internet	wants fewer graphics-too slow	8
10	Brookfield	CT	06830	203	Newspaper	ad too small	9
11	Jaffrey	NH	03452	603	Magazine	likes ad in hiking magazine	10
12	Chicago	IL	60614	312	Magazine	no comments	11
13	Salem	MA	01970	508	KWIN Radio	intrigued by announcer	12
14	Cambridge	MA	02138	617	Yellow Pages	found under "sporting goods"	13
15	Rio Rancho	NM	87124	505	Magazine	likes graphics	14
16	Salem	MA	01970	508	Magazine	thought ad not descriptive enough	15
17	Durango	CO	81301	303	Yellow Pages	found under "adventure tours"	16
18	Rio Rancho	NM	87124	505	Internet	likes Web page	17

FIGURE H-13: List sorted alphabetically by last name

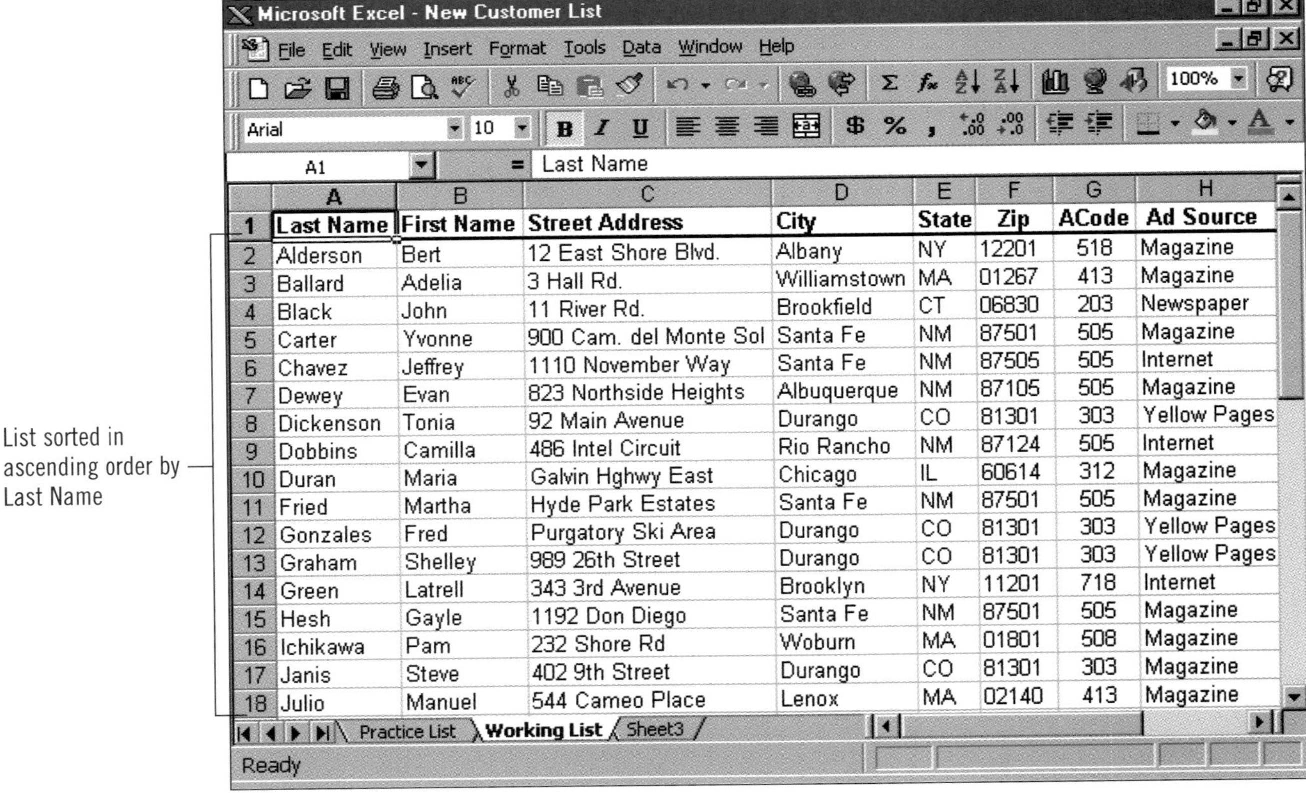

	A	B	C	D	E	F	G	H
1	**Last Name**	**First Name**	**Street Address**	**City**	**State**	**Zip**	**ACode**	**Ad Source**
2	Alderson	Bert	12 East Shore Blvd.	Albany	NY	12201	518	Magazine
3	Ballard	Adelia	3 Hall Rd.	Williamstown	MA	01267	413	Magazine
4	Black	John	11 River Rd.	Brookfield	CT	06830	203	Newspaper
5	Carter	Yvonne	900 Cam. del Monte Sol	Santa Fe	NM	87501	505	Magazine
6	Chavez	Jeffrey	1110 November Way	Santa Fe	NM	87505	505	Internet
7	Dewey	Evan	823 Northside Heights	Albuquerque	NM	87105	505	Magazine
8	Dickenson	Tonia	92 Main Avenue	Durango	CO	81301	303	Yellow Pages
9	Dobbins	Camilla	486 Intel Circuit	Rio Rancho	NM	87124	505	Internet
10	Duran	Maria	Galvin Hghwy East	Chicago	IL	60614	312	Magazine
11	Fried	Martha	Hyde Park Estates	Santa Fe	NM	87501	505	Magazine
12	Gonzales	Fred	Purgatory Ski Area	Durango	CO	81301	303	Yellow Pages
13	Graham	Shelley	989 26th Street	Durango	CO	81301	303	Yellow Pages
14	Green	Latrell	343 3rd Avenue	Brooklyn	NY	11201	718	Internet
15	Hesh	Gayle	1192 Don Diego	Santa Fe	NM	87501	505	Magazine
16	Ichikawa	Pam	232 Shore Rd	Woburn	MA	01801	508	Magazine
17	Janis	Steve	402 9th Street	Durango	CO	81301	303	Magazine
18	Julio	Manuel	544 Cameo Place	Lenox	MA	02140	413	Magazine

Excel 97

Sorting a List by Multiple Fields

You can sort lists by as many as three fields by specifying **sort keys**, the criteria upon which the sort is based. To perform sorts on multiple fields, you must use the Sort dialog box, which you access through the Sort command on the Data menu. Evan wants to sort the records alphabetically by state first, then within the state by Zip code.

1. Click the **name box list arrow**, then click **Database**
   The list is selected. Because you want to sort the list by more than one field, use the Sort command on the Data menu.
2. Click **Data** on the menu bar, then click **Sort**
   The Sort dialog box opens, as shown in Figure H-14. You want to sort the list by state and then by Zip code.
3. Click the **Sort by** list arrow, click **State**, then click the **Ascending option button**, if necessary
   The list will be sorted alphabetically in ascending order (A–Z) by the State field. Next, define a second sort field for the Zip code.
4. Click the top **Then by list arrow**, click **Zip**, then click the **Descending option button**
   You also could sort by a third key by selecting a field in the bottom Then by list box.
5. Click **OK** to execute the sort, press **[Ctrl][Home]**, then scroll through the list to see the result of the sort
   The list is sorted alphabetically by state in ascending order, then within each state by Zip code in descending order. Compare your results with Figure H-15. Notice that Massachusetts, New Mexico, and New York have multiple Zip codes.
6. Return to cell A1, then save the workbook

QuickTip

You can specify a capitalization sort by clicking Options in the Sort dialog box, then clicking the Case sensitive box. When you choose this option, lowercase entries precede uppercase entries.

FIGURE H-14: **Sort dialog box**

Sort

Sort by — First sort field

Last Name ▾ ◉ Ascending ○ Descending

Then by — Second sort field

◉ Ascending ○ Descending

Then by — Third sort field

◉ Ascending ○ Descending

My list has

◉ Header row ○ No header row

Options... OK Cancel

Fields on which the sort will be based

Indicates field name labels will not be included in sort

FIGURE H-15: **List sorted by multiple fields**

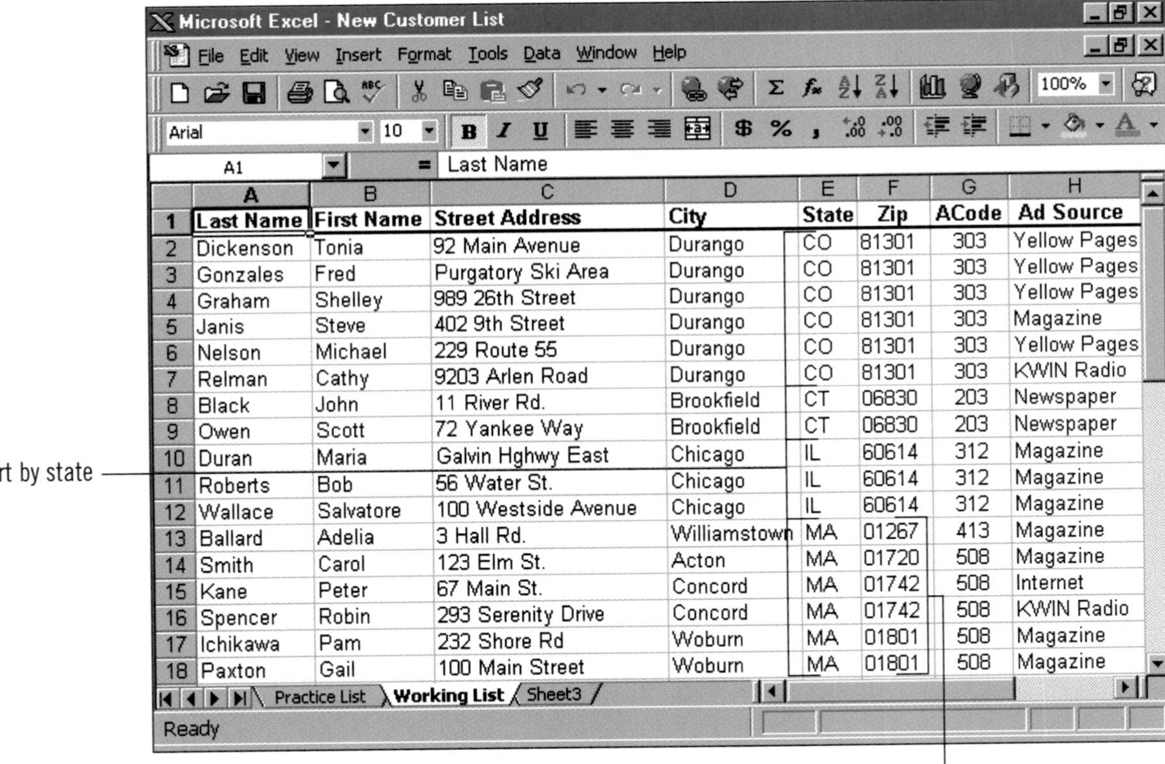

Microsoft Excel - New Customer List

File Edit View Insert Format Tools Data Window Help

A1 = Last Name

	A	B	C	D	E	F	G	H
1	Last Name	First Name	Street Address	City	State	Zip	ACode	Ad Source
2	Dickenson	Tonia	92 Main Avenue	Durango	CO	81301	303	Yellow Pages
3	Gonzales	Fred	Purgatory Ski Area	Durango	CO	81301	303	Yellow Pages
4	Graham	Shelley	989 26th Street	Durango	CO	81301	303	Yellow Pages
5	Janis	Steve	402 9th Street	Durango	CO	81301	303	Magazine
6	Nelson	Michael	229 Route 55	Durango	CO	81301	303	Yellow Pages
7	Relman	Cathy	9203 Arlen Road	Durango	CO	81301	303	KWIN Radio
8	Black	John	11 River Rd.	Brookfield	CT	06830	203	Newspaper
9	Owen	Scott	72 Yankee Way	Brookfield	CT	06830	203	Newspaper
10	Duran	Maria	Galvin Hghwy East	Chicago	IL	60614	312	Magazine
11	Roberts	Bob	56 Water St.	Chicago	IL	60614	312	Magazine
12	Wallace	Salvatore	100 Westside Avenue	Chicago	IL	60614	312	Magazine
13	Ballard	Adelia	3 Hall Rd.	Williamstown	MA	01267	413	Magazine
14	Smith	Carol	123 Elm St.	Acton	MA	01720	508	Magazine
15	Kane	Peter	67 Main St.	Concord	MA	01742	508	Internet
16	Spencer	Robin	293 Serenity Drive	Concord	MA	01742	508	KWIN Radio
17	Ichikawa	Pam	232 Shore Rd	Woburn	MA	01801	508	Magazine
18	Paxton	Gail	100 Main Street	Woburn	MA	01801	508	Magazine

Practice List | Working List | Sheet3

Ready

First sort by state

Second sort by Zip code within state

Specifying a custom sort order

You can identify a custom sort order for the field selected in the Sort by box. To do this, click Options in the Sort dialog box, click the First key sort order list arrow, then click the desired custom order. Commonly used custom sort orders are days of the week (Mon, Tues, Wed, and so forth) and months (Jan, Feb, Mar, and so forth), where alphabetic sorts do not sort these items properly.

Excel 97

Printing a List

If a list is small enough to fit on one page, you can print it as you would any other Excel worksheet. However, if you have more columns than can fit on a portrait-oriented page, try setting the page orientation to landscape. Because lists often have more rows than can fit on a page, you can define the first row of the list (containing the field names) as the **print title**. Most lists do not have any descriptive information above the field names on the worksheet. To augment the information contained in the field names, you can use headers and footers to add identifying text, such as the list title or report date. If you want to exclude any fields from your list report, you can hide the desired columns from view so that they do not print. Evan has finished updating his list and is ready to print it. He begins by previewing the list.

1. Click the **Print Preview button** on the Standard toolbar
   Notice that the status bar reads Page 1 of 2. You want all the fields in the list to fit on a single page, but you'll need two pages to fit all the data. So you set the page orientation to landscape and adjust the Fit to options.
2. From the Print Preview window, click **Setup**, click the **Page tab**, under Orientation click the **Landscape option button**, under Scaling click the **Fit to option button**, double-click the **tall box** and type **2**, then click **OK**
   The list still does not fit on a single page. Check to see what is on page 2.
3. Click **Next**
   Because the records on page 2 appear without column headings, you can set up the first row of the list, containing the field names, as a repeating print title.
4. Click **Close** to exit the Print Preview window, click **File** on the menu bar, click **Page Setup**, click the **Sheet tab**, under Print titles click the **Rows to repeat at top box**, then click any cell in row 1
   When you select row 1 as a print title, Excel automatically inserts an absolute reference to a beginning and ending row to repeat at the top of each page—in this case, the print title to repeat beginning and ending with row 1. See Figure H-16.
5. Click **Print Preview**, click **Next** to view the second page, then click **Zoom** to get a closer look
   Setting up a print title to repeat row 1 causes the field names to appear at the top of each printed page. Next, change the header to reflect the contents of the list.
6. Click **Setup**, click the **Header/Footer tab**, click **Custom Header**, click the **Center section box**, type **Nomad Ltd—New Customer List**
7. Select the header text in the Center section box, click the **Font button**, change the font size to **14** and the style to **Bold**, click **OK**, click **OK** again to return to the Header/Footer tab, then click **OK** to preview the list
   Page 2 of the report appears as shown in Figure H-17.
8. Save, print, then close the workbook

QuickTip

You can print multiple ranges in your worksheets at the same time by clicking the Print area box in the Sheet tab of the Page Setup dialog box. Then simply drag to select areas in the worksheet you wish to print.

FIGURE H-16: Sheet tab of the Page Setup dialog box

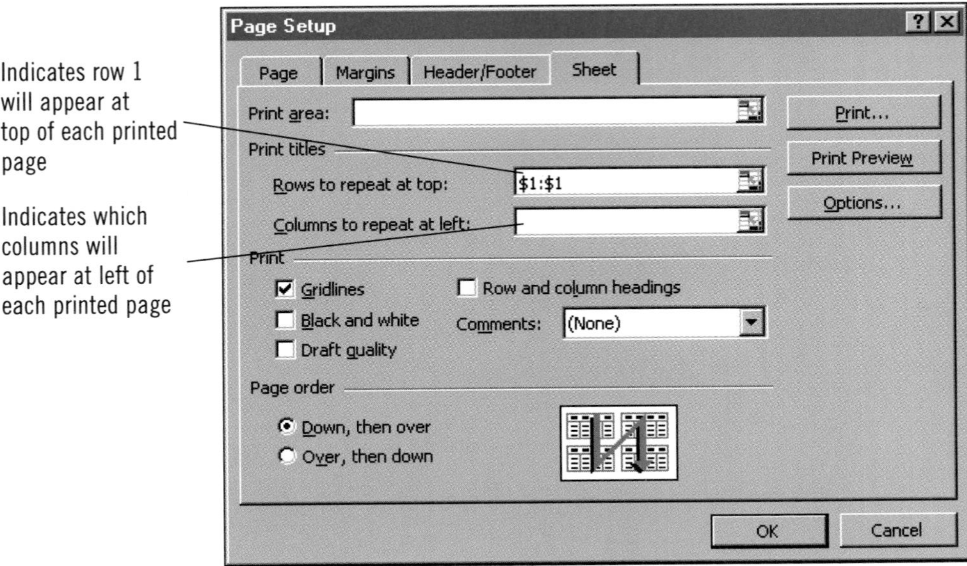

FIGURE H-17: Print Preview window showing page 2 of completed report

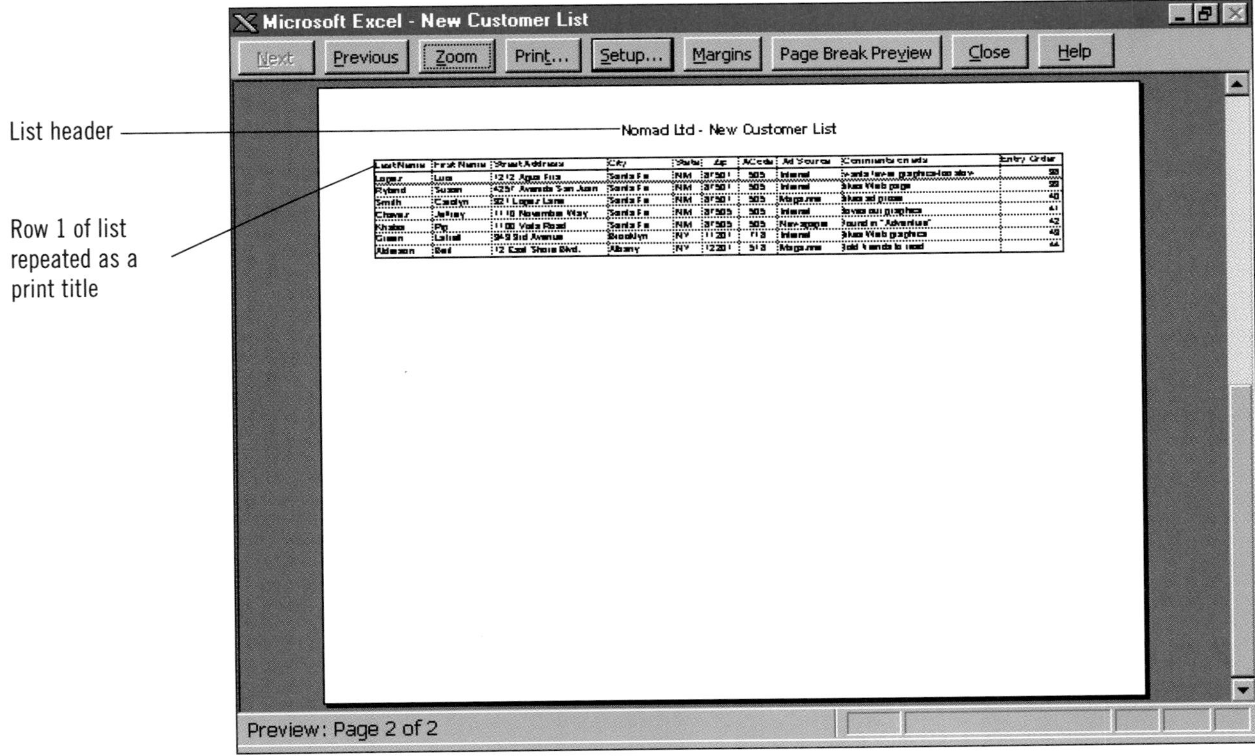

Setting page printing order

You can control the order Excel creates pages from your worksheet in the Sheet tab of the Page Setup dialog box. See the Page order option in Figure H-16. Normally, Excel prints pages by selecting a pageful of data going down the rows first, then across columns. You also can print by first filling pages going across the columns and then down the rows.

Practice

► Concepts Review

Label each of the elements of the Excel screen shown in Figure H-18.

FIGURE H-18

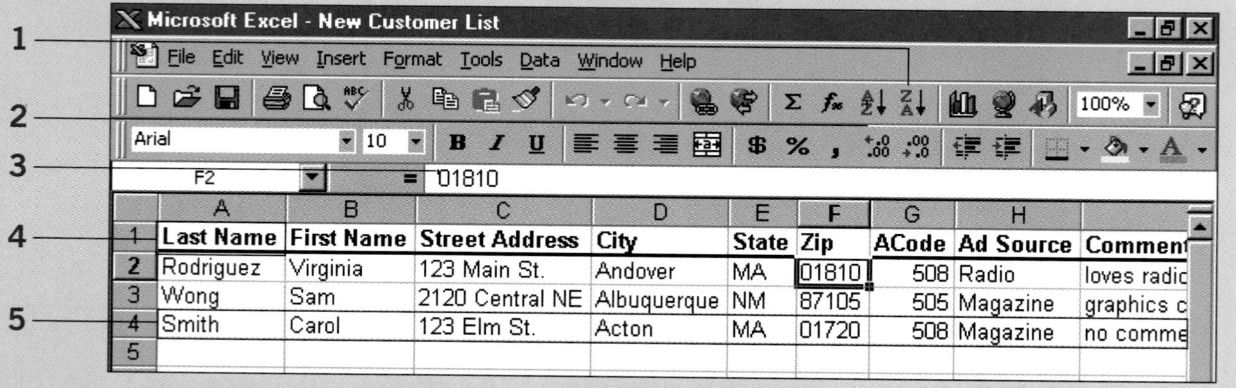

Match each statement with the term it describes.

6. **Arrange records in a particular sequence**
7. **Organized collection of related information in Excel**
8. **Row in an Excel list**
9. **Type of software used for lists containing more than 65,536 records**
10. **Label positioned at the top of the column identifying data for that field**

a. List
b. Record
c. Database
d. Sort
e. Field name

Select the best answer from the list of choices.

11. **Which of the following Excel sorting options do you use to sort a list of employee names in A-to-Z order?**
    a. Ascending
    b. Absolute
    c. Alphabetic
    d. Descending

12. **Which of the following series is in descending order?**
    a. 4, 5, 6, A, B, C
    b. C, B, A, 6, 5, 4
    c. 8, 7, 6, 5, 6, 7
    d. 8, 6, 4, C, B, A

13. Once the _____________ is defined, any new records added to the list using the data form are included in the _____________.

- **a.** Database, database
- **b.** Data form, data form
- **c.** Worksheet, worksheet
- **d.** List range, list range

14. When printing a list on multiple pages, you can define a print title containing repeating row(s) to

- **a.** Include appropriate fields in the printout.
- **b.** Include field names at the top of each printed page.
- **c.** Include the header in list reports.
- **d.** Exclude from the printout all rows under the first row.

Skills Review

1. Create a list.

- **a.** Create a new workbook, then save it as "M.K. Electric Employee List".
- **b.** In cell A1, type the title "M.K. Electric Employees".
- **c.** Enter the field names and records using the information in Table H-4.
- **d.** Apply bold formatting to the field names.

TABLE H-4

Last name	First name	Years	Position	Pension	Union
Smith-Hill	Janice	8	Office Manager	Y	N
Doolan	Mark	3	Customer Service	N	N
Coleman	Steve	4	Senior Installer	N	Y
Quinn	Jamie	7	Junior Installer	N	Y
Rabinowicz	Sarah	11	Field Manager	Y	Y

- **e.** Center the entries in the Years, Pension, and Union fields.
- **f.** Adjust the column widths to make the data readable.
- **g.** Save, then print the list.

2. Add records with the data form.

- **a.** Select all the records in the list, including the field names, then define the range as "Database".
- **b.** Open the data form and add a new record for David Gitano, a newly hired junior installer at M.K. Electric. David is not eligible for the employee pension, but he is a member of the union.
- **c.** Add a new record for George Worley, the company's new office assistant. George is not eligible for the employee pension, and he is not a union member.
- **d.** Save the list.

3. Find and delete records.

- **a.** Find the record for Jamie Quinn.
- **b.** Delete the record.
- **c.** Save the list.

4. Sort a list by one field.

- **a.** Select the Database list range.
- **b.** Sort the list alphabetically in ascending order by last name.
- **c.** Save the list.

5. Sort a list by multiple fields.

- **a.** Select the Database list range.
- **b.** Sort the list alphabetically in ascending order first by union membership and then by last name.
- **c.** Save the list.

6. Print a list.

- **a.** Add a header that reads, "Employee Information".
- **b.** Print the list, then save and close the workbook.
- **c.** Exit Excel.

Independent Challenges

1. Your advertising firm, Personalize IT, specializes in selling specialty items imprinted with the customer's name and/or logo such as hats, pens, and T-shirts. Plan and build a list of information with a minimum of 10 records using the three items sold. Your list should contain at least five different customers. (Some customers will place more than one order.) Each record should contain the customer's name, item sold, and its individual and extended cost. Enter your own data and make sure you include at least the following list fields:

- Item—Describe the item.
- Cost-Ea.—What is the item's individual cost?
- Quantity—How many items did the customer purchase?
- Ext. Cost—What is the total purchase price?
- Customer—Who purchased the item?

To complete this independent challenge:

1. Prepare a list plan that states your goal, outlines the data you'll need, and identifies the list elements.
2. Sketch a sample list on a piece of paper, indicating how the list should be built. What information should go in the columns? In the rows? Which of the data fields will be formatted as labels? As values?
3. Build the list first by entering the field names, then by entering the records. Remember you will invent your own data. Save the workbook as "Personalize IT".
4. Reformat the list, as needed. For example, you might need to adjust the column widths to make the data more readable. Also, remember to check your spelling.
5. Sort the list in ascending order by Item, then by Customer, then by Quantity
6. Preview the worksheet; adjust any items as needed; then print a copy.
7. Save your work before closing.
8. Submit your list plan, preliminary sketches, and final printouts.

2. You are taking a class titled "Television Shows: Past and Present" at a local community college. The instructor has provided you with an Excel list of television programs from the '60s and '70s. She has included fields tracking the following information: the number of years the show was a favorite, favorite character, least favorite character, the show's length in minutes, the show's biggest star, and comments about the show. The instructor has included data for each show in the list. She has asked you to add a field (column label) and two records (shows of your choosing) to the list. Because the list should cover only 30-minute shows, you need to delete any records for shows longer than 30 minutes. Also, your instructor wants you to sort the list by show name and format the list as needed prior to printing. Feel free to change any of the list data to suit your tastes and opinions.

To complete this independent challenge:

1. Open the workbook titled XL H-2, then save it as "Television Shows of the Past".
2. Using your own data, add a field, then use the data form to add two records to the list. Make sure to enter information in every field.
3. Delete any records having show lengths other than 30. (*Hint*: Use the Criteria data form to set the criteria, then find and delete any matching records.)

4. Make any formatting changes to the list as needed.
5. Save the list prior to sorting.
6. Sort the list in ascending order by show name.
7. Preview, then print the list. Adjust any items as needed so that the list can be printed on a single page.
8. Sort the list again, this time in descending order by number of years the show was a favorite.
9. Change the header to read "Television Shows of the Past: '60s and '70s".
10. Preview, then print the list.
11. Save the workbook.

3. You work as a sales clerk at Nite Owl Video. Your roommate and co-worker, Albert Lee, has put together a list of his favorite movie actors and actresses. He has asked you to add several names to the list so he can determine which artists and what kinds of films you enjoy most. He has recorded information in the following fields: artist's first and last names, life span, birthplace, the genre or type of roles the artist plays most (for example, dramatic or comedic), the name of a film for which the artist has received or been nominated for an Academy Award, and finally, two additional films featuring the artist. Using your own data, add at least two artists known for dramatic roles and two artists known for comedic roles.

To complete this independent challenge:

1. Open the workbook titled XL H-3, then add at least four records using the criteria mentioned above. Remember, you are creating and entering your own movie data for all relevant fields.
2. Save the workbook as "Film Star Favorites". Make formatting changes to the list as needed. Remember to check your spelling.
3. Sort the list alphabetically by Genre. Perform a second sort by Last Name.
4. Preview the list, adjust any items as needed, then print a copy of the list sorted by Genre and Last Name.
5. Sort the list again, this time in descending order by the Life Span field, then by Last Name.
6. Print a copy of the list sorted by Life Span and Last Name.
7. Save your work, then submit your printouts.

4. Because Web users are located all over the world, you can use the World Wide Web (WWW) to locate almost any type of information, in just about any country around the globe. Travel information is especially helpful when you are planning vacations. You have decided to travel to Hawaii for one month over the summer. Your choice of accommodations includes a condominium close to the beach with full kitchen facilities. Use your choice of search engines on the WWW to locate information on condo rentals in Hawaii, and then build an Excel list with the information you gather.

To complete this independent challenge:

1. Open a new workbook, then save it as "Hawaiian Vacation".
2. Create a list with the following field names: Complex Name, Island, Ocean View?, Peak Season Rate, Off-Season Rate (rates per night), Max # of Bedrooms, On-Site Pool?, On-Site Golf?, Air Conditioning?, and Web Site Address.
3. Log on to the Internet and use your Web browser to go to http://www.course.com. From there, click the link Student Online Companions, then click the Excel link for Unit H.
4. Use any combination of the following sites to search for and compile your data: Yahoo!, WebCrawler, or Alta Vista. (*Hint:* When using Web search engines, the + (plus sign) before a word means that the word must appear in the Web document. Therefore, a suggested search string would be +Hawaii +Condo +Rentals.) Be sure to gather information on 10 different possible vacation sites (minimum 10 records). While on the Web, print at least two graphics of sites chosen to accompany your worksheet data.
5. Add the Web data as records in your list.
6. Format the worksheet as desired to increase readability.
7. Save and print the workbook, then submit your printouts.

► Visual Workshop

Create the worksheet shown in Figure H-19. Save the workbook as "Famous Jazz Performers". Once you've entered the field names and records, sort the list by Contribution to Jazz and then by Last Name. Change the page setup so that the list is centered on the page horizontally and the header reads "Famous Jazz Performers". Preview and print the list, then save the workbook. Submit your printouts.

FIGURE H-19

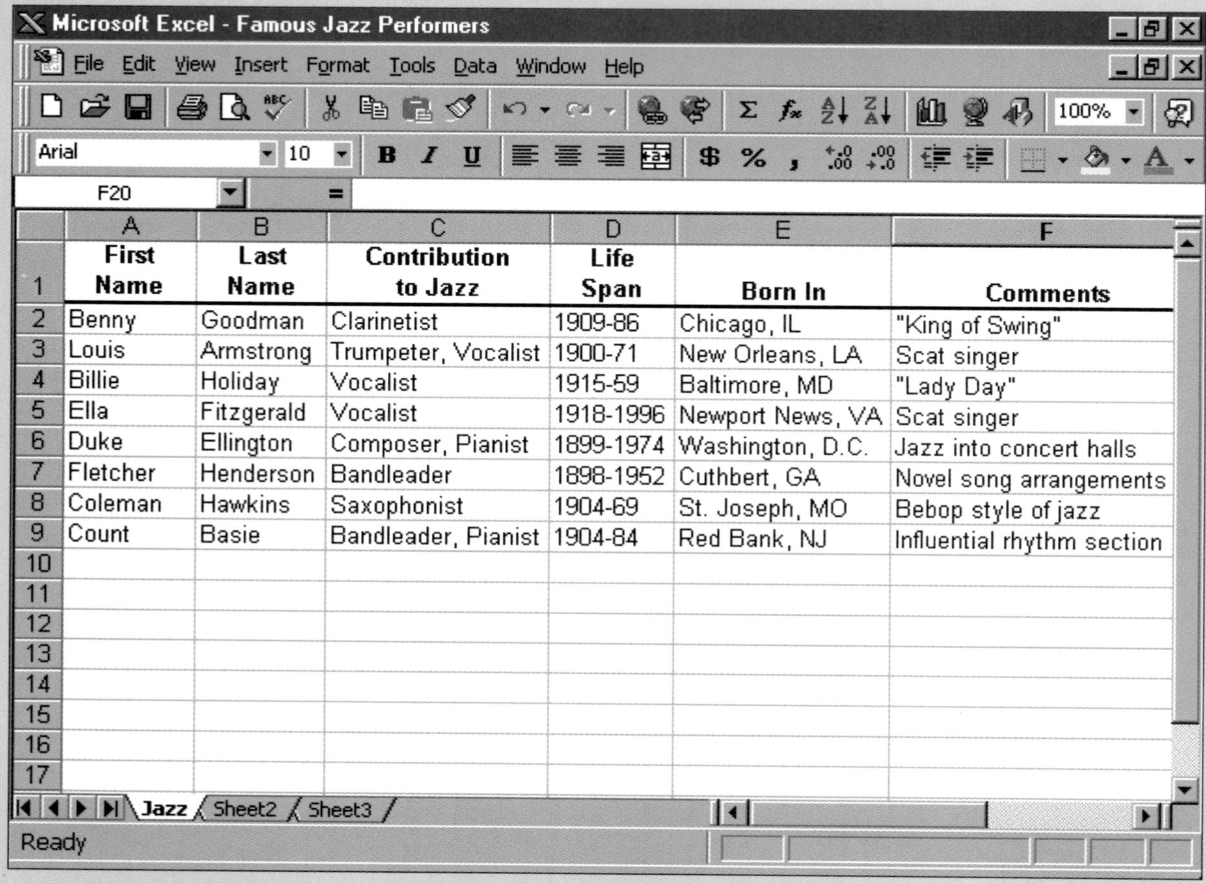

	A	B	C	D	E	F
1	First Name	Last Name	Contribution to Jazz	Life Span	Born In	Comments
2	Benny	Goodman	Clarinetist	1909-86	Chicago, IL	"King of Swing"
3	Louis	Armstrong	Trumpeter, Vocalist	1900-71	New Orleans, LA	Scat singer
4	Billie	Holiday	Vocalist	1915-59	Baltimore, MD	"Lady Day"
5	Ella	Fitzgerald	Vocalist	1918-1996	Newport News, VA	Scat singer
6	Duke	Ellington	Composer, Pianist	1899-1974	Washington, D.C.	Jazz into concert halls
7	Fletcher	Henderson	Bandleader	1898-1952	Cuthbert, GA	Novel song arrangements
8	Coleman	Hawkins	Saxophonist	1904-69	St. Joseph, MO	Bebop style of jazz
9	Count	Basie	Bandleader, Pianist	1904-84	Red Bank, NJ	Influential rhythm section
10						
11						
12						
13						
14						
15						
16						
17						

Integration

Exploring

Integration: Word, Excel, and Internet Explorer

Objectives

- Modify a Word document
- Enhance Excel data
- Modify a Web document

The skills you have developed in Word and Excel make your work more efficient and your documents and worksheets more professional. You can use elements from Word and Excel to create an effective Web document. Keith Watchman, Manager of Nomad Ltd's Bookkeeping Department, is preparing information for Nomad's efforts to acquire one of three companies. Because his co-workers use Microsoft Office 97 Professional, Keith will be able to combine their files with his own files easily.

Modifying a Word Document

Nomad's Board of Directors is planning to increase its product line by acquiring an existing company. Three prospective companies have been identified, and preliminary information has been obtained about each. 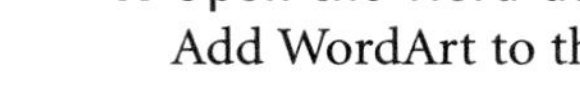 Keith Watchman has gathered the financial information on the prospective companies and is preparing information to present to the company Board members, accountants, and legal staff. A member of Keith's department has started a memo that Keith will use as a cover letter, incorporating spreadsheet data, for the project.

1. Open the Word document INT D-1, then save it as **Bookkeeping Memo**
   Add WordArt to the document to make it more attractive.
2. Delete the WordArt placeholder in the document, then create your own WordArt that reads "Bookkeeping Department," similar to the sample shown in Figure D-1
3. Enter information in the TO: and RE: sections of the memo using Figure D-1 as a guide
   You received background information on each of the three companies, portions of which you want to include in your memo.
4. Open the document INT D-2, then save it as **Preliminary Research**
   Start the memo with an introductory paragraph, followed by the board's analysis of the three companies.
5. In the Bookkeeping Memo, replace the "Enter text here" placeholder with a short introductory paragraph of your own, then copy the **three bulleted items** from the Preliminary Research document into the memo
   To back up the proposal, add a section to the memo summarizing the financial data you've gathered.
6. Open the Excel workbook INT D-3, then save it as **Acquisition Data**
7. In the **Bookkeeping Memo**, write a paragraph introducing the acquisition data, copy the annual totals for each company into the memo, then format the table appropriately
   Compare your memo to the sketch in Figure D-2. Now, print and save the file.
8. Save, preview, and print the **Bookkeeping Memo**, then close Word

QuickTip
You can use the Insert menu or a button on the Drawing toolbar to insert WordArt.

FIGURE D-1: Bookkeeping Memo with WordArt

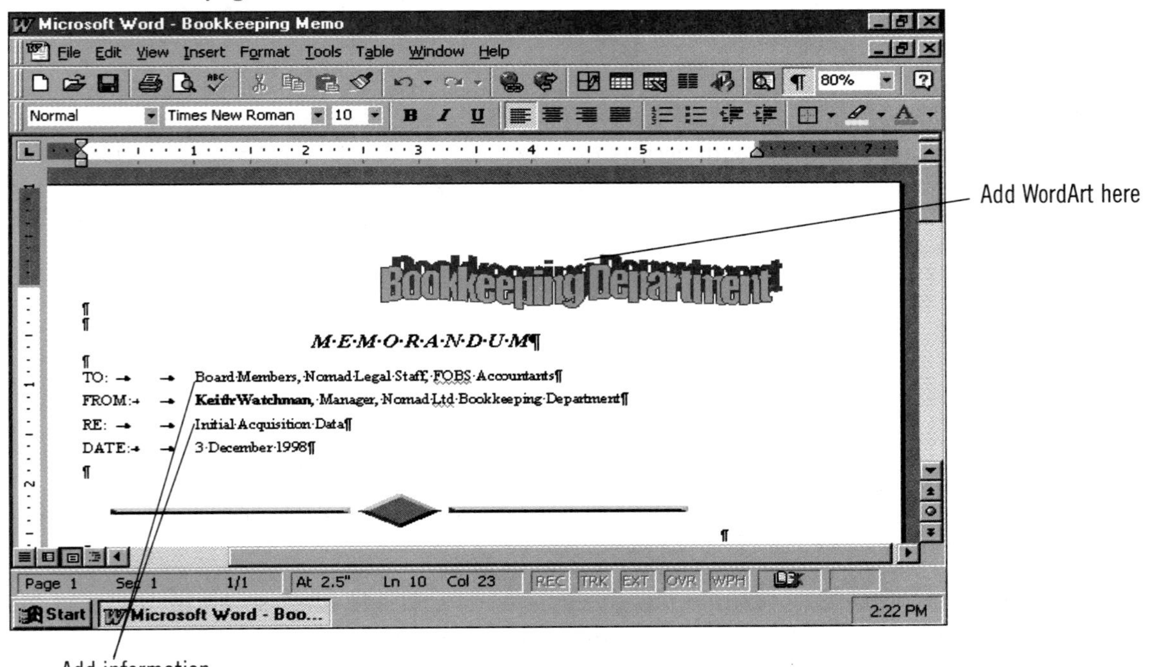

FIGURE D-2: Sample sketch of page layout

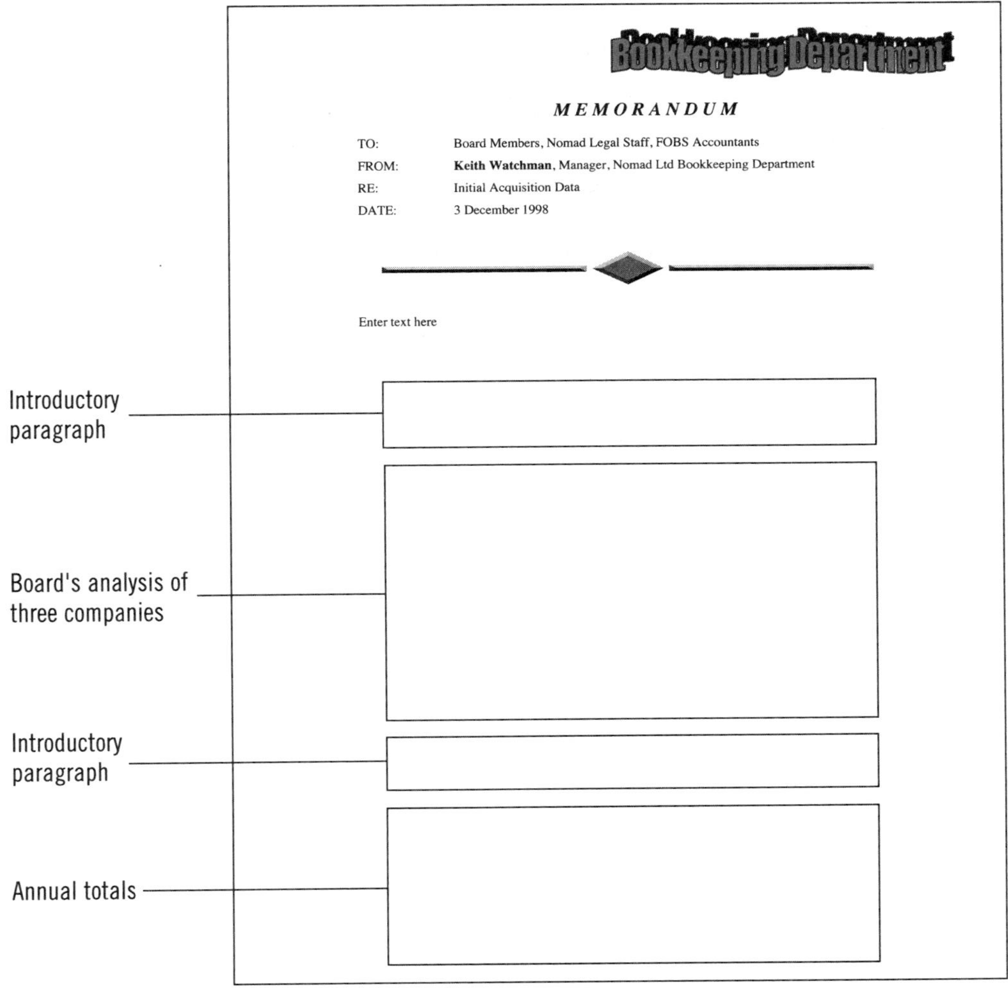

Enhancing Excel Data

Keith wants to increase the effectiveness of the financial data for each of the three companies under consideration. To do this, he'll format the data more attractively and convert the information to a chart. Keith decides to summarize the data in the Acquisition Data workbook on a single sheet. To call attention to the data, he'll use the Drawing toolbar and other techniques to format and annotate the information. Also he wants to create a chart for each company that will make the data more meaningful.

Steps

1. **Activate the Acquisition Data workbook**
   Create a summary page on a new sheet that contains all the data for each of the three companies.
2. **Insert a worksheet, rename the sheet Summary, create links so all the data on all the sheets is visible, then resize columns as necessary**
   See Figure D-3. Enhance the data using AutoFormats and the Drawing toolbar.
3. **Apply an AutoFormat of your choice to the data on the Summary sheet, then add annotations (circles, arrows, and text) where appropriate**
   Now you are ready to create charts for the data. You want the charts to appear on a new first sheet in the workbook, instead of on the Summary sheet.
4. **Insert a worksheet, then rename the sheet Charts**
   You want to create charts that illustrate the sales history of each company.
5. **Create one 3-D column chart for each company's data**
   Include any chart enhancements you feel are appropriate. Compare your work to Figure D-4. Next, you want to create a report that prints only the sheets containing the charts and the summary information.
6. **Use the Report Manager to create a report titled Graphic Summary that includes the Summary and Charts sheets and is numbered continuously**
7. **Save the workbook, then print the Graphic Summary report**

The Report Manager is an Excel feature that will only be available if it has been installed. See your instructor if this feature is not available.

FIGURE D-3: Summary sheet in Acquisition Data workbook

Results of linking formulas

Microsoft Excel - Acquisition Data

B4 = ='Campin" Cuisine'!B4

	A	B	C	D	E	F	
1	Sales Data						
2							
3	Campin' Cuisine	FY 93	FY 94	FY 95	FY 96	FY 97	Tota
4	Quarter 1	440,827.66	470,202.22	476,942.66	482,923.44	520,894.78	1,
5	Quarter 2	443,679.36	462,300.12	476,811.71	495,873.20	490,720.35	1,
6	Quarter 3	450,090.52	470,881.09	492,511.83	500,972.55	501,682.45	1,
7	Quarter 4	481,478.04	473,823.31	485,762.39	511,426.90	482,933.71	1,
8	Total	1,816,075.58	1,877,206.74	1,932,028.59	1,991,196.09	1,996,231.29	9,
9							
10	Chewy Treats	FY 93	FY 94	FY 95	FY 96	FY 97	Tota
11	Quarter 1	798,572.33	800,428.03	823,731.86	820,443.56	800,437.96	4,
12	Quarter 2	803,822.08	762,993.10	803,675.82	870,469.43	770,694.88	4,
13	Quarter 3	800,485.32	797,452.83	799,673.41	805,843.21	870,456.82	4,
14	Quarter 4	780,573.11	820,622.34	856,743.02	862,943.66	935,620.77	4,
15	Total	3,183,452.84	3,181,496.30	3,283,824.11	3,359,699.86	3,377,210.43	16,
16							
17	Health & Goodness	FY 93	FY 94	FY 95	FY 96	FY 97	Tota

Summary / Campin' Cuisine / Chewy Treats / Health &

Ready NUM

Start | Microsoft Excel - Acq... 3:08 PM

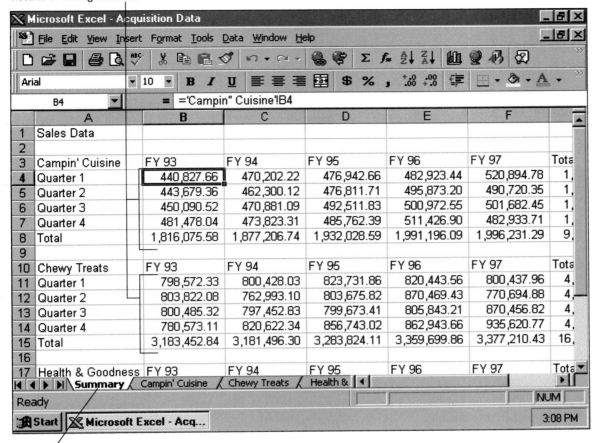

Newly added sheet

FIGURE D-4: Sample financial data charts

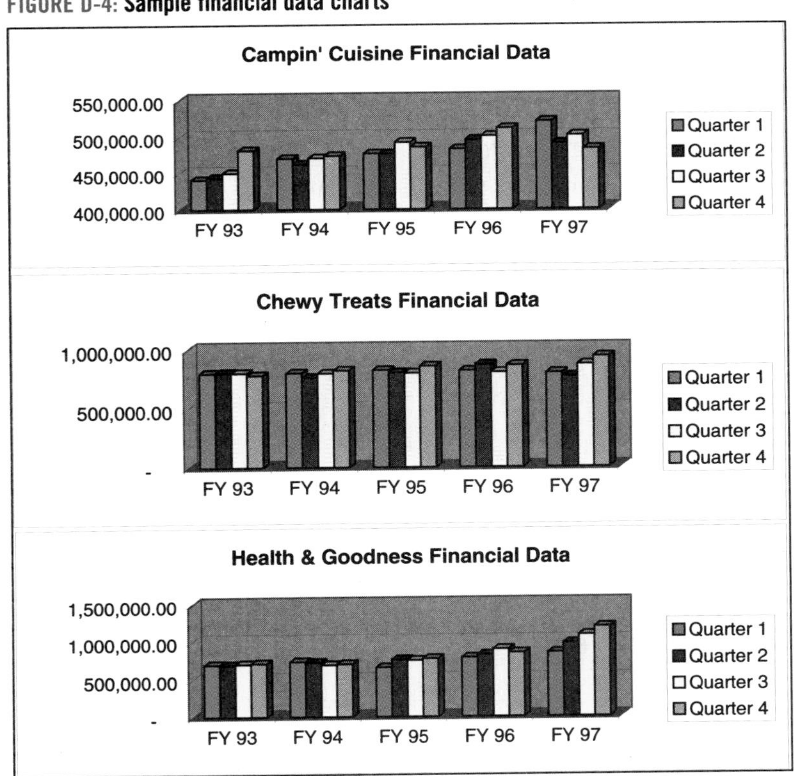

Modifying a Web Document

Because Nomad Ltd wants to keep its employees up-to-date on the impending acquisition, the Nomad Webmaster has established a page that the bookkeeping department maintains to make sure employees have current information. Nomad employees read this page to keep current on acquisition news. Keith will incorporate Excel charts from his memo into his department's existing Web page.

Steps

1. Open the Word HTML document INT D-4, then save it as **Acquisition Updates**
   First, replace a placeholder with explanatory text.
2. Select the text **Type some text**, then type **Sales histories of potential acquisitions**
   Compare your document to Figure D-5.
   Next, you copy Excel charts from the Acquisition Data workbook into this page.
3. Activate the Charts sheet in the **Acquisition Data workbook**
   Use the Copy button to copy the Campin' Cuisine chart.
4. Click the Campin' Cuisine chart, then click the **Copy button** on the Standard toolbar
   Once you have copied data to the Clipboard, you can paste it into another document using the Paste button.
5. Activate the **Acquisition Updates** document, select the line containing **Copy Campin' Cuisine chart here**, then click the **Paste button** on the Standard toolbar
6. Replace the remaining chart placeholders with the charts in the Acquisition Data workbook
   Once the charts are pasted in the Web page, save your work.
7. Click the **Save button** on the Standard toolbar
   With your work saved, preview the modified page using your Web browser, Microsoft Internet Explorer.
8. Click the **Web Page Preview button** on the Standard Web toolbar, then click the **Print button** on the Internet Explorer toolbar
   Compare your printout to Figure D-6.

FIGURE D-5: Web page with text added

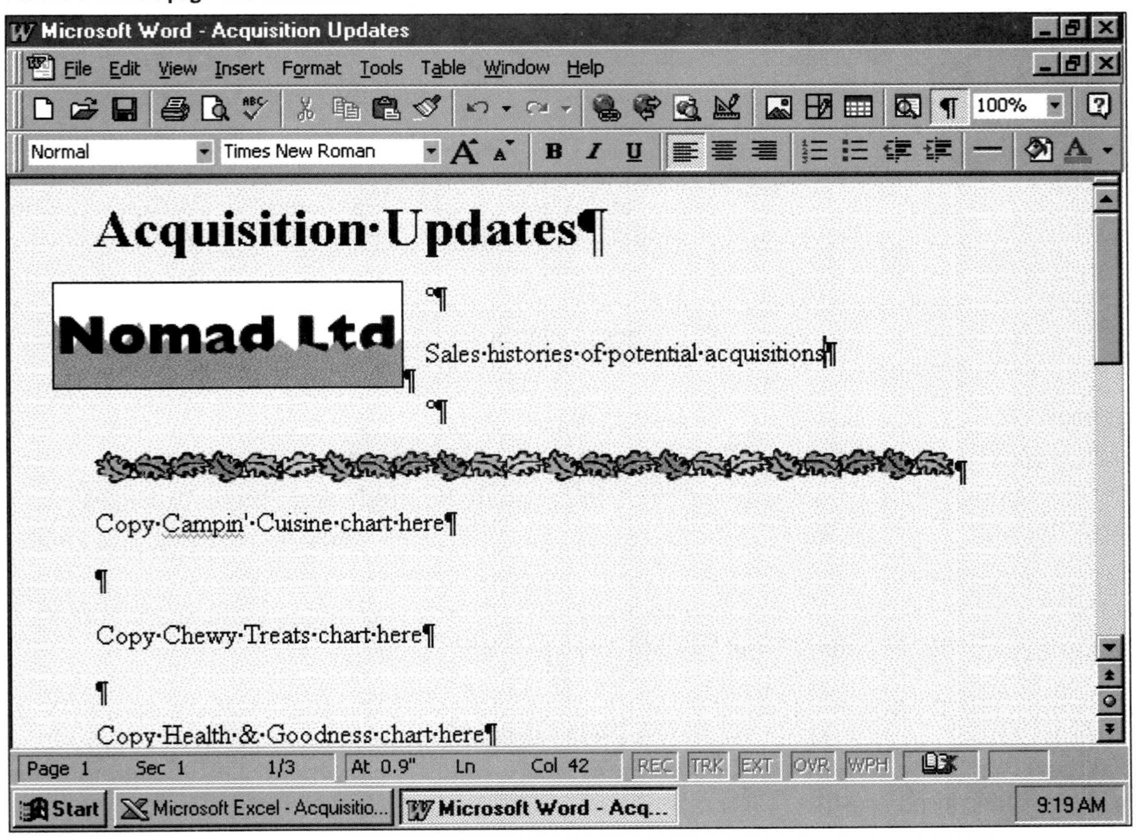

FIGURE D-6: Printed Web page

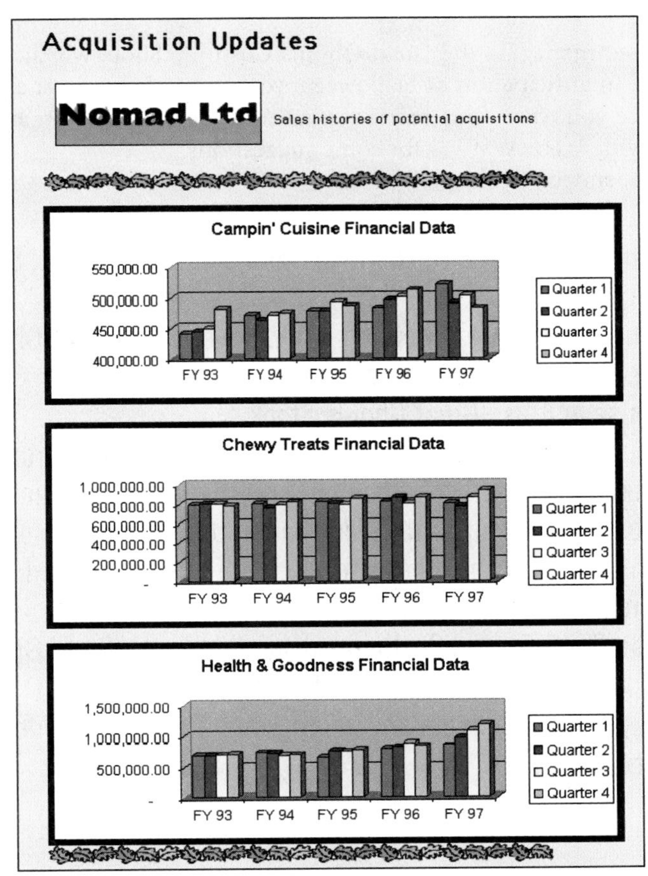

Integration

Independent Challenges

1. You've decided to act on your lifelong interest in botany and start your own floral shop called My Green Thumb. During your initial discussion with a banker from Big Bucks Bank, you were asked to submit a budget of anticipated expenses and revenues, as well as a one-page proposal outlining your plans for building the business. You are seeking a $25,000 startup business loan, which your banker assured you should be approved. Because the bank has Internet access, you've decided to create a Web page and include a printout of it in your loan application.

To complete this independent challenge:

1. Open the workbook INT D-5, then save it as "My Green Thumb Budget."
2. Create your own expense data using this workbook as a guide. Add more expenses if you wish.
3. Sort the expenses alphabetically, then create formulas to calculate quarterly and annual expenses.
4. Rename Sheet 2 "Income." Create a worksheet that calculates anticipated monthly, quarterly, and annual revenue.
5. Create a letterhead document for your company, then save it as "My Green Thumb Letterhead." Create a WordArt company logo for the letterhead, and include any applicable Clipart.
6. Use the letterhead to write your proposal, and save it as "My Green Thumb Proposal."
7. Compose a cover letter to the bank titled "Big Bucks Bank Cover Letter."
8. Create a Web page using the Web Page Wizard called "My Green Thumb web page." Add the logo you created and any other information or artwork to make the page look professional.
9. Save, preview, then print the documents you created.
10. Submit your printed materials.

2. Recently, you started managing the Great Ghouls Costume Shop, which rents costumes to both groups and individuals. In anticipation of Halloween, you've decided to host a gala costume party for current customers. Since you want your customers to come as their favorite horror show characters, you search the World Wide Web (WWW) for some suggestions.

To complete this independent challenge:

1. Create a Word document that contains a list of 15 costumes your company carries. Save the document as "Great Ghouls Costumes."
2. Create a Word document that announces your Halloween party. Save it as "Great Ghouls Costume Party." Add Clipart and WordArt to make the document more attractive.
3. Open the workbook INT D-6, then save it as "Great Ghouls Stock."
4. Log on to the Internet and use your Web browser to go to http://www.course.com. From there, click Student Online Companions, click the link for this textbook, then click on the Integration link for Unit D.
5. Use any of the following sites to compile your data about characters in horror movies: Shrine to Jason, Psycho, the Hannibal Lecter Home Page, or any other site you can find with related information.
6. Use information on the Web to create a list of costumes.
7. Copy the list of costumes from the Great Ghouls Costumes document to the Great Ghouls Stock workbook.
8. Supply in-stock and rental-fee figures, then format the data attractively.
9. Create a Web page to advertise your shop. Include any appropriate artwork and information.
10. Save, preview, then print your documents.
11. Submit your printed materials.

Modifying
a Database Structure

Objectives

- ► **Examine relational database requirements**
- ► **Plan a table**
- ► **Create new tables**
- ► **Create one-to-many relationships**
- ► **Delete fields**
- ► **Define field properties**
- ► **Define date/time field properties**
- ► **Define field validation properties**

In this unit, you will add new tables to an existing database and link them in one-to-many relationships to create a relational database. You will also modify several field **properties** such as field formatting and field validation to increase data entry accuracy. Michael Belmont has decided to expand the use of Access within Nomad to track customer, tour, and sales information. Because a single table database will not meet all of his needs, he will use multiple tables of data and link them together to create a relational database.

Access 97

Examining Relational Database Requirements

A **relational database** is a collection of related tables that share information. The goals of a relational database are to satisfy dynamic information management needs and to eliminate duplicate data entry wherever possible. After analyzing Nomad's sales transactions, Michael begins to see repeat customers. The Customers table shown in Figure E-1 allows Michael to sort and retrieve specific information on customers and tours very quickly, but does not have an easy way to track more than one sale to the same customer. The following list of database concepts will guide Michael's actions as he moves from a single table of data to the powerful relational database capabilities provided by Access.

A relational database is based on multiple tables of data. Each table should be based on only one subject.

Right now the Customers table in the Nomad database actually contains three subjects: Customers, Tours, and Sales. Michael knows that duplicate data across records of a table is a clue that a database needs to be redesigned into multiple tables. By breaking out each of these subjects into its own table, Michael will eliminate redundant data and increase the flexibility of his database.

Each record in a table should be uniquely identified with a key field or key field combination.

A **key field** is a field which contains unique information for each record. Typically, a customer table contains a Customer Identification (CustID) field to uniquely identify each customer. While using the customer's last name as the key field might accommodate a small database, it would be a poor choice and bad database design because it won't allow the user to enter two customers with the same last name.

Tables in the same database should be related, or linked, through a field common to each table in a one-to-many relationship.

To tie the information from the Customers table to the Sales table, the CustID field would need to be in both tables. Because the CustID field is a key field in the Customers table, this side of the relationship is the "one" side. Because the CustID field may be listed many times in the Sales table to record multiple sales to the same customer, this side of the relationship is the "many" side. Linking tables together with a common field in this manner is called creating a **one-to-many relationship** and is shown in Figure E-2.

FIGURE E-1: The datasheet of the Customers table

Customers : Table

CustID	First	Last	Street	City	State	Zip	Tour	Date	Birth Date
1	Ginny	Braithwaite	3 Which Way	Salem	MA	01970	Road Bike	6/15/96	1/10/60
10	Virginia	Rodarmor	123 Main Street	Andover	MA	01810	Bungee	9/20/96	1/6/70
11	Kristen	Reis	4848 Ashley	Fontanelle	IA	50810	Big Sky	1/10/97	3/18/68
12	Tom	Reis	4848 Ashley	Fontanelle	IA	50810	Big Sky	1/10/97	7/3/65
13	Mark	Eagan	987 Lincoln	Schaumberg	IL	44433	Big Sky	1/10/97	1/29/60
14	Peg	Fox	125 Maple	Des Moines	IA	50625	Big Sky	1/10/97	4/10/59
15	Ron	Fox	125 Maple	Des Moines	IA	50625	Big Sky	1/10/97	8/28/87
16	Amanda	Fox	125 Maple	Des Moines	IA	50625	Big Sky	1/10/97	1/30/88
17	Rebecca	Gross	123 Oak	Bridgewater	KS	50837	Road Bike	6/15/96	9/20/62
2	Robin	Spencer	293 Serenity Dr.	Concord	MA	01742	Mt. Bike	9/26/96	1/30/52
3	Camilla	Dobbins	486 Intel Circuit	Rio Rancho	NM	87124	Road Bike	6/15/96	3/15/65
4	Pip	Khalsa	1100 Vista Road	Santa Fe	NM	87505	Mt. Bike	9/26/96	4/16/69
5	Kendra	Majors	530 Spring Street	Lenox	MA	02140	Bungee	9/20/96	5/4/70
6	Tasha	Williams	530 Spring Street	Lenox	MA	02140	Road Bike	6/15/96	5/8/71
7	Fred	Gonzales	Purgatory Ski Area	Durango	CO	81301	Mt. Bike	6/15/96	6/10/60
8	John	Black	11 River Road	Brookfield	CT	06830	Road Bike	6/15/96	7/15/65
9	Scott	Owen	72 Yankee Way	Brookfield	CT	06830	Bungee	9/20/96	3/15/65
*									

Record: 1 of 17

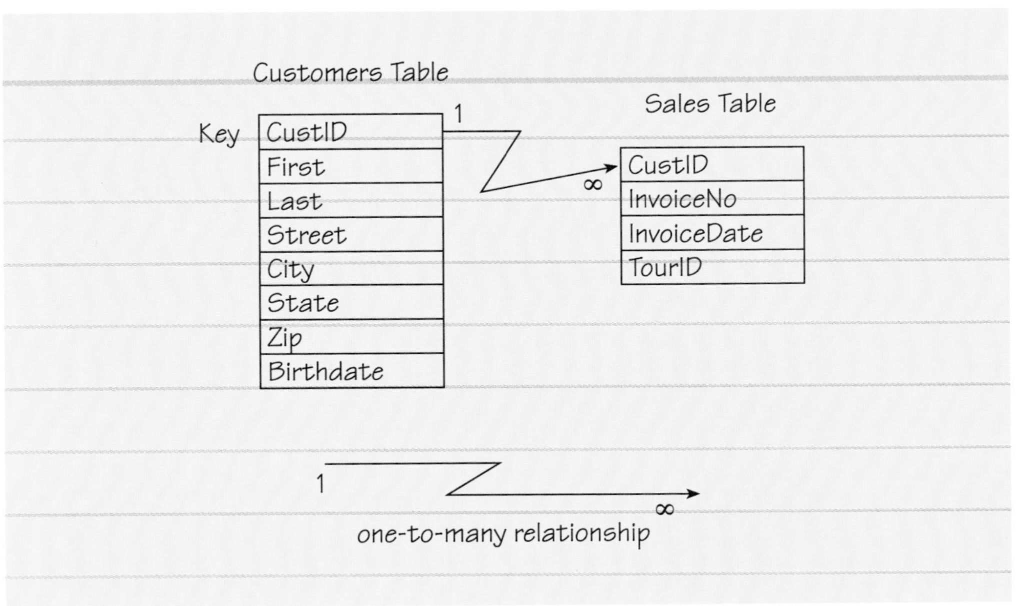

FIGURE E-2: A relational database with two tables

Access 97

Planning a Table

Careful planning is crucial to successful relational database design and creation. Not only is duplicated data error-prone, but it limits the query and reporting capabilities of the overall database. Once you understand the concepts and goals of a relational database, you'll often need to redistribute the fields of the database into new tables. Michael realizes that the current single-table database provides no way to track additional sales to existing customers without duplicating all of the customer's demographic data such as name and address. Michael decides to get some advice on how to redesign his database from a database expert.

Details

List all of the fields of data that need to be tracked

Typically, these fields are already present in existing tables or paper reports. Still, it is a good idea to document each field on a single sheet of paper in order to examine all fields at the same time. This is the appropriate time to determine if there are additional fields of information that do not currently exist on any report, but that should be tracked for future purposes. Michael decides that in addition to the existing fields in the Customers table he would also like to start tracking tour cost, tour sales price, invoice date, tour handicap accessibility, and tour difficulty.

Group fields together in subject matter tables

The new Nomad database will track sales to customers, a common use for a relational database in business. It will contain three tables: Customers, Tours, and Sales.

Identify key fields that exist in tables

Each table should include a key field or key field combination in order to uniquely identify each record. Each customer, tour, and sale must be uniquely identified. Michael will use the CustID field in the Customers table, the TourID field in the Tours table, and the InvoiceNo field in the Sales table to handle this requirement.

The linking field should be the only field that is duplicated in two tables. For clarity, give the linking field the same name in both tables.

Link the tables with a one-to-many relationship via a common field

Information from linked tables can be pulled together for one common report. By adding the CustID field to the Sales table, Michael has created a common field in both the Customers and Sales tables that can serve as the link between them. Similarly, by adding the TourID field to the Sales table, Michael has created a common field in both the Sales and Tours tables that can serve as the link. For a valid one-to-many relationship, the linking field must be designated as the key field in the "one" side of the one-to-many relationship. The final sketch of Michael's redesigned relational database is shown in Figure E-3.

FIGURE E-3: Final sketch of the redesigned relational database

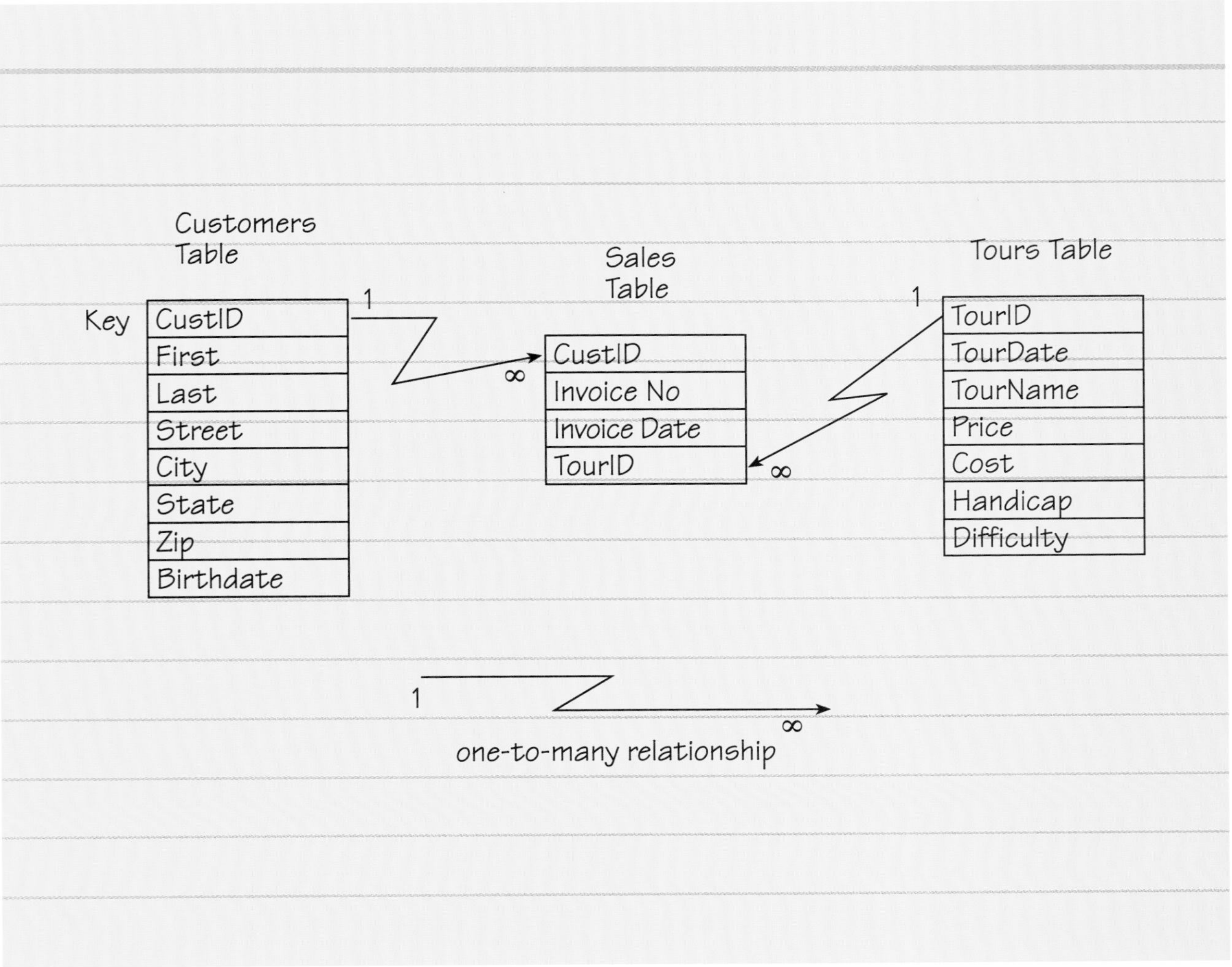

Customers Table

Key	
Key	CustID
	First
	Last
	Street
	City
	State
	Zip
	Birthdate

Sales Table

CustID
Invoice No
Invoice Date
TourID

Tours Table

TourID
TourDate
TourName
Price
Cost
Handicap
Difficulty

Customers.CustID 1 → ∞ Sales.CustID; Tours.TourID 1 → ∞ Sales.TourID

1 → ∞ one-to-many relationship

Key field combinations

Identifying a single key field may be difficult in some tables. Examine, for instance, a table that records employee promotions over time that includes three fields: employee number, date, and pay rate. None of the fields individually could serve as a valid key field because none are restricted to unique data. The employee number and date together, however, could serve as a valid **key field combination** since the employee number and date together would uniquely identify the record.

Access 97

Creating New Tables

Once you have developed a valid relational database design on paper, you are ready to define the tables in Access. All characteristics of a table including field names, data types, field descriptions, field properties, and key fields are designed in the table's **Design View**. In a relational database, it is important to define the length and data type of the linking field the same in both tables in order to create a successful link. Using his new database design, Michael will create the Sales and Tours tables.

1. Start Access and open the **Nomad-E** database on your Student Disk
2. Click the **Tables tab** in the database window if it is not already selected, then click **New**
   You will enter the fields directly into the table's Design View.
3. Click **Design View** in the New Table dialog box, then click **OK**
   First define the field names, data types, and other field properties of the new Sales table. Field names should be as short as possible, but long enough to be descriptive because the field name entered in a table's Design View is used as the default name for the field in all later queries, forms, and reports.
4. Type **CustID**, press **[Enter]**, press **t** to select the Text Data Type, and press **[Enter]** twice to bypass the Description column
5. Type the other fields and enter the data types as shown below:

Field Name	Data Type
InvoiceNo	**AutoNumber**
InvoiceDate	**Date/Time**
TourID	**Text**

6. Click **InvoiceNo** in the Field Name column, then click the **Primary Key button** on the Table Design toolbar
   The completed table Design View for the Sales table is shown in Figure E-4. Next, name, save, and close the Sales table.
7. Click the **Save button** on the Table Design toolbar, type **Sales** in the Table Name text box in the Save As dialog box, click **OK**, then click the **Close button** in the Sales: Table Design View window
   Sales is now displayed in the Tables tab, and it is a table in the Nomad-E database.
8. Click **New**, click **Design View**, click **OK**, then design the **Tours** table using the field information for the Tours table shown in Figure E-5
   Now that you have entered all the field information for the Tours table, name and save the table.
9. Click , type **Tours** in the Table Name text box in the Save As dialog box, click **OK**, then click the **Close button** in the Tours : Table Design View window
   Sales and Tours are now displayed in the Tables tab in the Nomad-E database.

QuickTip

You can press [Enter] or [Tab] to move to the next column in a table's Design View window.

Trouble?

If you clicked the Access program window Close button rather than the table's Close button, you closed the entire Nomad-E database. To continue work, simply start Access, open Nomad-E, and resume work.

FIGURE E-4: **Design View for the Sales table**

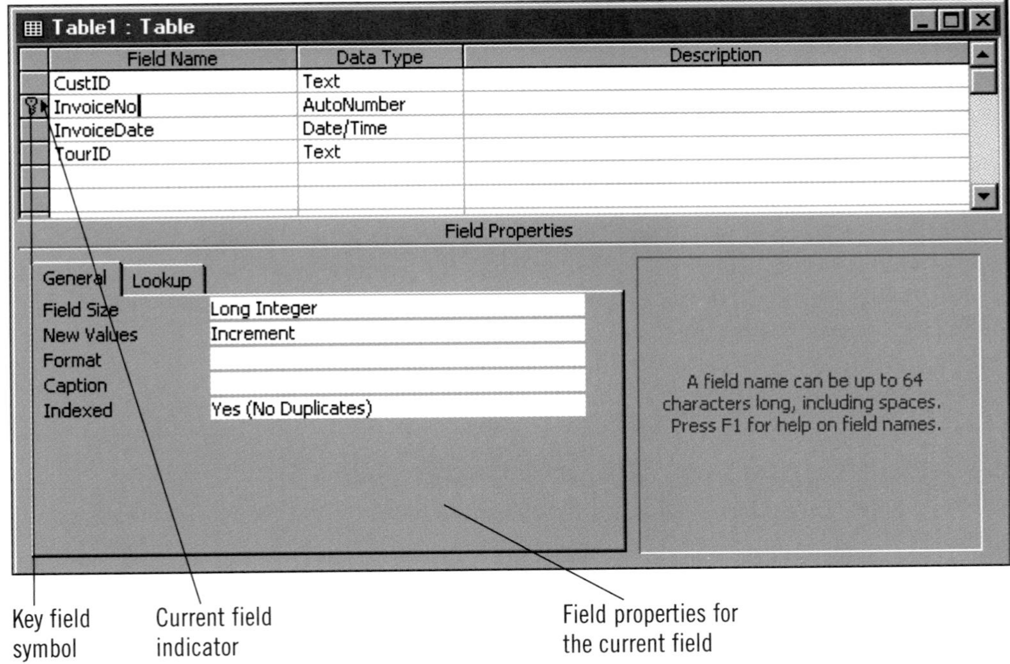

FIGURE E-5: **Design View for the Tours table**

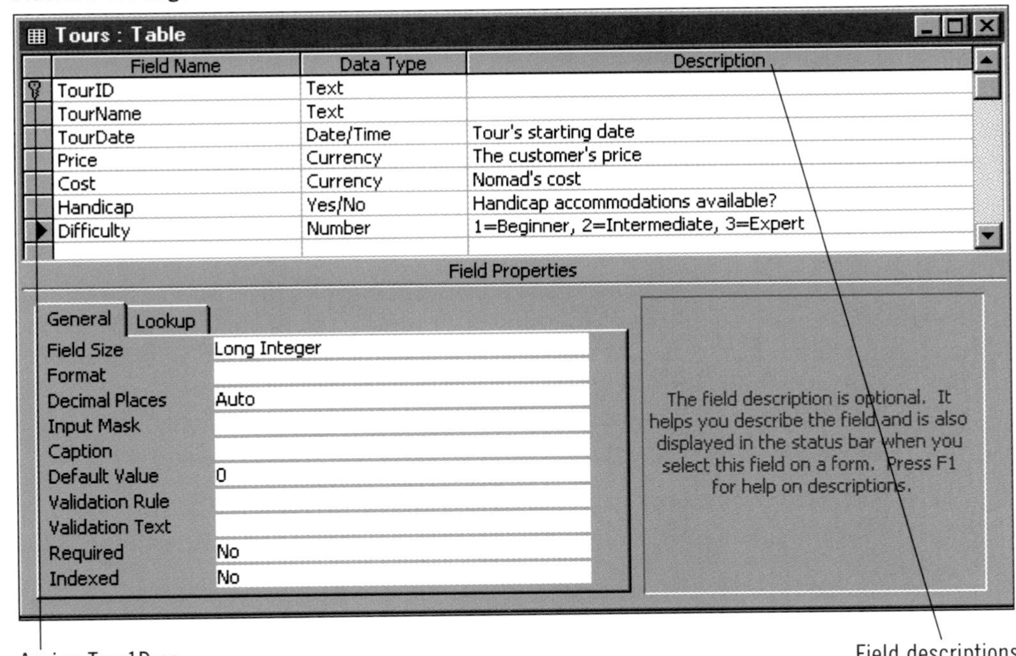

Assign TourID as the Primary key field

Linked tables

A **linked table** is a table created in another database product, or another application such as Excel, that is stored in a file outside of the open database. You can add, delete, and edit records in a linked table from within Access but you can't change its structure. An **imported table** creates a copy of the information from the external file, and places it in a new Access table in your database.

Access 97

Creating One-to-Many Relationships

Once the initial database design and table entry phase has been completed, you must identify which fields will link the tables in one-to-many relationships. Once the tables are linked, queries, reports, and forms can be designed with fields from multiple tables. Michael's initial database sketch revealed that the CustID field will link the Customer table to the Sales table and that the TourID field will link the Tours table to the Sales table. Michael will now define the one-to-many relationships between the tables of the Nomad database.

Steps

Trouble?

If the Show Table dialog box is not open, click the Show Table button on the Relationships toolbar.

Trouble?

If all of a table's field names are not displayed in the Relationships window, drag the bottom border of the table window until the scroll bar disappears and all fields are visible.

QuickTip

To delete a table from the Relationships window, click the table and press [Delete].

QuickTip

To print a copy of the Relationships window, press [Print Screen] while viewing the window, start an empty word processing document, paste, then print the document.

1. **Click the Relationships button on the Database toolbar**
   The Show Table dialog box opens and lists all three tables in the Nomad database on the Tables tab.
2. **Click Customers on the Tables tab if it is not already selected, click Add, click Sales, click Add, click Tours, click Add, then click Close**
   The field lists of all three tables have been added to the Relationships window with key fields in bold. Now Michael can create links between the tables.
3. **Maximize the window, then drag the CustID field from the Customers table to the CustID field in the Sales table**
   Dragging a field from one table to another in the Relationships window links the two tables with the chosen field and opens the Relationships dialog box shown in Figure E-6. **Referential integrity** between the tables helps insure data accuracy.
4. **Click the Enforce Referential Integrity check box in the Relationships dialog box, then click Create**
   The **one-to-many line** shows the linkage between the CustID field of the Customers table and the Sales table. The "one" side of the relationship is the unique CustID for each record in the Customers table. The "many" side of the relationship is identified by an infinity symbol pointing to the CustID field in the Sales table. This relationship allows repeat customer sales to be recorded in the Sales table without duplicating any of the static customer data in the Customers table. The only field that is duplicated is the data in the linking CustID field.
5. **Drag the TourID field from the Tours table to the TourID field in the Sales table**
   The TourID field will link the Sales table to additional information about each tour in the Tours table.
6. **Click the Enforce Referential Integrity check box in the Relationships dialog box, then click Create**
   The finished Relationships window with all of the field names displayed should look like Figure E-7. Close the Relationships window and save the layout changes.
7. **Click the Close button in the Relationships window, then click Yes**
   Michael is finished with the database today, so he'll close it.
8. **Click the Close button in the Nomad-E : Database window**

FIGURE E-6: Creating table relationships

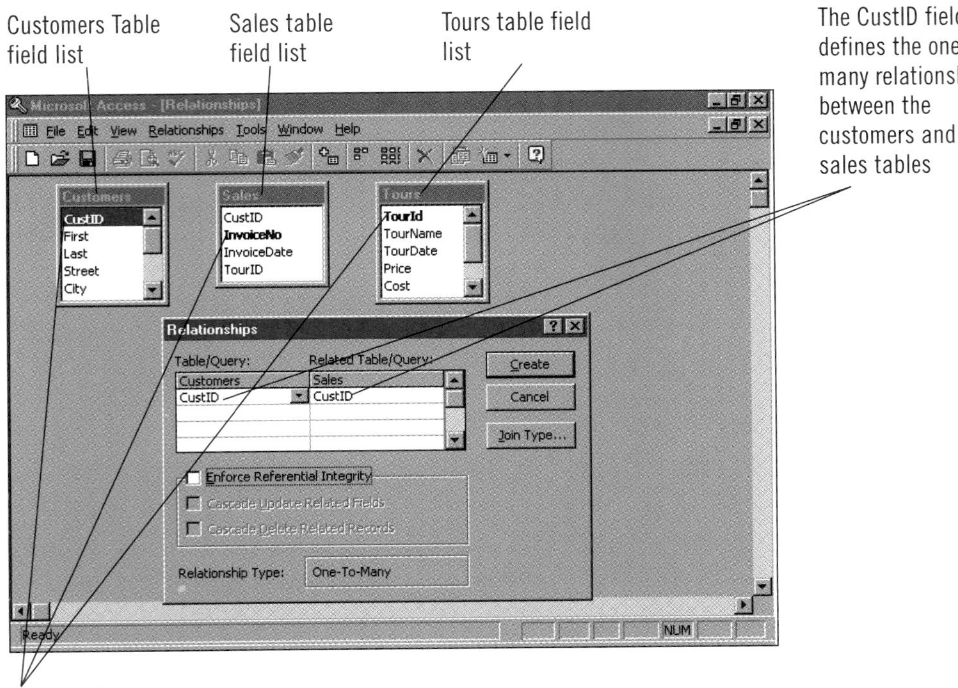

FIGURE E-7: The final Relationships window

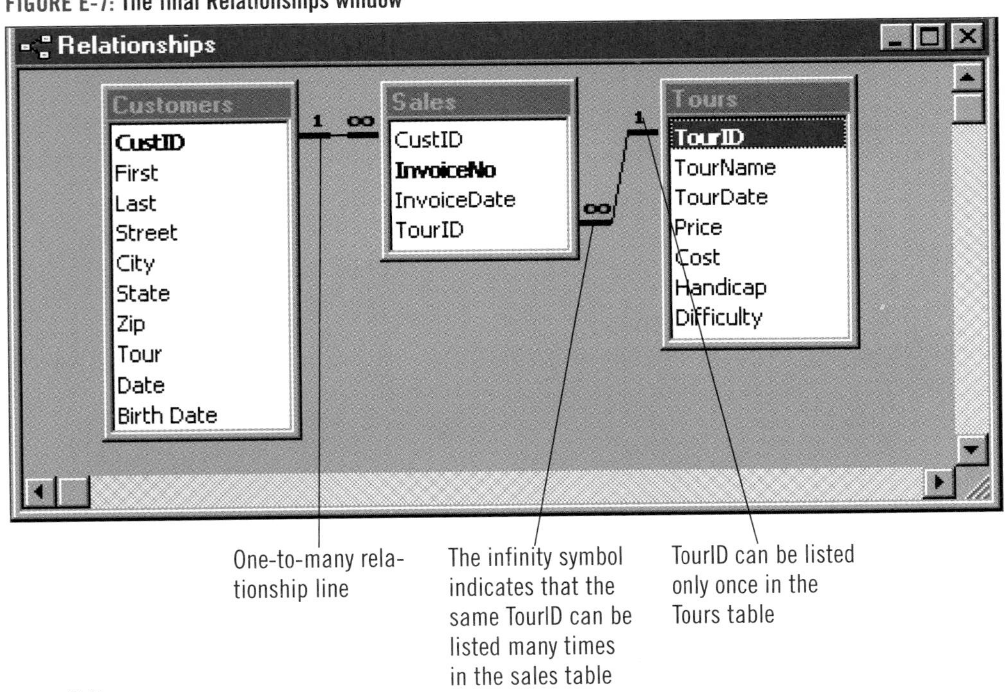

Why enforcing referential integrity is important

By using the **Enforce Referential Integrity** option, you are enforcing a set of rules to help maintain the accuracy of your database. In this case, referential integrity would not allow you to enter a CustID in the Sales table that had not already been entered in the Customers table. Similarly, you could not enter a TourID in the Sales table that had not already been entered in the Tours table. That way, you cannot record a sale to an unidentified customer or nonexistent tour.

Deleting Fields

Once a database is redesigned to handle relational data, there can be quite a bit of "cleanup" work to do. Changes to a table such as adding new fields, deleting unnecessary fields, or changing field properties are done in a table's Design View. When Michael redesigned his database, he moved the Tour information from the Customers table to the Tours table. In addition, he started tracking new fields that describe each tour such as Price, Cost, Handicap, and Difficulty. These changes created a considerable data entry project that Michael completed and saved as the database Nomad-E2.

Steps

1. Click the **Open Database button** on the Database toolbar and open the **Nomad-E2** database
   The Nomad-E2 database contains the data Michael entered in the Tours and Sales tables. In order to verify his work, he printed the datasheets from the Tours table shown in Figure E-8 and the Sales table shown in Figure E-9. Now that the tour and sales information is saved in the appropriate tables of the Nomad-E2 relational database, you can eliminate the Tour and Date fields from the Customers table.

2. Click the **Tables tab** in the Nomad-E2 : Database window if it is not already chosen, click the **Customers table**, then click **Design**

Trouble?

If the entire row isn't highlighted, you selected the field name rather than the field selector button to the left of the field name.

3. Scroll down the field names, click the **Tour field selector**, then press **[Delete]**
   Access warns you that deleting this field will delete all of the data in the field. Since this information has been safely entered in the Tours table, you can delete the field from the Customers table.

4. Click **Yes**

Trouble?

If you delete the wrong field, you can undo the action by clicking the Undo button . You can only undo your last action, however, so you must act immediately once the mistake occurs.

5. Repeat steps 3 and 4 to delete the **Date field** from the Customers table
   The new Design View of the Customers table should look like Figure E-10. Save the changes to the table.

6. Click the **Save button** on the toolbar

FIGURE E-8: Datasheet for the Tours table

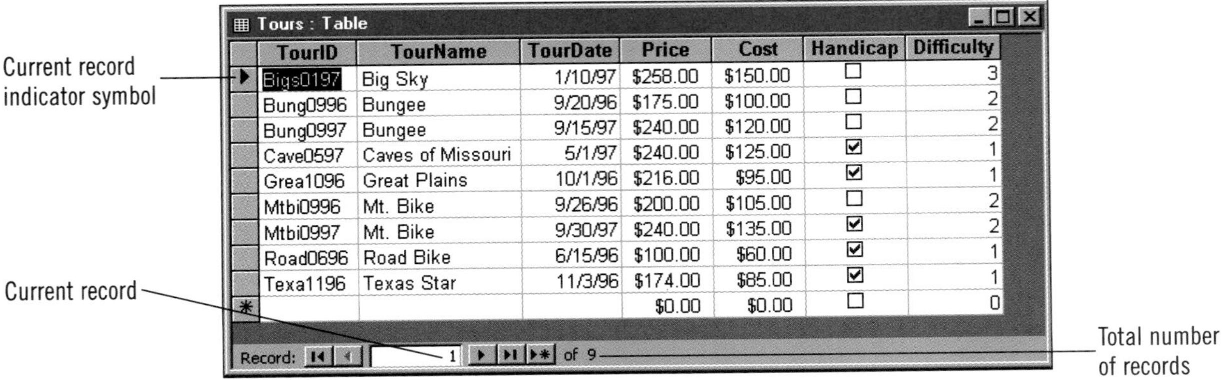

Tours : Table

TourID	TourName	TourDate	Price	Cost	Handicap	Difficulty
Bigs0197	Big Sky	1/10/97	$258.00	$150.00	☐	3
Bung0996	Bungee	9/20/96	$175.00	$100.00	☐	2
Bung0997	Bungee	9/15/97	$240.00	$120.00	☐	2
Cave0597	Caves of Missouri	5/1/97	$240.00	$125.00	☑	1
Grea1096	Great Plains	10/1/96	$216.00	$95.00	☑	1
Mtbi0996	Mt. Bike	9/26/96	$200.00	$105.00	☐	2
Mtbi0997	Mt. Bike	9/30/97	$240.00	$135.00	☑	2
Road0696	Road Bike	6/15/96	$100.00	$60.00	☑	1
Texa1196	Texas Star	11/3/96	$174.00	$85.00	☑	1
*			$0.00	$0.00	☐	0

Record: 1 of 9

FIGURE E-9: Datasheet for the Sales table

Sales : Table

CustID	InvoiceNo	InvoiceDate	TourID
1	1	5/1/96	Road0696
2	2	8/1/96	Mtbi0996
3	3	8/2/96	Bung0996
4	4	8/2/96	Mtbi0996
5	5	8/2/96	Bung0996
6	6	8/2/96	Bung0996
7	7	8/2/96	Mtbi0996
8	8	8/5/96	Mtbi0996
9	9	8/5/96	Bung0996
10	10	8/5/96	Mtbi0996
11	11	12/2/96	Bigs0197
12	12	12/2/96	Bigs0197
13	13	12/3/96	Bigs0197
14	14	12/3/96	Bigs0197
15	15	12/4/96	Bigs0197
16	16	12/4/96	Bigs0197
11	17	2/3/97	Bung0997
13	18	2/3/97	Bung0997
14	19	2/4/97	Mtbi0997
15	20	2/4/97	Mtbi0997
*	(AutoNumber)		

Record: 1 of 20

These sales represent repeat customers

FIGURE E-10: Design View of the final Customers table

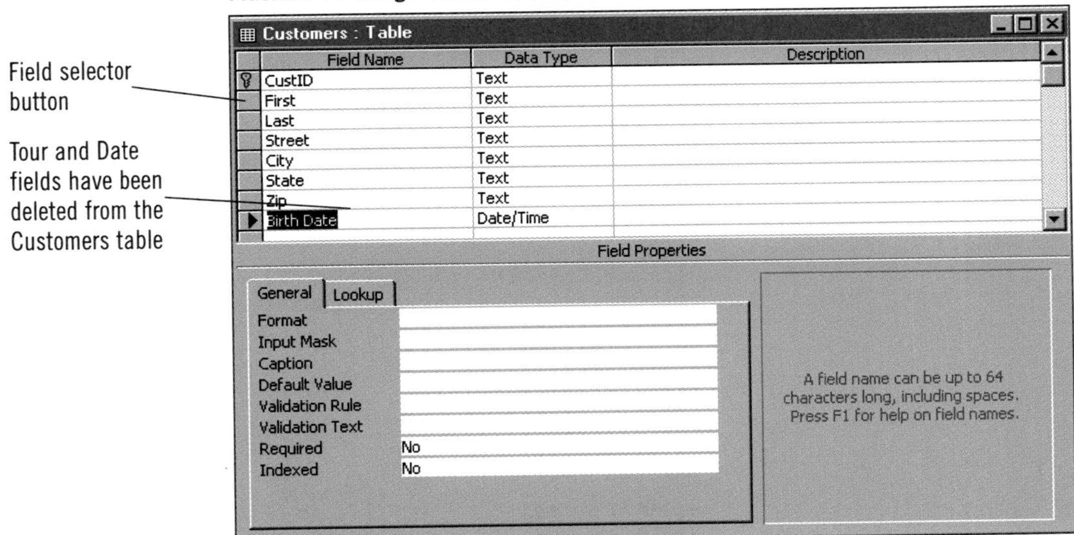

Access 97

Access 97

Defining Field Properties

Field properties are the characteristics that apply to each field in a table, such as field size, default value, or field formats. Modifying these properties helps insure database accuracy and clarity. Michael decides to make three field property changes in the Customers table. He will alter the field size, format, and default value properties for the State field.

QuickTip

Most field properties are optional, but if they require an entry, Access provides a default value.

1. Click each of the **field names** while viewing the Field Properties panel
   The Field Properties panel of a table's Design View changes to display the properties of the selected field. For example, when a field with a Text data type is selected, the Field Size property is visible. When a field with a Date/Time data type is selected, Access controls the Field Size property and therefore doesn't display it for the user.
2. Click the **State field name**
   Shorten the length of the Field Size for the State field in the Customers table to two characters since every state will be identified by its two-letter abbreviation.
3. Double-click **50** in the **Field Size Field Property text box** in the Field Properties panel, then type **2**
   Fifty is the default field size for a text field, but now the State field is limited to only two characters to prevent some keying errors. You will also force each entry in the State field to be uppercase letters, regardless of how the entry is typed.

QuickTip

The < (the less than sign) in the Format property forces all characters in the field to be lowercase letters.

4. Click in the **Format Field Property text box**, then type **>** (the greater than sign)
   The greater than sign forces all entries to be converted to uppercase characters. Since the majority of Nomad's new customers live in Iowa, designate IA as the default value for the State field.
5. Click in the **Default Value Field Property text box**, then type **IA**
   The Design View of the Customers table should now look like Figure E-11. Notice that the State field is chosen in the upper half of the window, and the Field Properties panel displays the properties that you have just changed.
6. Click the **Save button** on the Standard toolbar, then click **Yes** to continue when warned about losing data
   Since none of the entries in the State field were longer than two characters, you won't actually lose any data. Display the Customers table datasheet to see the effect of his property changes.
7. Click the **Datasheet View button** on the Table Design toolbar
   Notice that IA is entered as the default property for the next new record as shown in Figure E-12.

FIGURE E-11: The State field property changes

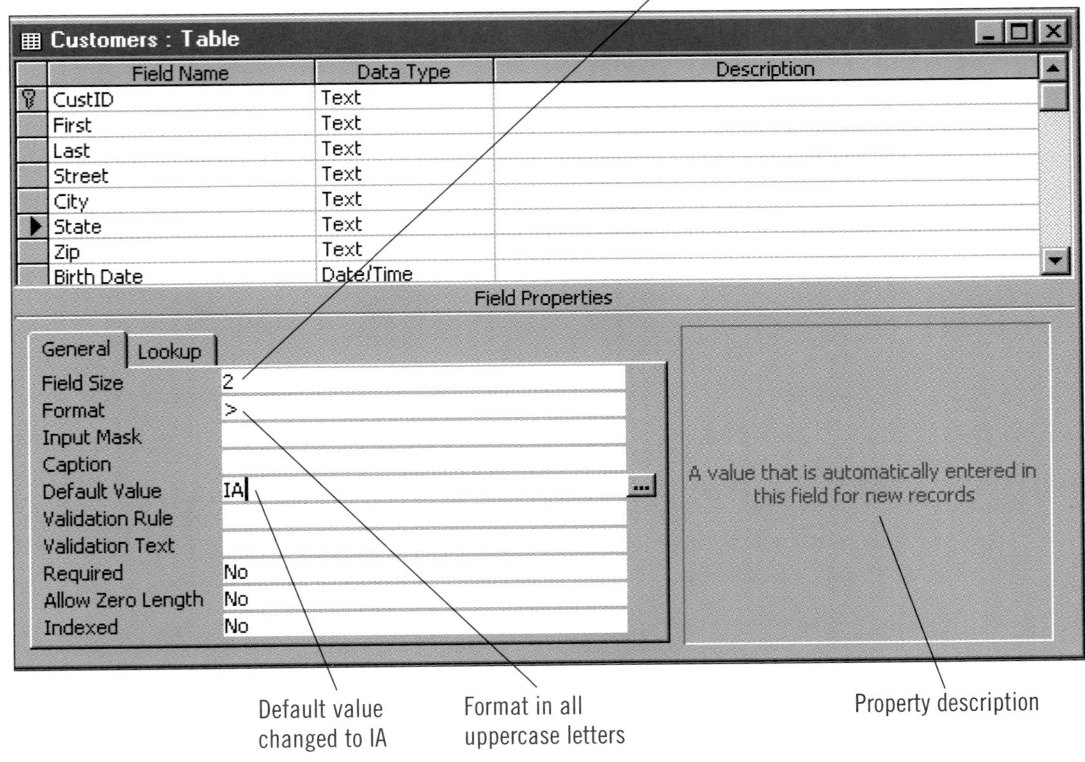

FIGURE E-12: The Customers table datasheet

Customers : Table

CustID	First	Last	Street	City	State	Zip	Birth Date
1	Ginny	Braithwaite	3 Which Way	Salem	MA	01970	1/10/60
10	Virginia	Rodarmor	123 Main Street	Andover	MA	01810	1/6/70
11	Kristen	Reis	4848 Ashley	Fontanelle	IA	50810	3/18/68
12	Tom	Reis	4848 Ashley	Fontanelle	IA	50810	7/3/65
13	Mark	Eagan	987 Lincoln	Schaumberg	IL	44433	1/29/60
14	Peg	Fox	125 Maple	Des Moines	IA	50625	4/10/59
15	Ron	Fox	125 Maple	Des Moines	IA	50625	8/28/87
16	Amanda	Fox	125 Maple	Des Moines	IA	50625	1/30/88
17	Rebecca	Gross	123 Oak	Bridgewater	KS	50837	9/20/62
2	Robin	Spencer	293 Serenity Dr.	Concord	MA	01742	1/30/52
3	Camilla	Dobbins	486 Intel Circuit	Rio Rancho	NM	87124	3/15/65
4	Pip	Khalsa	1100 Vista Road	Santa Fe	NM	87505	4/16/69
5	Kendra	Majors	530 Spring Street	Lenox	MA	02140	5/4/70
6	Tasha	Williams	530 Spring Street	Lenox	MA	02140	5/8/71
7	Fred	Gonzales	Purgatory Ski Area	Durango	CO	81301	6/10/60
8	John	Black	11 River Road	Brookfield	CT	06830	7/15/65
9	Scott	Owen	72 Yankee Way	Brookfield	CT	06830	3/15/65
*					IA		

Record: 1 of 17

State default value

Access 97

Access 97

Defining Date/Time Field Properties

The Date/Time format property allows the user to use predefined date and time formats or use custom formats. Michael is concerned about dates past the year 1999. He wants the database to display all dates with four digits for the year so there is no confusion regarding which century is being displayed. Michael will first make this change to the Customers table.

1. **Click the Design View button on the Table Datasheet toolbar to return to the table's Design View**

   You have to use a custom format for the Birth Date field because none of the predefined Date/Time formats match the format you want. For more information on predefined Date/Time formats, refer to Table E-1.

2. **Click the Birth Date field, then click the Format Field Property text box**

   The General Date format is the default. It is a combination of the predefined Short Date and Long Time settings. See Table E-1.

   To define a custom format, enter symbols that represent how you want the date to appear in the Format property text box.

3. **Type mm/dd/yyyy as shown in Figure E-13**

   Display the Customers table datasheet to see the effect of his property changes.

4. **Click the Datasheet View button on the Table Design toolbar, then click Yes to save the changes**

   Notice that all of the dates now display four digits as shown in Figure E-14.

5. **Click the Customers table datasheet Close button to close the window**

QuickTip

Press [F6] to move between the upper and lower parts of a table's Design View window.

Planning for the 21st Century

The General Date format assumes that dates between 1/1/30 and 12/31/99 are twentieth century dates (1930–1999), and those between 1/1/00 and 12/31/29 are twenty-first century dates (2000–2029). If you wish to enter dates outside these ranges, you must enter all four digits of the date.

FIGURE E-13: **The Birth Date field property change**

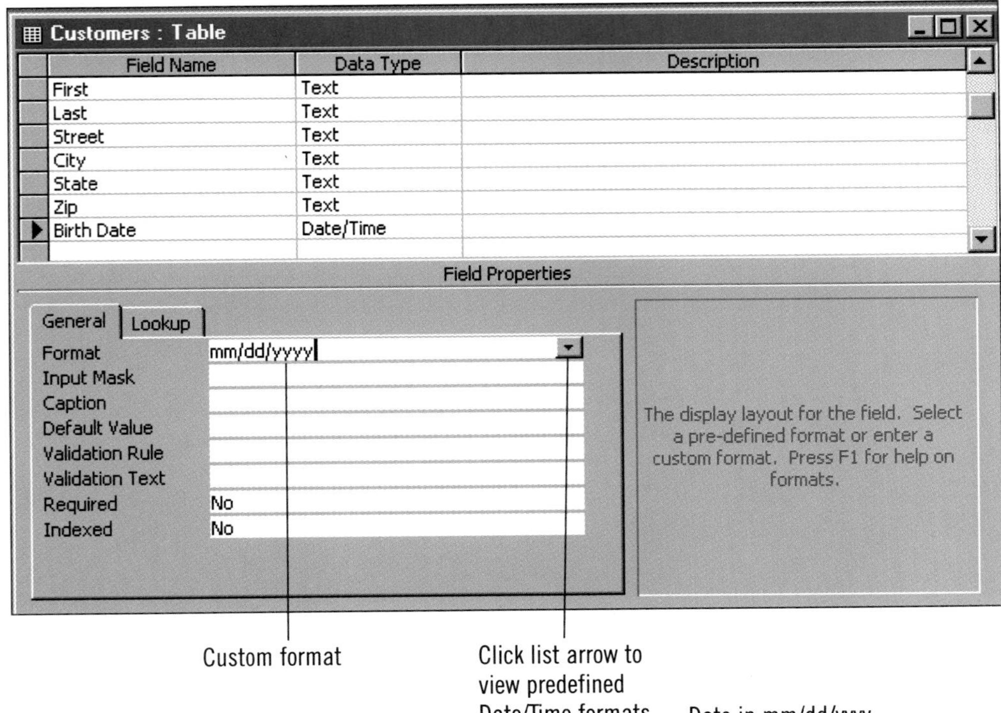

Date in mm/dd/yyyy format

FIGURE E-14: **The Customers table datasheet**

Customers : Table

CustID	First	Last	Street	City	State	Zip	Birth Date
1	Ginny	Braithwaite	3 Which Way	Salem	MA	01970	01/10/1960
10	Virginia	Rodarmor	123 Main Street	Andover	MA	01810	01/06/1970
11	Kristen	Reis	4848 Ashley	Fontanelle	IA	50810	03/18/1968
12	Tom	Reis	4848 Ashley	Fontanelle	IA	50810	07/03/1965
13	Mark	Eagan	987 Lincoln	Schaumberg	IL	44433	01/29/1960
14	Peg	Fox	125 Maple	Des Moines	IA	50625	04/10/1959
15	Ron	Fox	125 Maple	Des Moines	IA	50625	08/28/1987
16	Amanda	Fox	125 Maple	Des Moines	IA	50625	01/30/1988
17	Rebecca	Gross	123 Oak	Bridgewater	KS	50837	09/20/1962
2	Robin	Spencer	293 Serenity Dr.	Concord	MA	01742	01/30/1952
3	Camilla	Dobbins	486 Intel Circuit	Rio Rancho	NM	87124	03/15/1965
4	Pip	Khalsa	1100 Vista Road	Santa Fe	NM	87505	04/16/1969
5	Kendra	Majors	530 Spring Street	Lenox	MA	02140	05/04/1970
6	Tasha	Williams	530 Spring Street	Lenox	MA	02140	05/08/1971
7	Fred	Gonzales	Purgatory Ski Area	Durango	CO	81301	06/10/1960
8	John	Black	11 River Road	Brookfield	CT	06830	07/15/1965
9	Scott	Owen	72 Yankee Way	Brookfield	CT	06830	03/15/1965
*					IA		

Record: 1 of 17

TABLE E-1: **Predefined Date/Time Formats**

setting	examples	setting	examples
General Date (default)	4/3/97 5:34:00 PM	**Long Time**	5:34:23 PM
Long Date	Saturday, April 3, 1997	**Medium Time**	5:34 PM
Medium Date	3-Apr-97	**Short Time**	17:34
Short Date	4/3/97		

Defining Field Validation Properties

The **Validation Rule** and **Validation Text** field properties can help you eliminate unreasonable entries by establishing criteria for the entry before it is accepted into the database. For example, the Validation Rule property of a State field might be modified to allow only valid state abbreviations as entries. The Validation Text property is used to display a message when a user tries to enter data that doesn't pass the Validation Rule property for that field. Michael started his business in 1995. Therefore, it wouldn't make sense to enter any tours in the Tours table with dates earlier than 1995.

QuickTip

You must use the # (pound sign) to identify date criteria and use the double quote character to identify text criteria in a Validation Rule expression.

1. Click the **Tours table** in the Nomad-E2 database window, then click **Design**
2. Click the **TourDate field**, click the **Validation Rule text box** in the Field Properties panel, then type **>=#1/1/95#**
   This property forces all tour dates to be greater than or equal to 1/1/1995. See Table E-2 for more examples of validation rule expressions.
3. Click in the **Validation Text text box** in the Field Properties panel, then type **Date must be later than 1/1/1995**
   The Validation Text property will appear on the screen when the field entry does not pass the criteria specified in the Validation Rule property. The Design View of the Tours table should now look like Figure E-15. Save the changes to the Tours table.
4. Click the **Save button** on the Table Design toolbar, then click **Yes** when asked to test the existing data
   Since all dates in the TourDate field are more recent than 1/1/1995, there are no date errors in the current data and the table is saved. Michael will test the Validation Rule and Validation Text properties by trying to enter a pre-1995 date in the TourDate field of the Tours datasheet.
5. Click the **Datasheet View button** on the Table Design toolbar, press **[Tab]** twice to reach the **TourDate field**, type **1/1/94**, press **[Tab]**, then click **OK** to close the Validation Rule dialog box
   You know that the Validation Rule and Validation Text properties work properly, therefore close Access.
6. Press **[Esc]** to reject the invalid date entry, then click the **Close button** for the Access program window to close the database and program
   Since all changes to the objects and records within the database file are already saved, exiting the application does not open a Save dialog box.

FIGURE E-15: The TourDate field validation properties

TourDate field is chosen

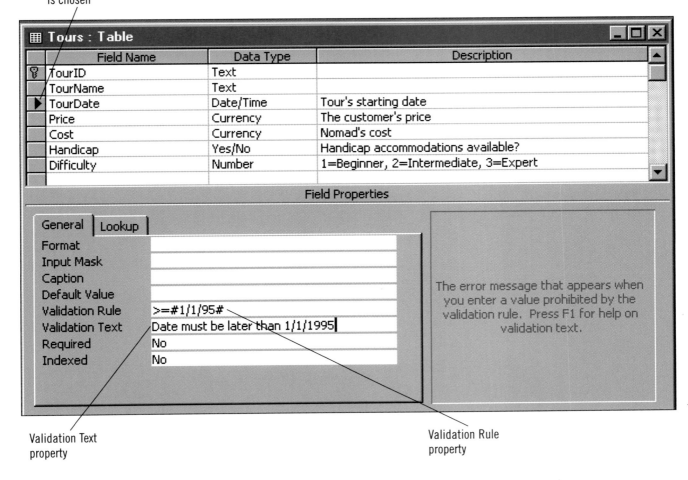

Tours : Table

Field Name	Data Type	Description
TourID	Text	
TourName	Text	
TourDate	Date/Time	Tour's starting date
Price	Currency	The customer's price
Cost	Currency	Nomad's cost
Handicap	Yes/No	Handicap accommodations available?
Difficulty	Number	1=Beginner, 2=Intermediate, 3=Expert

Field Properties

General | Lookup

Format	
Input Mask	
Caption	
Default Value	
Validation Rule	>=#1/1/95#
Validation Text	Date must be later than 1/1/1995
Required	No
Indexed	No

The error message that appears when you enter a value prohibited by the validation rule. Press F1 for help on validation text.

Validation Text property

Validation Rule property

Access 97

TABLE E-2: Validation Rule Expressions

data type	validation rule expression	description
Number or Currency	>0	The number must be positive
Number or Currency	>10 And <100	The number must be between 10 and 100
Number or Currency	10 Or 20 Or 30	The number must be 10, 20, or 30
Text	"IA" Or "NE" Or "MO"	The entry must be IA, NE, or MO
Date/Time	>=#1/1/93#	The date must be on or after 1/1/1993
Date/Time	>#1/1/80# And <#1/1/90#	The date must be between 1/1/1980 and 1/1/1990

Validation property rules

The Validation Rule property and Validation Text properties go hand in hand. If you omit the Validation Rule, no data validation is performed and the Validation Text property is meaningless. If you set the Validation Rule property, but not the Validation Text property, Access displays a standard error message when the validation rule is violated.

Practice

► Concepts Review

Identify each element of a table's Design View shown in Figure E-16.

FIGURE E-16

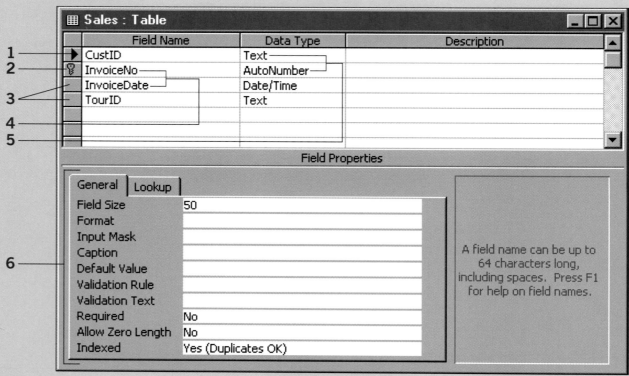

Match each term with the statement that describes its function.

7. Several tables linked together in one-to-many relationships
8. A field that holds unique information for each record in the table
9. Where all characteristics of a table including field names, data types, field descriptions, field properties, and key fields are defined
10. Characteristics that apply to each field of a table, such as field size, default values, or field formats
11. Helps you eliminate unreasonable entries by establishing criteria for the entry

a. Primary Key
b. Field Properties
c. Design View
d. Validation Rule and Validation Text
e. Relational database

Select the best answer from the list of choices.

12. Which of the following steps would probably help eliminate fields of duplicate data in a table?
- **a.** Redesign the database and add more tables.
- **b.** Redesign the database and add more fields.
- **c.** Change the formatting properties of the field in which the duplicate data existed.
- **d.** Change the validation properties of the field in which the duplicate data existed.

13. Which of the following is NOT defined in the table's Design View?
- **a.** Key fields
- **b.** Duplicate data
- **c.** Field lengths
- **d.** Data types

14. Which of the following is NOT a common Data Type?
- **a.** Text
- **b.** Alpha
- **c.** Number
- **d.** Date/Time

15. Which feature helps the database designer make sure that one-to-many relationships are preserved?
- **a.** Validation Text property
- **b.** Validation Rule property
- **c.** Field formatting
- **d.** Referential Integrity

16. Which character is used to identify dates in a validation expression?
- **a.** " (double quote)
- **b.** ' (single quote)
- **c.** # (pound sign)
- **d.** & (ampersand)

17. Which Format Property Option displays all characters in the field as uppercase?
- **a.** <
- **b.** >
- **c.** !
- **d.** @

▶ Skills Review

1. Examine relational database requirements.
- **a.** Examine your address book.
- **b.** Write down the fields you will need.
- **c.** Examine which fields contain duplicate entries.

2. Plan a table.

- **a.** Start Access.
- **b.** Use the Blank Database option button to create a new database file.
- **c.** Save the file as "Addresses-E" on your Student Disk.
- **d.** Click the Tables tab in the Database window, then click New.

3. Create new tables.

- **a.** Use Design View to create the new table with the following fields with the given data types.

First	Text
Last	Text
Street	Text
City	Text
State	Text
Zip	Text
Birthday	Date/Time

- **b.** Close the table, name, and save it as "Names".
- **c.** Do not define a primary key for Names.
- **d.** Reconsider what fields will contain duplicate data.
- **e.** Click the Tables tab in the Database window, then click New.
- **f.** Use Design View to create another new table with the following Text fields.
  Zip
  City
  State
- **g.** Identify Zip as the primary key.
- **h.** Close the table, then save it as "Zips".

4. Create one-to-many relationships.

- **a.** Click the Relationships button on the Database toolbar.
- **b.** Add both the Names and the Zips tables to the Relationships window.
- **c.** Drag the Zip field from the Zips table to the Zip field of the Names table to create a one-to-many relationship between these fields of the tables.
- **d.** Enforce referential integrity between the linking fields of the tables.
- **e.** Close the Relationships window, saving your layout changes.

5. Delete fields.

- **a.** Open the Names table in Design View.
- **b.** Click the City field selector button and delete the City field.
- **c.** Click the State field selector button and delete the State field.
- **d.** Close the Names table, saving the changes.

6. Define text field properties.

- **a.** Open the Zips table in Design View.
- **b.** Click the State field name and change the Field Size property to 2.
- **c.** Click the State field names Format property text box, then type > (greater than sign) to force all entries to uppercase letters.
- **d.** Close the Zips table, saving the changes.

7. **Define date/time field properties.**
   a. Open the Names table in Design View.
   b. Click the Birthday field names Format property text box, then type MM/DD/YYYY to display all dates with four-digit years.
   c. Close the Names table, saving the changes.

8. **Define field validation properties.**
   a. Note that this address listing will contain contacts from only three states: IA, KS, and MO.
   b. Open the Zips table in Design View.
   c. Click the State field name, click the Validation Rule property text box, then type ="IA" OR "KS" OR "MO".
   d. Note that this validation rule could be extended to accept more valid entries for all 50 states.
   e. Click the Validation Text text box, then type "State must be IA, KS, or MO".
   f. Close the Zips table, saving the changes.
   g. Print a copy of each table's datasheet in the Addresses-E database.

Independent Challenges

1. As the president of a civic organization, you have decided to launch a recycling campaign. Various clubs will gather recyclable trash and make deposits at recycling centers. You need to develop a relational database that tracks how much material has been taken to each of the centers, as well as the club that is responsible for the deposit. The following fields will be tracked in this database:

Club Information:
Name, Street, City, State, Zip, Phone, Club Number (a unique number to identify each club)
Deposit Information:
Date, Weight, Deposit Number (a sequential number for each drop off)
Recycle Center Information:
Name, Street, City, State, Zip, Phone, Center Number (a unique number to identify each recycling center)

To complete this independent challenge:

1. Plan the database.
   a. Sketch how the fields will be organized into three tables: Clubs, Deposits, and Recycling Centers.
   b. Determine if there are key fields in the tables.
   c. Determine how the tables should be linked using one-to-many relationships. This may involve adding a linking field to a table to establish the connection.
2. Create and save a database called "Cleanup-E".
3. Create the three tables in the Cleanup-E database using appropriate field names, data types, and key fields.
4. Create one-to-many relationships to link the tables. Be sure to enforce referential integrity as appropriate.
5. Print the Relationships window of the database using the [Print Screen] technique. Be sure that all fields of each table are visible.
6. Add a Validation Rule property to the Date field that only allows dates of 1/1/97 or later to be entered into the database. The property entry is >=#1/1/97#.
7. Add a Validation Text property to the Date field that states "Dates must be later than 1/1/1997".

2. You want to document the books you've read in a relational database. The following fields will be tracked:
Book Information:
Title, Category (such as Biography, Mystery, or Science Fiction), Rating (a numeric value from 1–10 that indicates how satisfied you were with the book), Date Read
Author Information (Note: If a book has more than one author, enter the name of the author listed first.):
First Name, Last Name, Author Number (a unique number to identify each author)

To complete this independent challenge:

1. Plan the database.
   a. Sketch how the fields will be organized into two tables: Books and Authors.
   b. Determine if there are key fields in the tables.
   c. Determine how the tables should be linked using one-to-many relationships. This may involve adding a linking field to a table to establish the connection.
2. Create and save a database called "Readings-E".
3. Create the three tables in the Readings-E database using appropriate field names, data types, and key fields.
4. Create the one-to-many relationship to link the tables. Be sure to enforce referential integrity as appropriate.
5. Print the Relationships window of the database using the [Print Screen] technique discussed in the Quick Tip of the "Creating one-to-many relationships" lesson. Be sure that all fields of each table are visible.
6. Change the field size of the author's First Name field and Last Name field to 25.

3. You work for a large medical clinic and wish to track the time physicians are spending on civic activities such as the Rural Outreach Program and the Low Income Health Screening Program. The database should track the date and number of hours each physician has logged with each program. The following fields will be tracked in this database:
Physician Information:
First Name, Last Name, Physician Number (a unique number to identify each physician)
Activity Information:
Date, Hours
Program Information:
Name, Program Number (a unique number to identify each program)

To complete this independent challenge:

1. Plan the database.
   a. Sketch how the fields will be organized into three tables: Physicians, Activities, and Programs
   b. Determine if there are key fields in the tables (*Hint*: The Activities table does not have a Key field.)
   c. Determine how the tables should be linked using one-to-many relationships. This may involve adding a linking field to a table to establish the connection.
2. Create and save a database called "Doctors-E".
3. Create the three tables in the Doctors-E database using appropriate field names, data types, and key fields.
4. Create one-to-many relationships to link the tables. Be sure to enforce referential integrity as appropriate.
5. Print the Relationships window of the database using the [Print Screen] technique discussed in the Quick Tip of the "Creating one-to-many relationships" lesson. Be sure that all fields of each table are visible.

4. You wish to find and document nine-digit ZIP codes for several addresses in a database. You know that nine-digit ZIP codes make the mail service more efficient because the nine digits specify the specific street address in addition to the city and state of the addressee.

To complete this independent challenge:

1. Log on to the Internet and use your browser to go to http://www.course.com. From there, click Student Online Companions, click Microsoft Office 97 Professional Edition – Illustrated: A Second Course, click the Access link for Unit E, then click the link for the United States Postal Service.
2. Read the homepage and click hypertext links to find the interactive ZIP+4 lookup service. (*Hint*: Finding the interactive ZIP+4 lookup service should take about two hypertext links.)
3. Use the Zip+4 Code Lookup page to find the ZIP+4 code for at least four addresses of friends or acquaintances and jot them down.
4. Plan a database to handle address information with ZIP+4 ZIP codes.
   a. Sketch how the fields will be organized into two tables: Names and Zips.
   b. Determine if there are key fields in the tables.
   c. Determine how the tables should be linked using one-to-many relationships. This may involve adding a linking field to a table to establish the connection.
5. Create and save a database called "Addresses9-E".
6. Create the two tables in the Addresses9-E database using appropriate field names, data types, and key fields. Recognize that this relational database is extremely similar to the one you created in the Skills Review with one exception: a ZIP code extension field needs to be added to the Names table.
7. Create the one-to-many relationship to link the tables. Be sure to enforce referential integrity as appropriate.
8. Print the Relationships window of the database using the [Print Screen] technique discussed in the Quick Tip of the "Creating one-to-many relationships" lesson. Be sure that all fields of each table are visible.
9. Open the Zips table in Datasheet View and enter the four ZIP codes, cities, and states that you researched on the Internet.
10. Print the Zips datasheet.
11. Open the Names table in Datasheet View and enter the four addresses that you researched on the Internet.
12. Print the Names datasheet.

Visual Workshop

Create a new database that includes the two tables, Alumni and Donations, shown in Figures E-17 and E-18. Give each of the fields a text Data Type, except for Value (use Currency) and Date (use Date/Time). Make sure that the Social Security Number is the key field in the Alumni table and links the Alumni table with the Donations table in a one-to-many relationship. Enforce referential integrity for the linking Social Security Number field between the tables. (*Hint:* The Donations table does not have a Key field.) Enter the records for both tables, then save and name the database "VW-E" on your Student Disk. Print the datasheets of both tables.

FIGURE E-17

Alumni : Table

First	Last	Street	City	State	Zip	Phone	SSN
Doug	Allen	888 Maple	Ames	IA	50010	515-555-8888	444-44-4444
Lisa	Eagan	777 Oak	Johnston	IA	50015	515-777-9999	111-11-1111
Kelsey	Wambold	555 Elm	Fontanelle	IA	50846	515-888-1111	222-22-2222
Aaron	Washington	222 Apple	Bridgewater	IA	50837	515-222-4444	333-33-3333

Record: 4 of 4

FIGURE E-18

Donations : Table

Value	Date	Type	SSN
$100.00	5/1/97	Art	111-11-1111
$200.00	5/1/97	Cash	222-22-2222
$500.00	5/2/97	Stock	333-33-3333
$50.00	6/2/97	Cash	111-11-1111
$1,000.00	6/2/97	Cash	444-44-4444
$500.00	6/2/97	Stock	333-33-3333
$500.00	7/1/97	Cash	444-44-4444
$500.00	7/1/97	Cash	333-33-3333
$0.00			

Record: 8 of 8

Creating
Multiple Table Queries

Objectives

- Create select queries
- Sort a query on multiple fields
- Develop AND queries
- Develop OR queries
- Develop calculated fields
- Add calculations on groups of records
- Develop crosstab queries
- Create update queries

In this unit, you will create **queries**, database objects that answer questions about the data by pulling fields and records that match specific criteria into a single datasheet. A **select query** retrieves data from one or more linked tables and displays the results in a datasheet. Queries can also be used to sort records, develop new calculated fields from existing fields, or develop summary calculations such as the sum or average of the values in a field. **Crosstab queries** present information in a cross tabular report, and **update queries** quickly change existing data in a table. Michael Belmont redesigned the Nomad database into multiple tables to eliminate redundant data entry. Michael will create select, crosstab, and update queries to display and change the data in his database.

Access 97

Creating Select Queries

Queries are developed by using the Query Wizard or by directly specifying requested fields and query criteria in **Query Design View**. The resulting query datasheet is not a duplication of the data that resides in the original table's datasheet, but rather, a logical view of the data. If you change or enter data in a query's datasheet, the data in the underlying table (and any other logical view) is updated automatically. Queries are often used to present and sort a subset of fields from multiple tables for data entry or update purposes. Michael creates a query to answer the question, "Who is buying what?" He pulls fields from several tables into a single query object which displays a single datasheet.

1. Start Access and open the **Nomad-F** database
2. Click the **Queries tab** in the Nomad-F: Database window, click **New**, click **Design View** in the New Query window, then click **OK**
   Use the Show Table dialog box to add the Tours table and the Customers table to the Query Design View. You also need to include the Sales table because it contains the linking fields that match specific customers to the specific tours they have purchased.
3. Click **Customers**, click **Add**, click **Sales**, click **Add**, click **Tours**, click **Add**, then click **Close**
   The Query Design View displays **field lists** for the three tables. Each table's name is in its field list title bar. Key fields are bold, and often serve as the "one" side of the one-to-many relationship between two tables. Relationships are displayed with **one-to-many join lines** between the linking fields as shown in Figure F-1. View the customer's last name in the query datasheet.
4. Drag the **Last field** in the Customers table field list to the Field cell in the first column of the Query design grid
   The order in which the fields are placed in the **Query design grid** will be their order in the datasheet. Select the First field from the Customers table, then add the TourName and TourDate fields from the Tours table.
5. Drag the **First field** from the Customers table to the Field cell in the second column, drag the **TourName field** from the Tours table to the Field cell in the third column, then drag the **TourDate field** from the Tours table to the Field cell in the fourth column
   You sort the datasheet by TourDate.
6. Click the **Sort cell** of the **TourDate field** in the Query design grid, click the **Sort list arrow**, then click **Ascending**
   The resulting Query design grid should look like Figure F-2.
7. Click the **Datasheet View button** on the Query Design toolbar
   The records of the datasheet are now listed in chronological order by TourDate as shown in Figure F-3. You scroll through the datasheet and notice that Mark Egan purchased two tours, and that his name has been incorrectly entered in the database. Change "Eagan" to the correct spelling "Egan" directly within the query datasheet.
8. Scroll and click before the **first letter A** of either **Eagan** in the Last column in the datasheet, press **[Delete]**, then click any other record in the datasheet
   The update shows that you are using a properly defined relational database and that any change to the data is automatically applied to all other occurrences of the customer's name.
9. Click the **Query datasheet Close button**, click **Yes** when prompted to save the changes, type **Customer Purchases** in the Query Name text box, then click **OK**
   The query is now saved and listed on the Queries tab in the Nomad-F: Database window.

Trouble?
Click the Show Table button on the Query Design toolbar to add table field lists to Query Design View. To delete a field list click the list and press [Delete].

QuickTip
Double-click the table's title bar to select all fields then drag them as a group to the grid if you want all fields in the resulting datasheet.

FIGURE F-1: **Query Design View**

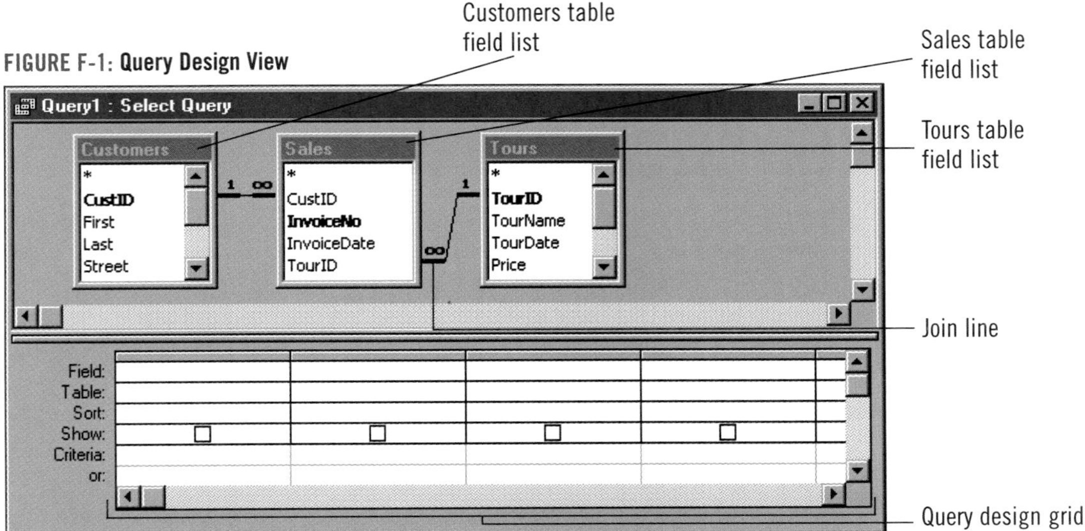

FIGURE F-2: **Completed Query design grid**

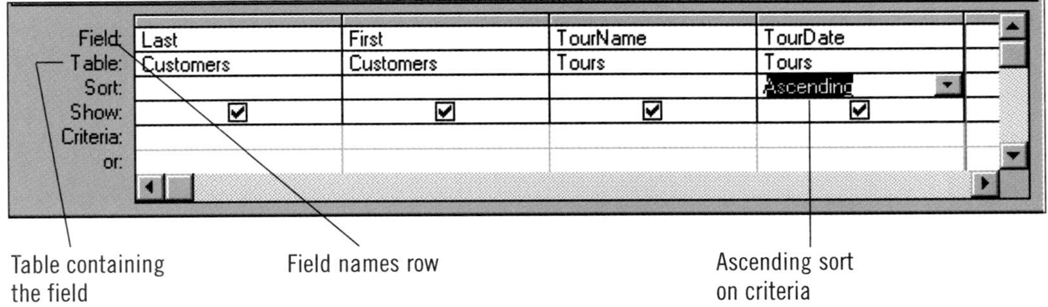

FIGURE F-3: **Datasheet sorted in ascending order by TourDate**

Query1 : Select Query

Last	First	TourName	TourDate
Braithwaite	Ginny	Road Bike	6/15/96
Owen	Scott	Bungee	9/20/96
Dobbins	Camilla	Bungee	9/20/96
Majors	Kendra	Bungee	9/20/96
Williams	Tasha	Bungee	9/20/96
Gonzales	Fred	Mt. Bike	9/26/96
Khalsa	Pip	Mt. Bike	9/26/96
Spencer	Robin	Mt. Bike	9/26/96
Black	John	Mt. Bike	9/26/96
Rodarmor	Virginia	Mt. Bike	9/26/96
Reis	Kristen	Big Sky	1/10/97
Fox	Amanda	Big Sky	1/10/97
Fox	Ron	Big Sky	1/10/97
Fox	Peg	Big Sky	1/10/97
Eagan	Mark	Big Sky	1/10/97
Reis	Tom	Big Sky	1/10/97
Eagan	Mark	Bungee	9/15/97

Record: 1 of 20

The difference between queries and filters

Use a **filter** to temporarily view or edit a subset of records when viewing a datasheet. Use a **query** to view the subset of records without first opening a specific table, to choose fields from multiple tables for the query, to control which fields from the subset of records appear in the results, or to perform calculations on values in fields.

Access 97

Sorting a Query on Multiple Fields

Sorting, or placing the records of a datasheet in either ascending or descending order, is a common task and can be specified in the Query design grid. Multiple sort fields determine the order in which records are displayed when two records contain the same data in the primary sort field. Michael wants to sort the Customer Purchases query on multiple fields to more clearly identify those customers who have purchased more than one tour. He needs an alphabetical listing of his tour sales by customers. Customers who have the same last name will be sorted by first name within last, and for those customers who have purchased more than one tour, the records need to be listed in chronological order by TourDate.

Steps 1234

1. Click the **Queries tab** in the Nomad-F : Database window if necessary, click **Customer Purchases**, then click **Design**
   The Query Design window of the Customer Purchases - Select Query opens. You want to show the First field in the first column, but make the Last field the primary sort field. Since Access sorts the fields in order from left to right, add the First field to the query grid twice. The first occurrence of the First field is used for display purposes. The second occurrence of the First field is used for sorting purposes.
2. Drag the **First field** from the Customer's field list to the first column of the Query design grid
   The Query design grid now has the fields First, Last, First. Use the Show checkboxes to specify this sorting.
3. Click the **First field Show checkbox** in the third column to deselect it
   Now that the grid includes all the fields needed to accommodate this datasheet, add the sort criteria.
4. Click the **Sort cell** of the **Last field** in the second column, click the **Sort list arrow**, click **Ascending**, then click the **Sort list arrow** for the **First field** in the third column, then click **Ascending**
   The new Query design grid is shown in Figure F-4. By setting up the Query design grid in this way, you specify the Last field as the primary sort field, the First field as the secondary sort field, and the TourDate field as the third sort field.
5. Click the **Datasheet View button** on the Query Design toolbar
   The resulting datasheet is shown in Figure F-5. Michael wants to use this information in an upcoming sales meeting, so print a copy of the datasheet.
6. Click the **Print button** on the Query Datasheet toolbar
   You review the printout, and verify that it has the information you need. Now you can save the Customer Purchases query.
7. Click the **Save button** on the Query Datasheet toolbar

Trouble?

If you drag a field from a Field list to the wrong column of the Query design grid, click the column selector and drag the column to its new location. Existing fields shift to make room for the inserted column.

FIGURE F-4: **Query design grid for a sort order that doesn't follow the order of the fields on the datasheet**

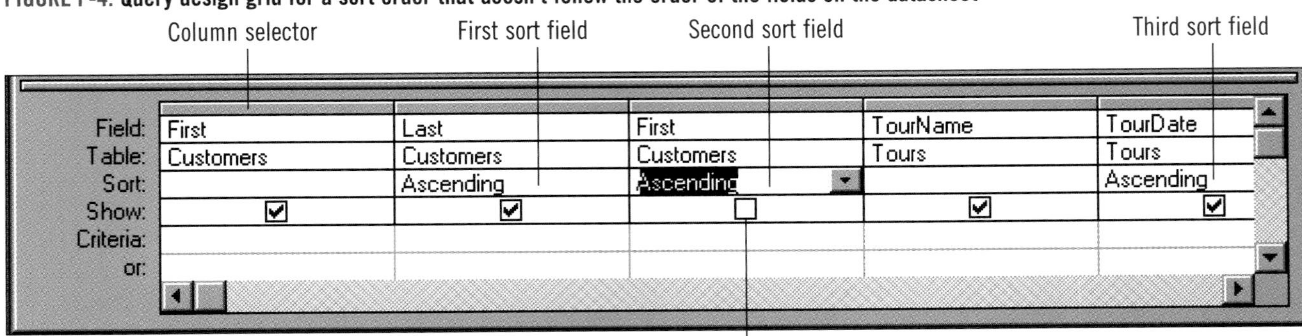

This column will not be displayed but is still used for sorting purposes

FIGURE F-5: **Customer Purchases query with three sort fields**

Secondary sort — Primary sort — Third sort field

Customer Purchases : Select Query

First	Last	TourName	TourDate
John	Black	Mt. Bike	9/26/96
Ginny	Braithwaite	Road Bike	6/15/96
Camilla	Dobbins	Bungee	9/20/96
Mark	Egan	Big Sky	1/10/97
Mark	Egan	Bungee	9/15/97
Amanda	Fox	Big Sky	1/10/97
Peg	Fox	Big Sky	1/10/97
Peg	Fox	Mt. Bike	9/30/97
Ron	Fox	Big Sky	1/10/97
Ron	Fox	Mt. Bike	9/30/97
Fred	Gonzales	Mt. Bike	9/26/96
Pip	Khalsa	Mt. Bike	9/26/96
Kendra	Majors	Bungee	9/20/96
Scott	Owen	Bungee	9/20/96
Kristen	Reis	Big Sky	1/10/97
Kristen	Reis	Bungee	9/15/97
Tom	Reis	Big Sky	1/10/97
Virginia	Rodarmor	Mt. Bike	9/26/96

Record: 1 of 20

Example of when the Second sort field is used

Example of when the Third sort field is used

Access 97

Developing AND Queries

Using Access you can query for specific records that match two or more criteria, or limiting conditions. **Criteria** are tests for which the record must be true to be selected for a datasheet. To create an **AND query** in which two or more criteria are present, enter the criteria for the fields on the same Criteria row of the Query design grid. If two AND criteria are entered for the same field, the AND operator separates the criteria in the Criteria cell for that field. Michael wants to send a special mailing to a subset of his customers who have recently purchased tours in Massachusetts. He creates an AND query because the State field must equal Massachusetts and the TourDate field must be greater than 09/01/96.

Steps

1. Click the **Design View button** on the Query Datasheet toolbar
   Instead of creating a query from scratch, modify the Customer Purchases query. The only additional field you have to add to the query is the State field.

2. Scroll and click the **State field** in the Customers table, then drag the **State field** to the fourth column in the Query design grid after the First field
   The TourName and TourDate fields move to the right to accommodate the new field in the grid. Next, enter the state criterion.

3. Click the **Criteria cell** of the **State field**, type **MA**, then click the **Datasheet View button** on the Query Design toolbar
   The resulting datasheet in Figure F-6 shows five customers from Massachusetts. Return to the Query design window to complete the second part of this query which involves selecting only those tour dates that are after 9/1/96. See Table F-1 for more information on using special comparison operators.

4. Click on the Query Datasheet toolbar, scroll in the grid to view the **TourDate field**, click the **Criteria cell** of the **TourDate field**, then type **>9/1/96**
   The resulting Query design grid is shown in Figure F-7. Notice that Access entered double quotes automatically around the text criterion in the State field. Access enters # (pound signs) around date criteria. Numeric criteria aren't surrounded by any special character.

5. Click on the Query Design toolbar
   Multiple criteria added to the same line of the Query design grid (AND criteria) must *each* be true for the record to be displayed in the resulting datasheet, therefore causing the resulting datasheet to display fewer records. In this case, the date criterion eliminated one record in the datasheet. Save this query with a different name.

6. Click **File** on the menu bar, click **Save As/Export** to save this query with a new name, type **MA after 9/1/96** in the New Name: text box, then click **OK**

QuickTip

To resize a column in the Query design grid, click the right boundary of the column selector then drag it left or right.

FIGURE F-6: Datasheet for MA query

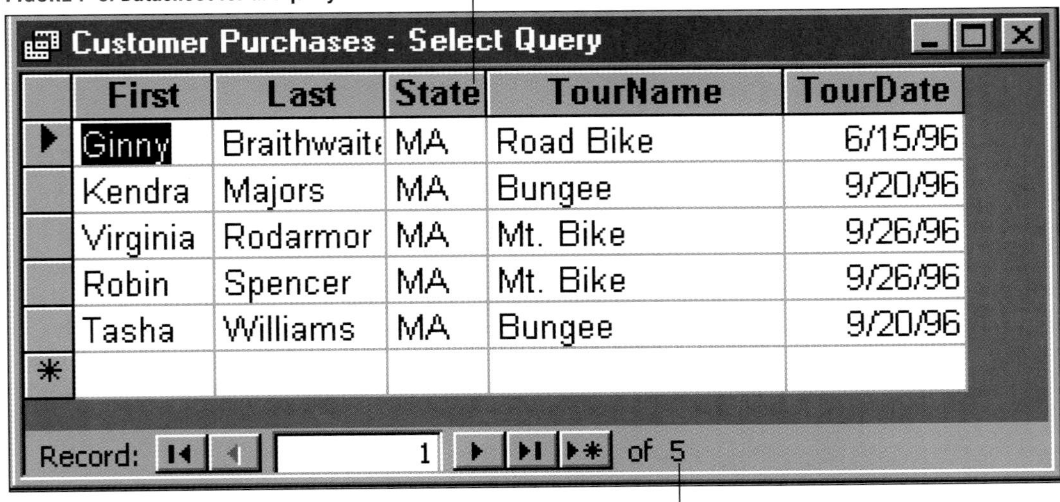

State = "MA"
Customer Purchases : Select Query
First
Last
State
TourName
TourDate
Ginny
Braithwaite
MA
Road Bike
6/15/96
Kendra
Majors
MA
Bungee
9/20/96
Virginia
Rodarmor
MA
Mt. Bike
9/26/96
Robin
Spencer
MA
Mt. Bike
9/26/96
Tasha
Williams
MA
Bungee
9/20/96
Record:
1
of 5
Total number of records

FIGURE F-7: Query design grid for AND query

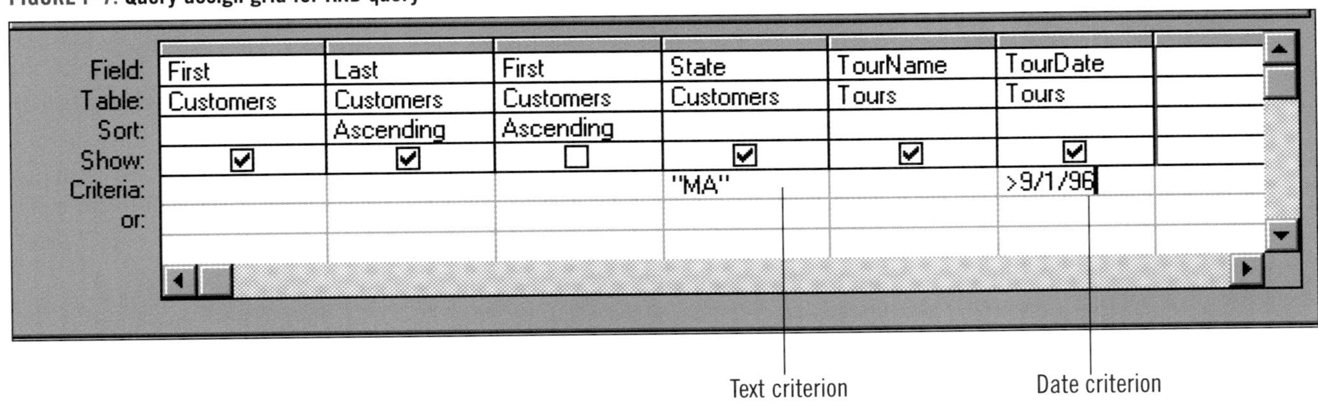

TABLE F-1: Comparison operators for the Criteria row of the Query design grid

operator	description	example	result
>	greater than	>50	Value exceeds 50
>=	greater than or equal to	>=50	Value is 50 or greater
<	less than	<50	Value is less than 50
<=	less than or equal to	<=50	Value is 50 or less than 50
<>	not equal to	<>50	Value is any number other than 50
Between...And	finds values between two numbers or dates	Between #2/2/95# And #2/2/98#	Dates between 2/2/95 and 2/2/98
In	finds a value that is one of a list	In(IA,KS,NE)	Value equals IA or KS or NE
Null	finds records which are blank	Null	No value has been entered
Is Not Null	finds records which are not blank	Is Not Null	Any value has been entered
Like	finds records that match the criteria	Like "A"	Value equals A
Not	finds records that do not match the criteria	Not "2"	Numbers other than 2

Access 97

Developing OR Queries

OR queries broaden the number of records that will be displayed because only one criterion joined by an OR operator needs to be true for the record to be displayed on the resulting datasheet. OR criteria are entered in the Query design grid on different lines. Each criteria line of the Query design grid is evaluated separately and the record must only be true for one row in order to be displayed in the datasheet. If two OR criteria are specified for the same field, they are separated by the **OR operator**. Michael decides to broaden the number of records in the query datasheet by adding OR criteria. Since new business is coming from the state of Iowa, he decides to add those customers from Iowa who purchased tours after 9/1/96 to his existing query.

Steps

1. **Click the Query Design View button on the Datasheet toolbar**
   To add OR criteria, enter criteria in the 'or' row of the Query design grid.
2. **Click the or State criteria cell below the MA entry, then type IA**
   If you don't put the date criteria into this row, the datasheet will pull all customers from Iowa, regardless of when their tour date occurred.
3. **Click then drag to select >#9/1/96#, right-click, click Copy, click the TourDate or criteria cell below the >#9/1/96# entry, right-click, then click Paste**
   The >#9/1/96 entry is copied to the or row in the TourDate field. If the record matches *either* row of the criteria grid, it is included in the query's datasheet. Figure F-8 shows the OR criteria in the Query design grid.
4. **Click the Datasheet View button on the Query Design toolbar**
   The resulting datasheet is shown in Figure F-9. All of the records contain State data of either MA or IA, and TourDate data after 9/1/96. Also, notice that the sort order (Last, First, TourDate) is still in effect. Save this query as a separate database object as well.
5. **Click File on the menu bar, click Save As/Export, type MA and IA after 9/1/96, then click OK**
   You have completed this query. Close the datasheet.
6. **Click the MA and IA after 9/1/96 datasheet Close button**
   The Nomad-F database Queries tab displays the new queries that you created.

QuickTip

If the criterion expression becomes too long to completely fit in a cell of the Query design grid, right-click the cell then click Zoom on the shortcut menu. The Zoom dialog box provides space to enter lengthy criteria expressions.

FIGURE F-8: Query design grid for OR query

Field:	First	Last	First	State	TourName	TourDate
Table:	Customers	Customers	Customers	Customers	Tours	Tours
Sort:		Ascending	Ascending			
Show:	☑	☑	☐	☑	☑	☑
Criteria:				"MA"		>#9/1/96#
or:				"IA"		>#9/1/96#

FIGURE F-9: Datasheet for OR query

Customer Purchases : Select Query

First	Last	State	TourName	TourDate
Amanda	Fox	IA	Big Sky	1/10/97
Peg	Fox	IA	Mt. Bike	9/30/97
Peg	Fox	IA	Big Sky	1/10/97
Ron	Fox	IA	Mt. Bike	9/30/97
Ron	Fox	IA	Big Sky	1/10/97
Kendra	Majors	MA	Bungee	9/20/96
Kristen	Reis	IA	Bungee	9/15/97
Kristen	Reis	IA	Big Sky	1/10/97
Tom	Reis	IA	Big Sky	1/10/97
Virginia	Rodarmor	MA	Mt. Bike	9/26/96
Robin	Spencer	MA	Mt. Bike	9/26/96
Tasha	Williams	MA	Bungee	9/20/96

Record: 1 of 12

Access 97

Using wildcard characters in query criteria

To search for a pattern, use a ? (question mark) to search for any single character and an * (asterisk) to search for any number of characters. Wildcard characters are often used with the Like operator. For example, the criterion Like "10/*/97" would find all dates in October of 1997 and the criterion Like "F*" would find all values that start with the letter F.

Access 97

Developing Calculated Fields

Arithmetic operators such as the ones shown in Table F-2 are used to create mathematical calculations in a query. Often these operators are used to develop a completely new field of information in a query. If you can calculate a new field of information based on existing fields in a database, never define it as a separate field in the table's Design View. The query method of creating the data ensures that the new field contains accurate, up-to-date information. Michael has decided to track profit (the difference between his cost and his price) per tour. To accomplish this, he creates a query that tells him how much profit he has realized for each tour booked.

Steps

1. **Click the Queries tab, if necessary, click New, click Design View, then click OK**
   You need the InvoiceNo, TourName, TourDate, Price, and Cost fields from the Sales and Tours tables to develop this query.
2. **Click Sales, click Add, click Tours, click Add, then click Close**
3. **Drag the InvoiceNo field from the Sales table to the first Field column of the Query design grid, drag the TourName field from the Tours table to the second Field column, then drag the TourDate field from the Tours table to the third Field column**
   A **calculated field** is created by entering a field name followed by a colon in the Field cell of the Query design grid followed by an expression. An **expression** is a combination of operators such as + (plus), - (minus), * (multiply), or / (divide), raw values (such as numbers or dates), functions, and fields that produce a result. Field names used in an expression are surrounded by square brackets.
4. **Click the blank Field cell of the fourth column, then type Profit:[Price]-[Cost]**
   The Query design grid should now look like Figure F-10. You further decide to sort the records from the most profitable sales transaction to the least profitable.
5. **Click the Sort cell of the Profit field, click the Sort list arrow, then click Descending**
   View this query to see the results of your work.
6. **Click the Datasheet View button on the Query design toolbar**
   The query's datasheet appears with the calculated field, Profit. The records are sorted from the highest to the lowest profit as shown in Figure F-11. You cannot enter information directly into the datasheet of a calculated field. The data shown in the Profit field is totally dependent upon the underlying fields of Price and Cost which are not displayed in this datasheet. To use this query at a meeting, print the resulting datasheet.
7. **Click the Print button on the Query Datasheet toolbar**
   You are done with this query. Close the datasheet.
8. **Click the Datasheet Close button, then click Yes when prompted to save changes**
9. **Type Profit by Sale as the query name, then click OK**

QuickTip

Double-click the thin black vertical line separating field names in the Query design grid or datasheet to make the column width automatically adjust to the widest entry in the column.

CLUES TO USE

Functions in calculated expressions

Functions can be used in expressions. You can develop a function to calculate information based on data in a record, or use a "built-in" function available within Access. The Date built-in function, for example, returns today's date and can be used in an expression or custom function to determine the number of days between today and another date.

FIGURE F-10: **A calculated field**

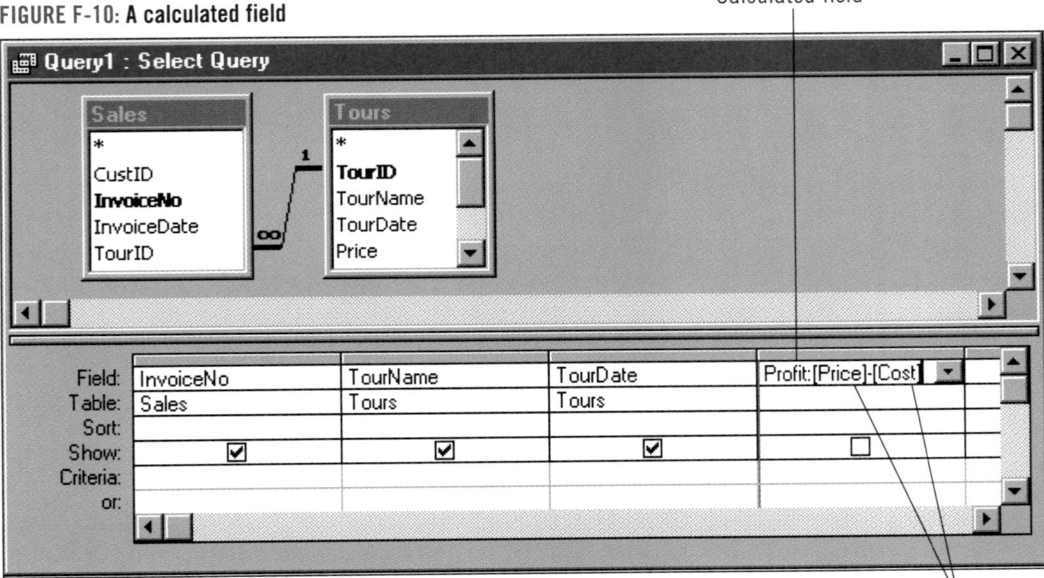

FIGURE F-11: **Datasheet sorted in descending order by Profit**

Double-click line to adjust column width automatically

Descending sort order

Query1 : Select Query

InvoiceNo	TourName	TourDate	Profit
17	Bungee	9/15/97	$120.00
18	Bungee	9/15/97	$120.00
12	Big Sky	1/10/97	$108.00
13	Big Sky	1/10/97	$108.00
11	Big Sky	1/10/97	$108.00
14	Big Sky	1/10/97	$108.00
15	Big Sky	1/10/97	$108.00
16	Big Sky	1/10/97	$108.00
20	Mt. Bike	9/30/97	$105.00
19	Mt. Bike	9/30/97	$105.00
10	Mt. Bike	9/26/96	$95.00
8	Mt. Bike	9/26/96	$95.00
7	Mt. Bike	9/26/96	$95.00
4	Mt. Bike	9/26/96	$95.00
2	Mt. Bike	9/26/96	$95.00

Record: 1 of 20

TABLE F-2: **Arithmetic operators**

operator	description
+	Addition
-	Subtraction
*	Multiplication
/	Division
^	Exponentiation

Access 97

Adding Calculations on Groups of Records

As your database grows, you probably will be less interested in individual records and more interested in information about groups of records. A query can be used to calculate information about a group of records by adding appropriate **aggregate functions** to the Total row of the Query design grid. Aggregate functions are summarized in Table F-3. Michael decides that he would like to have a total profit figure for each tour he has offered. This query first groups the records for each individual tour, and then calculates a total on the Profit field.

Steps

1. Click the **Profit by Sale** query on the Queries tab, then click **Design**
   Instead of creating this query from scratch, modify the existing Profit by Sale query.
2. Drag the **TourID field** from the Sales table to the second column of the Query design grid
   The fields move to the right to accommodate the move. The records will be grouped by TourID and summarized by Profit. The InvoiceNo field is not required for this query.
3. Click the **InvoiceNo field column selector**, then press **[Delete]**
   Deleting the field from the Query design grid does not affect the data in the underlying table. Next, add the Total row to the Query design grid.
4. Click the **Totals button** on the Query Design toolbar
   By default, the entry for each field of the new Total row is Group By. To get a total profit for each TourID, change the Group By function to Sum for the Profit column.
5. Click the **Total cell** of the **Profit field**, click the **Group By list arrow**, then click **Sum**
   The Query design grid now looks like Figure F-12.
6. Click the **Datasheet View button** on the Query Design toolbar
   As you can see from the resulting datasheet, Michael netted $648 from the 1/10/97 Big Sky tour. It was the most profitable tour when summarized across the database. Add a Count function to determine how many individual sales transactions are included in each summarized profit figure.
7. Click the **Design View button** on the Query Datasheet toolbar, click the **Total cell** of the **TourID field**, click the **Group By list arrow**, click **Count**, then click
   The resulting datasheet is shown in Figure F-13 and shows that six Big Sky tours were sold. Print the query.
8. Click the **Print button** on the Query Datasheet toolbar
   You add this datasheet to your Nomad file of printouts. Close and save the Profit by Sale query.
9. Click the **Profit By Sale Close button**, then click **Yes** to save the changes

QuickTip

Click the list arrow of the Top Values button on the Query design toolbar to quickly narrow the number of records in the resulting datasheet to the top 5, 25, 100, 5%, or 25% of the total records.

FIGURE F-12: Query design grid with Total row

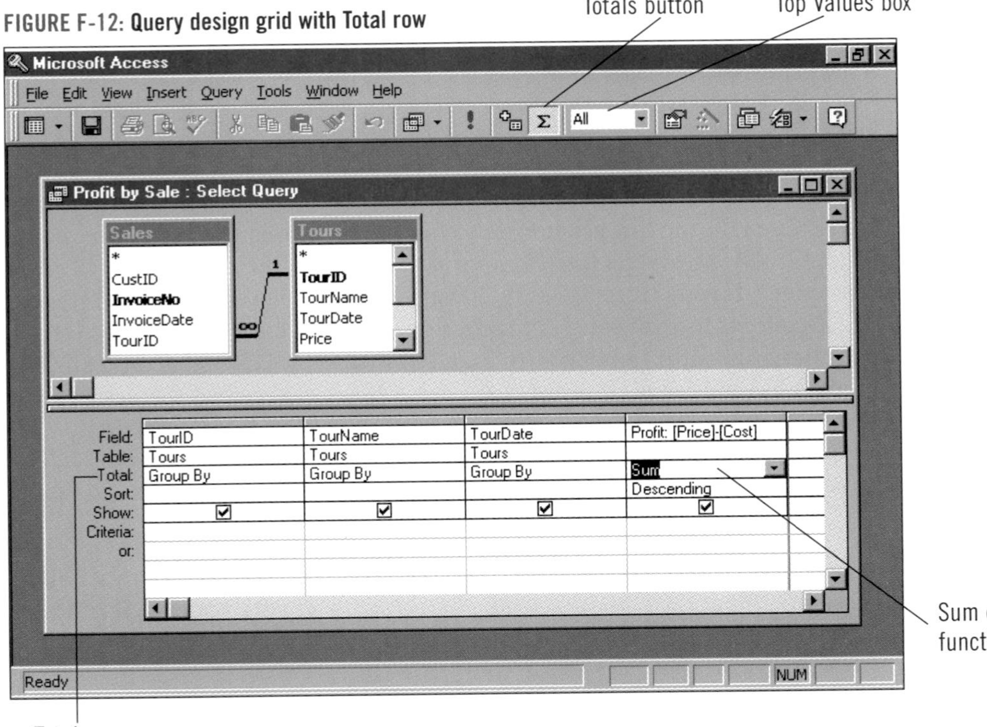

FIGURE F-13: Datasheet with Count and Sum functions

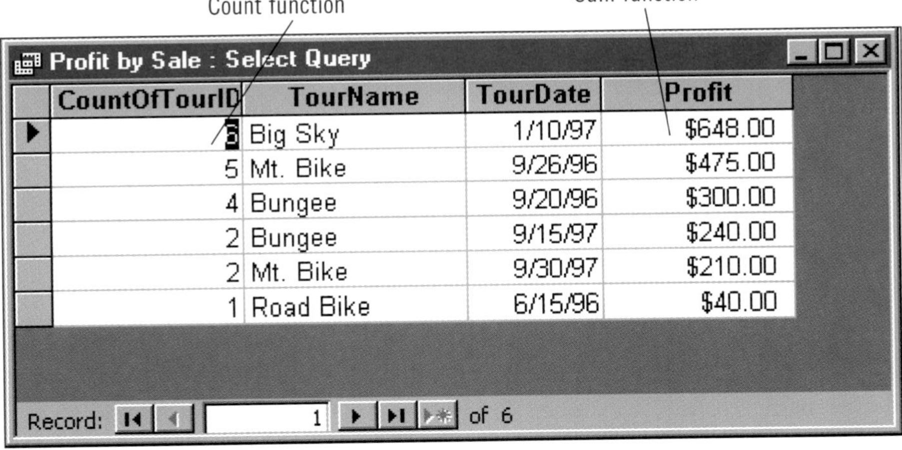

TABLE F-3: Aggregate functions

aggregate function	used to find the
Sum	total of values in a field
Avg	average of values in a field
Min	minimum value in the field
Max	maximum value in the field
Count	number of values in a field (not counting null values)
StDev	standard deviation of values in a field
Var	variance of values in a field
First	field value from the first record in a table or query
Last	field value from the last record in a table or query

Access 97

Developing Crosstab Queries

Crosstab queries provide another method to summarize data by creating a datasheet in which one or more fields are chosen for the row headings, another field is chosen for the column headings, and a third field, usually a numeric field, is summarized within the datasheet itself. You can create a crosstab query directly from a Query Design window or use the Crosstab Query Wizard. Michael needs to analyze his company's profit from a customer perspective. He creates a query that summarizes profit not only by TourID, but also by Customer so that he can develop marketing plans around his high-profit customers. Michael sketched the design for a final report in Figure F-14. Michael uses the Crosstab Query Wizard to guide his actions.

QuickTip

You can make any query into a crosstab query by choosing the Crosstab option from the Query type button on the Query toolbar.

Trouble?

If the Crosstab Wizard has been recently used, you may see different default options in each dialog box. Be sure to check each option as you move through the dialog boxes. Click the Back button to review previous dialog boxes. Be sure to double-check the query name and modify the default option if necessary.

1. **Click the Queries tab if necessary, click New, click Crosstab Query Wizard, then click OK**
   The first step to creating a crosstab query is to assemble the fields in a single query object. The Profit by Customer query will be used as the basis for the crosstab query. It contains the needed fields of CustID, Last, TourID, and Profit.

2. **Click the Queries option button, click Profit by Customer, then click Next >**
   Identify the CustID and Last fields as row headings.

3. **Click the CustID field, click the Add Selected Field button >, click the Last field, click >, then click Next >**
   The sample pane displays the results of your choices as you build the query. Next Michael identify the column heading field.

4. **Click the TourID field, then click Next >**
   Finally, identify the field which will be crosstabulated, and the aggregate function shown in Figure F-15.

5. **Click Profit, click Sum in the Functions column, then click Next >**
   Accept the default name Profit by Customer_Crosstab and view the crosstab query

6. **Click Finish, then click the datasheet Maximize button if necessary**
   The resulting datasheet for the Crosstab query is shown in Figure F-16. You could switch to Query Design View and sort this query by Profit or enter limiting criteria as with any other query. In this case though, just print a copy of the crosstab datasheet for a future meeting.

7. **Click the Print button on the Query Datasheet toolbar, click the Crosstab query datasheet Close button**

Types of Query Wizards

The Simple Query Wizard is another way to create a select query rather than use the Query Design View. The Find Duplicates Query Wizard is used to determine whether a table contains duplicate values in one or more fields. The Find Unmatched Query Wizard is used to find records in one table that don't have related records in another table.

FIGURE F-14: Sketch of a crosstab query

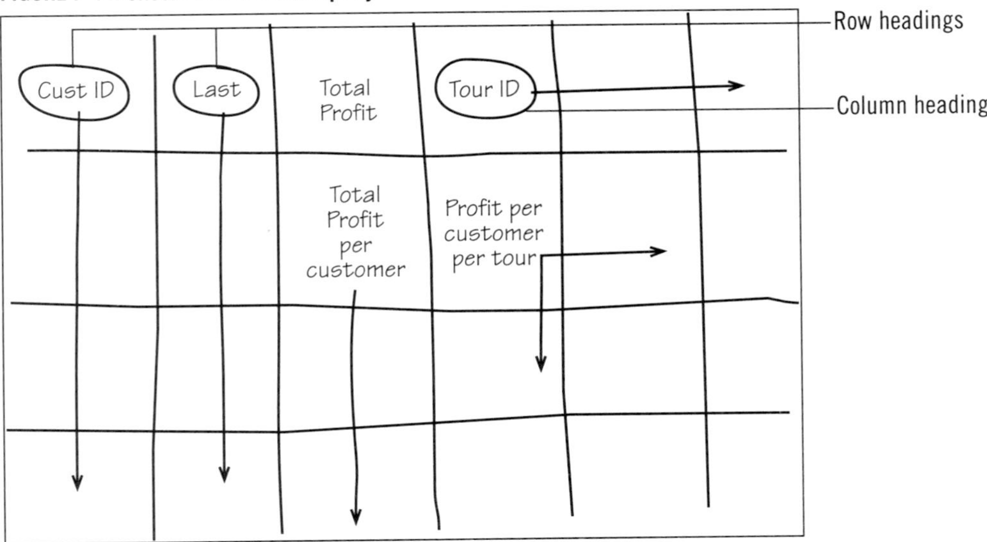

FIGURE F-15: Crosstab Query Wizard

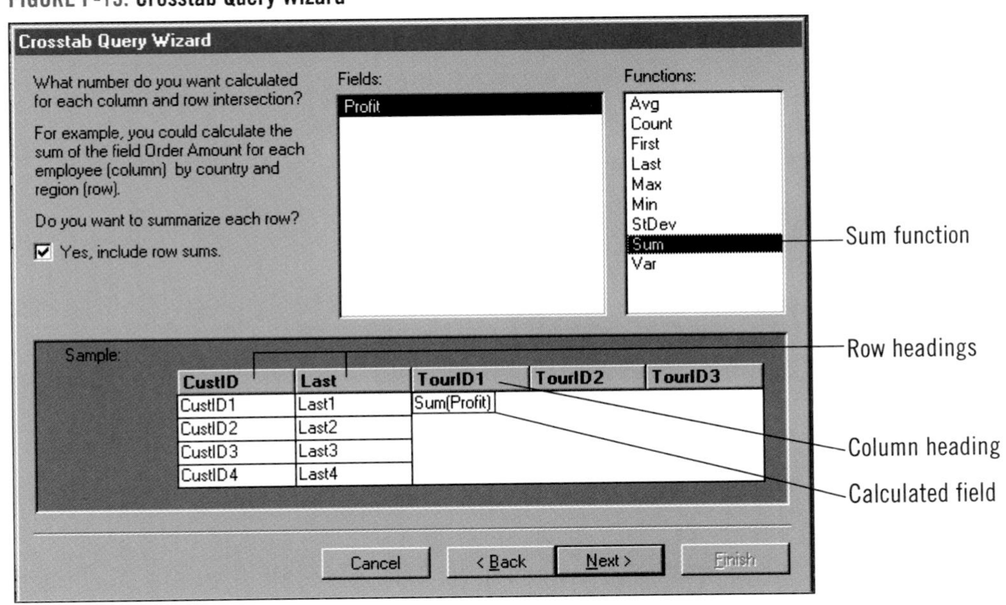

FIGURE F-16: Crosstab query datasheet

CustID	Last	Total Of Profit	Bigs0197	Bung0996	Bung0997	Mtbi0996	Mtbi0997
1	Braithwaite	$40.00					
10	Rodarmor	$95.00				$95.00	
11	Reis	$228.00	$108.00		$120.00		
12	Reis	$108.00	$108.00				
13	Egan	$228.00	$108.00		$120.00		
14	Fox	$213.00	$108.00				$105.00
15	Fox	$213.00	$108.00				$105.00
16	Fox	$108.00	$108.00				
2	Spencer	$95.00				$95.00	
3	Dobbins	$75.00		$75.00			
4	Khalsa	$95.00				$95.00	
5	Majors	$75.00		$75.00			
6	Williams	$75.00		$75.00			
7	Gonzales	$95.00				$95.00	
8	Black	$95.00				$95.00	
9	Owen	$75.00		$75.00			

Record: 1 of 16

Datasheet View NUM

Total profit per customer

Column headings

Row headings

Access 97

Access 97

Creating Update Queries

Update queries allow you to select a group of records then update all of them with one action. For example, you may wish to delete a group of records with a **Delete** query, change the value of a field with a basic Update query, or add several records to an existing table with an **Append** query. An update query starts as a select query with an Update to row added to the Query design grid. Table F-4 shows examples of update formulas. Michael wants to increase the prices of all 1997 tours by 20%.

Steps

1. Click the **Queries tab**, click **New**, click **Design View**, then click **OK**
   The only table you need for this update query is the Tours table.
2. Click **Tours**, click **Add**, then click **Close**
   You need the TourDate field in order to select 1997 tours and the Price field to increase the data in that field by 20%. You have to insert the Price field in the first column in the Query design grid, and the TourDate field in the second column in the Query design grid.
3. Double-click the **Price field**, then double-click the **TourDate field**
   Specify that only those tours with dates on or after 1/1/97 are chosen.
4. Click the **Criteria cell** of the **TourDate field**, then type **>=1/1/97**
   Change the select query into an update query.
5. Click the **Query Type button list arrow** on the Query Design toolbar, then click **Update Query**
   The Sort and Show rows of the Query design grid changes to an Update To row where the formula for the new updated value is entered.
6. Click the **Update To cell** of the **Price field**, then type **[Price]*1.2**
   This formula will update the current prices of all tours selected by 20%. The Query Design grid now looks like Figure F-17.
7. Click the **Run button** on the Query Design toolbar to update the database, click **Yes** when asked if you want to update 4 rows, click the **Datasheet View button** on the Query Design toolbar, click the **Restore Window button**.
   The resulting datasheet of the update query is shown in Figure F-18. Since you don't want to inadvertently run the query again and increase prices a second time, do not save the query.
8. Click the **Access Close button**, click **No** when prompted to save the changes to the query, close the database, then close Access
   Michael can use this information to project higher profit margins for Nomad.

Trouble?

Don't click the Run button twice or you will update the Price field of the chosen records by 20% a second time.

FIGURE F-17: **Query Design View of an update query**

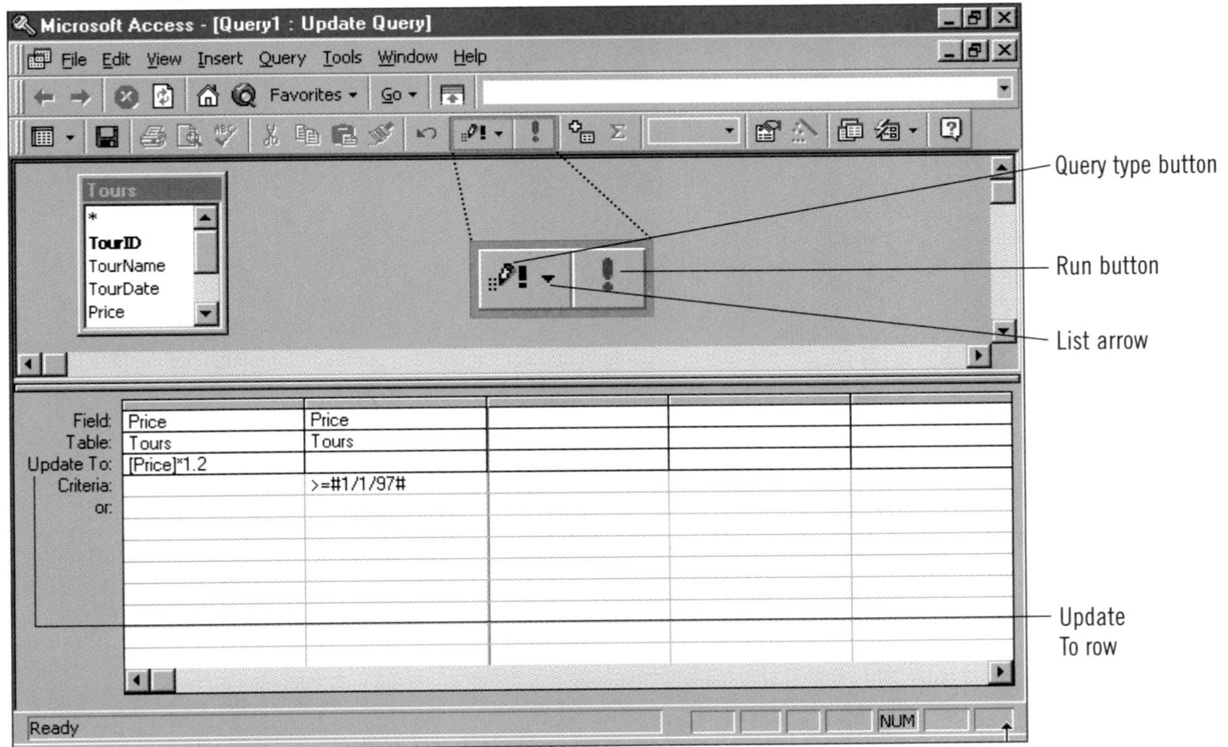

FIGURE F-18: **Datasheet of an update query after running the update**

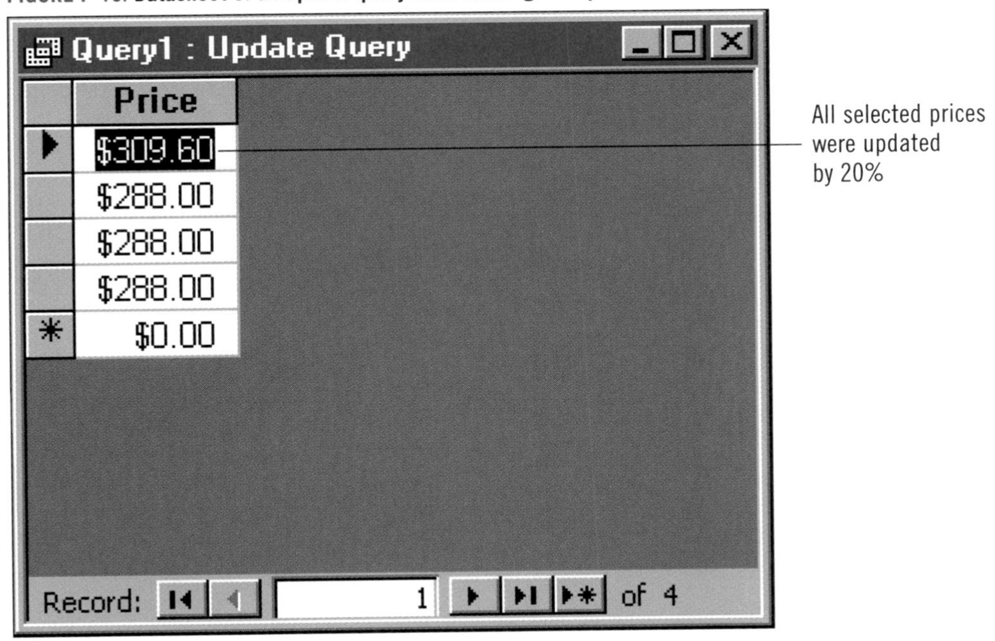

TABLE F-4: **Update query formulas and results**

update formula	result
"Vice President"	Changes the values of the chosen field to the text Vice President
#1/1/98#	Changes the values of the chosen field to the date 1/1/98
7	Changes the values of the chosen field to 7
[Cost]*1.05	Updates the values of the chosen field to five percent more than the current value of the Cost field

Practice

► Concepts Review

Identify each element of a table's Design View shown in Figure F-19.

FIGURE F-19

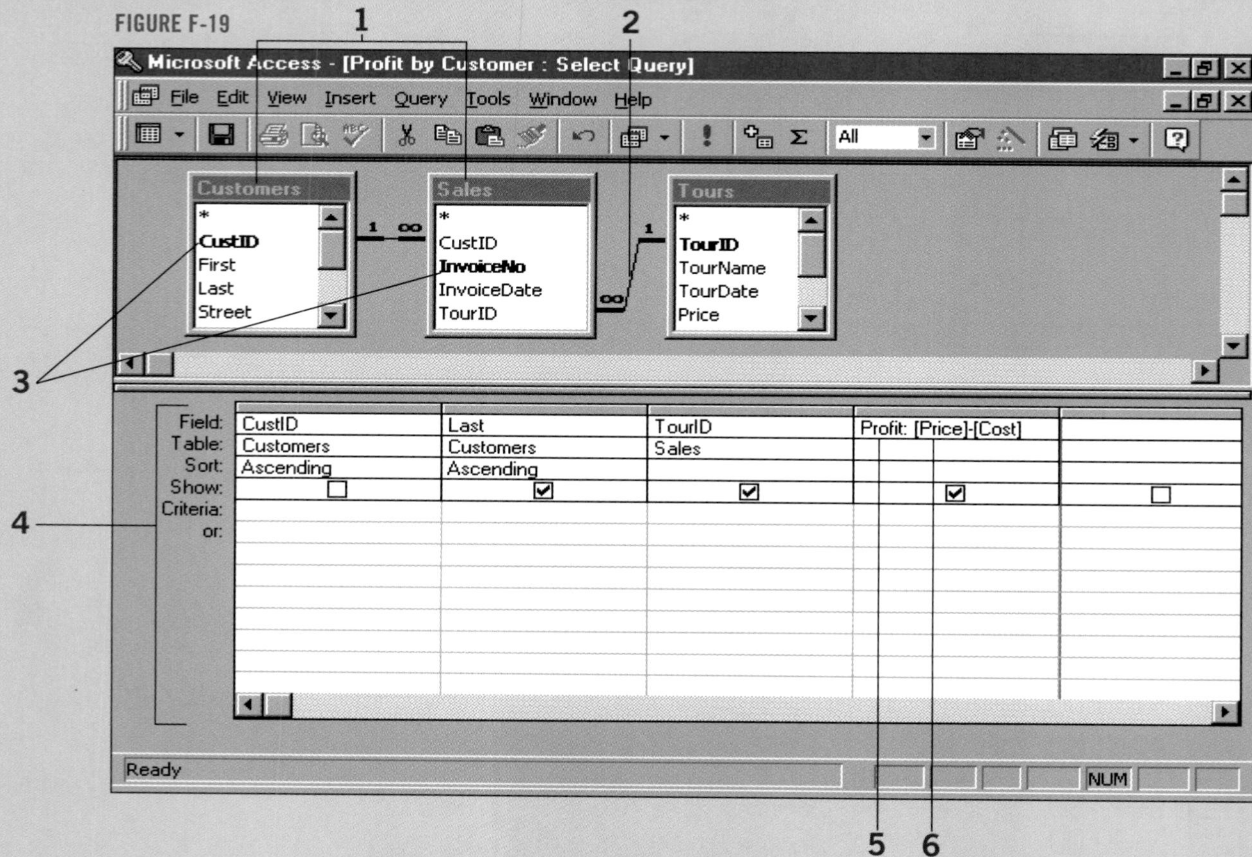

Match each term with the statement that describes its function.

7. Placing the records of a datasheet in a certain order
8. Used to create mathematical calculations in a query
9. A database object that answers questions about the data
10. Conditions that select only certain records
11. Operator used to combine two expressions

a. Query
b. Arithmetic operators
c. And
d. Sorting
e. Criteria

Select the best answer from the list of choices.

12. The query datasheet can best be described as:

- **a.** A duplication of the data in the underlying table's datasheet.
- **b.** A logical view of the selected data from an underlying table's datasheet.
- **c.** A separate file of data.
- **d.** A second copy of the data in the underlying tables.

13. Queries are often used to:

- **a.** Create copies of database files.
- **b.** Eliminate the need to build multiple tables.
- **c.** Create option boxes and list boxes from which to choose field values.
- **d.** Present a subset of fields from multiple tables.

14. When you update data in a table that is displayed in a query:

- **a.** You must also update the query.
- **b.** You must relink the query to the table.
- **c.** The data is automatically updated in the query.
- **d.** You have the choice whether you want to update the data in the query or not.

15. To assemble several fields from different tables, use a(n):

- **a.** Select Query.
- **b.** Update Query.
- **c.** Delete Query.
- **d.** Append Query.

16. The order in which records are sorted is determined by:

- **a.** The order in which the fields are listed in the underlying table.
- **b.** The alphabetic order of the field names.
- **c.** The left-to-right position of the fields in the Query grid.
- **d.** Ascending fields are sorted first in the Query grid. Descending fields are sorted second.

17. Crosstab queries are used to:

- **a.** Summarize information based on fields in the column and row headings of the report.
- **b.** Update several records at the same time.
- **c.** Select fields for a datasheet from multiple tables.
- **d.** Calculate price increases on numeric fields.

Skills Review

1. **Create select queries using multiple tables**
   a. Start Access and open the database Addresses-F.
   b. Create a new select query using Design View using both the Names and Zips tables.
   c. Add the following fields to the Query design grid in this order:
   First, Last, Street, and Zip from the Names table
   City and State from the Zips table
   d. Save the query as "Basic Address List", view the datasheet, print the datasheet, then close the query.

2. **Sort a query on multiple fields**
   a. Think about how you would modify the "Basic Address List" query so that it is sorted in ascending order by Last, then by First, but do not change the order of the fields in the resulting datasheet.
   b. Add another First field to the right of the Last field in the Query design grid to make the first three fields in the Query design grid First, Last, and First.
   c. Add the ascending sort criteria to the second column and third column fields, and uncheck the Show check-box in the third column.
   d. Save the query as "Sorted Address List", view the datasheet, print the datasheet, then close the query.

3. **Develop AND queries**
   a. Think about how you would modify the "Basic Address List" query so that only those people from IA with a last name that starts with "F" are chosen.
   b. Enter F* (the asterisk is a wildcard) as the criterion for the Last field to choose all people whose last name starts with F. Enter IA as the criterion for the State field.
   c. Be sure to enter the criteria on the same line in the Query design grid to make the query an AND query.
   d. Save the query as "Iowa F Names", view the datasheet, print the datasheet, and close the query.

4. **Develop OR queries**
   a. Modify the "Iowa F Names" query so that only those people from IA with a last name that starts with "F" or "B" are chosen.
   b. Enter the OR criterion B* on the or row for the Last field in the Query design grid. Access will assist you with the syntax for this type of criterion and enters "Like B*" in the cell when you click elsewhere in the grid.
   c. Be sure to reenter the IA criterion on the or row for the State field in the Query design grid to make sure that your query doesn't display all names that start with B, but only those who live in Iowa.
   d. Save the query as "Iowa B or F Names", view the datasheet, print the datasheet, then close the query.

5. **Develop calculated fields**
   a. Plan how you might create a new select query using Design View using just the Names table to determine the number of days old each person is based on the information in the Birthday field.
   b. Add the following fields from the Names table to the Query design grid in this order:
   First, Last, Birthday
   c. Create a calculated field called "Days Old" in the fourth column of the Query design grid with the expression
   Days Old:Date()-[Birthday]
   (Note: Date() is an Access function that always represents today's date.)
   d. Save the query as "Days Old", view the datasheet, print the datasheet, then close the query.

6. Add calculations on groups of records

   a. Create a new select query using Design View, then add the Names and Zips tables.
   b. Add the following fields:
   Zip from the Names table
   City and State from the Zips table
   c. Add the Total row to the Query design grid and change the function from Group By to Count for the Zip field
   d. Save the query as "Count Zip", view the datasheet, print the datasheet, then close the query.

7. Develop crosstab queries

   a. Use the Crosstab Query Wizard to create a new crosstab query that counts the number of people who live in each City and State.
   b. Use the Basic Address List query as the basis for the new crosstab query.
   c. Select City as the row heading and State as the column heading.
   d. Count the First field for the calculation within the crosstab datasheet.
   e. Name the query "Crosstab of Cities and States".
   f. View, Save, print, then close the datasheet.

8. Create update queries

   a. Think about how you would create a new select query using Design View to update the city "Overland Park" to the correct post office designation of "Shawnee Mission."
   b. Use Design View to design a new query.
   c. Add just the Zips table to the Query design grid.
   d. Add the City field from the Zip table to the query.
   e. Click Query on the menu bar, then click Update Query.
   f. In the Criteria cell, enter "Overland Park".
   g. In the Update To cell, enter "Shawnee Mission".
   h. Run the query to update the record that contains the Overland Park entry in the City field.
   i. Save the query as "Shawnee Mission".
   j. Close the database, then exit Access.

Independent Challenges

1. As the president of a civic organization, you have developed a database that tracks donations of recyclable material called Cleanup-F. Now that several deposits have been made and recorded, you wish to query the database for several different listings that are needed for the next meeting.

To complete this independent challenge:

1. Start Access and open the database Cleanup-F.
2. Create a query that pulls the following fields into a datasheet and print the datasheet.
   Name (of Clubs), Deposit Date, Weight, Name (of Recycle Centers)
   Call the query "Deposits by Club".
3. Modify Deposits by Club so that it is sorted ascending by club Name, and then ascending by Deposit Date. Print the datasheet and save the query as "Deposits Sorted by Club then Date".
4. Modify Deposits Sorted by Club then Date to eliminate both the deposit Date and Name (of Center) fields. Then, group the records by club Name and total the Weight. Print the datasheet and save the query as "Total Weight by Club".

5. Modify Total Weight by Club so that the records are sorted from the highest total deposit weight to the lowest. Print the datasheet and save the query as "Sorted Total Weight by Club".
6. Create a new query that pulls the following fields with the given criteria into a datasheet.
   Fields: Name (of Center), deposit Date, Weight
   Criteria: Recycle Center Name = East Side
   Sorting: Sort ascending by deposit Date
7. Save the query with the name "East Side Deposits", view, then print the datasheet.
8. Close the database and exit Access.

2. Now that you've developed a relational database that documents the books you've read called Readings-F, your friends are starting to ask for recommended reading lists. You wish to query your book database to satisfy the requests of your friends.

To complete this independent challenge:

1. Start Access and open the database Readings-F.
2. Create a query that pulls the following fields into a datasheet:
   Title, Category, Rating, and Last Name
   Print the datasheet, save, and name the query "Books I've Read".
3. Modify Books I've Read so that it is sorted in a descending order on Rating and then in an ascending order by Last Name. Print the datasheet and name the query "Books I've Read Sorted by Rating and Author".
4. Use the Crosstab Query Wizard and the Books I've Read query to find out how many books you've read within each category by each author. Use Last Name as the row heading field, Category as the column heading field, and count the Title field within the body of the Crosstab report. Print the datasheet and name the query "Crosstab of Authors and Categories".
5. Modify the Books I've Read Sorted by Rating and Author query so that only fiction books with a rating of 7 or above are displayed.
6. Save the query as "Top Fiction Books", then print the datasheet.
7. Close the database and exit Access.

3. You have recently helped the medical director of a large internal medicine clinic put together and update a database called Doctors-F that tracks extra-curricular activities. You wish to query the database for specific listings of information to present to the committee responsible for philanthropic activities.

To complete this independent challenge:

1. Start Access and open the database Doctors-F.
2. Create a query that pulls the following fields into a datasheet:
   First Name, Last Name, Date, Hours, and Name (of Program)
   Save the query as "Physician Activities", then print the datasheet.
3. Modify Physician Activities so that it is sorted ascending by Last Name and then ascending by Date. Print the datasheet and name the query "Physician Activities Sorted by Name and Date".
4. Modify the Physician Activities Sorted by Name and Date query to eliminate the Date and Name fields. Then, group the records by Last Name and First Name and subtotal them by Hours. Print the datasheet and save the query as "Total Physician Hours".
5. Modify Total Physician Hours so that the records are listed from the physician who has volunteered the most time to the least. Print the datasheet and save the query as "Total Physician Hours Sorted from High to Low".

6. Create a new query that pulls the following fields with the given criteria into a datasheet:
   Fields: Name (of program), Last Name, Date, Hours
   Criteria: Hours are greater than 2 and Program equals "Heart Healthy" or Hours are greater than 2 and Program equals "Diabetes Campaign"
   Sorting: Sort ascending by Name then Last Name
7. Save the query as "Heart and Diabetes", then print the datasheet.
8. Create a new query that pulls the Program Name field from the Programs table and updates any occurrences of "Elderly Outreach" to "Senior Outreach".
9. Save the query as "Elderly to Senior".
10. Create a new query that pulls the First Name field and Last Name field from the Physicians table. Make the First Name field the first column and the Last Name field the second column. Sort by Last Name, then by First Name.
11. Add the Hours field to the third column of the grid of the new query.
12. Add a calculated field to the fourth column of the grid that calculates the total time spent by the staff during the activity. The total time is calculated as three times the hours spent by the physician to account for the hours spent by the physician, the nurse, and the aide. The entry in the fourth column should be as follows:
    Total Staff:[Hours]*3
13. Save the query as "Total Time."
14. Close the database and exit Access.

4. You are interested in finding out about technical jobs currently available at IBM. Using information about job openings posted at IBM's Web site, you have started an Access database that you can query for the opportunities that most interest you.

To complete this independent challenge:

1. Log on to the Internet and use your browser to go to http://www.course.com. From there, click Student Online Companions, click the link for this textbook, then click the Access link for Unit F.
2. Use the IBM Employment site to find out what jobs are posted on the web page, and print at least two pages of the web site.
3. Open the IBM-F database.
4. Using the information you printed from IBM's site, enter two new records into the Job Listing Query.
5. Create a new query that first displays the Category field from the Category table, second displays the Job Title from the Job Titles table, and third shows the Job Reference # field from the Job Titles table.
6. Having recently read an article about job prospects for developers, you decide to determine how many of the job postings in the database match this title. Modify the query by entering "Developers" in the Criteria cell of the Job Title field.
7. Sort the records ascending by the Category field.
8. Resize the columns of the resulting datasheet so that all the information in each column is displayed.
9. Save the query as "Developers Query", print the datasheet, close the datasheet and database, then exit Access.

► Visual Workshop

Open the VW-F database and create a new query as shown in Figure F-20. Notice that the records are sorted alphabetically by last name and the total value of their donations is summarized in the SumOfValue field. Save the query as "Summarized Donations" then print the datasheet.

FIGURE F-20

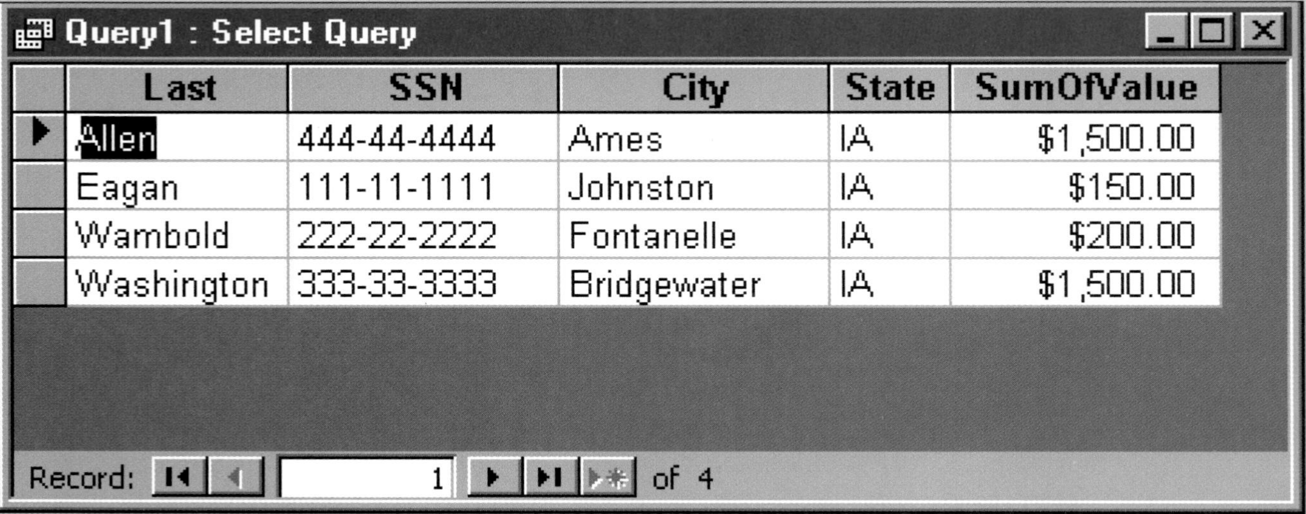

Last	SSN	City	State	SumOfValue
Allen	444-44-4444	Ames	IA	$1,500.00
Eagan	111-11-1111	Johnston	IA	$150.00
Wambold	222-22-2222	Fontanelle	IA	$200.00
Washington	333-33-3333	Bridgewater	IA	$1,500.00

Developing
Forms with Subforms

Objectives

- Create a form from multiple tables
- Move and resize controls
- Add labels and format controls
- Sort records within a form
- Find records within a form
- Filter records within a form
- Change the default value of a form control
- Add list boxes

Adding new records or modifying existing data in a database must be easy and straightforward. A datasheet is often too cumbersome or complex for extensive data entry purposes. A **form** overcomes these obstacles by allowing you to present fields in any logical or useful screen arrangement. Also, forms allow you to add **controls** such as field labels, field text boxes, list boxes, and option buttons to help identify the data on the form. Michael wants to develop forms that match Nomad's source documents, the paper documents on which data is initially recorded. Entering data through well-designed forms will encourage fast, accurate data entry and will shield the data entry person from the complexity of tables, queries, and datasheets.

Creating a Form from Multiple Tables

A form displays the fields of a table or query in an arrangement that you design, and can be based on one of five general layouts: Columnar, Tabular, Datasheet, Chart, and PivotTable. See Table G-1 for more information on the different form layouts. Once the form is created, the design can be changed. Michael will develop a sales transaction form that Nomad employees can use to record additional tour sales including customer and invoice information at the time of the sale. The form requires fields from both the Customers and Sales tables in the Nomad database.

Steps

1. Start Access and open the **Nomad-G** database
2. Click the **Forms tab** in the Nomad-G : Database window, click **New**, click **Form Wizard** in the New Form dialog box, then click **OK**
   The **Form Wizard**, as shown in Figure G-1, prompts you to select the fields, layout, and style of the form. You use the Form Wizard to select all the fields from both the Customers and Sales tables which are not currently gathered in any single query object.
3. Click the **Select all fields button** [>>] to select all fields from the Customers table, click the **Tables/Queries list arrow**, click **Table: Sales**, click the **Select all fields button** [>>], then click [Next >]
   Next, you must decide how to view the data. Arranging the form by Customers places the customer information at the top of the form, and places invoice and tour information in a subform. A **subform** links multiple records from one table (Sales) to a single record of another table (Customers). It is especially effective when you want to show data from tables with a one-to-many relationship.
4. If necessary, click **by Customers**, click the **Form with subform(s) option button**, then click [Next >]
   Next, choose a tabular form layout then choose a Standard style in the following dialog box.
5. Click the **Tabular option button**, click [Next >], click **Standard**, then click [Next >]
   Form names appear on the Forms tab and should be descriptive so you can identify the forms at a later time. Change the default form name and accept the default subform name.
6. Type **Customer Form** in the Form: text box, click [Finish], then click the **Customer Form Maximize button**
   The form is shown in Figure G-2. By placing the customer information in the main form and the sales information in the subform, you can show multiple sales transactions for the same customer on the same form.

Using AutoForm

The **AutoForm** option creates the specified type of form for the chosen table or query. To quickly create a columnar form, click the table or query object with the fields you wish the form to contain, click the New Object button on the Database toolbar, then click AutoForm.

FIGURE G-1: **Form Wizard**

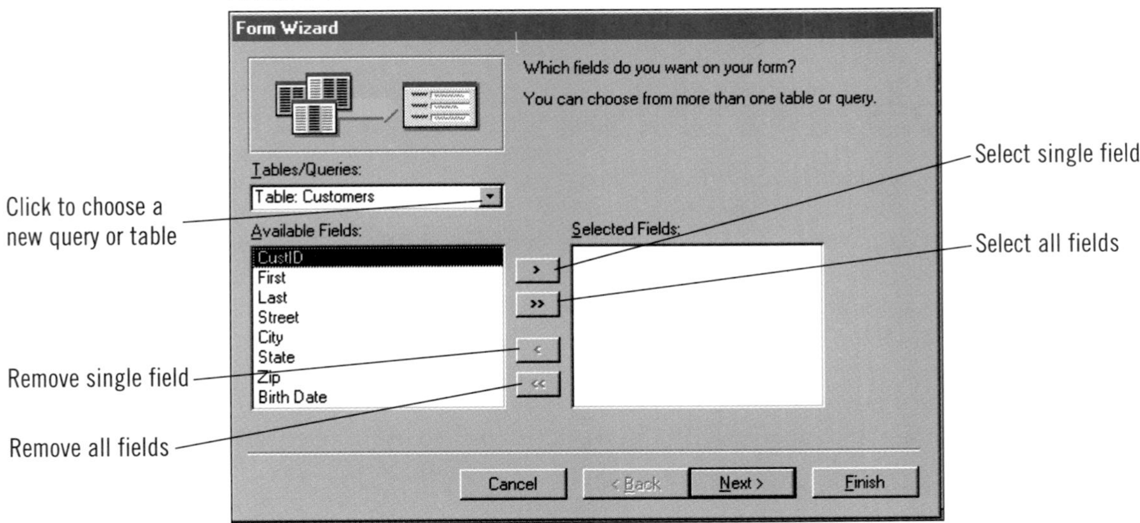

FIGURE G-2: **Customer Form**

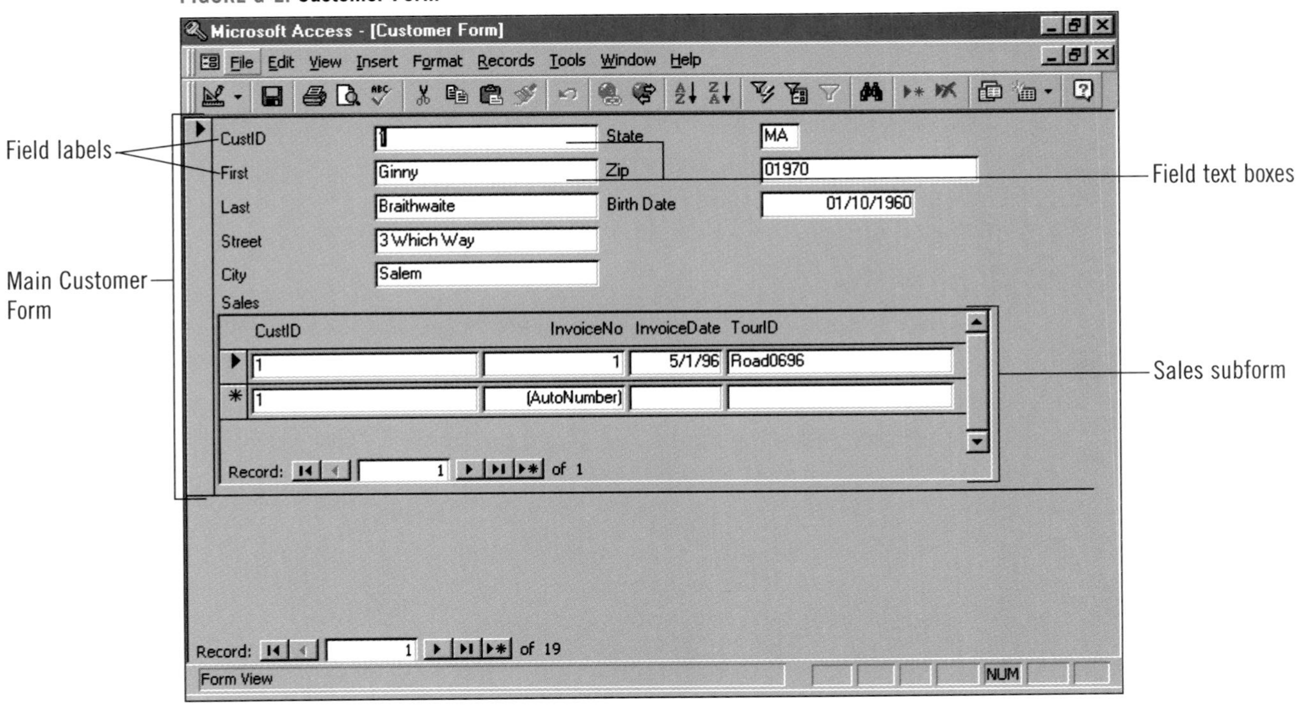

TABLE G-1: **Form layouts**

layout	description
Columnar	Each field appears on a separate line with a label to its left, one record for each screen
Tabular	Each field appears as a column heading and each record as a row; displays multiple records just like a datasheet, but provides more design control and flexibility; for example, you could change elements such as colors, fonts, headers, or footers
Datasheet	Each field appears as a column heading and each record as a row; the datasheet layout displays multiple records, but formatting options, except for resizing columns, are limited
Chart	Numeric fields are present in a chart (graph) format
PivotTable	Fields are chosen for column and for row headings, and a field is summarized in the intersection of the appropriate column and row in a cross-tabular format

Access 97

Moving and Resizing Controls

Even though the Form Wizard sets up a workable form, some rearrangement and resizing of the fields is often necessary for the form to best meet your needs. Form elements are called **controls** and can be bound or unbound. An **unbound control** is not linked to the data of any table; it exists only within the form itself. Field labels are the most common unbound control, but other types include clipart, lines, and instructional labels. **Bound controls** are linked to data in underlying tables. The most common bound control is a field text box. Check boxes, list boxes, and option buttons can also be bound controls. When you add a field to a form, Access automatically adds both an unbound control (the descriptive field label) and a bound control (a field text box). Michael rearranges and modifies the controls on the form to better suit his data entry needs.

Steps

Trouble?

If the Toolbox covers the form, drag the Toolbox title bar to the right edge of the window so the entire form is visible.

1. Click the **Design View button** on the Form View toolbar

   Use Design View to move, delete, or add any elements to the form. The fields from the Customer table appear in the upper half of the form, and a large control to designate the size and position of the Sales Subform appears in the lower half. Delete the unnecessary labels from the form.

Trouble?

If you select the wrong label, click it again while holding [Shift] to deselect it and retain the other selections.

2. Click the **First label**, press and hold **[Shift]**, click the **Last label**, click the **Street label**, click the **City label**, click the **State label**, click the **Zip label**, then release **[Shift]**

   Pressing [Shift] while clicking the second and subsequent controls allows you to select multiple controls at the same time as shown in Figure G-3.

3. Press **[Delete]**

   Deleting the labels does not affect the data displayed on the form in the field text boxes.

QuickTip

The Object list box on the left edge of the Formatting (Form/Report) toolbar always displays which control is currently selected on the form. In addition, you can select a control by clicking the Object list arrow, then clicking the desired control from the list.

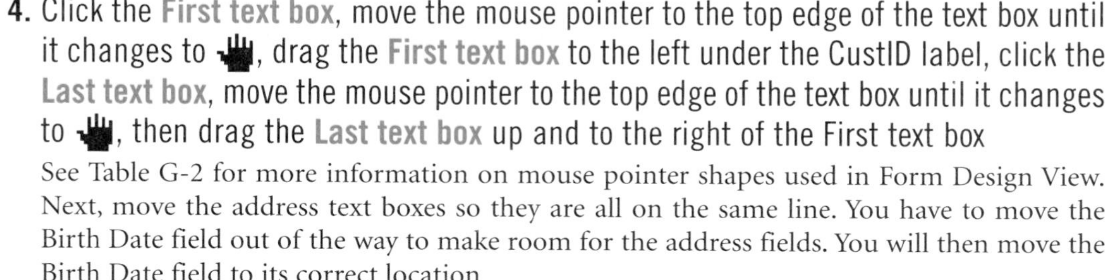

4. Click the **First text box**, move the mouse pointer to the top edge of the text box until it changes to , drag the **First text box** to the left under the CustID label, click the **Last text box**, move the mouse pointer to the top edge of the text box until it changes to , then drag the **Last text box** up and to the right of the First text box

   See Table G-2 for more information on mouse pointer shapes used in Form Design View. Next, move the address text boxes so they are all on the same line. You have to move the Birth Date field out of the way to make room for the address fields. You will then move the Birth Date field to its correct location.

5. Move the **Birth Date text box** down and to the right to an empty space on the form, then move the **Street, City, State,** and **Zip** to the positions shown in Figure G-4

   You want the Birth Date field label and text box next to the CustID field.

QuickTip

You can press and hold [Ctrl] while pressing an arrow key to move objects very small distances (less than a grid mark).

6. Click the **Birth Date text box**, move the mouse pointer to the top edge of the text box until it changes to , then drag the **Birth Date text box** to the right of the CustID field

   The CustID and Zip text boxes are wider than necessary.

7. Click the **CustID text box**, press and hold **[Shift]**, click the **Zip text box**, move the mouse pointer to the **middle resize handle** on the right side of the Zip text box; drag to the left to the **4.5" mark** on the ruler

   The new form design organizes the information logically, without the unnecessary labels.

Time To

- Save
- Close

8. Click the **Form View button** on the Form Design toolbar

   Compare your screen to the form shown in Figure G-5. Now you can save and close the new form.

FIGURE G-3: Form Design View

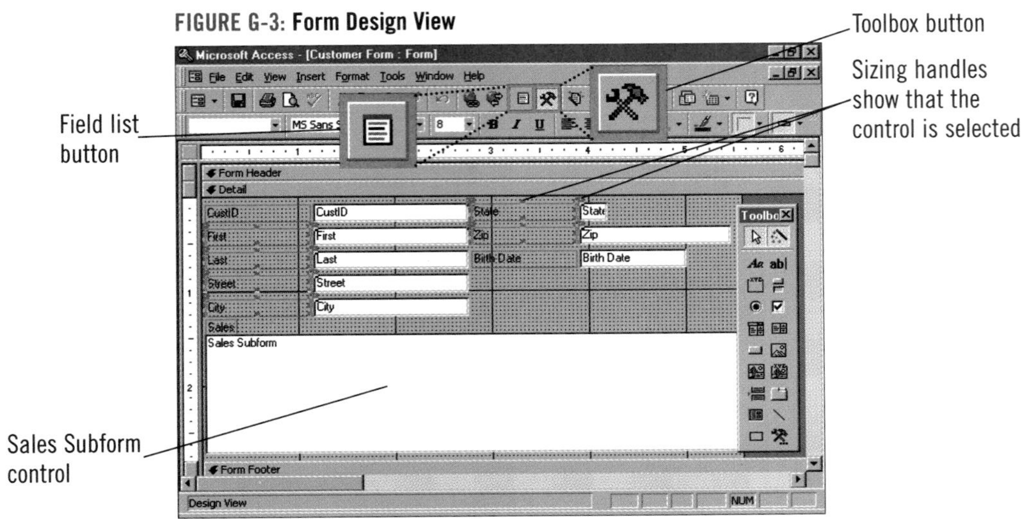

FIGURE G-4: Customer Form after fields are moved

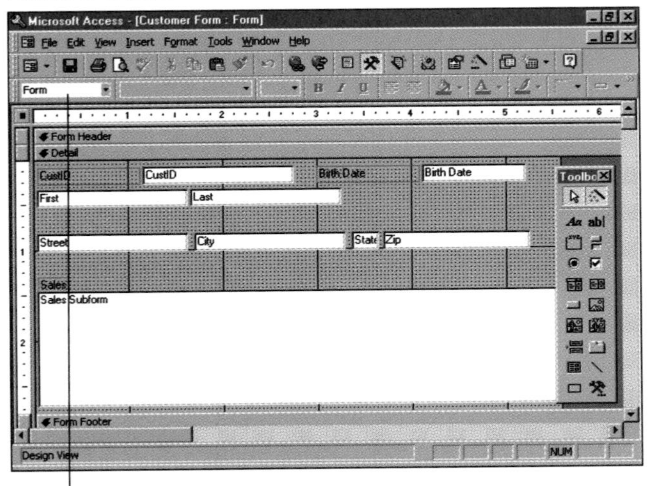

FIGURE G-5: Final Customer Form

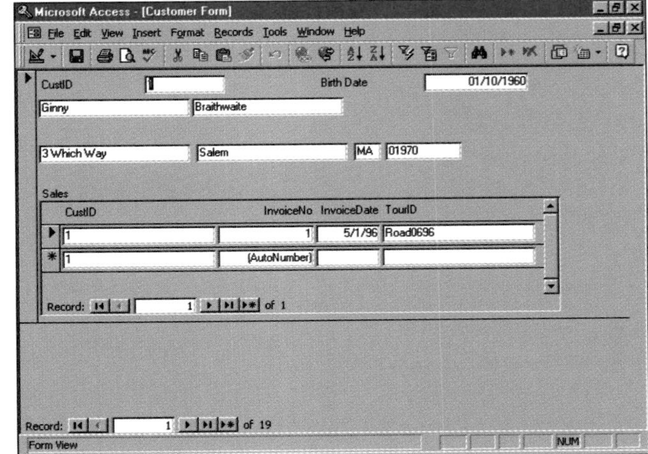

Access 97

TABLE G-2: Mouse pointer shapes used in Form Design View

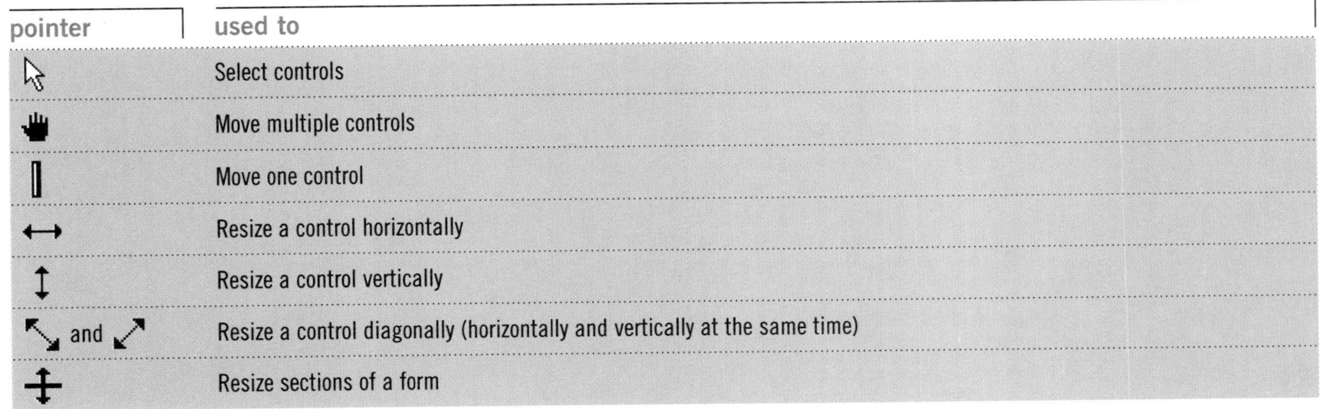

pointer	used to
(arrow)	Select controls
(hand)	Move multiple controls
(pointing hand)	Move one control
↔	Resize a control horizontally
↕	Resize a control vertically
↘ and ↗	Resize a control diagonally (horizontally and vertically at the same time)
(resize section)	Resize sections of a form

Access 97

Adding Labels and Formatting Controls

Even though unbound controls such as field labels and lines help identify and organize related information on a form, sometimes more descriptive labels are necessary. Formatting, enhancing the appearance of controls, can also improve a form's readability. The **Formatting** (Form/Report Design) toolbar provides the most popular formatting options for changing a label's border, font name, font size, or color. Formatting options that are not available on the toolbar must be changed through the control's property sheet. Michael decides to add a label to the Detail section of the form. See Table G-3 for more information on form sections. He will also change the label alignment so labels are positioned closer to the field text boxes they describe. His first step will be to add a label to identify the address information, then he'll realign the labels closer to their corresponding text boxes.

Steps

1. Click **Customer Form** on the Forms tab if necessary, click **Design**, click the **Label tool** in the Toolbox, click above the **address text fields at 5/8" on the ruler**, then type **Address Information:**

   Select both the CustID and Birth Date labels so that you can change the alignment property on both labels at the same time.

2. Click the **CustID label**, press and hold **[Shift]**, click the **Birth Date label**, then release **[Shift]**

   You want to right-align these labels. Since the Formatting toolbar doesn't contain a right-alignment button, make the change on the property sheet for these controls.

3. Click the **Properties button** on the Form Design toolbar, click the **Format tab**, scroll to display the **Text Align property**, click the **Text Align text box**, click the **Text Align list arrow**, then click **Right**

   The title bar of the property sheet displays the selected control's name. In this case, multiple controls are selected. The Customer Form should look like Figure G-6. Close the property sheet and view this form.

4. Click the **Properties button** on the Formatting toolbar, then click the **Form View button** on the Formatting toolbar

   The CustID and Birth Date labels are right aligned on the form.

5. Click the **Save button** on the Form View toolbar

   The final Customer Form should look like Figure G-7.

QuickTip

Click the Properties button to toggle the form property sheet on or off.

Trouble?

If you move, resize, or change a property of the wrong control, click the Undo button to undo your last action.

TABLE G-3: Form sections

section	description
Detail	Appears once for every individual record
Form Header	Appears at the top of the form and often contains a label with the form's title
Form Footer	Appears at the bottom of the form and often contains a label with instructions on how to use the form
Page Header	Appears at the top of a printed form with information such as page numbers or dates. The Page Header and Page Footer sections can be added to the form by clicking View on the menu bar, then clicking Page Header/Footer
Page Footer	Appears at the bottom of a printed form with information such as page numbers or dates

FIGURE G-6: **Customer Form with label and alignment changes**

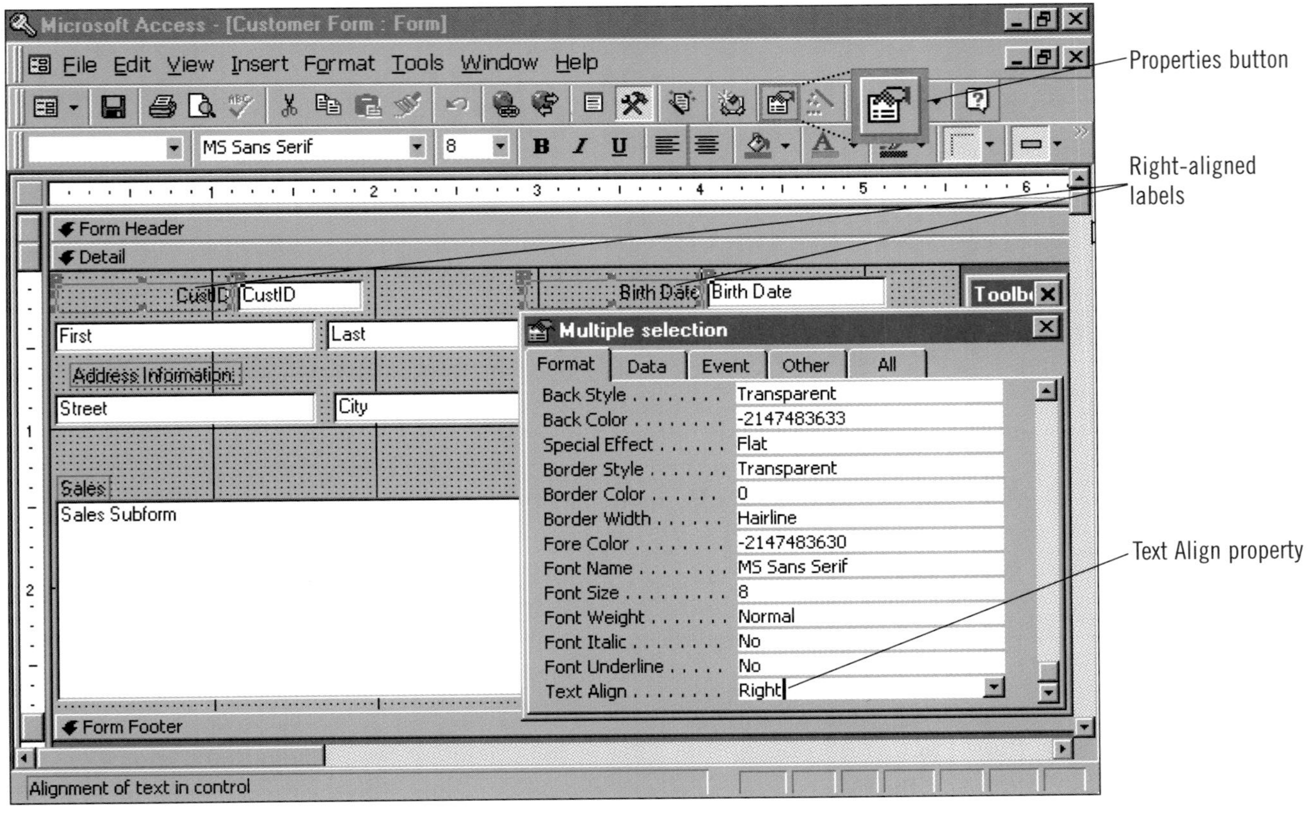

FIGURE G-7: **Customer Form**

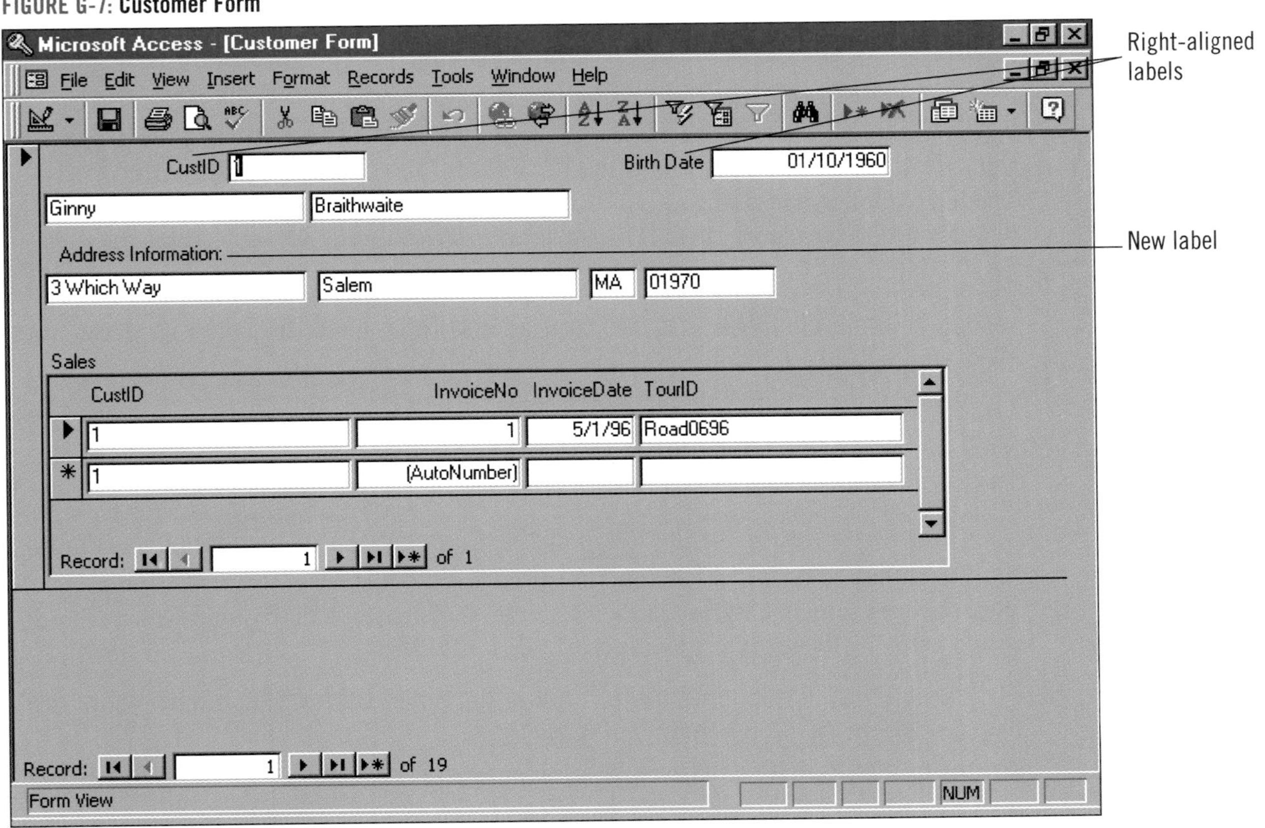

Access 97

Access 97

Sorting Records within a Form

Once a form is created, you can **sort** the records the same way that you sort within a datasheet. This is helpful to the user who entered data using a form, but needs to order the records in a certain way to make sure that the same customer is not being added to the database. If the form is based on a query that has already specified a sort order, the records will appear in that order when the form is opened but can be resorted at any time. Advanced sorts using more than one field in the sort order can be applied directly within the form by using the Advanced Filter/Sort option. Now that Michael has developed the Customer Form to record sales, he will use the Sort features to reorder the records within the form. He wants to analyze his customers based on their age, so he decides to sort the customers on the Birth Date field.

Steps

1. Click the **Birth Date text box**, then click the **Sort Descending button** on the Form View toolbar
   Amanda Fox is displayed as the record with the highest birth date (she is the youngest in the database) as shown in Figure G-8. Notice that two sets of **record navigation buttons** are displayed, one for the form, and one for the subform. The navigation buttons for the subform control the sales records for each customer. Use the main form record navigation buttons to move between customer records.
2. Click the **Next record button** in the Customer form navigation buttons
   Ron Fox, the next customer's record, should be displayed in the Customer Form. Ron Fox has two sales records in the Sales subform. Sort the records by name.
3. Click the **Last text box (Fox)**, then click the **Sort Ascending button** on the Form View toolbar
   John Black is displayed as the first record. You can further sort the records using both the First and Last fields. Since the buttons on the toolbar only accommodate a single-field sort, use the Advanced Filter/Sort option to sort on two fields.
4. Click **Records** on the menu bar, point to **Filter**, then click **Advanced Filter/Sort**
   The filter window opens so you can sort the records on the form using multiple fields. The filter window is very similar to the Query design grid and already shows the Last sort criterion.
5. Click the **First field** in the Customers field list window, drag it to the **Field cell** of the second column, click the **Sort cell** for the First field, click the **Sort list arrow**, then click **Ascending**
   The finished filter window should look like Figure G-9.
6. Click the **Apply Filter button** on the Filter/Sort toolbar
   The Customer form is displayed in Form View with the sort applied.
7. Click the **Next record button** in the Customer Form navigation buttons six times to move to record 7 for Ron Fox
   When two customers have the same last name, the First field determines which record is sorted first. Use the form to enter another sale for Ron Fox.
8. Click in the first blank **InvoiceDate field** in the Sales subform (in a new record row), type **7/1/98**, press **[Tab]**, then type **Bung0998**
   The forms work well for entering new sales for existing customers.
9. Click the **Save button** on the Form View toolbar

QuickTip

Double-click a field in the field list to move it to the next available column in the grid.

QuickTip

Type a record number in the record indicator box and press [Enter] to quickly move to that record in the database.

FIGURE G-8: Form sorted descending by Birth Date

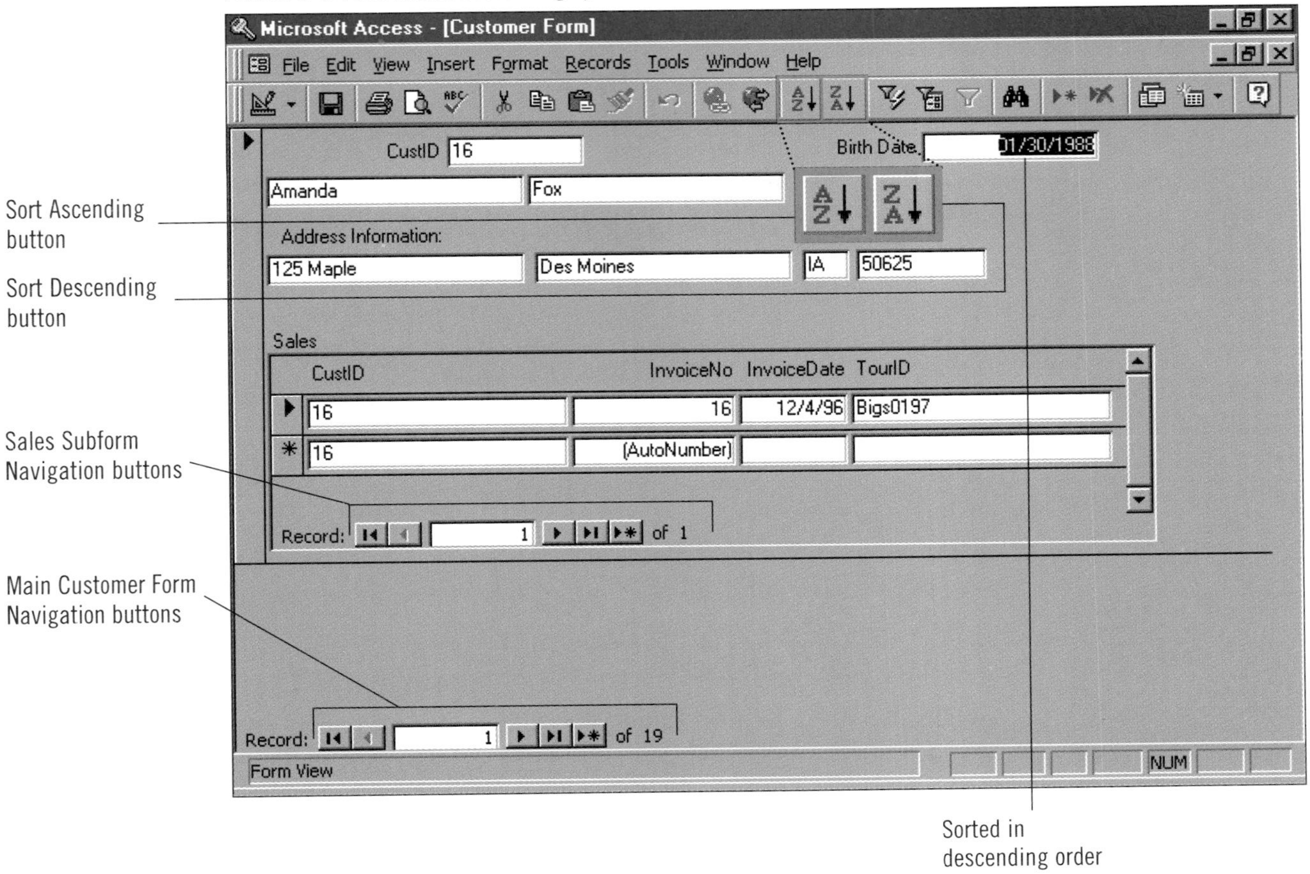

Sort Ascending button

Sort Descending button

Sales Subform Navigation buttons

Main Customer Form Navigation buttons

Sorted in descending order

FIGURE G-9: Filter window

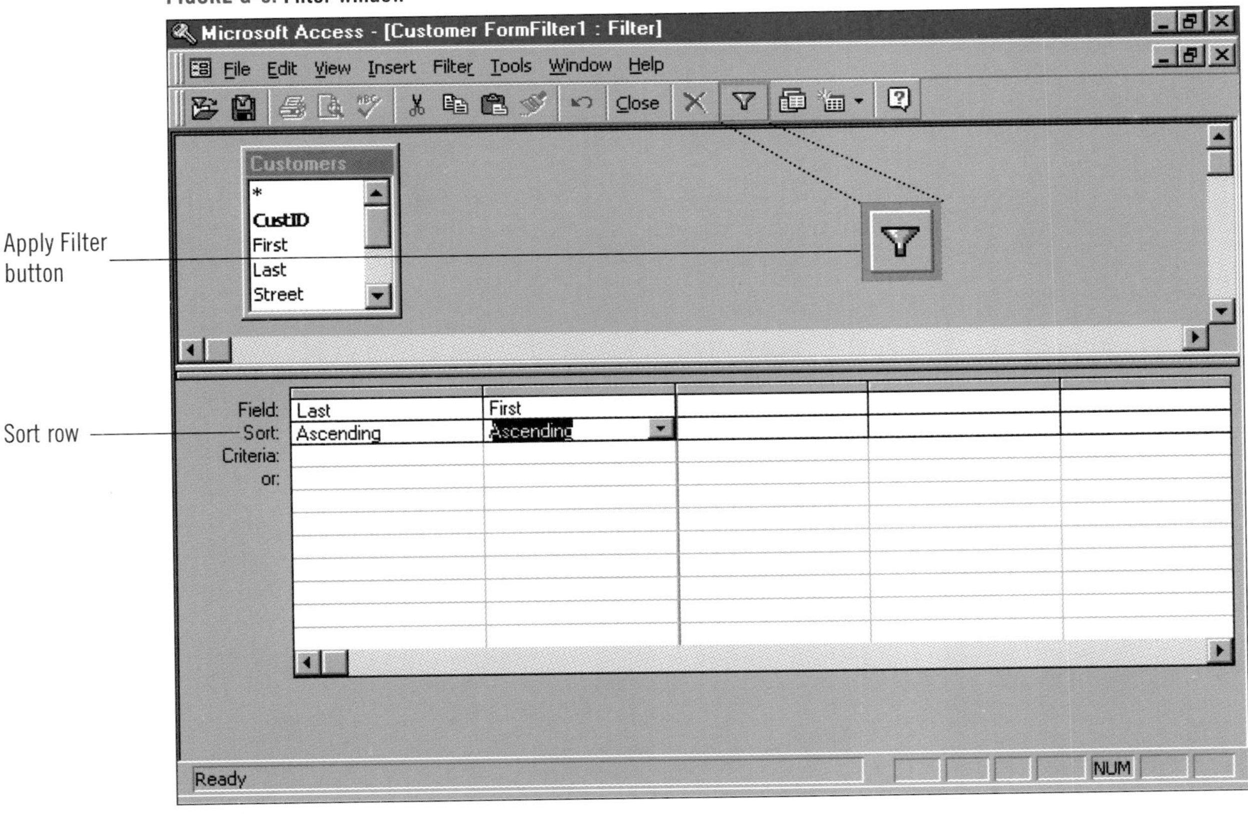

Access 97

Access 97

Finding Records within a Form

Access has a **Find** feature that allows you to search for a text string in any field. With the Find dialog box, you can locate specific records or find certain values within fields. You can navigate through records as Access finds each occurrence of the item you're looking for. If you want to replace certain values that you find, use the **Replace** feature found on the Edit menu. Michael will use the Find feature to answer questions about his customers and sales. Michael is making a presentation in Des Moines, Iowa, and wants to find all customers from that state.

Steps 1 2 3 4

1. Click **IA** in the **State field** in the Customer Form, then click the **Find button** on the Form View toolbar
   The Find in field dialog box opens as shown in Figure G-10. The options in the Find dialog box allow you to customize the search.
2. Type **IA** in the Find What text box, then click **Find First**
   The Amanda Fox record is the first one that matches the find criteria.
3. Click **Find Next** three times to find Fritz Friedrichsen's record, then click **Close**
   Fritz Friedrichsen just booked a tour, so record the sale to Fritz in the subform.
4. Click in the **InvoiceDate field** in the Sales subform, type **7/1/98**, press **[Tab]**, then type **Bung0998** in the TourID text box
   The sale is recorded as shown in Figure G-11. Next, find all customers who live in Des Moines.
5. Click the **Fontanelle** in the City field, click , type **Des Moines**, then click **Find First** in the Find dialog box
   Amanda Fox is the first customer in the database who lives in Des Moines.
6. Click **Find Next**, then view each found record until you have reached the end of the records
   A dialog box indicating that you have finished searching the records appears when you have found all of the records that match the find criteria. You should have found three customers who live in Des Moines.
7. Click **OK** in the Search item not found warning message dialog box
   You found what you needed, so close the Find in field dialog box.
8. Click **Close**

FIGURE G-10: **Find dialog box**

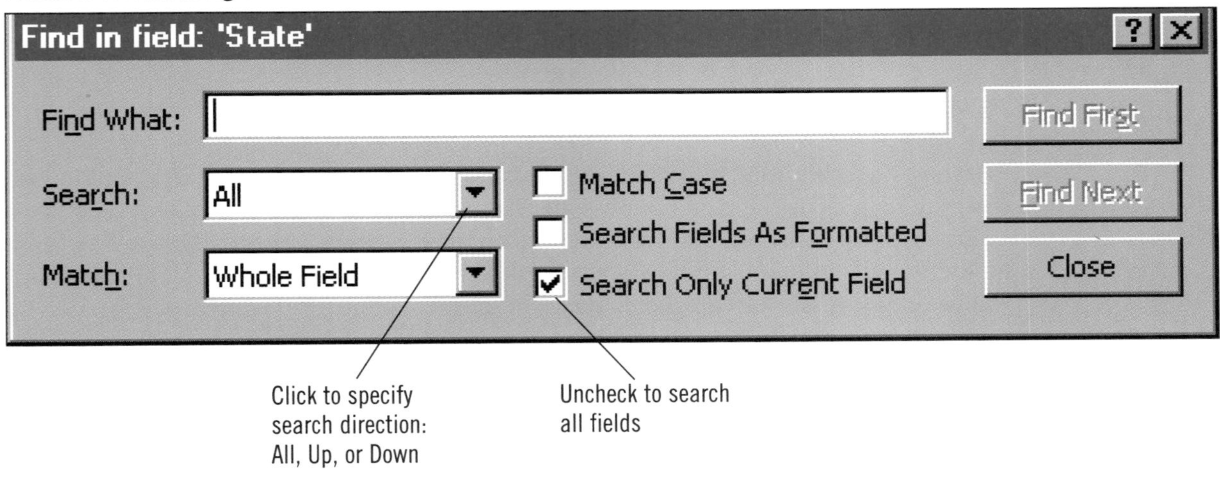

Find in field: 'State'
Find What:
Search:
All
Match:
Whole Field
Match Case
Search Fields As Formatted
Search Only Current Field
Find First
Find Next
Close
Click to specify search direction: All, Up, or Down
Uncheck to search all fields

FIGURE G-11: **Adding a sale using the Customer Form**

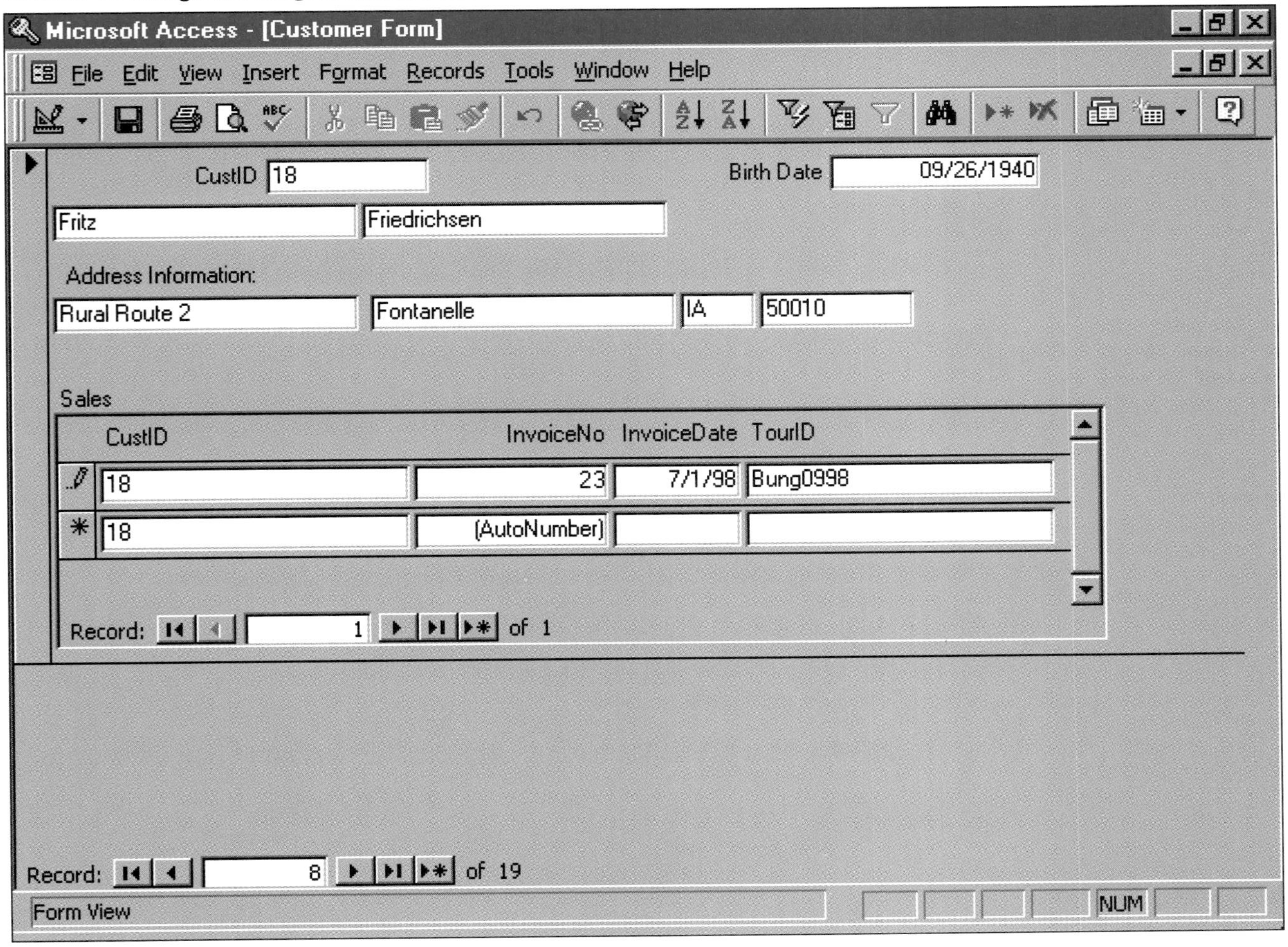

Microsoft Access - [Customer Form]
File Edit View Insert Format Records Tools Window Help
CustID 18
Birth Date 09/26/1940
Fritz
Friedrichsen
Address Information:
Rural Route 2
Fontanelle
IA
50010
Sales
CustID
InvoiceNo
InvoiceDate
TourID
18
23
7/1/98
Bung0998
18
(AutoNumber)
Record: 1 of 1
Record: 8 of 19
Form View
NUM

Access 97

Filtering Records within a Form

Filtering is another way to locate the records that match certain criteria, but filtering is more powerful than using the Find button. Filtering presents ALL of the records that meet the specified criteria instead of just the first or next record that meets the criteria. Michael wants to filter for all customers from Massachusetts because he knows that several new exciting tours will be offered in the New England area from the fall of 1998 through the winter of 1999.

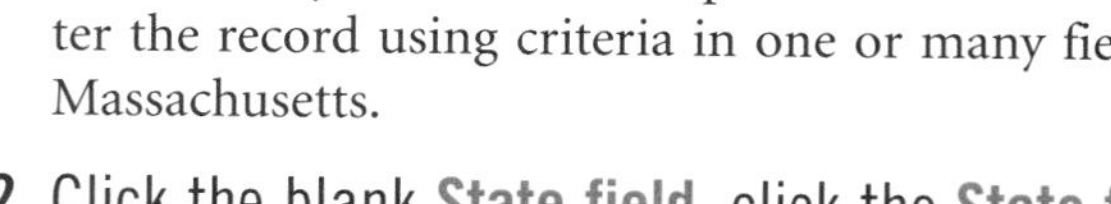

Steps

QuickTip

Click the Filter by Selection button to apply a filter that finds the records based on the information in the current field.

Trouble?

If this filter does not show four customers, return to the Filter by Form window to see if a criterion has been entered into the wrong field. Be sure to check each Or tab as well.

1. Click the **Filter By Form button** on the Form View toolbar
   The Filter by Form window opens as shown in Figure G-12. Filter by Form allows you to filter the record using criteria in one or many fields. Filter for all the customers who live in Massachusetts.
2. Click the blank **State field**, click the **State field list arrow**, click **MA**, then click the **Apply Filter button** on the Filter/Sort toolbar
   The navigation buttons indicate that five customers match this filter criterion. The next question is to find all customers over 30 years of age that live in Massachusetts or Connecticut.
3. Click on the Form View toolbar, click the **Birth Date field**, then type **<1/1/67**
   This entry will find all Massachusetts customers who turned 30 before 1/1/97. To find the customers who live in Connecticut, you must enter this "OR" criterion on another part of the filter screen.
4. Click the **Or tab** for the Customer Form, click in the **Birth Date field**, type **<1/1/67**, click the **State field list arrow**, click **CT**, then click on the Filter/Sort toolbar
   This filter found four customers as shown in Figure G-13. Print the results of this filter to be able to use this information at a later time.
5. Click the **Print Preview button** on the Form View toolbar, then click the **Next page button**
   You view the four forms on the screen, and they look just fine.
6. Click the **Print button** to print the records
   Now, close the Print Preview window and remove the filter.
7. Click **Close** on the Print Preview toolbar to return to the Customer Form, then click the **Remove Filter button** on the Form View toolbar
   Now you can save then close the form.
8. Click the **Save button** on the toolbar, then click the **Customer Form Close button**

FIGURE G-12: Filter by Form

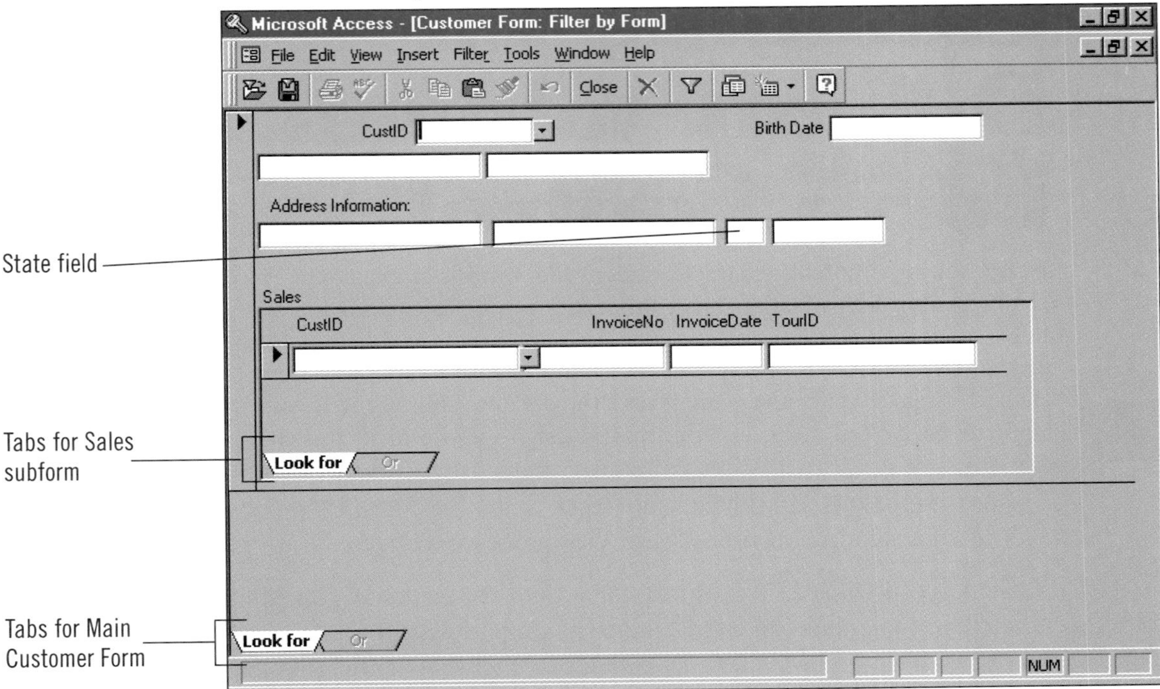

FIGURE G-13: Filtered Customer Form

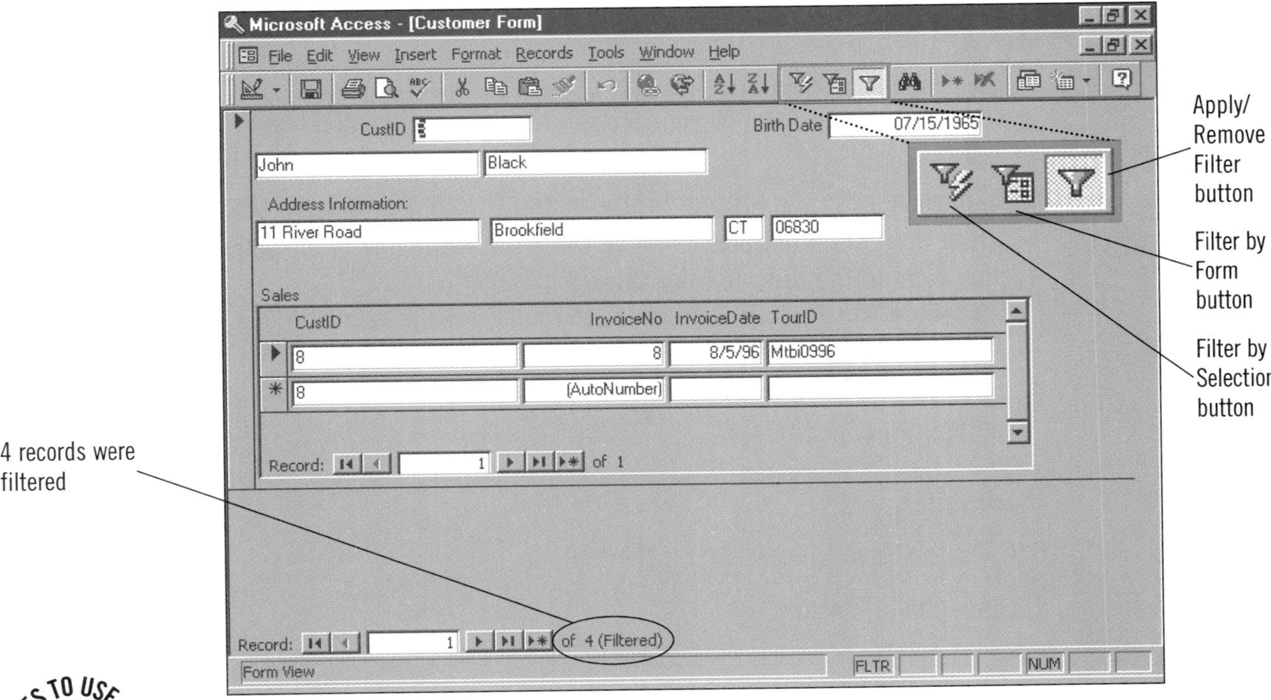

CLUES TO USE

Filtering with complex criteria expressions

When criteria are entered in more than one field of the Filter by Form window, both criteria must be true for the record to be displayed. These are called AND criteria. To enter OR criteria, in which only one or another set of criteria must be true for a record to be displayed, use the Or tab at the bottom of the Filter by Form window. You can use wildcard characters such as the asterisk * for multiple characters and the question mark ? for single characters with either AND or OR criteria. These criteria evaluation rules are exactly the same as those used to evaluate criteria in the Query design grid.

Access 97

Changing the Default Value of a Form Control

Properties are simply the characteristics of the controls on the Form. You change the properties of a control in Form Design View. Properties can be as basic as the control's color, text alignment, or default value, or as complex as branching to a different form when the control is clicked. The control's property sheet is a comprehensive list of the control's properties. Michael wants to make the current date the default value of the InvoiceDate field on the Sales subform. He'll open the Sales Subform in Design View to make this change.

Steps

1. Click the **Forms tab** if necessary, click **Sales Subform**, then click **Design**
   The Sales Subform opens in Design View as shown in Figure G-14.
2. Click the **InvoiceDate text box**, click the **Properties button** on the Form Design toolbar, then click the **Data tab** on the property sheet
   The Data tab of the InvoiceDate properties sheet shows properties that have to do with the source, validation, and default value of the data that can be entered in the InvoiceDate text box. Change the default value of this text box to display today's date. This will eliminate extra data entry on the Customer Form.
3. Click in the **Default Value text box**, then click the **Expression Builder button** ...
   The Expression Builder dialog box opens as shown in Figure G-15. Use the Expression Builder dialog box to guide your actions to build an expression that results in a single value. In this case, the expression is a single function, =Date(), that returns today's date.
4. Double-click the **Functions folder** in the first list box, click the **Built-In Functions folder** in the first list box, click the **Date/Time** category in the second list box, double-click **Date** in the third list box, then click **OK**
   The =Date() expression is added as the value for the Default Value property. To see the change on the Sales Subform, open the Sales Subform in Form View.
5. Click the **Form View button**, then press **[Ctrl][End]** to move to the last field of the last record
   The default InvoiceDate is today's date confirming that the changes to the form were successful.
6. Click the **Save button** on the toolbar
7. Close the subform

CLUES TO USE

Inherited properties

If you change a control's property setting on a form, the change doesn't affect the underlying query or table. Likewise, if you change the property setting for a field in a table or query after you've created a form that uses the field, the property setting for the control on the form isn't updated; you must do this manually. There are exceptions to the last rule, however. If you change the Default Value, Validation Rule, or Validation Text properties in a table's Design View, these changes will be enforced in any controls based on these fields later.

FIGURE G-14: **Sales subform in Form Design View**

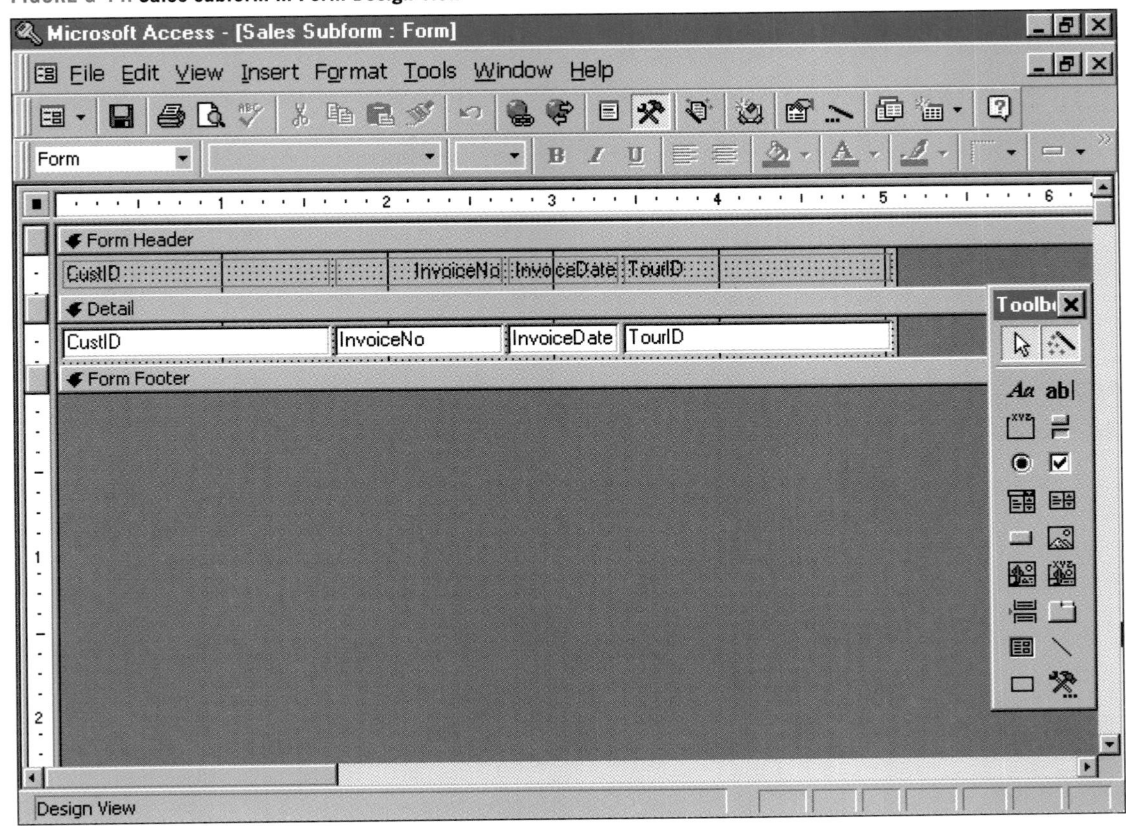

FIGURE G-15: **Expression Builder dialog box**

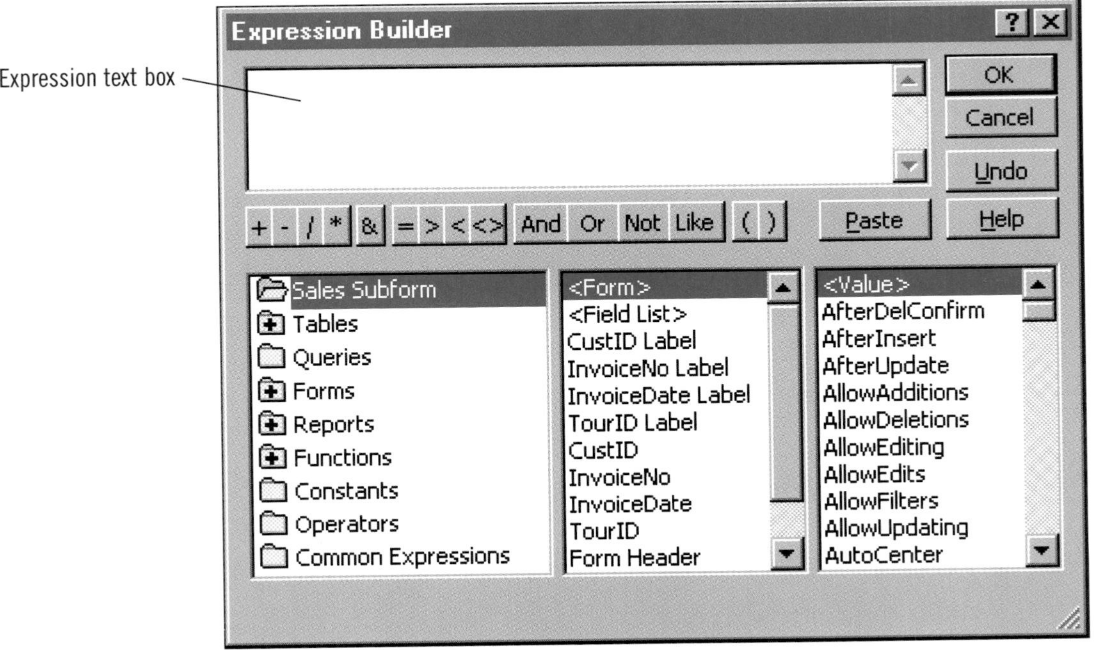

Access 97

Adding List Boxes

By default, fields are added to a form as bound text boxes, but sometimes other controls such as list boxes, combo boxes, or options buttons would handle the data entry process easier or faster for a particular field. Both the **list box** and **combo box** controls provide a list of values from which the user can choose an entry. A combo box also allows the user to make an entry from the keyboard, so it is really a list box plus a text box combined. 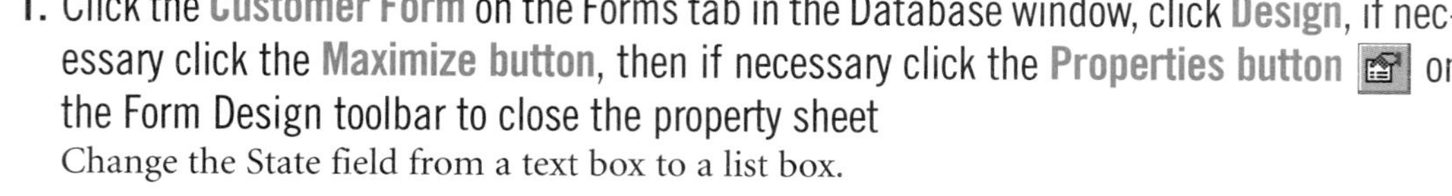 Michael realizes that it would be easier to choose an appropriate entry from the State field from a list. He has added a States table to the database. The States table has two fields: the two-letter state abbreviation and state description. He also developed a query that sorts the states alphabetically called "States sorted ascending." Michael will change the State field on the Customer Form to a list box bound to the state query.

QuickTip

Double-click a control to access its property sheet.

Trouble?

Be sure to change the Row Source property instead of the Control Source property. The Control Source property controls what underlying field in a table or query is updated. The Row Source property controls what items are displayed in the list box.

Trouble?

If the text box is not wide enough, click the Design View button and resize the control.

1. Click the **Customer Form** on the Forms tab in the Database window, click **Design**, if necessary click the **Maximize button**, then if necessary click the **Properties button** on the Form Design toolbar to close the property sheet
   Change the State field from a text box to a list box.
2. Right-click the **State field text box**, point to **Change To**, then click **List Box**
   When you create a list box that looks up values, you need to decide where the data for the list will come from. Change the Row Source property for the list box to handle this requirement.
3. Click the **Properties button** on the Form Design toolbar, click the **Data tab** if necessary, click the **Row Source text box**, click the **list arrow**, then choose **States sorted ascending** as shown in Figure G-16
   List boxes need more width to display the information than text boxes. Therefore move the Zip text box to the right, and resize the new State list box.
4. Click the **Properties button** to close the property sheet, click the **Zip text box field**, move the mouse pointer to the top edge of the Zip field until it changes to, then drag the field to the right side so that the left edge of the field rests at the **4" mark** on the ruler
   With the Zip field moved to the right, you have room to make the State list box wider and shorter so that it doesn't overlap with the Sales Subform control.
5. Click the **State list box**, position the mouse pointer on the lower-right corner resize handle until it changes to ↗, then drag the **list box control** up and right so that the list box control fills the area above the Sales Subform and to the left of the Zip text box as shown in Figure G-17
   View the changed Customer Form.
6. Click the **Form View button** on the toolbar
   The final Customer Form is shown in Figure G-18. The first customer lives in Salem, MA. To change the state data for any record, you can simply scroll to the appropriate entry in the list box and click the state abbreviation desired. Done for the day, save then close the Customer Form, then exit Access.
7. Click the **Save button**, click the Customer Form **Close button**, then click the **Access Close button**

FIGURE G-16: **Property sheet for State list box**

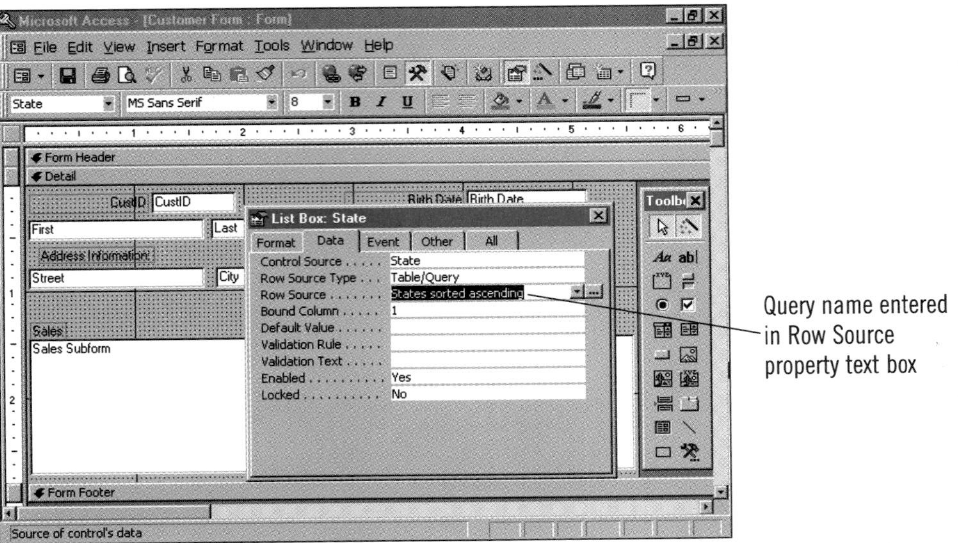

FIGURE G-17: **Resized State list box**

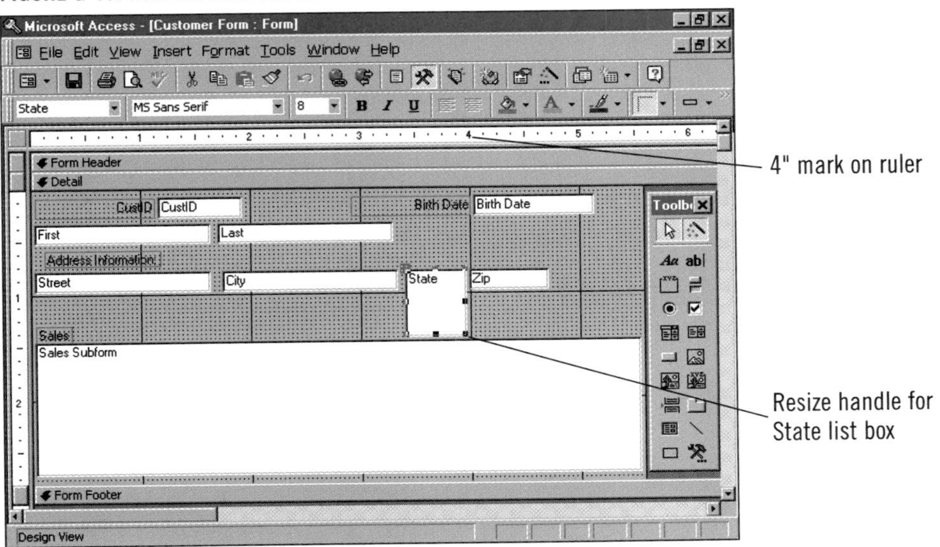

FIGURE G-18: **Customer Form with State list box**

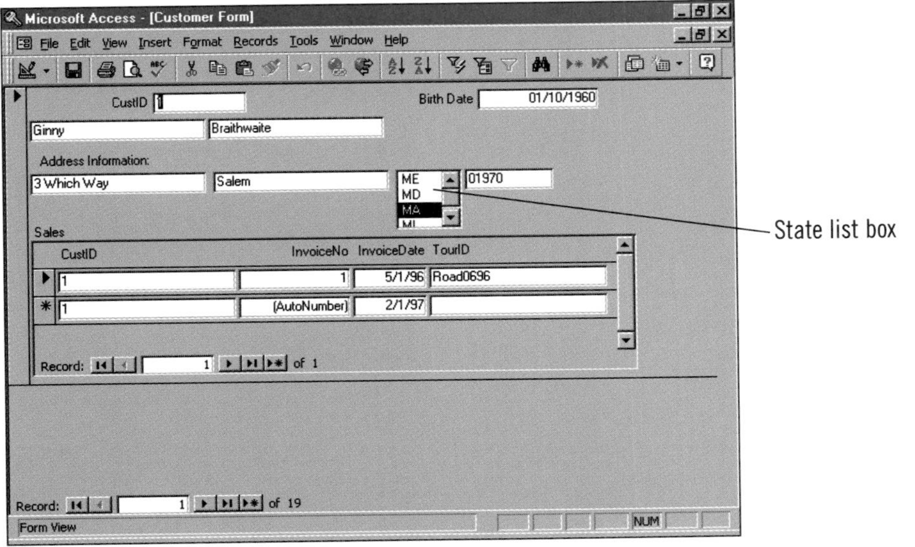

Access 97

Practice

► Concepts Review

Identify each element of a form's Design View shown in Figure G-19.

FIGURE G-19

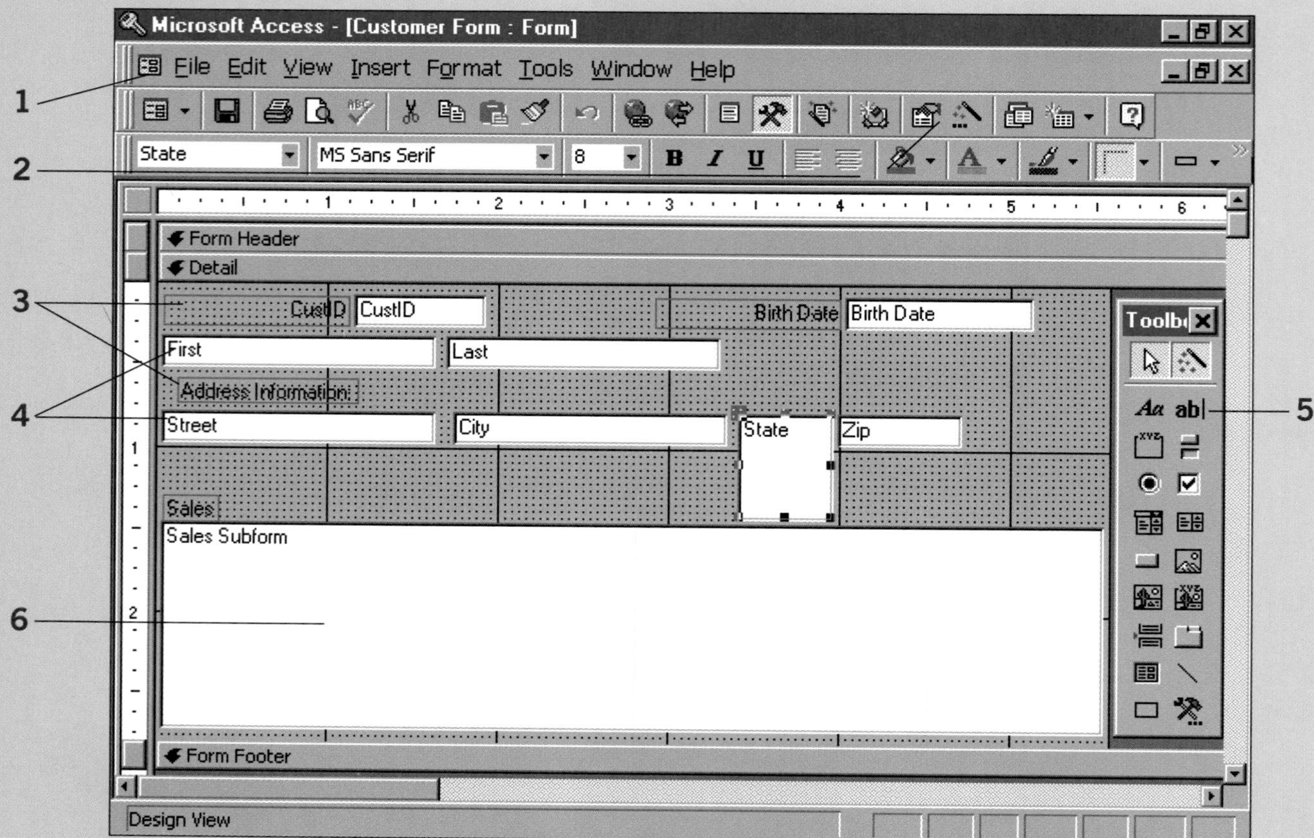

Match each term with the statement that describes its function.

7. Elements you add to a form such as labels, text boxes, and list boxes
8. An Access object that allows you to present the fields of one record in almost any screen arrangement you desire
9. The ability to locate specific subsets of records
10. Form elements that are linked to data in underlying tables and therefore change when the form switches from record to record
11. An element on a form that is not linked to the data of any table or query

a. Bound control
b. Controls
c. Filter
d. Form
e. Unbound control

Select the best answer from the list of choices.

12. To select records based on criteria, you should use which feature?
- **a.** Filter
- **b.** Find
- **c.** Form Wizard
- **d.** Sort

13. Which of the following is the most common type of bound control?
- **a.** Option group
- **b.** List box
- **c.** Text box
- **d.** Label

14. Which of the following is the most common type of unbound control?
- **a.** Check box
- **b.** Field label
- **c.** List box
- **d.** Combo box

15. To quickly access a new blank record to enter new data, use which buttons?
- **a.** Toolbox
- **b.** Form Design View toolbar
- **c.** Record Navigation
- **d.** Formatting toolbar

16. To view multiple linked records of one table simultaneously with a single record of another table in a form use a:
- **a.** Subform
- **b.** List box
- **c.** Design template
- **d.** Link control

► Skills Review

1. **Create a form from multiple tables.**
   - **a.** Start Access and open the database Addresses-G.
   - **b.** Create a new form using the Form Wizard.
   - **c.** Add all the fields from both the Names and the Zips tables. By choosing all of the fields from both tables, you'll be adding the linking Zip field from both tables. When the Form Wizard is complete, you'll notice the Zip field from the Zips table in the main form and the Zip field in the Names table in the subform.
   - **d.** View the data with the Form with subform option by Zips.
   - **e.** Choose a Tabular layout and a Colorful 1 style.
   - **f.** Title the Form "Names within Zips" and the subform "Names Subform".
   - **g.** View the form, then close the form.

2. **Move and resize controls.**
   - **a.** Open the Names Subform in Design View.
   - **b.** In the Detail section, select the first four field text boxes: First, Last, Street, and Zip and narrow them to about half of their current width. Repeat this process in the Form Header section for the first four labels: First, Last, Street, and Zip.
   - **c.** In the Detail section, individually move the Last, Street, Zip, and Birthday text boxes left. All of the five text box controls in the Detail section should fit between the 0" and 5" marks on the ruler. Repeat this process in the Form Header section for the labels.
   - **d.** Save and close the Names Subform.
   - **e.** Open the Names within Zips form to view the changes to the Names Subform within the main form. You should be able to see all five fields of the subform clearly.

3. **Add labels and formatting controls.**
   - **a.** Open the Names within Zips form in Design View.
   - **b.** Add a label in the upper-right corner of the form with the text, "This form is used to enter new zip codes and contact information."
   - **c.** Select all of the labels (Zip, City, and State) on the form, and right align the text within the control by changing the Text Align property to Right in the property sheet.
   - **d.** Close the property sheet.
   - **e.** View the form.

4. **Sort records within a form.**
   - **a.** Open the Names within Zips form in Form View.
   - **b.** Sort the records in ascending order by City. Print the first record using the Selected Records option on the Print dialog box. Click File on the menu bar, click Print to open the Print dialog box, click Selected Records, then click OK.
   - **c.** Sort the records in ascending order by State. Print the first record.
   - **d.** Using the Advanced Filter/Sort option from the Filter option of the Records menu, further refine the sort to first sort ascending by State and then ascending by Zip. Print the first two records.

5. Find records within a form.
   a. Click the State text box then click the Find button on the toolbar.
   b. Enter MO in the Find What text box, then click Find First to find the first record with the State equal to MO.
   c. Print the record.
   d. Close the Find dialog box.

6. Filter records within a form.
   a. Use the Filter by Form button to filter for records where the Zip equals 50837. Apply the filter.
   b. Print the record.
   c. Use the Filter by Form button to filter for all contacts where the birth dates are before 1/1/55 (less than 1/1/55).
   d. Print the first record.

7. Change the default value of a form control.
   a. Open the Names within Zips form in Design View.
   b. Open the property sheet for the State text box and change the Default Value property to IA.
   c. Open the Names within Zips form in Form View, click the New Record button to move to a blank record at the end of the datasheet, enter 50846 in the Zip text box, then enter Fontanelle in the City text box.
   d. Print the record. It should show the default IA entry in the State field even though you didn't directly enter this data on the form.

8. Add list boxes.
   a. Open the Names within Zips form in Design View.
   b. Right-click the State text box, then click Change to change the State text box to a list box.
   c. Change the Row Source property of the State list box to the States table. (The States table was added to the Addresses-G database for this exercise.)
   d. Widen and shorten the State list box so that you can clearly see the entries in Form View and so that the list box doesn't overlap the Names subform.
   e. Save the changes to the form.
   f. Print the first record.
   g. Close the database and exit Access.

► Independent Challenges

1. As the president of a civic organization, you have developed a database that tracks donations of recyclable material called Cleanup-G. Now that several deposits have been made and recorded, you wish to develop a form to record the deposits.

To complete this independent challenge:

1. Start Access and open the database Cleanup-G.
2. Using the Form Wizard, create a form/subform based on the Deposits By Club query.
3. Use all four fields in the form, and view the form by Clubs.
4. Use a datasheet layout, and a Colorful2 style.
5. Name the form "Deposits By Clubs Form" and the subform "Deposits Subform".
6. Filter the form so that only those deposits of 50 pounds or greater are displayed.
7. Sort the resulting records in descending order on club name and print the first record.
8. Close the database and exit Access.

2. Now that you've developed a relational database that documents the books you've read called Readings-G, you'd like to develop a form to quickly enter new records.

To complete this independent challenge:

1. Start Access and open the database Readings-G.
2. Using the Form Wizard, create a form/subform using all the fields of both the Books and Authors tables.
3. View the data by Authors.
4. Use a datasheet layout, and an Evergreen style.
5. Name the form "Books within Authors" and the subform "Books Subform".
6. Open the Books Subform in Design View, then narrow the Category and Author Number text boxes in the Detail section and the Category and Author Number labels in the Form Header section to about half of their current size.
7. Move the text boxes in the Detail section and the labels in the Form Header section so that they all fit within the first five inches of the form.
8. Save and close the subform.
9. Return to the Books within Authors form and filter the form so that only Non-Fiction books are displayed.
10. Print the first record.
11. Close and save the form.
12. Close the database and exit Access.

3. You have recently helped the medical director of a large internal medical clinic put together and update a database called Doctors-G that tracks extra-curricular activities. You wish to develop a form to use as a data entry mechanism for the database.

To complete this independent challenge:

1. Start Access and open the database Doctors-G.
2. Using the Form Wizard, create a form/subform using all the fields from the Physicians and Activities tables, and only the Program Name field from the Programs table.
3. View the data by Physicians.
4. Use a datasheet layout, and a Stones style.
5. Name the form "Activities by Physician" and the subform "Activities Subform".
6. Open the Activities Subform in Design View, then delete the Physician Number and Program Number text boxes in the Detail section. Also, delete the Physician Number and Program Number labels in the Form Header section.
7. Move the Name label and Name text box next to the Hours label and text box so that all of the remaining controls in the Activities Subform fit within the first three inches of the form.
8. Save and close the subform.
9. Return to the Activities by Physician form and sort it in ascending order by First Name within Last Name.
10. Print the first record.
11. Close and save the form, then close the database and exit Access.

4. Your dance club is making a trip to the famous Alberto's Nightclub, and has asked you to develop a small Access database to track the special events that Alberto's Nightclub offers. You've called the database Alberto-G. Now you'll go to the Alberto's Nightclub web site to find out what events are offered for this week and will add the information into the database using a form you've already developed. Then you will sort, filter, and query the information for various requests from dance club members.

To complete this independent challenge:

1. Log on to the Internet and use your browser to go to http://www.course.com. From there, click Student Online Companions, click the link for this text, then click the Access link for Unit G.
2. Use the Alberto's Nightclub site to find out what events are being offered for the week, and print the web page.
3. Start Access, then open the Alberto-G database.
4. Enter the week's event information into the Days of the Week form. The Days of the Week form is a form that contains a subform of events linked to the main form by the day of the week. The first event for Monday has already been entered. Leave this event in the database as an example of how to enter the event information and simply add the rest of the current week's events that you found on the web site.
5. Print the Monday record from the Days of the Week form.
6. Sort the records alphabetically on the Theme field and print the first record.
7. Filter the records so that only the Salsa themes are showing. Print the Salsa records.
8. Find the records who have a teacher named "DJ Polo." Print the DJ Polo records.
9. Create a query that sorts the Theme Name field in the Themes table in an ascending order and call it "Sorted Themes".
10. Delete the Theme text box in the Days of the Week form. Add the Theme field back to the form as a list box that uses the Sorted Themes query as the source of the information.
11. Resize the Theme list box so that it doesn't overlap with the Events Subform.
12. Close and save the form.
13. Close the database and exit Access.

Visual Workshop

Open the VW-G database and create a new form/subform as shown in Figure G-20. Use all of the fields in both the Alumni and Donations tables. Notice that the labels in the main form have been right aligned.

FIGURE G-20

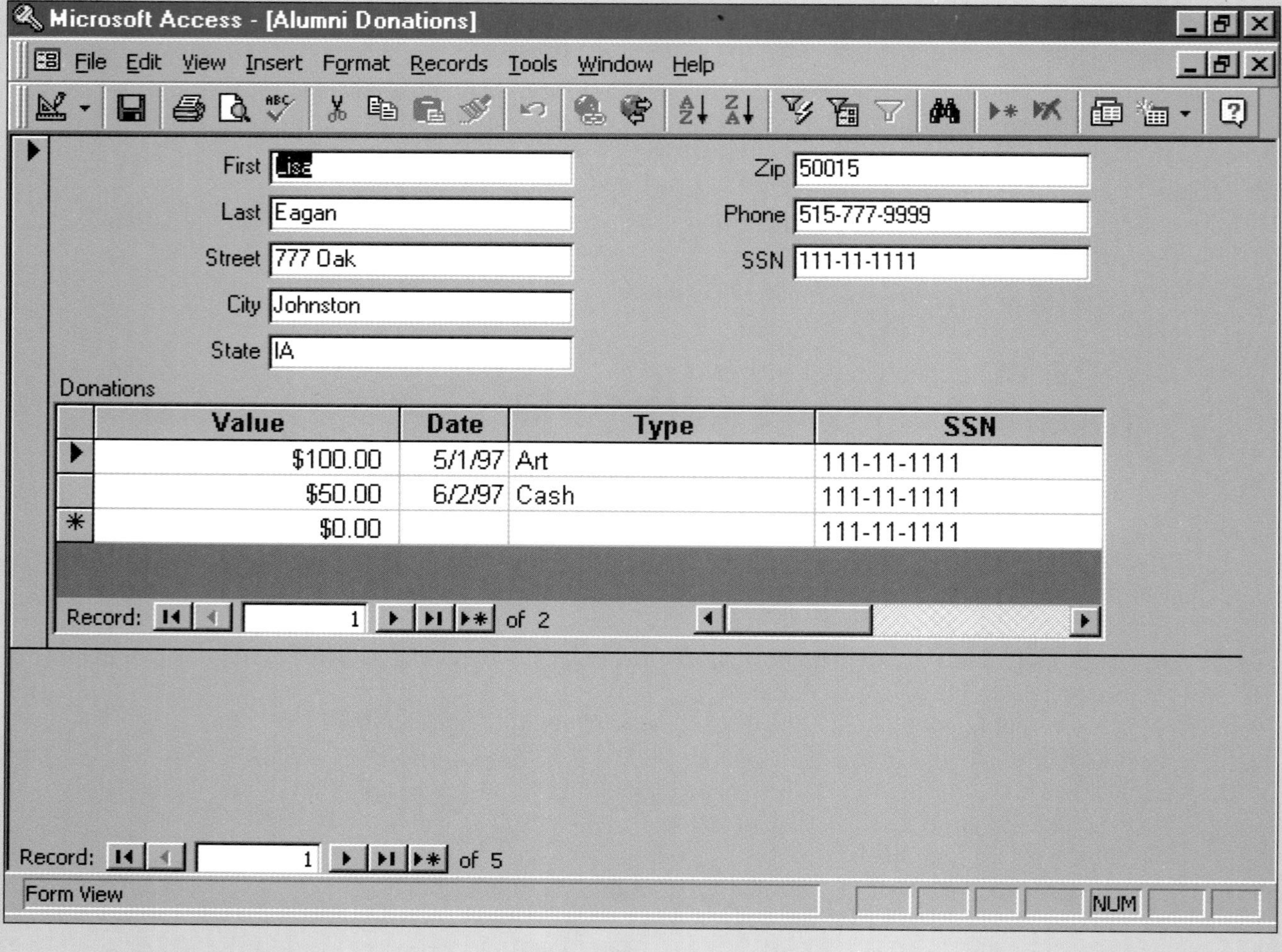

Microsoft Access - [Alumni Donations]

File Edit View Insert Format Records Tools Window Help

First	Lisa
Last	Eagan
Street	777 Oak
City	Johnston
State	IA
Zip	50015
Phone	515-777-9999
SSN	111-11-1111

Donations

	Value	Date	Type	SSN
▶	$100.00	5/1/97	Art	111-11-1111
	$50.00	6/2/97	Cash	111-11-1111
*	$0.00			111-11-1111

Record: 1 of 2

Record: 1 of 5

Form View NUM

Creating
Complex Reports

Objectives

- ► Create a report from a query
- ► Use report sections
- ► Use group headers
- ► Add calculations to group footers
- ► Modify control alignment
- ► Add graphics to reports
- ► Use color
- ► Add special effects

Although you can print data in forms and datasheets, **reports** give you more control over how data is displayed and greater flexibility in presenting summary information such as subtotals on groups of records. Reports are often used to distribute information in formal presentations or meetings. Since a report definition (the report object) can be saved, it can be developed once but used many times to produce a paper report. Printed reports always reflect the most up-to-date data in a consistent format each time they are printed. As with form designs, report designs allow you to add bound controls such as text boxes and unbound controls such as lines, graphics, or labels. Michael's datasheet and form printouts have been very valuable; however, he wants to create more professional documents that include subtotals on groups of records to share with potential investors. In addition, he wants the reports to contain clip art images, various colors, and advanced formatting enhancements.

Access 97

Creating a Report from a Query

The **Report Wizard** provides an interactive way to select fields from multiple tables or queries for a report. It also asks questions regarding how you want the records of the report to be grouped and formatted. **Grouping** provides a way to sort records so that summary statistics can be applied to a group of records that meet certain criteria. Grouping is not allowed within a form object. Another way to differentiate between a form and report object is to think about the primary purpose of the object. Forms are used for effective data entry. Reports provide effective printed output. A potential investor has asked for a report showing sales and profit information for each tour. Michael will use the Report Wizard to create the report.

Steps

1. Start Access and open the **Nomad-H** database, click the **Reports tab** in the Nomad-H : Database window, then click **New**
   The options in the New Report dialog box are very similar to those used to develop a form. Design View allows you to manually add controls to the report. AutoReport creates reports based on the chosen object with predefined settings.
2. Click **Report Wizard** in the New Report dialog box, then click **OK**
3. Click the **Tables/Queries: list arrow**, then click **Query: Profits**
   The Profits query has the four fields needed for this report as shown in Figure H-1.
4. Click the **Select all fields button** [>>], then click [Next >]
   The next wizard dialog box determines how the records are displayed.
5. Click **by Tours**, then click [Next >]
   Since the records are already grouped by individual tour, you don't need to establish further grouping levels.
6. Click [Next >]
   The next wizard dialog box determines how the records within the detail section of the report are sorted. Choose to sort the invoices in ascending order.
7. Click the **first list arrow**, click **InvoiceNo**, then click [Next >]
   Finally, choose the layout, orientation, style, and title for the report.
8. Click the **Block Layout option button**, verify that the **Portrait Orientation option button** is selected, click [Next >], click the **Corporate** style, click [Next >], type **Profit by Tour Report** as the report title, click [Finish], then **Maximize** the report window
   Print Preview of the Profit by Tour Report is shown in Figure H-2. Print Preview won't allow you to make any changes to the report, but does allow you to see exactly how your report will print. Refer to Table H-1 for more information on the buttons on the Print Preview toolbar.

QuickTip

If you can't see the entire report, scroll to see all the records and fields. Click on the report to reduce the printout to show an entire printed page on the screen. To magnify a portion of the report on the screen, click on the part of the report you wish to magnify.

FIGURE H-1: **Report Wizard**

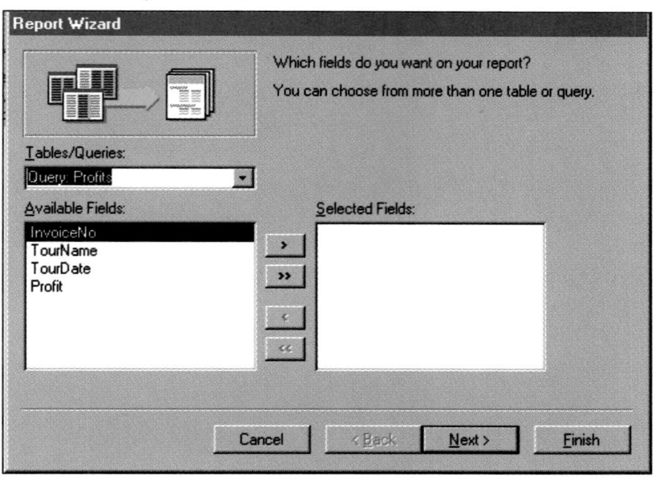

FIGURE H-2: **Print Preview**

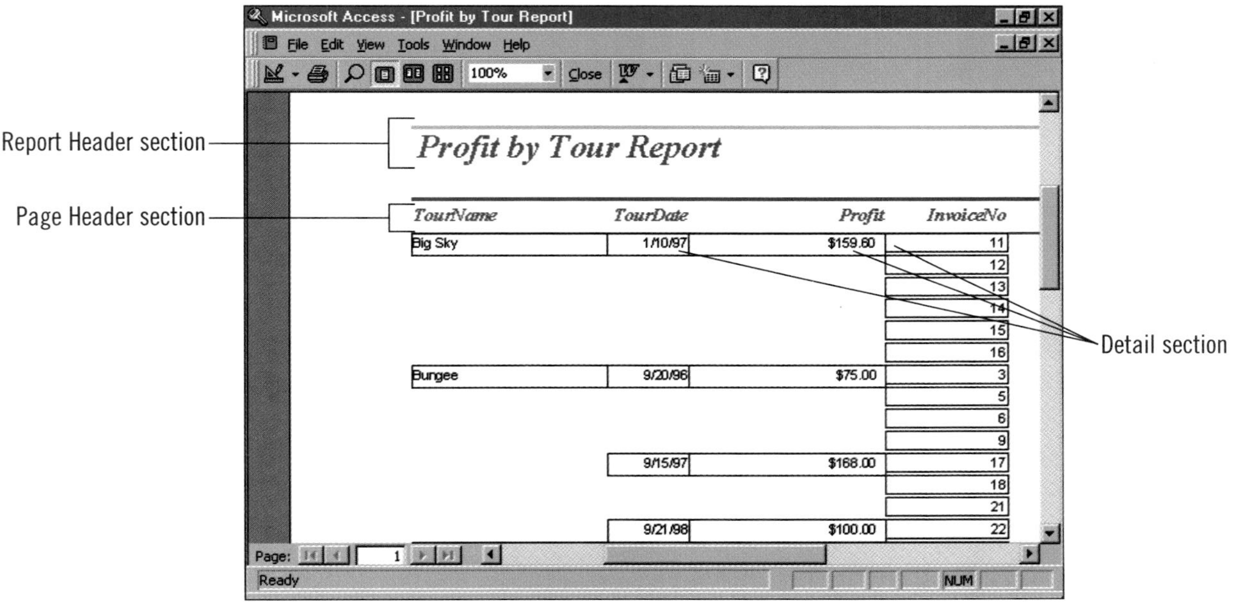

TABLE H-1: **Buttons on the Print Preview toolbar**

name	button	description
Print		Send a copy of the report to the default printer
Zoom		Toggles the print preview screen between 100% zoom and fit one page zoom
One page		Adjusts the zoom (magnification) level to fit one page of the report on the screen
Two pages		Adjusts the zoom level to fit two pages of the report on the screen
Multiple Pages		Displays multiple full pages in a matrix (2 rows by 3 columns, for example)
Zoom control	Fit	Adjusts the zoom level by clicking the list arrow and choosing the desired percentage
Close window	Close	Closes the print preview screen and displays the report's Design View
OfficeLinks		Sends the report to Word or Excel by clicking the list arrow and clicking Word or Excel
Database Window		Displays the database window which lists all objects in the database
New Object		Creates a new database object
Office Assistant		Provides Help topics or tips to help you complete a task

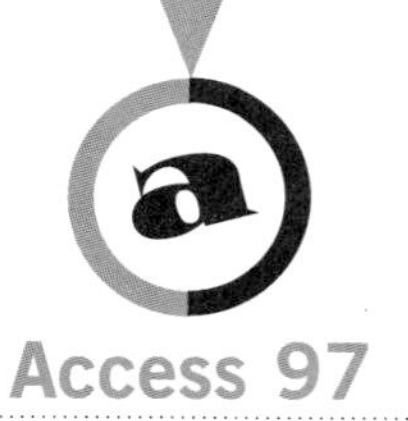

Using Report Sections

Just as Form Design View is used to modify forms, Report Design View is used to modify reports. Report Design View consists of **sections** (designated areas of the report design) in which controls and formatting specifications are placed. Because reports allow more sophisticated analysis of groups of records, the sections become very important design elements. See Table H-2 for a description of the different sections of a report. Michael wants to add the company name, "Nomad Ltd," to the top of the first page of the report. He'll switch to Report Design View to add the label to the appropriate section of the report's Design View.

Steps

1. Click the **Design View button** on the Print Preview toolbar to close the Print Preview window
   The Profit by Tour Report Design View is shown in Figure H-3. Each report consists of several sections that determine how the final report will print. Because the underlying records are grouped by TourName, this report also contains a group header section.
2. Click the **Label tool** on the Toolbox, click in the **Report Header section** at the 4" mark on the ruler, then type **Nomad Ltd**
   The label you add to the Report Header section will print only at the top of the first page of the report. Next, expand the Report Footer section.
3. Position the mouse pointer at the **bottom of the Report Footer section bar**, then drag the **resize pointer** as shown in Figure H-4 down 1/2 inch
   Add a descriptive label to the Report Footer section that identifies the author of the report. Since the label is in the Report Footer section, it will print once at the end of the last page of the report.
4. Click the **Label tool** on the Toolbox, click in the **Report Footer section** at the 1" mark on the ruler, then type **Report Created by Michael Belmont**
   To see the work you have done, view the report.
5. Click the **Print Preview button** on the Report Design toolbar, scroll to observe the new labels, then click the **One Page button** on the Print Preview toolbar
   The entire page of the report is now in the Print Preview window as shown in Figure H-5. Close the Print Preview window.
6. Click to return to Design View
7. Click the **Save button** on the toolbar to save the report

Trouble?

If the Toolbox isn't displayed, click the Toolbox button to display it.

TABLE H-2: Report sections

section	description
Report header	Appears only at the top of the first page of the report and usually contains the report name or company logo
Page header	Appears at the top of every page (but below the report header on the first page) and usually contains field labels
Group header	Appears at the beginning of a group of records ("Group" is replaced by the field name)
Detail	Appears once for every record in the underlying datasheet and usually contains bound field text boxes
Group footer	Appears at the end of each group of records ("Group" is replaced by the field name)
Page footer	Appears at the bottom of each page and usually contains the current date and page number
Report footer	Appears at the end of the last page of the report, before the page footer

FIGURE H-3: **Report Design View**

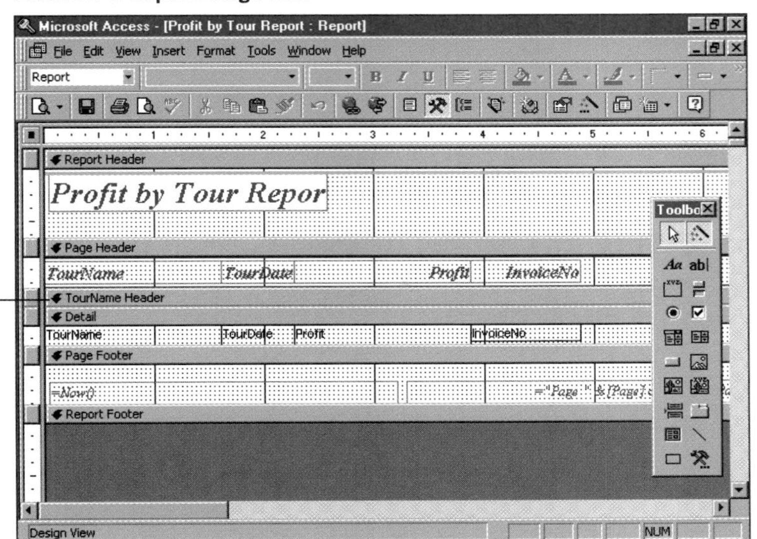

FIGURE H-4: **Resizing report sections**

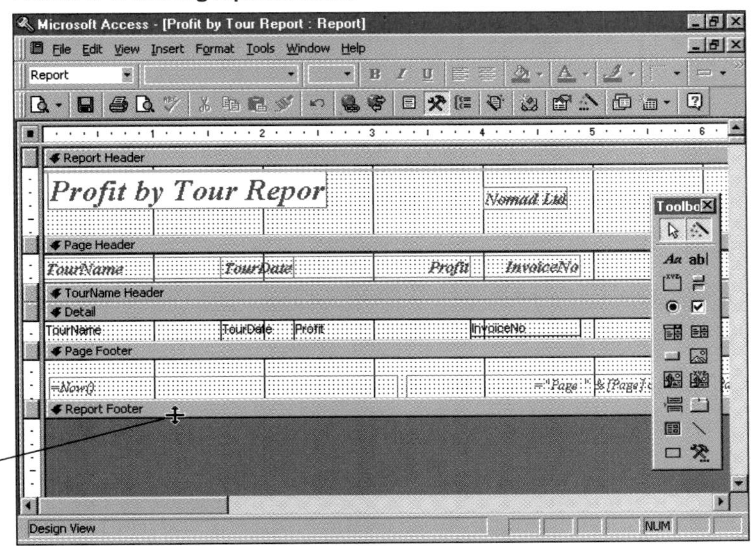

FIGURE H-5: **Print Preview at One Page Magnification**

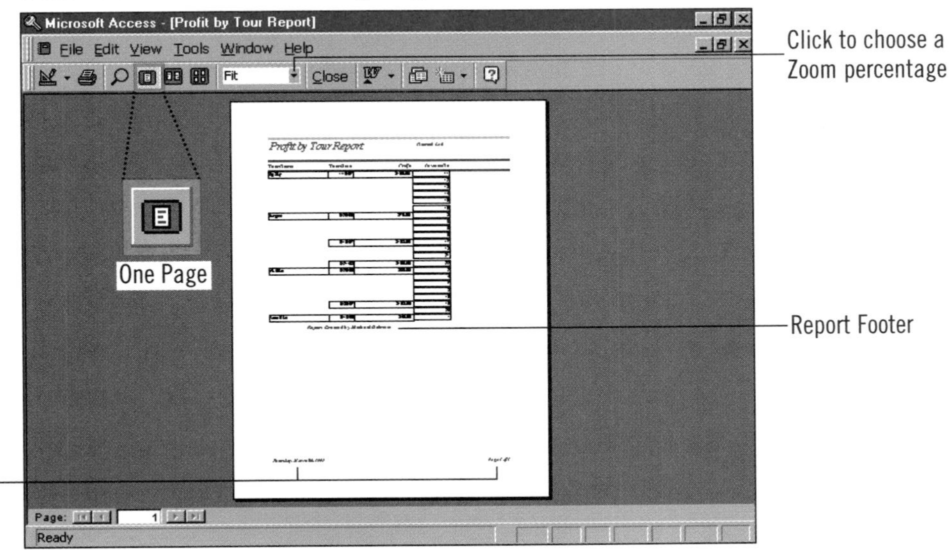

Using Group Headers

A **group header** appears on its own line on a report just before the Detail section of a new group of records. Use the group header to display information that applies to the group of records. For example, you can include a field text box control that displays the name of the field by which the records are grouped. After reviewing the Profit by Tour Report, Michael decides to expand the report to make it easier to read. Michael will move the TourName text box to the TourName group header section rather than have this print on the same line as the TourDate, Profit, and InvoiceNo fields in the Detail section. He will also reformat the TourName text box control to make each new tour group more prominent on the report.

Steps

1. Position the mouse pointer on the **section divider bar** between the TourName Header section and the Detail section, then drag down to the top of the Page Footer section
   Now that the TourName Header section is opened, you can move the TourName control from the Detail section to the TourName Header section.
2. Click the **TourName text box** in the Detail section, position the mouse pointer at the top edge of the control when it changes to , then drag the **TourName text box** straight up into the TourName Header section as shown in Figure H-6
   With the TourName text box still selected, you will reformat the control to enhance the TourName section and make the report easier to read.
3. Click the **Line/Border Color list arrow** on the Formatting (Form/Report) toolbar, click **Transparent**, click the **Font Size list arrow** on the Formatting (Form/Report) toolbar, then click **10**
   In addition to removing the border and increasing the font size, change the text color and attributes.
4. Click the **Font/Fore Color button** on the Formatting (Form/Report) toolbar, click the **Bold button**, then click the **Italic button**
   View the report to verify that you have increased the visibility of the TourName field by formatting it as red, bold, italic text in the TourName header section.
5. Click the **Print Preview button**
   Adjust the view to see the report in the window at 100% view.
6. Click the **Zoom list arrow** on the Print Preview toolbar, click **100% View**, then scroll to observe the new labels
   The final report is shown in Figure H-7. Notice that the TourDate and Profit text box controls don't appear for each record in the Detail section even though the controls appear in the Detail section. The Hide Duplicates property has been set to "Yes" for the TourDate and Profit text box controls in this report, and therefore this field prints only once for the group of records that have duplicate values in these fields.
7. Click **Close** on the Print Preview toolbar
8. Click the **Save button** on the toolbar to save the report

FIGURE H-6: Moving report controls

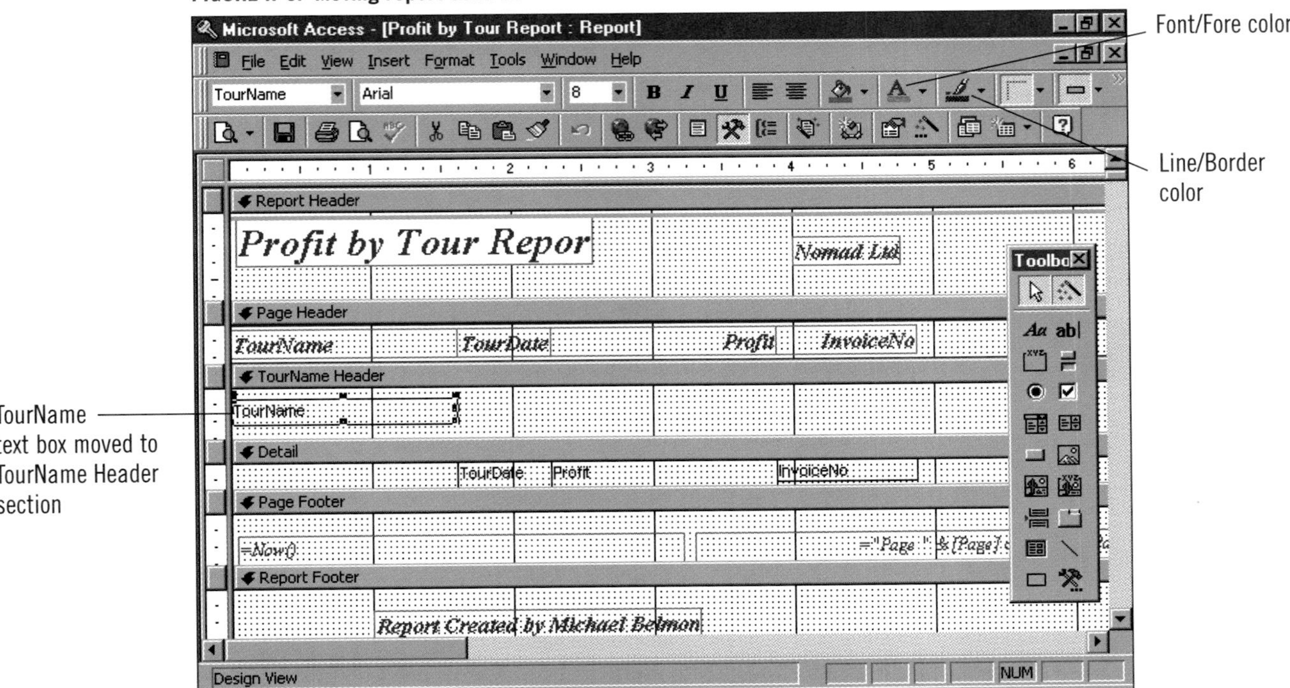

FIGURE H-7: Print Preview of a report with a group header section

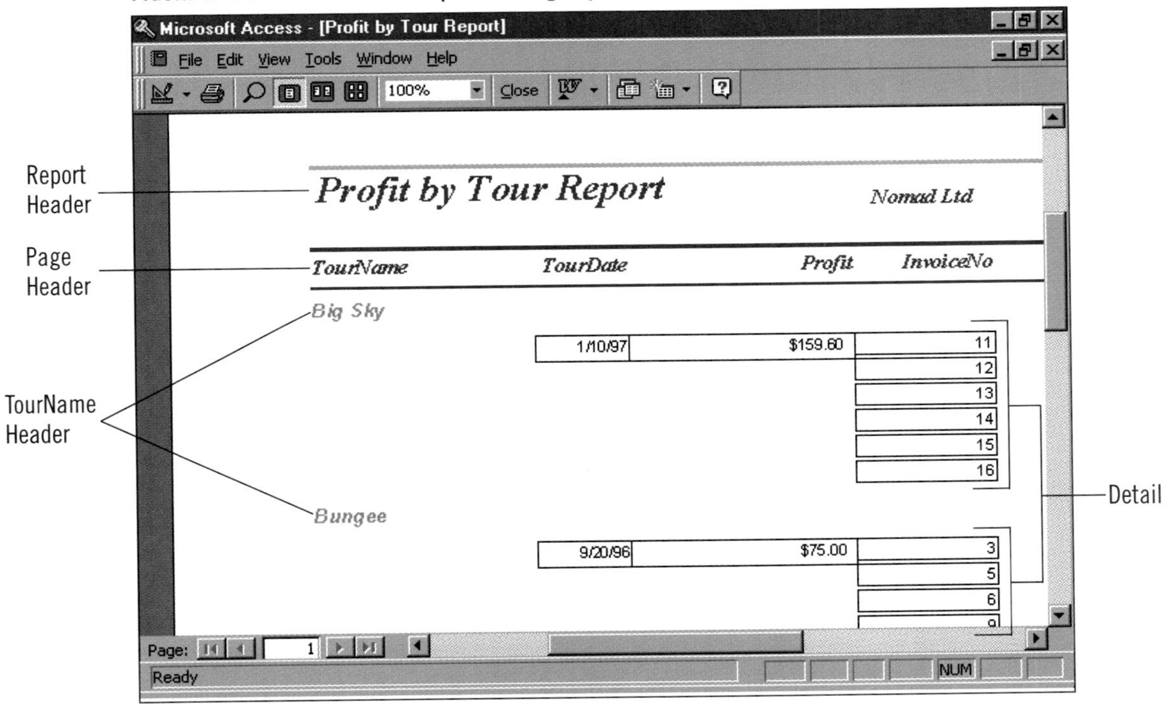

Hide Duplicates property

The Hide Duplicates property hides multiple occurrences of the same data for the fields in the Detail section of the report. To view or change the Hide Duplicates property, click the field in Report Design View, click the Properties button on the toolbar, then click the Format tab.

Adding Calculations to Group Footers

A **group footer** appears on its own line on a report just below the Detail section of a group of records. **Calculated expressions**, bound report controls that total groups of records, are often added to the group footer to total or count the records within the group. Michael decides to add a total profit figure and count the number of tours sold after each unique group of records. Michael will place these two calculated expressions in the TourDate group footer.

Steps

1. Click the **Sorting and Grouping button** on the Report Design toolbar, verify that the **TourName field** is selected, click the **Group Footer text box**, click the **Group Footer property list arrow**, then click **Yes**

   The Sorting and Grouping dialog box shown in Figure H-8 controls how the records are sorted as well as whether or not the group header and footer sections appear for each sort field. Now that a TourName Footer section has been opened on the report, you will add a text box to the section to hold the calculated expression that totals the profits.

Trouble?

Be sure to click the Text Box button, NOT the Label button to insert a text box.

2. Click to close the Sorting and Grouping dialog box, click the **Text Box button** on the Toolbox, then click in the **TourName Footer** section just below the Profit text box in the Detail section

   With the unbound text box in place, access the Control Source property for the new text box and enter the appropriate expression that will calculate the total profit.

3. Click the **Properties button** on the Report Design toolbar, verify that the **Data tab** is selected, click the **Control Source property text box**, then type **=Sum([Profit])**

   The expression is shown in Figure H-9. Next, close the property sheet and delete the unnecessary label control that was automatically added to the left of the text box control.

Trouble?

The label control on your screen may or may not be labeled Text 16. It won't affect your work if it is a different number.

4. Click to close the property sheet, click the new **label control**, then press **[Delete]**

   In addition to adding up the profits per tour, you can count the number of sales that contributed to that profit figure. Rather than type a new expression, copy the existing text box control in the TourName footer, paste it in the section, then edit the Control Source property so that it counts the InvoiceNo field rather than sums the Profit field.

5. Click the **=Sum([Profit]) text box**, right-click, click **Copy**, click at the 1" mark on the ruler in the TourName Footer, right-click, then click **Paste**

   Now that the text box with the calculated expression has been duplicated, edit the expression to count the number of invoices, and position the control under the InvoiceNo field.

QuickTip

Clicking inside a text box control and editing the expression accomplishes the same task as changing the expression in the Control Source property of the property sheet.

6. Click and drag to select **=Sum([Profit])** inside the **new control**, then type **=Count([InvoiceNo])**, click outside the control, click to select the **new control**, position the mouse pointer at the **top edge of the control** until it changes to, then drag the **=Count control** to the right of the =Sum control so that it is directly below the InvoiceNo field

   View the report to see the changes you made.

7. Click the **Print Preview button**, then scroll to view the total profit and number of invoices

   The updated report is shown in Figure H-10. Close the Print Preview window.

8. Click **Close** on the Print Preview toolbar

   Now you can save the report.

9. Click the **Save button** on the toolbar to save the report

FIGURE H-8: Sorting and Grouping dialog box

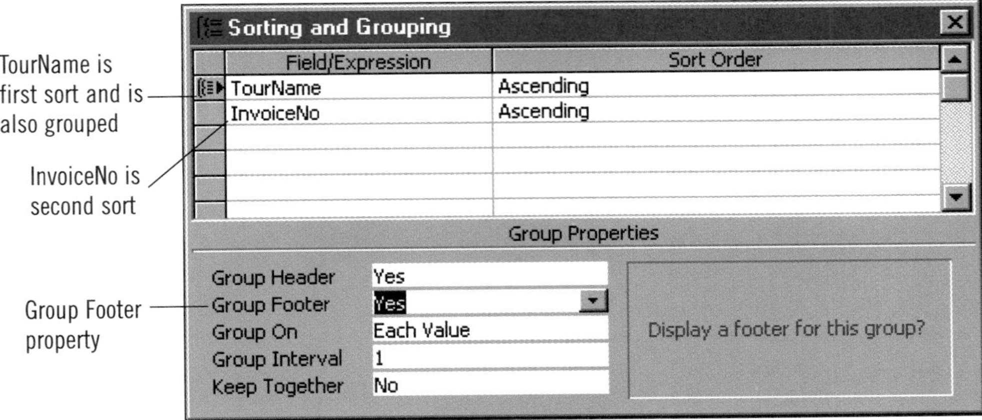

FIGURE H-9: Entering a calculated expression

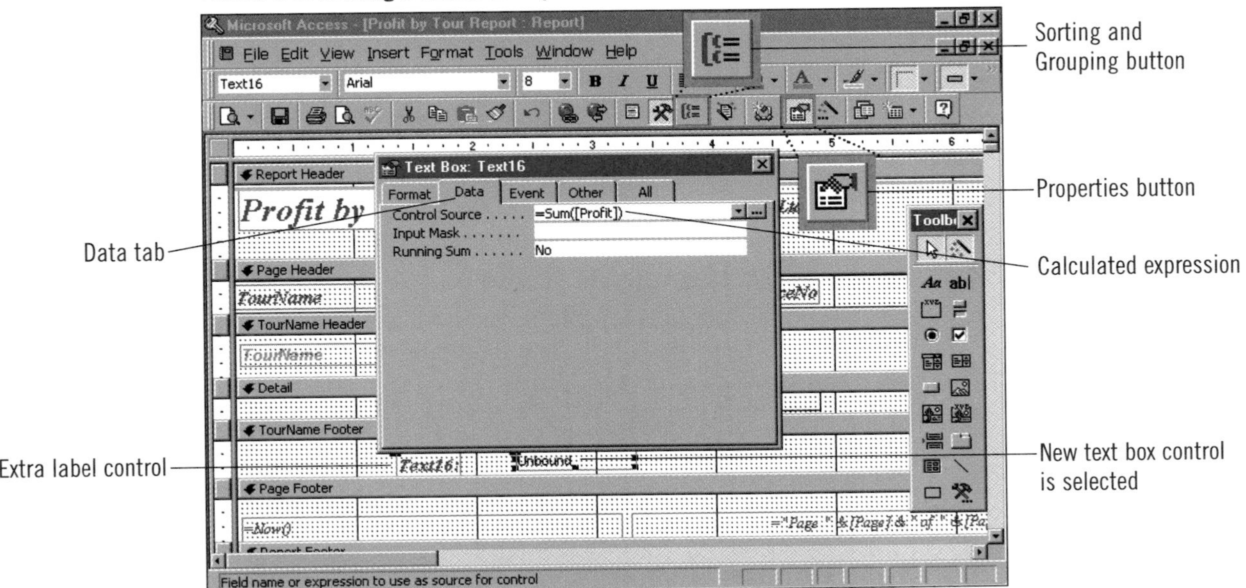

FIGURE H-10: Print Preview of a report with calculated expressions in the group footer

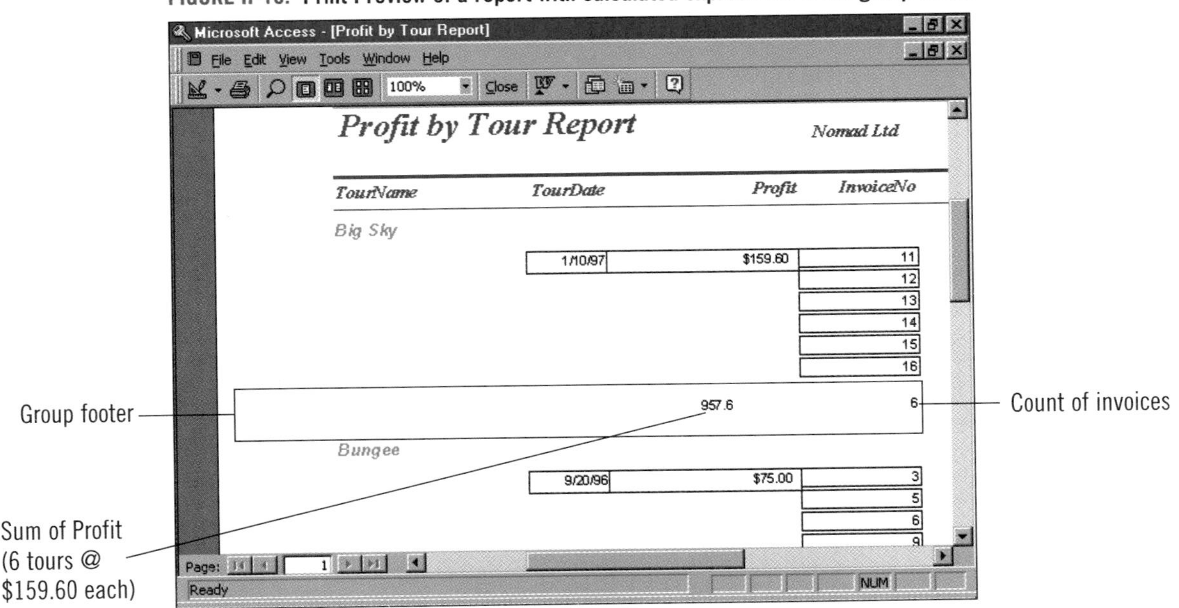

Access 97

Modifying Control Alignment

By default, the information displayed within a single numeric or currency field is right aligned and the information within a text field is left aligned. Another type of alignment involves aligning the edges of multiple controls with respect to each other. For example, the text boxes in the TourName Footer section would look better if they were precisely aligned underneath the information they summarize in the Detail section. See Table H-3 for more information on aligning controls with respect to each other. Michael wants to format and align the new text boxes in the TourName Footer section to make the report clearer. He aligns the new expressions under their respective columns and also modifies the summarized Profit text box to appear with a currency format.

Steps 1 2 3 4

1. Click the **InvoiceNo text box** in the Detail section, press and hold **[Shift]**, click the **=Count([InvoiceNo]) expression** in the TourName Footer section, release **[Shift]**, click **Format** on the menu bar, point to **Align**, then click **Right**
   Now that the InvoiceNo fields are right aligned with respect to each other, align the Profit fields.
2. Click the **Profit text box** in the Detail section, press and hold **[Shift]**, click the **=Sum([Profit]) expression** in the TourName Footer section, release **[Shift]**, click **Format** on the menu bar, point to **Align**, then click **Right**
   In addition to aligning the controls, format the =Sum([Profit]) expression as currency.
3. Click in the TourName Footer section to cancel the current selection, click the **=Sum([Profit]) expression**, click the **Properties button** on the Report Design toolbar, click the **Format tab**, click the **Format text box**, click the **Format property list arrow**, scroll and click **Currency**, then click the to close the property sheet
   Add a descriptive label in the TourName Footer section so that the reader can clearly understand that this part of the report shows summary statistics.
4. Click the **Label tool** on the Toolbox, click near the top at the left edge in the **TourName Footer section**, type **Summarized profit and count statistics:**, then click outside the control
   Your screen should look like Figure H-11. Finally, add a line below the calculated expressions to further differentiate between the groups of records.
5. Click the **Line tool** in the Toolbox, click below the new label in the **TourName Footer section** at the left edge of the report, then drag + to the right to the 5" mark on the ruler
   Look at the report in Print Preview to see the work you have done.
6. Click the **Print Preview button** on the Report Design toolbar
   The horizontal lines add definition to the different sections of the report. They make it easier to understand which records are summarized in the TourName footer.
7. Click the **Print button** on the Print Preview toolbar
   The final report is shown in Figure H-12. Close the Print Preview window and save the report.
8. Click **Close** on the Print Preview toolbar, click the **Save button** on the Report Design toolbar, then click the **Profit by Tour Report Close button**

QuickTip

Press and hold [Shift] while creating a line to make it perfectly horizontal or vertical.

FIGURE H-11: **Modifying controls in Report Design View**

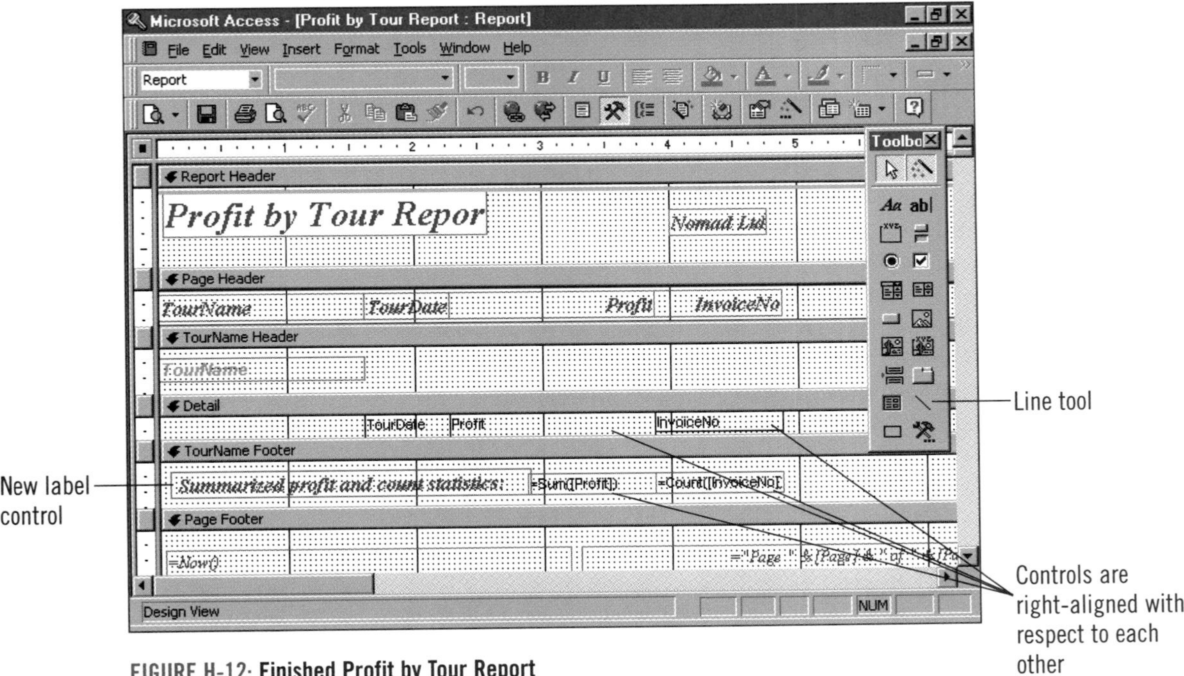

FIGURE H-12: **Finished Profit by Tour Report**

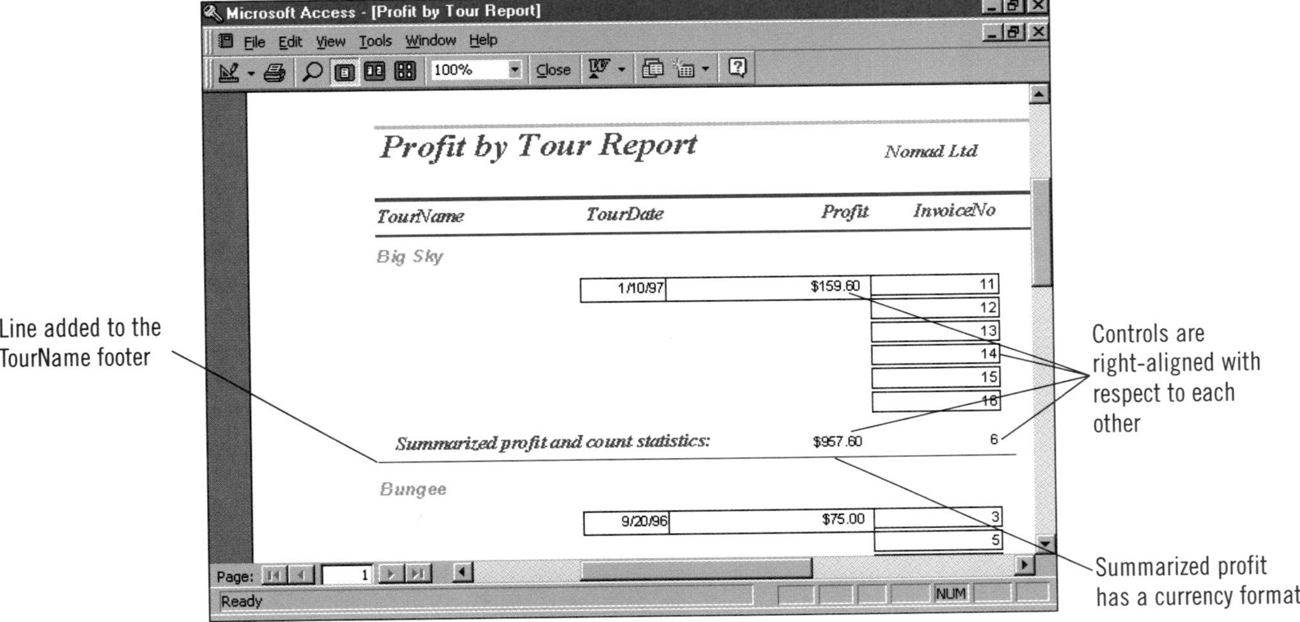

TABLE H-3: **Aligning controls with respect to each other**

menu option	description
Format|Align|Left	Aligns the left edges of the selected controls with the left edge of the leftmost control in the selection
Format|Align|Right	Aligns the right edges of the selected controls with the right edge of the rightmost control in the selection
Format|Align|Top	Aligns the top edges of the selected controls with the top edge of the topmost control in the selection
Format|Align|Bottom	Aligns the bottom edges of the selected controls with the bottom edge of the bottommost control in the selection
Format|Align|Grid	Aligns the upper-left corner of each selected control to the nearest point on the grid

Adding Graphics to Reports

Graphics refers to any non-text or non-numeric element such as lines, clipart, or boxes placed in the report. Lines and boxes are usually added to increase the report's clarity and professionalism. Clipart is usually added to create visual interest in a report that might otherwise be dull with just numbers and text. When you use the AutoReports or Reports Wizard, Access automatically adds lines to certain sections of the Report Design View to differentiate the sections and make it easier to read. Michael wants to create an attractive Tours Report listing all of Nomad's past and present tours as a customer handout. Michael will use the AutoReport: Tabular option and then add a clipart image to the Report Header section.

Steps

1. Click the **Reports tab** if necessary, click **New**, click **AutoReport: Tabular**, click the **Choose the table or query where the object's data comes from list arrow**, click **Tours**, then click **OK**
   The **AutoReport: Tabular** option automatically creates a tabular report as shown in Figure H-13 with all the fields of the Tours table and opens in Print Preview mode. After scrolling through the report, you decide to delete the Cost field (you don't want the customer to see this field!)
2. Click the **Design View button** on the Print Preview toolbar, scroll to the right, click the **Cost label** in the Page Header section, press and hold **[Shift]**, click the **Cost text box** in the Detail section, release **[Shift]**, then press **[Delete]**
   With the Cost information eliminated, you can move the Handicap label to the left.
3. Click the **Handicap label** in the Page Header section, point to the edge so the mouse pointer changes to, then drag to the left so that the Handicap label is centered over the checkmark in the Detail section
   The realigned label is shown in Figure H-14. Now you can add a clipart image to enhance the Report Header section.
4. Click the **Image button** on the Toolbox, then click at the 6" mark in the **Report Header**
   The Insert Picture dialog box opens, allowing you to select the clipart image you wish to add to the report.
5. Click the **Preview button** on the Insert Picture dialog box toolbar, click the folders as needed to position the Look in: box to the drive letter with the MS Office folder, double-click the **MS Office folder**, double-click the **clipart folder**, scroll, then click the **Buttrfly.wmf** file as shown in Figure H-15, then click **OK**
   The butterfly clipart image was added to the report view; print the report.
6. Click the **Print Preview button** then click the **Print button** on the Print Preview toolbar
   The final report is shown in Figure H-16. The butterfly adds an interesting visual touch to an otherwise basic report. After looking over all your enhancements, close the Print Preview window.
7. Click **Close** on the Print Preview toolbar
   Save the report, naming it Tours Report.
8. Click the **Save button** on the Report Design toolbar, then type **Tours Report** in the Name text box, then click **OK**
   Now you can close the report.

Trouble?

If the Handicap field appears on the report as a textbox displaying "Yes" or "No" instead of a checkbox, change it to a checkbox in Design View. Delete the Handicap textbox in the report's Detail section, click, drag the Handicap field from the field list back to the same location. The new Handicap field appears as a checkbox. Delete the attached new "Handicap" label.

Time To

✓ Close the report

FIGURE H-13: AutoReport created from the Tours table

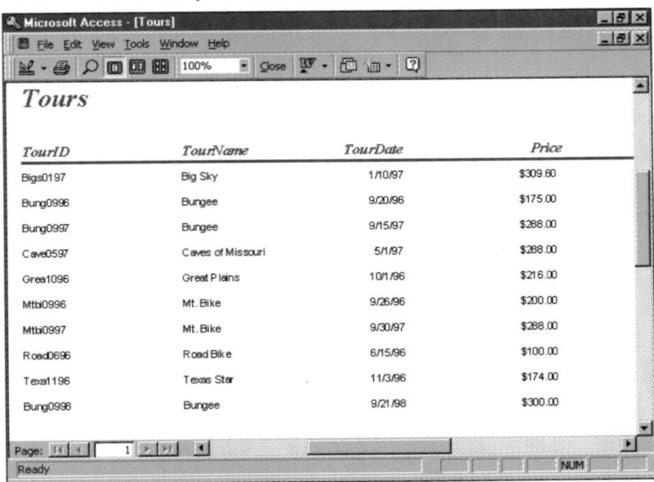

FIGURE H-14: Moving controls

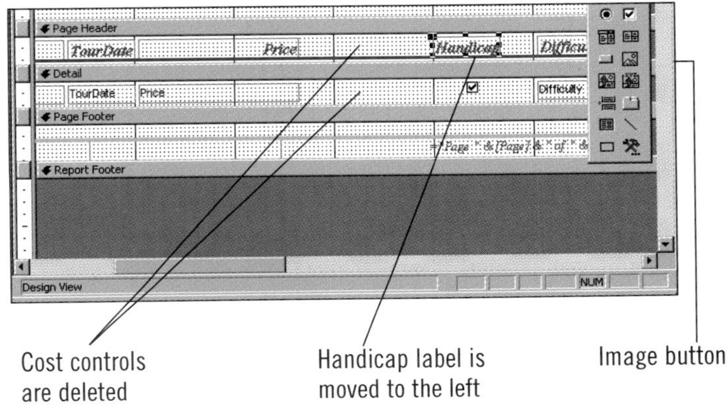

FIGURE H-15: Insert Picture dialog box

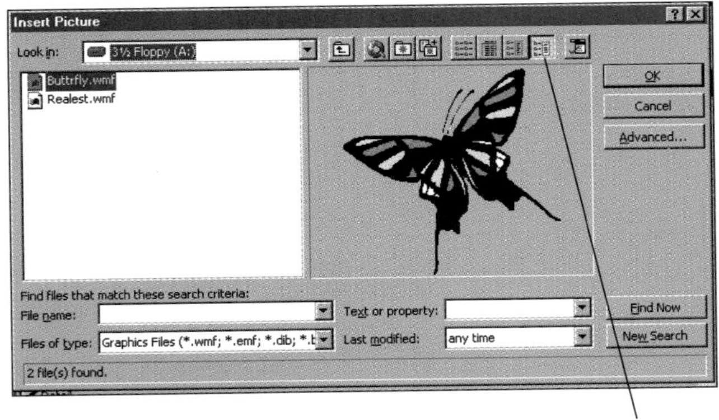

FIGURE H-16: Final report with clipart

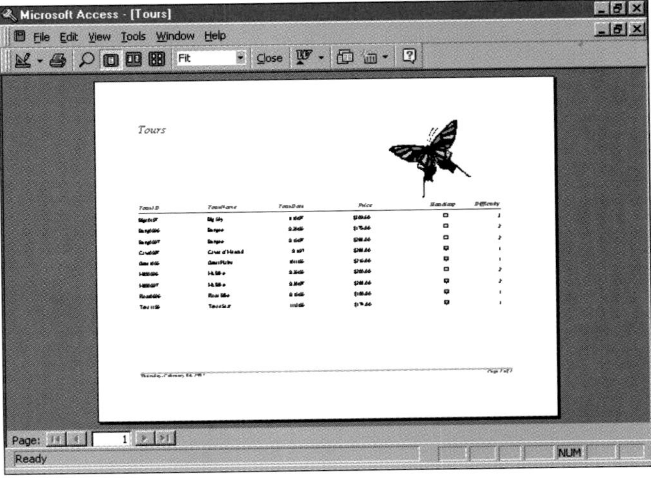

CLUES TO USE

Graphic image files supported by Access

You can insert many popular graphic file formats into a form or report. You don't need a separate graphic filter to insert the following graphic file formats: Enhanced Metafile (.emf), Windows Bitmap (.bmp, .rle, .dib), Windows Metafile (.wmf) and Icon (.ico) graphics. Metafiles scale better than bitmaps because they're made up of lines rather than patterns of individual dots.

Access 97

Using Color

Discriminate use of color can enhance any report. Access allows you to change several colors of a report including the borders, text, and backgrounds by using the buttons on the Formatting (Form/Report) toolbar. Michael just purchased a new color laser printer for Nomad and has decided to add color to the Tours Report. Specifically, he'll change text, background, and border colors to highlight the most important information on the report.

Steps

1. Click **Tours Report** on the Reports tab, then click **Design**
2. Click the **Tours label** in the Report Header section, press and hold **[Shift]**, click the **TourName label** in the Page Header section, click the **TourName text box** in the Detail section, release **[Shift]**, then click the **Font/Fore Color button** on the Report Design toolbar
   The text color changes to bright red. Now that you have accented the most important words of the report with red text, add a background color to the TourDate information.
3. Click the **TourDate label** in the Page Header section, press and hold **[Shift]**, click the **TourDate text box** in the Detail section, release **[Shift]**, click the **Fill/Back Color list arrow** on the Report Design toolbar, then click the **light gray color box** (the last color box in the fourth row)
   The Report Design View now looks like Figure H-17. Next, add one more accent color to the report. Border the Difficulty field with the same dark blue color displayed in many of the labels.
4. Scroll and click the **Difficulty text box** in the Detail section, click the **Line/Border list arrow** on the Report Design toolbar, then click the **dark blue box** (the sixth color box in the first row)
   Review the changes, then preview and print the report.
5. Click the **Print Preview button**, then click the **Print button** on the Print Preview toolbar
   The final report is shown in Figure H-18.
6. Close the Print Preview window, then save the report

How to create custom colors

If you change a control's property setting on a report, the change doesn't affect the underlying query or table. Likewise, if you change the property setting for a field in a table or query after you've created a report that uses the field, the property setting for the control on the report isn't updated; you must do this manually. There are exceptions to the last rule, however. If you change the Default Value, Validation Rule, or Validation Text properties in a table's Design View, these changes will be enforced in any controls based on these fields later.

FIGURE H-17: Changing control colors

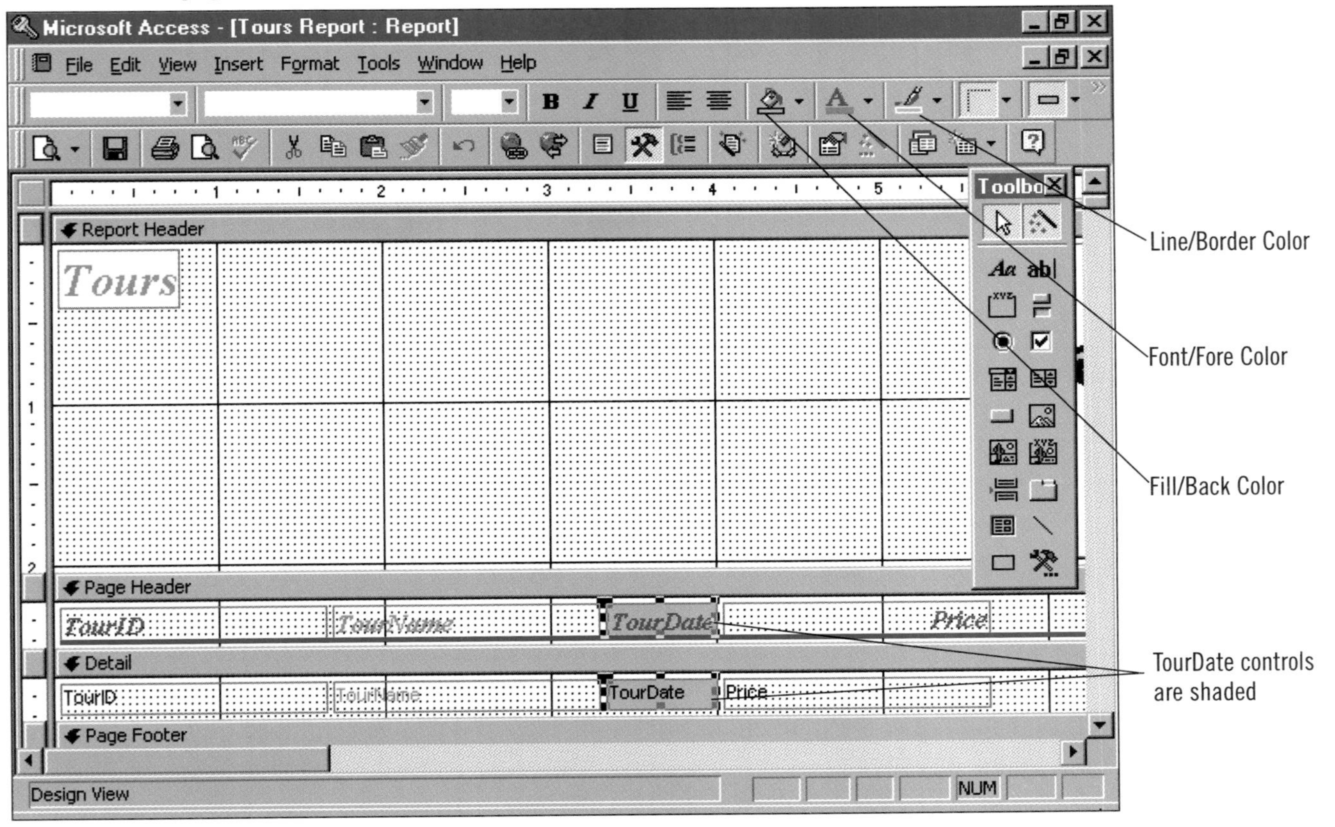

FIGURE H-18: Finished report with color accents

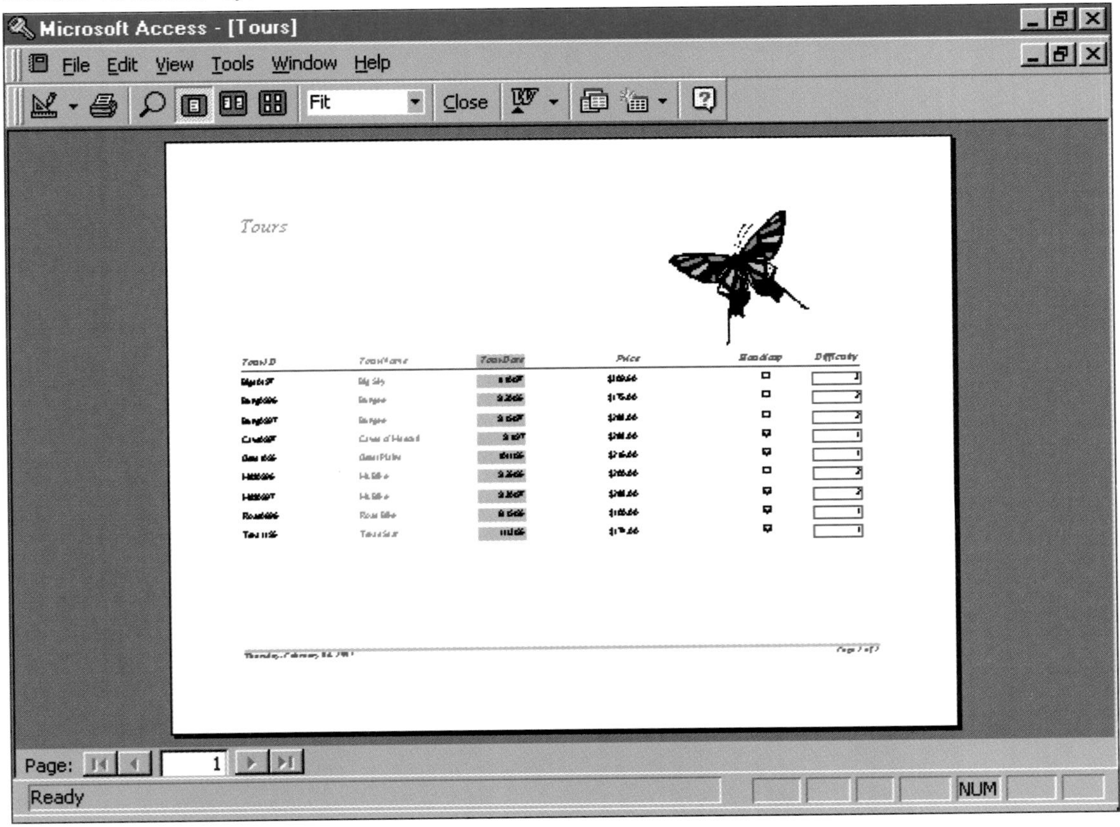

Access 97

Adding Special Effects

You can add raised, sunken, shadowed, etched, or chiseled **special effects** to controls by changing the settings of the Special Effect property. The sunken special effect is often used to make a button look indented. The raised special effect makes a button look not indented. The shadowed effect is especially attractive for titles, and the etched and chiseled special effects create interesting borders. Refer to Table H-4 for an example of each of the special effects. Michael wants to add some special effects to the Tours report to continue to enhance its appearance. He'll add a shadowed effect to the title and a chiseled effect to the Price fields.

Steps

1. Click the **Design View button** to view the report's design, click the **Tours label** in the Report Header section, click the **Special Effect list arrow** on the Report Design toolbar, then click the **Special Effect: Shadowed button**
   The shadowed special effect requires more width than a default flat look. Therefore widen the Tours label to make sure it has enough room to look proper on the report.
2. Position the mouse pointer on the **middle**, **right sizing handle** until it changes to ↔, then drag to the right so that the right edge of the label control is aligned with the 1" mark on the ruler
   Now add a chiseled effect to the Price text box.
3. Click the **Price text box** in the Detail section, click the **Special Effect list arrow** then click the **Special Effect: Chiseled button**
4. Click the **Print Preview button** on the Report Design toolbar
   The final report is shown in Figure H-19. The shadowed effect on the title really draws attention to that area of the report. The chiseled effect helps keep the information in the TourDate column aligned with the information in the Price column. Satisfied with the changes, print a hard copy of the report.
5. Click the **Print button** on the Print Preview toolbar
   Done for the day, save and close the report, then exit Access.
6. Click **Close** on the Print Preview toolbar to close the Print Preview window
7. Save the report, close the report, then exit Access

FIGURE H-19: Tours Report with special effects

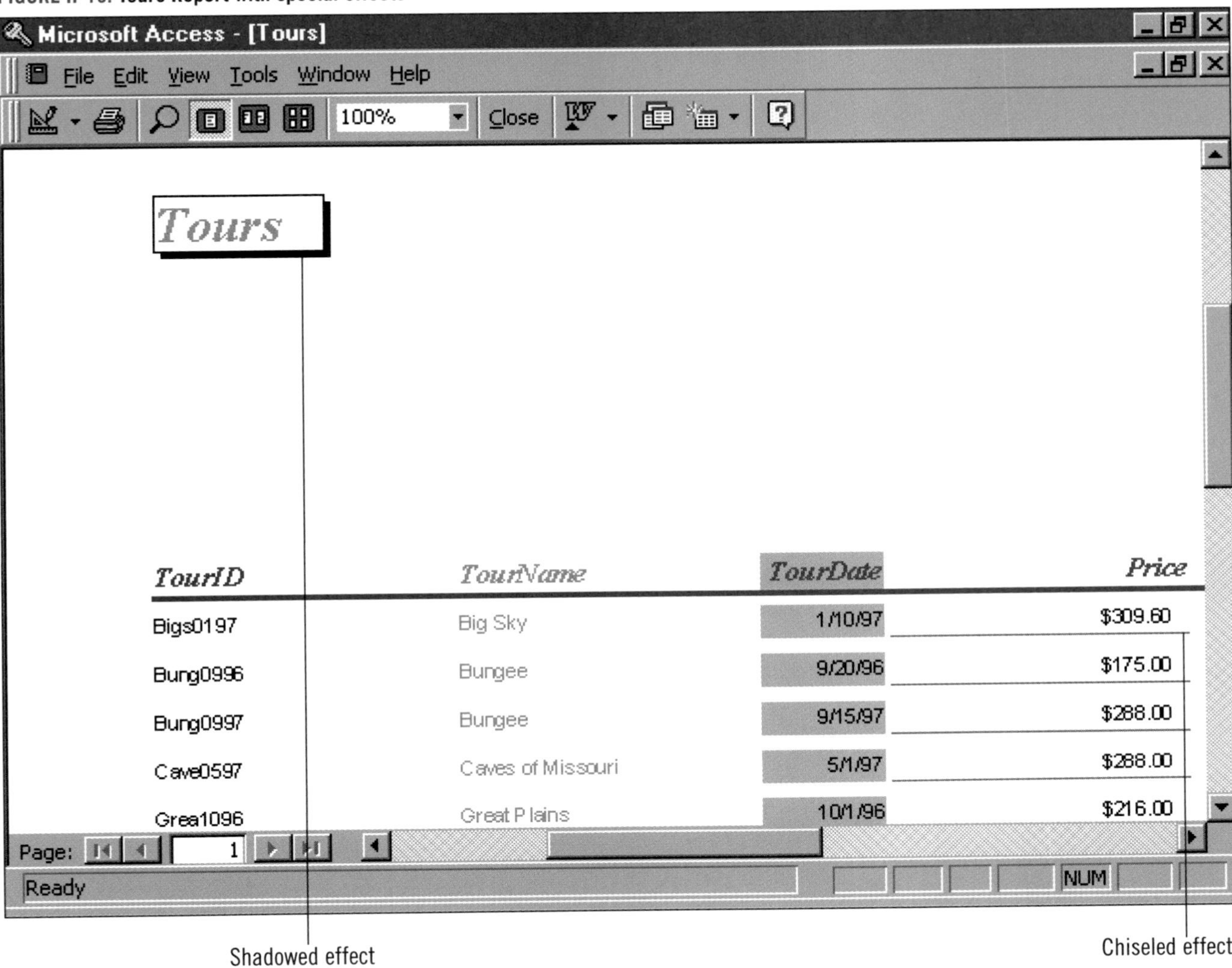

Shadowed effect

Chiseled effect

Access 97

TABLE H-4: Special effects

special effect	sample
Flat	Alaska
Raised	Alaska
Sunken	Alaska
Etched	Alaska
Shadowed	Alaska
Chiseled	Alaska

Practice

► Concepts Review

Identify each element of a form's Design View shown in Figure H-20.

FIGURE H-20

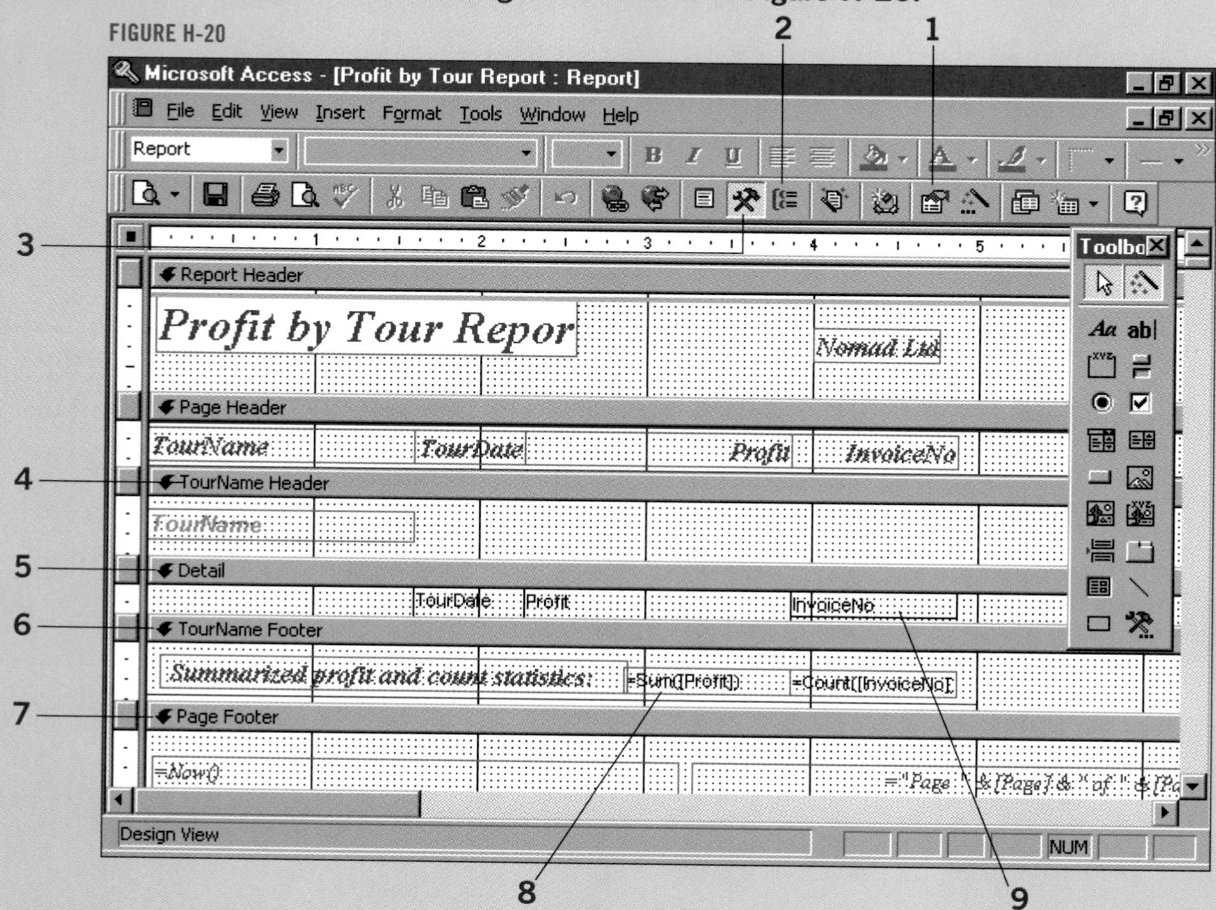

Match each term with the statement that describes its function.

10. An entry in an unbound text box that returns a value such as the sum or count of a field
11. Automatically creates a columnar or tabular report
12. The database objects most likely used to distribute information in formal presentations or meetings
13. Sorting records in a certain order, and distinguishing them with an identifying header and/or footer in the body of the report
14. Sunken, etched, or chiseled "looks" added to a report control
15. A report section that appears just before the Detail section
16. A report section that appears just after the Detail section
17. A report section that appears once for every record
18. An element such as a line or clipart placed on the report

- **a.** Group header
- **b.** Group footer
- **c.** Calculated expressions
- **d.** Reports
- **e.** Grouping
- **f.** Detail section
- **g.** Special effects
- **h.** Graphic
- **i.** AutoReport

Select the best answer from the list of choices.

19. Which of the following is a benefit of reports over forms?
- **a.** Reports allow you to add calculations on groups of records.
- **b.** Reports allow you to add bound or unbound controls.
- **c.** Reports allow you to sort records.
- **d.** Reports allow you to add graphic images such as lines and clipart.

20. Which of the following is NOT a valid report section?
- **a.** Report Header
- **b.** Group Header
- **c.** Detail
- **d.** Summary

21. Which of the following report sections would you probably use to add group calculations?
- **a.** Page Header
- **b.** Detail
- **c.** Group Footer
- **d.** Summary

22. Which of the following calculated expressions displays the correct syntax to return the total of the values in the Cost field?
- **a.** =Total((Cost))
- **b.** =Sum(Cost)
- **c.** =Total([Cost])
- **d.** =Sum([Cost])

23. Which of the following is NOT a valid color property?
- **a.** Interior Color
- **b.** Fill/Back Color
- **c.** Font/Fore Color
- **d.** Line/Border Color

Skills Review

1. **Create a report from a query.**
   a. Start Access and open the database Addresses-H.
   b. Begin to create a Report using the Report Wizard based on the Basic Address List query.
   c. Add all the fields from the Basic Address List query.
   d. View the data within the report by Zips but do not include any additional grouping levels.
   e. Sort the records in ascending order by Last within the groups.
   f. Choose an Outline 1 layout, a Landscape orientation, and a Soft Gray Style.
   g. Title the Report "Address Report by City".
   h. Print the Address Report by City.

2. **Use report sections.**
   a. Open the Address Report by City report in Design View.
   b. Expand the Page Header section about one half inch.
   c. Add the descriptive label "Report is sorted by City, then by Last" to the left edge of the Page Header section.
   d. Save the report.

3. **Use group headers.**
   a. View the Address Report by City report in Design View.
   b. In the City Header section, move the State text box to the right of the City text box.
   c. Delete the State label.
   d. In the City Header section, move the City label, City text box, and State text box down so that the bottom edge of the three controls rests slightly above the Last, First, and Street labels.
   e. Save the report.

4. **Add calculations to group footers.**
   a. View the Address Report by City report in Design View.
   b. Use the Sorting and Grouping button to access the properties for the City group, and display the group footer for this section.
   c. In the City Footer section, use the label tool to add the label "Count of addresses in this city:" to the left edge of the section.
   d. In the City Footer section, use the text box tool to add an unbound text box at the 3" mark.
   e. Modify the Control Source property of the new text box to the following expression: =Count([Last]) to count the number of entries in the Detail section for each city.
   f. In the City Footer section, delete the extra label.
   g. Move and resize the controls as necessary.
   h. Save and print the report.

5. Modify control alignment.

a. Open the Address Report by City report in Design View.
b. Resize the City label in the City Header so that the right edge ends at the 0.75" mark on the ruler.
c. In the City Header, move the City text box to the left by dragging the upper left corner of the control so that the left edge is even with the Last label beneath it.
d. In the City Header, make sure that the City text box and the Last label are left aligned with respect to each other. Several horizontal lines surround the Last, First, and Street labels in the City Header section. Don't forget about the Undo button if your alignment commands go awry.
e. In the City Header, resize the City text box so that the right edge is even with the Last label beneath it.
f. In the City Header, move the State text box so that the left edge is even with the First label beneath it.
g. In the City Header, make sure that the State text box and the First label are left aligned with respect to each other.
h. Save the report and print it.

6. Add report graphics.

a. View the Address Report by City report in Design View.
b. In the Report Header section, add an appropriate image control to the 5" mark.
c. Insert the Realest.wmf picture in the image control. It should be found in the C:\MSOFFICE\CLIPART folder. If you can't find this image, insert another one of your choice.
d. Save and print the report.

7. Use color.

a. View the Address Report by City report in Design View.
b. In the City Header section, select the City label, City text box, and State text box and apply a red text color to the controls.
c. In the Detail section, select the Last, First, and Street text boxes and apply a bright blue border to the controls.
d. In the Detail section, select the Last text box and apply a light gray fill color to the control.
e. Save and print the report.

8. Add special effects.

a. View the Address Report by City report in Design View.
b. In the Report Header section, select the Address Report by City label and apply a raised special effect.
c. In the City Header section, select the City label and apply an etched special effect.
d. Save, print, and close the report.
e. Close the database and exit Access.

Independent Challenges

1. As the president of a civic organization, you have developed a database that tracks donations of recyclable material called Cleanup-H. Now that several deposits have been made and recorded, you wish to create several reports.

To complete this independent challenge:

1. Start Access and open the Cleanup-H database.
2. Use the Reports Wizard to develop a report from the Deposits by Club query.
3. Use all the fields in the query and view the information by Recycle Centers.
4. Do not add any additional grouping levels, sort the records in ascending order by Date, use an Outline 1 layout, use a portrait orientation, and specify a Casual style.
5. Name the report "Recycle Center Deposits".
6. Modify the Recycle Centers.Name label in the Recycle Centers.Name Header section so that the label only displays "Recycle Centers".
7. Using the Reports Wizard, develop another report on the Deposits by Club query with the same choices except for the following: view the information by Clubs and name the report "Club Deposits".
8. Modify the Clubs.Name label in the Clubs.Name Header section so that the label only displays "Clubs."
9. Print both reports and note the differences in the way the records are grouped.
10. Close the database and exit Access.

2. Now that you've developed a relational database that documents the books you've read called Readings-H, you'd like to develop a couple of reports to professionally display the information.

To complete this independent challenge:

1. Start Access and open the Cleanup-H database.
2. Use the Reports Wizard to develop a report from the Books I've Read query.
3. Use all the fields in the query, view the data by Authors, don't add further grouping levels, sort the records by Title, use a Block layout, use a portrait orientation, and apply a Bold style.
4. Title the report "Books I've Read Report".
5. Change the text color of the label in the Report Header section to black.
6. Change the Line/Border color of all of the lines in the Report Header and Page Header section to red.
7. Apply bold formatting to the Last Name text box in the Detail section.
8. Apply a shadowed special effect to the label in the Report Header section. Be sure to widen the label to accommodate for the special effect.
9. Print and save the report.
10. Close the database and exit Access.

3. You have recently helped the medical director of a large internal medical clinic put together and update a database that tracks extra-curricular activities called Doctors-H. You wish to develop a report of activities in the database.

To complete this independent challenge:

1. Start Access and open the Cleanup-H database.
2. Use the Reports Wizard to develop a report from the Physician Activities query.
3. Use all the fields in the query, view the data by Physicians, do not add any more grouping levels, sort the fields by date, use a Stepped Layout, use a portrait orientation, and apply a Formal style.

4. Title the report "Physician Activities Report".
5. Open the First Name Footer section and add an unbound text box to the section.
6. Modify the Control Source property of the text box to be the expression =Sum([Hours]).
7. Modify the label in the First Name Footer section to read "Total Number of Hours Volunteered", and make sure it is positioned just to the left of the new expression text box.
8. Make sure the new label and text box in the First Name Footer section are top aligned with respect to each other.
9. Make sure the Hours label in the Page Header, the Hours text box in the Detail section, and the new expression text box in the First Name Footer are all right aligned as well as right aligned with respect to each other.
10. Add a line control at the bottom of the First Name Footer section that stretches from the 0" to the 6" mark on the ruler.
11. Save and print the report.
12. Close the database and exit Access.

4. You are considering attending Keller Graduate School of Management to obtain an MBA after you finish your undergraduate degree. You'd like to analyze the courses Keller offers by discipline (information systems, marketing, management, and so on) to determine if they have the depth and breadth of electives you desire. You have started an Access database called MBA-H to record Keller's courses. Now you need to return to Keller's home page to find the current listing of information systems courses and add them to your database before you can build a report that analyzes the courses by discipline.

To complete this independent challenge:

1. Log on to the Internet and use your browser to go to http://www.course.com. From there, click Student Online Companions, click the link for this textbook, then click the Access link for Unit H.
2. Print the pages (about five) describing the MBA courses available from Keller Graduate School of Management.
3. Log off the Internet and open the MBA-H database.
4. Add the five elective Information Systems courses to the courses table.
5. Use the Report Wizard and create a report using all the fields from the Courses Sorted Alphabetically within Discipline query, group the records by Disciplines Name, sort ascending on Course Number, use a Stepped layout, use a portrait orientation, apply the Formal style, and name the report "KGSM Courses Report".
6. Add a Discipline Name group footer then add a control that counts the number of offerings within each discipline within the footer. Align the counting control under the Course Number column and make sure that a descriptive label clarifies the expression.
7. Add a horizontal line at the bottom of the Discipline Name Footer to help separate the groups of records.
8. Add a shadow effect to the label in the Report Header.
9. Preview the report and make sure that all labels print clearly. (*Hint:* You may have to adjust the labels in the various headers.)
10. Save and print the report.
11. Close the database and exit Access.

► Visual Workshop

Open the VW-H database and create a new report as shown in Figure H-21. The report is based on the Donations Query, viewed by Alumni, further sorted by Value, given a Stepped layout, a portrait orientation, and a Corporate style. Also, notice that the Value field is summarized for each donor and a horizontal line separates the donors.

FIGURE H-21

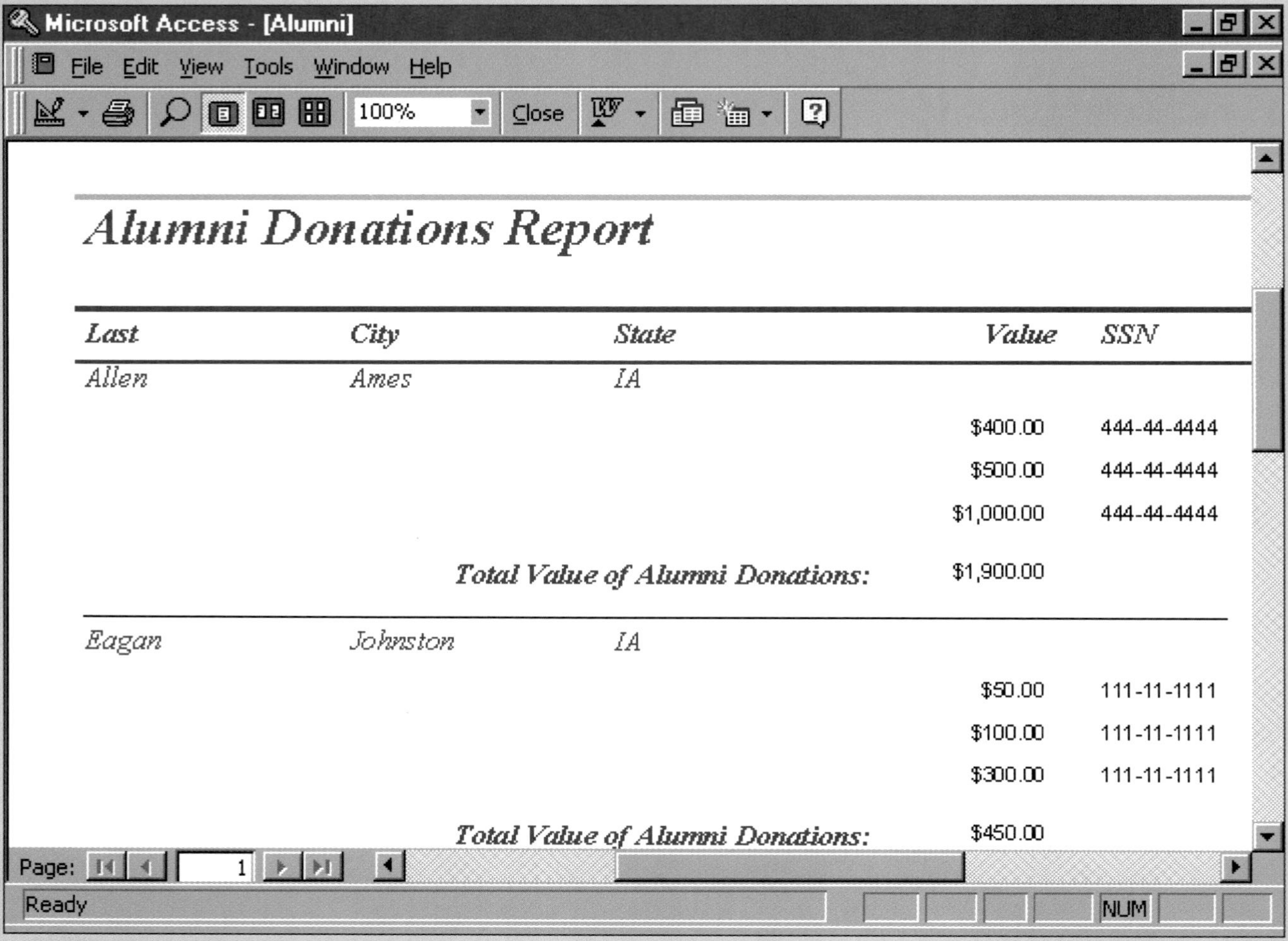

Microsoft Access - [Alumni]

File Edit View Tools Window Help

100% Close

Alumni Donations Report

Last	*City*	*State*		*Value*	*SSN*
Allen	*Ames*	*IA*			
				$400.00	444-44-4444
				$500.00	444-44-4444
				$1,000.00	444-44-4444
			Total Value of Alumni Donations:	$1,900.00	
Eagan	*Johnston*	*IA*			
				$50.00	111-11-1111
				$100.00	111-11-1111
				$300.00	111-11-1111
			Total Value of Alumni Donations:	$450.00	

Page: 1

Ready NUM

Exploring

Integration: Word, Excel, and Access

Objectives

- ► Copy an Access table into Word
- ► Sort Access data in Excel
- ► Embed an Excel chart in Word

Integrating data from multiple programs allows you to combine information from a variety of sources with valuable analytical tools and features. Nomad Ltd's bookkeeping manager, Keith Watchman, has learned that his company is close to deciding which new company it will acquire. Keith's department has been asked for further background information. Although this information is readily available, it should undergo some analysis and manipulation before it is presented to the board of directors and Nomad's accountants.

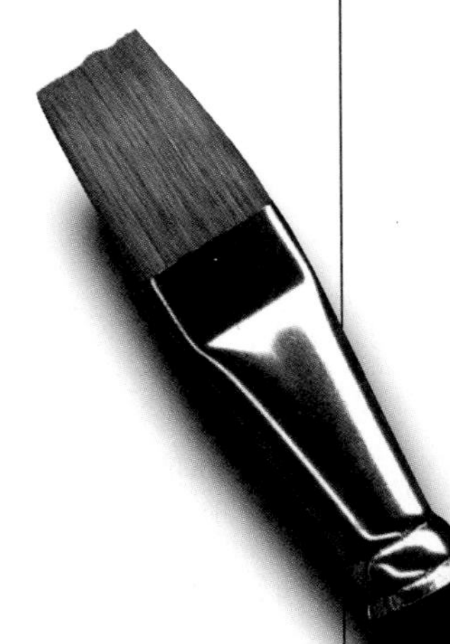

Integration

Copying an Access Table into Word

Although the company has not made a final decision, Nomad's first acquisition choice is Health & Goodness Inc. Nomad's accounting firm, FOBS, wants an analysis of the sample product line. Keith has examined the H&G products database and is analyzing it. Using Word, he will include a cover letter to the accountants that outlines the data analysis. Using the bookkeeping department's standard memo document, Keith writes a brief synopsis of the data from the Access database and encloses a short list of sample products.

Steps 1 2 3 4

1. Open INT E-1; in the RE: memo block, type **Acquisition Analysis**, then save the document as **Cover Letter to FOBS**
   Once the memo document is open, open the Access database table containing the needed records.
2. Open the **H&G Products** database, then open the **Sample Product Line table**
   The table containing sample items in the H&G product line appears. Move some of the fields to the end of the table because you don't need them now.
3. Move the **Product ID** and **Serial Number fields** so they appear at the far right of the table, then maximize the table and resize the fields so that all the data is visible
   As you review the table, you realize that you don't need to see all the fields. Create a query that retrieves only the necessary information.
4. Create a query called **Product Listing** that displays the fields in the following order: **Product Name**, **Product Description**, **Unit**, and **Unit Price**
   Next, modify the query so the records display in a particular order.
5. Sort the records in descending order by Product Description, then in ascending order by Product Name
   Compare your queried table to that shown in Figure E-1. The resulting list of products is too long to include in the memo, so you decide to filter it by adding criteria to the query.
6. Modify the query to include only those products that have a Product ID of FO-01 or FO-02, *but do not display this field*, then save this query as **Product Listing Short List**
   The modified query retrieves 12 records. You are ready to include this data in your memo.
7. Spell-check the document, copy the **Product Listing Short List** into the Cover Letter to FOBS document, then format the table using AutoFormat
   Compare your document to Figure E-2. Once the table data is incorporated into the memo, write a short introductory paragraph.
8. Replace the **Enter text here: placeholder** with a brief paragraph that introduces the table data, then save, preview, and print the **Cover Letter to FOBS**

QuickTip

"Suppliment" and "tomatos" are misspellings and will be corrected using the Spell Check feature.

FIGURE E-1: Queried Access table

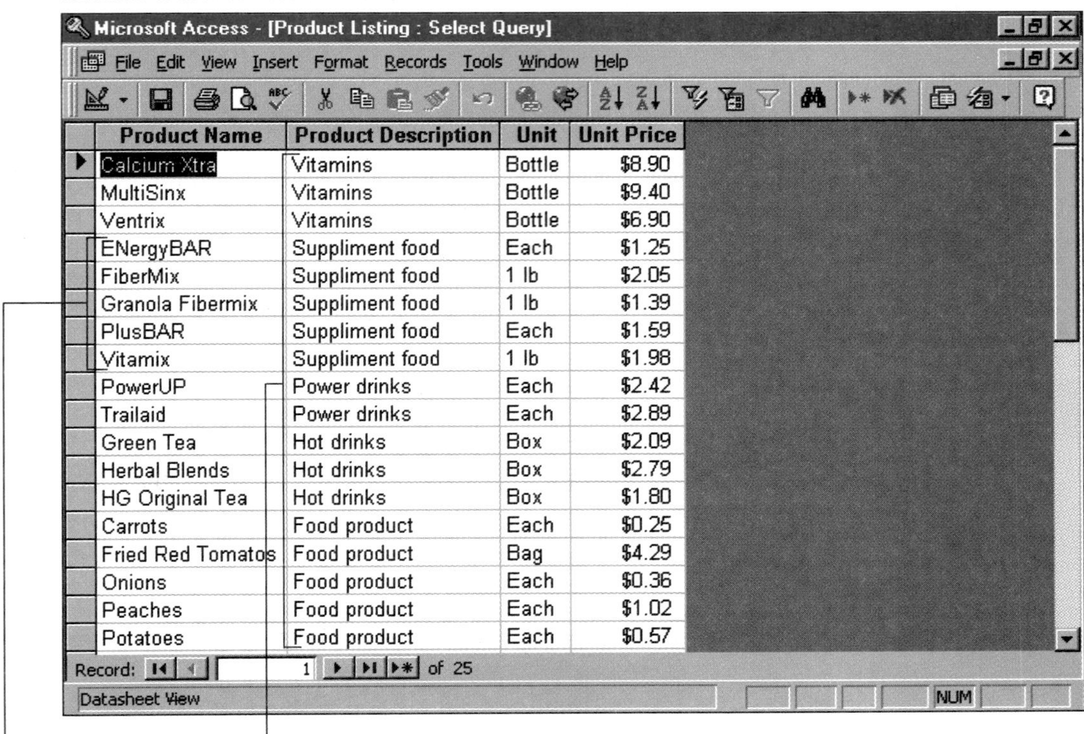

FIGURE E-2: Access data in Word document

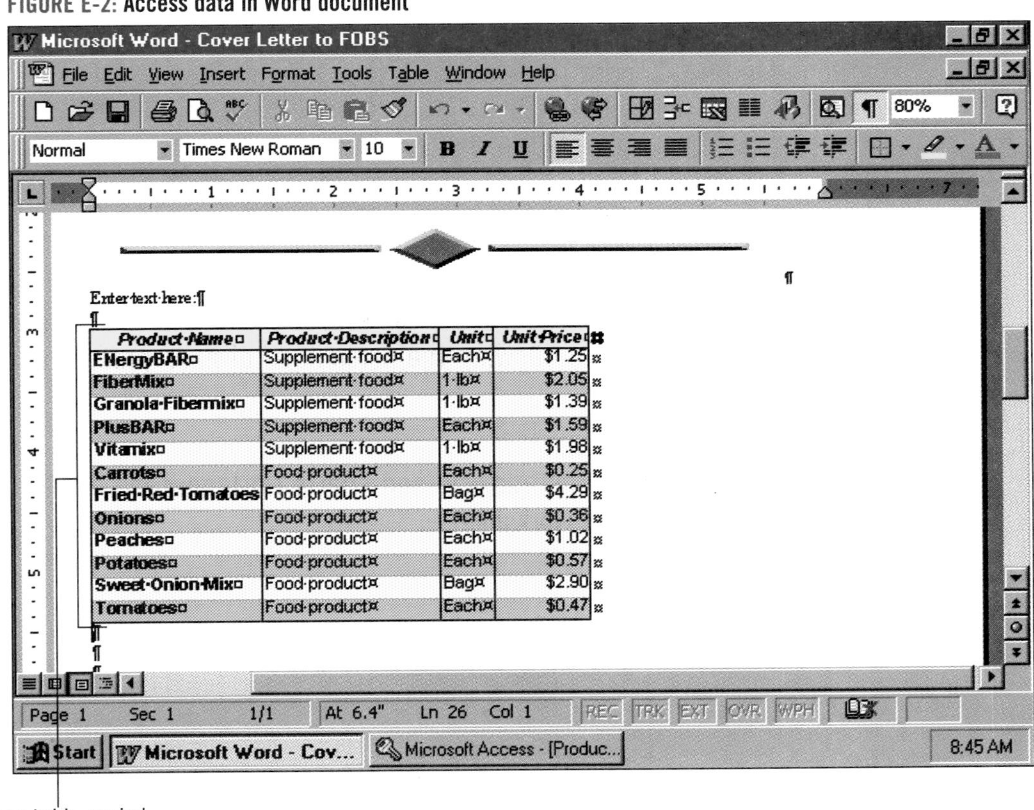

Sorting Access Data in Excel

Keith will forward the information in the Access table to Nomad's accounting firm. He thinks the raw data will be stronger if it is accompanied by a product analysis. Keith will submit an analysis determining which sample products require the longest lead time. First, he'll create an Access query to retrieve the data, and then he'll use an Excel worksheet to analyze it.

Steps

1. **Create a query of the Sample Product Line table that includes the following fields: Product Name, Product Description, Unit, Reorder Level, and Lead Time**
   The query displays all the fields Keith needs for his analysis. Next, Keith adds sort criteria to the query.
2. **Sort the query in ascending order by Product Name, then save it as Product Shipping Analysis**
   You can copy datasheet information to Excel using the copy/paste method or by selecting the query in the Database window, clicking the Office Links list arrow button on the Database toolbar, then clicking Analyze It with MS Excel.
3. **Copy the query datasheet to a blank Excel workbook, then save the workbook as Product Shipping Analysis**
   Use the AutoFilter to apply criteria to the data quickly.
4. **Use AutoFilter to produce a list of products that require "2 days" lead time, as shown in Figure E-3, print the worksheet, then turn off the AutoFilter**
   AutoFilter reveals that only 6 of the 25 products need a two-day lead time. You think that a summary of the sample data information is needed.
5. **Create equations beneath the current data that determine the number of products by the lead time they require, as shown in Figure E-4**
   Chart the analysis to add emphasis to it.
6. **Create two charts of the analysis: one showing the lead times required (by product description), and the other showing the percentage of each product description in the sample**
   Compare your results to Figure E-4.
7. **Save, preview, and print the analysis and charts (in landscape orientation) in the Product Shipping Analysis worksheet**

FIGURE E-3: **AutoFiltered data in Excel**

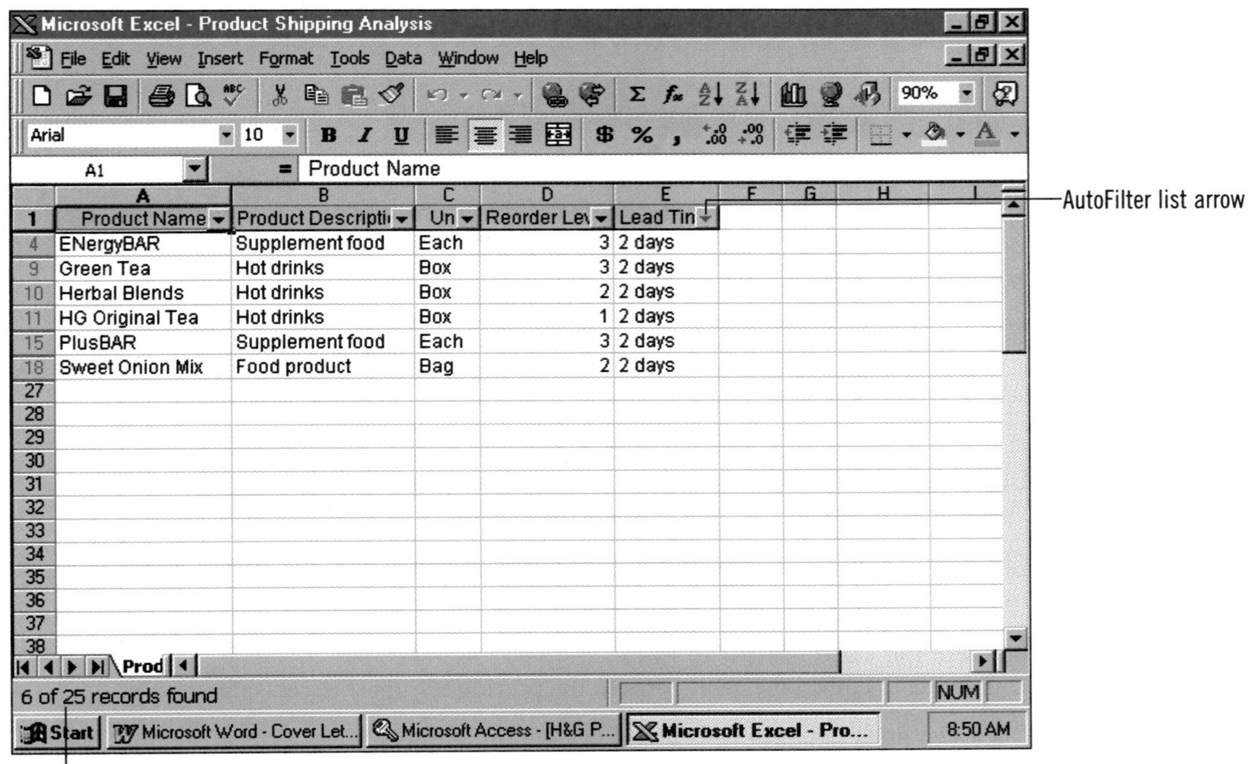

FIGURE E-4: **Analysis and charts of Access table in Excel**

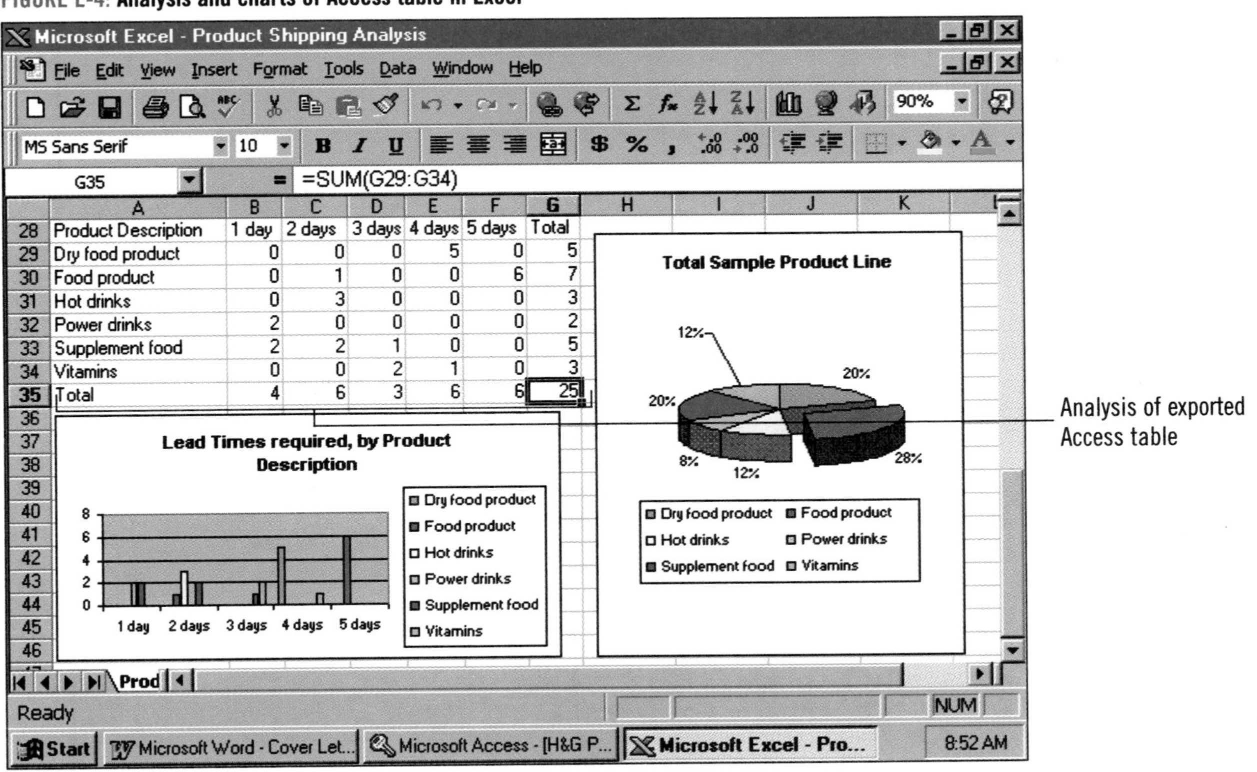

Integration

Embedding an Excel Chart in Word

Documentation of mathematical data has more impact if text or numbers are accompanied by illustrations, such as charts. Keith decides to include one of the charts he created. Instead of just copying and pasting the chart, however, he'll embed it. That way, if the data changes, his memo will be updated automatically.

Steps

1. **Click the chart containing the percentage of each product description**
   Once the chart is selected, copy it to the Clipboard.
2. **Click the Copy button on the Standard toolbar**
   In order to embed the chart, return to the Word document.
3. **Activate the Cover Letter to FOBS**
   You decide to embed the chart beneath the previously copied Access table.
4. **Click two lines beneath the copied Access table query**
   Embedding the chart means that the data in the memo will be identical to the data in the Excel chart.
5. **Use the Paste Special command to embed the chart**
   You decide to add descriptive text that wraps to the right of the chart.
6. **Add a descriptive paragraph that wraps to the right of the chart**
   Compare your document to Figure E-5.
7. **Save the document, then close Word, Access, and Excel**

FIGURE E-5: Word document with embedded Excel chart

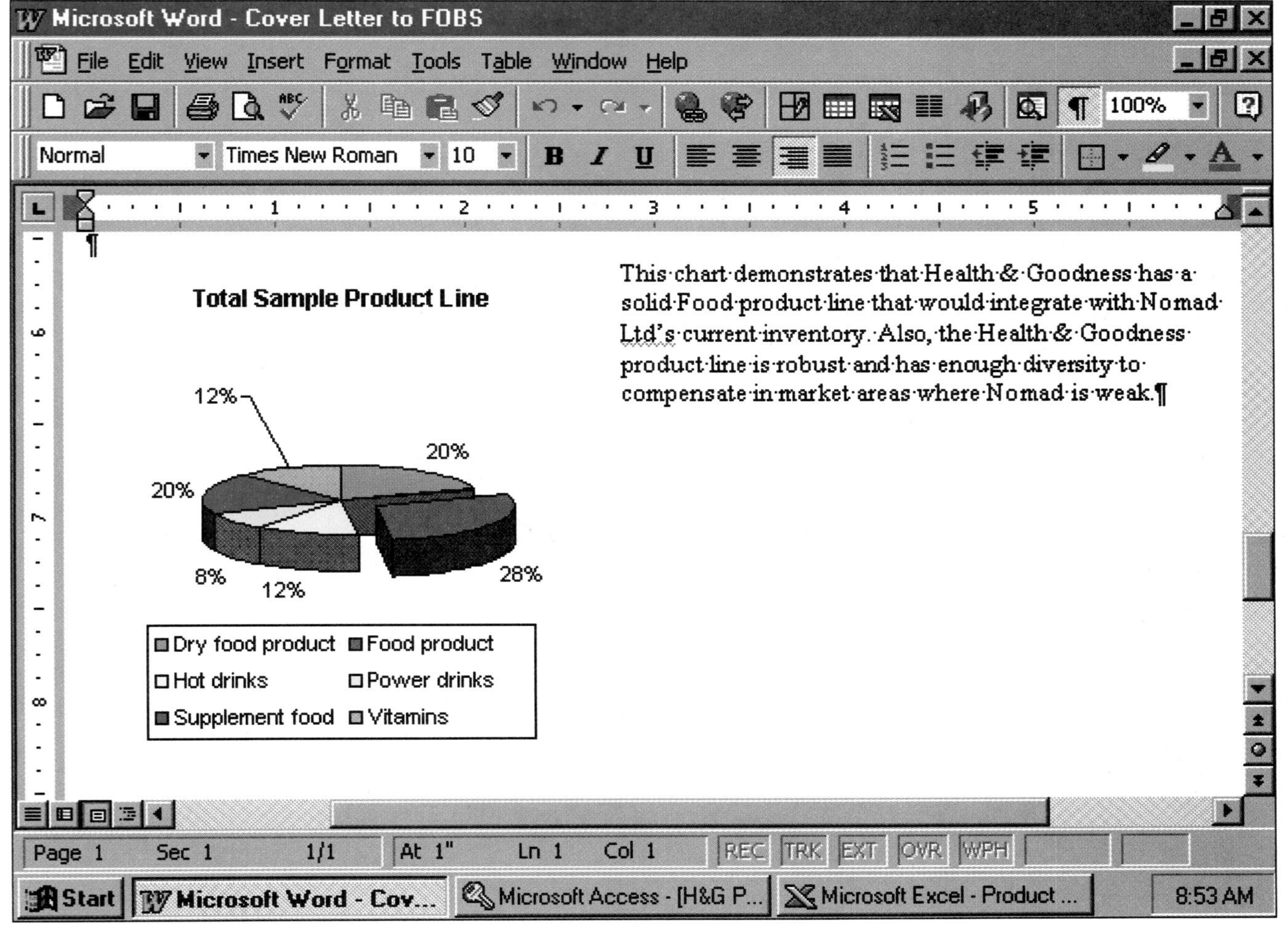

Integration

Practice

► Independent Challenges

1. The Big Bucks Bank approved you for a $25,000 business loan to start your new floral shop, My Green Thumb. Your company is thriving, and your inventory is expanding. Because the loan enabled you to purchase a computer containing Microsoft Office, you're interested in sending your current customers a copy of your inventory list.

To complete this independent challenge:

1. Using the My Green Thumb database file, create at least 15 items in the Product Line table.
2. Create a query called "In-Stock Items" that sorts products in ascending order and retrieves all products that have more than five items in stock.
3. Copy the results of the In-Stock Items query to a new Excel workbook.
4. Use AutoFormat to make the data more attractive.
5. Create a new table within the database file titled "Customers," then add five customer records.
6. Create a Word document titled "Letter to Green Thumb Customers" that tells customers about the list of in-stock products.
7. Merge the Customer table with the Letter to Green Thumb Customers.
8. Print the results of the mail merge, then submit your printed materials.

2. You have recently started a business called Mega-Web Sites using your personal computer (PC). This business will track Web sites pertaining to American history. Your subscribers want to be kept current on the best Web sites for a variety of historic events.

To complete this independent challenge:

1. Log on to the Internet and use your web browser to go to http://www.course.com. From there, click Student Online Companions, click the link for this textbook, then click the Integration link for Unit E.
2. Use any of the following sites to compile your data: the Library of Congress, the FDR Library, the LBJ Library and Museum, the John F. Kennedy Library, or any other site where you can find related information.
3. Create a database that contains a Web Site table with at least 10 historic Web sites in it. Save the database file as "Mega Web Sites."
4. Create a table called "Customers," and add at least five records.
5. Create a relationship between the Customers and Web Site tables.
6. Create a query that displays Web sites requested by each customer.
7. Copy the resulting datasheet into an Excel workbook titled "Web Site Info."
8. Use the AutoFilter to determine which Web sites are the most popular.
9. Create a short Word document titled "Historic Web Sites" that records your findings.
10. Combine the data compiled in Excel into the Word document.
11. Print the Web Site Info document, then submit your work.

Customizing
Your Presentation

Objectives

- Understand PowerPoint masters
- Format master text
- Change master text indents
- Add footers to slides
- Adjust text objects
- Use advanced drawing tools
- Use advanced formatting tools
- Use the Style Checker

Design features such as text spacing and color are some of the most important qualities of a professional-looking presentation. When preparing a presentation, however, it is also important to make design elements consistent throughout a presentation to hold the reader's attention and to avoid confusing the reader. PowerPoint helps you achieve the look you want by providing ways to customize and enhance your slides, notes pages, and handouts. Carrie Armstrong, the new executive assistant to the president of Nomad Ltd, is working on a presentation that the president will give to the company as part of the annual report. After receiving feedback from the president, she revises her presentation by customizing the format of her slides and by enhancing her graphics.

PowerPoint 97

Understanding PowerPoint Masters

Presentations in PowerPoint uses slide **masters**, templates for all of the slides in the presentation. Three of the PowerPoint views have a corresponding master view—Slide Master view for Slide view, Notes Master view for Notes Pages view, and Handout Master view for Slide Sorter view. Slide view actually has two master views; the second view, called the Title Master, allows you to customize just the title slide of your presentation. Formatting changes and design elements that you place on the slide master appear on every slide in the presentation (except for the title slide). When you insert an object, or change a text attribute in one of the text placeholders on the master slide, the change appears in all the slides of the corresponding view. For example, you could insert a company e-mail address in the upper right corner of the Slide Master and that address would then appear on every slide in your presentation. Carrie wants to make a few changes to the presentation design, so she opens her presentation and examines the Slide Master.

Steps

1. Start PowerPoint, open the presentation **PPT E-1**, save it as **97 Annual Report Revised Version**, then to make sure your screen matches the figures in this book, make sure the Zoom text box is **36%**, click the **Restore Window button** in the Presentation window, click **Window** on the menu bar, then click **Fit to Page**
   The title slide of the presentation appears. Switch to the Title Master to view the master elements.
2. Press **[Shift]**, then click the **Slide View button**
   The presentation's Title Master and the Master toolbar appear. Examine the placeholder elements of the Title Master and then switch to the Slide Master view.
3. Drag the **vertical scroll box** to the top of the scroll bar
   The Slide Master appears. Notice that the Slide Master displays a **Master title placeholder**, and a **Master text placeholder** as shown in Figure E-1. These placeholders control the format for each title text object and main text object for each slide in the presentation after Slide 1. Figure E-2 shows Slide 2 of the presentation. Examine Figures E-1 and E-2 to better understand the relationship between Slide Master view and Slide view.

QuickTip

In Slide Master view, click New Title Master on the Common Tasks toolbar to add a Title Master to a presentation that does not have one.

Details

The Master title placeholder, labeled "Title Area for AutoLayouts," in Figure E-1 indicates the title text object's position, font size, style, and color as shown in Figure E-2.

The Master text placeholder, labeled "Object Area for AutoLayouts" determines the characteristics for the main text objects on all the slides in the presentation as shown in Figure E-2. Notice how the bullet levels in the main text object of Figure E-2 compare with the corresponding bullet levels of the Master text placeholder in Figure E-1.

FIGURE E-1: **Slide Master view**

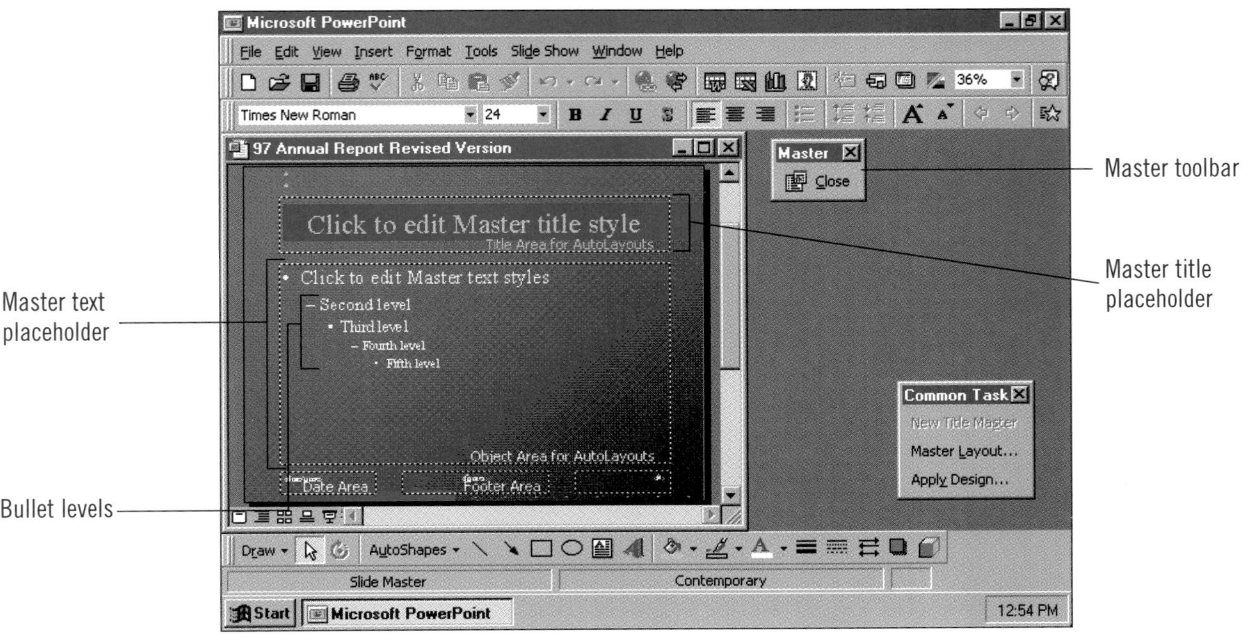

FIGURE E-2: **Slide view**

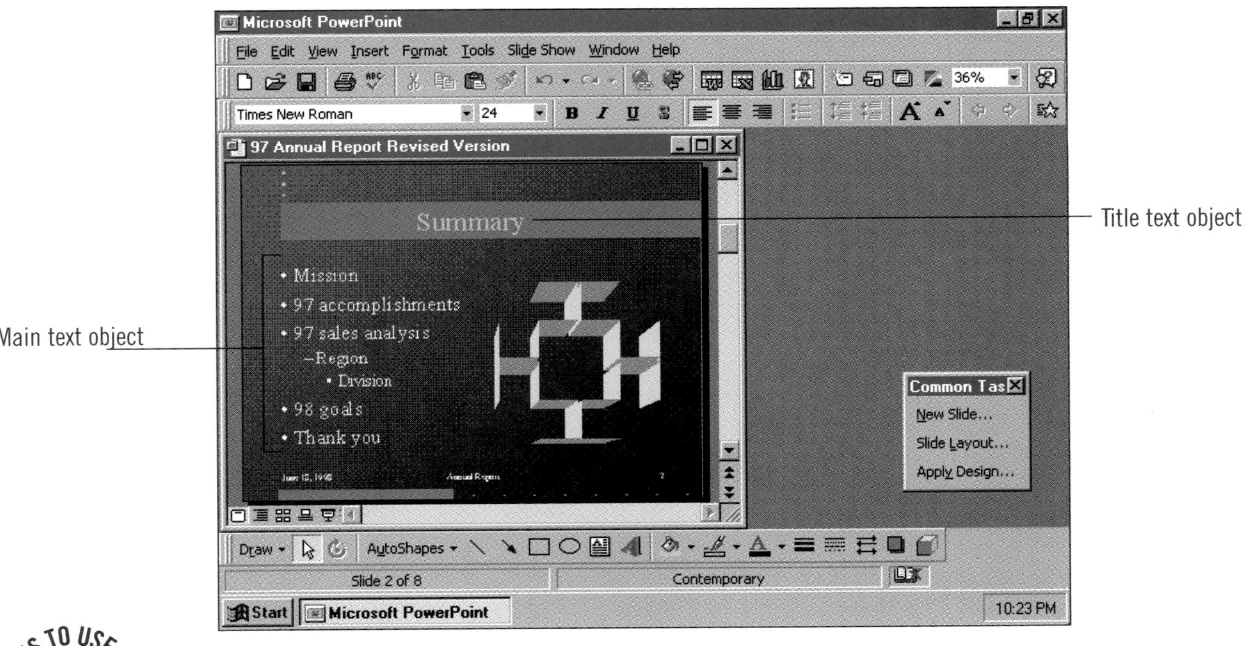

CLUES TO USE

Changing the Master Layout

When you are in Slide Master view, the Slide Layout command on the Common Tasks toolbar changes to Master Layout. Clicking Master Layout opens the Master Layout dialog box as shown in Figure E-3. If you happen to delete a master placeholder or if one doesn't appear in a master view, use the Master Layout dialog box to reapply a master placeholder. Each master view has its own Master Layout dialog box.

FIGURE E-3: **Master Layout dialog box**

Master Layout
Placeholders
Title
Text
Date
Slide number
Footer
OK
Cancel

Formatting Master Text

Formatting text in a master view works the same as it does in a normal view, but remember that PowerPoint applies the changes you make in the master view to the whole presentation. This is a convenient way to change a feature of your entire presentation without having to change each slide. It also ensures that you don't use a mixture of fonts throughout the presentation. For example, if your presentation is part of a marketing campaign for a travel tour to the Middle East, you may decide to switch the title text font of the entire presentation from the standard Times New Roman font to a scripted font. You can change text color, style, size, and bullet type in the master view. Carrie decides to make a few formatting changes to the text of her Slide Master.

1. **Make sure the Slide Master is still visible**
2. **Move I anywhere in the first line of text in the Master text placeholder, then click**
   The insertion point appears. To make the formatting changes to the whole line of text, you don't have to select the line; just click to insert the insertion point. Make the first line of text stand out by making it bold and adding a shadow.

Trouble?
Make sure you check the shadow button on the formatting toolbar, not on the Drawing toolbar.

3. **Click the Bold button B on the Formatting toolbar, then click the Shadow button S on the Formatting toolbar**
   The first line of text becomes bold with a shadow. Now, change the bullet symbol in the second line of text of the master text placeholder.
4. **Right-click anywhere in the second line of text in the Master text placeholder, then click Bullet on the pop-up menu**
   The Bullet dialog box opens displaying the current bullet symbol. Choose a different bullet symbol for this line of text.

QuickTip
The size of a bullet looks best if it is the same size or smaller than the text it is identifying.

5. **Click the Bullets from list arrow, then click Monotype Sorts**
   The available bullet choices change.
6. **Click the "X" in the first row as shown in Figure E-4, click the Color list arrow, then click the dark yellow square**
   You can now apply the new bullet to the line of text.
7. **Click OK, then click in a blank area of the Presentation window**
   Compare your screen to Figure E-5. Switch to Slide view to see how the changes you've made look on the slide.

Time To
✓ Save

8. **Click the Slide View button, then click the Next Slide button**
   Slide 2 appears.

FIGURE E-4: Bullet dialog box

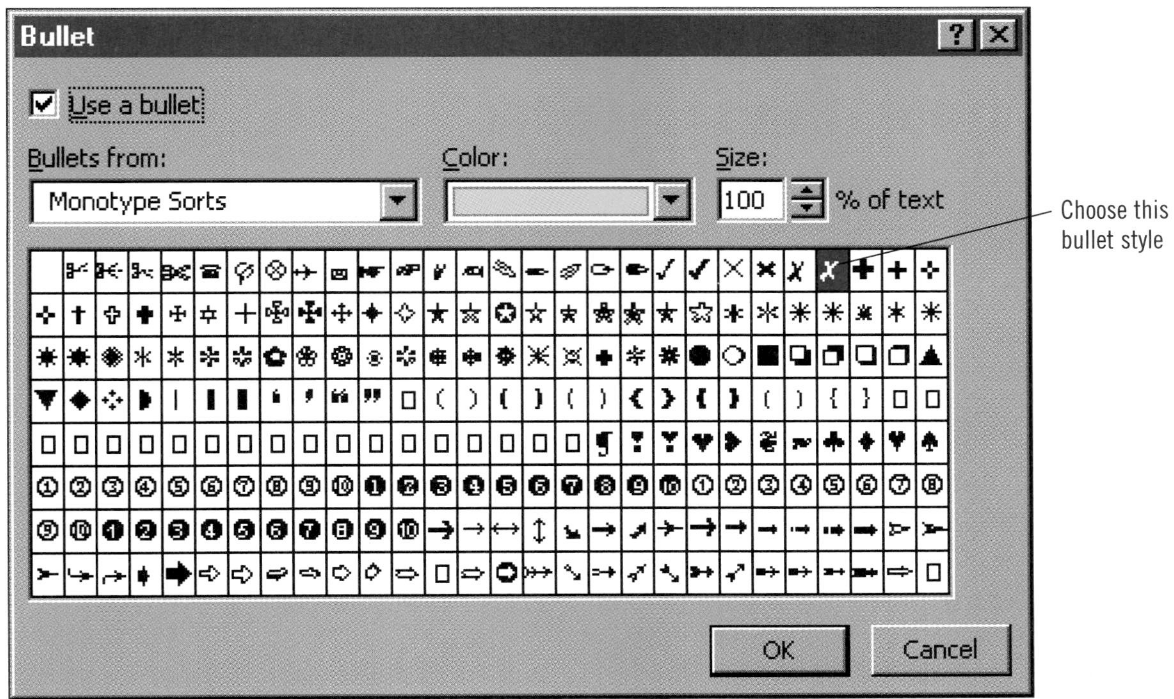

FIGURE E-5: Slide Master showing formatted text

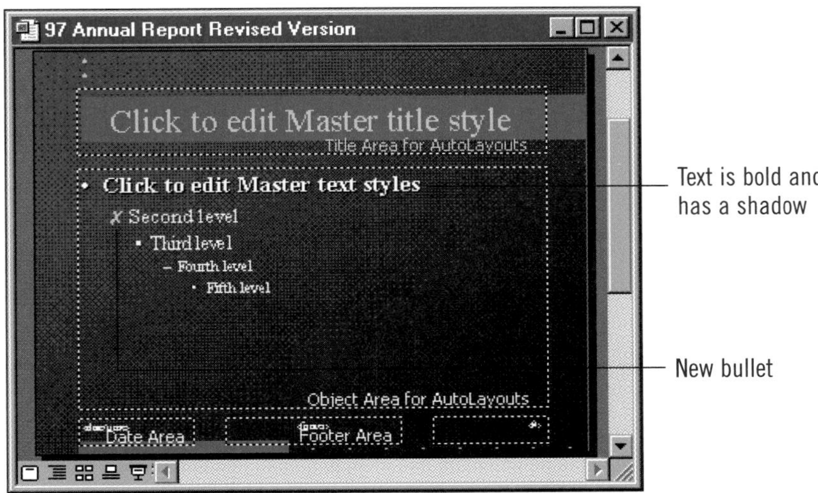

Exceptions to the Slide Master

If you change the format of text on a slide and then apply a template to the presentation, the slide that you formatted retains the text formatting changes you made. These format changes that differ from the Slide Master are known as **exceptions**. Exceptions can only be changed on the individual slides where they occur. For example, you might change the font and size of a particular piece of text on a slide to make it stand out and then you decide later to add a different template to your presentation. The piece of text you formatted before you applied the template is unaffected by the new template. This text formatting is an exception.

PowerPoint 97

PowerPoint 97

Changing Master Text Indents

The master text placeholder in every presentation has five levels of text, called **indent levels**. You can use the horizontal slide ruler to control the space between the bullets and the text or to change the position of the whole indent level. Each indent level is represented by two small triangles called **indent markers** that identify the position of each indent level in the master text placeholder. Table E-1 gives a brief description of the symbols on the horizontal ruler. Carrie decides to change the distance between the bullet symbols and the text in the first two indent levels of her presentation to emphasize the bullets.

Steps

1. **Click View on the menu bar, point to Master, then click Slide Master**
   Slide Master view appears. Now, display the rulers for the Master text placeholder to change the first two indent levels.
2. **Click anywhere in the master text placeholder to place the insertion point, click View on the menu bar, then click Ruler**
   PowerPoint displays the rulers and indent markers for the Master text placeholder. Notice that the indent markers for each indent level are set so that the first line of text, in this case the bullet, begins to the left of subsequent lines of text. This is a **hanging indent** and is commonly used for bulleted text. Figure E-6 illustrates how a hanging indent looks in a main text object. Change the distance between the bullet symbol and the text in the first indent level.
3. **Position the pointer over the bottom indent marker (triangle) of the first indent level, then drag to the right to the ½" mark**
   Compare your screen to Figure E-7. Now, move the bottom indent marker of the second indent level to change the distance between the bullet symbol and the second level of text.
4. **Position the pointer over the bottom indent marker of the second indent level, then drag to the right until the ruler looks like Figure E-8**
   Compare your screen to Figure E-8. Now, hide the rulers and check your work.
5. **Click the right mouse button in a blank area of the Presentation window, then click Ruler**
   Switch to Slide view and check your work.
6. **Click Close on the Master toolbar**
   Slide 2 appears, showing the results of changing the indent markers in the master text placeholder. Save your work.
7. **Click the Save button on the Standard toolbar**

Trouble?

If you accidentally drag an indent marker into another marker, the second indent marker moves along with the first until you release the mouse. Click the Undo button to restore the indent levels to their original position.

TABLE E-1: Indent Markers

symbol	name	function
▽	Top indent marker	Controls the position of the first line of text in an indent level
△	Bottom indent marker	Controls the position of subsequent lines of text in an indent level
▭	Margin marker	Moves both indent markers of an indent level at the same time

FIGURE E-6: Example of hanging indent

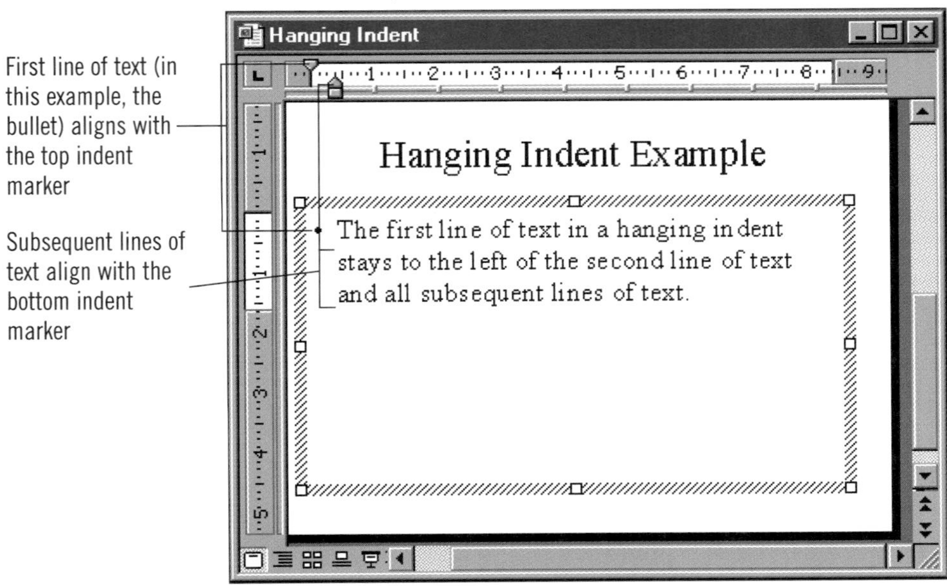

FIGURE E-7: Slide Master with first level bottom indent marker moved

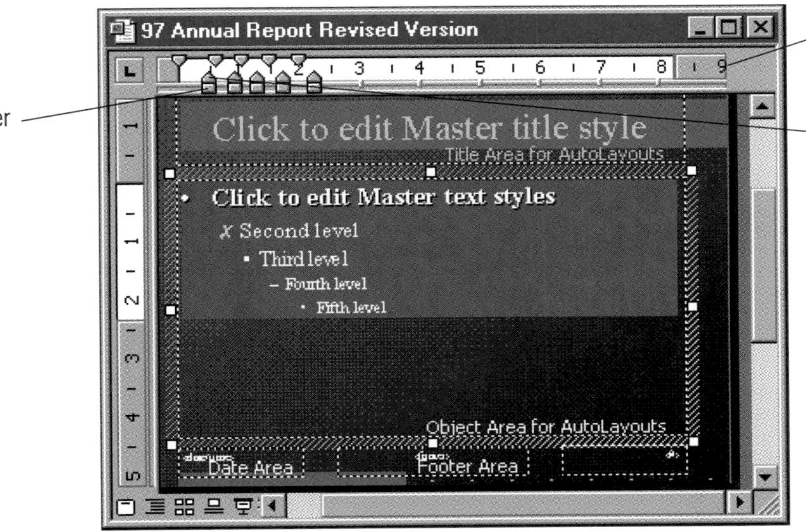

FIGURE E-8: Slide Master with changed indent markers

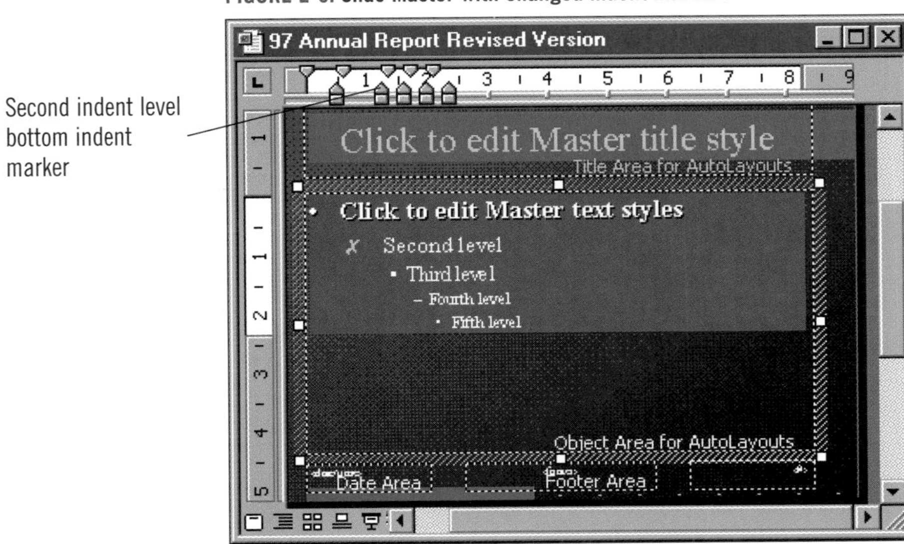

PowerPoint 97

PowerPoint 97

Adding Footers to Slides

Each Slide Master and Title Master has preset placeholders for footer text, the date and time, and the slide number. To place text in the placeholders, you use the Header and Footer dialog box. You can also add the page number to the Handouts and Speaker's Notes. Carrie uses the preset placeholders to identify her slides and make them easier to navigate through during the presentation.

Steps 1 2 3 4

QuickTip

To add other background items such as lines, shapes, or pictures to a master view, display the master view and then add the background item directly to the master slide.

1. Click **View** on the menu bar, then click **Header and Footer**
   The Header and Footer dialog box opens with the Slide tab on top. You can use this dialog box to insert the date and time, slide number, and footer text into a presentation. Notice that the left and middle placeholders in the Preview box are shaded. The left placeholder will contain the date. The middle placeholder contains footer text.
2. In the Include on slide section, make sure the **Date and time check box** and the **Fixed option button** are selected, click in the **Fixed text box**, then type **June 18, 1998**
   Now add a slide number to the presentation.
3. In the Include on slide section, click the **Slide number check box**
   This places a slide number in the bottom right corner of each slide in the presentation. The right placeholder is now shaded in the Preview box.
4. In the Include on slide section, click the **Footer check box** to select it, click in the **Footer text box**, if necessary, then type **Annual Report**
5. Click the **Don't show on title slide check box**
   Because the title slide is the first slide in the presentation, there is no reason to include the footer information on it. Compare your dialog box to Figure E-9.
6. Click **Apply to All**
   Notice that the footer information appears on the slide, as shown in Figure E-10. Now review the presentation in Slide Show view to make sure the footer information looks good.
7. Click the **Slide Show button**, then click the mouse button to advance through each slide in the presentation
   Slide Show view opens to Slide 2. The footer information you added looks good on all slides. Save your presentation.
8. Click the **Save button** on the Standard toolbar

FIGURE E-9: Header and Footer dialog box

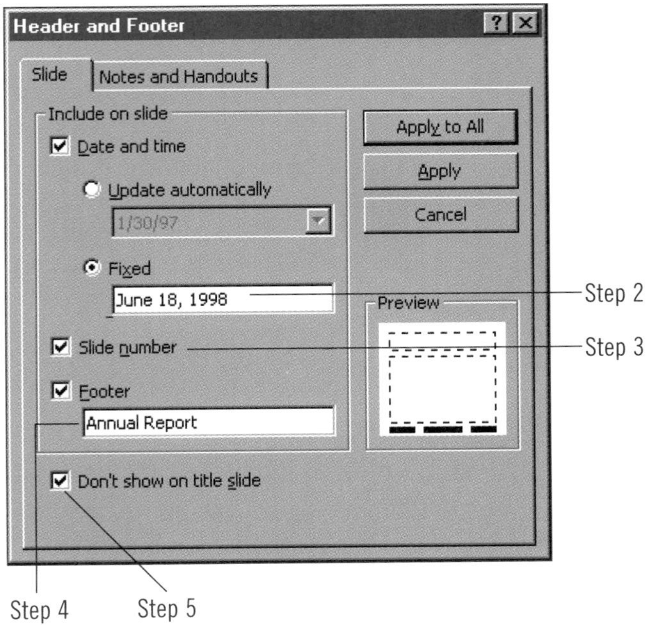

FIGURE E-10: Slide showing completed footer information

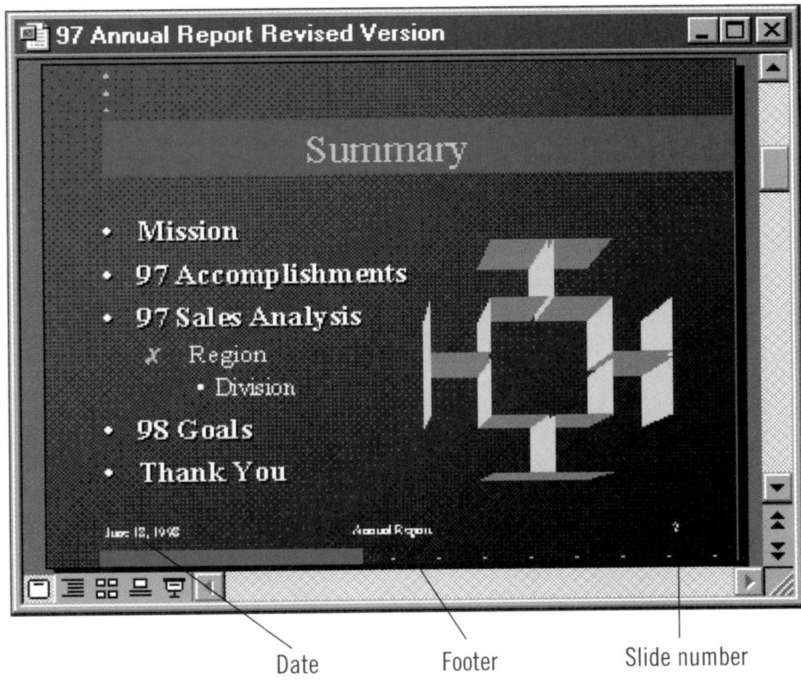

Objects on the Slide Master

The text placeholders on the Slide Master and Title Master can be manipulated the same way text placeholders on slides are manipulated; you can resize and move them. You can also add additional background objects to the Slide Master. If you add an object to the Slide Master, it will appear on every slide in the presentation behind the text and objects you place on the slides. To add an object to the Slide Master, simply add the AutoShape, clip art, picture, or other object the same way you add objects to other slides in a presentation.

Adjusting Text Objects

You have complete control over the placement of your text in PowerPoint. With the **text anchor** feature, you can adjust text position within text objects or adjust shapes to achieve the best look. If you want your text to fill more or less of the slide, you can adjust the spacing between lines of text. Carrie decides that the sailboat image clutters the last slide in her presentation. She will delete it, then adjust the text position and line spacing to give the slide a more open and polished look.

Steps

1. Drag the **vertical scroll box** to the last slide in the presentation, click the sailboat image, press **[Delete]**, click **Slide Layout** on the Common Tasks toolbar, select the **Bulleted List AutoLayout**, then click **Apply**
   Give this slide a cleaner look by moving the text anchor to the center.
2. Press **[Shift]**, right-click the **main text object**, click **Format AutoShape** on the pop-up menu, then click the **Text Box tab**
   The Format AutoShape dialog box opens, similar to Figure E-11. To center the text at the top of the text box, change the text anchor point to top centered.
3. Click the **Text anchor point list arrow**, click **Top Centered**, click **Preview**, then drag the **dialog box title bar** to the bottom portion of the screen
   The text moves to the center of the text object. Now, adjust the size of the text box to fit the text.
4. Drag the dialog box back up the screen, click the **Resize autoshape to fit text check box**, then click **OK**
   The shape of the text box resizes to fit the size of the text object. Now, adjust the spacing between the lines of text and between each paragraph in the main text object so that there is less empty space on the slide.
5. Click **Format** on the menu bar, then click **Line Spacing**
   The Line Spacing dialog box opens, similar to Figure E-12. First, to emphasize the paragraphs in the text object, change the space after each paragraph.
6. In the After paragraph section, click the **up arrow** until 0.15 appears, click **Preview**, then drag the dialog box out of the way, if necessary
   The space, or leading, after each paragraph increases. **Leading** is the vertical space between lines of text. Decrease the leading between the text lines.
7. In the Line spacing section, click the **down arrow** until 0.7 appears, then click **Preview**
   The line spacing between the text lines decreases.
8. Click **OK**, then click in a blank area of the presentation window to deselect the main text object
   Compare your screen to Figure E-13.

To quickly change line spacing, select the text object, then click the Increase Paragraph Spacing button or Decrease Paragraph Spacing button on the Formatting toolbar.

✔ Save

FIGURE E-11: Format AutoShape dialog box

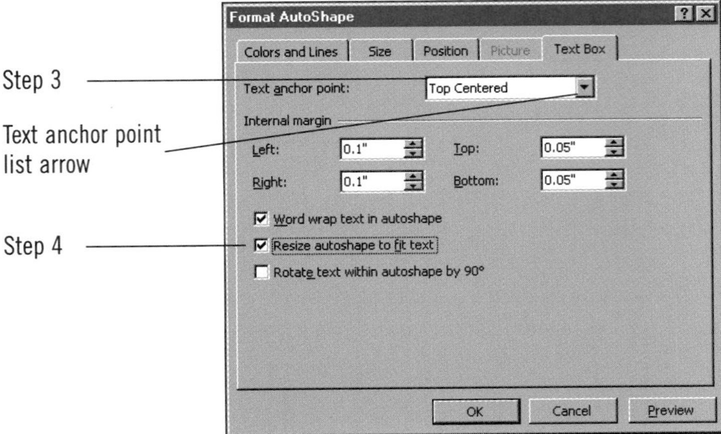

FIGURE E-12: Line Spacing dialog box

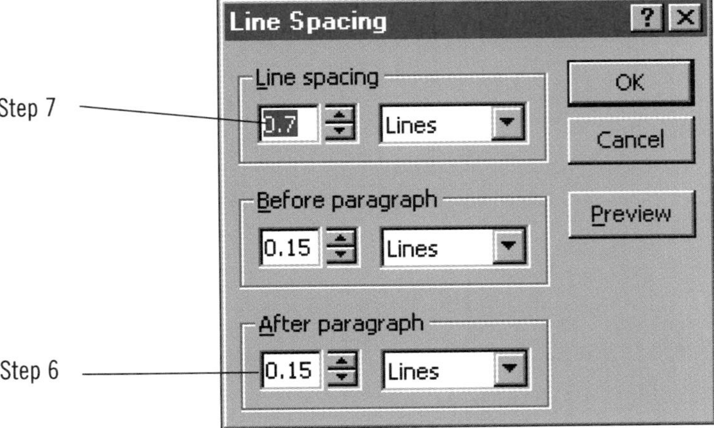

FIGURE E-13: Slide showing formatted text object

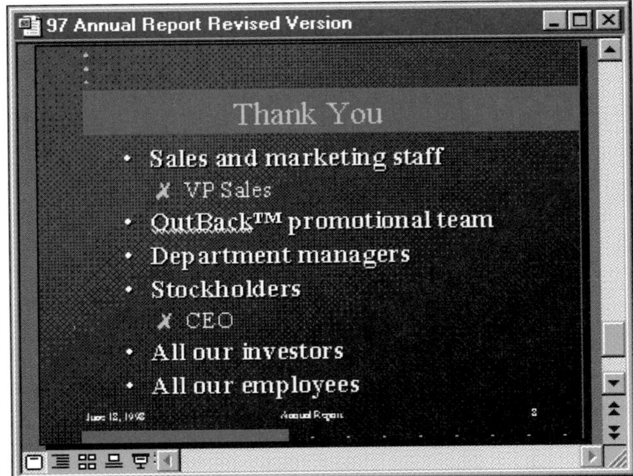

Changing margins around text in shapes

You can also use the Text anchor point command to change the margins around a text object to form a shape that suits the text better. Right-click the shape, click Format AutoShape, click the Text Box tab, then adjust the Internal margin settings. Click Preview to see your changes before you apply them to the shape.

PowerPoint 97

Using Advanced Drawing Tools

PowerPoint has a number of powerful drawing tools on the AutoShapes menu to help you draw all types of shapes. For example, the Curve drawing tool allows you to create a freeform curved line, the Arc tool helps you draw smooth curved lines and pie-shaped wedges, and the Connector line tools allow you to connect objects on your slide with a line. Once you have drawn a shape, you can format and rearrange it to create the effect you want. Carrie uses the Arc tool and a Connector line tool to complete the diagram on the slide.

Steps

1. Click the **Previous Slide button** to move to Slide 7
   Slide 7 appears. Select the Arc tool to draw an arrow between the objects in the diagram.
2. Click the **AutoShapes menu button** on the Drawing toolbar, point to **Basic Shapes**, then click the **Arc button**
3. Position + on the left center edge of the object labeled "Objectives," and then drag down to the top center of the object labeled "Planning," as shown in Figure E-14
   The direction in which you drag the arc determines whether the arc opens up or down and the distance you drag the arc determines its size. To constrain the arc to a proportional size, press [Shift]. Next, extend the arc.
4. Drag the bottom adjustment handle to the right so it becomes a half circle, then drag the lower middle sizing handle down so that the end of the arc touches the middle of the object labeled "Engineering"
   The adjustment handle determines the length of the arc; the sizing handle changes its size. Now, format the arc to match the other arc on the slide.
5. Click the **Line Style button** on the Drawing toolbar, then click the **4½ pt** line style
   The line style of the arc changes to a thicker weight.
6. Click the **Arrow Style button** on the Drawing toolbar, then click **Arrow Style 5**
   An arrowhead appears on the arc. The direction in which you drag the arc determines the direction of the arrowhead. Now, send the arc behind the cube.
7. Click the **Draw menu button** on the Drawing toolbar, point to **Order**, click **Send to Back**, then click a blank area of the slide
   Draw a connector line between two of the objects.
8. Click the **AutoShapes menu button** on the Drawing toolbar, point to **Connectors**, then click the **Straight Double-Arrow Connector button**
   The pointer changes to +.
9. Move + to the right side of the "Planning" object until it changes to ⌖, click to place the left side of the connector line, position ⌖ on the left side of the "Manufacturing" object, then click to place the right side of the connector line
   Format the connector line so it looks similar to the other lines on the slide.
10. Click , click **4½ pt**, then click in a blank area of the Presentation window
    Compare your screen to Figure E-15.

QuickTip

To change the default attributes of a particular AutoShape, format the AutoShape, select it, click Draw on the Drawing toolbar, then click Set AutoShape Defaults.

Time To

✓ Save

FIGURE E-14: Slide showing drawn arc object

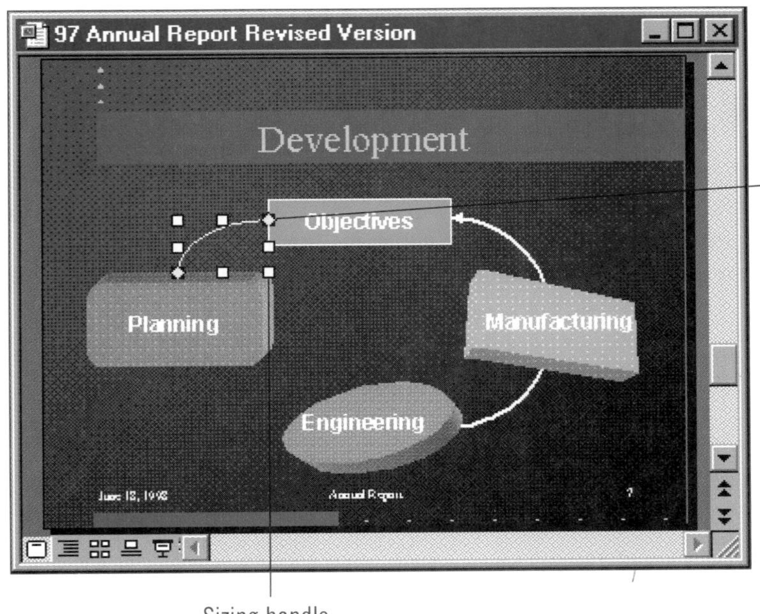

FIGURE E-15: Slide showing formatted arc and connector line

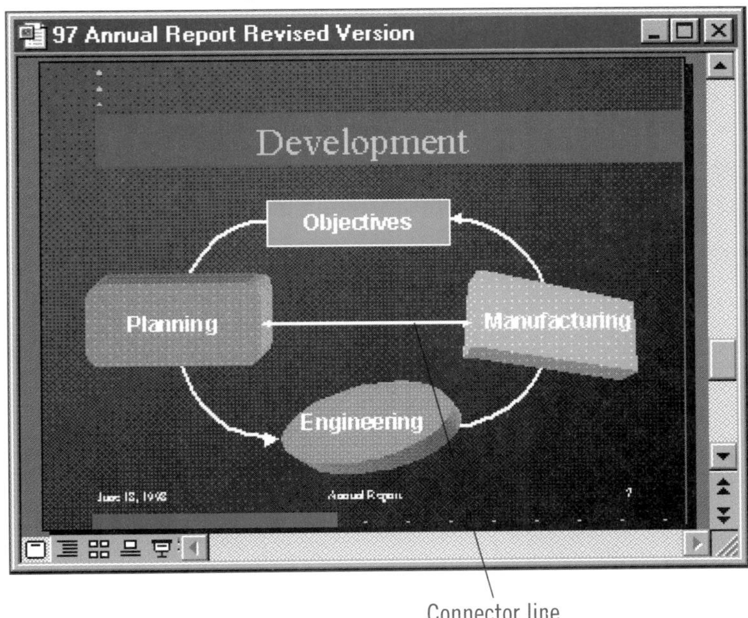

CLUES TO USE

Drawing a freeform shape

A **freeform** shape can consist of straight lines, freehand (or curved) lines, or a combination of the two. To draw a freeform shape, click the AutoShapes menu button, point to Lines, then click the Freeform button . Drag the mouse to draw the desired shape (the cursor changes to a pencil), then double-click when you are done. To draw a straight line with the Freeform tool, click where you want to begin the line, move the mouse and click again to end the line, then double-click to deactivate the Freeform tool. To edit a freeform object, right-click the object, then click Edit Points on the pop-up menu.

Using Advanced Formatting Tools

With PowerPoint's advanced formatting tools, you can change formatting attributes such as fill texture, 3-D effects, and shadow for text and shapes. If you like the attributes of an object, you can use the Format Painter feature to pick up the attributes and apply them to another object. Carrie wants to use the advanced formatting tools to enhance the diagram on the slide.

1. Click the rectangle labeled "Planning"
   Make sure the rectangle is selected and not the word "Planning."
2. Right-click the object, click **Format AutoShape** on the pop-up menu, click the **Colors and Lines tab**, click the **Color list arrow** in the Fill section, then click **Fill Effects**
   The Fill Effects dialog box opens.
3. Click the **Texture tab**, click the **White marble square**, then click **OK** twice
   Now, change the 3-D settings for the object.
4. Click the **3-D button** on the Drawing toolbar, then click **3-D Settings**
   The 3-D Settings toolbar opens.
5. Click the **Depth button** on the 3-D Settings toolbar, then click **72 pt.**
   The depth of the 3-D effect lengthens. Now, change the direction of the 3-D effect.
6. Click the **Direction button** on the 3-D Settings toolbar, then click the left effect in the top row
   The 3-D effect changes to the bottom of the object. Now, change the direction of the lighting on the object.
7. Click the **Lighting button** on the 3-D Settings toolbar, click the middle effect in the right column, then click the 3-D Settings toolbar **Close button**
   Now, copy the formatting attributes of the selected rectangle to the other three objects on the slide.
8. Double-click the **Format Painter button** on the Standard toolbar, click the other three objects, click again, then click in a blank area of the slide
   When you use the Format Painter tool, it picks up the attributes of the object that is selected and copies them to the next object that you click. Now, all the objects on the slide have the same fill effect. Compare your screen to Figure E-16. Next, run through the slide show, then switch to Slide Sorter view and evaluate your presentation.
9. Press **[Ctrl][Home]** to move to Slide 1, click the **Slide Show button**, press **[Spacebar]** or click the left mouse button to run through the presentation, click the **Slide Sorter View button**, then maximize the Presentation window
   Compare your screen to figure E-17.
10. Save your changes, then print the presentation as **Handouts (2 per page)**

FIGURE E-16: Slide showing formatted objects

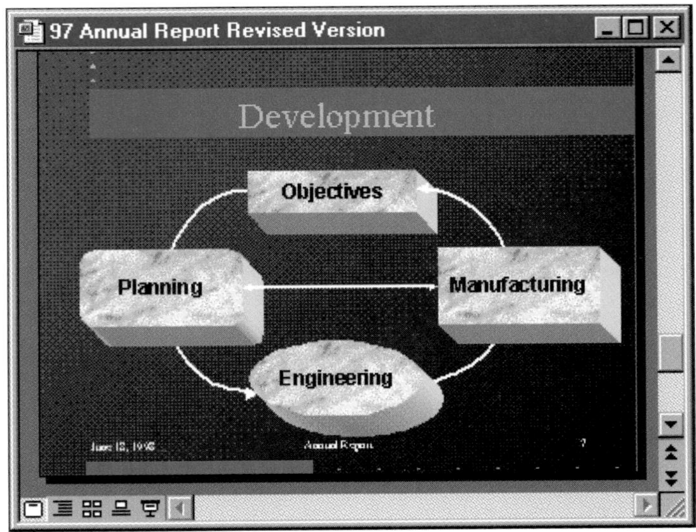

FIGURE E-17: Final presentation in Slide Sorter view

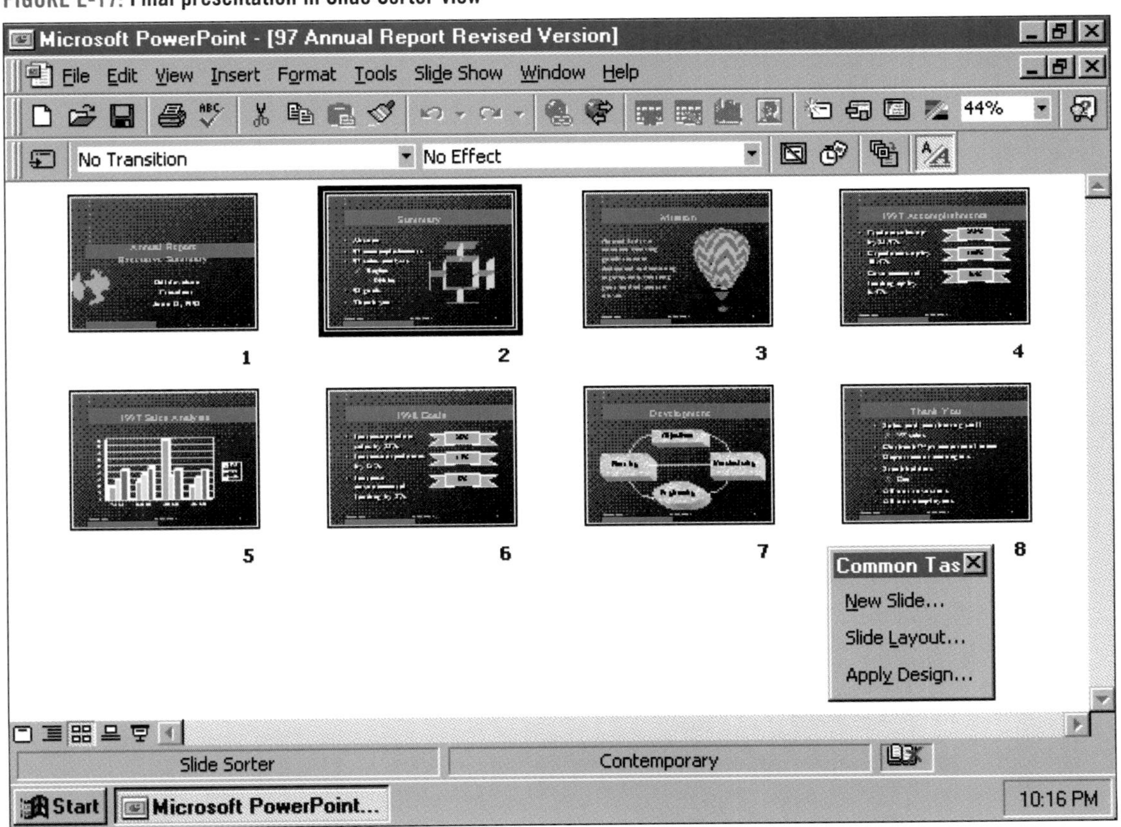

CLUES TO USE

Applying a color scheme to another presentation

If you develop a custom color scheme that you like, you can use the Format Painter tool to apply it to another presentation. To apply a color scheme from one presentation to another, open each presentation in Slide Sorter view. Select a slide in the presentation with the color scheme, click the Format Painter button on the Standard toolbar, then click each slide that you want to change in the other presentation.

PowerPoint 97

Using the Style Checker

To help you correct common design mistakes, the Style Checker feature in PowerPoint reviews your presentation for typical errors such as incorrect font sizes, use of too many fonts, excess words, errors in punctuation, and other readability problems. The Style Checker then suggests ways to improve your presentation. Carrie knows it's easy to overlook mistakes while preparing a presentation, so she uses the Style Checker to look for errors she may have missed.

Steps

1. **Click Tools on the menu bar, then click Style Checker**
   The Style Checker dialog box opens. Review the options before you begin the Style Checker.
2. **Click Options, review the options on the Case and End Punctuation tab, then click the Visual Clarity tab**
   The Style Checker Options dialog box displays the current option settings for visual clarity. Change several of these options.
3. **Adjust the settings in the Style Checker Options dialog box so that your screen matches Figure E-18**
   When the Style Checker begins, it will ensure that the text style on the slides matches the descriptions in this dialog box.
4. **Click OK**
   To speed up the Style Checker, turn off the spelling.
5. **In the Check for section of the Style Checker dialog box, click the Spelling check box to clear it, then click Start**
   The Style Checker Summary dialog box opens, displaying progress information as PowerPoint checks the presentation style. The Style Checker finds four inconsistencies as shown in Figure E-19. Click OK to complete the style check, then review the slides that the Style Checker identified.
6. **Click OK, click the Slide View button then drag the verticle scroll box to Slide 2, Slide 4, Slide 6, and Slide 8 to review each slide**
   The Style Checker is helpful for identifying potential errors, but you are not required to make changes to your presentation based on the summary. The four slides with potential errors all look fine and are easy to read.
7. **Close your presentation without saving the changes**

FIGURE E-18: **Style Checker Options dialog box**

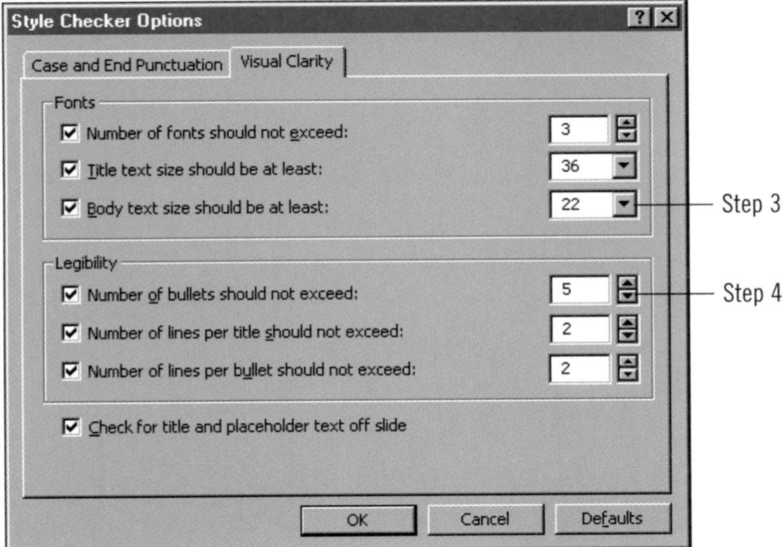

FIGURE E-19: **Style Checker Summary dialog box**

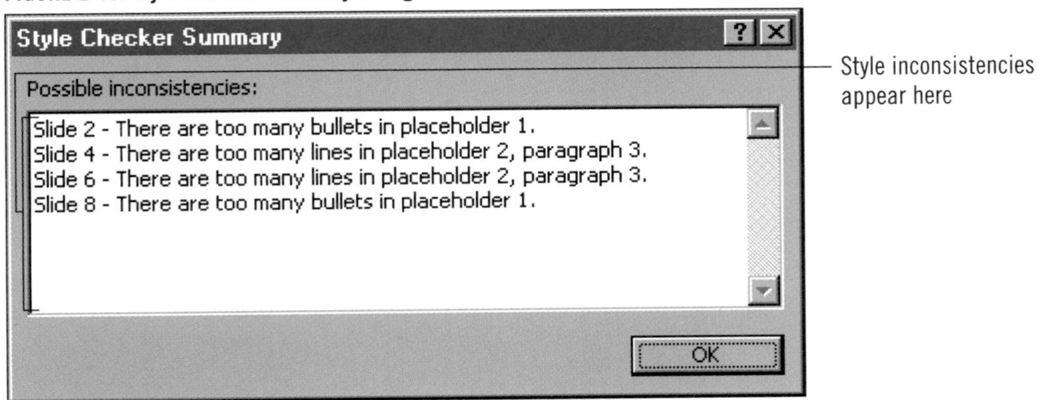

PowerPoint 97

Understanding Style Checker Options

The Style Checker is helpful, however, it may make some changes that you don't expect. Figure E-20 shows the Case and End Punctuation tab in the Style Checker Options dialog box. For example, notice that the Body text style is set to Sentence case. This option treats each line of text as a sentence and therefore removes uppercase letters in the middle of a line. If you run Style Checker, be sure to review your slides for any unexpected changes.

FIGURE E-20: **Case and End Punctuation tab in Style Checker Options dialog box**

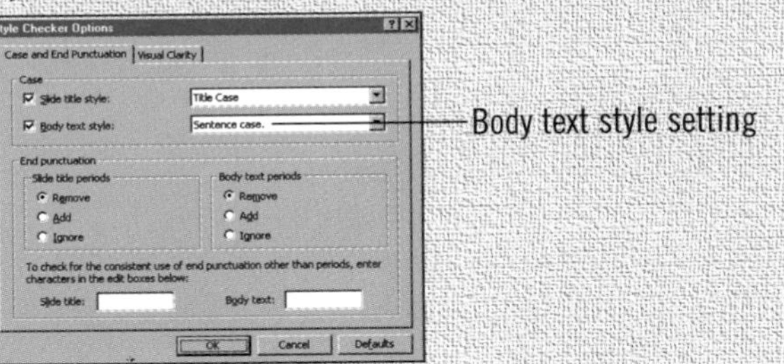

Practice

► Concepts Review

Label each of the elements of the PowerPoint window shown in Figure E-21.

FIGURE E-21

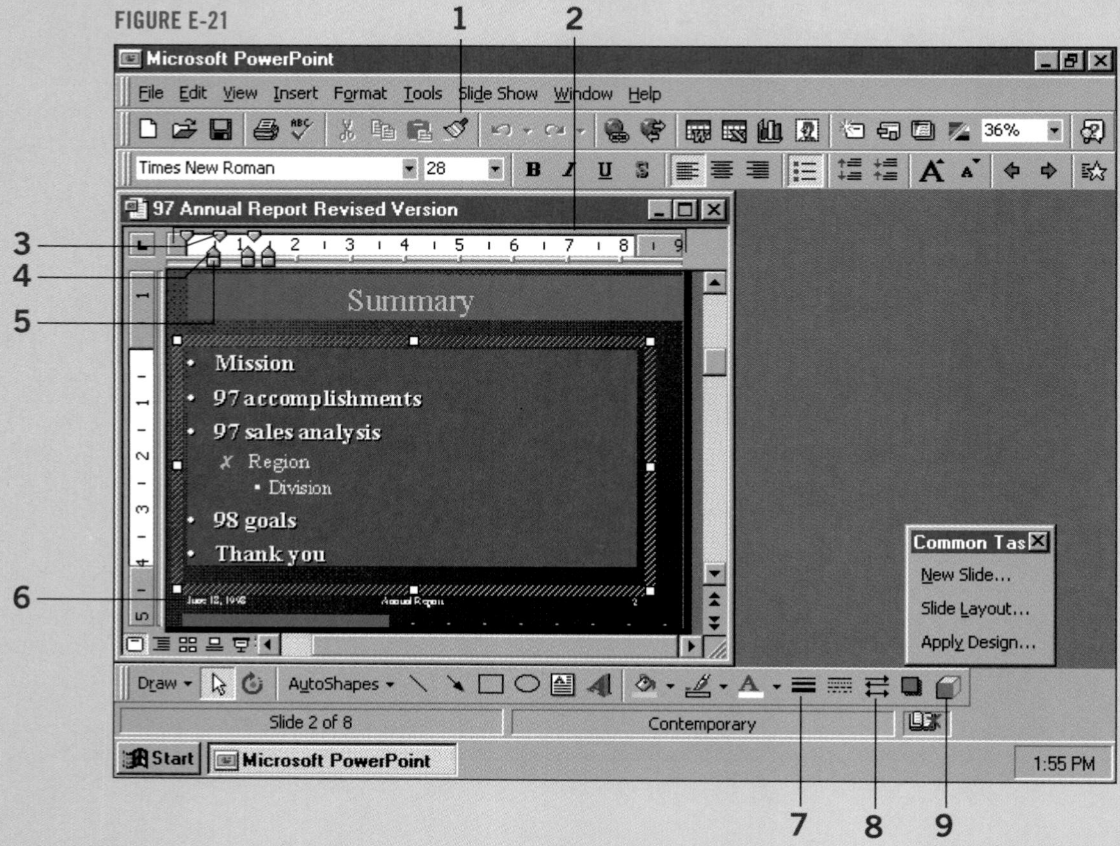

Match each of the terms with the statement that describes its function.

10. Each master text placeholder has five levels of text called
11. Moves the whole indent level
12. Controls subsequent lines of text in an indent level
13. A template for all the slides in a presentation
14. Adjusts the distance between text lines
15. Adjusts the position of text in a text object

a. Line spacing
b. Indent levels
c. Text anchor
d. Margin marker
e. Master
f. Bottom indent marker

Select the best answer from the list of choices.

16. Each line of text is identified on the ruler with
    a. Indent markers
    b. Indent levels
    c. Text levels
    d. Ruler markers

17. **A hanging indent is an indent in which the**
    - **a.** First line of text is to the right of subsequent lines of text
    - **b.** First line of text is to the left of subsequent lines of text
    - **c.** The bullet symbol is to the left of the first line of text
    - **d.** The bullet symbol is to the right of the first line of text

18. **Inserting a background item on the Slide Master**
    - **a.** Changes all views of your presentation
    - **b.** Is only seen on the title slide
    - **c.** Is a simple way to place an object on every slide of your presentation
    - **d.** Does not affect the slides of your presentation

19. **Which of the following does the Style Checker not check for?**
    - **a.** Case and punctuation in the presentation
    - **b.** A specified text font size
    - **c.** Title text that is off the slide
    - **d.** Incorrect color scheme colors

20. **What is leading?**
    - **a.** Vertical space between text lines
    - **b.** Horizontal space between lines of text
    - **c.** Diagonal space between text characters
    - **d.** Vertical space between text characters

► Skills Review

1. **Format master text.**
    - **a.** Start PowerPoint and open the presentation PPT E-2, then save it as Apparel Presentation.
    - **b.** Click the Next Slide button.
    - **c.** Switch to Slide Master view, then click anywhere in the first line of text in the Master text placeholder.
    - **d.** Click the Bold button on the Formatting toolbar.
    - **e.** Click Format on the menu bar, then click Bullet.
    - **f.** Use bullets from Monotype Sorts, click the second bullet from the left in the fourth row, then click the Size up arrow until 75 appears.
    - **g.** Click the Color list arrow, click the second color cell from the right, then click OK.
    - **h.** Click anywhere in the second line of text.
    - **i.** Click the Italic button on the Formatting toolbar.
    - **j.** Click the Font list arrow on the Formatting toolbar, then click Arial.
    - **k.** Click the Save button on the Standard toolbar.

2. Change master text indents.

a. With the insertion point still in the Master text placeholder, click View on the menu bar, then click Ruler.

b. Move the indent markers and margin markers of all the indent levels to match Figure E-22.

FIGURE E-22

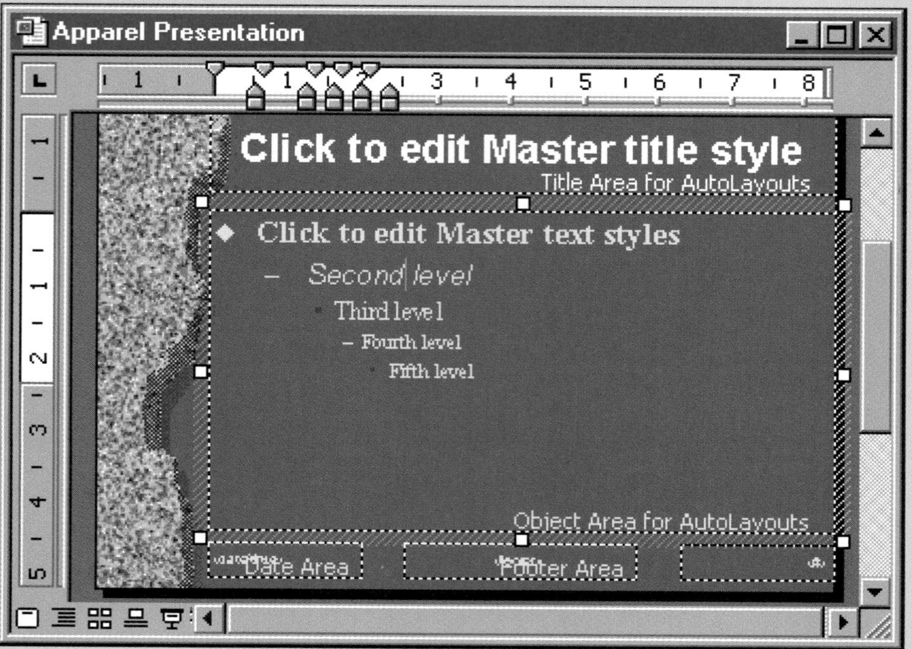

c. Right-click in a blank area of the presentation window, then click Ruler.

d. Click the Slide View button, then click the Save button on the Standard toolbar.

3. Add footers to slides.

a. Click View on the menu bar, then click Header and Footer.

b. Click the Date and time check box.

c. Click the Update automatically option button, click the Update automatically list arrow, then click the fourth option in the list.

d. Click the Slide number check box.

e. Click the Don't show on title slide check box.

f. Click the Notes and Handouts tab.

g. Click the Update automatically option button, click the Update automatically list arrow, then click the fifth option in the list.

h. In the Header text box, type "Apparel Division Report."

i. Click Apply to All.

j. Click the Notes Page View button. Notice the header and date information.

k. Click the Slide View button, then save your changes.

4. Adjust text objects.

a. Right-click anywhere in the main text object on Slide 2, then click Format AutoShape on the pop-up menu.

b. Click the Text Box tab.

c. Click the Text anchor point list arrow, click Middle, then click Preview.

d. In the Internal margin section, click the Left up arrow until 0.5 appears, then click Preview.

e. Click the Resize autoshape to fit text check box, then click Preview.

f. Click OK.

g. Move the pointer over the edge of the main text object, then click to select the entire object.

h. Click Format on the menu bar, then click Line Spacing.
i. In the Before paragraph section, click the up arrow until 0.3 appears, then click Preview.
j. Click OK.
k. Press ↑ four times to move the main text object up, then click the Save button on the Standard toolbar.

5. Use advanced drawing tools.

a. Drag the vertical scroll box to Slide 5.
b. Click the AutoShapes menu button on the Drawing toolbar, point to Connectors, then click the Elbow Connector button.
c. Position the cursor on the left side of the "Product Idea" diamond, then drag a connector line to the left side of the Review 1 diamond.
d. Click the AutoShapes menu button on the Drawing toolbar, point to Connectors, then click Straight Connector.
e. Position the cursor over the right side of the Review 1 diamond, then drag the connector line to the left side of the Review 2 diamond.
f. Click the AutoShapes menu button on the Drawing toolbar, point to Connectors, then click the Elbow Arrow Connector button.
g. Position the pointer over the right side of the Review 2 diamond, then drag the connector line to the point on the right side of the Product Idea diamond.
h. Press [Shift], then click the other two connector lines.
i. Click the Line Style button on the Drawing toolbar, click 3 pt, then click in a blank area of the slide.
j. Click the right connector line, click the Arrow Style button on the Drawing toolbar, then click More Arrows.
k. In the Arrows section, click the End size list arrow, click Arrow R Size 8, then click OK.
l. Click in a blank area of the slide, then save your changes.

6. Use advanced formatting tools.

a. Drag the vertical scroll box to Slide 1.
b. Press [Shift], right-click the text object in the lower right corner of the slide, then click Format AutoShape.
c. In the Fill section, click the Color list arrow, then click Fill Effects.
d. In the Colors section, click the One Color button, then click the Color1 option list arrow.
e. Click the second color cell from the right, then click the Light scroll arrow four times.
f. In the Variants section, click the bottom left variant, click OK, then click OK again.
g. Double-click the Format Painter button on the Standard toolbar, then drag the vertical scroll box to Slide 5.
h. Click each of the diamond objects, click the Format Painter button on the Standard toolbar, then click a blank area of the slide.
i. Press [Shift], click the Product Idea diamond object, click the 3-D button on the Drawing toolbar, then click the 3-D Style 14 button.
j. Click the 3-D button on the Drawing toolbar, then click 3-D Settings.
k. Click the Tilt Down button twice, then click the 3-D Settings toolbar Close button.
l. Double-click the Format Painter button on the Formatting toolbar, click the other two diamond objects, then click the Format Painter button again.
m. Select the three connector lines, then drag them slightly to the left so they connect the three objects.
n. Click in a blank area of the slide, then save your changes.

7. Use the Style Checker.

a. Click the Next Slide button.
b. Click Tools on the menu bar, then click Style Checker.
c. Click Options, then click the Visual Clarity tab.
d. In the Fonts section, double-click the number in the Title text size should be at least text box, then type "44".
e. In the Legibility section, click the Number of bullets should not exceed down arrow until 4 appears.
f. Click OK, deselect the Spelling check box, then click Start.

g. As the Style Checker finds inconsistencies, click Change to change them. Notice that your presentation changes.
h. Read the Style Checker Summary dialog box. Notice that the title text font is too small based on your adjustment to the Style Checker.
i. Click OK, press [Shift], then click the Slide View button.
j. Click anywhere in the Master title placeholder, then click the Increase Font Size button on the Formatting toolbar, then click the Slide View button.
k. Turn the Spelling option off and run the Style Checker again. Notice that the title text font size is no longer listed in the summary dialog box.
l. Click OK, then scroll through the presentation. Change the subtitle on the title slide so it is "A Nomad Ltd Division".
m. Save the presentation, print the presentation as Handouts (3 slides per page), then close the presentation.

Independent Challenges

1. You are the owner of Premier Catering in New York City. You have built your business on banquets, private parties, wedding receptions, and special events over the last five years. To expand, you decide to cater to the local business community by offering executive meals and business luncheons. Use PowerPoint to develop a presentation that you can use to gain corporate catering accounts.

In this independent challenge, you will create an outline and modify the look of a presentation. Create your own material to complete the slides of the presentation. Assume the following about Premier Catering:

- Premier Catering has eight full-time employees and 10 part-time employees.
- Premier Catering handles catering jobs from 10 people to 1000 people.
- Premier Catering is a full-service catering business providing cost estimates, set-up, complete preparation, service personnel, and clean up.

To complete this independent challenge:

1. Open the file PPT E-3, then save it as Premier.
2. Think about the results you want to see, the information you need, and how you want to communicate the message.
3. Switch to Outline view and create a presentation outline. As you type, misspell words so PowerPoint can automatically correct them as you type.
4. Customize your presentation by formatting the Slide Master.
5. Use PowerPoint's advanced drawing and formatting tools to give your presentation a unique look.
6. Switch to the last slide and change the text anchor and line spacing to create the best look.
7. Review the Style Checker options and then check the style of the presentation.
8. Print and submit the slides of your final presentation.

2. You are the finance director at Splat Records in Los Angeles, California. Splat Records specializes in alternative music. As an emerging record company, your business is looking for investment capital to expand its talent base and increase sales. It is your responsibility to develop the outline and basic look for a standard presentation that the president can present to various investors.

In this independent challenge, you will complete an outline and choose a custom background for the presentation. You'll need to create a presentation consisting of at least six slides. Assume the following about Splat Records:

- Splat Records has been in business for six years.
- Splat Records currently has 12 recording contracts. Splat wants to double that during the next year and a half.
- Splat Records has two superstar recording groups at the present time: RIM and Blacknight.

To complete this independent challenge:

1. Open the file PPT E-4, then save it as Splat.
2. Think about the results you want to see, the information you need, and how you want to communicate the message.

3. Enter text into the title and main text placeholders of the slides. As you type, misspell words so PowerPoint can automatically correct them as you type.
4. Use advanced drawing and formatting tools to create a unique look.
5. Check the style of the presentation.
6. Print and submit the slides of your final presentation.

3. You work for Graphics +, a small multimedia software company in Silicon Valley that develops games and entertainment applications. Your primary job is to promote your company's computer software ideas to different venture capitalists and to secure money to develop products. Develop a 10- to 15-slide presentation that promotes a software product idea. Use PowerPoint clip art and shapes to enhance your slides. Use one of PowerPoint's templates or design one of your own. You can use one of the following three ideas that Graphics + has been developing, or you can develop one of your own.

1. "Cavern Adventures," an interactive game in which you lead a group of thrill seekers on one of 10 different cave adventures throughout the world
2. "Posse," an interactive game that puts you in one of six different historical situations, where you lead a "posse" of people chasing after a convicted murderer
3. "Spies," an adventure game in which you are a spy for the Axis Powers or the Allies during World War II; assume there are six different situations to choose from for each political side

Create your own company information, but assume the following:

- The product is designed for adults and children ages 13 and up.
- The cost of product development is estimated to be $250,000. Development time is four months.
- The retail price of the final product is designed to be $50, given the current product development cost estimate. For every $10,000 increase in product development cost, the base retail price goes up $2.
- The final presentation will be shown as a static presentation using color overheads.

To complete this independent challenge:

1. Think about the results you want to see, the information you need to create the slide presentation, and the message you want to communicate.
2. Plan the story line of the software product using five or more slides. Plan the beginning and ending slides. What do you want your audience to know about the product idea?
3. Use clip art, shapes, and a shaded background to enhance the presentation. Change the bullet and text formatting in the master text and title placeholders to fit the subject matter.
4. Save the presentation as Graphics
5. Submit your presentation plan and print the final slide presentation.

4. You are the vice president of sales for Redwood Timber Products Inc, a company based in Northern California that harvests redwood trees and sells a number of redwood products. As the vice president of sales, one of your responsibilities is to nurture and develop new business contacts with foreign countries. You are going to give a presentation at an international timber conference in Portland, Oregon, where many prospective foreign buyers will be in attendance.

Plan and create a 10- to 15-slide presentation that focuses on Redwood Timber Products Inc. Redwood Timber Products has been in business for over 75 years and employs a 320-person work force. Develop your own content, but assume the following:

- Redwood Timber Products harvests 75,000 acres per year and replants with 92,000 acres per year.
- Redwood Timber Products can harvest and deliver 400,000 tons of timber per month overseas.
- Redwood Timber Products uses Pacific Shipping Inc to deliver timber to overseas locations.
- Timber prices range from $10 to $16 per board foot depending on the size and grade (or quality) of the lumber. Lumber grades are designated with numbers as follows: "1" for top grade, "2" for middle grade, and "3" for bottom grade.
- Many of the attendees at the conference are from Middle Eastern countries.

The presentation will be shown with a projection screen and will last approximately 30 minutes.
To complete this independent challenge:

1. Think about the results you want to see, the information you need to create the slide presentation, what type of message you want to communicate, and the target audience.
2. Use the AutoContent Wizard to help you start an outline.
3. Log on to the Internet and use your browser to go to http://www.course.com. From there, click Student Online Companions, click the link for this textbook, then click the PowerPoint link for Unit E. Use the link there to research shipping costs, and include this information in your presentation.
4. Use clip art or pictures to enhance the presentation. Use culturally relevant symbols to appeal to your audience. Add or create a shaded background template for the presentation.
5. Format the content, then save the presentation as Redwood.
6. Submit your presentation plan and print the final slide presentation.

Visual Workshop

Create two slides that look like the examples in Figures E-23 and E-24. Save the presentation as New Products. Save and print the Slide view of the presentation. Submit the final presentation output.

FIGURE E-23:

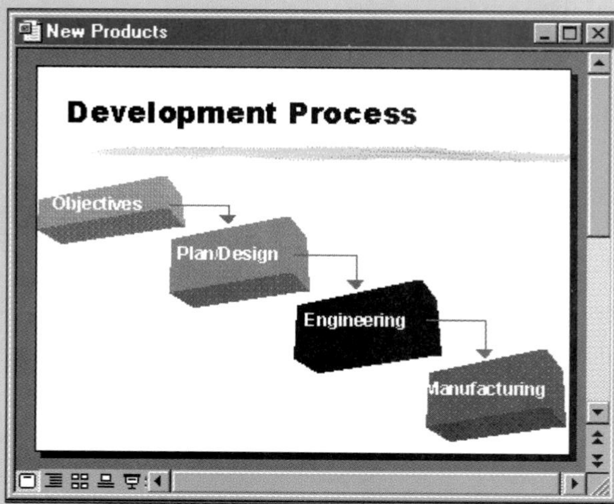

FIGURE E-24:

Enhancing
Charts

Objectives

- Insert data from a file into a datasheet
- Format a datasheet
- Change a chart's type
- Customize a chart's 3-D view
- Customize a chart
- Work with chart elements
- Embed and format an organizational chart
- Modify an organizational chart

A PowerPoint presentation is a visual communication tool. A slide that delivers information with a relevant graphic object has a more lasting impact than a slide with plain text. Graphs and charts often communicate information more effectively than words. Microsoft Graph and Microsoft Organization Chart are built-in PowerPoint programs that allow you to easily create and embed charts in your presentation. In this unit, Carrie Armstrong updates the data and enhances the appearance of a Microsoft Graph chart, and then creates and formats an organizational chart showing the top company structure at Nomad Ltd.

Inserting Data from a File into a Datasheet

With Microsoft Graph, you can enter your own data into a datasheet using the keyboard or you can import existing data from a spreadsheet program like Microsoft Excel. The sales manager gave Carrie sales data in an Excel file. Carrie wants to insert this data as a chart on Slide 6. To do this, she will open Graph and import the updated data from Excel.

1. **Start PowerPoint and open the presentation PPT F-1, save it as 97 Annual Report Revised Version 2, make sure the zoom is set for 36%, click the Restore Window button in the Presentation window, click Window on the menu bar, then click Fit to Page**
   Move to Slide 6 to make changes to the chart on the slide.
2. **Drag the vertical scroll box to Slide 6, then double-click the chart object**
   Insert the data into the Graph datasheet from your Excel worksheet.
3. **Click the first cell (upper left corner) in the datasheet**
   This indicates where the imported data will appear in the datasheet.
4. **Click the Import File button on the Graph Standard toolbar**
   The Import File dialog box opens.
5. **Locate the worksheet file PPT F-2, then click Open**
   The Import Data Options dialog box opens. All the options are correctly marked, so just click OK.
6. **Click OK**
   Compare your screen to Figure F-1. The chart changes to reflect the new data you inserted into the datasheet. The data in Column D does not need to be included in the chart, so you can exclude it.
7. **Double-click the Column D control box**
   Control boxes are the gray boxes located along the edges of the datasheet, as shown in Figure F-2. The data in column D are grayed out, indicating that they're excluded from the datasheet and will not be displayed in the chart. To include data that you've previously excluded, double-click the control box again. Next, save your changes.
8. **Click the Save button on the Standard toolbar**

QuickTip

You can change Graph options, such as how empty cells are plotted in the chart or the color of chart fills and lines, by choosing Options from the Tools menu.

FIGURE F-1: Datasheet showing imported data

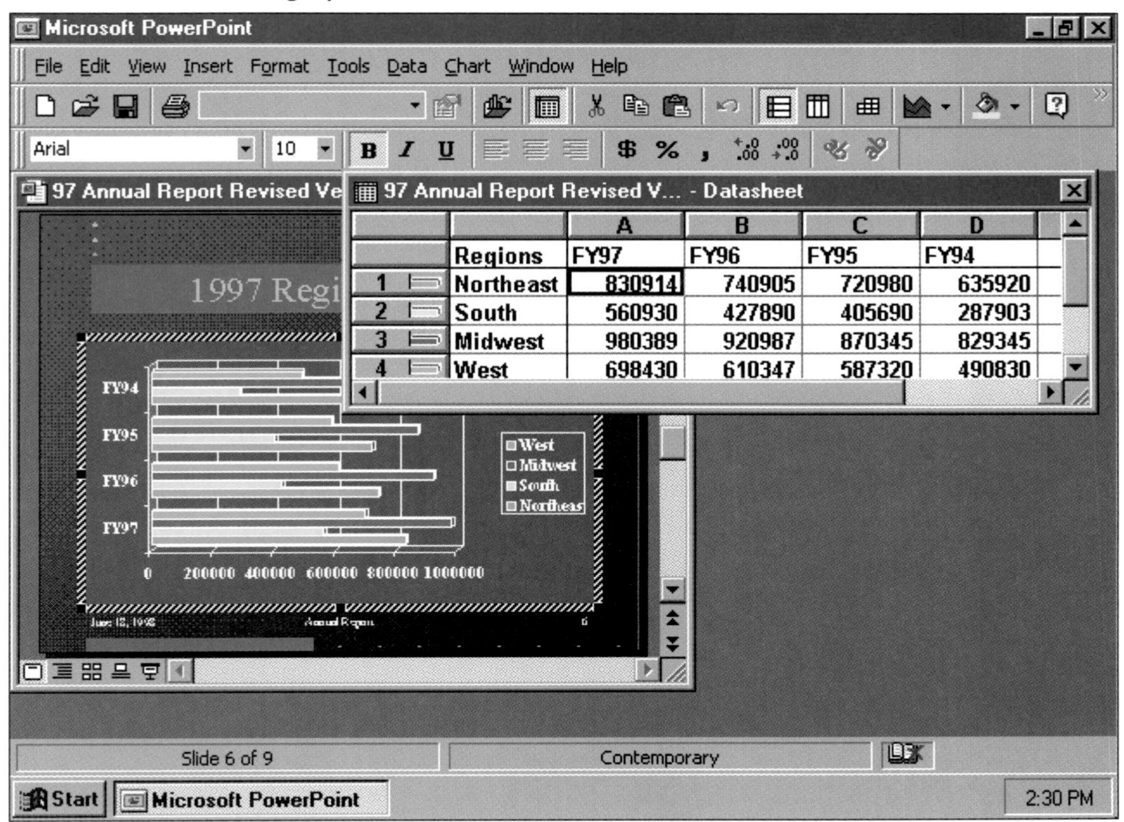

		A	B	C	D
	Regions	FY97	FY96	FY95	FY94
1	Northeast	830914	740905	720980	635920
2	South	560930	427890	405690	287903
3	Midwest	980389	920987	870345	829345
4	West	698430	610347	587320	490830

FIGURE F-2: Datasheet showing excluded column

97 Annual Report Revised V... - Datasheet

		A	B	C	D
	Regions	FY97	FY96	FY95	FY94
1	Northeast	830914	740905	720980	635920
2	South	560930	427890	405690	287903
3	Midwest	980389	920987	870345	829345
4	West	698430	610347	587320	490830

Column D control box

Data series and data series markers

Each column or row of data in the datasheet is called a **data series.** Each data series has corresponding **data series markers** in the chart, which are graphical representations such as bars, columns, or pie wedges. Figure F-3 shows how each number in the West data series row appears in the chart.

FIGURE F-3: Graph chart and datasheet

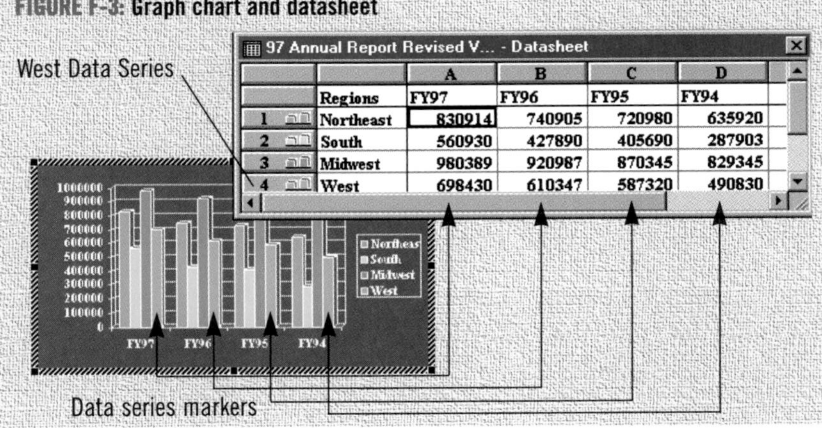

		A	B	C	D
	Regions	FY97	FY96	FY95	FY94
1	Northeast	830914	740905	720980	635920
2	South	560930	427890	405690	287903
3	Midwest	980389	920987	870345	829345
4	West	698430	610347	587320	490830

PowerPoint 97

Formatting a Datasheet

Once you've imported the data from another file, it can be helpful to modify and format the datasheet to make your data easier to view and manipulate. With Graph, you can make simple formatting changes to the font, number format, and column size in your datasheet. To format the data in the datasheet, you must first select the data. 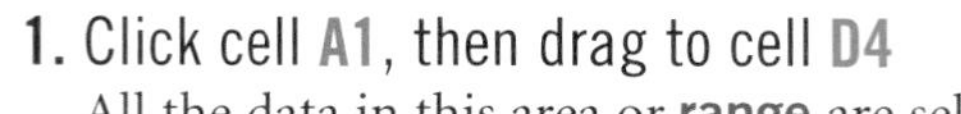 In this lesson, Carrie changes the size of the chart and the number format to display the sales numbers correctly, then she changes the chart to show the sales by region rather than by year.

Steps

Trouble?
If you can't see all the rows and columns, resize the datasheet window.

1. **Click cell A1, then drag to cell D4**
   All the data in this area or **range** are selected.
2. **Right-click the selection, then click Number on the pop-up menu**
   The Format number dialog box opens. The Category list on the left side of the dialog box displays the format categories. Change the datasheet numbers to the Currency format.
3. **In the Category list box, click Currency**
   Notice the sample number format at the top of the dialog box that shows you how the selected format code will display your data. Compare your Format number dialog box to Figure F-4.

QuickTip
To quickly change the number format to Currency, click the Currency Style button $ on the Graph Formatting toolbar.

4. **Click OK**
   The data in the datasheet and in the chart change to the new number format. Graph cannot display the numbers properly, however, because the new format increased the number of placeholders that each number has. Change all the column widths so the data can be displayed properly.
5. **With all the columns still selected, click Format on the menu bar, click Column Width, then click Best Fit**
   The column widths increase to accommodate the Currency format. Now, eliminate the numbers after the decimal point.

QuickTip
To increase the column width to fit the widest cell of data in a column, double-click ✣ over the control box border.

6. **Click the Decrease Decimal button on the Graph Formatting toolbar twice, then click anywhere in the datasheet**
   This chart would be more helpful if it displayed the Regions along the y-axis.
7. **Click Data on the menu bar, then click Series in Columns**
   The column icons now appearing in the column control boxes change to indicate that the data is shown in a series by column. Compare your datasheet to Figure F-5.
8. **Click the Close button in the datasheet**
   The datasheet closes, but Graph is still open. Save your changes.
9. **Click the Save button on the Standard toolbar**

FIGURE F-4: Format number dialog box

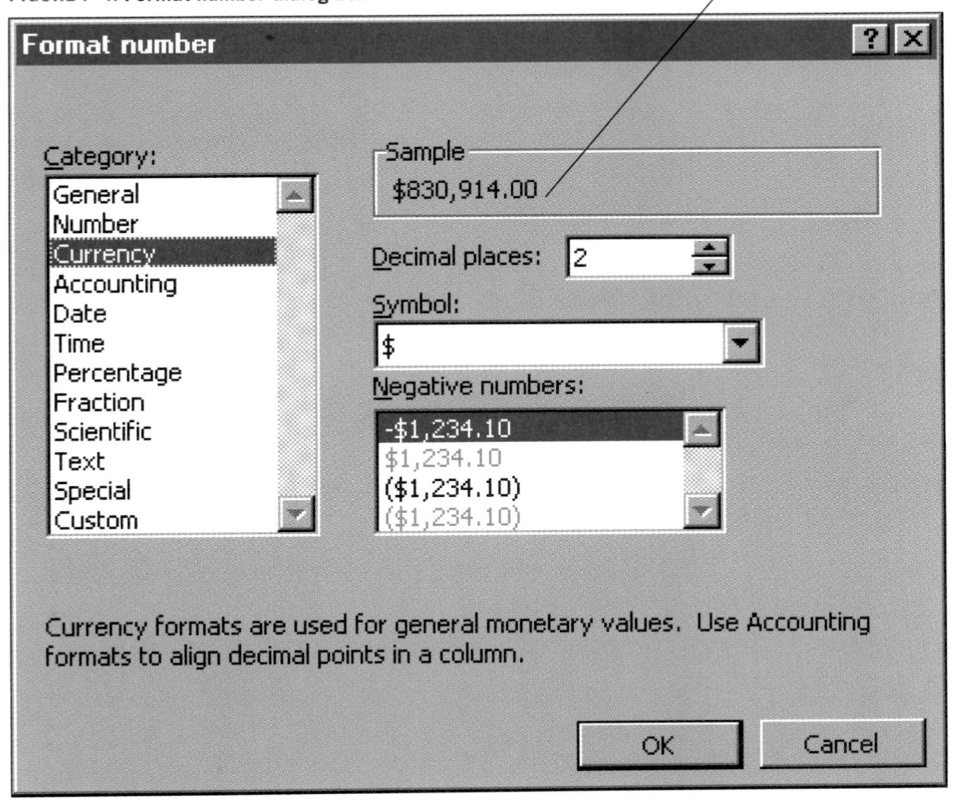

FIGURE F-5: Datasheet showing formatted data

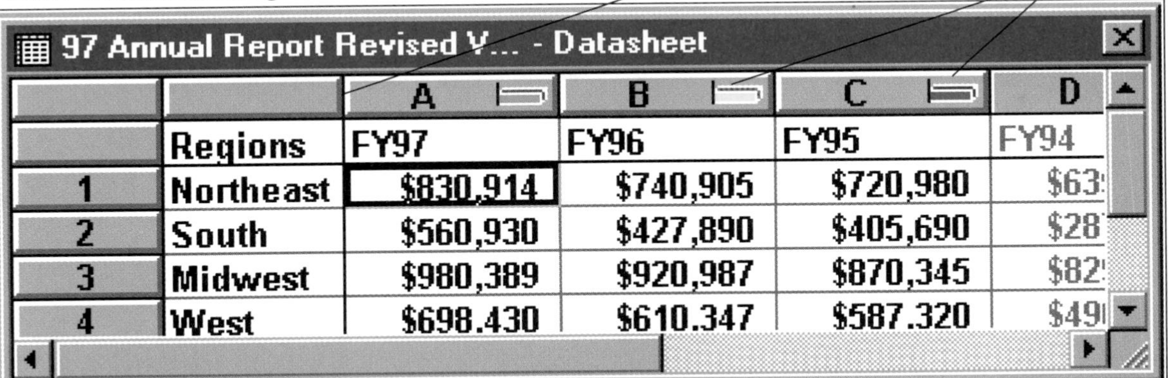

Formatting: datasheets and charts

You can format data in both datasheets and in charts created by Graph. Sometimes it's easier to view the numbers in the datasheet after they have been formatted; other times, you may want to manipulate the numbers after they have been placed into a chart to get a better picture. After you've formatted the data in the datasheet, the formatting changes will be reflected in the chart; however, formatting changes made to the data in the chart will not be reflected in the datasheet.

PowerPoint 97

Changing a Chart's Type

Each chart has a specific type that defines how the chart graphically displays the data from the datasheet. There are over 20 chart type categories, including two-dimensional and three-dimensional graphs. Some of the most common chart types are area, bar, column, line, and pie charts. The type of chart you choose depends on the amount of information you have and how it's best displayed. For example, a chart with more than six or seven data series does not fit well in a pie chart. You can change a chart type quickly and easily by using the Chart Type command on the Chart menu. Carrie decides that a column chart on Slide 6 would communicate the information more clearly than a bar chart.

Steps 1 2 3 4

1. **With the chart still selected and Graph still open, click Chart on the menu bar, then click Chart Type**
   The Chart Type dialog box opens. Change the chart from a three-dimensional bar chart to a three-dimensional column chart.
2. **In the Chart type section, click Column, in the Chart sub-type section, click the sub-type shown in Figure F-6, then click OK**
   Now, customize the chart format by changing the column positions.
3. **Click the Chart Objects list arrow on the Standard toolbar, click Series "FY97", click Format on the menu bar, then click Selected Data Series**
   The Format Data Series dialog box opens as shown in Figure F-7. Change the color of the data series to green.
4. **In the Area section, click the green square in the second row, third column, then click the Options tab**
   The Options tab contains three sizing options that change the way the chart appears. **Gap depth** changes the size of the base area, or **floor**, of the chart; **Gap width** changes the distance between each group of data series; and **Chart depth** changes the size of the data series markers on the chart. Now, change the way the chart appears.
5. **Double-click the Gap depth text field, type 100, then click OK**
   Notice that the data series changes to a green color and the size of the chart floor enlarges. Go back now and change the other two chart sizing options.
6. **Right-click one of the columns in the FY97 data series, then click Format Data Series on the pop-up menu**
   The Format Data Series dialog box opens. Change the Gap width and Chart depth options.
7. **Double-click the Gap width text field, then type 200**
8. **Double-click the Chart depth text field, type 250, then click OK**
9. **Click the Save button on the Graph Standard toolbar**
   Compare your chart to Figure F-8.

QuickTip

To easily change your chart's type, click the Chart Type button on the Graph Standard toolbar.

FIGURE F-6: **Chart Type dialog box**

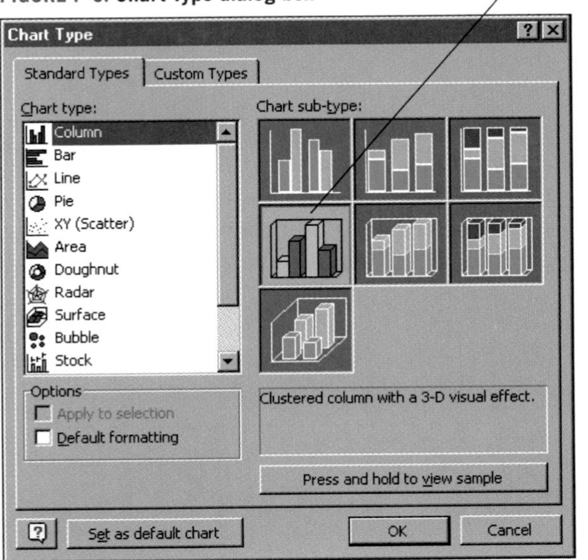

FIGURE F-7: **Format Data Series dialog box**

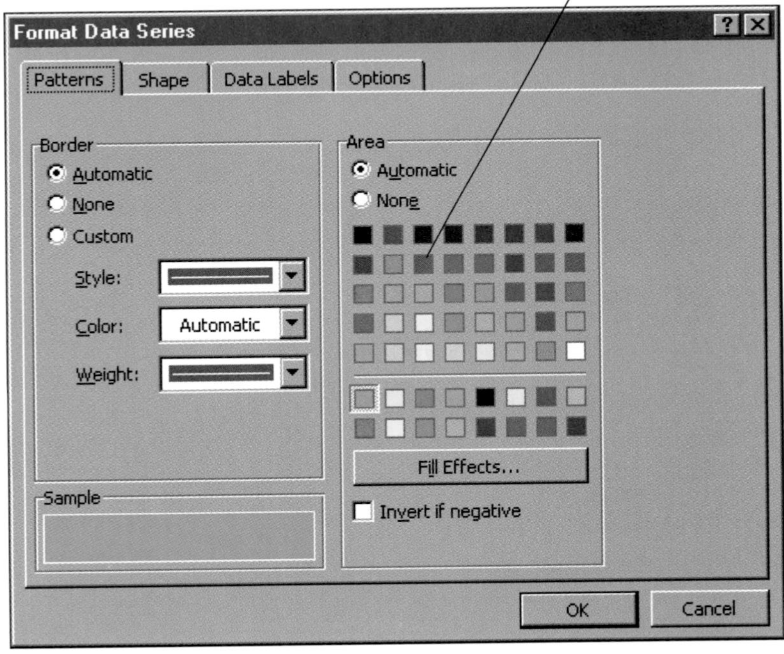

FIGURE F-8: **Formatted chart**

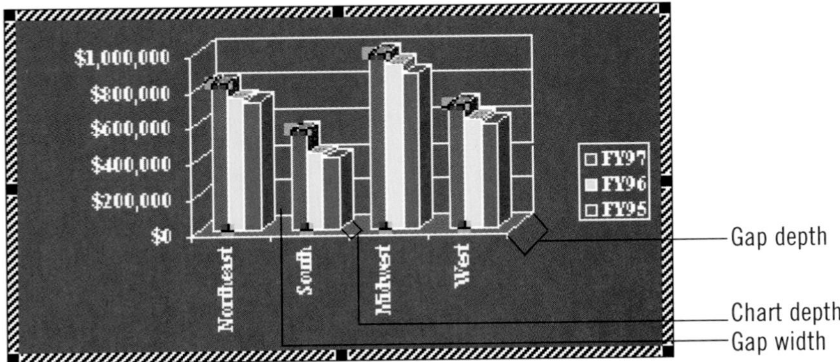

PowerPoint 97

PowerPoint 97

Customizing a Chart's 3-D View

In Graph, every two-dimensional and three-dimensional chart format has a default position setting that determines the chart's placement on the slide. The 3-D formatting options allow you to creatively display your chart on the slide. Refer to Table F-1 for a description of the most common 3-D view options. One format option that you can change on most 3-D charts is the **elevation** or angle at which you view the chart. By changing the elevation, you can view a chart from above or below. Another option you can change is the **rotation** of the chart. This allows you to rotate that chart around so that you can get a clearer view of the data that interests you. Carrie experiments with the 3-D options by changing the elevation and rotation of her chart.

Steps

1. Click **Chart** on the menu bar, then click **3-D View**
   The 3-D View dialog box opens, as shown in Figure F-9. Change the elevation of the chart.
2. Click the **Elevation up arrow** twice, then click **Apply**
   The elevation setting changes to 25. Notice that the chart in the Preview box changes to show you how the chart looks with the new elevation setting. To see the changes on your slide, drag the dialog box up.
3. Drag the 3-D View dialog box up by its title bar until you see the chart in Slide 6
   Now, rotate the chart to the left to give it a more dramatic appearance.
4. Click the **Rotation left arrow** twice, then click **Apply**
   The rotation setting changes to 40. The new rotation setting moves the chart around to the left, which displays more of the side of the data series columns. To see how the perspective feature changes the chart format, you'll need to clear the Right angle axes check box.
5. Click the **Right angle axes check box** to clear it
   Notice that the Perspective option appears and the Preview box changes to show the default perspective setting. Change the perspective of the chart.
6. Click the **Perspective down arrow** until 50 appears, then click **Apply**
   The chart appears farther away. Turning the Right angle axes option off drastically changes the way this particular chart looks, so turn the option back on to reset the chart.
7. Click the **Right angle axes check box**, then click **Apply**
   The chart looks best with the current settings.
8. Click **OK**
   Compare your screen to Figure F-10. Save your changes.
9. Click the **Save button** on the Standard toolbar

QuickTip

Click Default in the 3-D View dialog box to return your chart to its original settings.

FIGURE F-9: 3-D View dialog box

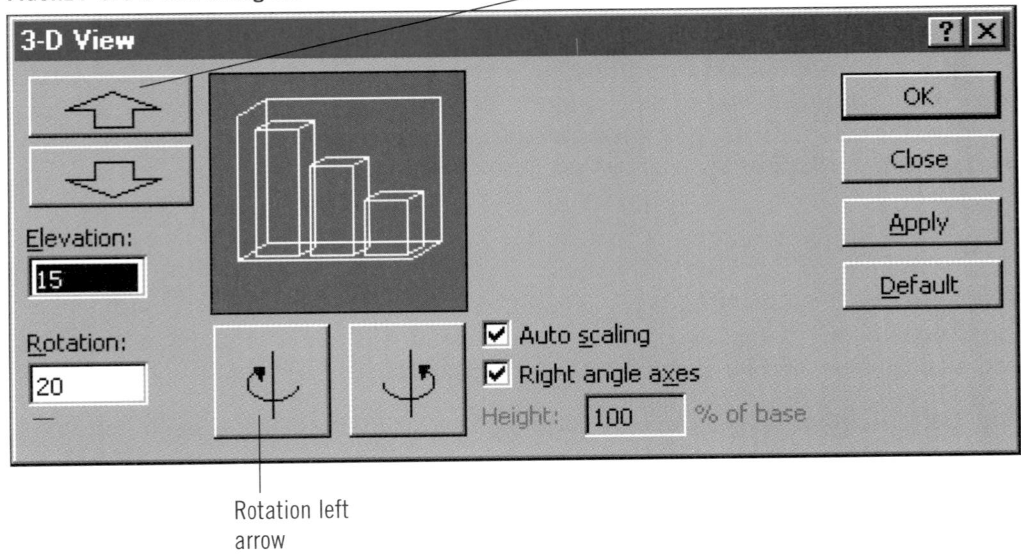

FIGURE F-10: Formatted Chart

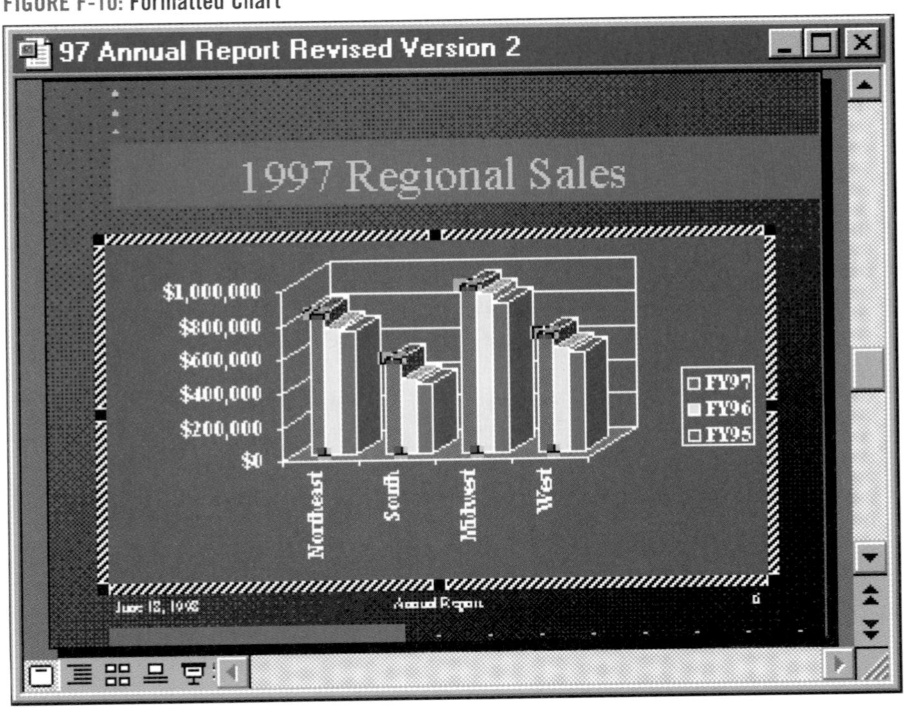

TABLE F-1: Understanding the 3-D View options

option	definition
Elevation	Controls the height or angle from which you view the chart; the elevation ranges from +90 degrees to -90 degrees
Rotation	Controls the horizontal rotation of the plot area; you can rotate your graph from 0 degrees to 360 degrees
Auto Scaling	Controls the scale of a chart automatically; helps keep the size of the chart proportional when changing a two-dimensional chart to a three-dimensional chart
Right Angle Axes	Controls the orientation of the axes; when this option is checked, the axes of the chart appear at right angles to each other
Perspective	Controls the distance perspective; the higher the perspective, the farther away the chart appears; only available when the Right Angle Axes option is turned off

Customizing a Chart

Graph provides many advanced formatting options so that you can customize your chart to emphasize the information you think is important. For example, you can add gridlines to a chart, change the color or pattern of data markers, and format the axes. Carrie wants to improve the appearance of her chart, so she makes several formatting changes.

Steps

1. Click **Chart** on the menu bar, then click **Chart Options**
   The Chart Options dialog box opens. First, add major and minor gridlines to the x-axis. Gridlines help separate and clarify the data series markers.

2. Click the **Gridlines tab** in the Category (X) axis section, click the **Major gridlines check box**, then click the **Minor gridlines check box**
   Gridlines appear on the floor and back of the chart in the Preview box. Compare your screen to Figure F-11. Adding minor gridlines increases the number of gridlines in the chart. Now, add the data table to the chart.

3. Click the **Data Table tab**, click the **Show data table check box**, then click **OK**
   Adding the data table dramatically decreased the size of the chart, so undo your last action.

4. Click **Chart** on the menu bar, click **Chart Options**, click the **Show data table check box** to deselect it, then click **OK**
   Next, add data labels to one of the data series to make the series easier to identify.

5. Double-click one of the **FY97 data markers** in the chart, click the **Data Labels tab** in the Format Data Series dialog box, click the **Show value option button**, then click **OK**
   Each data marker's value from the datasheet is displayed, as shown in Figure F-12. Now, finish the formatting of the chart by modifying the z-axis. In a three-dimensional chart, the vertical axis is the z-axis.

6. Right-click one of the **values** on the z-axis, click **Format Axis** on the pop-up menu, then click the **Scale tab**
   The Scale tab in the Format axis dialog box opens. Change the major unit number to better display the values on the z-axis.

7. Double-click **200000** in the Major unit text field, type **100000**, then click **OK**
   Notice that the values on the z-axis change to the new unit scale. Now, check to see how your chart looks on the slide.

8. Click a blank area of the slide
   Compare your screen to Figure F-13.

Trouble?

If the incorrect formatting dialog box opens, you double-clicked the wrong chart element. Close the dialog box, then double-click the correct chart element.

Time To

✓ Save

FIGURE F-11: Chart options dialog box

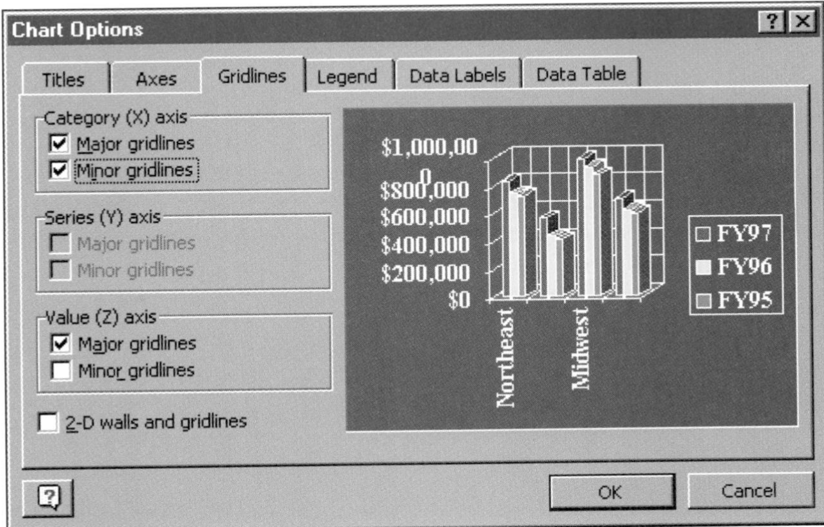

FIGURE F-12: Chart showing data marker labels

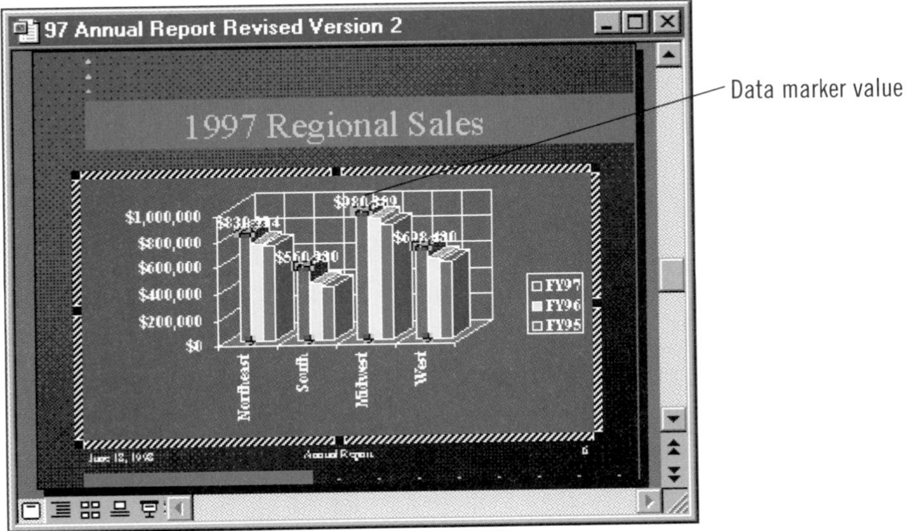

FIGURE F-13: Modified chart

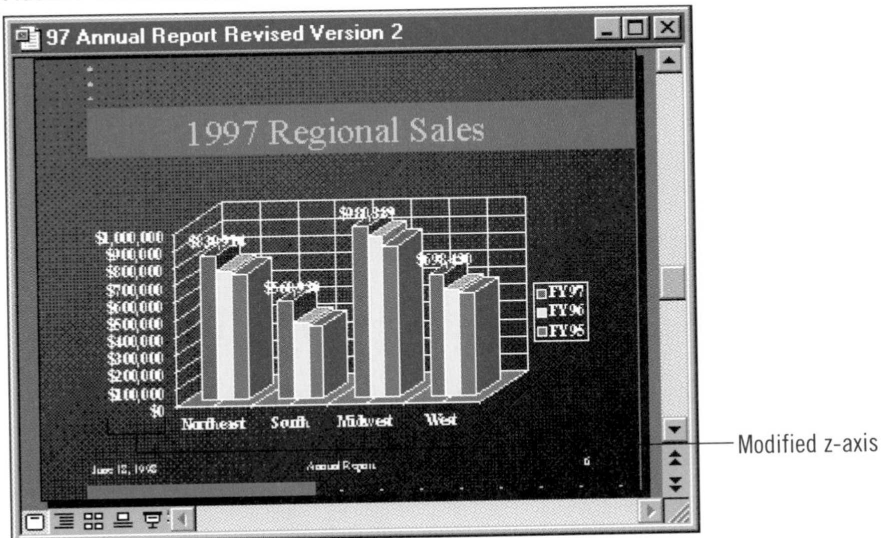

Working with Chart Elements

Chart elements are objects you can add and format to help display or highlight certain information in your chart. Chart elements include legends, arrows, shapes or lines, text objects, and chart titles. Carrie decides to add a text object and an arrow to draw attention to particularly strong sales from the Midwest sales region.

1. Double-click the **Graph chart object**
   Graph opens and displays the chart from the previous lesson. Display the Graph Drawing toolbar, then add a text object to the chart.
2. Right-click the **Graph Formatting toolbar**, click **Drawing** on the pop-up menu, then click the **Text Box button** on the Drawing toolbar
   The pointer changes to +. Due to the limited blank space in the chart, create the text box over the top of the chart.
3. Position + over the top right side of the chart, drag to create a text box, then type **Over Goal**
   Compare your screen to Figure F-14. After typing the text into the text box, it's apparent that the text is difficult to read. Change the color and size of the text.
4. Drag I over the text to select it, click **Format** on the menu bar, then click **Text Box**
   The Format Text Box dialog box opens.
5. Click the **Color list arrow**, click the **red box** in the last row, scroll down the **Size list**, click **22**, click **OK**, then click in a blank area of the chart
   Now, draw an arrow to connect the new text object to a data marker in the chart.
6. Click the **Arrow button** on the Drawing toolbar, position + to the left of the word "Over," then drag an arrow to the top of the Midwest data markers
   Modify the arrow slightly to make it stand out better.
7. Click the **Arrow Style button** on the Drawing toolbar, click **More Arrows**, then in the Line section, click the **Color list arrow**
   Change the arrow line color to yellow and change the arrow format.
8. Click one of the **yellow boxes** in the color palette, click the **Weight up arrow** until **2 pt** appears, then click **OK**
9. Click a blank area of the slide, then click the **Save button** on the Standard toolbar
   Compare your screen to Figure F-15.

Trouble?

If the text object is not where you want it, refer to the Clues to Use, then reposition the object.

Trouble?

Resize the text box if necessary to accommodate the larger font size.

FIGURE F-14: Chart showing new text object

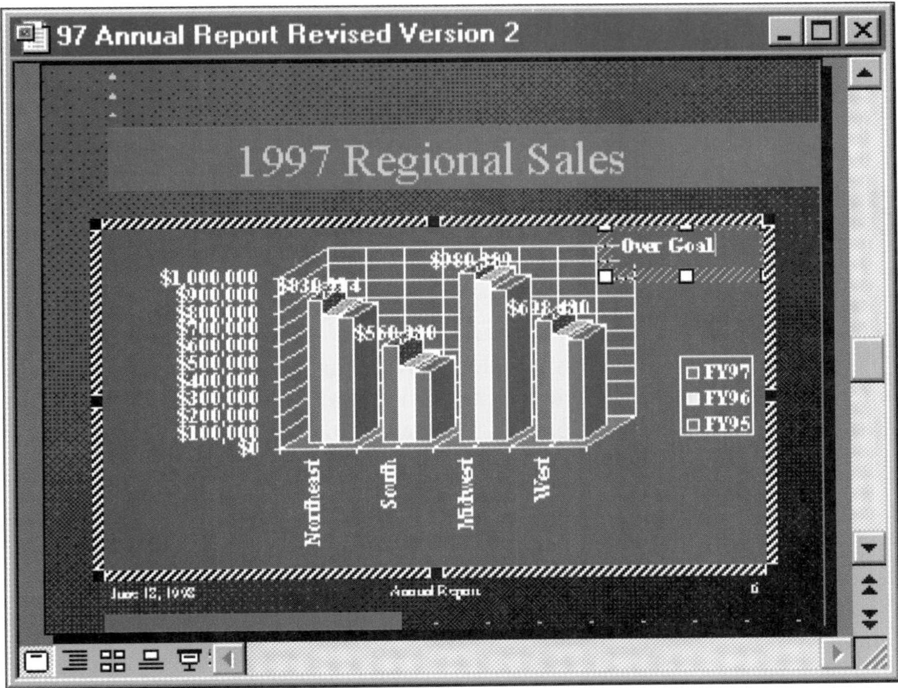

FIGURE F-15: Chart showing added elements

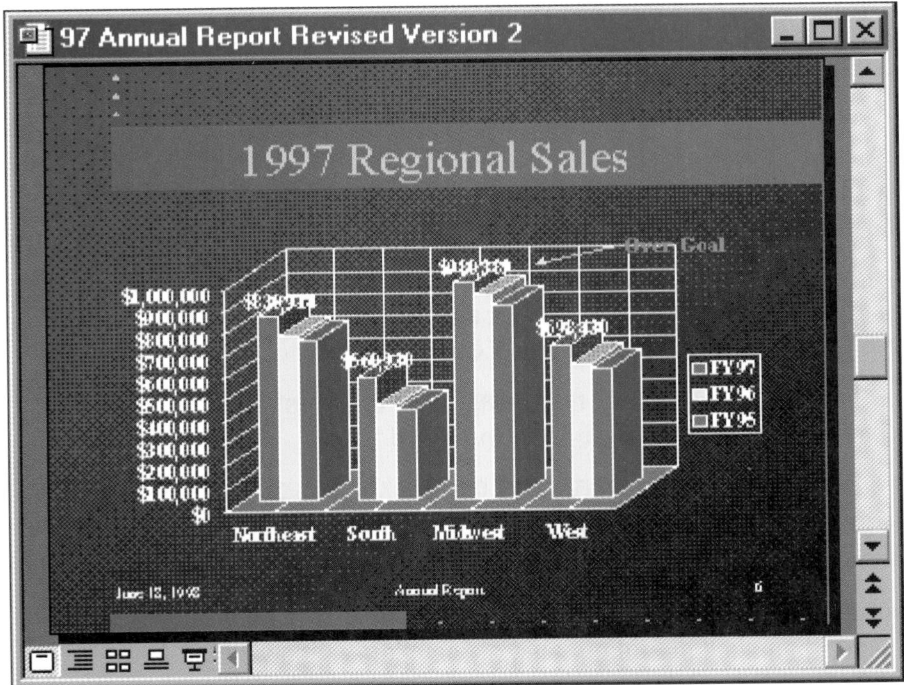

Moving and sizing chart elements

To move a chart element, such as an arrow or legend, you must first select the object to display its resize handles, then drag the object to a new location. Make sure that the cursor is over the border when you drag, not over the resize handle. To change the size of a chart element, click the object to display its resize handles, then drag a resize handle.

PowerPoint 97

Embedding and Formatting an Organizational Chart

You can create an organizational chart by using the Object command on the Insert menu or by changing the layout of your slide to the Organization Chart slide AutoLayout. Once you open Microsoft Organization Chart, a series of connected boxes called **chart boxes** appears. Each chart box has placeholder text that you replace with the names and titles of people in your organization. Carrie is satisfied with her graph and now turns her attention to creating an organizational chart showing Nomad's top management structure. Follow Carrie as she creates a basic organizational chart.

1. Drag the vertical scroll box to Slide 8, click **New Slide** on the Common Tasks toolbar, click the **Organization Chart AutoLayout**, then click **OK**
   A new slide appears displaying the Organization Chart placeholder. Use the Organization Chart placeholder to insert a new organizational chart.
2. Type **Nomad Ltd**, then double-click the **org chart placeholder**
   The text you type is entered into the title placeholder and the default organizational chart appears in a separate window, as shown in Figure F-16. The default organizational chart displays a chart title and four chart boxes. The open chart box at the top of the window is a **Manager chart box** and the three chart boxes below it are **Subordinate chart boxes**. Notice that the Manager chart box is selected and ready to accept text.
3. Type **Bill Davidson**, press **[Tab]**, type **President**, then click a blank area of the Organization chart window
   Now fill in the three subordinate chart boxes.
4. Enter the information in the Subordinate chart boxes shown in Figure F-17
   Click each chart box to enter the first line of text, then press [Tab] to move from line to line. Now, format the chart boxes using Organization Chart's formatting tools.
5. Click **Edit** on the Organization Chart menu bar, point to **Select**, then click **All**
   All the chart boxes are selected and ready to be formatted.
6. Click **Boxes** on the Organization Chart menu bar, click **Color**, click the fifth color cell from the left in the top row, then click **OK**
   The chart boxes change to a deep blue color. Now change the chart box connector line style.
7. Click **Lines** on the Organization Chart menu bar, point to **Thickness**, click the third line in the menu, then click in a blank area of the chart window
   Notice that the connector line between the chart boxes is thicker. Now embed the organizational chart in your slide.
8. Click **File** on the menu bar, then click **Exit and Return to 97 Annual Report Revised Version 2**
   A Microsoft Organization Chart alert box opens to confirm your desire to update your slide with the organizational chart.
9. Click **Yes** to update the presentation, then click a blank area of the Presentation window
   Compare your screen to Figure F-18.

QuickTip

You can also press [Enter] to move to the next placeholder in a chart box.

Time To

✓ Save

FIGURE F-16: Default organizational chart

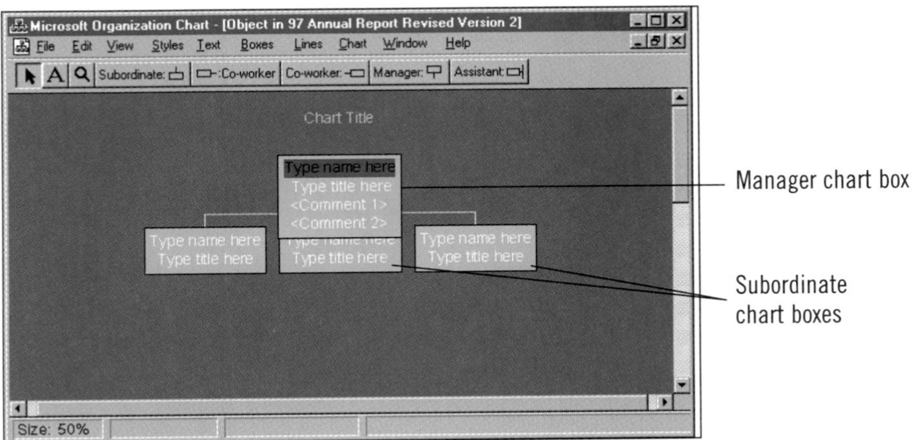

FIGURE F-17: Organizational chart showing filled-in chart boxes

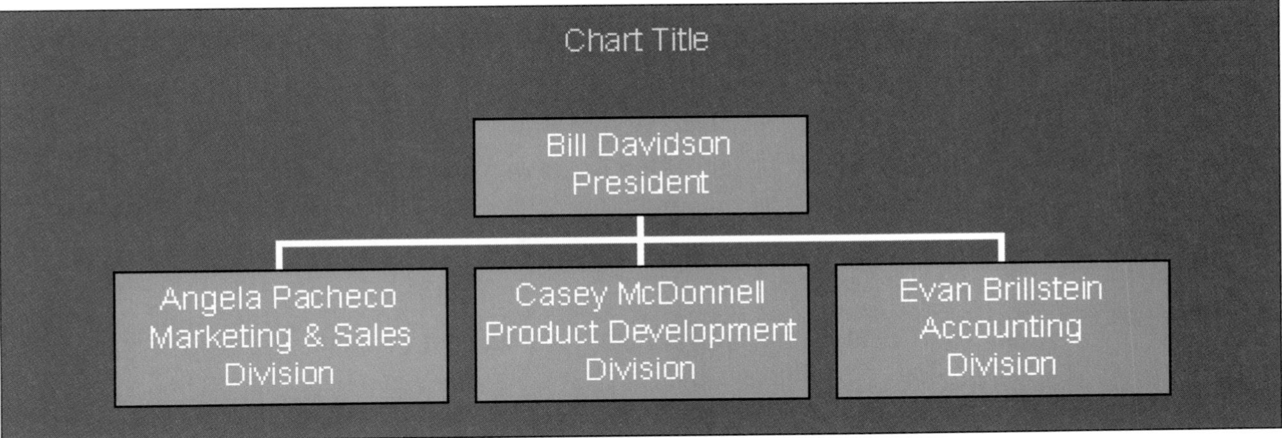

FIGURE F-18: Organizational chart embedded on the slide

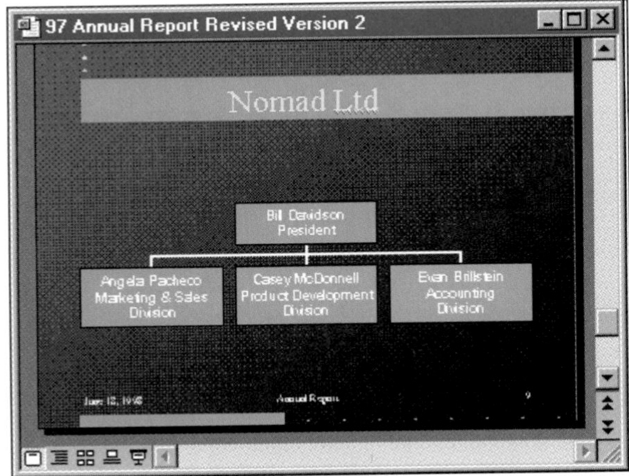

Changing chart styles

In Organization Chart you can change the way chart boxes are grouped together by clicking a group style on the Styles menu. Figure F-20 illustrates how each Styles button displays subordinate chart boxes relative to the Manager chart box.

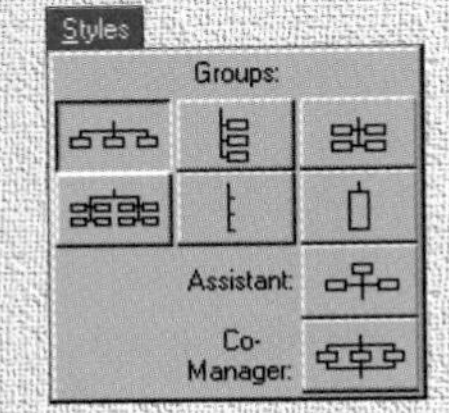

FIGURE F-19: Styles Menu

PowerPoint 97

PowerPoint 97

Modifying an Organizational Chart

If the organizational chart you want to create requires more than the four default chart boxes, you can add up to nine chart boxes in a row and thirteen chart boxes in a column to accommodate more information. Note, however, that each chart box you add automatically decreases the size of all the chart boxes so that the organizational chart fits on the slide. After you add all the chart boxes you need for your chart, you can rearrange them as desired. Carrie needs to add two chart boxes to her organizational chart.

1. Double-click the **organizational chart**
   The Organization Chart window opens, displaying the organizational chart you created in the last lesson. Maximize the window to make it easier to work with all the chart boxes.
2. Click the **Microsoft Organization Chart window Maximize button**
   The Organization Chart window fills the screen. Now, add a co-worker chart box.
3. Click the **Right Co-worker button** [Co-worker:] on the Organization Chart toolbar
   The pointer changes to
4. Click the **Evan Brillstein chart box**, type **Michael Belmont**, press **[Tab]**, type **Travel**, press **[Tab]**, type **Division**, then click in a blank area of the Organization Chart window
   Compare your screen to Figure F-20. Now, add a subordinate chart box to the chart.
5. Click the **Subordinate button** [Subordinate:] on the Organization Chart toolbar, then click the **Michael Belmont chart box**
   A small blank chart box appears.
6. Type **Barry Cheda**, press **[Tab]**, type **Executive Director**, then click in a blank area of the Organization Chart window
   Change the placement of the Michael Belmont chart box to another position on the chart.
7. Drag the **Michael Belmont chart box** on top of the Casey McDonnell chart box until the pointer changes to ⇦, release the mouse button, then click in a blank area of the Organization Chart window
   You may have to experiment with the placement of the chart box until the pointer changes to ⇦ . Compare your organizational chart to Figure F-21. Notice that the subordinate chart box moves with the Co-worker chart box to the new location in the chart. When you move a chart box, all of its subordinate chart boxes move with it, which makes it easy to rearrange the organizational chart. See Table F-2 for an explanation of chart box placement arrows.
8. Click **File** on the menu bar, then click **Exit and Return to 97 Annual Report Revised Version 2**, click **Yes** to update the presentation, click a blank area of the Presentation window, click **Slide Layout** on the Common Tasks toolbar, then click **Reapply**
9. Click the **Slide Sorter View button** , then click the **Maximize button** in the Presentation window
   Compare your screen to Figure F-22.

QuickTip

See the Organization Chart on-line Help for information on keyboard commands you can use to create and edit chart boxes.

Trouble?

When you move a chart box, make sure the correct placement arrow appears before you release the mouse button.

Time To

- Save
- Run the slide show
- Print handouts (3 slides per page)
- Close the presentation

FIGURE F-20: **Organizational chart showing new co-worker chart box**

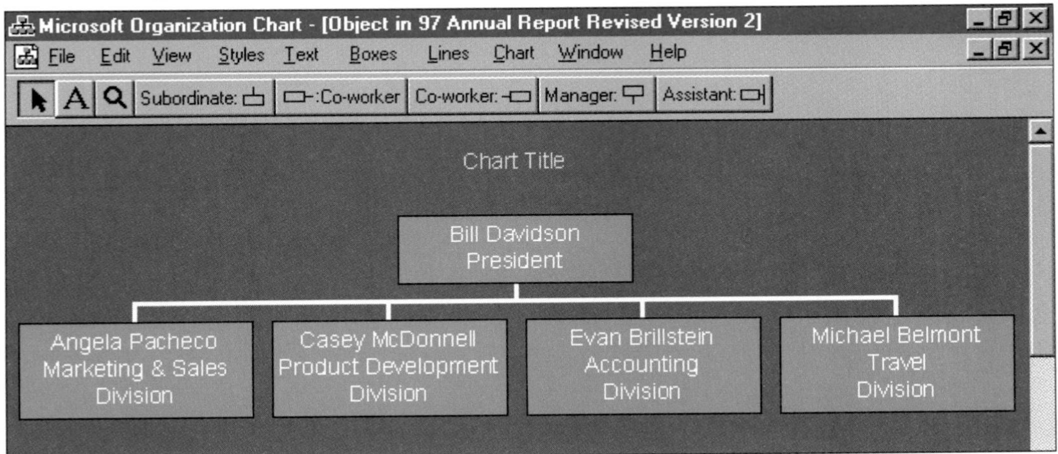

FIGURE F-21: **Organizational chart showing rearranged chart boxes**

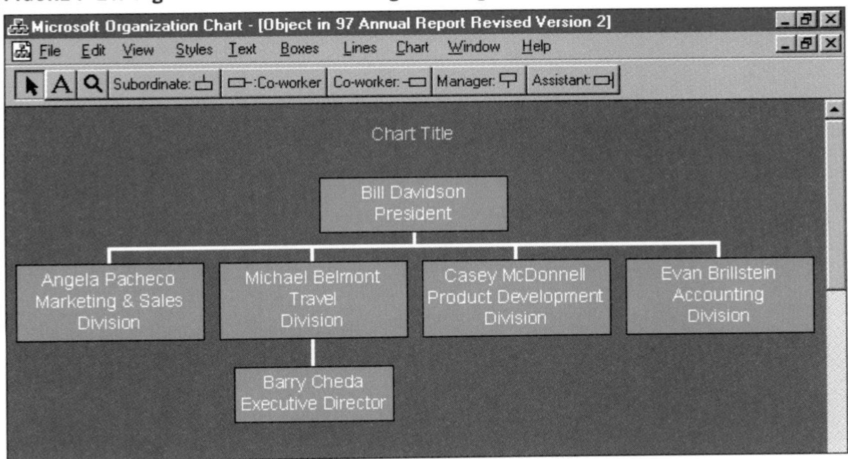

FIGURE F-22: **Final presentation in Slide Sorter view**

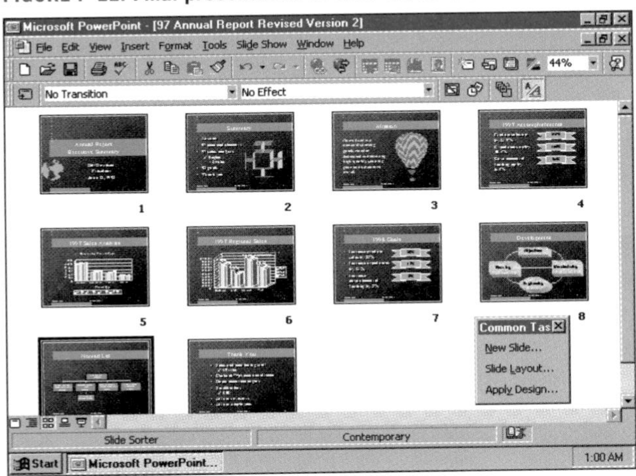

TABLE F-2: **Chart box placement arrows**

arrow	placement
⇨	Places a chart box to the right of another chart box
⇦	Places a chart box to the left of another chart box
┴	Places a chart box below another chart box

PowerPoint 97

Practice

► Concepts Review

Label each of the elements of the PowerPoint window shown in Figure F-23.

FIGURE F-23

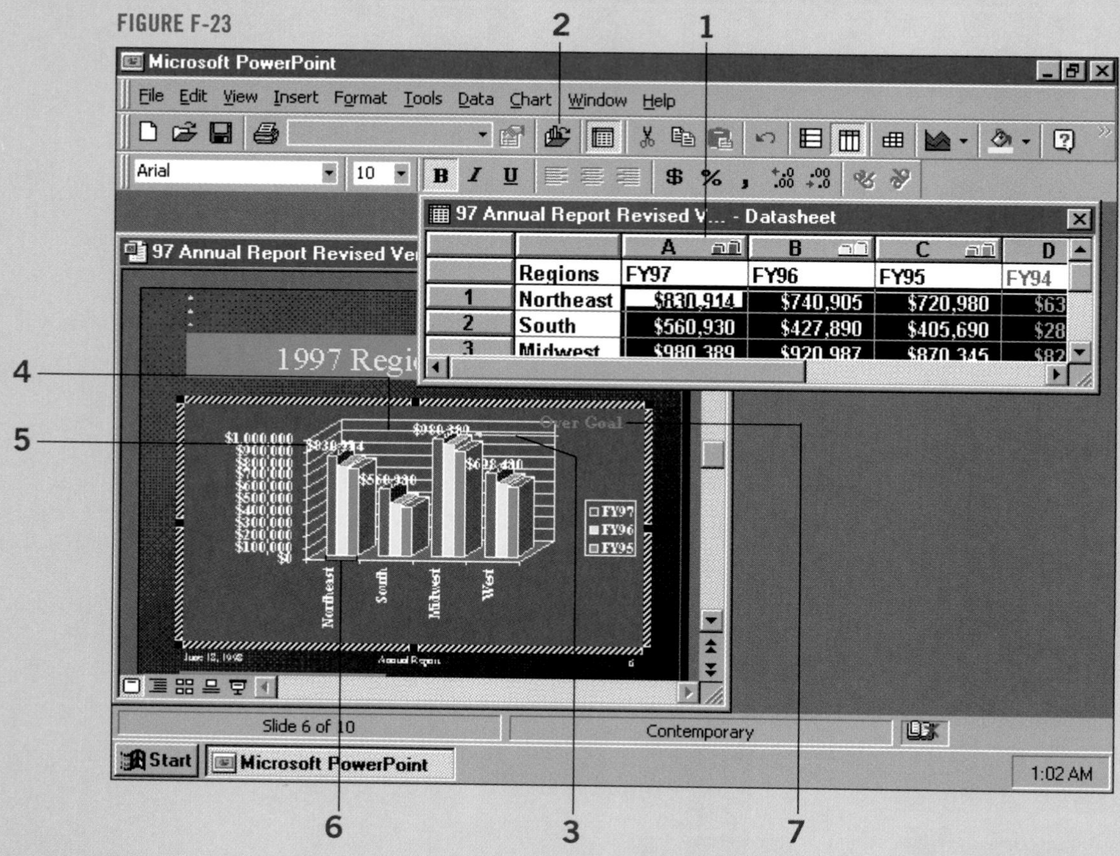

Match each of the terms with the statement that describes its function.

8. A row or column of data in a datasheet
9. How a chart graphically displays data
10. Graphical representation of a data series
11. Size of a chart floor
12. The angle at which you view a chart
13. Distance between each data series group

a. Data series markers
b. Chart type
c. Data series
d. Elevation
e. Gap width
f. Gap depth

Select the best answer from the list of choices.

14. In Graph, clicking a column control box
   a. Selects all column data markers in a chart
   b. Selects an entire column of data in the datasheet
   c. Switches the chart format to 3-D column
   d. Controls the format of the datasheet

15. **Which of the following statements about Graph charts is incorrect?**
    a. There are two-dimensional and three-dimensional chart type categories.
    b. You can change the size and format of data markers.
    c. You can format every element of a chart.
    d. The type of chart you choose does not depend on the data you have.

16. **What does the elevation option in the 3-D View dialog box control?**
    a. The angle of the chart
    b. The rotation of the chart
    c. The perspective of the chart
    d. The dimension of the chart

17. **Which of the following is true about an organizational chart?**
    a. You can create a chart by using the Organization Chart command on the Insert menu.
    b. The default organizational chart displays two subordinate chart boxes.
    c. Adding chart boxes to your chart increases the size of all the chart boxes.
    d. Chart boxes have placeholder text that you type over.

18. **Based on what you know of organizational charts, which of the following data would best fit in an organizational chart?**
    a. A company's division structure
    b. A company's database mailing list
    c. A company's annual financial numbers
    d. Spreadsheet data

Skills Review

1. **Insert data from a file into a datasheet.**
    a. Start PowerPoint and open the presentation PPT F-3, then save it as OutBack Report.
    b. Drag the vertical scroll box to Slide 3, then double-click the Graph chart.
    c. Click the first cell.
    d. Click the Import File button on the Graph Standard toolbar.
    e. Locate the file PPT F-4, then click Open.
    f. Make sure "Sheet 1" is selected, then click OK.
    g. Double-click the Column A control box. Column A is excluded from the datasheet and does not appear in the chart.
    h. Double-click the Column A control box again.

2. **Format a datasheet.**
    a. Click cell A1, drag to cell D4 to select the range, right-click the selection, then click Number on the pop-up menu.
    b. In the Category list box, click Accounting.
    c. Click the Decimal places down arrow twice to remove the places after the decimal point.
    d. Click OK.
    e. Select all the columns in the datasheet, click Format on the menu bar, click Column Width, click Best Fit, then click anywhere in the datasheet.
    f. Click the datasheet Close box, then click the Save button.

3. **Change a chart's type.**
   a. Right-click a blank area of the chart, then click Chart Type on the pop-up menu.
   b. Click the Custom Types tab, then click each of the chart types in the Chart type list box. Notice how each chart type displays your data.
   c. Click the Standard Types tab, click the Cylinder chart type, then click OK.
   d. Click the Chart Objects list arrow, then click Series "Outlets".
   e. Click Format on the menu bar, then click Selected Data Series.
   f. Click the Options tab.
   g. Double-click the Gap depth text field, then type "50".
   h. Double-click the Gap width text field, then type "175".
   i. Double-click the Chart depth text field, type "350" then click OK.

4. **Customize a chart.**
   a. Right-click a blank area of the chart, then click Chart Options on the pop-up menu.
   b. Click the Gridlines tab.
   c. In the Category (X) axis section, click the Major gridlines check box, then click the Minor gridlines check box.
   d. In the Value (Z) axis section, click the Major gridlines check box, then click OK.
   e. Right-click the Z-axis (Value Axis), then click Format Axis.
   f. Click the Scale tab, double-click the Major Unit text field, then type "300".
   g. Click the Font tab, then in the Size list box, click 20.
   h. Click OK.
   i. Right-click the X-axis (Category Axis), then click Format Axis.
   j. Click the Font tab, then in the Size list box, click 16.
   k. Click OK.
   l. Right-click an Outlets data series marker (dark blue), then click Format Data Series.
   m. In the Area section, click the tan color cell (sixth row, sixth column), then click OK.
   n. Save your changes.

5. **Work with chart elements.**
   a. Right-click the legend, then click Format Legend on the pop-up menu.
   b. Click the Font tab, then in the Size list box, click 16.
   c. Click the Patterns tab, then in the Area section, click Fill Effects.
   d. Click the Texture tab, click the Green marble square, then click OK.
   e. Click the Placement tab, click the Top radio button, then click OK.
   f. Click the Chart Objects list arrow on the Graph Standard toolbar, then click Plot Area.
   g. Drag the left bottom corners of the plot area.
   h. Right-click the Formatting toolbar, then click Drawing on the pop-up menu.
   i. Click the Text Box button on the Drawing toolbar, position the cursor near the top of the chart over the West data series markers, then drag a text box.
   j. Type Sales Goal Reached, then select the text.
   k. Right-click the selection, then click Format Text Box on the pop-up menu.
   l. Click the Color list arrow, click the red color cell in the last row, then click OK.
   m. Press [Shift], right-click the selection box of the text object, then click Format Text Box on the pop-up menu.
   n. Click the Font tab, click the Background list arrow, click Automatic, then click OK.
   o. Click anywhere in the chart to deselect the text object, then, if necessary, resize the text object and drag it to a better position in the chart.

6. **Customize a chart's 3-D view.**
   a. Right-click a blank area of the chart, then click 3-D View.
   b. Drag the 3-D View title bar to the top of the screen until you see the chart.
   c. Click the Elevation up arrow until 25 appears.
   d. Click the Rotation left arrow until 40 appears, then click Apply.
   e. Click OK.
   f. Click in a blank area of the slide, then click the Save button on the Standard toolbar.

7. **Embed and format an organizational chart.**
   a. Click the Next Slide button.
   b. Click Slide Layout on the Common Tasks toolbar, click the Organization Chart AutoLayout, then click Apply.
   c. Double-click the Organization Chart placeholder, then click the Organization Chart window Maximize button.
   d. Type "Tanya Bryceson," press [Tab], then type "Division Manager."
   e. In the Subordinate chart boxes, type the names and titles shown in Table F-3.

TABLE F-3

W. Paul Jones III	Sherline Montgomery	David Von Rotz
Accounting Manager	Design Manager	Product Manager

   f. Click Edit on the menu bar, point to Select, then click Lowest Level.
   g. Click Boxes, point to Border Style, then click the third line style down in the first column.
   h. Click the Manager chart box, click Boxes on the menu bar, point to Border Style, then click the fourth line style down in the first column.
   i. Click File on the menu bar, then click Exit and Return to Outback Report.
   j. Click Yes to update the presentation, click a blank area of the Presentation window, then save your changes.

8. **Modify an organizational chart.**
   a. Double-click the organizational chart.
   b. Click the Organization Chart window Maximize button.
   c. Click the Assistant button on the Organization Chart Standard toolbar, then click the Tanya Bryceson chart box.
   d. Type "Lisa Musante," press [Tab], then type "Special Assistant."
   e. Add a Subordinate chart box to each manager chart box.
   f. In the Subordinate chart boxes, type the names and titles shown in Table F-4.

TABLE F-4

Robert Garcelon	Lori Heredia	Wendy Peterson
Account Specialist	Style Designer	Finance Supervisor

   g. Click in a blank area of the Organization Chart window.
   h. Drag the David Von Rotz chart box over the W. Paul Jones III chart box, then place the David Von Rotz chart box to the left of the W. Paul Jones III chart box.
   i. Drag the Wendy Peterson chart box over the Robert Garcelon chart box, then place the Wendy Peterson chart box to the right of the Robert Garcelon chart box.
   j. Click File on the menu bar, then click Exit and Return to Outback Report.
   k. Click Yes to update the presentation.
   l. Click Slide Layout on the Common Tasks toolbar, then click Reapply.
   m. Click the Slide Sorter View button, then run through your slide show in Slide Show view.
   n. Save your changes, print Slides 3 and 4, then close the presentation.

Independent Challenges

1. You work for Larsen Concepts, a business consulting company that helps small and medium-sized businesses organize or restructure themselves to be more efficient and profitable. You are one of six senior consultants who work directly with clients. To prepare for an upcoming meeting with executives at ComSystems, a mobile phone communications company, you create a brief presentation outlining Larsen's typical investigative and reporting techniques, past results versus the competition, and the company's business philosophy.

The following is a sample of the type of work you perform as part of your duties at Larsen: You usually investigate a client's business practices for two weeks and analyze all relevant records. Once the initial investigation stage is complete, you submit a client recommendation report to your boss that describes the known problem areas, the consequences of the problems, the reasons for the problems, the recommended solutions, the anticipated results for each solution, the anticipated cost to the client for each solution, and Larsen's final professional recommendation. After the client recommendation report is approved by your boss, you prepare a full report for the client. If the client approves a particular plan, you develop a maintenance schedule (usually one year or less) to make sure the plan is implemented correctly.

To complete this independent challenge:

1. Open the file PPT F-5, then save it as Larsen Presentation.
2. Think about the results you want to see, the information you need, and how you want to communicate the message. Sketch how you want your presentation to look.
3. Create two organizational charts on Slides 3 and 4. Use the information above to create two flow charts (Phase 1 and Phase 2) showing the various stages of investigation and reporting.
4. Create a Graph chart on Slide 5 that shows how Larsen compares with two competitors. For example, you might illustrate the satisfaction level of Larsen clients compared to its competitors' clients.
5. Add supplemental objects to enhance the presentation.
6. Format the text on the slides. Modify the master views to achieve the look you want.
7. Add a template and shaded background to finish the presentation.
8. Spell check the presentation.
9. Print the slides of the presentation, then submit your presentation plan and printouts.

2. This year you have been selected by your peers to receive a national teaching award for the educational program for handicapped children that you created in your home state of Connecticut. In accepting this award, you have the opportunity to give a presentation describing your program's results since its introduction. You will give the presentation at an educator's convention in Washington, D.C.

Plan and create a color slide presentation describing your results. Create your own data, but assume the following:

- Over the last four years, 3,548 children in 251 classrooms throughout Connecticut participated in your program.
- Children enrolled in your program have shown at least a 7% improvement in skills for every year the program has been in effect.
- Children ages 4 through 16 have participated in the program.
- Money to fund the program comes from the National Education Association (NEA) and the State of Connecticut Public Schools Department. The money goes to each participating school district in the state.
- Funding per child is $2,867.45 per school year. Funding for children in the regular public school system is $3,950 per year.

To complete this independent challenge:

1. Think about the results you want to see, the information you need to create the slide presentation, and how your message should be communicated.
2. Create a color slide presentation using Microsoft Graph and Microsoft Organization Chart to build some of your slides. Think about how you can effectively show information in a chart.
3. Use clip art, shapes, and a shaded background to enhance the presentation. Change the bullet and text formatting in the master text and title placeholders to fit the subject matter.
4. Save the presentation as Teaching Award.
5. Submit your presentation plan and print the final slide presentation.

3. LabTech Industries is a large company that develops and produces technical medical equipment and machines for operating and emergency rooms around the United States. You are the business manager for the company and one of your assignments is to prepare a presentation for the stockholders on the profitability and efficiency of each division in the company.

Plan and create a slide presentation that shows all the divisions and divisional managers of the company. Also, graphically show how each division performed in relation to its previous year's performance. Create your own content but assume the following:

- The company has seven divisions: Administration, Accounting, Sales and Marketing, Research and Development, Product Testing, Product Development, and Manufacturing.
- Four divisions increased productivity by at least 12%.
- The presentation will be given in a boardroom using a projector.

To complete this independent challenge:

1. Think about the results you want to see, the information you need to create the slide presentation, what type of message you want to communicate, and the target audience.
2. Use Outline view to create the content of your presentation.
3. Use Microsoft Graph and Microsoft Organization Chart to create charts to help display the information you want to communicate.
4. Use clip art, pictures, or a shaded background to enhance the presentation.
5. Format the content, then save the presentation as LabTech Industries.
6. Submit your presentation plan and print the final slide presentation.

4. You are in your first year of graduate school where you are earning a Masters in Business Administration (MBA). The final project in your first semester sales and marketing class is to create a sales or marketing presentation and then present it to the entire class during finals week. You decide to use PowerPoint to help you create a professional-looking presentation.

In this independent challenge, you'll need to develop a presentation that convinces your audience that they need to have the product you are selling. Create your own information using the basic presentation provided on your Student Disk. Assume the following about this final project assignment: (1) Your presentation topic is on a new type of pen computing software called NotesWriter produced by Romedia. NotesWriter is a word-processing program for a Windows-compatible computer with an integrated pen or an attached tablet (personal communicator) with a pen. You can create, edit, and send handwritten notes, faxes, e-mail notes, and other messages using this software. (2) The primary feature of NotesWriter is its ability to allow the user to write and edit naturally with a pen and then send the note as a fax or an e-mail message. (3) The assignment requires a 6- to 10-slide presentation that adequately explains the topic.

To complete this independent challenge:

1. Open the file PPT F-6, then save it as NotesWriter.
2. Think about the results you want to see, the information you need, and how you want to communicate the message. Plan the presentation using an outline.
3. Log onto the Internet and use your browser to go to http://www.course.com. From there, click Student Online Companions, click the link for this textbook, then click the PowerPoint link for Unit F. Use the links you find there to research data on pen commuting products to use in your presentation.
4. Use the information on the second and third slides to create charts.
5. Add between 3 and 5 slides to the presentation that adequately explain the product features, the target market, and the market need.
6. Enhance the presentation with objects, a shaded background, or other items that improve the look of the presentation.
7. Add a template and then change the master views, if necessary, to fit your information.
8. Spell-check the presentation.
9. Print the slides of the presentation, then submit your presentation plan and printouts.

► Visual Workshop

Create two slides that look like the examples in Figures F-24 and F-25. Save the presentation as Semiphore. Save and print Slide view of the presentation. Submit the final presentation output.

FIGURE F-24

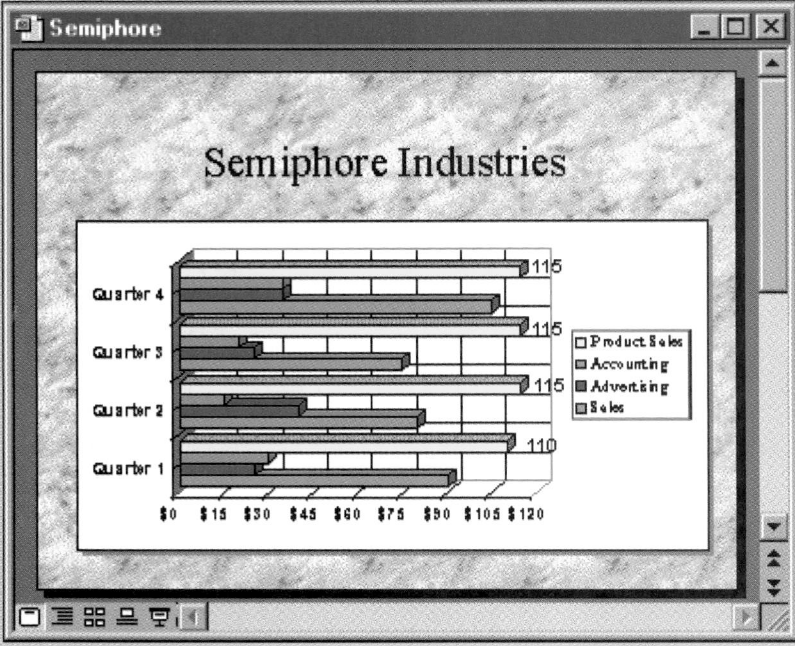

FIGURE F-25

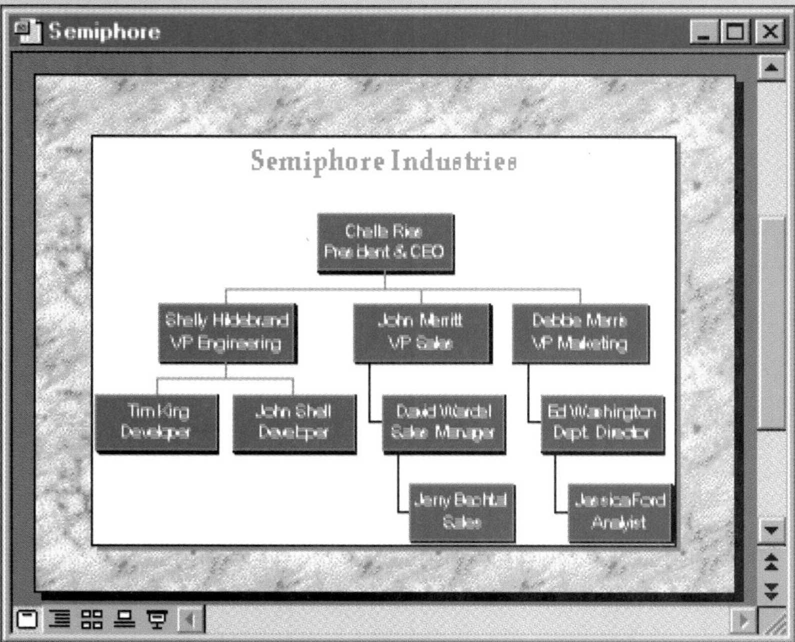

Working with Embedded and Linked Objects and Hyperlinks

Objectives

- Embed a picture
- Embed a table
- Embed a worksheet
- Link an Excel worksheet
- Update a linked Excel worksheet
- Insert a movie
- Insert a sound
- Insert a hyperlink

PowerPoint offers many ways to add graphic elements to a presentation. In this unit you will learn how to embed or link objects created in other programs. **Embedded** and **linked** objects are created in another program, known as a **source program**, and then stored in or linked to the PowerPoint presentation. In this unit, Karen Craig, the executive director for New Directions, Nomad Ltd's travel subsidiary, creates a brief presentation using embedded and linked objects that outlines a new product proposal for a magazine on a CD-ROM called *CD Travel™ Magazine*. When Karen is finished with her presentation, she will give it to Carrie Armstrong, who plans to link it to the Annual Report Executive Summary presentation.

PowerPoint 97

Embedding a Picture

There are several methods for inserting pictures into PowerPoint slides. You can enbed over 20 different types of pictures using the Insert Picture command. As you work with pictures, especially photographs, be aware that frequently a presentation's color scheme will not match the colors in the picture. In order to make the picture look good in the presentation, you may need to customize the presentation's color scheme, recolor the picture, or change the presentation's template. Karen wants to embed a picture in a slide. She will make sure that the photo-graph looks good with the slide color scheme.

Steps 1 2 3 4

1. **Start PowerPoint, open the presentation PPT G-1, save it as CD Travel, click the Restore Window button in the Presentation window, click Window on the menu bar, then click Fit to Page**
   Move to Slide 2 to embed a picture.
2. **Click the Next Slide button, click Insert on the menu bar, point to Picture, click From File, select the file PPT G-2, then click OK**
   A picture of a tropical island harbor appears in the middle of the slide and the Picture toolbar opens. Resize the picture and position it on the slide.
3. **Drag the picture to the right side of the slide, drag the picture's resize handles to match the size of Figure G-1, then click on a blank area of the Presentation window**
   Compare your screen to Figure G-1. The current color scheme is a little dark for the picture, so experiment with a different color scheme for this slide.
4. **Right-click a blank area of the Presentation window, then click Slide Color Scheme on the pop-up menu**
   The Color Scheme dialog box opens. Notice that there are six standard color schemes to choose from. Experiment with the standard color schemes to see if any look good with the picture.
5. **Drag the Color Scheme dialog box title bar to the upper right corner of the PowerPoint window so that you can see part of the picture**
6. **In the Color schemes section, click each standard color scheme option, then click Preview**
   As you click a color scheme option and then click Preview, the color scheme is applied to the slide. The middle color scheme in the bottom row fits best with the color and contrast of the picture.
7. **In the Color Schemes section, click the middle color scheme option in the bottom row, then click Apply**
   Make sure you do not click Apply to All. The color scheme for slide 2 changes, as shown in Figure G-2. Save your changes.
8. **Click the Save button on the Standard toolbar**

Trouble?

If your picture size doesn't look like the picture in Figure G-1, drag the resize handle again until the picture matches the figure.

FIGURE G-1: Slide showing resized picture

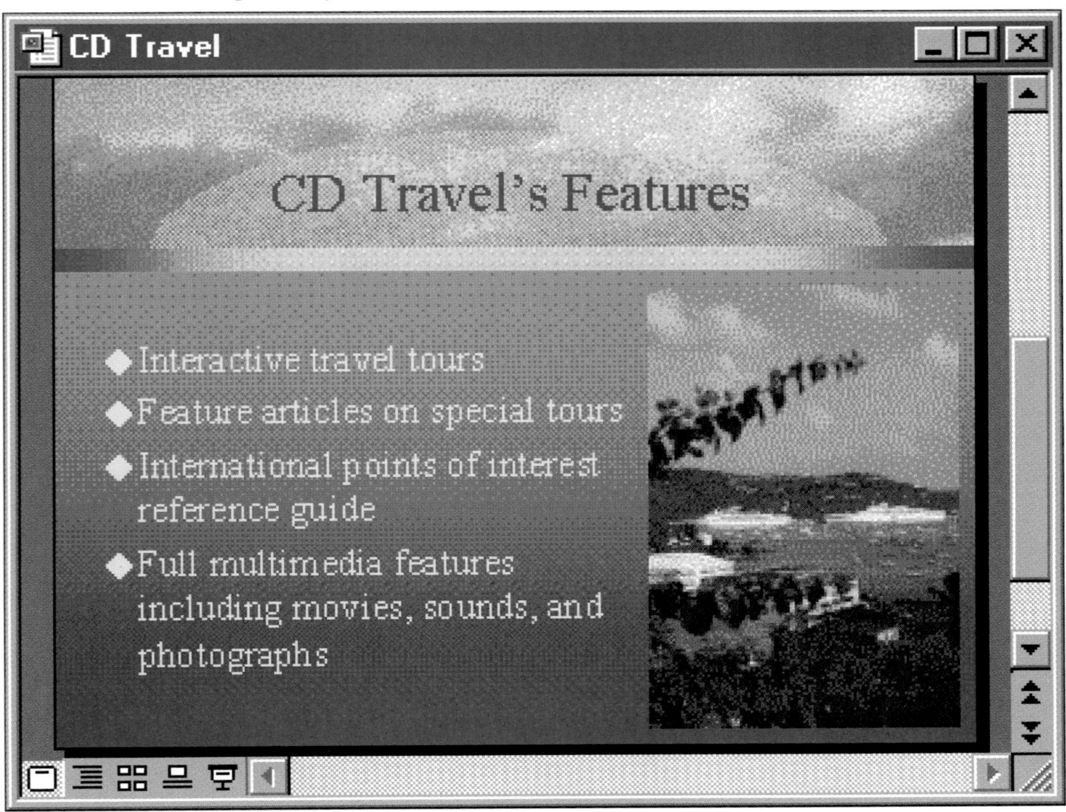

FIGURE G-2: Slide showing new color scheme

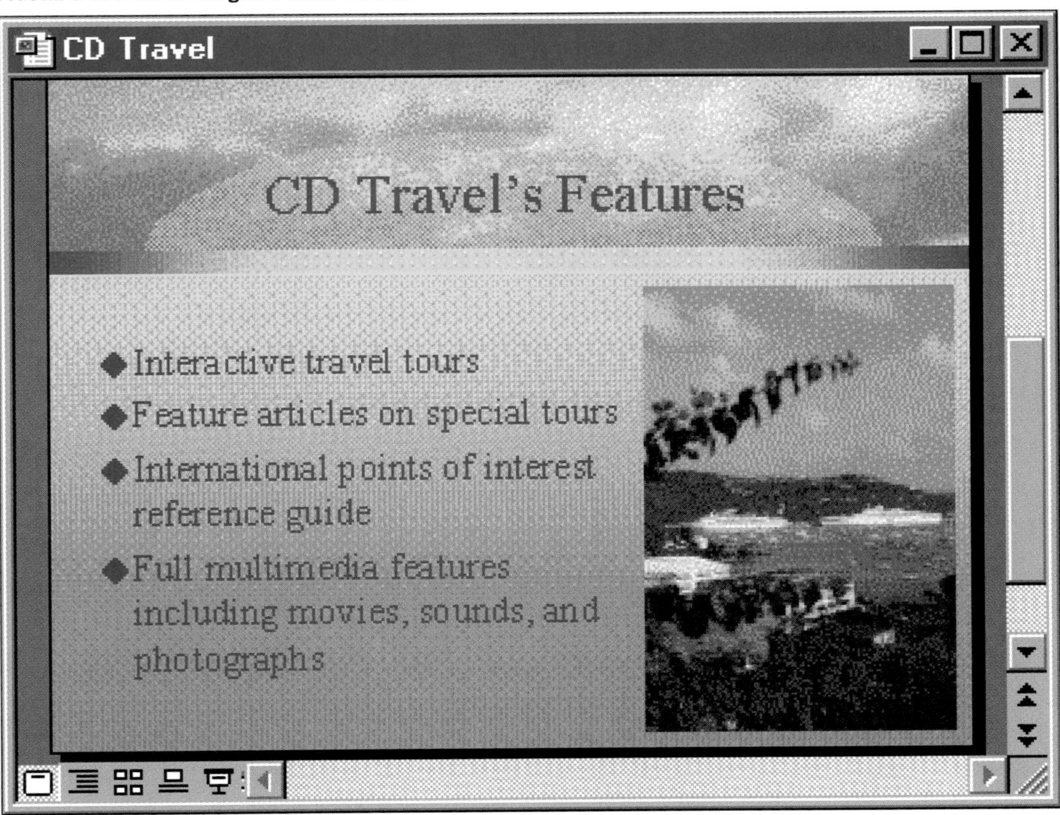

PowerPoint 97

Embedding a Table

Sometimes a table is the best way to provide information in an organized and concise manner. You create tables in PowerPoint by embedding a Microsoft Word table in your PowerPoint slide. You can use formatting features of both Word and PowerPoint to call attention to important information and to make the table visually appealing. Karen decides to add a new slide with a table showing competitive market analysis information for *CD Travel Magazine.*

Steps

1. Click **New Slide** on the Common Tasks toolbar, click the **Title Only AutoLayout**, then click **OK**
   A new Slide 3 appears. Now create the table for the presentation.
2. Click the **Insert Microsoft Word Table button** on the Standard toolbar, then drag to create a **6 × 4 Table**, as shown in Figure G-3
   Microsoft Word opens and displays a blank table with six rows and four columns in the middle of the slide. Notice that the Microsoft Word menu bar and toolbars replace PowerPoint's menu bar and toolbars. Increase the size of the table to accommodate the information you will enter.
3. Resize the table object so it occupies most of the slide as shown in Figure G-4, then enter the data shown in Figure G-4 into your blank table
4. Click in a blank area of the Presentation window, double-click the table object to open Word again and redisplay the table, then use ⟷ to drag each **column marker** on the horizontal ruler so that the words wrap as shown in Figure G-4
   Use the Tab key to move from cell to cell in your table. If necessary, use the vertical scroll bar to view the last line of the table. Now format the table using Microsoft Word formatting features.
5. Click **Table** on the menu bar, then click **Table AutoFormat**, in the Formats section click **Simple 2**, then click **OK**
   The new table format adds lines to the table and changes the row and column headings to bold. The horizontal and vertical table lines may not appear in Slide view. They should appear in Slide Show view. Now change the text alignment of Columns 2 through 4.
6. Drag to select **Columns 2 through 4**, click the **Center button** on the Formatting toolbar, then adjust column widths as necessary to accomodate the new formatting
   The data in Columns 2 through 4 move to the center of the cells. Compare your screen to Figure G-4. Next, add a fill color to the table so it is easier to see.
7. Click in a blank area of the Presentation window, click the table once to select it, click the **Fill color list arrow** on the Drawing toolbar, then click the **light purple box** labeled **Follow Fills Scheme Color**
   The table fills with the purple color. Now move and resize the table.
8. Drag the table to the lower section of the slide, drag the table's resize handles so the table fills as much of the lower section as possible, leaving about ¼" of space above and below it, then drag the table to center it horizontally on the slide
   Complete this slide by adding a title.
9. Click the **title placeholder**, type **Market Research Analysis**, click in a blank area of the Presentation window, then click the **Save button** on the Standard toolbar
   Compare your screen to Figure G-5.

QuickTip

You can also embed a Word table by choosing the Table AutoLayout.

Trouble?

If your insertion point scrolls out of view as you are entering the data, resize the columns before you enter the rest of the data.

Trouble?

If the table has extra blank space on the bottom or the sides, or if it is very small, double-click the table and drag the borders of the table object to eliminate extra space between the table and the object borders. Double-click the table, then click it once and resize it as necessary.

FIGURE G-3: Insert Microsoft Word Table button selected

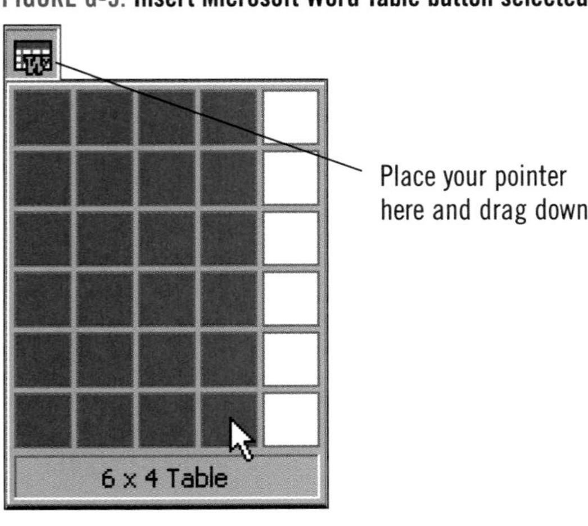

FIGURE G-4: Formatted Microsoft Word table

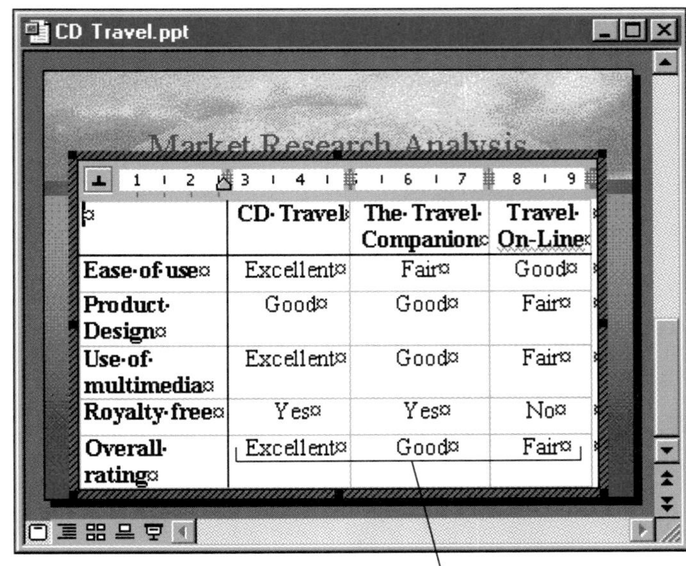

FIGURE G-5: Slide showing embedded table

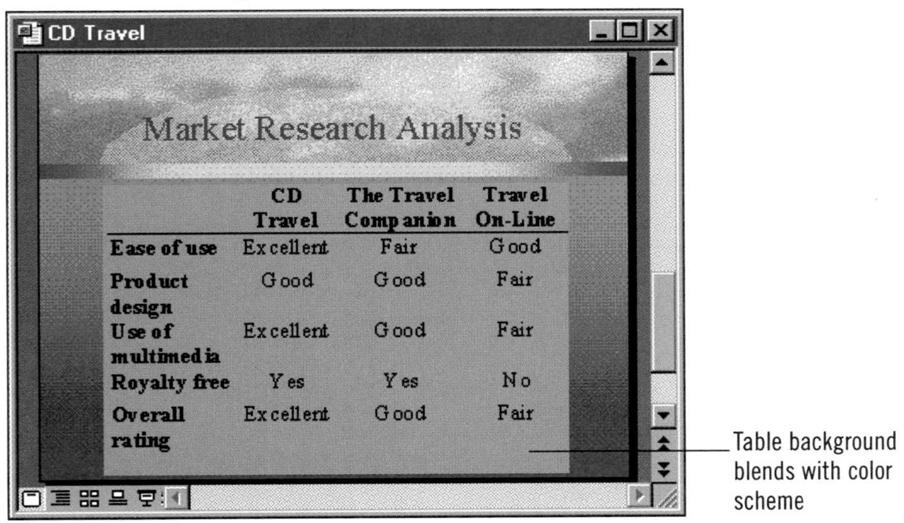

Exporting a presentation to Microsoft Word

Sometimes you need the features of a word-processing program like Word to create detailed speaker's notes or handouts. Using the PowerPoint Send To command, you can copy or link a presentation into a Microsoft Word document. Click File on the menu bar, point to Send to, and then click Microsoft Word. In the Send To dialog box, shown in Figure G-6, select one of the layout options. A new Word document opens with your embedded presentation, using the layout you selected. If you plan to modify the presentation, click the Paste link option button.

FIGURE G-6: Send To dialog box

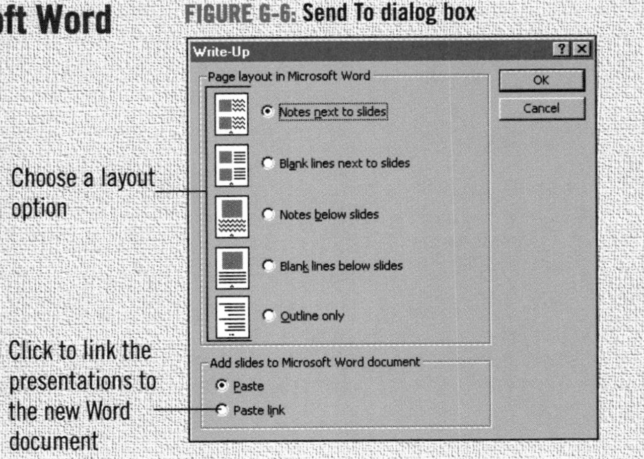

Embedding a Worksheet

Sometimes a spreadsheet is the best way to present information that PowerPoint is not designed to create. For example, you may need to show an income and expense summary for each quarter of the year. For large amounts of data, it's easier to create a worksheet using a spreadsheet program. Then you can embed the workbook file in your PowerPoint presentation, and edit it using Excel tools. Excel is the workbook file's source program, the program in which the file was created. PowerPoint is the **target program.** Karen created an Excel workbook with the budget allocation data for *CD Travel Magazine.* She wants to include this worksheet in her presentation, so she embeds the workbook in a slide.

Steps

1. Click **New Slide** on the Common Tasks toolbar, click the **Object AutoLayout**, then click **OK**
   A new Slide 4 appears. Before you embed the workbook file, create a title for the new slide.
2. Type **Budget Allocation**, then click in a blank area of the Presentation window
   Now that the title is in place, embed the Excel workbook file.
3. Double-click the **object placeholder**, and in the Insert Object dialog box, click the **Create from file option button**, click **Browse**, locate the file **PPT G-3**, click **OK**, then click **OK** in the Insert Object dialog box
   The worksheet containing the budget allocation data appears on the slide. Notice that the Total row is not filled in yet. Because the worksheet is embedded, you can edit the worksheet using Excel tools. Use the Microsoft Excel Sum **function** (a presupplied formula) to automatically calculate the category totals.
4. Double-click the spreadsheet to open Microsoft Excel, click cell **B5**, click the **AutoSum button** Σ on the Excel Formatting toolbar, then press **[Tab]**
   The total, 115,000, appears in cell B5, which is the total of the Phase 1 category. Now copy the formula to enter the totals for the other three categories.
5. Click cell **B5**, then drag the selection handle in the lower right corner of cell **B5** (you might need to scroll the worksheet down to see it) to cell **E5**
   The total for each column appears, because you have copied the sum formula you entered in B5. Now format the headings in bold.
6. Drag to select cells **A2** through **A5**, press and hold **[Ctrl]**, select cells **B1** through **E1**, click the **Bold button** B on the Formatting toolbar, then click any cell to deselect the cells
   The column and row headings are now bold, as shown in Figure G-7. The original Budget Allocation worksheet, however, remains in its original form, without the totals and the new formatting. You have edited only the copy of the worksheet you embedded in the presentation. Now redisplay PowerPoint and fill the embedded spreadsheet with a color that matches the presentation color scheme.
7. Click in a blank area of the Presentation window to redisplay PowerPoint, click the **worksheet object** once, then click the **Fill color button** on the Drawing toolbar
   The embedded worksheet fills with the same color you used to fill the embedded table in the last lesson. Resize the worksheet object.
8. Drag the lower corners of the embedded worksheet so it fills the width of the slide, then click a blank area of the Presentation window to deselect the object
   Compare your screen to Figure G-8.

QuickTip

To edit or open an embedded object in your presentation, the object's source program must be available on your computer or network.

Time To

✔ Save

FIGURE G-7: Formatted Excel worksheet

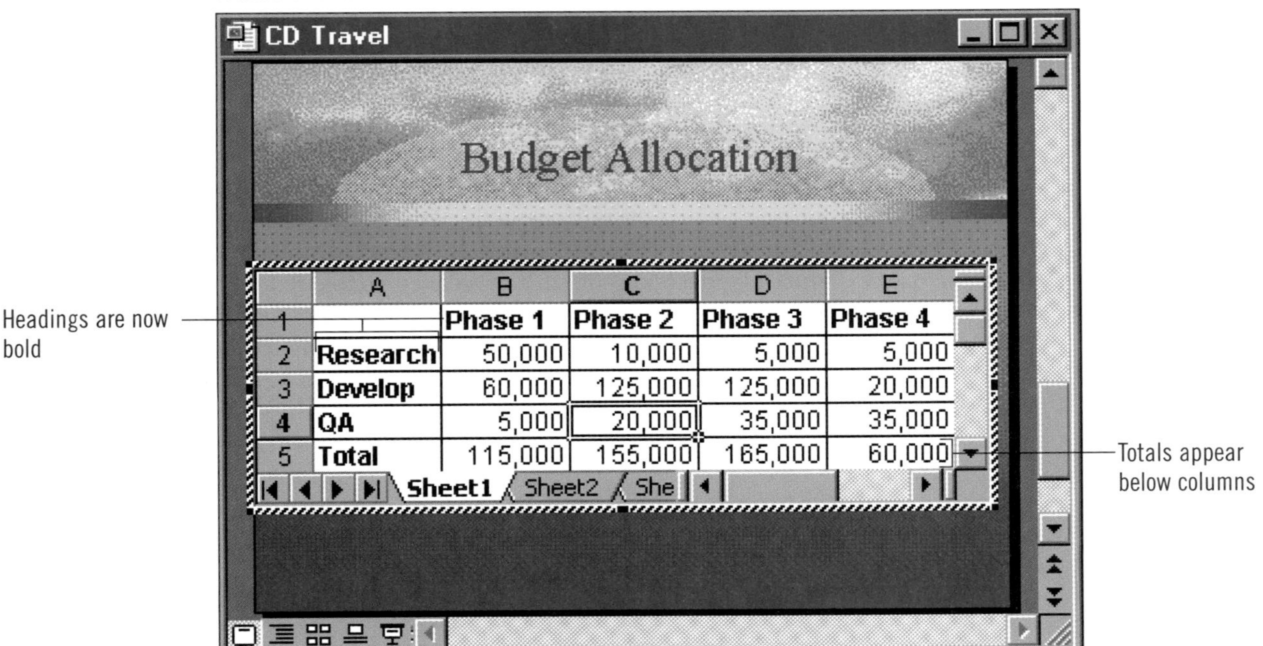

	A	B	C	D	E
1		Phase 1	Phase 2	Phase 3	Phase 4
2	Research	50,000	10,000	5,000	5,000
3	Develop	60,000	125,000	125,000	20,000
4	QA	5,000	20,000	35,000	35,000
5	Total	115,000	155,000	165,000	60,000

FIGURE G-8: Embedded Microsoft Excel worksheet on slide

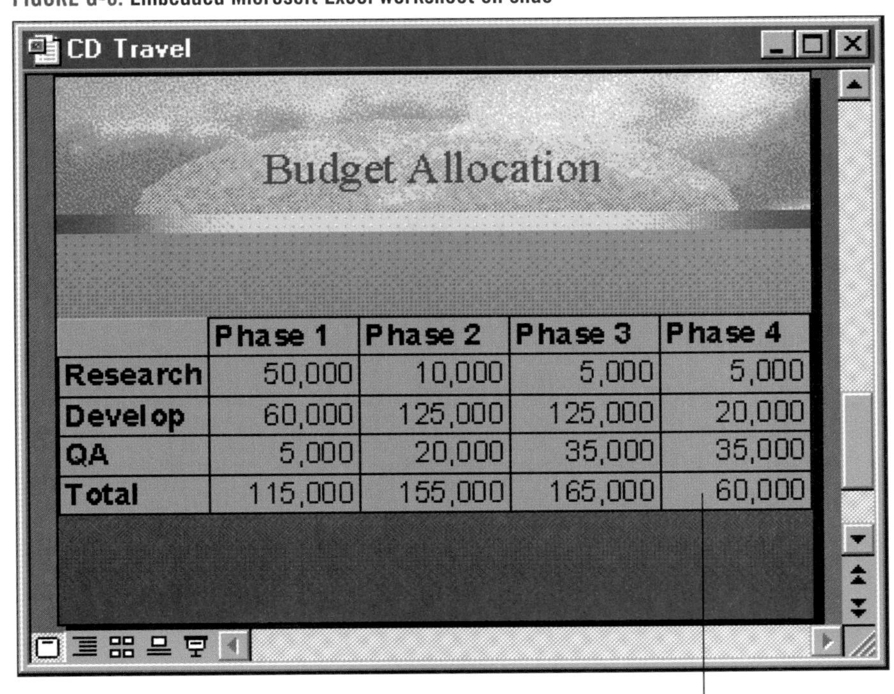

	Phase 1	Phase 2	Phase 3	Phase 4
Research	50,000	10,000	5,000	5,000
Develop	60,000	125,000	125,000	20,000
QA	5,000	20,000	35,000	35,000
Total	115,000	155,000	165,000	60,000

CLUES TO USE

Embedding part of a worksheet

You can copy and paste only part of a worksheet into a PowerPoint slide. Open the Excel workbook and copy the cells you want to include in your presentation. Open the PowerPoint presentation, and paste the cells on a slide. To edit the information, double-click the pasted copy to open Excel, and edit it with Excel tools as you did in this lesson.

Linking an Excel Worksheet

Objects like Excel worksheets can also be connected to your presentation by establishing a **link** between the source file that created the object and the PowerPoint presentation that displays the object. When you link an object to a PowerPoint slide, a representation (picture) of the object, not the actual object itself, appears on the slide. Unlike an embedded object, a linked object is stored in its source file, not on the slide. When you link an object to a PowerPoint slide, any changes made to the source file are automatically reflected in the linked representation in your PowerPoint presentation. Use linking when you want to include an object, such as an accounting spreadsheet, that may change over time and when you want to be sure your presentation contains the latest information. See Table G-1 for suggestions on when to use embedding and linking. Some of the objects that you can link to PowerPoint include movies, Microsoft Excel worksheets, and PowerPoint slides from other presentations. Karen needs to link to her presentation an Excel worksheet created by the Accounting Department manager earlier in the year.

Steps 1 2 3 4

1. Click **New Slide** on the Common Tasks toolbar, make sure the **Object AutoLayout** is selected, click **OK**, then type **Division Annual Budget** in the title placeholder
   Next, link a worksheet to the new slide to show the New Directions annual budget for 1998.
2. Double-click the **object placeholder**
   The Insert Object dialog box opens.
3. Click the **Create from file option button**, click **Browse**, locate the file **Division Budget**, click **OK**, then click the **Link check box** to select it
   Compare your screen to Figure G-9.
4. Click **OK**
   The image of the linked worksheet appears on the slide. Add a background fill to the worksheet object.
5. With the worksheet still selected, click the **Fill Color list arrow** on the Drawing toolbar, then click the **pink box** on the far right
   A background fill color appears behind the worksheet, as shown in Figure G-10. Now save and close the presentation.
6. Click the **Save button** on the Standard toolbar, then click the Presentation window **Close button**
   PowerPoint remains open but the Presentation window closes.

TABLE G-1: Embedding vs. linking

embed	link
When you are the only user of an object and you want the object to be a permanent part of your presentation	When you want your object to always have the latest information from its source file
When you don't want to create a separate file for your object	When the object's source file is shared on a network or when other users have access to the file and can change it
When you want to access the object in its source program in the future, even when the original file is not available	When you want to keep your presentation file size small
When you want to update the object manually while working in PowerPoint	

FIGURE G-9: Insert Object dialog box

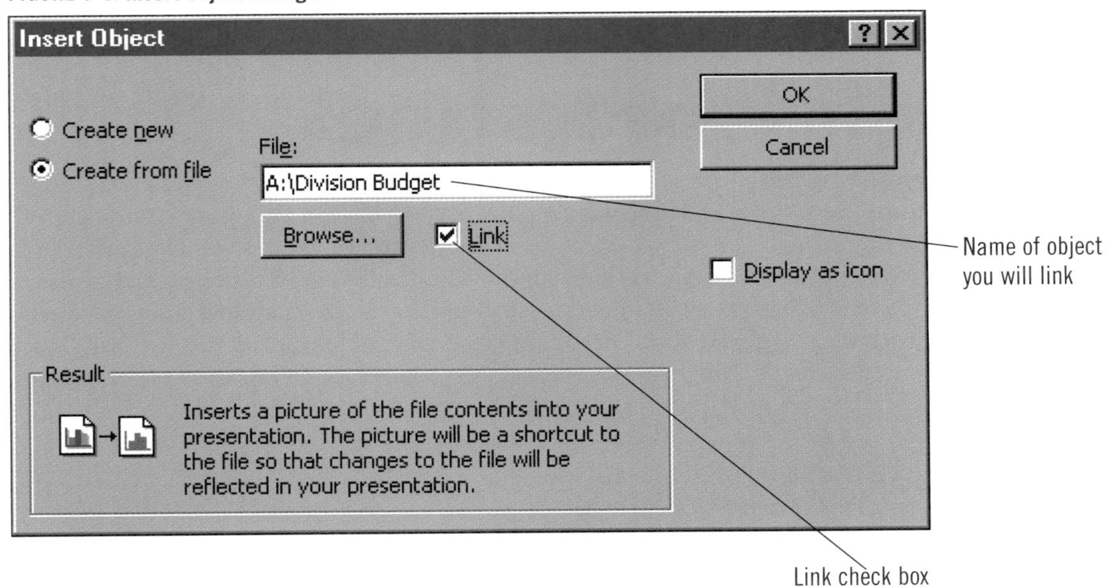

FIGURE G-10: Linked worksheet with background fill color

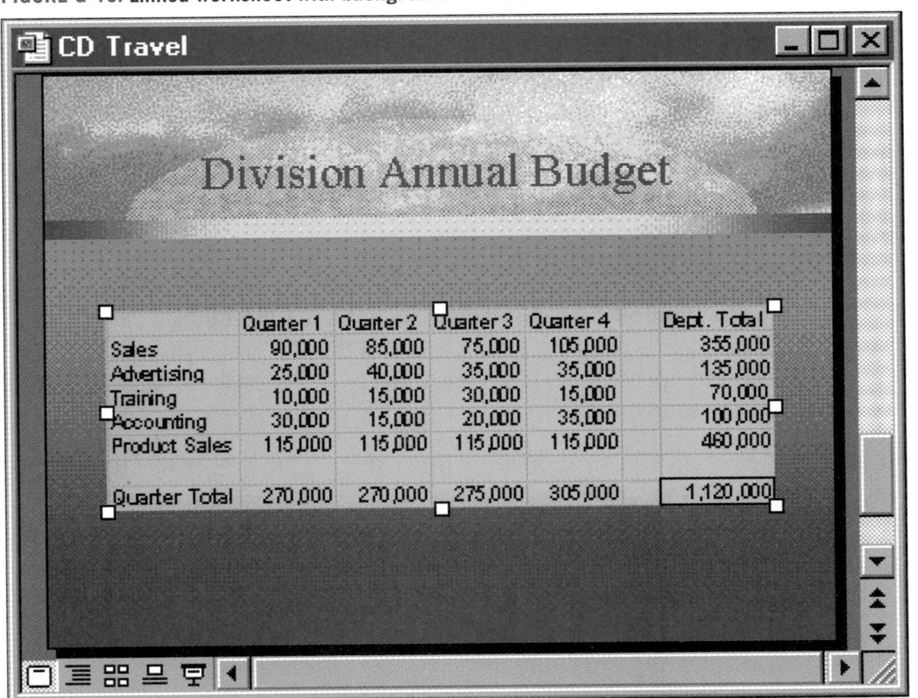

CLUES TO USE

Linking objects using Paste Special

You can also link an object or selected information from another program into PowerPoint by copying and pasting the information. This technique is useful when you want to link part of a worksheet rather than the entire file. For example, you may want to link a worksheet from a Microsoft Excel workbook that contains both a worksheet and a chart. To link just the worksheet, open the Microsoft Excel workbook file that contains the worksheet, select the worksheet, then copy it to the Clipboard. Open the PowerPoint presentation, click Edit on the menu bar, click Paste Special, click the Paste link option button, then click OK.

PowerPoint 97

Updating a Linked Excel Worksheet

To edit or change the information in a linked object, you must open the object's source program. For example, you must open Microsoft Word to edit a linked Word table or you must open Microsoft Excel to edit a linked Excel worksheet. You can open the Source program by double-clicking the linked object in the PowerPoint slide as you did with embedded objects or by clicking the Start menu, which you will do here. When you work in the source program, you can close your PowerPoint presentation or leave it open. Karen needs to update some of the data in the Microsoft Excel worksheet, so she opens Excel, changes some data, and then updates the linked object in PowerPoint.

1. Click the **Start** button on the taskbar, point to **Programs**, and click **Microsoft Excel**
   The Microsoft Excel program opens.
2. On the Microsoft Excel Standard toolbar, click the **Open button**, locate the file **Division Budget**, then click **Open**
   The Division Budget worksheet opens. Insert the updated figures for the Sales budget.
3. Click cell **E2**, type **95000**, click cell **C2**, type **80000**, then press **[Enter]**
   The Department Total for Sales is automatically recalculated and now reads $340,000 instead of $355,000. Now close Microsoft Excel and return to the linked worksheet in PowerPoint.
4. Click the **Close button** in the Microsoft Excel program window, then click **Yes** to save the changes
   Microsoft Excel closes and the PowerPoint window appears.
5. Click on the Standard toolbar, locate the file **CD Travel**, then click **Open**
   A Microsoft PowerPoint message box opens, telling you that the CD Travel presentation has links and asking if you want to update them. See Figure G-11. This message appears whether or not you have changed the source file.
6. Click **OK**, restore your Presentation window to the size used in this book, then drag the vertical scroll box to **Slide 5**
   Compare your screen to Figure G-12. The linked Excel worksheet shows the new Department Total for Sales, $340,000. The changes you made in Excel were automatically made in this linked copy when you reopened the worksheet. Save your changes.
7. Click the **Save button** on the Standard toolbar

QuickTip

To open or edit a linked object in your presentation, the object's source program and source file must be available on your computer or network.

FIGURE G-11: **PowerPoint update links message box**

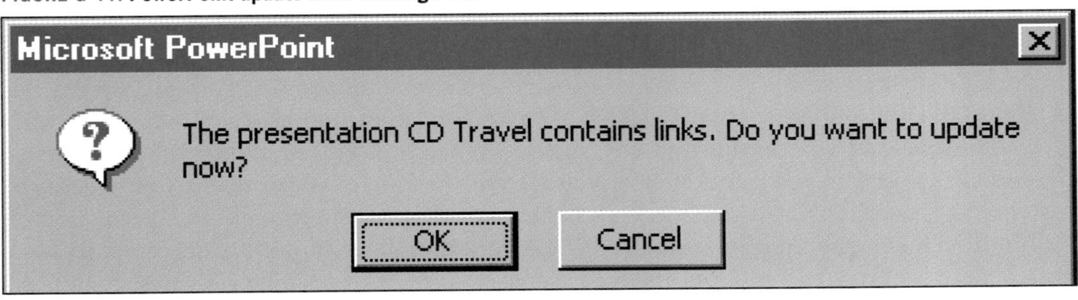

FIGURE G-12: **Slide showing updated linked worksheet**

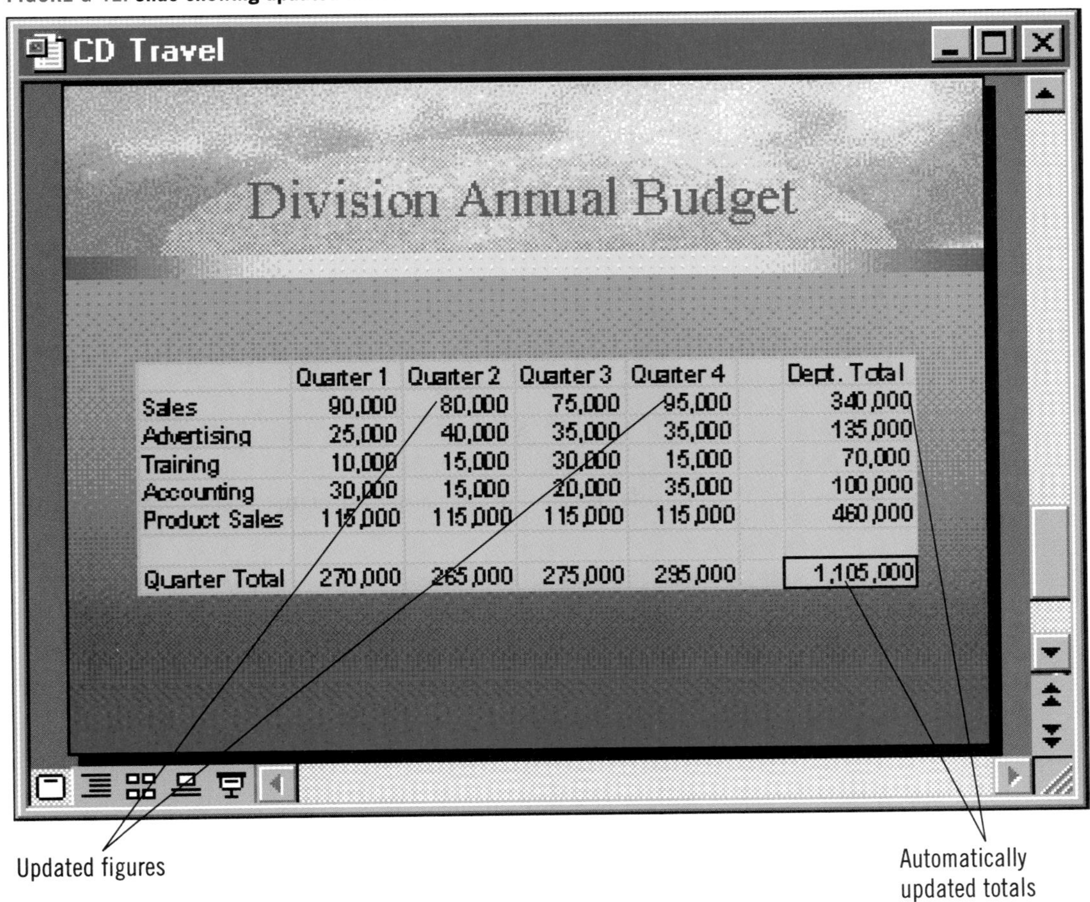

	Quarter 1	Quarter 2	Quarter 3	Quarter 4	Dept. Total
Sales	90,000	80,000	75,000	95,000	340,000
Advertising	25,000	40,000	35,000	35,000	135,000
Training	10,000	15,000	30,000	15,000	70,000
Accounting	30,000	15,000	20,000	35,000	100,000
Product Sales	115,000	115,000	115,000	115,000	460,000
Quarter Total	270,000	265,000	275,000	295,000	1,105,000

Updated figures

Automatically updated totals

Updating links when both files are open

You do not have to close the target file to update the links. If you change the source file, when you switch back to the presentation file, the link will be updated. If you want to update the links manually, click Edit on the menu bar, then click Links to open the Links dialog box. See Figure G-13. If the Manual check box is selected, the links in the target file will not be updated unless you select the link in this dialog box and click Update Now.

FIGURE G-13: Links dialog box

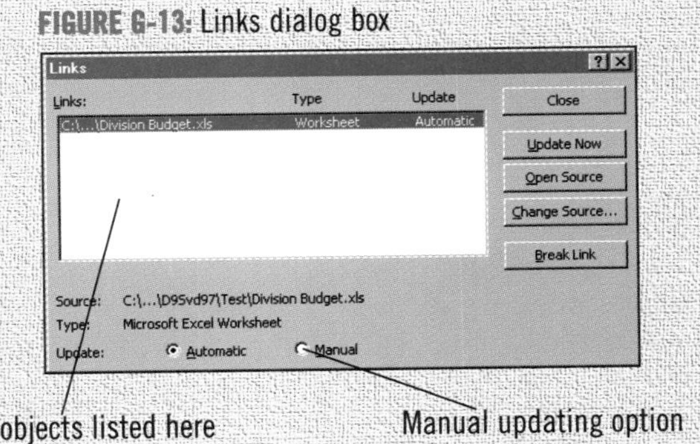

Linked objects listed here

Manual updating option

PowerPoint 97

Inserting a Movie

In your presentations, you may want to use special effects to illustrate a point or capture the attention of your audience. Microsoft Media Player, a video editing program that comes with PowerPoint, allows you to run and edit movies. When you embed a movie, it becomes a PowerPoint object, so you can change or edit it to fit the style of your presentation. There are two basic types of movies: digital video and animation. **Digital video** refers to a live-action or full-motion movie captured by a video camera. An **animation** is a movie that sets graphics (clip art or drawn objects) in motion. Karen continues developing her presentation by embedding an animated movie and then changing its playback options.

Steps

QuickTip

You can also use the Text and Media Clip Auto Layout to insert a movie on a slide.

1. Click **New Slide** on the Common Tasks toolbar, click the **Text & Object AutoLayout**, click **OK**, then type **International Distribution** in the title placeholder
   Before embedding the animation, enter the main points for the slide in the main text placeholder.
2. Click the main text placeholder, type **United States**, press **[Enter]**, type **Western Europe**, press **[Enter]**, type **Australia**, press **[Enter]**, type **Asia**, press **[Enter]**, type **South America**, then resize and reposition the text object on the slide so it appears as shown in Figure G-14
   Now embed the animation.
3. Double-click the **object placeholder**, click the **Create from file option button**, click **Browse**, select the file **PPT G-4**, click **OK**, then click **OK**
   The movie appears on the right side of the slide, as shown in Figure G-14. Play the movie to make sure it works properly.
4. Double-click the **movie object**
   The Globe movie plays once through. You can modify an embedded movie the same way you modify any embedded file. Change some playback options now.
5. Right-click the **movie object**, then click **Edit Video Clip Object** on the pop-up menu
   The Microsoft Media Player program window opens, as shown in Figure G-15. You can easily edit your movie with the Microsoft Media Player control bar that appears below the menu bar.
6. Click **Edit** on the menu bar, then click **Options**
   The Options dialog box opens. First, hide the movie control bar so it won't show while the movie plays.
7. In the OLE Object section, click the **Control Bar On Playback check box** to deselect it
   You can set the movie to play continuously until you stop it, and to rewind to the beginning after you stop it.
8. Click the **Auto Repeat check box** to select it, click **OK**, then click in a blank area of the Presentation window
   The Microsoft Media Player program window closes. Notice that the movie control bar is no longer visible. Resize the movie object so it occupies more of the slide.
9. Drag the corner resize handles and reposition the movie object so it fills the right half of the slide
   Now, run the movie again to view the changes.
10. Double-click the **movie object**, view the movie for a while, click in a blank area of the Presentation window to stop the movie, then click the **Save button** on the Standard toolbar

Trouble?

If your movie object seems small, reapply the Text & Object AutoLayout using the Slide Layout button on the Common Tasks toolbar.

FIGURE G-14: Slide showing embedded movie object

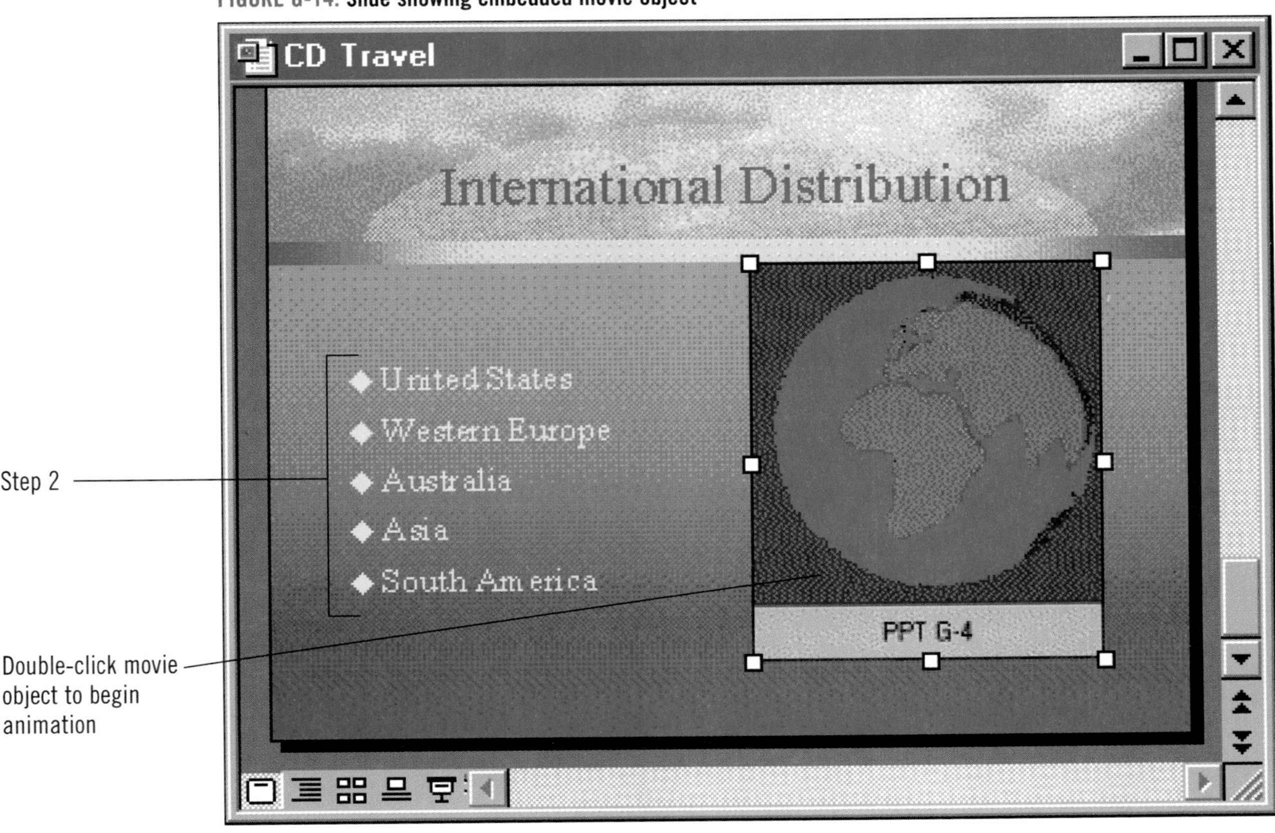

FIGURE G-15: Microsoft Media Player program window

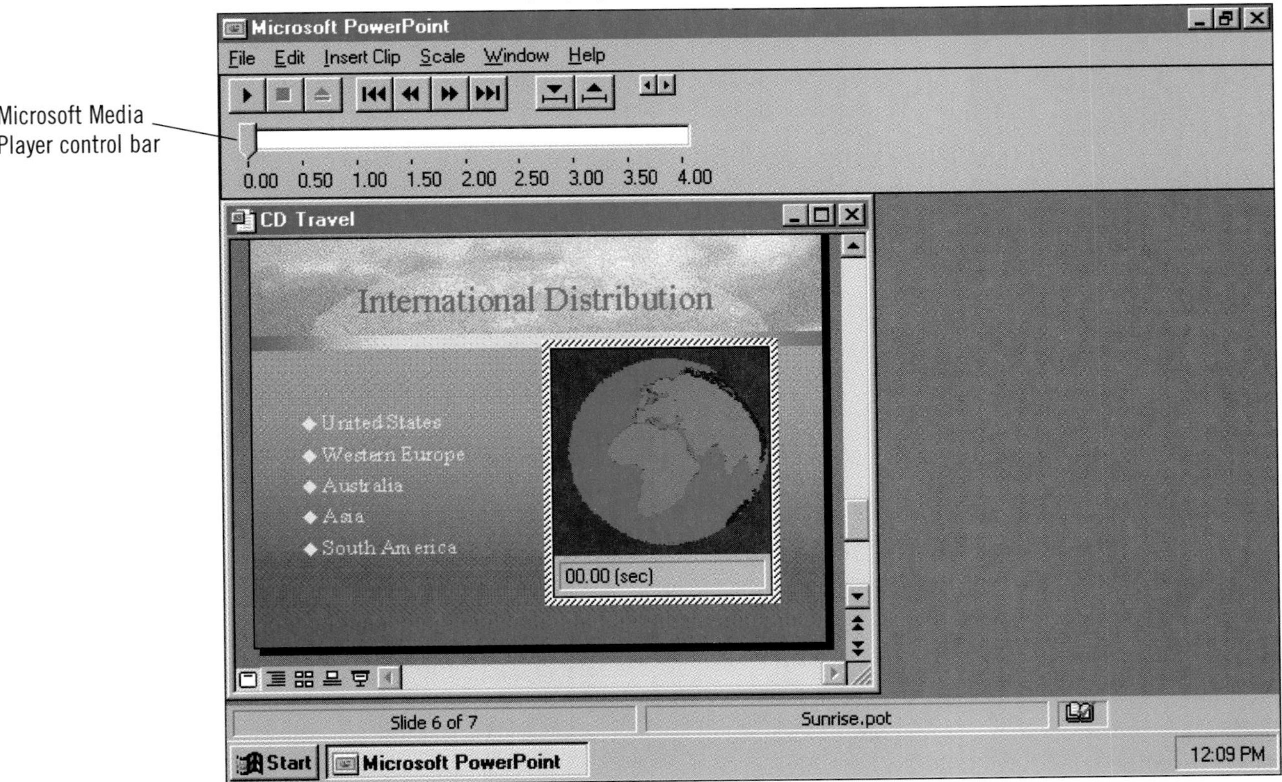

PowerPoint 97

Inserting a Sound

PowerPoint allows you to embed sounds in your presentation just as you embed movies. When adding sounds to your presentation, it is a good idea to think about how a sound can help you present your message. Use sound to enhance the message of a slide. For example, if you are creating a presentation about a raft tour of the Colorado River, you might embed a river sound on a slide showing a photograph of people white-water rafting. You can embed several different types of sounds in your presentation, but you'll need a sound card and speakers installed on your computer to play the sounds. In this lesson, Karen embeds a sound on Slide 2 of her presentation to enhance the picture on the slide.

Steps

1. **Drag the vertical scroll box to Slide 2**
2. **Click Insert on the menu bar, point to Movies and Sounds, then click Sound from File**
   The Insert Sound dialog box opens.
3. **Select the file PPT G-5, then click OK**
   A small sound icon appears on the slide, as shown in Figure G-16. Enlarge the icon so it is easier to see.
4. **Click Format on the menu bar, click Picture, then click the Size tab**
   The Size tab opens in the Format Picture dialog box.
5. **In the Scale section, double-click the Height setting and type 150, then click OK**
   The sound icon enlarges to 150% of its original size. Now move the sound icon down to the bottom of the slide.
6. **Drag the sound icon to the lower-right corner of the Presentation window**
   Compare your screen to Figure G-17. Now play the sound.
7. **Double-click the sound icon**
   The sound of a camera clicking plays. Save your changes.
8. **Click the Save button on the Standard toolbar**

Trouble?

The sound icon you see may be different from the one illustrated in Figure G-16, depending on your sound card software.

Trouble?

If you do not hear a sound, your computer may not have a sound card installed. See your instructor or technical support person for help.

CLUES TO USE

Inserting sounds and movies from the Clip Gallery

You can also insert sounds and movies from the Microsoft Clip Gallery. Make sure the Office 97 CD-ROM is in the CD drive or that all the clip art images from the Office 97 CD-ROM have been imported to the Clip Gallery. Click Insert on the menu bar, point to Movies and Sounds, click Movie from Gallery or click Sound from Gallery, select the clip you want to include in the presentation, then click Insert. If you insert movies and sounds using this method, the Office 97 CD-ROM must be in the CD drive. If PowerPoint cannot find the file, then you need to locate it manually.

FIGURE G-16: Slide showing small sound icon

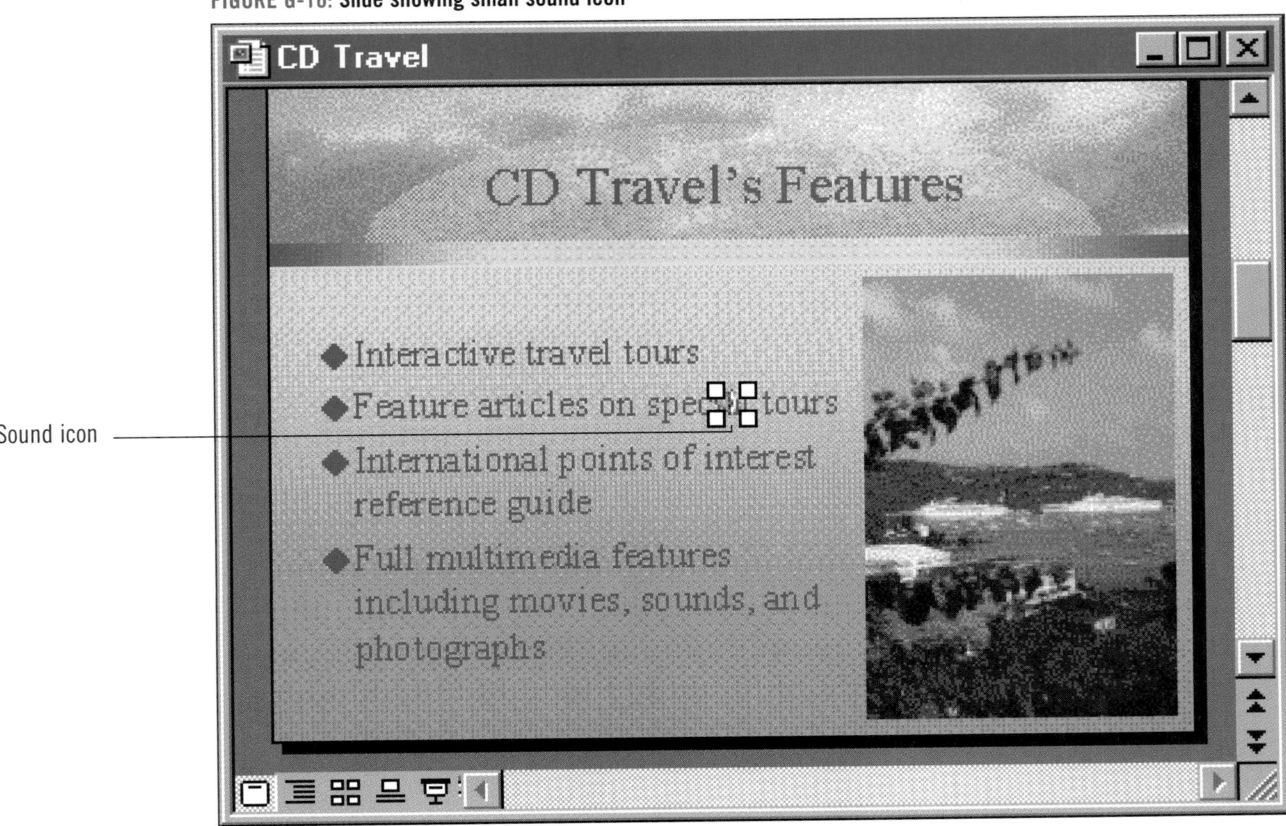

FIGURE G-17: Slide showing scaled and repositioned sound icon

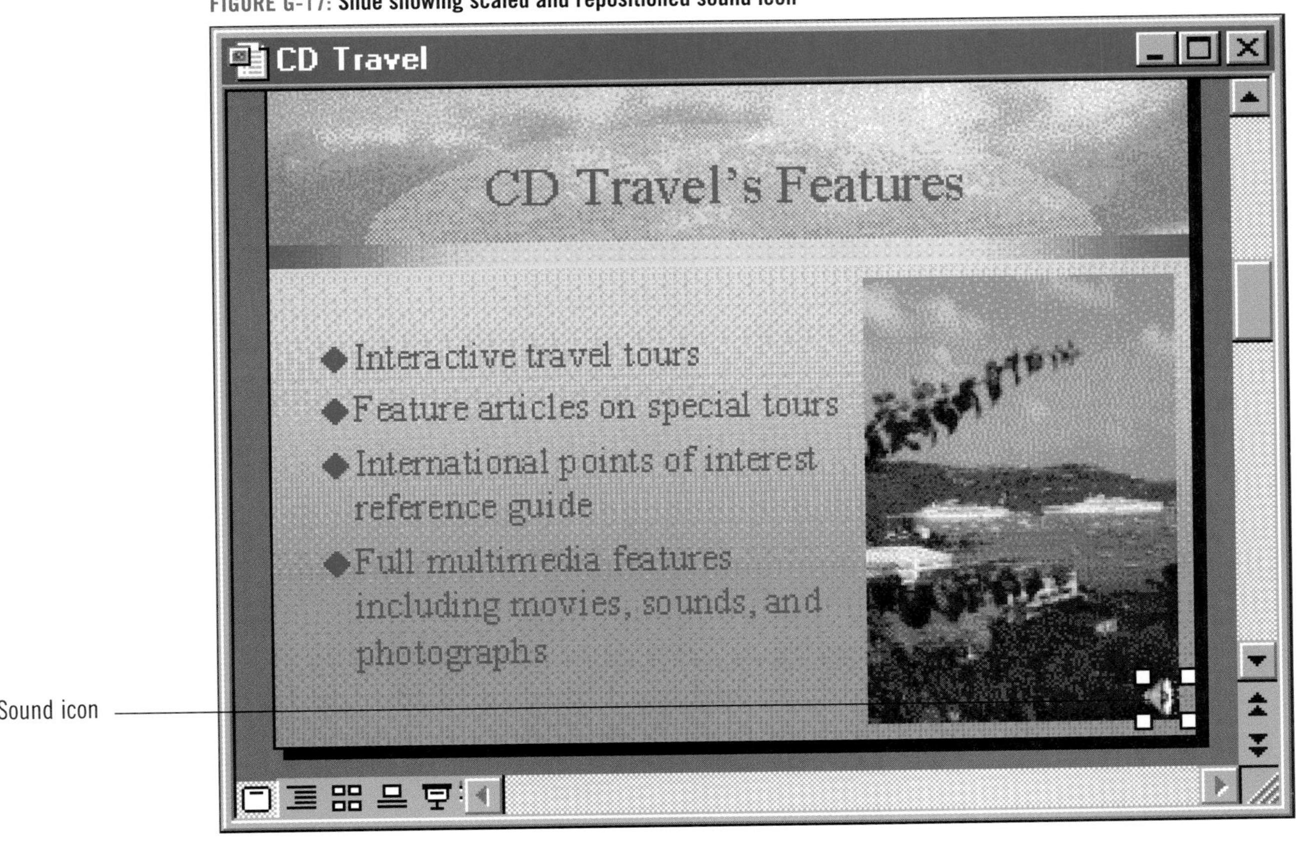

PowerPoint 97

Inserting a Hyperlink

Often you will want to display a document that either won't fit on the slide, or that is too detailed for your presentation. In these cases, you can insert a **hyperlink**, which is a specially formatted word, phrase, or graphic that you click during your slide show to "jump to," or display, another document. The **target document**, the file your hyperlink displays on the screen when you click it, can be a Word, Excel, or Access file, another slide in your current presentation, another PowerPoint presentation, or an address on the World Wide Web. Inserting a hyperlink is similar to linking because you can change the object in the source program after you click the hyperlink. Karen decides to use a hyperlink to display a recent product review, which is in a Word document.

Steps

1. Go to **Slide 6**, click **New Slide** on the Common Tasks toolbar, click the **Bulleted List AutoLayout**, click **OK**, then type **Product Reviews** in the title placeholder
   Enter the names of three magazines that have recently reviewed *CD Travel Magazine.*
2. Click the main text placeholder, type **Travel World**, press **[Enter]**, type **Armchair Traveler**, press **[Enter]**, and type **Vacation Monthly**
   Now format the text box.
3. Click the border of the text box to select the entire text object, click the **Font Size list arrow**, click **48**, drag the lower-right corner of the text box up and to the left to resize it to fit the text, and then center the text box on the slide
   To be able to click on a magazine name to display the review during the slide show, make the second magazine title a hyperlink to the review from that magazine.
4. Highlight **Armchair Traveler**, click the **Insert Hyperlink button** on the Standard toolbar, click **Browse** at the top of the dialog box, locate the file **PPT G-6**, click **OK**, click **OK** in the Insert Hyperlink dialog box, then click in a blank area of the Presentation window
   Now that you have made the magazine title a hyperlink, the title automatically changes to hyperlink formatting, which is underlined blue text. Change the background color of the slide, so the blue text will be more readable.

QuickTip

The hyperlink will only take you to the target document when you are in slide show view.

5. Right-click in a blank area of the Presentation window, click **Slide Color Scheme** on the pop-up menu, click the **Standard tab**, click the scheme with the dark pink background in the bottom row on the left, then click **Apply**
   Make sure you do not click Apply to All. The hyperlink is now visible on the slide. See Figure G-18. Now test the hyperlink.
6. Click the **Slide Show button**, then click the **Armchair Traveler hyperlink**
   The Word document containing the review appears on the screen in Full Page View. See Figure G-19. The Web toolbar appears at the top of the screen. Now return to the presentation.
7. Click the **Back button** on the Web toolbar
   The Product Reviews slide reappears in slide show view. The hyperlink is now light purple, indicating that the hyperlink has been used.
8. Click once to end the slide show, press **[Ctrl][Home]**, click the **Slide Sorter View button**, then click the **Maximize button** in the Presentation window
   Compare your screen to Figure G-20. Evaluate the presentation, then save and print it.
9. Run through the entire slide show making sure you click the Sound icon on Slide 2, the Movie object on Slide 6, and the hyperlink on Slide 7, spell-check the presentation, save your changes, print the slides of the presentation, close the presentation, right-click the Word program button on the taskbar, then click **Close** on the pop-up menu

FIGURE G-18: The hyperlink to the product review

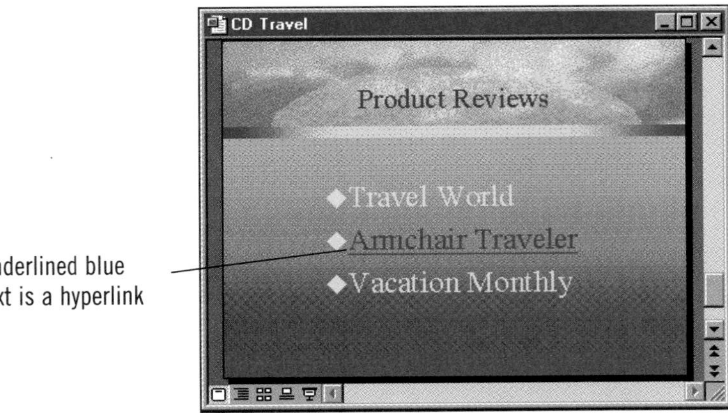

Underlined blue text is a hyperlink

FIGURE G-19: The product review displays during the slide show

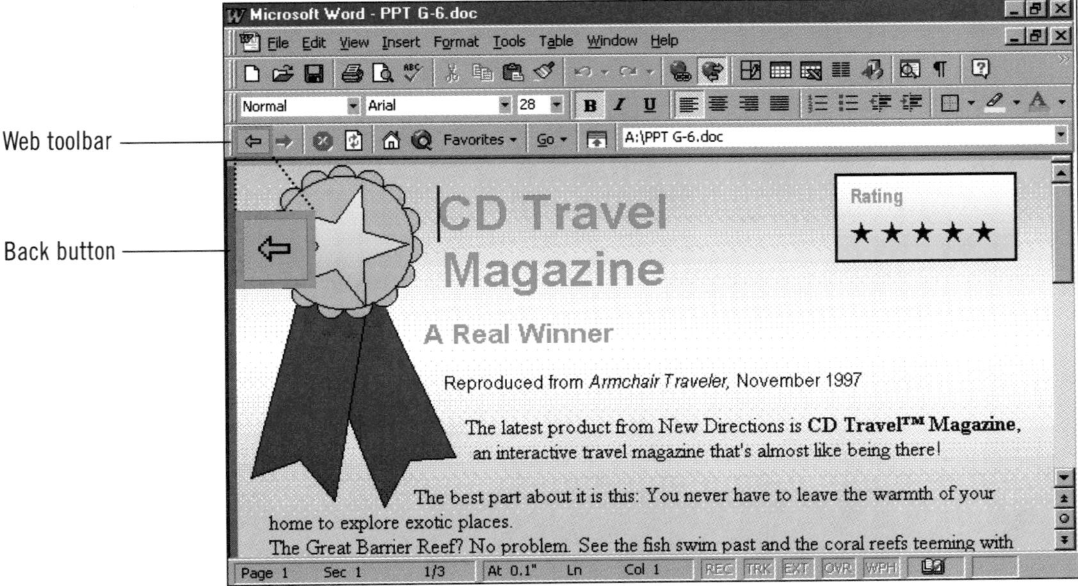

Web toolbar

Back button

FIGURE G-20: Final presentation in Slide Sorter view

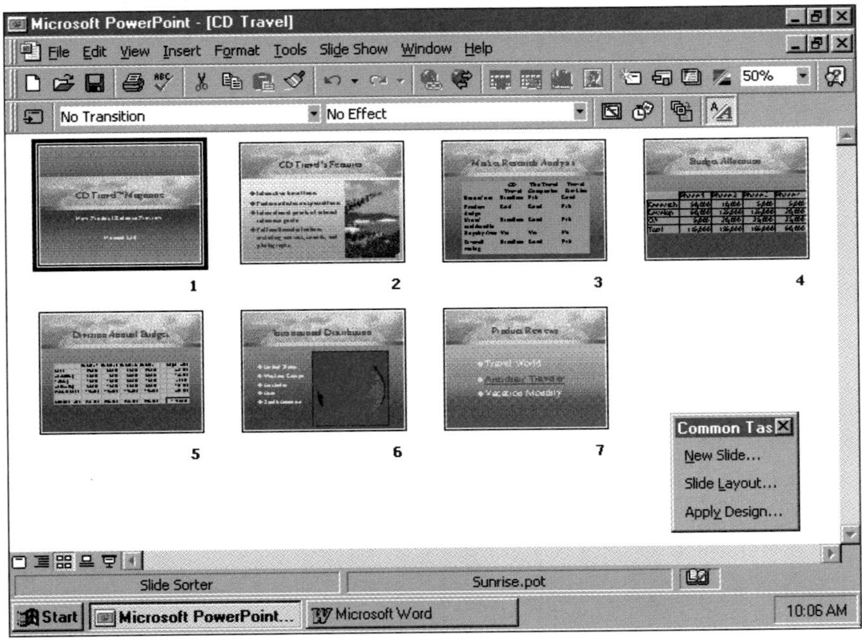

PowerPoint 97

Practice

► Concepts Review

Label each of the elements of the PowerPoint window shown in Figure G-21.

FIGURE G-21

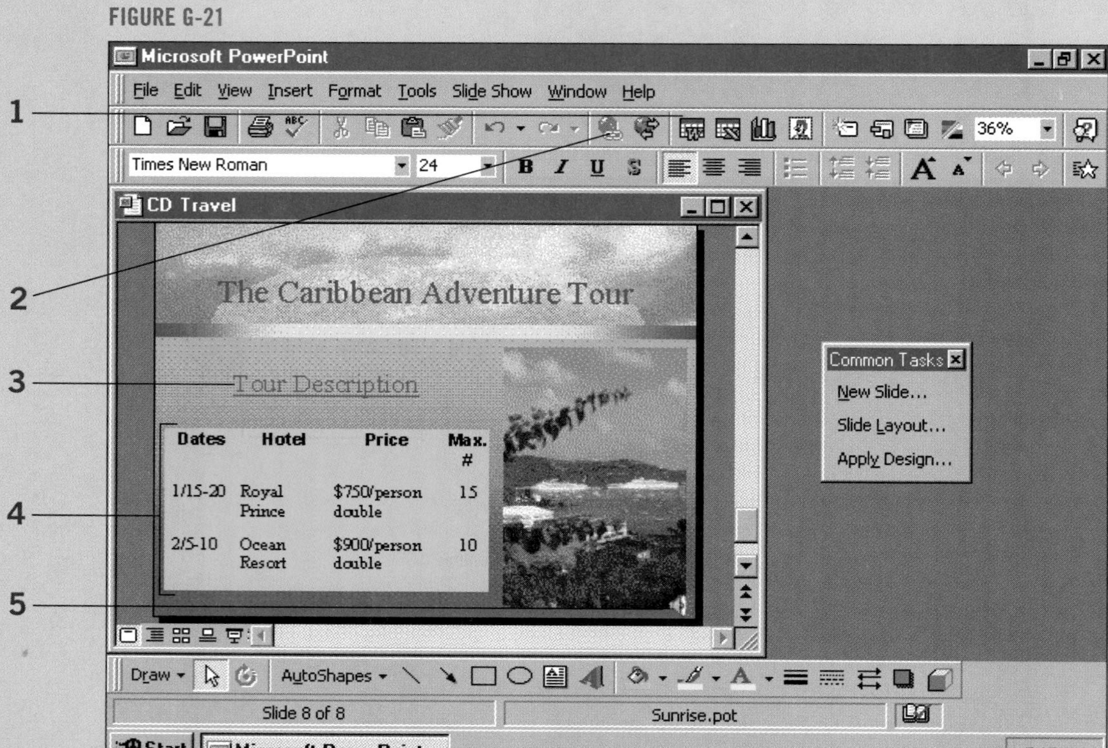

Match each of the terms with the statement that describes its function.

6. An object created in another program and then stored in PowerPoint
7. The program in which an embedded object is created
8. A scanned photograph or piece of line art
9. A word or object you click to display another file
10. The connection between a source file and a PowerPoint presentation

a. Picture
b. Embedded object
c. Link
d. Source program
e. Hyperlink

Select the best answer from the list of choices.

11. Which of the following objects are you able to embed into PowerPoint?
    a. Digital movies
    b. Photographs
    c. Microsoft Excel worksheets
    d. All of the above
12. Which statement about embedded objects is false?
    a. You can format embedded objects in their source program.
    b. Embedded objects are not dependent on a source file.
    c. Embedded objects are not a part of the presentation.
    d. Embedded objects increase your presentation file size more than linked objects do.

13. Which statement about linked objects is true?
- **a.** To edit a linked object, you must open its source file.
- **b.** A linked object is an independent object embedded directly to a slide.
- **c.** You can access a linked object even when the source file is not available.
- **d.** A linked object substantially increases the size of your presentation file.

► Skills Review

If you complete all of the exercises in this unit, you may run out of space on your Student Disk. To make sure you have enough disk space, please copy files PPT G-7, PPT G-8, PPT G-9, and ND Profit onto a new disk and use the new disk to complete the rest of the exercises in this unit. If you do not have access to the Office 97 CD-ROM or if the complete set of clip art images has not been imported to the Clip Art Gallery, then you should also copy the files PPT G-2, PPT G-4, and PPT G-5.

1. Embed a picture.
- **a.** Start PowerPoint, open the presentation PPT G-7, then save it as New Directions 97.
- **b.** Click the Next Slide button twice.
- **c.** Click Insert on the menu bar, point to Picture, then click Clip Art.
- **d.** Click the Pictures tab, click the Sports & Leisure category, click the photo of the rock climber, then click Insert. (If this image is not available, use the Insert Picture From File command and insert the file PPT G-2 again.)
- **e.** Click the Crop button on the Picture toolbar, position the cropping tool pointer over the right middle sizing handle, drag the handle to the left to crop out the right half of the picture, then click the Crop button to deselect it.
- **f.** Drag the picture to the right side of the slide, resize the picture so it is slightly taller than the bulleted list, then use the [Arrow] keys on the keyboard to make minor adjustments to the picture's position.
- **g.** Click the More Contrast button on the Picture toolbar three times to make the image in the photo stand out more.
- **h.** Save your changes.

2. Embed a table.
- **a.** Click the Previous Slide button, click New Slide on the Common Tasks toolbar, click the Title Only AutoLayout, then click OK.
- **b.** Type "New Directions at a Glance."
- **c.** Click the Insert Microsoft Word Table button on the Standard toolbar and drag to select a 5 x 3 table.
- **d.** Enter the information shown in Figure G-22. Don't worry about the column widths now.

FIGURE G-22

Adventure	Sailing	International Tours
Kayaking	Hawaii	Trans-Siberian Railway
Alaskan Lakes	South China Sea	China
U.S. by Air	Black Sea	African Safari
Hot Air Balloon	World Tour	Black Forest

- **e.** Click in the Presentation window, then double-click the table to redisplay it.
- **f.** Drag to select all three columns, then click the Center button on the Formatting toolbar.

g. Click Table on the menu bar, click Table AutoFormat, click Simple 3, then click OK.
h. Drag the column dividers so that the columns are sized as in Figure G-22, then resize the table object border so it fits the table as closely as possible.
i. Click in a blank area of the Presentation window, resize the table so it fills the lower portion of the slide, then drag the table so it is centered below the slide title.
j. With the table still selected, click the Fill Color list arrow, and select the turquoise box on the far right.
k. Click the Save button on the Standard toolbar.

3. Embed a worksheet.

a. Drag the vertical scroll box to Slide 4.
b. Click New Slide on the Common Tasks toolbar, click the Object AutoLayout, then click OK.
c. Type "Projected Division Income."
d. Double-click the object placeholder, click the Create from file option button, then click Browse.
e. Locate the file PPT G-8, then click OK twice.
f. Double-click the worksheet, click cell B4, click the AutoSum button on the Excel Standard toolbar, then press [Tab].
g. Drag to select cells B4 through E4, click Edit on the menu bar, point to Fill, then click Right.
h. Leave cells B4 to E4 selected, hold down [Ctrl], drag to select cells B1 through E1, release [Ctrl], and click the Bold button on the Formatting toolbar.
i. Drag to select cells B1 through E1, then click the Center button in the Formatting toolbar.
j. Click on the slide outside the worksheet, then click the worksheet and drag its lower-right resize handle until the worksheet is almost as wide as the slide.
k. Reposition the worksheet using the keyboard arrow keys, so it is centered horizontally and vertically.
l. With the worksheet selected, click the Fill Color button on the Drawing toolbar.
m. Save your changes.

4. Link an Excel worksheet.

a. Click New Slide on the Common Tasks toolbar, click the Object AutoLayout, then click OK.
b. Type "Projected Division Profit."
c. Double-click the object placeholder, click the Create from file option button, then click Browse.
d. Locate the file ND Profit, click OK, click the Link check box, then click OK.
e. Drag the object's lower resize handles so that it fills the slide width.
f. Use the keyboard arrow keys to reposition the object so it is centered horizontally.
g. With the worksheet still selected, click the Fill Color button on the Drawing toolbar.
h. Save and close the New Directions 97 presentation.

5. Update a linked Excel worksheet.

a. Click the Start button on the taskbar, point to Programs, then click Microsoft Excel.
b. On the Excel Standard toolbar, click the Open button, locate the file ND Profit, then click Open.
c. Click cell B2, type "2550900," then press [Enter].
d. Click cell D3, type "95000," click cell B4, type "220300," click cell D7, type "1780800," then press [Enter].
e. Click the Excel Program window Close button, then click Yes to save the changes.
f. Click the Open button on the PowerPoint Standard toolbar, locate the file New Directions 97, then click Open.
g. Click OK to update the linked object.
h. Drag the vertical scroll box to Slide 6. View your changes.
i. Click the linked worksheet, click Edit on the menu bar, click Links, examine the link information, then click Close.
j. Save the presentation.

6. Embed a movie.

a. Drag the vertical scroll box to Slide 2.
b. Click Insert on the menu bar, point to Movies & Sounds, then click Movie from Gallery.
c. Scroll down to find the Globe movie, select it, then click Insert. (If this movie is not available, insert the movie file PPT G-4.)

d. Double-click the movie object.
e. Right-click the movie object, then click Edit Movie Object.
f. Click the Loop until stopped check box, then click OK.
g. Click in a blank area of the Presentation window, then resize the movie object so it fills the right side of the screen.
h. Double-click the movie object, click outside the movie object, then save the presentation.

7. **Embed a sound.**
   a. Click the Next Slide button twice.
   b. Click Insert on the menu bar, point to Movies and Sounds, then click Sound from Gallery.
   c. Click the Charge sound, then click Insert. (If this sound is not available, insert the sound file PPT G-5.).
   d. Click Format on the menu bar, click Picture, click the Size tab.
   e. In the Scale section, double-click the Height setting, type "150", then click OK.
   f. Drag the sound icon to the bottom right of the slide.
   g. Double-click the sound icon to test it.
   h. Click the Save button on the Standard toolbar.
8. **Insert a hyperlink.**
   a. Drag the vertical scroll bar to the last slide in the presentation, click New Slide on the Common Tasks toolbar, click the Bulleted List AutoLayout, and click OK.
   b. Type "Testimonials" in the Title placeholder.
   c. Click the main text placeholder and type "George Sanders, Medford, Oregon," and press [Enter].
   d. Type "Jorge Fonseca, Orem, Utah."
   e. Click the edge of the main text placeholder, click the Font Size list arrow, and click 48.
   f. Drag the lower-right corner of the text box up and to the left to resize it to fit the text, and then center the text box on the slide using the keyboard arrow keys.
   g. Highlight the text in the George Sanders bullet, click the Insert Hyperlink button on the Standard toolbar, and, under Link to file or URL, click Browse.
   h. Select the file PPT G-9, click OK, then click OK again.
   i. Click on the slide outside the text box.
   j. Click the Slide Show button, then click the hyperlink.
   k. After you view the Testimonial, click the Back button on the Web toolbar.
   l. Click the slide background to leave Slide Show view, then save the presentation.
   m. Run the spell checker, view the entire presentation in Slide Show view, print the slides, close the presentation, right-click the Word program button on the taskbar, then click Close on the pop-up menu.

Independent Challenges

1. Quincy Engineering is a mechanical and industrial design company that specializes in designing manufacturing plants in the United States and Canada. Most of the work that Quincy Engineering does is refitting manufacturing plants that are old and outdated. As the company financial analyst, you have been asked by Quincy Engineering's board of directors to investigate and report on a possible contract to design and build a large manufacturing plant in Brazil. Because Quincy Engineering has never worked overseas, the board of directors wants to make sure that they can make a minimum profit on the deal. It is your job to provide a recommendation to the board.

In this challenge, you'll need to enhance the presentation to make it look professional. Create your own information using the basic presentation provided and assume the following about Quincy Engineering:

- The Brazilian company can offer a contract for no more than $23 million for this entire project.
- The new manufacturing plant in Brazil will be 75,000 square feet in size. The projected cost for Quincy Engineering to design and build the plant in Brazil is $350.00 per square foot based on a four-phase schedule; planning and design, site acquisition and preparation, construction phase 1, and construction phase 2.
- Factors that helped determine Quincy Engineering's cost to build the plant include: Quincy Engineering payroll

for 15 people in the United States and payroll for 10 people in Brazil for 18 months; materials cost; hiring of one construction company in the United States and two in Brazil to construct the plant; travel and lodging costs.

- The board of directors requires at least a 4% profit margin to go ahead with a proposal.

To complete this independent challenge:

1. Open the file PPT G-10, then save it as Quincy 1.
2. Think about what results you want to see, what information you need to create the slide presentation, and how your message should be communicated. In order for your presentation to be complete, it must include the following objects: (1) embedded Word table; (2) embedded Excel worksheet; (3) linked table, worksheet, chart, or other object; (4) embedded picture; and (5) hyperlink.
3. Use Microsoft Word and Microsoft Excel to embed, link, or hyperlink objects into your presentation. Use the preceding assumptions to develop related information that would be appropriate for a table or worksheet.
4. All slides should be titled and have main text where appropriate.
5. The last slide in the presentation should be your recommendation to pursue the contract or not, based on the financial data you present.
6. Submit your presentation plan and print the final slide presentation.

2. You are the director of operations at The Franklin Group, a large investment banking company in Texas. Franklin is considering merging with Redding Industries Inc, a smaller investment company in Arizona, to form the tenth largest financial institution in the United States. As the director of operations, you need to present some financial projections regarding the merger to a special committee formed by Franklin to study the proposed merger.

Create your own information using the basic presentation provided on your Student Disk. Assume the following facts about the merger between Franklin and Redding:

- Franklin earned a $19 million profit last year. Projected profit this year is $26 million. Projected profit next year with the merger with Redding is $36 million. Franklin's operating expenses run about $30 million a year. Redding's operating expenses run about $19 million a year.
- Redding earned $8 million in profit last year. Projected profit this year is $10 million. Projected profit next year with the merger is $18 million.
- Franklin has an 18% share of the market without Redding. Redding has a 6% share of the market without Franklin. Combined, the companies would have a 24% share of the market.
- With the merger, Franklin would need to cut $7.6 million from its annual operating costs and Redding would need to cut $2 million from its annual operating costs.

To complete this independent challenge:

1. Open the file PPT G-11, then save it as Merger.
2. Think about what results you want to see, what information you need to create the slide presentation, and how your message should be communicated. In order for your presentation to be complete, it must include the following objects: (1) embedded Word table; (2) embedded Excel worksheet; (3) linked table, worksheet, chart, or other object; (4) embedded picture; and (5) a hyperlink.
3. Use Microsoft Excel to embed or link a worksheet to your presentation. Use the preceding assumptions to develop related information that would be appropriate for a worksheet. For at least one worksheet, use the profit and operating expense figures to create your own revenue figures. (Revenue minus operating expenses equals profit.)
4. Use Microsoft Word to create a table showing market share analysis between Franklin, Redding, and two other companies that you create. Illustrate the market share figures with and without the merger.
5. All slides should be titled and have main text where appropriate. Create slides as necessary to make the presentation complete.
6. Create another slide or presentation that you can branch to your presentation.
7. Submit your presentation plan and print the final slide presentation.

3. You are the communications director at Johnson & Associates, a large advertising agency in southern Florida. One of your company's clients is New Directions, the travel subsidiary of Nomad Ltd. One of your jobs is to create a sales presentation for the New Directions account that promotes New Directions' new products and tours for 1998. The presentation will be shown to large groups at the annual travel trade show held every year in Miami, Florida.

Plan and create a presentation that promotes New Directions' products and tours. Use the information you know about New Directions from this unit as a basis for your presentation. You may want to open the presentations you created in this unit for more information. Create your own data, but assume the following:

- New Directions is offering four new international tours for 1998: (1) Trans-Siberian Railway; (2) China; (3) African Safari; and (4) the Black Forest.
- New Directions wants to vigorously promote its Adventure tour series. The new Adventure tours for 1998 include: the Colorado River Kayak tour; the Yosemite Rock Climbing tour; the Southern States Hot-Air Balloon tour; the US by Air tour; and the Alaskan Lakes tour.
- New products include: the *CD Travel Magazine*; the *Travel Encyclopedia*; and the *Traveler's Handbook*.

To complete this independent challenge:

1. Think about what results you want to see, what information you need to create the slide presentation, and how your message should be communicated. In order for your presentation to be complete, it must include the following objects: (1) embedded Word table; (2) embedded Excel worksheet; (3) linked table, worksheet, chart, or other object; (4) embedded picture; (5) embedded movie and sound; and (6) a hyperlink.
2. Use the information provided and the information in the presentations you created in this unit to help you develop the content for your presentation. Use the movies and sounds provided for you with the student files for this text, or if you have access to the Microsoft Office CD-ROM, choose another appropriate movie (and sound) to embed into your presentation. (Feel free to embed another movie or sound if you have access to other media sources.)
3. Use Microsoft Word and Microsoft Excel to embed, link, or hyperlink objects into your presentation. Use the preceding assumptions to develop related information that would be appropriate for a table or worksheet.
4. All the slides should be titled and have main text where appropriate.
5. Create another slide or presentation that you can branch to from your presentation. To help you create a branch, you can customize the New Directions 97 presentation you created in the Skills Review portion of this unit.
6. Add a template, background shading, or other enhancing objects to make your presentation look professional.
7. Save the presentation as Johnson Presentation.
8. Submit your presentation plan and print the final slide presentation.

4. You have just been promoted to the position of sales manager at DWImports, a U.S. company that exports goods and professional services to companies in Japan, South Korea, China, and the Philippines. One of your new responsibilities is to give a presentation at the biannual finance meeting showing how the Sales Department performed during the previous six-month period.

Plan and create a short slide presentation (six to eight slides) that illustrates the Sales Department's performance during the last six months. Identify the existing accounts (by country) and then identify the new contracts acquired during the last six months. Create your own content, but assume the following:

- The majority of goods and services being exported are: food products (such as rice, corn, and wheat); agriculture consulting; construction engineering; and industrial designing and engineering.
- The company gained five new accounts in China, South Korea, and the Philippines.
- The Sales Department showed a $5 million profit for the first half of the year.
- Department expenses for the first half of the year were $3.5 million.
- The presentation will be given in a boardroom using a projection machine.

To complete this independent challenge:

1. Think about what results you want to see, what information you need to create the slide presentation, and how your message should be communicated. In order for your presentation to be complete, it must include the following objects: (1) embedded Word table; (2) embedded Excel worksheet; (3) linked table, worksheet, chart, or other object; (4) embedded picture; (5) embedded movie and sound; and (6) hyperlink.
2. Use the movies and sounds provided for you on your Student Disk, or if you have access to the Microsoft Office CD-ROM, choose another appropriate movie (and sound) to embed into your presentation. (Feel free to embed another movie or sound if you have access to other media sources.)

3. Use Microsoft Word and Microsoft Excel to embed, link, or hyperlink objects into your presentation. Use the preceding assumptions to develop related information that would be appropriate for a table or worksheet.
4. Log on to the Internet and use your browser to go to http://www.course.com. From there, click Student Online Companions, click the link for this textbook, then click the PowerPoint link for Unit G. Use the link there to find relevant information about trade between the U.S. and the Asia-Pacific area, and any issues that might have influenced the sales climate during the last six months.
5. All the slides should be titled and have main text points where appropriate.
6. Add a template, background shading, or other enhancing objects to make your presentation look professional.
7. Save the presentation as Imports.
8. Submit your presentation plan and print the final slide presentation.

► Visual Workshop

Create two slides that look like the examples in Figures G-23 and G-24. Save the presentation as Year End Report. Save and print Slide view of the presentation. Submit the final presentation output.

FIGURE G-23

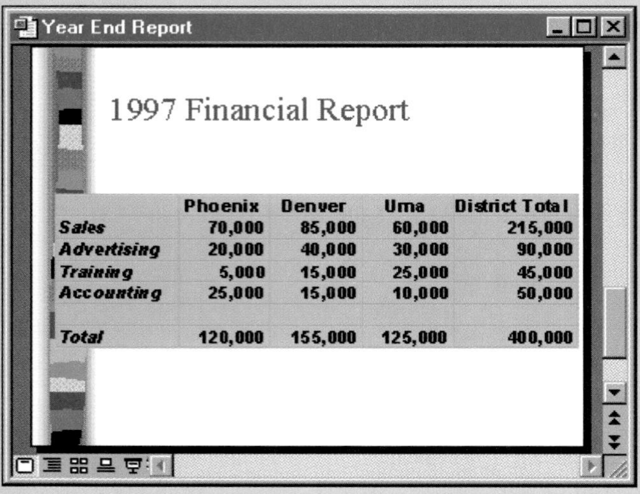

FIGURE G-24

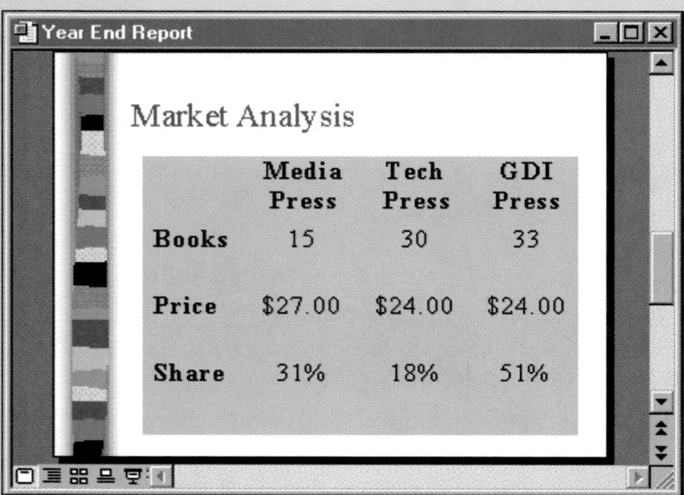

Using
Slide Show Features

Objectives

- Animate charts and sounds
- Set up a slide show
- Create a custom show
- Hide a slide during a slide show
- Use the Meeting Minder
- Rehearse slide timings
- Use the Pack and Go Wizard
- Use the Microsoft PowerPoint Viewer

After all the work on your presentation is complete, you need to produce the final output that you will use when you give your presentation. You probably have realized by now that PowerPoint offers several options for your presentation output. You can create 35mm slides, overhead transparencies, audience handouts, or you can show your presentation on a computer using Slide Show view. Slide Show view turns your computer screen into a projector that displays your slides one by one in an **on-screen presentation.** Carrie Armstrong finishes the Annual Report Executive Summary by adding special effects. She then produces an on-screen presentation to show Bill Davidson, the president of Nomad Ltd.

PowerPoint 97

Animating Charts and Sounds

As you know, you can animate text and objects in PowerPoint by determining how and when bullets or pictures appear during a slide show. You can add more interest to your slide shows by animating charts, sounds, and videos. For example, instead of displaying the entire chart at one time, you can animate the individual bars in a bar chart and specify when you want them to appear. Then you can add a sound effect to accompany the appearance of each one. You can animate sounds and videos to play at predetermined times during and after each slide. Carrie added a sound icon to Slide 5, the slide containing the bar chart of the 1997 Sales Analysis. Now she'd like to animate the bar chart and add the embedded applause sound effect on that slide.

Steps 1 2 3 4

1. Start PowerPoint, open the presentation **PPT H-1**, save it as **97 Annual Report Final Version**, make sure the Presentation window is at **36% zoom**, click the **Restore Window button** in the Presentation window, click **Window** on the menu bar, then click **Fit to Page**
   First, you'll animate the chart and an embedded sound on Slide 5.
2. Drag the vertical scroll bar to go to **Slide 5**, click the chart to select it, click **Slide Show** on the menu bar, click **Custom Animation**, then click the **Chart Effects tab**
   The Custom Animation dialog box opens, similar to Figure H-1. You'll animate each data series in the chart to "dissolve in" gradually, accompanied by the sound of a cash register.
3. In the Introduce chart elements list box, select **by Series**; in the top Entry animation and sound list box, select **Dissolve**; and in the bottom Entry animation and sound list box, select **Cash Register**
   Compare your screen to Figure H-1.
4. Click **Preview** and watch the Preview window to see how the chart will appear with the settings you've chosen
   Now set the timing so that each chart element appears three seconds after the previous one.
5. Click the **Timing tab**, in the Start animation section, click the **Automatically option button**, change the setting to **3** seconds after previous event, then click **OK**
   Now add the embedded applause sound to the slide animation.
6. Right-click the **sound icon**, click **Custom Animation** on the pop-up menu, then click the **Play Settings tab**
   Set the applause sound animation effect so that it plays after the chart animation has finished, hide the sound icon, and pause the slide show while the embedded sound plays.
7. Click to select the check boxes for **Play using animation order** and **Hide while not playing**, and make sure that the **Pause slide show option button** is selected
   See Figure H-2. Now set the applause sound to play 2 seconds after the chart appears.
8. Click the **Timing tab**, click the **Automatically option button** in the Start animation section, change the setting to **2 seconds**, click **OK**, then deselect the icon
   See Figure H-3. Now view the slide show to see the full effect of your changes. Several of the slides have transition and animation effects already applied to them.
9. Press **[Ctrl][Home]**, click the **Slide Show button** , click the left mouse button to advance through the slide show, making sure you wait to view the animation effects on each slide

Trouble?

If your computer does not have a sound card, you will not be able to hear the sound effects. You can still continue with the lesson.

QuickTip

Use animations to emphasize only the most important points in your presentation. Too many animations and sounds will distract audience attention from your message.

Time To

✔ Save

FIGURE H-1: Chart Effects tab in the Custom Animation dialog box

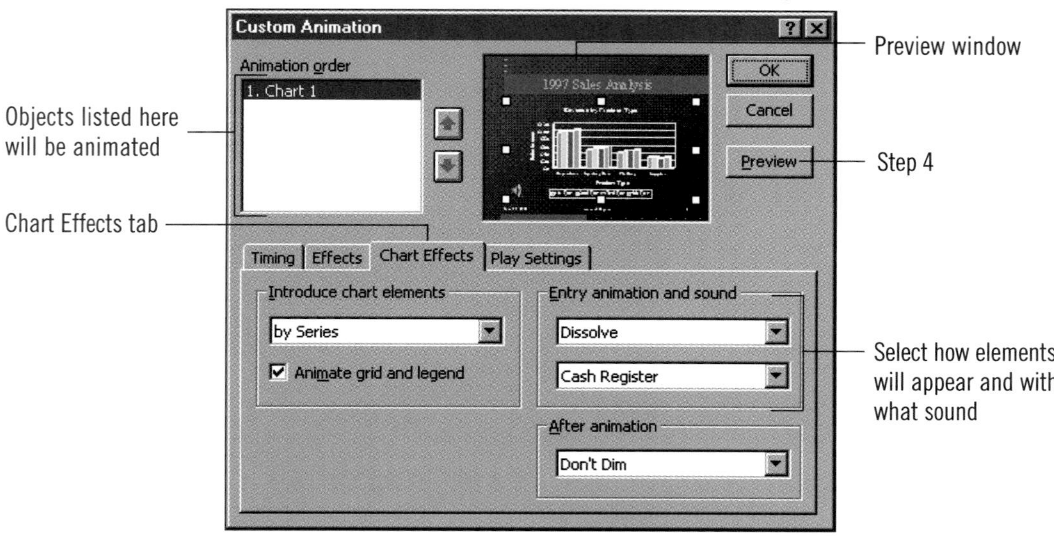

FIGURE H-2: Play Settings tab in the Custom Animation dialog box

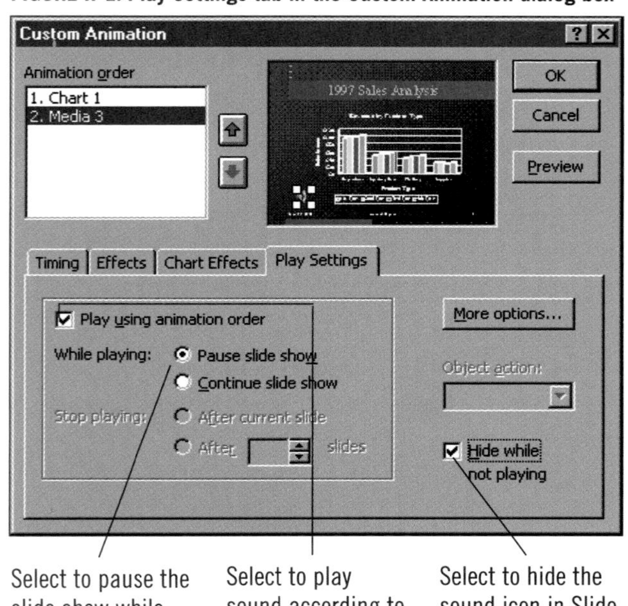

FIGURE H-3: Final chart

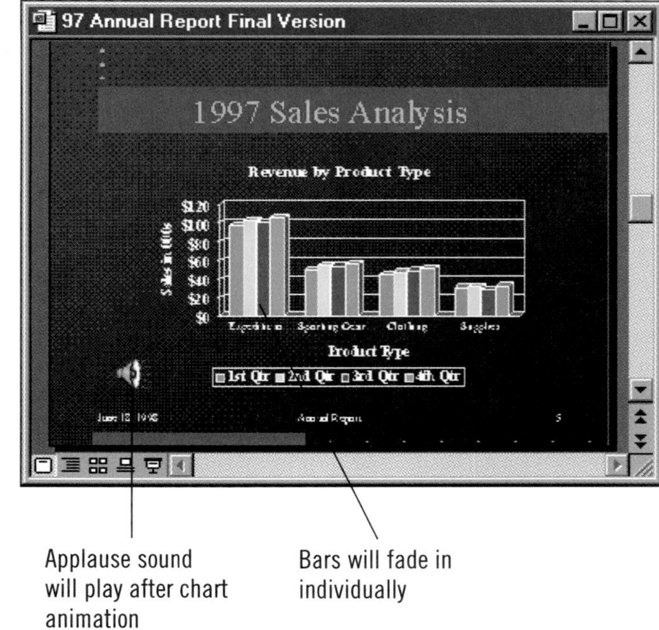

PowerPoint 97

Adding voice narrations

If your computer has a sound card and a microphone, you can record a voice narration that plays with your slide show. To record a voice, click Slide Show on the menu bar, then click Record Narration. If you want the recording to be linked to the presentation, click the Link narrations in check box. If you do not select this option, the recording will be embedded in the presentation. Then start recording.

PowerPoint 97

Setting Up a Slide Show

With PowerPoint, you can create a slide show that runs automatically. Viewers can then watch the slide show individually on a public computer at a convention or a trade show on a free-standing computer called a **kiosk**. You can create a self-running slide show that loops, or runs through the entire show, without users touching the computer. You can also let viewers advance the slides at their own pace by pressing the spacebar, clicking the mouse, or clicking an on-screen control button called an Action button. Carrie prepares the Annual Report presentation so shareholders can view it at a table during the open house after Bill Davidson's presentation.

Steps 1 2 3 4

QuickTip

When you set up a slide show in a public area, you should think about where you'll set up the show, who will monitor the area, and how to prevent viewers from changing the presentation.

Trouble?

Although transition icons appear in Slide Sorter view, the settings in the Set Up Show dialog box override the transition effects. If you want, you can reapply the transition effects to the slides.

QuickTip

You must be in Slide Show view to use the hyperlink buttons.

1. Click **Slide Show** on the menu bar, click **Set Up Show**, and under Show Type, click the **Browsed at a kiosk (full screen) option button** to select it
   The Set Up Show dialog box opens, similar to Figure H-4. When the kiosk option is selected, the slide show will run continuously until you press [Esc] to end the show. Include all the slides in the presentation, and have PowerPoint advance the slides at time intervals you set.
2. In the Slides section, make sure the **All option button** is selected, and in the Advance slides section, click the **Using timings, if present option button**
   Compare your screen to Figure H-4. Next, specify that you want a 5 second pause between slides.
3. Click **OK**, click the **Slide Sorter View button**, press **[Ctrl][A]** to select all the slides, click **Slide Show** on the menu bar, click **Slide Transition**, in the Advance section, click the **Automatically after check box** to select it, type **5**, then click **Apply to All**
   The slide show will now display the slides automatically using the timing you entered, and it will not advance if someone clicks the mouse or presses [Spacebar].
4. Click the **Slide Show button**, view the self-running presentation through to the end, let it start again, and then press **[Esc]**
   Now set up a show that lets users click a button to move to the next slide.
5. Click **Slide Show** on the menu bar, click **Set Up Show**, in the Advance slides section, click the **Manually option button**, then click **OK**
   Now place a button on each slide that is actually a hyperlink to the next slide.
6. Double-click Slide 1, click **Slide Show** on the menu bar, point to **Action Buttons**, click the **Action Button: Forward or Next button**, and drag the pointer to draw a button in the lower right corner of Slide 1
   The Action Settings dialog box opens. See Figure H-5.
7. Make sure the **Hyperlink to option button** is selected and that **Next Slide** is selected in the list box, then click **OK**
   Compare your screen to Figure H-6. Now copy the hyperlink button to all the slides.
8. With the button selected, press **[Ctrl][C]** to copy it, click the **Next Slide button**, press **[Ctrl][V]** to paste the button on Slide 2, then repeat for each slide that follows
   Now view the slide show using the hyperlink buttons to move from slide to slides.
9. Press **[Ctrl][Home]**, click the **Slide Show button**, click the **hyperlink buttons** to move from slide to slide, then press **[Esc]** after you have viewed the last slide
   Make sure you wait for the animated objects to appear on the slides. There are some tasks you can't do during a slide show with the kiosk setting active, so turn this feature off for now.
10. Click **Slide Show** on the menu bar, click **Set Up Show**, click the **Presented by a speaker (full screen option button)**, click **OK**, then save your changes

FIGURE H-4: **Set Up Show dialog box**

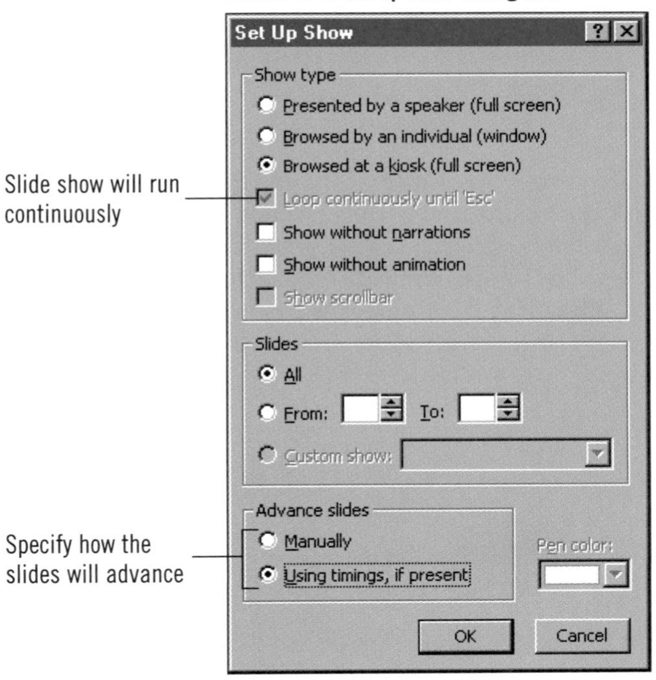

FIGURE H-5: **Action Settings dialog box**

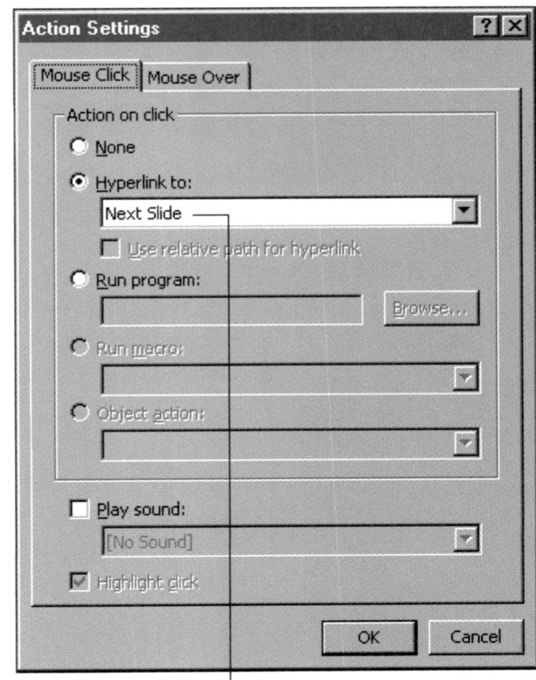

FIGURE H-6: **Slide 1 with the hyperlink button to the next slide**

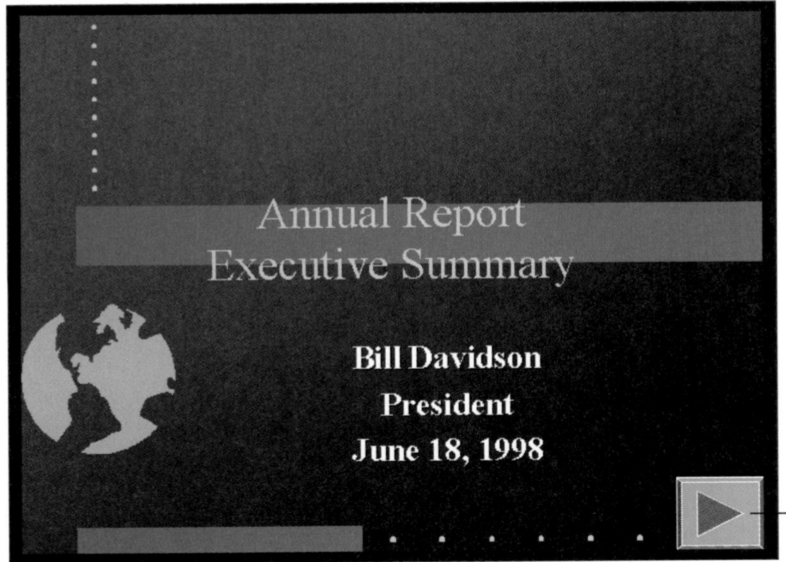

PowerPoint 97

Presenting a slide show on two screens

PowerPoint lets you connect two computers so you can control a slide show on one computer while showing it on another. The speaker can view the presentation on a laptop computer, while the audience views a computer with a large-screen monitor. To do this, you connect the two computers with a special cable, and install PowerPoint 97 on both computers. During the presentation, you can use the Slide Navigator and other tools available on the slide show pop-up menu that help you manage your slide show on the speaker's computer screen, without displaying them on the audience monitor.

Creating a Custom Show

Often when you create a slide show, you need to create a custom version of it for a different audience or purpose. For example, you might create a 20-minute presentation about a new product to show to potential customers who will be interested in the product features and benefits. Then you could create a 5-minute version of that same show for an open house for potential investors, containing only selected slides from the longer show. Bill Davidson wants a reduced version of the slide show that he can present to the sales force, so Carrie creates a custom slide show containing only the slides relating to sales goals and performance.

Steps

1. **Click Slide Show on the menu bar, click Custom Shows, then click New in the Custom Shows dialog box**
   The Define Custom Show dialog box opens, with the slides in your current presentation in the Slides in presentation list box on the left. Select the slides that give information about sales.
2. **Click Slide 3. Mission, press and hold [Shift], click Slide 7. 1998 Goals to select Slides 3 through 7, then click Add**
   The five selected slides move to the Slides in custom show list box, indicating that they will be included in the new presentation. See Figure H-7.
3. **Select the existing text in the Slide show name text box, then type Sales Presentation**
   Now change the slide order in the custom show.
4. **In the Slides in custom show list, click the Mission slide, click the Slide Order down arrow 4 times to move the Mission slide to the bottom of the list, then click OK**
   The Custom Shows dialog box lists your new presentation. Preview the custom show, which starts with the 1997 Accomplishments slide and ends with the Mission slide.
5. **Click Show, view the slide show, clicking the hyperlink button to move from slide to slide; when you reach the Mission slide, press [Esc] to end the custom show**
   Because the slide show is not set up to loop continuously, clicking the hyperlink button on the Mission slide doesn't do anything.
6. **Click Close in the Custom Shows dialog box**
   You return to the presentation in Slide view. Now view the custom show, starting at the title slide, as the president would at the actual presentation to the sales force. To show a custom slide show, you must first open the show you used to create it. You then go to the custom show, which is not saved as a separate slide show on your disk, even though you assigned it a new name.
7. **Press [Ctrl][Home] to go to Slide 1, click the Slide Show button, right-click the slide, point to Go, point to Custom Show, then click Sales Presentation as shown in Figure H-8**
8. **Use the hyperlink buttons to move from slide to slide and press [Esc] after viewing the Mission slide**
   Now print the slides in the custom show and save your changes.
9. **Click the Save button on the Standard toolbar, click File on the menu bar, click Print, click the Custom Show option button, make sure Sales Presentation is listed in the list box, click the Print what list arrow, select Slides (without animations), then click OK**

Trouble?

If you right-click the title slide and no shortcut menu appears, you probably forgot to return the Set Up Show option to Presented by a speaker (full screen). Press [Esc], click Slide Show on the menu bar, click Set Up Show, and select that option now.

FIGURE H-7: Define Custom Show dialog box

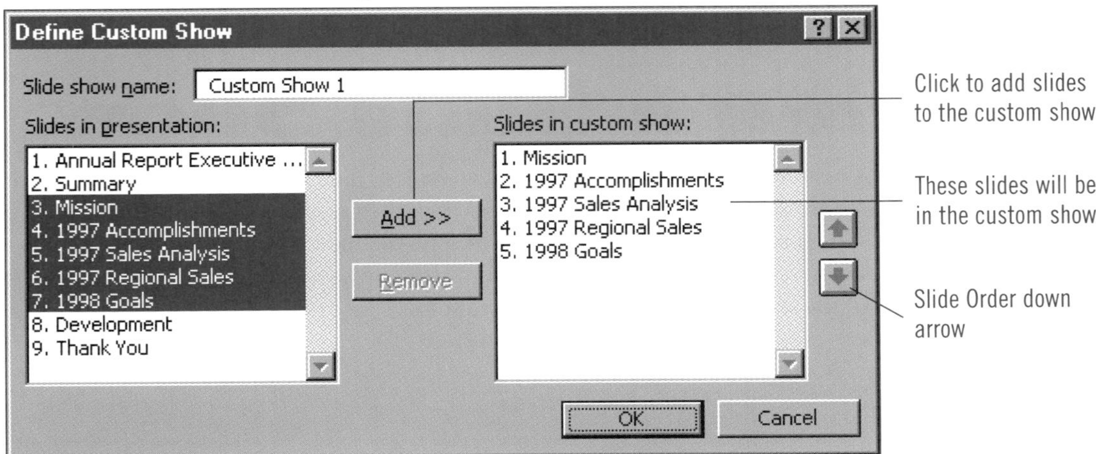

FIGURE H-8: Switching to the custom slide show

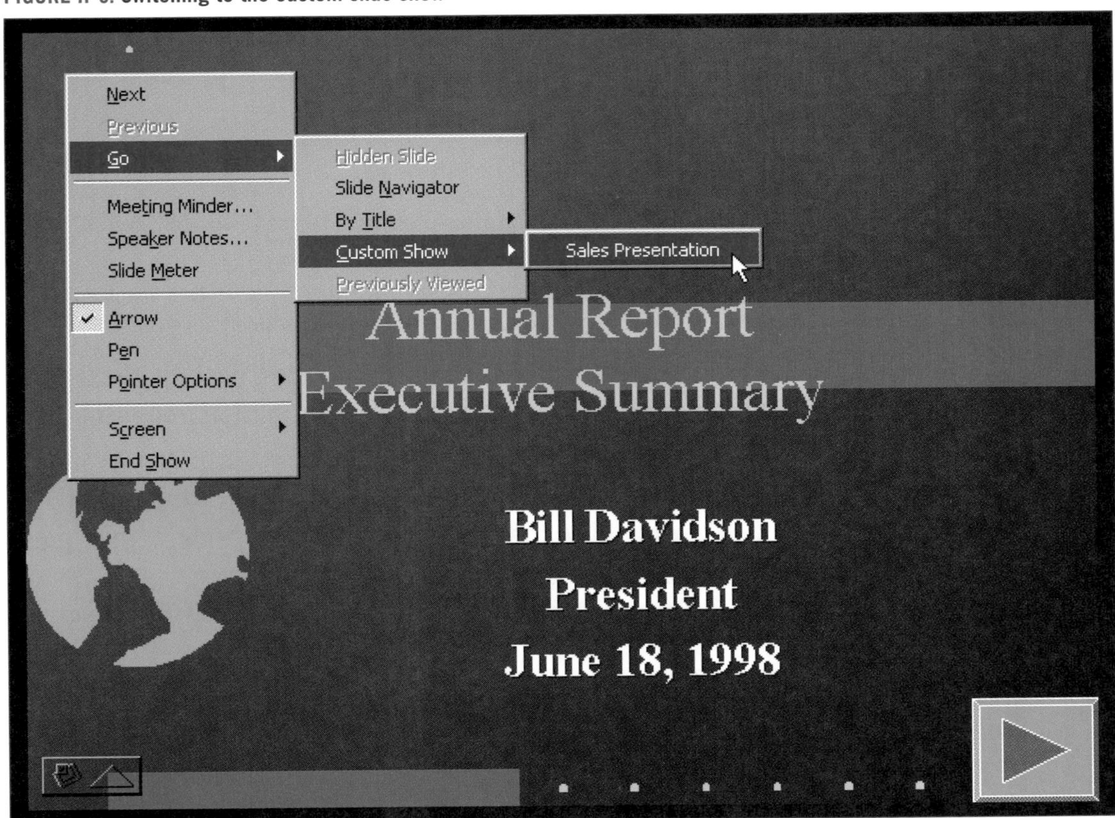

Using action buttons to hyperlink to a custom slide show

You can also use action buttons to switch from the "parent" show to the custom show. Click Slide Show on the menu bar, point to Action Buttons, and choose any action button. Drag the pointer to draw a button on the slide, in the Action Settings dialog box, select Custom Show in the Hyperlink list box. Select the name of the custom show to which you want to hyperlink and click OK. When you run the show, click the hyperlink button you created to run the custom show.

PowerPoint 97

Hiding a Slide During a Slide Show

Another method of customizing a slide show for an audience is to hide slides you don't need or want to see. Hidden slides are not deleted from the presentation; they just don't appear during a slide show. You know a slide is hidden when there is a line through the slide number in Slide Sorter view. Carrie decides to learn how to hide slides so she can quickly teach the president in case he wants to hide any of the slides when he gives the presentation.

Steps

1. Click the **Slide Sorter View button**, and click **Slide 8**
   The presentation appears in Slide Sorter view, and Slide 8 is selected.
2. Click the **Hide Slide button** on the Slide Sorter toolbar
   The slide number under Slide 8 now has the hide symbol on it, as shown in Figure H-9. To test the Hide Slide feature, view Slides 7, 8, and 9 in Slide Show view.
3. Click **Slide Show** on the menu bar, then click **Set Up Show**
   The Set Up Show dialog box opens, similar to Figure H-10.
4. In the Slides section, type **7** in the From box, make sure **9** appears in the To box, compare your screen to Figure H-10, then click **OK**
   Before you can display the slide show without Slide 8, you must first delete the hyperlink buttons you inserted earlier, since they will override the slide sequence that you set here.
5. Double-click **Slide 1**, click the hyperlink button, press **[Delete]**, click the **Next Slide button**, and repeat the procedure to delete the hyperlink button from each slide in the presentation
   Now run slides 7 through 9 in Slide Show view.
6. Click the **Slide Show button**, view the animation effects on Slide 7, then press **[Spacebar]** once to move to Slide 9
   PowerPoint displays Slide 7, skips over Slide 8, and shows Slide 9. Replay the same slide show, but this time display Slide 8.
7. Press **[PgUp]** twice to redisplay Slide 7, press **[H]** to display Slide 8, then press **[Spacebar]** to display Slide 9
   Pressing [H] tells PowerPoint to display Slide 8. Now turn the Hide Slide feature off.
8. Press **[Esc]**, click the **Slide Sorter View button**, click **Slide 8**, then click
   The Hide symbol no longer appears over the slide number. Now reset the slide show setup so that the entire show will display in Slide Show view.
9. Click **Slide Show** on the menu bar, click **Set Up Show**, in the Slides section click the **All option button**, click **OK**, then click the **Save button** on the Standard toolbar
   The next time you run the slide show, all the slides will appear.

QuickTip

To hide a slide in Slide view, click Hide Slide on the Slide Show menu.

QuickTip

To display a hidden slide during a slide show, you can also right-click the slide before the hidden one, point to Go on the pop-up menu, then click Hidden slide.

FIGURE H-9: Slide showing Hide symbol

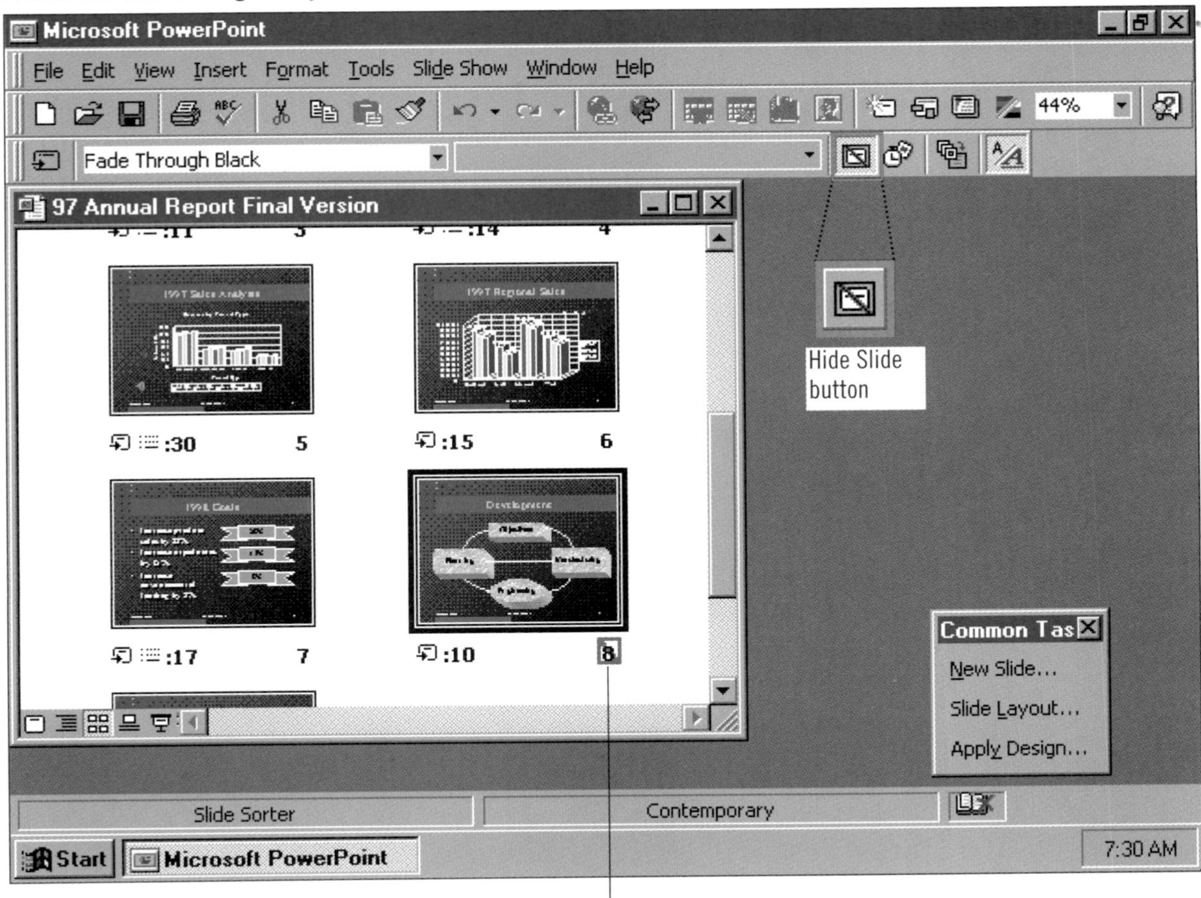

FIGURE H-10: Set Up Show dialog box

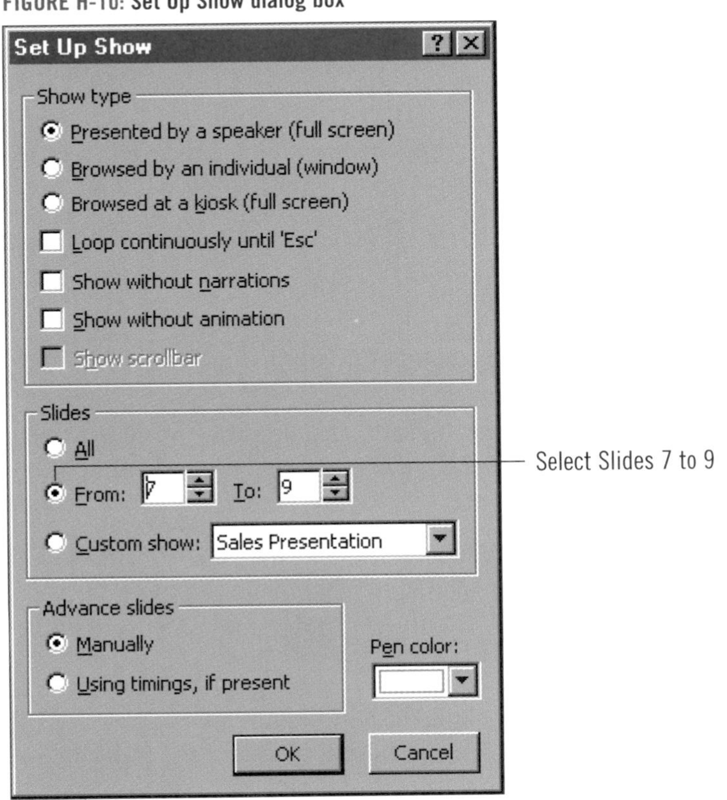

PowerPoint 97

PowerPoint 97

Using the Meeting Minder

Occasionally, it's helpful to assign tasks or take notes as you present a slide show to make sure people follow up on meeting items. PowerPoint makes that task easy with the Meeting Minder. The Meeting Minder is a dialog box you use in Slide Show view to enter information related to the slides in your presentation. The action items you enter are automatically added to a new slide at the end of your presentation. You can export the action items to a Microsoft Word document to edit them or to make them part of another document. Carrie practices adding action items with the Meeting Minder so she can teach the president how to use it.

Steps 1 2 3 4

1. **Click the Slide View button, then press [Ctrl][Home] to go to Slide 1**
   Slide 1 appears. Enter an action item.
2. **Click the Slide Show button, right-click the slide, click Meeting Minder on the pop-up menu, then click the Action Items tab**
   The Meeting Minder dialog box opens and displays the Action Items tab, similar to Figure H-11. Enter an action item that will help with meeting follow-up.
3. **Type 1. Review meeting minutes with president, press [Tab], type Carrie in the Assigned To text box, double-click the Due Date text box, type 6/22/98, compare your screen to Figure H-11, then click Add**
   The action item you entered appears in the list box on the Action Items tab. If you were to enter any more action items, they would be added to this list.
4. **Click OK**
   Now view the last slide to make sure the item was added to a new slide at the end of the presentation.
5. **Right-click the slide, point to Go on the pop-up menu, point to By Title, then click 10 Action Items on the list of slides**
   The new Action Items slide appears, with the action item you entered in the Meeting Minder. See Figure H-12. Now export your meeting notes to a Microsoft Word document.
6. **Right-click the slide, select Meeting Minder on the pop-up menu, click the Action Items tab, then click Export**
   The Meeting Minder Export dialog box opens.
7. **Make sure that the Send meeting minutes and action items to Microsoft Word check box is selected, then click Export Now**
   Microsoft Word starts and opens a new Word document containing your Meeting Minder action items. See Figure H-13. You can edit and print this document just as you would any Word document. Now print and save the document, then return to your PowerPoint presentation.
8. **Click the Print button on the Word Standard toolbar, click the Close button in the Word program window, click Yes to save the document, then save it as Action Items to the drive and folder where you are storing the files for this unit**
   Your PowerPoint presentation reappears in Slide Show view.
9. **Click the left mouse button once to end the slide show**
   If PowerPoint on your computer is set to show a black slide at the end of the presentation, then you will need to click twice to end the slide show.

Trouble?

If you receive an error message telling you that PowerPoint will be shut down, click Close to exit, restart the program, open 97 Annual Report Final Version, and start this lesson again. If it happens a second time, try restarting your computer.

FIGURE H-11: Meeting Minder dialog box

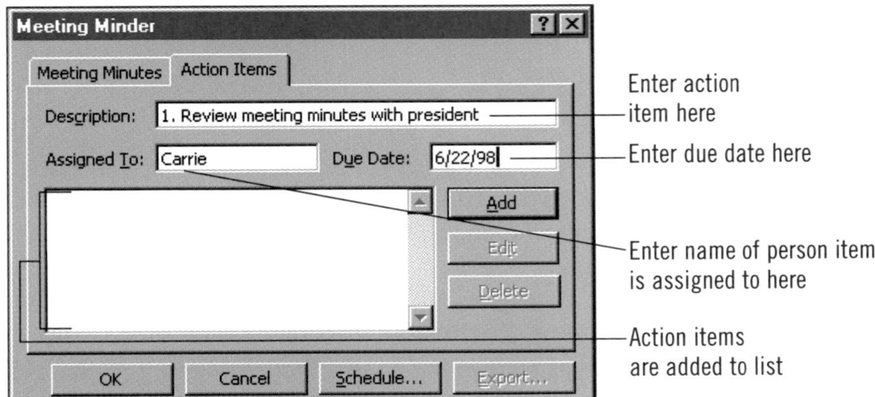

FIGURE H-12: New Action Items slide at end of presentation

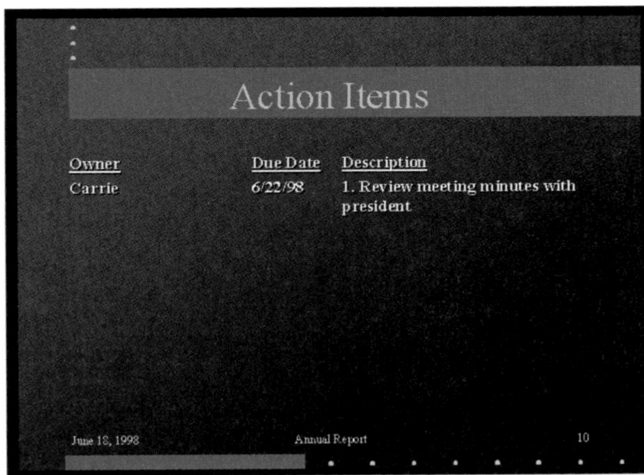

FIGURE H-13: Action Items after exporting to Microsoft Word

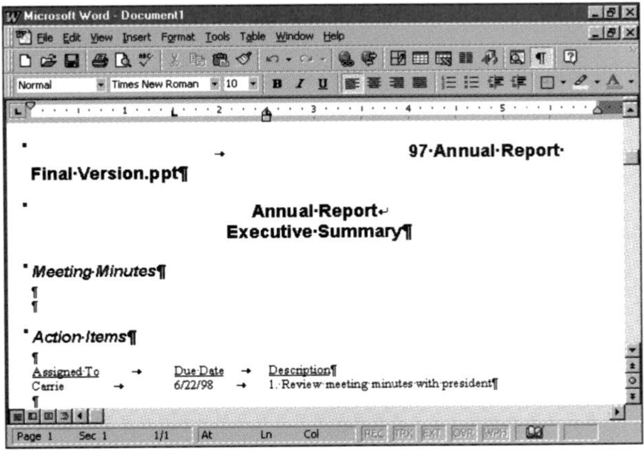

Keeping track of Meeting Minutes and Speaker Notes

You can also use the Meeting Minder to keep a record of meeting minutes you type during the slide show. Right-click any slide in Slide Show view, click Meeting Minder, click the Meeting Minutes tab, then type notes in the text box. You can export meeting minutes to Microsoft Word the same way you export action items. You can also create speaker notes by clicking the Speaker Notes command on the Slide Show view pop-up menu. Type any items you want to remember, and they will automatically be transferred to the Speaker Notes section of that slide.

Rehearsing Slide Timings

Whether you are creating a self-running slide show or you're planning to talk about the slides as they appear, you should rehearse the slide timings, the amount of time each slide stays on the screen. Your presentation will be smoother if you rehearse your slide show and set an appropriate slide timing for each slide. If you assign slide timings to your slides without actually running through the presentation, you will probably discover that the timings do not allow enough time for each slide or point in your presentation. To set accurate slide timings, use PowerPoint's Rehearse Timings feature. As you run through your slide show, the Rehearsal dialog box shows you how long the slide stays on the screen. As soon as you decide enough time has passed, click the mouse to move to the next slide. Carrie learns how to rehearse slide timings so she can show the president, who might want to set appropriate slide timings while he rehearses.

Steps

1. **Click the Slide Sorter View button, then click Slide 1**
   Before you continue through the steps of the lesson, you may want to read the steps and comments that follow first, so you are aware of what happens during a slide show rehearsal.
2. **Click the Rehearse Timings button on the Slide Sorter toolbar**
   Slide Show view opens, displaying Slide 1. The Rehearsal dialog box appears in the lower-right corner of the screen, as shown in Figure H-14.
3. **When you feel an appropriate amount of time has passed for the presenter to speak and for the audience to view the slide, click the Forward arrow in the Rehearse dialog box or click your mouse anywhere on the screen**
   Slide 2 appears.
4. **Click the Forward arrow at an appropriate interval after all the information on Slide 2 appears, then click the Forward arrow again to view Slide 3**
5. **Continue through the rest of the slides in the presentation**
   Be sure to leave enough time to present the contents of each slide thoroughly. At the end of the slide rehearsal, a Microsoft PowerPoint message box opens asking if you want to save the slide timings. If you save the timings, the next time you run the slide show, the slides will appear automatically at the intervals you specified during the rehearsal.
6. **Click Yes to save the timings**
   A second message box opens. This message box asks if you want to review your timings in Slide Sorter view.
7. **Click Yes to review the timings, then click the Presentation window Maximize button**
   Slide Sorter view appears showing the new slide timings, as shown in Figure H-15. Your timings will be different. Run the slide show to see how the new slide timings work. When you run the slide show, it will run by itself, using the timings you rehearsed. The rehearsed timings override any previous timings you set.
8. **Click the Slide Show button, view the presentation with your timings, then save your changes**
   Now print the slide show as Handouts (6 slides per page)
9. **Click File on the menu bar, click Print, click the All option button, click the Print what list arrow, click Handouts (6 slides per page), then click OK**

QuickTip

If you are called away during the rehearsal and too much time has elapsed, click Repeat to restart the timer for that slide.

To override slide timings, click your mouse to advance to the next slide or open the slide show pop-up menu.

FIGURE H-14: Rehearsal dialog box

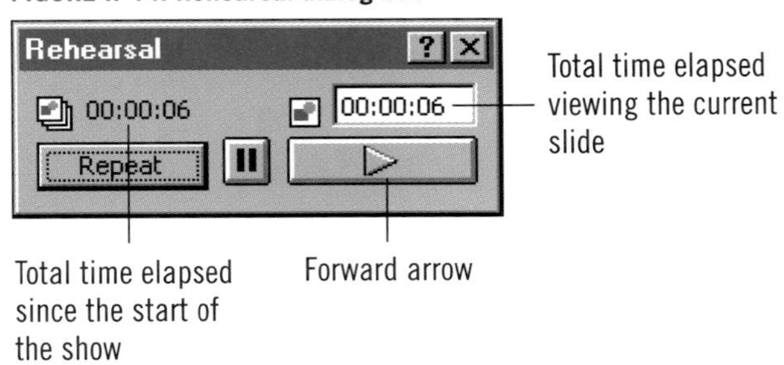

FIGURE H-15: Final presentation in Slide Sorter view showing new slide timings

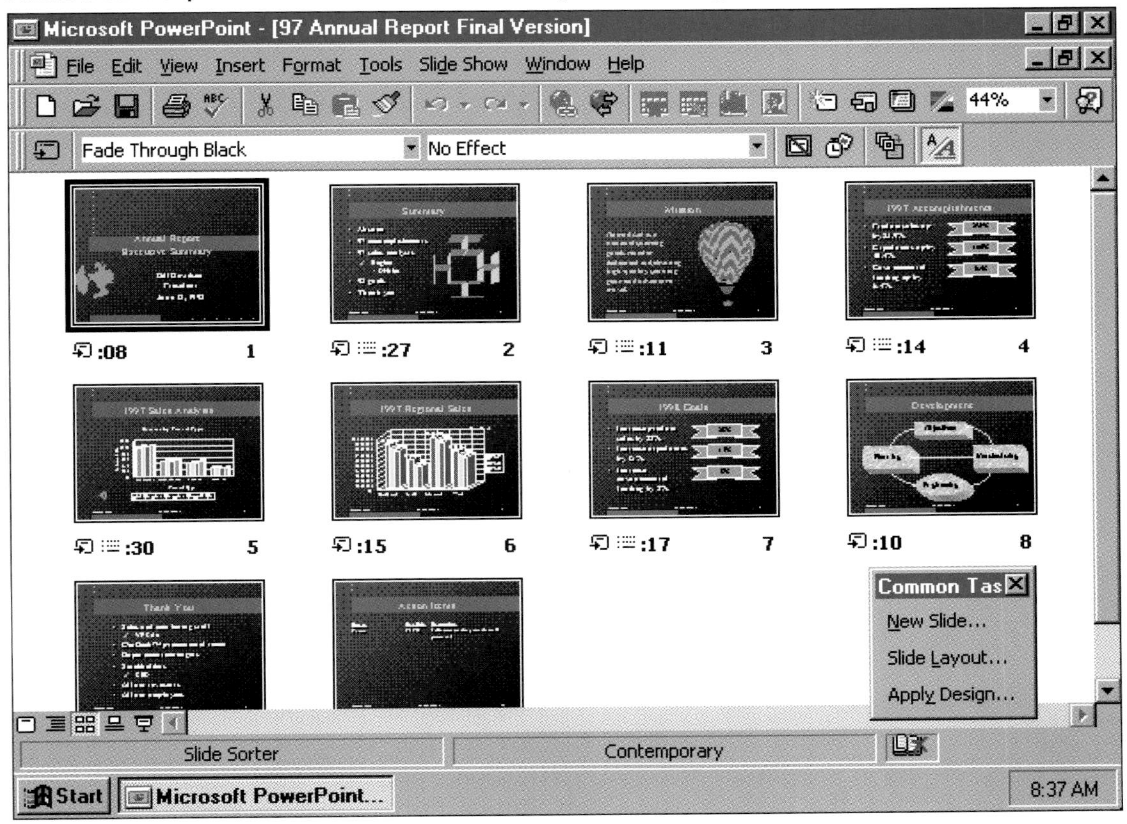

CLUES TO USE

Using the Slide Meter

The Slide Meter measures the time you take to present the information on the slide in relation to the rehearsed slide timing you set. You can use the Slide Meter while practicing your presentation to help determine if your rehearsed slide timings are accurate. To open the Slide Meter, switch to Slide Show view, right-click, then click Slide Meter on the pop-up menu. The Slide Meter dialog box opens, as shown in Figure H-16, and immediately begins recording the slide time. If you need to make adjustments to a slide time, you can open the Slide Transition dialog box and make the changes there.

FIGURE H-16: Slide Meter dialog box

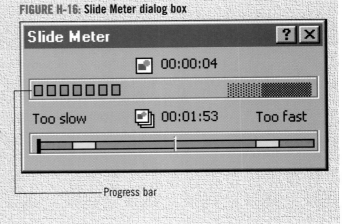

PowerPoint 97

Using the Pack and Go Wizard

Occasionally you need to present your slide show using another computer. To transport everything to the new computer, you use the Pack and Go Wizard. The Pack and Go Wizard compresses and packages all the necessary files (such as your presentation, embedded objects, linked objects, and fonts) that you'll need to take a presentation on the road. You can also package the PowerPoint Viewer. PowerPoint Viewer is a program that allows you to view a slide show even if PowerPoint is not installed on the computer. Carrie packages the Annual Report presentation using the Pack and Go Wizard.

1. **Create a new folder on your hard drive called PackNGo**
   When you run the Pack and Go Wizard, you will save your packaged presentation in this new folder. You will delete this folder from your hard drive at the end of the next lesson. PowerPoint Viewer is available in several versions. Older versions of the Viewer will not run PowerPoint 97 presentations. Save your presentation as a PowerPoint 95 & 97 Presentation so that the steps in this lesson will work no matter which version of the Viewer you have.
2. **Click File on the menu bar, click Save As, in the Save As dialog box, change the Save in list box to the PackNGo folder on your hard drive, click the Save as type list arrow, click PowerPoint 95 & 97 Presentation, edit the File name so it is 97 Annual Report Viewer Version, then click Save**
   Now open the Pack and Go Wizard.
3. **Click File on the menu bar, click Pack and Go, read the screen, then click Next**
   The Pick files to pack screen in the Pack and Go Wizard dialog box opens, as shown in Figure H-17. You indicate here which presentation you would like to package.
4. **Make sure the Active presentation check box is selected, then click Next**
   The Choose destination screen opens. Select the PackNGo folder on your hard drive as the destination for the packaged presentation.
5. **Click the Choose destination option button, click Browse, locate and click the PackNGo folder, then click Select**
   See Figure H-18. In the Links screen, you'll include the TrueType fonts in your packaged presentation and any linked files. Although your presentation doesn't include any linked files, leave this option checked whenever you're not sure if there are linked files.
6. **Click Next, make sure the Include linked files checkbox is selected, click the Embed TrueType fonts check box to select it, then click Next**
   The Viewer screen in the Wizard opens. You want to package the PowerPoint Viewer with your presentation so you can run it from any compatible computer. The PowerPoint Viewer program is available on the Office 97 CD-ROM.
7. **Insert the Office 97 CD-ROM into the disk drive, click the Viewer for Windows 95 or NT option button, click Next, read the Finish screen, then click Finish**
   The Pack and Go Wizard packages the Annual Report presentation. After the presentation is packaged, a message box opens telling you that the Pack and Go Wizard has finished.
8. **Click OK**
   Now close PowerPoint.
9. **Close the presentation, then exit PowerPoint**

QuickTip

If your original presentation is on your hard disk, you can place the packaged version directly on a floppy disk. If the presentation is too big for one disk, PowerPoint 97 lets you save across multiple floppy disks.

Trouble?

If you are working on a network, ask your instructor where you can locate the PowerPoint Viewer file. You can also download the latest version of Viewer from the Product News link on the Microsoft Web Site (http://www.microsoft.com).

FIGURE H-17: Pick files to pack screen in the Pack and Go Wizard

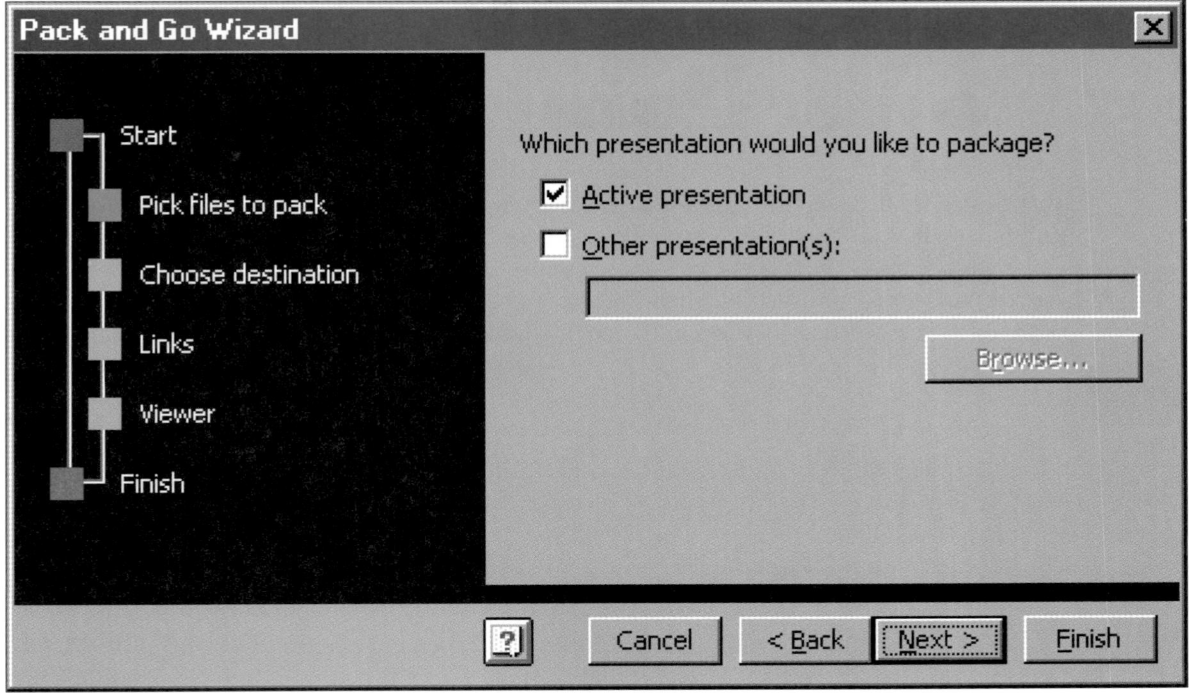

FIGURE H-18: Choose destination screen in the Pack and Go Wizard

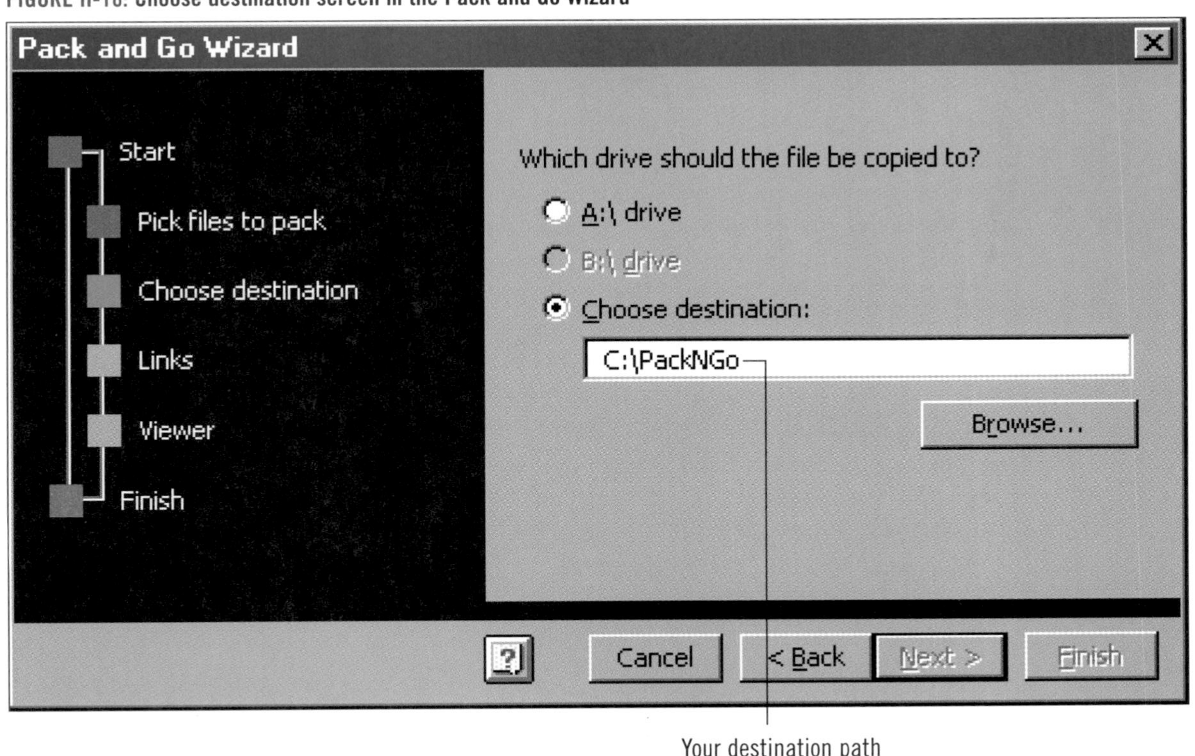

Your destination path may be different

PowerPoint 97

PowerPoint 97

Using the Microsoft PowerPoint Viewer

The Microsoft PowerPoint Viewer is a program that displays a slide show on compatible computers that do not have PowerPoint installed. All you need to show a presentation using the Viewer is a computer running Windows 95 or Windows NT, a copy of PowerPoint Viewer, and the PowerPoint presentation itself. The content of a presentation can't be altered using the Viewer. PowerPoint Viewer is a free program distributed by Microsoft that can be copied onto any compatible computer. Carrie practices locating and using the PowerPoint Viewer to show her presentation.

Steps

1. **Open the PackNGo folder you created in the previous lesson**
   The Pack and Go Wizard supplies a special setup program that automatically decompresses the packaged file.
2. **Double-click the Pngsetup icon in the PackNGo folder window**
   The Pack and Go Setup dialog box appears. Indicate the destination folder for your extracted file.
3. **In the Destination folder text box, click after the backslash, type the path to your PackNGo folder ending with the folder name PackNGo (the same way it appears in the Source Folder line), click OK, click Yes to unpack the presentation to the PackNGo directory, then click OK in the warning box that opens**
   The presentation you previously saved as a PowerPoint 95 and 97 presentation has been overwritten with the newly unpacked files. Next a message box opens telling you that the installation was successful and asking if you want to view the slide show.
4. **Click Yes**
   When you use Viewer, preview your slide show before the actual presentation to make sure everything works the way you expect. The Viewer displays the Annual Report presentation without opening PowerPoint. The presentation runs with the slide timings set during the rehearsal. When the presentation is complete, the presentation and the Viewer close. Now change the settings so that you can advance the slides manually.
5. **In the PackNGo folder window, double-click the Ppview32 icon**
   The Microsoft PowerPoint Viewer dialog box opens, similar to Figure H-19.
6. **Select the file 97 Annual Report Viewer Version**
   A preview of the Annual Report presentation appears in the Preview window. Now tell the Viewer that you want to have access to the pop-up menu and end with a black slide. Since this will not be a kiosk presentation, you won't need to protect it with a password.
7. **Select the check boxes Popup Menu on Right Mouse Click, Show Popup Menu Button, and End With Black Slide**
   Ending with a black slide is a visual cue to the audience that the presentation is ending. Now change the way the slides advance.
8. **Click the Show SlideShow Dialog check box, then click Show**
   The Advanced Slide Show Settings dialog box opens, similar to figure H-20.
9. **Click the Manual Advance option button, click Show, then click the left mouse button to progress through the slide show**
   PowerPoint Viewer displays your show. The timing of the animated objects' appearance on the slides was overridden by selecting the Manual Advance option in the Advanced Slide Show Settings dialog box. After you view the last slide, you are returned to the Microsoft PowerPoint Viewer dialog box.
10. **Click Exit, then delete the PackNGo folder and its contents from the hard drive**

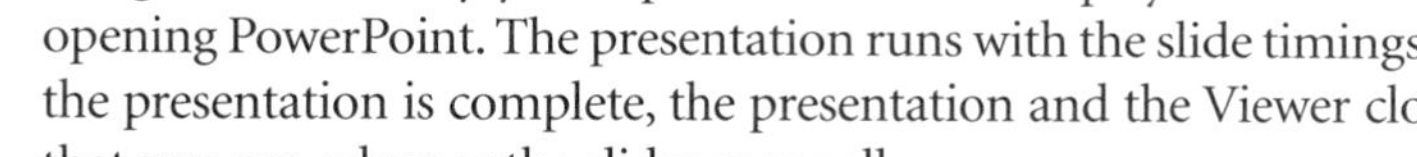

Trouble?

You may see messages that the Viewer cannot play the sound you embedded. Click OK and continue.

Trouble?

If you see a truncated file name, for example 97annu~1, in the PowerPoint viewer dialog box, select it and continue with the steps.

FIGURE H-19: Microsoft PowerPoint Viewer dialog box

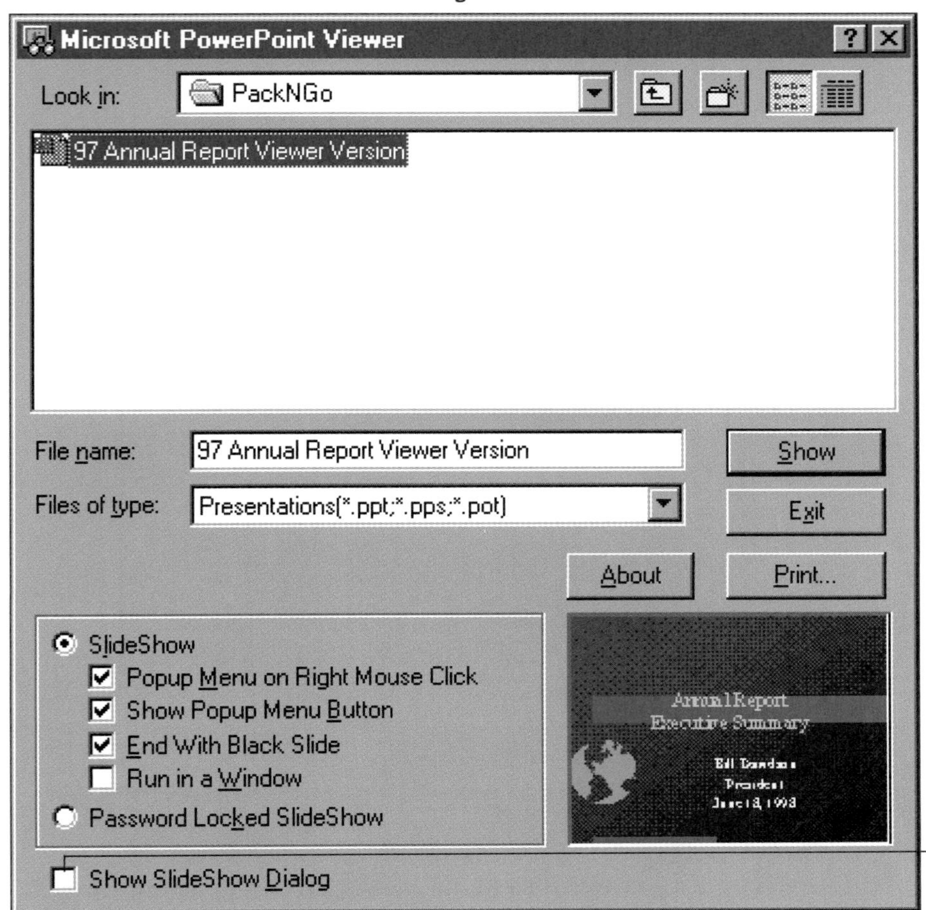

Click to show only selected slides or to change slide advance method

FIGURE H-20: Advanced Slide Show Settings dialog box

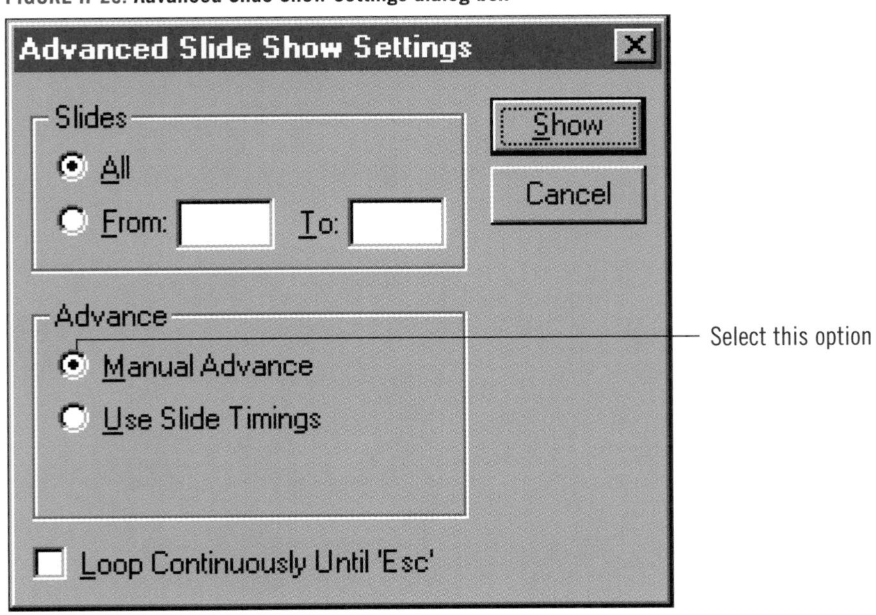

Select this option

PowerPoint 97

Practice

Concepts Review

Label each of the elements of the PowerPoint window shown in Figure H-21.

FIGURE H-21

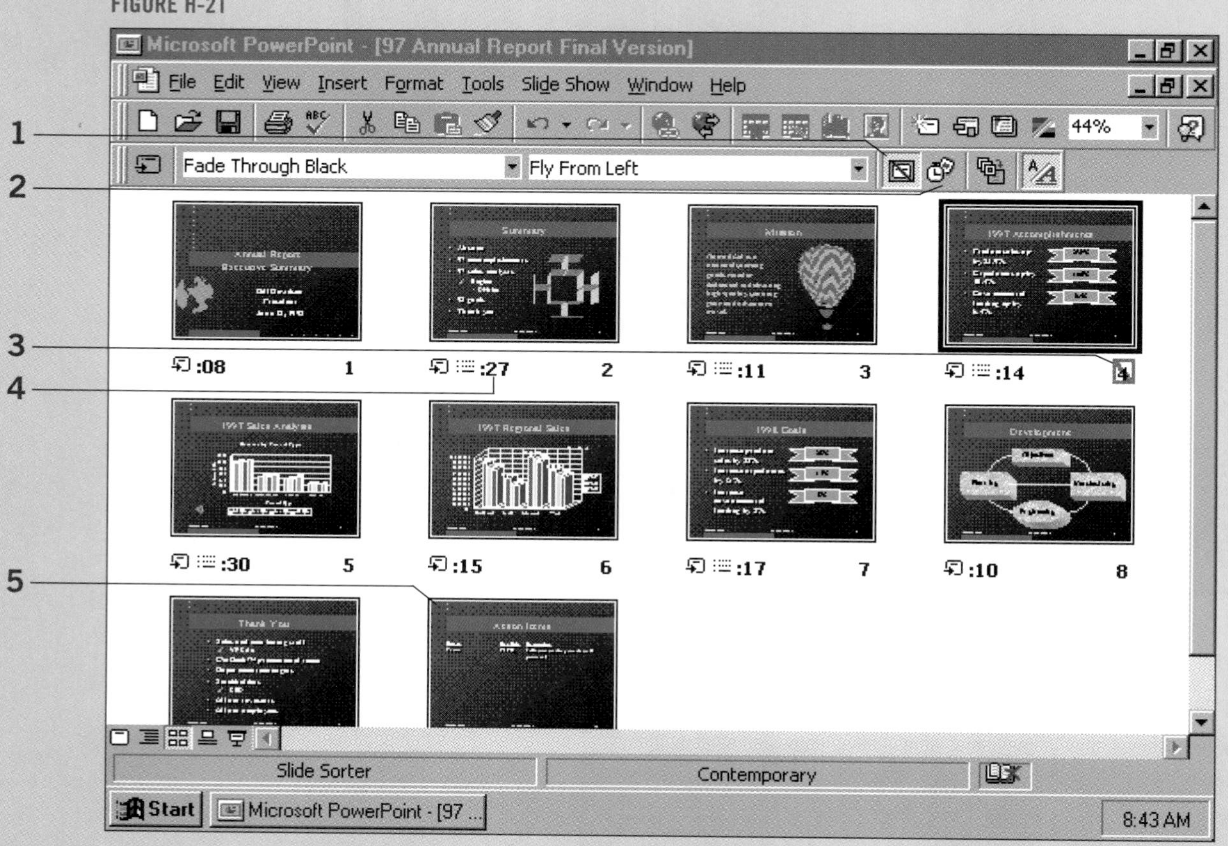

Match each of the terms with the statement that describes its function.

6. A presentation created from selected slides in another presentation
7. Program that runs a slide show on other computers
8. A free-standing public computer that runs a slide show
9. A dialog box that lets you keep track of meeting minutes and action items during a slide show
10. Packages a presentation to take it on the road

a. Microsoft PowerPoint Viewer
b. kiosk
c. custom show
d. Pack and Go Wizard
e. Meeting Minder

Select the best answer from the list of choices.

11. In Slide Sorter view, what does a box with a line through it indicate when it is over a slide number?
    a. The slide is first in the presentation.
    b. The slide is deleted.
    c. The slide appears last in a slide show.
    d. The slide won't appear in a slide show.

12. Which of the following is not a Meeting Minder feature?
- **a.** You can enter text directly to the notes pages of your presentation.
- **b.** You can export text to Microsoft Word.
- **c.** You can enter text that is placed on a new slide in your presentation.
- **d.** You can print the text you enter in the Meeting Minder.

13. Which of the following statements is true about rehearsing your slide timings?
- **a.** Rehearsing the slides in your presentation gives each slide the same slide timing.
- **b.** During a rehearsal, you have no way of knowing how long the slide stays on the screen.
- **c.** If you give your slides random slide timings, you may not have enough time to adequately view each slide.
- **d.** If you rehearse your presentation, someone on another computer can set the slide timings.

14. When you want to have a slide show run continuously and automatically at a kiosk, you should
- **a.** Use the Set Up Show dialog box to choose the appropriate settings
- **b.** Click Custom Animation on the Slide Show menu, and choose the Automatically option button
- **c.** Insert hyperlink buttons on all the slides
- **d.** Add a voice narration and save the presentation using the Pack and Go Wizard

Skills Review

1. Animate charts and sounds
- **a.** Open the presentation PPT H-2, and save it as Division Final.
- **b.** Go to Slide 6 and click the sound icon to select it.
- **c.** Click Slide Show on the menu bar, click Custom Animation, and click the Timing tab.
- **d.** Click the Animate option button, then click the Automatically option button, then set the timing to 1 second.
- **e.** Click the Play Settings tab, select the check boxes Play using animation order and Hide while not playing.
- **f.** Select the Pause slide show option button, then click OK.
- **g.** Right-click the chart to select it, click Custom Animation on the pop-up menu, then click the Timing tab.
- **h.** Click the Animate option button, click the Automatically option button, then set the timing to 2 seconds.
- **i.** Click the Chart Effects tab, in the Introduce chart elements list box, select by Category, in the top Entry animation and sound list box, select Wipe Down, then in the bottom list box, select Drum Roll.
- **j.** Click Preview, watch the Preview box, watch the Preview box, then click OK.
- **k.** Save your changes, click the Slide Show button, view the animation effects, then press [Esc].

2. Set up a slide show
- **a.** Click Slide Show on the menu bar, click Set Up Show, then click the Browsed at a kiosk (full screen).
- **b.** In the Advance Slides section, click the Using timings if present option button, then click OK.
- **c.** Switch to Slide Sorter view, select all the slides, click Slide Show on the menu bar, click Slide Transition, click the Automatically after check box, set the timing to 3 seconds, then click Apply to All.
- **d.** Run the slide show all the way through, then press [Esc] to end the presentation.
- **e.** Click Slide Show on the menu bar, click Set Up Show, then click the Manually option button.
- **f.** Click the Presented by a speaker (full screen) option button, then click OK.
- **g.** Move to Slide 1 in Slide view, click Slide Show on the menu bar, point to Action Buttons, click the Action Button: Forward or Next button, then drag to draw the button on Slide 1 in the lower right corner.
- **h.** In the Action Settings dialog box, click OK.
- **i.** Copy the action button to the Clipboard, then paste it onto all of the slides except the last one.
- **j.** Move to Slide 6, click Slide Show on the menu bar, point to Action Buttons, click the Action Button: Back or Previous button, then drag to draw the button in the lower left corner of Slide 6. Resize the button so it is the same size as the button you created in step g.
- **k.** In the Action Settings dialog box, click OK.

l. Copy the button to the Clipboard, then copy it to all of the slides except the first one.
m. Press [Ctrl][Home], then run through the slide show using the hyperlink buttons you inserted. Move forward and backward through the presentation, watching the animation effects as they appear.
n. When you have finished viewing the slide show, press [Esc] to end the show, then save your changes.

3. **Create a custom show**
   a. Click Slide Show on the menu bar, click Custom Shows, then click New
   b. Click Slide 3, press and hold [Shift], click Slide 5, then click Add.
   c. Select the Adventure Tours slide in the Slides in custom show list, then click the Slide Order up arrow.
   d. Select the existing text in the Slide show name text box, type New Customer Presentation, then click OK.
   e. Click Show, click the hyperlink buttons to move among the three slides, then click [Esc] to end the slide show.
   f. Click Close in the Custom Shows dialog box.
   g. Move to Slide 1, click the Slide Show button, right-click Slide 1, point to Go, point to Custom Show, then click New Customer Presentation.
   h. View the custom slide show, press [Esc] to end the show, then save your changes.
4. **Hide a slide during a slide show**
   a. Delete the hyperlink buttons from all the slides.
   b. Click the Slide Sorter View button.
   c. Click Slide 2, then click the Hide Slide button on the Slide Sorter toolbar.
   d. Click Slide Show on the menu bar, click Set Up Show, in the Slides section, type 1 in the From box, type 3 in the To box, then click OK.
   e. Click the Slide Show button, then click through the selected slides. Slide 2 does not appear in the slide show.
   f. Click the Slide Show button, press [H], then view the animation on Slide 2.
   g. Move through the rest of the slide show, select Slide 2, then click the Hide Slide button on the Slide Sorter toolbar.
   h. Click Slide Show on the menu bar, click Set Up Show, click the All option button, then click OK.
5. **Use the Meeting Minder**
   a. Click Slide 1, then click the Slide Show button.
   b. Click the left mouse button to move to Slide 2, and wait for the animation effects to appear.
   c. Right-click, click Meeting Minder, then click the Meeting Minutes tab.
   d. In the text box, type the following items. (Press [Enter] after typing each sentence.)
      "Research the type of tour and the target audience."
      "Explore the tour features: projected costs, special equipment, weather considerations, profit margin."
      "Promote and advertise the tour."
   e. Click the Action Items tab.
   f. Type "1. Review tour philosophy with sales staff", press [Tab], type [Your First Name] in the Assigned To text box, press [Tab], change the Due Date to one week from today's date, click Add, then click OK. (Note: The Assigned To text box will accept a maximum of 10 characters.)
   g. Click the left mouse button once, then open the Meeting Minder again.
   h. Click the Action Items tab, then type "2. Review Int. tours figures for 1997", enter your name and the date as described in step f, click Add, then click OK.
   i. Click through the rest of the presentation until Slide 7 appears.
   j. Open the Meeting Minder, click the Action Items tab, click Export, then click Export Now.
   k. Save the Microsoft Word document as ND Action, print the document, then exit Word.
   l. Click your mouse once to end the slide show.
6. **Rehearse slide timings**
   a. Click Slide 1, then click the Rehearse Timings button on the Slide Sorter toolbar.
   b. Click through the presentation setting new slide timings, then save your new timings and review them.
   c. Save your changes.

   d. Click File on the menu bar, click Print, click the Custom Show option button, click the Print what list arrow, select Slides without animations, then click OK.
   e. Open the Print dialog box again, and print all the slides as Handouts (3 slides per page).

7. Use the Pack and Go Wizard

   a. Create a new folder on your hard drive and name it PackNGo2.
   b. Click File on the PowerPoint menu bar, click Save As, change the Save in list box to the PackNGo2 folder, click the Save as type list arrow, click PowerPoint 95 & 97 Presentation, edit the file name so it is Division Final Viewer Version, then click Save.
   c. Click File on the menu bar, click Pack and Go, then click Next.
   d. In the Pick files to pack screen, make sure the Active presentation check box is selected, then click Next.
   e. In the Choose destination screen, click the Choose destination option button, click Browse, locate and click the PackNGo2 folder on the hard drive, click Select, then click Next.
   f. In the Links screen, click the Embed TrueType Fonts check box, then click Next.
   g. Make sure the Office 97 CD-ROM is in the disk drive, then in the Viewer screen, click the Viewer for Windows 95 or NT option button, click Next, then click Finish.

8. View a packaged presentation

   a. Open PackNGo2 folder, double-click the Pngsetup file, then in the Destination Folder text box, type the path to your PackNGo2 folder ending with the name "PackNGo2".
   b. Click OK, then click OK again.
   c. Click Yes to show your packaged presentation, then view the slide show. (You may not be able to play the sounds or the movie.)
   d. Double-click the Pptview32 icon in the PackNGo2 folder.
   e. Select the file Division Final Viewer Version (the file name may be truncated).
   f. Select the following check boxes: Popup Menu on Right Mouse Click, End With Black Slide, and Show SlideShow Dialog, then click Show.
   g. Click the Manual Advance option button, then click Show.
   h. Click the left mouse button or press [Spacebar] to move through the slide show.
   i. Click Exit, then delete the PackNGo2 folder from your hard drive.

Independent Challenges

1. If you complete all of the exercises in this unit and the Skills Review, you may run out of space on your Student Disk. If so, copy the files referenced in the Independent Challenges to a new disk. You work for Pacific Tours, an international tour company that provides specialty tours to destinations in the Pacific Ocean region. You have to develop presentations that the sales force can use to highlight different tours at conferences and meetings.

In this challenge, you will use some of PowerPoint's advanced slide show features such as slide builds and interactive settings to finish the presentation you started. Create at least two additional slides for the basic presentation provided on your Student Disk using your own information. Assume the following about Pacific Tours:

- Pacific Tours has a special (20% off regular price) on tours to Bora Bora and Tahiti during the spring of 1998.
- Over the years, Pacific Tours has built a successful business selling tour packages to the major islands of the Pacific: Philippines, Japan, Australia, and New Zealand.

To complete this independent challenge:

1. Open the file PPT H-3, then save it as South Pacific.
2. Use the assumptions provided to help you develop additional content for your presentation. Use pictures, movies, and sounds provided on the Office 97 CD-ROM or from other media sources to complete your presentation.
3. Animate the chart and have an appropriate sound effect play as each chart element appears.
4. Create a custom version of the show that can be shown at a trade show kiosk.
5. Rehearse slide timings.
6. Use the Meeting Minder to create Action Items that could result from your presentation.
7. Package your presentation, then use the viewer to present your packaged presentation to the class.
8. Submit your presentation plan and print the final slide presentation and all related documents.

2. You work for WorldWide Travel Services, a travel service company. WorldWide Travel is a subsidiary owned by Globus Inc. Every year in October, WorldWide Travel needs to report to Globus Inc on the past year's activity.

Create your own information using the basic presentation provided on your Student Disk. Assume the following:

- WorldWide purchased major routes from Canada to Asia and the Far East from Canadian AirTours.
- WorldWide's operating expenses run $6 million a quarter.
- Ten new tour packages to Eastern Europe were created this year. Two of the new tours are The Great Wall Tour and The Trans-Siberian Rail Tour.
- WorldWide added 30 employees during the year.

To complete this independent challenge:

1. Open the file PPT H-4, then save it as WorldWide.
2. Use the assumptions provided to help you develop additional content for your presentation. Use pictures, movies, and sounds provided on the Office 97 CD-ROM or from other media sources to complete your presentation.
3. Animate the chart, and have an appropriate sound effect play as each chart element appears.
4. Rehearse slide timings.
5. Create a version of your show to run continuously at a conference kiosk, using the timings that you rehearsed.
6. Create a custom version of the show for a specific audience of your choice, with only selected slides, and rearrange the order of the slides appropriately.
7. Use the Meeting Minder to create meeting minutes, then export the minutes to Microsoft Word. Save the Word document as WorldWide Minutes.
8. Package your presentation, then use the Viewer to present your packaged presentation to the class.
9. Submit your presentation plan and print the final slide presentation and all related documents.

3. You are the assistant director of operations at American Shipping Line Inc, an international marine shipping company based in San Francisco, California. American Shipping handles 65% of all the trade between Asia, the Middle East, and the West Coast of the United States. You need to give a quarterly presentation to the company's operations committee that outlines the type and amount of trade American Shipping handled during the previous quarter.

Plan and create a 10- to 15-slide presentation that details the type of goods American Shipping carried, how much was carried, what companies (foreign and domestic) purchased goods, what companies (foreign and domestic) sold goods, and how much revenue American Shipping earned. You also need to identify the time it took to deliver the goods to their destinations and the delivery cost. Create your own content, but assume the following:

- American Shipping hauled cars and trucks from Tokyo to San Francisco during the last quarter. A car carrier ship can hold 143 cars or 126 trucks.
- American Shipping hauled large tractor equipment and parts made by Caterpillar Tractor and Massey-Ferguson. One shipload went to South Korea and one load went to Saudi Arabia.
- Typical household goods carried by American Shipping include electronic equipment, appliances, toys, and furniture.
- The cost of hauling goods by ship is $3,380 a ton. American Shipping owns five cargo ships that can operate at one time. All five ships were in operation during the last quarter.
- American Shipping hauled a total of 980,000 tons during the last quarter.

To complete this independent challenge:

1. Use clip art or shapes to enhance your presentation.
2. Use the assumptions provided to help you develop the content for your presentation. Use movies and sounds provided on the Office 97 CD-ROM or from other media sources to complete your presentation.
3. Use Word and Excel to embed or link objects into your presentation. Use the preceding assumptions to develop related information that would be appropriate for a table or worksheet.
4. Set transitions and animations, and rehearse slide timings.
5. Use the Meeting Minder to create action items and then export the items to Microsoft Word.
6. Save the presentation as Shipping.
7. Package your presentation, then use the Viewer to present your packaged presentation to the class.
8. Submit your presentation plan and print the final slide presentation and all related documents.

4. You work for Discover Industries, an aerospace and defense contractor in Maryland. You need to prepare a presentation to present to the U.S. Congress outlining your company's competency and ability to build a permanent space station.

Plan and create a slide show presentation that gives a general outline of Discover's space station production plan. Create your own information, but assume the following:

- The space station production costs for the first year are estimated at $25 billion. Each year after the first, until the project is completed, is estimated to cost $16 billion. The space station would take eight years to build. Discover could begin production in 1999.
- Discover Industries has three production facilities: in Livermore, California; Tulsa, Oklahoma; and Bremerton, Washington. The California production facility produces rocket propulsion and satellite systems. The Oklahoma production facility produces the space station module (frame, structure, and furnishings). The Washington production facility produces the communication, directional guidance, and living environment systems.
- Aerospace Systems Inc is the subcontractor that Discover Industries uses to assemble and deliver the space station to orbit. Estimated cost to assemble and deliver the space station to orbit is $215 billion. It will take approximately 14 space shuttle payloads over a two-and-a-half-year period to get the entire space station into orbit.

To complete this independent challenge:

1. Use the assumptions provided to help you develop the content for your presentation. Use movies and sounds provided on the Office 97 CD-ROM or from other media sources to complete your presentation.
2. Log on to the Internet and use your browser to go to http://www.course.com. From there, click Student Online Companions, click the link for this textbook, then click the PowerPoint link for Unit H. Use the link there to find information, photographs, videos, and sound to enhance your presentation. (The videos may be very large files.)
3. Use Word and Excel to embed, link, or hyperlink objects into your presentation. Use the preceding assumptions to develop related information that would be appropriate for a table or worksheet.
4. Create and add a chart with information about Discover, and animate the chart elements. Make the appearance of each chart element be accompanied by an appropriate sound effect.
5. Add a template, background shading, or other enhancing objects to make your presentation look professional.
6. Rehearse slide timings.
7. Create Action Items and then export the items to Microsoft Word. Print the Action Items.
8. Save the presentation as Space.
9. Package your presentation, then use the Viewer to present your packaged presentation to the class.
10. Create a custom version of the slide show that will run continually at a kiosk at a company meeting.
11. Create a custom version of the slide show for an audience of your choice.
12. Submit your presentation plan and print the final slide presentation and all related documents.

► Visual Workshop

Create the slides shown in Figures H-22 and H-23. The clip art is on the Office 97 CD-ROM. Set transitions, animations, and slide timings. Insert a hyperlink and create a target slide for the hyperlink to jump to. Create a title slide. Adjust the background of all the slides to match the figures. Submit the final presentation output.

FIGURE H-22

FIGURE H-23

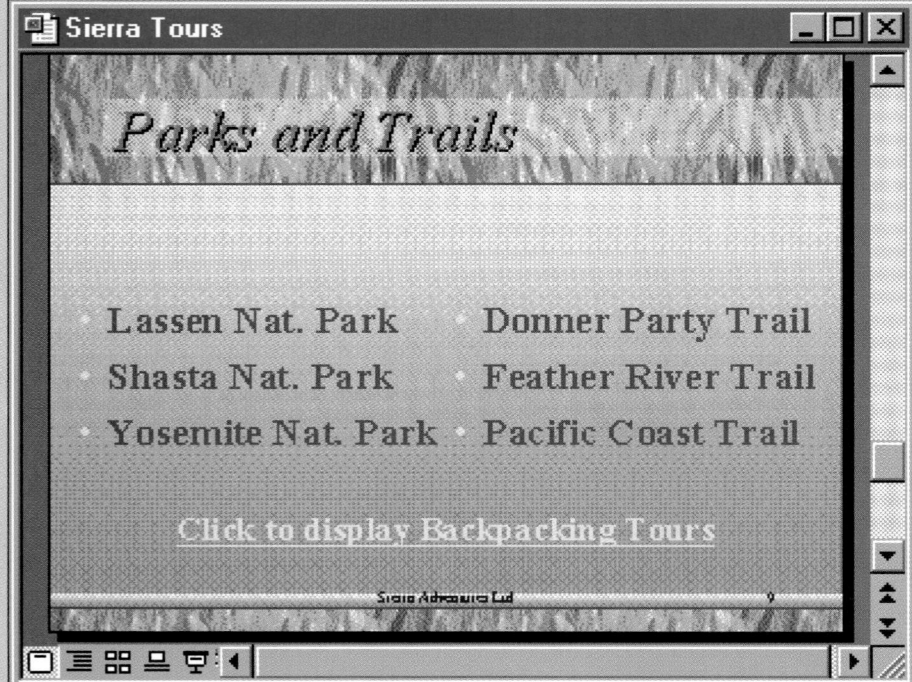

Exploring

Integration: Office 97 Professional

Objectives

- ► Create a presentation using a Word outline
- ► Add a Word table and Excel worksheet to slides
- ► Create relationships in Access
- ► Analyze Access data in Excel
- ► Export an Access table into Word
- ► Import Excel data into PowerPoint

As the previous units have explained, Microsoft PowerPoint provides the necessary tools to create great-looking presentations. With Microsoft Office, you can use not only PowerPoint's built-in tools, but all the formatting and data analysis tools available in Microsoft Word, Excel, and Access as well to create professional, integrated presentations. While developing a presentation, it's helpful to use information you or someone else has created in other Microsoft Office programs. Because PowerPoint is a part of Microsoft Office, you can exchange files or data easily between Word, Excel, Access, and PowerPoint.

In this integration unit, Nomad Ltd is preparing to acquire Health & Goodness Inc, a dry foods corporation located in Santa Fe, New Mexico. You will help Chris Weaver of Nomad Ltd as he develops three presentations in PowerPoint using information from Access, Excel, and Word for Nomad's president, Bill Davidson.

Creating a Presentation Using a Word Outline

Once you've created an outline in Word, it's easy to build a PowerPoint presentation. This is a time-saving technique when you're using content from an existing Word document, or if you prefer creating your initial outline in Word. Then, you can focus on formatting and enhancing your presentation using PowerPoint. To get started, Chris creates a presentation using a Word outline that gives a summary of the Health & Goodness Inc (H&G) acquisition. Because this presentation is for the company division heads, it does not need to be detailed, but it should be informative and complete. To complete the presentation, Chris adds a template, plans the design of each slide, formats each slide, then sets slide builds, transitions, slide timings, and interactive settings.

Steps

1. **Open a blank PowerPoint presentation, then save it as Nomad 1**
   A blank presentation appears. Now, insert an outline from Word that you will use as the basis for the presentation.

2. **Insert the document INT F-1 into your presentation, then in Outline view make any needed changes to the text**
   Compare your screen to Figure F-1. Fill in the blank areas in the outline with your own content. You may want to change the outline flow or create some additional information about H&G that would help the target audience. Use Outline view to finalize the presentation content. Now, move to Slide view and organize the contents of each slide in the presentation.

3. **Switch to Slide view, apply a template, then plan how you want each slide in the presentation to look**
   Use the sample sketch in Figure F-2 to help design your presentation. Take some time and look through the PowerPoint templates to the one that fits the presentation. If you don't like any of the standard templates, create one or modify an existing PowerPoint template. If you modify a PowerPoint template, make sure you rename the template and save it as a presentation template to your My Integration Files folder. During this design phase, decide how you can use clipart, drawn objects, tables, charts, sounds, movies, headers and footers, or other enhancing objects to communicate your message effectively. Analyze the content of each presentation slide to see if a chart, table, or other object could better communicate the topic you are presenting.

4. **Adjust each slide in the presentation based on your design decisions**
   You may need to change a slide's AutoLayout (for example, so the slide can accommodate a picture, chart, or movie), change master text indents, change the anchor point or spacing of text, or customize master placeholders.

QuickTip
For a dramatic 3-D effect, shade a slide background in one direction, then shade objects or shapes in another direction.

FIGURE F-1: Inserted Word outline in PowerPoint

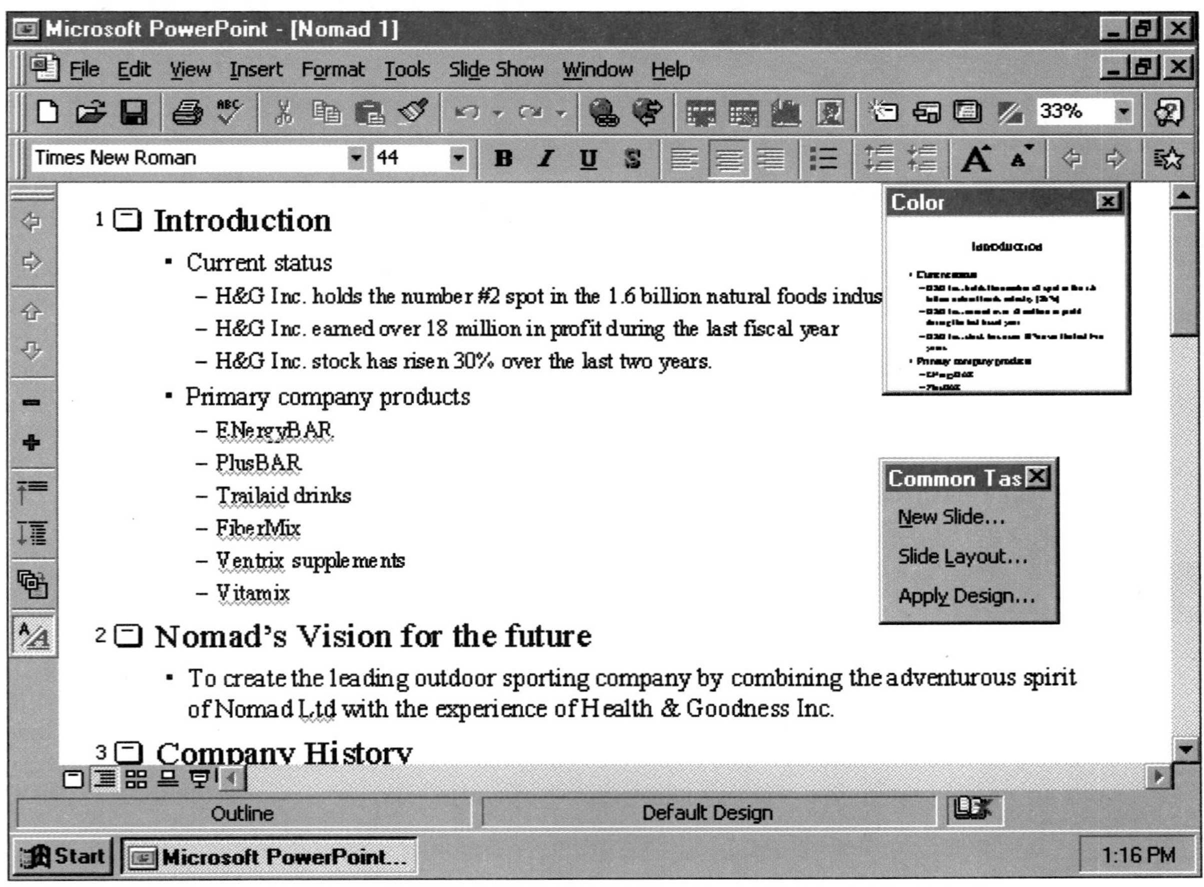

FIGURE F-2: Sample presentation sketch

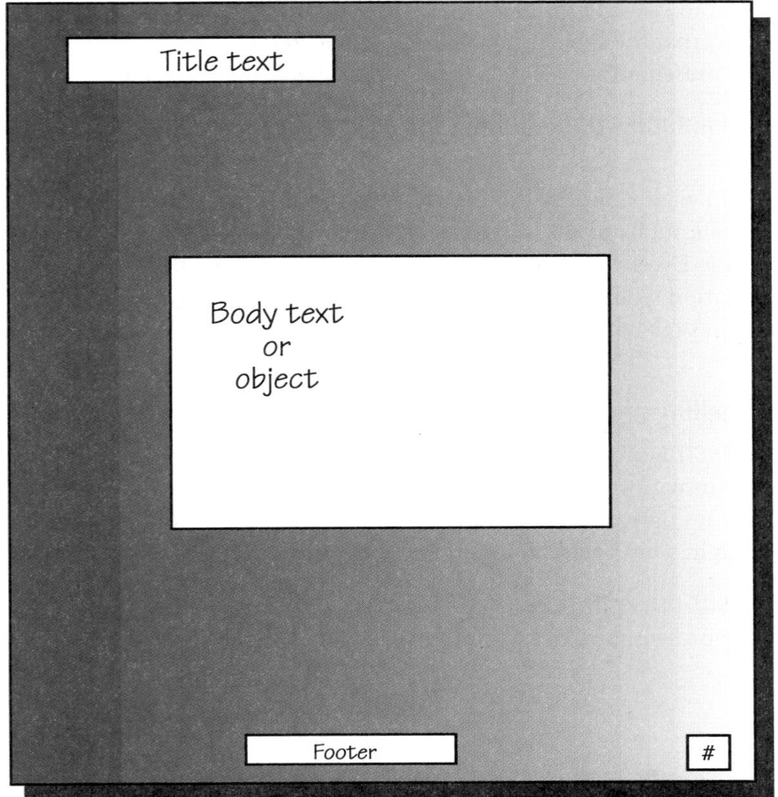

Adding a Word Table and Excel Worksheet to Slides

After you have adjusted the design of your slides, you can fine-tune each slide one at a time by adding objects and changing slide and text formatting. Sometimes, when you insert content or an outline from another source such as Microsoft Word, the text or data doesn't fit the slide design or look good in its current form. Then you need to change the slide layout or the way text or data appears on the slide to achieve a certain look. At this stage, you also will decide about adding data from other applications such as Microsoft Excel to help communicate your message. Chris finishes this presentation by customizing some of the content, embedding an Excel worksheet, then setting slide show features.

Steps

1. **Add or create objects that enhance your presentation slides**
   Use clipart, drawn objects, photographs, animation movies, digital movies, or sound to enhance your presentation. If necessary, change an object's appearance to better fit the slide color scheme or design. Be careful not to overload your presentation with too many objects; you don't want your audience distracted from the message of your presentation.

2. **Convert the text relating to H&G's primary products to an embedded Word table**
   The easiest way to convert text in PowerPoint to a Word table is to cut the text from the slide, then paste it into a Word document. Because you want to convert the text on the slide to an embedded table, first insert a Word document into your slide using the Insert Object command, then paste the text from PowerPoint to the Word document. Once the text is in Word, convert it to a table style, format the table using Word's formatting tools, then exit Word to embed the table into your presentation. Refer to the sample table shown in Figure F-3.

3. **Add a new slide called Financial Data to the presentation, then create and embed an Excel worksheet**
   Use the Excel worksheet in Figure F-4 as the basis for your data. Use formulas and the AutoSum button to calculate totals in the worksheet. Format the worksheet using Excel's formatting tools. Embed the Excel worksheet in your presentation. Once the worksheet is embedded in your presentation, you may need to scale it so it's easier to see and position it on the slide. Use PowerPoint's formatting tools to enhance the worksheet so it stands out on the slide.

4. **Finish by checking for spelling errors, then set builds, transitions, slide timings, and interactive settings for each slide in the presentation**
   Set build options in the Animation Settings dialog box for titles, main text objects, and objects. Set interactive settings options for objects you want to interact with during the slide show. For example, you might want to edit or open an embedded chart.

5. **Save, print, then close your presentation**
   Be prepared to justify your presentation design and revisions.

FIGURE F-3: Word table sketch

Product	Units Sold	Total
1. ENergyBAR	467,390 ea	$ 584,237.50
2. Trailaid drinks	187,932 ea	$ 543,123.48
3. Ventrix	59,035 btl	$ 407,341.50
4. PlusBAR	210,968 ea	$ 335,439.12
5. FiberMix	35,621 lbs	$ 73,023.05
6. Vitamix	19,004 lbs	$ 37,627.92

FIGURE F-4: Excel worksheet

H&G Sales Data					
	FY 93	FY 94	FY 95	FY 96	FY 97
Quarter 1	$ 693,427.83	$ 732,956.16	$ 657,933.84	$ 784,690.32	$ 848,925.77
Quarter 2	$ 688,475.09	$ 725,632.88	$ 759,437.22	$ 823,485.12	$ 973,204.72
Quarter 3	$ 700,925.98	$ 690,427.76	$ 750,832.09	$ 893,862.45	$ 1,078,940.92
Quarter 4	$ 710,473.88	$ 701,533.25	$ 770,428.10	$ 846,327.09	$ 1,186,358.32
Total	$ 2,793,302.78	$ 2,850,550.05	$ 2,938,631.25	$ 3,348,364.98	$ 4,087,429.73
5 yr Total					$ 16,018,278.79

Creating Relationships in Access

When the data you need for your presentation already exists in an Access database, you can import it into your PowerPoint presentation. You can manipulate Access data to get exactly the information you need by creating relationships between tables, then importing the information into Excel for analysis and formatting. The president of Nomad, Bill Davidson, needs to give a presentation to Nomad's Board of Directors that focuses on the benefits of acquiring H&G. The presentation should include information on H&G's top four clients. To complete this presentation, Chris uses the presentation he created for the company division heads in the last project as the basis for a new one. To get the appropriate information for this project, Chris creates a relationship between two Access tables, queries the database, analyzes the data in Excel, then imports it into a PowerPoint presentation.

Steps

1. **Open the Access database H&G Inc**
   You need to extract client and product sales information from the second quarter of 1995 for your presentation. The database that H&G provided Nomad does not include a client table, so you add one.

2. **Add a new table to the H&G Inc database, then save it as Customer List**
   Refer to Figures F-5 and F-6 for help in creating the new table. Remember to define the length and data type of the fields exactly as you see them in Figure F-6 to link the tables successfully. The Customer ID field in this table will link to the Customer ID field in the H&G 1997 Sales table. You need to link the tables to create a query for the presentation.

3. **Create a one-to-many relationship between the H&G Inc tables**
   Identify the common field in each table in the database that will link the tables. To ensure data integrity, make sure you enforce referential integrity between the tables. When you have successfully linked the tables, you will see a one-to-many line between the Customer List table and the H&G 1997 Sales table and between the H&G 1997 Sales table and the H&G Products table. Now you create a query with the database tables to determine which clients are purchasing H&G's primary products.

4. **Create a query using all three H&G Inc tables, use the fields in Table F-1, sort in ascending order by Company Name field, then save it as Customer Comparison**
   Use the Query Design View to create your query. Add the H&G Inc database tables to the Query Design View; then, if necessary, rearrange each table's field list to view its contents. Arrange the fields in a logical manner based on how you want the table to look. You might want to review the table in Query View to see how the finished table will look.

5. **Export the Customer Comparison query to Microsoft Excel, then save it as Customer Comparison**
   Excel creates a worksheet that displays the Customer Comparison query from Access. Now that you have imported the information, you can close Access.

FIGURE F-5: **Customer List Table in Design view**

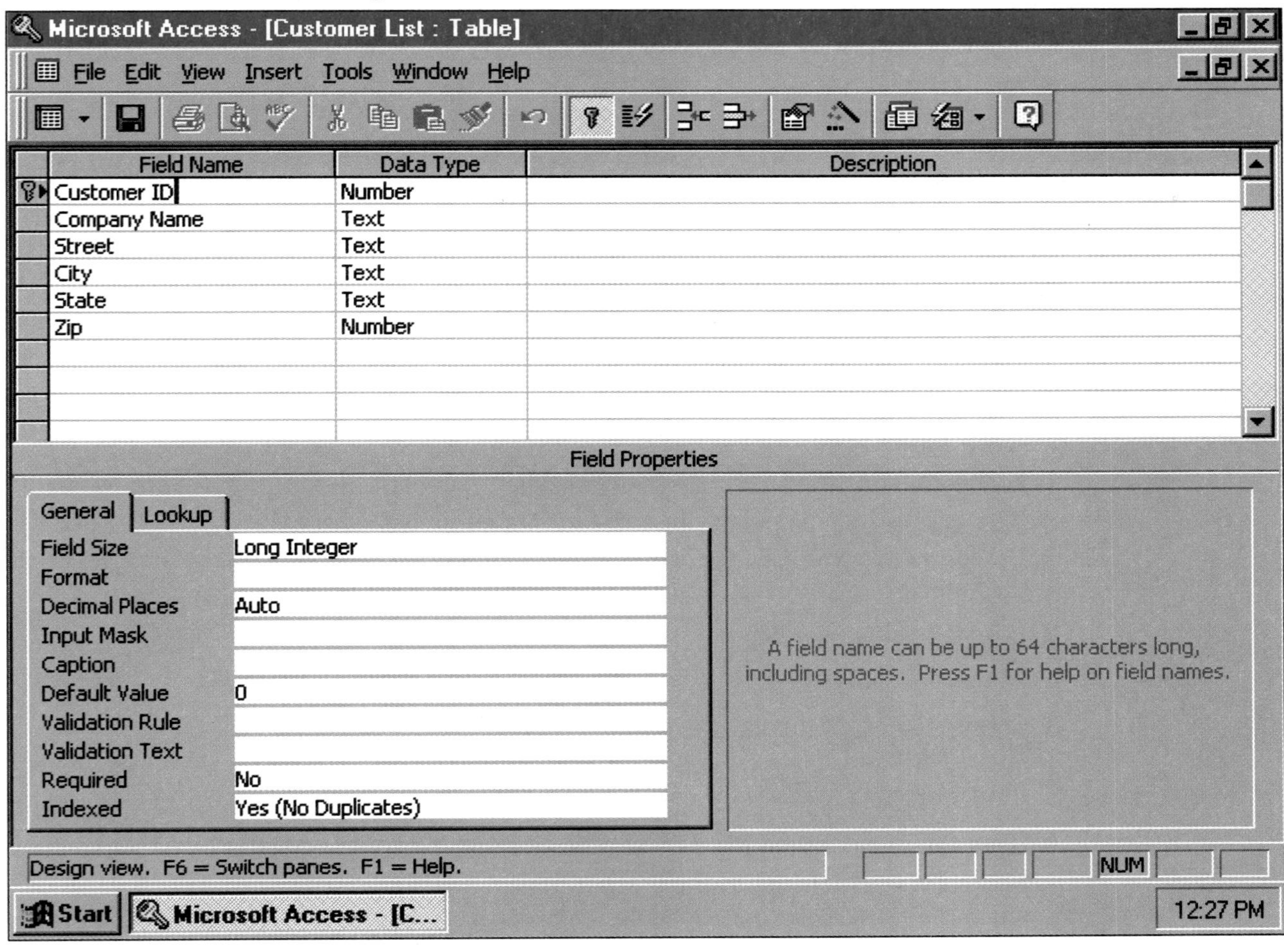

FIGURE F-6: **Customer List Table**

Customer ID	Company Name	Street	City	State	Zip
1889	CO-OP USA	8723 Front St.	L.A.	CA	93902
2459	Western Foods Inc.	One High Ave.	Vancouver	WA	94532
3409	Chestnut Stores	3489 Haber Rd. Suite #34	Southfork	MI	19011
12384	Natural Products Inc.	9490 Mission Ave.	Berkeley	CA	90345
23429	Company Square	21120 46th Ave. Flr #12	New York	NY	20090
58938	All Natural Company	6422 Forest St.	Dun Glen	NV	82353
0					0

TABLE F-1: **Customer Comparison query fields**

table field list name	fields in list
Customer List	Customer ID, Company Name
H&G 1997 Sales	Units Sold, Unit Price
H&G Products	Product ID, Product Name

Analyzing Access Data in Excel

Importing the database information into Excel allows Chris to analyze and format the data before exporting it to PowerPoint. For this presentation to the Board of Directors, Chris wants some specific information on H&G's top four clients. He finishes by adding a total column to the Excel worksheet, formatting the worksheet, analyzing the data, charting the analyzed data, and then embedding four charts in his PowerPoint presentation.

Steps 1 2 3 4

1. **Add a column titled Total to the worksheet, calculate the total amounts for each H&G client, then calculate the total for the entire worksheet**
   Use formulas to calculate the figures in the Total column, then format the worksheet using the AutoFormat feature. Now analyze each client's numbers using your Excel skills.
2. **Create a table that determines sales for each product**
   Use sorting or AutoFilter to create data similar to that shown in Figure F-7.
3. **Create a chart to display the data**
   Figure F-8 shows how a typical chart might display this data. Format the chart using Excel's formatting tools. Analyze the data to find the four largest clients.
4. **Open the presentation INT F-2, save it as Nomad 2, then embed a chart for each of the four largest clients in the presentation**
   Once the PowerPoint presentation is open, insert four new slides after the Primary Company Products slide, where you can embed the Excel charts. Remember, if you want to embed just the chart from an Excel worksheet that contains both data and a chart, you can copy and embed the chart alone. Now you have successfully moved data from Access to Excel, then to PowerPoint.
5. **Finish the presentation by checking for spelling errors; then set builds, transitions, slide timings, and interactive settings for the slides in your presentation**
   You may also need to enhance the presentation with objects or color, such as background shading or a template. Organize or restructure the presentation, if necessary.
6. **Save, print, then close your presentation**
   Be prepared to justify your decisions about this presentation.

FIGURE F-7: Sample Excel data

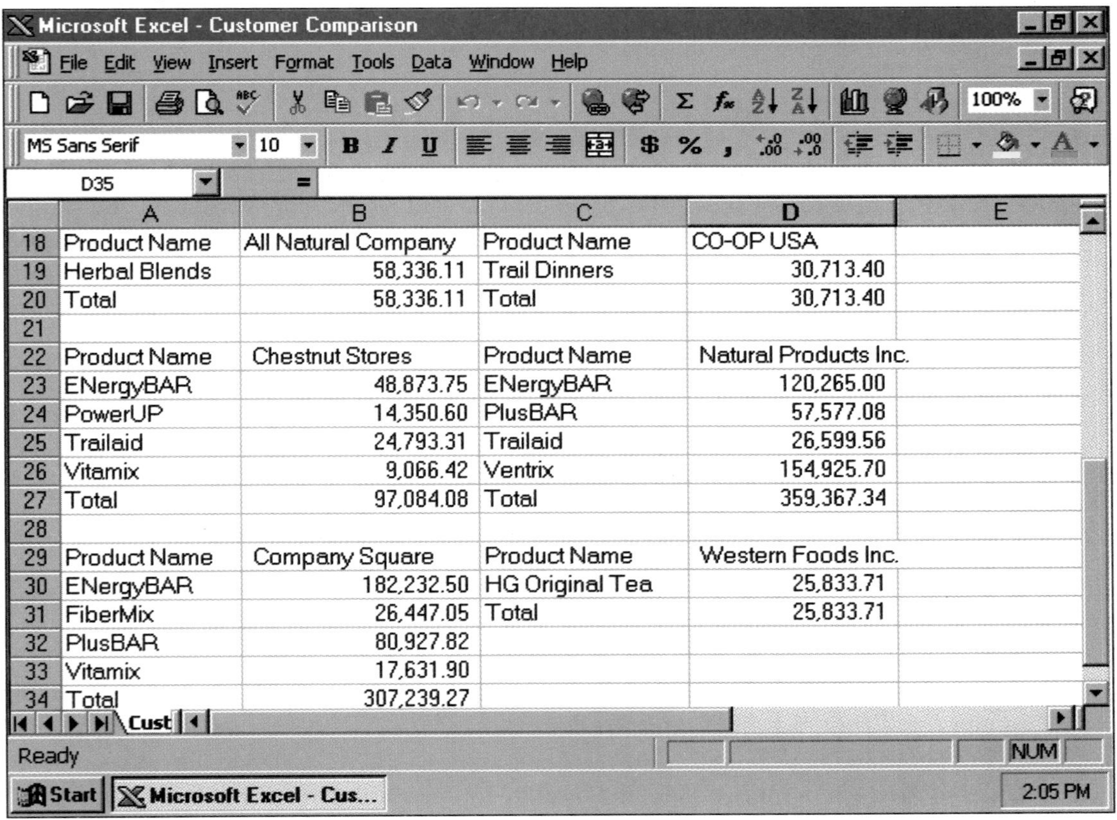

	A	B	C	D	E
18	Product Name	All Natural Company	Product Name	CO-OP USA	
19	Herbal Blends	58,336.11	Trail Dinners	30,713.40	
20	Total	58,336.11	Total	30,713.40	
21					
22	Product Name	Chestnut Stores	Product Name	Natural Products Inc.	
23	ENergyBAR	48,873.75	ENergyBAR	120,265.00	
24	PowerUP	14,350.60	PlusBAR	57,577.08	
25	Trailaid	24,793.31	Trailaid	26,599.56	
26	Vitamix	9,066.42	Ventrix	154,925.70	
27	Total	97,084.08	Total	359,367.34	
28					
29	Product Name	Company Square	Product Name	Western Foods Inc.	
30	ENergyBAR	182,232.50	HG Original Tea	25,833.71	
31	FiberMix	26,447.05	Total	25,833.71	
32	PlusBAR	80,927.82			
33	Vitamix	17,631.90			
34	Total	307,239.27			

FIGURE F-8: Sample chart

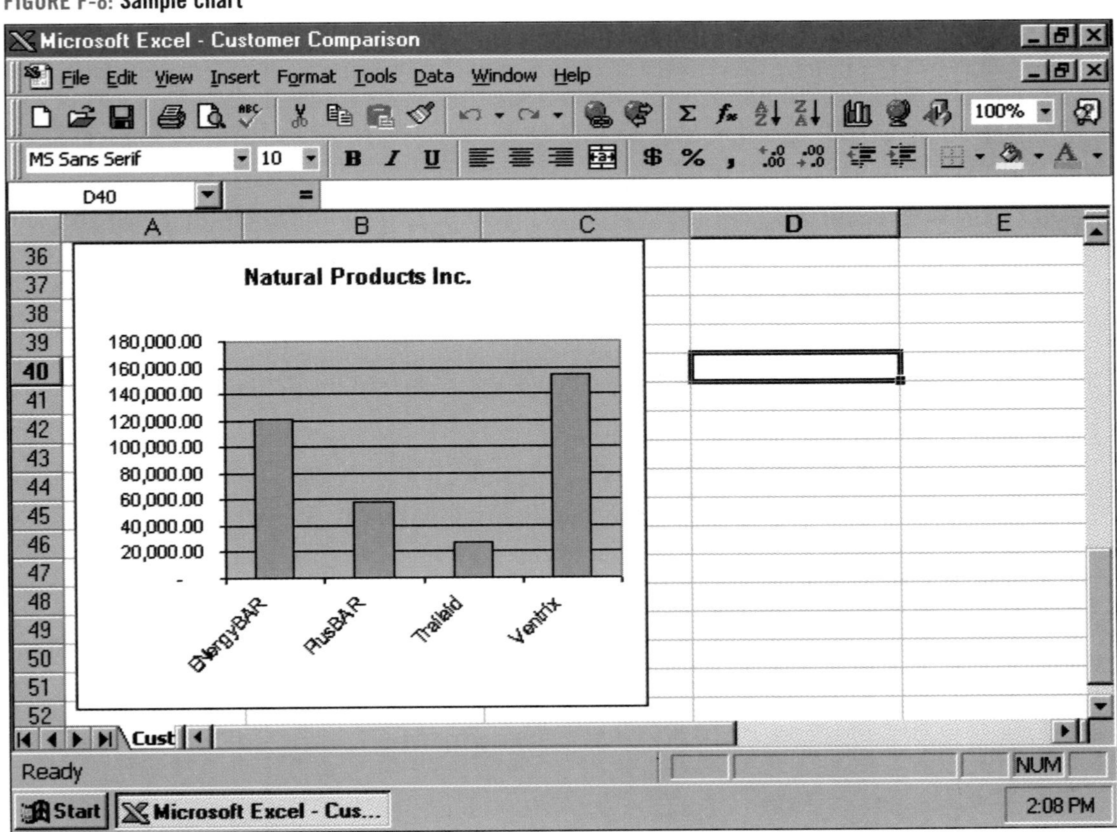

Integration

Exporting an Access Table into Word

Choosing the right Microsoft Office program for the job is an important part of creating integrated presentations. Your work will be easier and your end results more polished if you choose the right tools. Before Nomad's Board of Directors can begin negotiations to purchase H&G, Nomad's stockholders need to vote on the acquisition proposal. Chris develops a presentation describing H&G's customer and client base. To complete this presentation, he first creates a table in Word and then links it to his presentation. Chris then imports data from Excel into Microsoft Graph and embeds a chart in his presentation. He finishes by making any necessary changes to the slides.

Steps

1. **Open the Access database H&G Inc.**
   You need to create a detailed list of H&G's products for the stockholder's presentation, so you decide to create a Word table from the H&G Products table.

2. **Export the H&G Products table to Word, then split the table in half and save the documents as Product table 1 and Product table 2**
   Figure F-9 shows how a published Access table appears in Word. Divide the table into two tables so they will fit on two slides in PowerPoint. Keep both documents open, and format the tables using Word's formatting features. After you publish the table to Word, close Access to free up your computer's memory.

3. **Enhance each table using Word features**
   Switch to Page Layout view and, if necessary, add the Drawing toolbar to your screen. You might want to reposition each table on the page, then add a callout explaining part of the table or add a text label that identifies the table. Also, you could add WordArt or a graphic to the table. Close Word when you are finished formatting the tables.

4. **Open the presentation INT F-3, save it as Nomad 3, then link each table you created in Word to a new slide in the presentation**
   Create two new slides before the Primary Company Products slide in the presentation, then link Product table 1 and Product table 2 to the slides. Crop and scale each of the tables to fit the slide. Depending on how you formatted the tables in Word, you may need to open the tables and edit them in Word to enhance their appearance in the presentation. Now import data from Excel into Microsoft Graph to create a chart.

5. **Open the worksheet INT F-4, save it as ENergyBAR, filter the worksheet for the ENergyBAR records, then create a new workbook with the ENergyBAR records called ENergyBAR shortlist**
   Compare your ENergyBAR shortlist worksheet to Figure F-10. You want to create a chart in PowerPoint using the client information relating to the ENergyBAR product. Close Excel and save the changes to your new worksheet, then turn off AutoFilter in the ENergyBAR workbook.

FIGURE F-9: **Published Access table in a Word document**

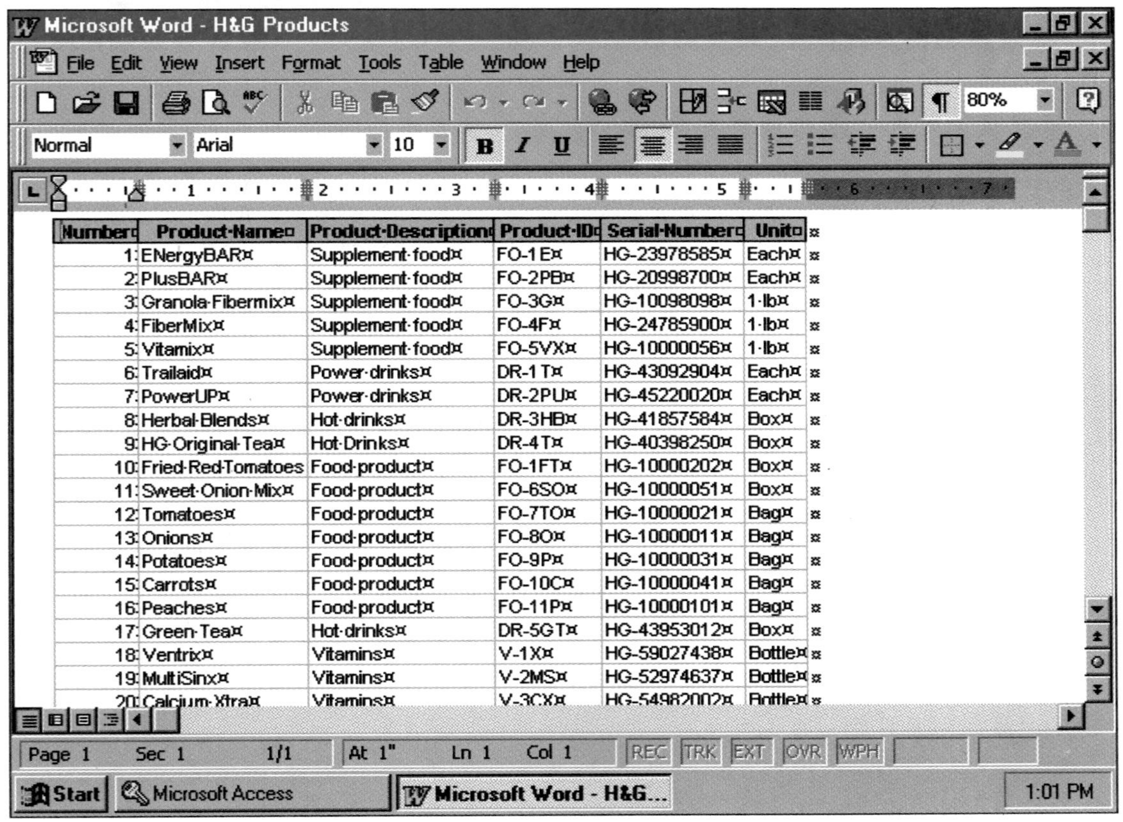

Number	Product Name	Product Description	Product ID	Serial Number	Unit
1	ENergyBAR	Supplement food	FO-1E	HG-23978585	Each
2	PlusBAR	Supplement food	FO-2PB	HG-20998700	Each
3	Granola Fibermix	Supplement food	FO-3G	HG-10098098	1 lb
4	FiberMix	Supplement food	FO-4F	HG-24785900	1 lb
5	Vitamix	Supplement food	FO-5VX	HG-10000056	1 lb
6	Trailaid	Power drinks	DR-1T	HG-43092904	Each
7	PowerUP	Power drinks	DR-2PU	HG-45220020	Each
8	Herbal Blends	Hot drinks	DR-3HB	HG-41857584	Box
9	HG Original Tea	Hot Drinks	DR-4T	HG-40398250	Box
10	Fried Red Tomatoes	Food product	FO-1FT	HG-10000202	Box
11	Sweet Onion Mix	Food product	FO-6SO	HG-10000051	Box
12	Tomatoes	Food product	FO-7TO	HG-10000021	Bag
13	Onions	Food product	FO-8O	HG-10000011	Bag
14	Potatoes	Food product	FO-9P	HG-10000031	Bag
15	Carrots	Food product	FO-10C	HG-10000041	Bag
16	Peaches	Food product	FO-11P	HG-10000101	Bag
17	Green Tea	Hot drinks	DR-5GT	HG-43953012	Box
18	Ventrix	Vitamins	V-1X	HG-59027438	Bottle
19	MultiSinx	Vitamins	V-2MS	HG-52974637	Bottle
20	Calcium Xtra	Vitamins	V-3CX	HG-54982002	Bottle

FIGURE F-10: **ENergyBAR shortlist worksheet**

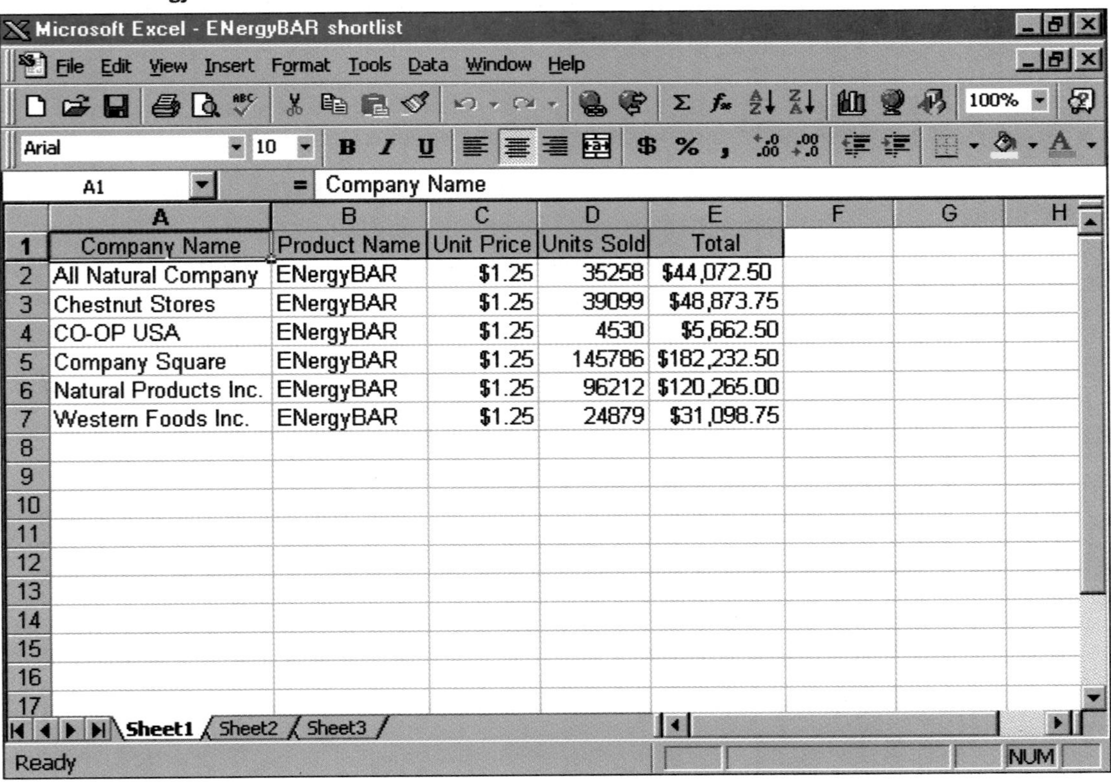

	A	B	C	D	E
1	Company Name	Product Name	Unit Price	Units Sold	Total
2	All Natural Company	ENergyBAR	$1.25	35258	$44,072.50
3	Chestnut Stores	ENergyBAR	$1.25	39099	$48,873.75
4	CO-OP USA	ENergyBAR	$1.25	4530	$5,662.50
5	Company Square	ENergyBAR	$1.25	145786	$182,232.50
6	Natural Products Inc.	ENergyBAR	$1.25	96212	$120,265.00
7	Western Foods Inc.	ENergyBAR	$1.25	24879	$31,098.75

Importing Excel Data into PowerPoint

An easy way to create a chart in PowerPoint is to import existing data from Excel into PowerPoint using Microsoft Graph. Once you import data into Microsoft Graph and create a chart for your presentation, you don't need to use Excel to change or modify the chart. Chris finishes his work on this presentation by importing data from Excel into Microsoft Graph and then embedding the chart to a new slide. Chris evaluates the presentation to make sure it's organized and complete, then creates handouts in Word.

Steps

1. **Insert a new slide after the Primary Company Products slide, then create and format a Graph chart showing the ENergyBAR shortlist data**
   Use the AutoLayout button to apply the appropriate slide layout. Remember to clear the default data out of the datasheet before you import the new data from the ENergyBAR worksheet. Compare your Microsoft Graph datasheet to Figure F-11. Arrange the datasheet so the chart shows the company names, units sold, and the total. Experiment with the chart's type and 3-D view to determine the best format. Set chart options, such as chart subtype, gap depth, chart depth, gap width, and gridlines. Format the chart's data markers, data labels, and the axis. Add and format chart elements, such as a text box, an arrow, a legend, or shapes. Refer to Figure F-12 for a sample Microsoft Graph chart showing the data from the ENergyBAR shortlist worksheet. When you are finished formatting your chart, add any finishing touches to the rest of the presentation.

2. **Review the presentation, then make changes as necessary**
   You might use clipart, drawn objects, photographs, animation movies, digital movies, or sound to enhance your presentation. If necessary, change an object's appearance to better fit with the slide color scheme or slide design. Make sure the content of the presentation flows logically and is complete. You may need to add some of your own content or remove some to complete the presentation. Remember, this presentation is designed to convince the stockholders of Nomad Ltd to purchase Health & Goodness Inc.

3. **Finish the presentation by checking for spelling errors, then set builds, transitions, slide timings, and interactive settings for the presentation slides**
   To make it easy for the stockholders to follow the president as he gives the presentation, you make handouts in Word. You decide to use the Write Up feature in PowerPoint to create and link your presentation to Word because Word allows more than one slide on a handout page.

4. **Create linked handouts in Word, then save your Word document as Nomad Handouts**

5. **Save and print your presentation, then print the Word handouts**
   Be prepared to justify your presentation strategy.

FIGURE F-11: Microsoft Graph datasheet showing imported Excel data

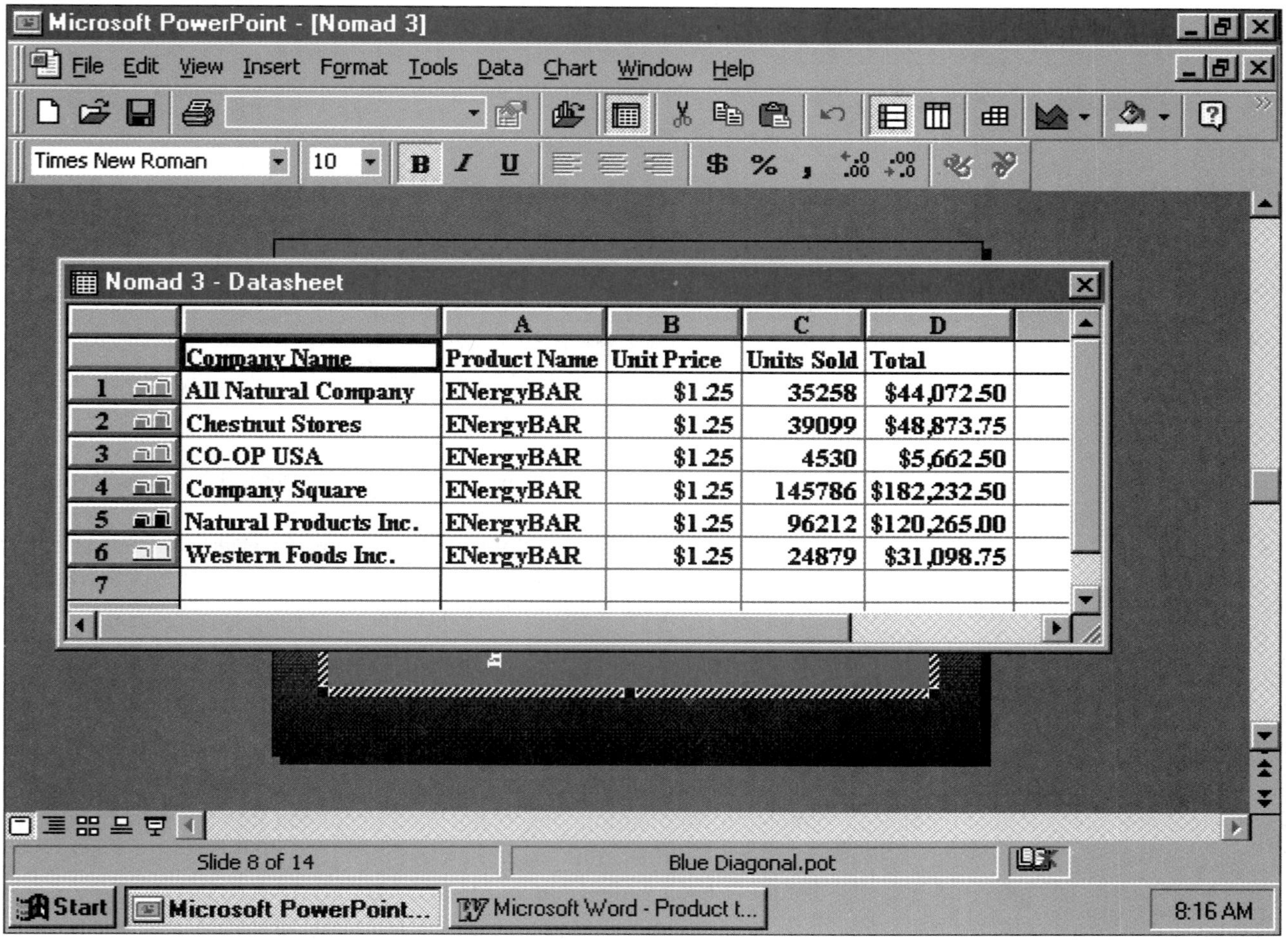

Microsoft PowerPoint - [Nomad 3]
File Edit View Insert Format Tools Data Chart Window Help
Times New Roman
10
Nomad 3 - Datasheet
A B C D
Company Name | Product Name | Unit Price | Units Sold | Total
1 All Natural Company | ENergyBAR | $1.25 | 35258 | $44,072.50
2 Chestnut Stores | ENergyBAR | $1.25 | 39099 | $48,873.75
3 CO-OP USA | ENergyBAR | $1.25 | 4530 | $5,662.50
4 Company Square | ENergyBAR | $1.25 | 145786 | $182,232.50
5 Natural Products Inc. | ENergyBAR | $1.25 | 96212 | $120,265.00
6 Western Foods Inc. | ENergyBAR | $1.25 | 24879 | $31,098.75
7
Slide 8 of 14
Blue Diagonal.pot
Start
Microsoft PowerPoint...
Microsoft Word - Product t...
8:16 AM

FIGURE F-12: Sample Microsoft Graph chart

Nomad 3
H&G's ENergyBAR
$182,232.50
145786

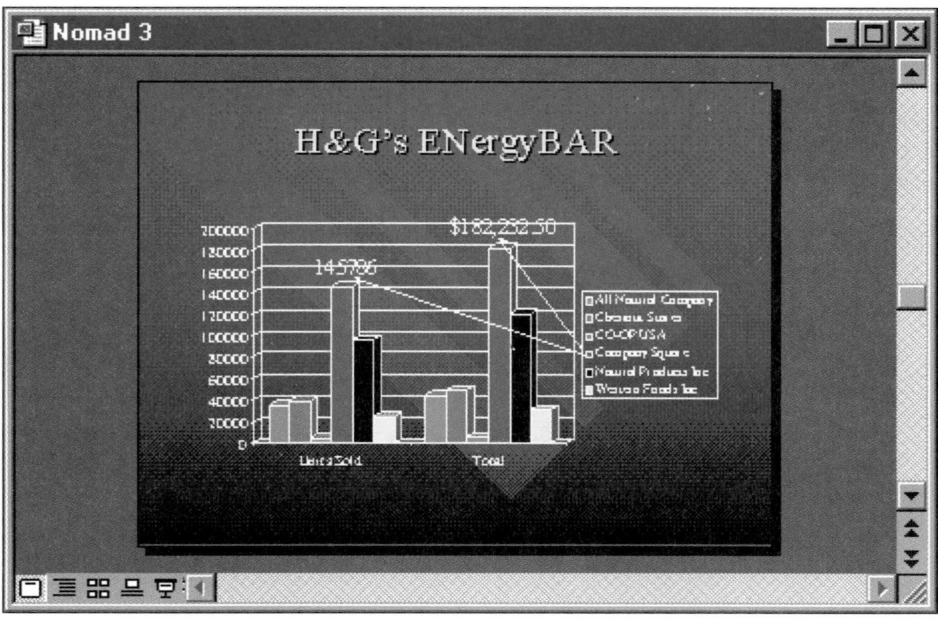

Independent Challenges

1. You are a marketing analyst at Davis Press, a publishing company that produces many top-rated magazines. Recently, you were asked to research a marketing strategy for a new sports magazine that will compete with magazines such as *Sports Illustrated.* You decide to use PowerPoint to develop a presentation that you can use to illustrate your research findings and marketing recommendations.

To help you complete this independent challenge, a partially completed Word document is provided. You will complete the Word outline and then use it as the outline for a new PowerPoint presentation. Assume the following information to be true as you complete the Word outline and create a presentation:

- The name of the new magazine is *AllSports.*
- Currently, there are only three magazines that have some of the features that the new *AllSports* magazine will contain.
- *AllSports* should appeal to both men and women ages 25–55.
- *AllSports* should have articles on major field sports—for example, football, baseball, and basketball—and hobbyist sports, such as fishing and hunting.
- The magazine will focus on sports analysis and the people behind the sports.

To complete this independent challenge:

1. Open the Word document INT F-5, then save it as "AllSports Outline."
2. Review the partially completed Word document, then replace the italicized text with your own content.
3. Add information that would strengthen your presentation to the Word outline.
4. Create a new presentation using your completed Word outline. Insert the Word document into PowerPoint. Consider the results you want and how you need to adjust the text in PowerPoint.
5. Preview the presentation and plan the design of each slide. Change the slide layout, if necessary.
6. Add a template or a shaded background. Customize an existing presentation template, or create one of your own.
7. Add or create objects to enhance the slides of your presentation. Analyze each slide to see if an object can enhance the text on that slide.
8. Embed the following Word table from PowerPoint using the Insert Microsoft Word Table button:

	AllSports	*Sports Illustrated*	*Sportsman*
Type of coverage	All sport types	Major sports	Hobbyist sports
Coverage focus	Analytical, personal	Analytical	Personal
Coverage appeal	Nondiscriminatory	Male, 20s–40s	Male, 40s–60s

9. Use your own information to add one more magazine examples and two more categories to the table.
10. Format the table using Word's formatting tools, embed the table into PowerPoint, then format the table in PowerPoint.
11. Spell-check the presentation, then save it as "AllSports Magazine."
12. Set slide builds, slide timings, slide transitions, and interactive settings to all the slides.
13. Print your final presentation slides.
14. Submit the printed output and a slide show of the presentation to your instructor.

2. You are the controller for Health & Goodness Inc. (H&G), a dry foods company. In relation to the impending sale of H&G to Nomad Ltd, you must give a detailed presentation to the chief financial officer and the financial board on the revenue generated by all of H&G's clients during the last quarter. The information you give to the board will be used to help determine relevant issues regarding H&G's sale.

In this independent challenge you will analyze an Excel worksheet and then embed seven charts that you create into a PowerPoint presentation. Your presentation should be at least 10 slides long. Use the Excel worksheet provided for you to help you complete your presentation.

To complete this independent challenge:

1. Open the Excel worksheet INT F-6, then save it as "**H&G Sale.**"
2. Review the partially completed Excel worksheet. You'll need to create a separate chart for each client.
3. Create an analysis of the data similar to what is shown in Figure F-13.
4. Create similar analyses of the worksheet data that enable you to design charts of each client's total product revenue, as well as the total revenue of all the clients.
5. Format each chart using Excel's formatting tools.
6. Open a new PowerPoint presentation, then save it as "H&G Financial Review."
7. You may want to use the AutoContent wizard to help with the basic content of your presentation. Consider the results you want to see in PowerPoint and how you need to design the slides of the presentation. Remember, this is primarily a financial presentation showing revenue figures from Excel.
8. Preview the presentation and plan the design of each slide. Change the slide layout, if necessary. If you used the AutoContent Wizard in Step 6, change the sample text.
9. Add a template or a shaded background, if necessary. Customize an existing presentation template, or create one of your own.
10. Switch to Excel, and embed each chart in a different slide in PowerPoint.
11. Add or create objects to enhance the slides of your presentation. Analyze each slide to see if an object can enhance the text on that slide.
12. Spell-check the presentation.
13. Set slide builds, slide timings, slide transitions, and interactive settings for all the slides.
14. Print your final presentation slides.
15. Submit the printed output and a slide show of the presentation to your instructor.

FIGURE F-13

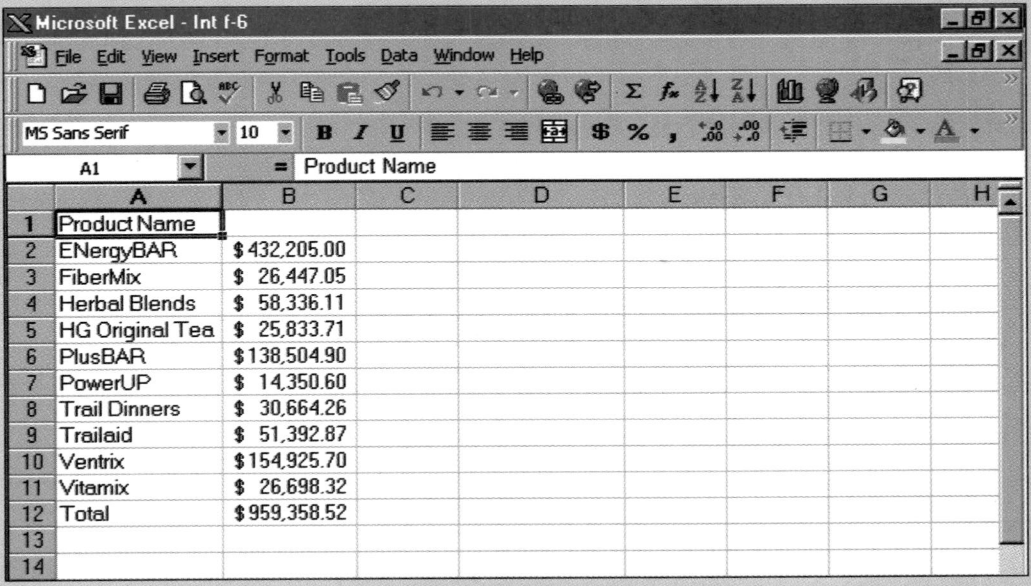

Microsoft Excel - Int f-6

File Edit View Insert Format Tools Data Window Help

MS Sans Serif 10

A1 = Product Name

	A	B	C	D	E	F	G	H
1	Product Name							
2	ENergyBAR	$432,205.00						
3	FiberMix	$ 26,447.05						
4	Herbal Blends	$ 58,336.11						
5	HG Original Tea	$ 25,833.71						
6	PlusBAR	$138,504.90						
7	PowerUP	$ 14,350.60						
8	Trail Dinners	$ 30,664.26						
9	Trailaid	$ 51,392.87						
10	Ventrix	$154,925.70						
11	Vitamix	$ 26,698.32						
12	Total	$959,358.52						
13								
14								

3. Your investment group, High Rollers, has been asked to prepare a presentation based on current stock market research. To do this, you've decided to utilize the World Wide Web (WWW) and your Microsoft Office skills.

To complete this independent challenge:

1. Log on to the Internet and use your web browser to go to http://www.course.com. From there, click Student Online Companions, click the link for this textbook, then click on the Integration link for Unit F.
2. Use any of the following sites to research current investment opportunities: New York Stock Exchange, American Stock Exchange, the NASDAQ, or any other site you can find with related information.
3. Create a database called "High Rollers Data" that contains information on at least 10 stocks of interest. The stocks do not have to have the same focus (e.g., technology, medicine, or entertainment) but should include a category field that defines it. Also, include a field that contains the current cost per share.
4. Export the table to Excel, and save the workbook as "High Rollers Info."
5. Create a column that calculates the cost of 15 shares of each stock, then chart the data in this new column.
6. Create a Word outline that will be the basis for your presentation to the club and will discuss your stock recommendations. The outline should contain at least six slides. Save the outline as "High Rollers Outline."
7. Open a new PowerPoint presentation, and save it as "High Rollers Presentation."
8. Import the "High Rollers Outline" into the "High Rollers Presentation."
9. Add the Excel chart to one of the slides.
10. Set slide builds, slide timings, slide transitions, and interactive settings for all the slides.
11. Spell-check the presentation.
12. Print the slides of your final presentation.
13. Submit the printed output and a slide show of the presentation to your instructor.

Glossary

Alignment The horizontal position of text within the width of a line or between tab stops; for example, left, center, or right.

AutoCorrect A feature that automatically corrects a misspelled word. Word provides several entries for commonly misspelled words, but you can add your own.

AutoFormat A feature that improves the appearance of a document by applying consistent formatting and styles based on a default document template or a document template you specify. The AutoFormat feature also adds bullets to lists and symbols for trademarks and copyrights where necessary.

AutoText entry A stored text or graphic you want to use again.

Border A straight vertical or horizontal line between columns in a section, next to or around paragraphs and graphics, or in a table. You can assign a variety of widths to a border.

Bullet A small graphic, usually a round or square dot, often used to identify items in a list.

Callout A graphic element used to label or point to an item in a document. It consists of text and a line pointing to the item.

Character style A stored set of text format settings.

Clipboard A temporary storage area for cut or copied text or graphics. You can paste the contents of the Clipboard into any Microsoft program file. The Clipboard holds the information until you cut or copy another piece of text or a graphic.

Cut To remove selected text or a graphic from a document so you can paste it to another place in the document or to another document. The cut information is placed in a temporary storage area called the Clipboard. *See also* Clipboard.

Data source The document containing the variable information to be used with the mail merge feature.

Field Variable information in a document that is supplied by a file or by Word. In a mail merge operation, individual items (such as a name or state) are stored in fields in the data source. A merge field inserted in the main document (such as a form letter) instructs Word to provide that field's contents from the data source. A Word field is variable information provided by Word. For example, if you insert the Filename field in a footer, the document's filename appears in the footer.

Font A collection of characters (letters, numerals, symbols, and punctuation marks) with a specific design. Arial and Times New Roman are examples of font names.

Font effects Refers to enhanced formatting you can apply to text, such as Shadow, Engraved, all caps, and hidden, among others.

Font size Refers to the physical size of text, measured in points (pts). The bigger the number of points, the larger the font size.

Font style Refers to whether text appears as bold, italicized, or underlined, or any combination of these formats.

Footer The text that appears at the bottom of each printed page of a document.

Format The way text appears on a page. In Word, a format comes from direct formatting and the application of styles. The four types of formats are character, paragraph, section, and document.

Formatting toolbar A bar that contains buttons and options for the most frequently used formatting commands.

global template In Word, a template with the filename NORMAL.DOT that contains default menus, AutoCorrect entries, styles, and page setup settings. Documents use the global template unless you specify a custom template. *See also* template.

Graphic A picture, chart, or drawing in a document.

Graphic object An element in a document that can be moved, sized, and modified without leaving Word.

Hanging indent A paragraph format in which the first line of a paragraph starts farther left than the subsequent lines.

Header The text that appears at the top of each printed page of a document.

Indent The distance between text boundaries and page margins. Positive indents make the text area narrower than the space between margins. Negative indents allow text to extend into the margins. A paragraph can have left, right, and first-line indents.

Landscape A term used to refer to horizontal page orientation; it is the opposite of "portrait," or vertical, orientation.

Line break A mark inserted where you want to end one line and start another without starting a new paragraph.

Line spacing The height of a line of text, including extra spacing. Line spacing is often measured in lines or points.

Mail merge The process of creating personalized form letters or labels by combining boilerplate text with variable information.

Main document In the mail merge process, the main document is the document containing the boilerplate text; the text that is the same in each version of the merged document.

Margin The distance between the edge of the text in the document and the top, bottom, or side edges of the page.

Normal view The view you see when you start Word. Normal view is used for most editing and formatting tasks.

Page break The point at which one page ends and another begins. A break you insert (created by pressing [Ctrl] + [Enter]) is called a "hard break"; a break determined by the page layout is called a "soft break". A hard break appears as a dotted line and is labeled Page Break. A soft break appears as a dotted line without a label.

Page Layout view A view of a document as it will appear when you print it. Items such as headers, footnotes, and framed objects appear in their actual positions and can be dragged to new positions. You can edit and format text in page layout view.

Paragraph style A stored set of paragraph format settings.

Paste To insert cut or copied text into a document from the temporary storage area called the Clipboard.

Point size A measurement used for the size of text characters. There are 72 points per inch.

Portrait A term used to refer to vertical page orientation; it is the opposite of "landscape", or horizontal, orientation.

Record The entire collection of fields related to an item or individual contained in the data source.

Redo The ability to repeat reversed actions or changes, usually editing or formatting actions. Only reversed changes can be repeated with the redo feature.

Repetitive text Text that you use often in documents.

Resize The ability to change the size of an object (such as framed text or a graphic) by dragging sizing handles located on the sides and corners of the selected object.

Resolution Refers to the size of your monitor's screen display. Resolution is measured in pixels; a typical resolution is 640 x 480. The illustrations in this book were taken on a computer with these resolutions. Because a higher resolution results in more space visible on the screen and smaller text, your screen might not exactly match the illustrations in this book. You can change the resolution of the monitor using the Control Panel on the Start menu.

Sans serif font A font whose characters do not include serifs (the small strokes at the ends of the characters). Arial is a sans serif font.

ScreenTip When you place the pointer over a button, the name of the button is displayed and a brief description of its function appears in the status bar.

Section A part of a document separated from the rest of the document with a section break. By separating a document into sections, you can use different page and column formatting in different parts of the same document.

Selection bar An unmarked column at the left edge of a document window used to select text with the mouse. In a table, each cell has its own selection bar at the left edge of the cell.

Serif font A font that has small strokes at the ends of the characters. Times New Roman and Palatino are serif fonts.

Shading The background color or pattern behind text or graphics.

Soft return A line break created by pressing [Shift] + [Enter]. This creates a new line without creating a new paragraph.

Style A group of formatting instructions that you name and store and can modify. When you apply a style to selected characters and paragraphs, all the formatting instructions of that style are applied at once.

Style Gallery A feature that allows you to examine the overall formatting and styles used in a document template. With the Style Gallery, you can also preview your document formatted in the styles from a selected template.

Template A special kind of document that provides basic tools and text for creating a document. Templates can contain the following elements: styles, AutoText items, macros, customized menu and key assignments, and text or graphics that are the same in different types of documents.

Text flow Refers to paragraph formatting that controls the flow of text across page breaks. Controlling text flow prevents awkward breaks within paragraphs or ensures that related paragraphs appear together on the same page.

Vertical ruler A graphical bar displayed at the left edge of the document window in the page layout and print preview views. You can use this ruler to adjust the top and bottom page margins as well as to change row height in a table.

Excel 97

Glossary

Add-in An additional utility program that comes with Excel but is not automatically installed during a standard installation.

Alignment The horizontal position of cell contents; for example, left, center, or right.

Argument A value, range of cells, or text used in a macro or function. An argument is enclosed in parentheses; for example, =SUM(A1..B1).

Ascending Order Data organized from A to Z or 0 to 9.

Attribute A styling feature such as bold, italics, and underlining that can be applied to cell contents.

AutoCalculate area The area in the status bar that displays the sum (or function of your choice) of the values in the selected range.

AutoSum A feature that automatically calculates worksheet totals accessed by a button on the Standard toolbar.

Border Edges of a selected cell or area of cells in a worksheet. Lines and color can be applied to borders.

Cell The intersection of a column and row.

Cell address Unique location identified by intersecting column and row coordinates.

Cell pointer A highlighted rectangle around a cell that indicates the active cell.

Cell reference The address or name of a specific cell; cell references can be used in formulas and are relative or absolute.

Check box A square box in a dialog box that can be clicked to turn an option on or off.

Clear A command on the Edit menu used to erase a cell's contents, formatting, or both.

Clipboard A temporary storage area for cut or copied text or graphics. You can paste the contents of the Clipboard into any Microsoft program file. The Clipboard holds the information until you cut or copy another piece of text or a graphic.

Close A command that puts a file away but keeps Excel open so that you can continue to work on other workbooks.

Copy A command that copies the selected information and places it on the Clipboard.

Criteria form A data entry window used to set search criteria in lists.

Custom view A set of display and/or print settings that you can name and save, then access at a later time.

Cut A command that removes the contents from a selected area of a worksheet and places them on the Clipboard.

Data entry area The cells in a protected (locked) worksheet that must be unlocked because you need to change them.

Data form A data entry window used to view or add records to a list.

Database A collection of information organized by fields and records. A telephone book, a card catalog, and a list of company employees are all lists.

Delete A command that removes cell contents from a worksheet.

Descending Order Data organized from Z to A or 9 to 0.

Dialog box A window that displays when you choose a command whose name is followed by an ellipsis (...). A dialog box allows you to make selections that determine how the command affects the selected area.

Dynamic Information that updates automatically when certain parts of the workbook change.

Edit A change made to the contents of a cell or worksheet.

External reference indicator An ! (exclamation point) within a formula indicating that the cell referenced is outside the active sheet.

Field A labeled column in a list; it contains the same kind of information for each record, such as a phone number.

Field name A column label that describes the field.

Fill handle Small square in the lower-right corner of the active cell used to copy cell contents.

Find A command used to locate information the user specifies.

Find & Replace A command used to find one set of criteria and replace it with new information.

Folder A section of a disk used to store workbooks, much like a folder in a file cabinet.

Font A collection of characters (letters, numerals, and punctuation marks) with a specific design. Arial and Times New Roman are font names.

Footer The text that appears at the bottom of each printed page of a worksheet; for example, the page number and the date.

Form A data entry window used when working with lists. *See also* **Data form** *and* **Criteria form**.

Format The appearance of text and numbers, including color, font, attributes, and worksheet defaults. *See also* **Number format**.

Formula A set of instructions that you enter in a cell to perform numeric calculations (adding, multiplying, averaging, etc.); for example, +A1+B1.

Formula bar The area below the menu bar and above the Excel workspace where you enter and edit data in a worksheet cell. The formula bar becomes active when you start typing or editing cell data. Includes an Enter button and a Cancel button.

Freeze To lock in specified columns and/or rows to assist in scrolling through large worksheets.

Function A special predefined formula that provides a shortcut for commonly used calculations; for example, AVERAGE.

Header The text that appears at the top of each printed page; for example, the report name and the date.

Insertion point Blinking I-beam that appears in the formula bar during entry and editing.

Label Descriptive text or other information that identifies the rows and columns of a worksheet. Labels are not included in calculations.

Landscape A term used to refer to horizontal page orientation; it is the opposite of "portrait," or vertical orientation.

Linking Referencing data between workbooks dynamically so that any changes made in one workbook are reflected immediately in another workbook.

List A collection of information organized by fields and records. A telephone book, a card catalog, and a list of company employees are all lists.

List range A range of a worksheet that organizes information into fields and records.

Locked cells Cells that are protected so that their contents cannot be altered.

Logical test When the condition is a question that can be answered with a true or false response.

Macro A set of recorded instructions that tell the computer to perform a task or series of tasks.

Macro code The Visual Basic programming language Excel uses to translate your keystrokes and commands into words.

Menu A group of related commands located under a single word on the menu bar. For example, basic commands (New, Open, Save, Close, and Print) are grouped on the File menu.

Menu bar The area under the title bar on a window. The menu bar provides access to most of the application's commands.

Module Workbook area where the macro program code is located.

Name A name assigned to a selected cell or range in a worksheet. *See also* **Range name**.

Name box The leftmost area in the formula bar that shows the cell reference or name of the active cell. For example, A1 refers to cell A1 of the active worksheet. You also can get a list of names in a workbook using the name list arrow.

Number format A format applied to values to express numeric concepts, such as currency, date, and percent.

Operators Perform mathematical functions.

Option button A circle in a dialog box that can be clicked when only one option can be chosen.

Order of precedence The order in which Excel calculates parts of a formula: (1) exponents, (2) multiplication and division, and (3) addition and subtraction.

Page Break Preview Allows you to view and change page breaks manually in the Print Preview window.

Pane A column or row that always remains visible.

Paste A command that moves information on the Clipboard to a new location. Excel pastes the formulas rather than the result, unless the Paste Special command is used.

Paste Special A command that enables you to paste formulas as values, styles, or cell contents.

Personal Macro Workbook A file in which to store commonly used macros.

Point A unit of measure used for fonts and row height. One inch equals 72 points.

Portrait A term used to refer to vertical page orientation; it is the opposite of "landscape," or horizontal, orientation.

Precedence The order in which Excel calculates parts of a formula: (1) exponents, (2) multiplication and division, and (3) addition and subtraction.

Print Preview window A window that displays a reduced view of area to be printed.

Print Title The first row of a list (containing the field names) that appears as descriptive information on all worksheet pages.

Protect An option that lets you prevent cells in a worksheet from being changed.

Range A selected group of adjacent cells.

Range format A format applied to a selected range in a worksheet.

Range name A name applied to a selected range in a worksheet.

Record Horizontal rows in a list that contain related information.

Reference Populate cell data using existing cell content. You do this by typing = (equal sign) and then selecting the desired cell(s).

Relative cell reference Use to indicate a relative position in the worksheet. This allows you to copy and move formulas from one area to another of the same dimensions. Excel automatically changes the column and row numbers to reflect the new position.

Report Manager An add-in program that lets you create reports containing multiple worksheets in a workbook.

Row height The vertical dimension of a cell.

Run To execute a macro.

Scroll bars Bars that display on the right and bottom borders of the worksheet window that give you access to information not currently visible in the current worksheet as well as others in the workbook.

Sheet A term used for a worksheet.

Sheet tab A description at the bottom of each worksheet that identifies it in a workbook. In an open workbook, move to a worksheet by clicking its sheet tab. *See* **Tab.**

Sort To rearrange rows of a worksheet, usually rows in a list, in a particular order. *See also* **Ascending order** *and* **Descending order**.

Sort key Any cell in a field by which a list or selected range is being organized.

Status bar The bar near the bottom of the screen that provides information about the tasks Excel is performing or about any current selections.

Tab A description at the bottom of each worksheet that identifies it in a workbook. In an open workbook, move to a worksheet by clicking its tab.

Tab scrolling buttons Enable you to move among sheets within a workbook.

Template A fill-in-the-blank worksheet(s) that can include any text, formatting, formulas, layout and other workbook elements. You open a template, fill in the missing information, then save the file as a regular workbook, leaving the template intact.

Toggle A button that can be clicked to turn an option on. Clicking again turns the option off.

Toolbar An area within the Excel screen which contains buttons that you can click to perform frequently used Excel tasks.

Values Numbers, formulas, or functions used in calculations.

View A set of display and/or print settings that you can name and save, then access at a later time. *See also* **Custom view.**

Wildcards Special symbols used when defining search criteria in the data form or Find dialog box. The question mark (?) wildcard stands for any single character. The asterisk (*) wildcard stands for any group of characters.

Wizard A series of dialog boxes that lists and describes all Excel functions and assists the user in function creation.

Workbook A collection of related worksheets contained within a single file.

Worksheet An electronic spreadsheet containing 256 columns by 65,536 rows.

Worksheet Menu Bar Also called the "menu bar"; a special toolbar that contains commands you use when working with worksheets.

Zoom Enables you to focus on a larger or smaller part of the worksheet in Print Preview.

Zoom box Option on the Standard toolbar that allows you to change the screen magnification percentage.

Glossary

Aggregate functions Functions such as Sum, Avg, and Min that are used in the Query Design grid to calculate statistics across several records.

AND query A query in which more than one criteria must be satisfied for the record to be displayed in the resulting datasheet. AND criteria are placed in the same row of the Query Design grid.

Append query An update query used to add records to an existing table.

AutoForm Wizards Options in the New Form dialog box that allow quick creation of tabular, columnar, or datasheet AutoForms.

AutoReport A report created with the New Object button on the toolbar. Access displays all fields and records in the selected table or query with field names used as labels.

AutoReport Wizard Two options in the New Report dialog box that allow quick creation of tabular or columnar AutoReports.

Bitmap A clip art or image file format that is made up of patterns of individual dots. The file type for bitmap files is usually .BMP.

Bound control A control on a form or report that is linked to a field in an underlying table or query.

Bound object frame A control on a form or report that is linked to images stored in a table.

Calculated expressions Bound report controls that total groups of records and are most likely placed in the group footer section of the report.

Calculated field Created in the Query Design grid by entering a field name followed by a colon in the Field cell followed by an expression such as New Price:[Price]*1.1

Cell The intersection of a row and a column.

Check box A square box on a dialog box or form used to indicate whether an option is selected (checked) or cleared (unchecked). Also used to indicate yes/no choices.

Clipboard A temporary storage area for cut or copied text or graphics, You can paste the contents of the Clipboard into any Microsoft program file. The Clipboard holds the information until you cut or copy another piece of text or a graphic.

Column A vertical stack of cells, usually representing the values for a database field.

Combo box A list box with the additional capability of allowing the user to type an entry from the keyboard.

Control A graphical object used on a form or report that displays data or other information.

Criteria A set of conditions used in a filter or query that selects a particular group of records.

Crosstab query A query that presents information in a cross-tabular report, usually with one field counted or summarized by rows and columns within the body of the report.

Data The information stored in a database.

Data type A specification that controls what kind of data a field can contain.

Database An organized collection of data for a specific purpose.

Database management system A computer program that organizes and manages data.

Database window The window that opens when you start an Access database. It lists all the objects contained in the database.

Dataset A set of records retrieved by applying a filter or running a query.

Datasheet Data from a table, form, or query displayed as rows and columns.

Delete query An update query used to delete a chosen subset of records.

Design grid The grid that you use to design a query or filter.

Design view A window that shows the structure of a table, form, query, or report.

Detail section The section of the report that prints once for each record in the underlying record set.

Expression A combination of values and functions that evaluates to a single result.

Field The part of a table that contains a particular type of data. Also used to name the column of cells containing a particular type of data.

Field list A window available in Design view to display all the fields in a table or query being used.

Field properties The qualities of a field that affect how it appears or what type of data it receives.

Field selector The gray bar at the top of a field column that selects the entire column.

Filter Criteria used to retrieve a specific set of records.

Find A feature that allows you to search for a string of characters in one or many fields.

Form An object, resembling a paper form, used for entering and editing single records.

Form view A window that displays the contents of a database in a form.

Function A preprogrammed mathematical activity that returns a value.

Graphic Any nontext or nonumeric element such as lines, clip art, or boxes placed in the report.

Group footer A section of a form or report that appears on its own line on a report just after the Detail section of a new group of records. Group footer sections are often used to add summary statistics to groups of records.

Group header A section of a form or report that appears on its own line on a report just before the Detail section of a new group of records.

Grouping A report feature that provides a way to sort records so that summary statistics can be applied to a group of records that meet a certain criteria.

Handle A small black square used to move or resize controls in Design view.

Help An online collection of information about Access that you reach from the Help menu.

Hide Duplicates property Hides multiple occurrences of the same data for the fields in the Detail section of the report.

Icon A small graphical representation of an object.

Imported table A new Access table in your database created from information copied from an external file.

Key Field A field that contains unique information for each record.

Key field combination Using two or more fields together as the key field for a record.

Label A control that displays unbound text on a form or report.

Linked table A table created in Excel or other database product that is stored in a file outside of the open database.

List box A box that displays a list of choices.

Menu A list of related commands displayed by clicking a menu name.

Menu bar The row at the top of a window that contains menu names.

Metafile A clip art or image file format that is made up of lines. The file type for metafiles is often .WMF or .EMF.

Move handle The large black square in the upper-left corner of a selected control that you drag to reposition the control.

Navigation buttons The arrows in the lower-left corner of a datasheet or form that are used to move through records.

Object The principal component of an Access database. Tables, forms, queries, reports, macros and modules are all referred to as "objects" in Access.

One-to-many relationship The link between two tables in which the "one" side of the relationship is a key field and the "many" side of the relationship allows the data in that field to be entered many times in that table.

Operators Instructions added to criteria to create new criteria conditions. Mathematical operators such as + (add), and * (multiply) can be used to calculate new criteria. Logical operators such as AND and OR can be used to create more complex criteria expressions.

Option button A button, typically part of a group, that selects an option. Only one option can be selected at a time.

OR query A query in which only one of two or more criteria rows must be satisfied for the record to be displayed in the resulting datasheet. OR criteria are placed on different rows in the Query Design grid.

Page footer The text that appears at the bottom of each page in printed output.

Page header The text that appears at the top of each page in printed output.

Pointer Used to select items; repositioned by movement of the mouse.

Primary key A field whose value uniquely identifies each record.

Print Preview An on-screen view of how an item will appear on paper.

Property An attribute of a object that you can change to control the object's appearance or behavior.

Property sheet The window that displays all the properties for the chosen control on a form or report.

Query A set of instructions used to extract specific records from a database. A "question" asked to the database.

Record All the pieces of information (fields) about one item. A row composed of fields in a datasheet.

Record number box The small box that displays the current record number in the lower-left corner of a datasheet or form.

Referential integrity A set of rules to help maintain the accuracy of a database. For example, enforcing referential integrity will not allow entry of records with data on the "many" side of a one-to-many relationship before the data is first recorded for the "one" side.

Relational database A database such as Access, where information is stored in tables that can be related to one another.

Relationship The connection between two or more tables established by fields common to two or more tables.

Replace A feature that allows you to search for a string of characters and replace it with a different entry.

Report An Access object that presents data selected and formatted for printed output.

Report window The window that presents reports in Design view.

Row A horizontal grouping of a record's data fields in a datasheet.

Row selector A gray box at the left edge of a datasheet that is used to select an entire row.

Run A command or button used to run a query.

Section A designated area of a form or report in which controls can be placed. For example, a Page Header section displays/prints at the top of every page, but a Report Header section displays/prints only at the top of the entire report.

Select query A query that creates a record set without changing any of the affected records.

Shortcut key A key or key combination that lets you carry out a command without opening a menu or using a button.

Shortcut menu A floating menu that opens when the right mouse button is clicked. Menu contents vary, depending on the task in process.

Sizing handle A small black square at the edge of a selected control that you drag to resize the control.

Sorting Placing the records in a certain order (such as ascending order) according to the data in the Lastname field.

Sort order The order that records are displayed in either-Ascending (A-Z) or Descending (Z-A).

Special effects Raised, sunken, shadowed, etched, or chiseled effects added to controls on forms or reports.

Status bar The gray bar across the bottom of the screen that shows supplementary information about commands or actions.

Subform A form contained inside another form.

Text box The most common type of bound control on a form or report. When using a form, the text box allows the user to make an entry for a record by typing information at the keyboard. When reading a report, the text box displays the information in the field on the report.

Toolbar The row of buttons just below the menu bar that provides shortcuts for frequently used commands.

Toolbox The tools used to place controls on a form or report in Design view.

Unbound control A control that is stored entirely in the design for a form or report. There is no link to data in a table.

Unbound object frame A frame containing an image that is stored entirely in the design for a form or report. There is no link to an image stored in the database.

Update query A query that updates the information in the resulting datasheet.

Validation properties Properties of a field that help you eliminate unreasonable entries in a field at the point of data entry.

Value The contents of a field.

View A window that lets you work with Access objects in a specific way, including Form view, Design view, and Report view.

Wizard A tool that helps you create objects such as tables, queries, and forms.

Zoom box A dialog box that lets you view and edit the full contents of an entry that is too large to be viewed in a single cell.

Glossary

Active cell A selected cell in a Graph datasheet.

Adjustment handle A small diamond positioned next to a resize handle that changes the dimension of an object.

Animation A movie that sets graphics or drawn objects to motion.

AutoLayout A predesigned slide layout that contains placeholder layouts for titles, main text, clip art, graphs, and charts.

Cell A rectangle in a Graph datasheet where you enter data.

Chart The component of a graph that graphically portrays your Graph datasheet information.

Chart box The text box in an organizational chart.

Chart depth A chart-sizing option that changes the size of the data series markers.

Chart elements Objects you can add to a chart to help display or highlight certain information.

Chart type Defines how a chart graphically displays data from a datasheet.

Clip art Professionally designed pictures that come with PowerPoint.

Clipboard A temporary storage area for cut or copied text or graphics. You can paste the contents of the Clipboard into any Microsoft program file. The Clipboard holds information until you cut or copy another piece of text or a graphic.

Control boxes The gray boxes located along the left and top of a Graph datasheet.

Data series A row or column of data in a datasheet.

Data series markers The graphical representation, such as a bar or column, of a data series in a chart.

Datasheet The component of a graph that contains the information you want to display on your Graph chart.

Design Templates Prepared slide designs with formatting and color schemes that you can apply to an open presentation.

Digital video Live-action or full-motion video captured by a video camera.

Dotted selection box Indicates that an object is selected and can be modified.

Elevation A chart 3-D view option that changes the angle from which you view the chart.

Embedded object An object that is created in another application but is stored in PowerPoint. Embedded objects maintain a link to their original application for easy editing.

Exception A formatting change made on an individual slide that does not follow the Slide Master.

Folder A subdivision of a disk that works like a filing system to help you organize files.

Freeform A shape that has straight lines, curved lines, or a combination of the two.

Gap depth A chart-sizing option that changes the size of the chart floor.

Gap width A chart-sizing option that changes the distance between each group of data series markers.

Graph The datasheet and chart you create to graphically display information.

Grid Evenly spaced horizontal and vertical lines that do not appear on the slide.

Hanging indent A paragraph format in which the first line of a paragraph starts farther left than the subsequent lines.

Hyperlink A specially formatted word, phrase, or graphic that you click during a slide show to jump to or display another document.

Indent levels The text levels in a text placeholder.

Indent marker A small triangle that shows the position of an indent level.

Interactive settings Customized actions that you apply to objects to play during a slide show.

Leading The vertical space between lines of text.

Link The connection between an object and the source file where it is stored.

Main text placeholder A reserved box on a slide for the main text points.

Margin marker A small box on an indent level that enables you to move the whole indent level.

Master text placeholder The placeholder on the Slide Master that controls the formatting and placement of the Main text placeholder on each slide. If you modify the Master text placeholder, each Main text placeholder is affected in the entire presentation.

Master title placeholder The placeholder on the Slide Master that controls the formatting and placement of the Title placeholder on each slide. If you modify the Master title placeholder, each Title placeholder is affected in the entire presentation.

Object The component you place or draw on a slide. Objects are drawn lines and shapes, text, clip art, imported pictures, and embedded objects.

Organizational chart A diagram of connected boxes that shows reporting structure.

Picture Any piece or artwork, such as a scanned photograph, line art, or clip art that is created in another application and embedded into PowerPoint.

Placeholder A dashed line box in which you place text or objects.

PowerPoint Viewer A special application designed to run a PowerPoint slide show on any compatible computer that does not have PowerPoint installed.

ScreenTip When you place the pointer over a button, the name of the button is displayed and a brief description of its function appears in the status bar.

Slide icon A symbol used to identify a slide title in Outline view.

Source file The file where a linked object is stored.

Source program The original application where embedded and linked objects are created.

Target document The file your hyperlink displays on the screen when you click it.

Text anchor Adjusts the text position in text objects or shapes.

Text box A box within a dialog box where you type information needed to carry out a command.

Text object Any text you create with the Text Tool or enter into a placeholder. Once you enter text into a placeholder, the placeholder becomes a text object.

Timing The time a slide stays on the screen during a slide show.

Title The first line or heading in Outline view.

Title master The master view for the first slide in a presentation.

Title placeholder A reserved box on a slide for a presentation or slide title.

Title slide The first slide in your presentation.

Transition The effect that moves one slide off the screen and the next slide on the screen during a slide show. Each slide can have its own transition effect.

View PowerPoint has five views that allow you to look at your presentation in different ways. Each view allows you to change and modify the content of your presentation.

View buttons Appear at the bottom of the Presentation window. Allow you to switch between PowerPoint's five views.

Wizard A guided approach that steps you through creating a presentation. PowerPoint has two wizards, the AutoContent Wizard and the Pick a Look Wizard, that help you with the content and the look of your presentation.

Index

Index

D

E

Index

Index

▶M

▶N

▶O

Index

▶P

▶Q

▶R

S

►T

▶ U

▶ V

▶ W

Index

▶Y

▶Z